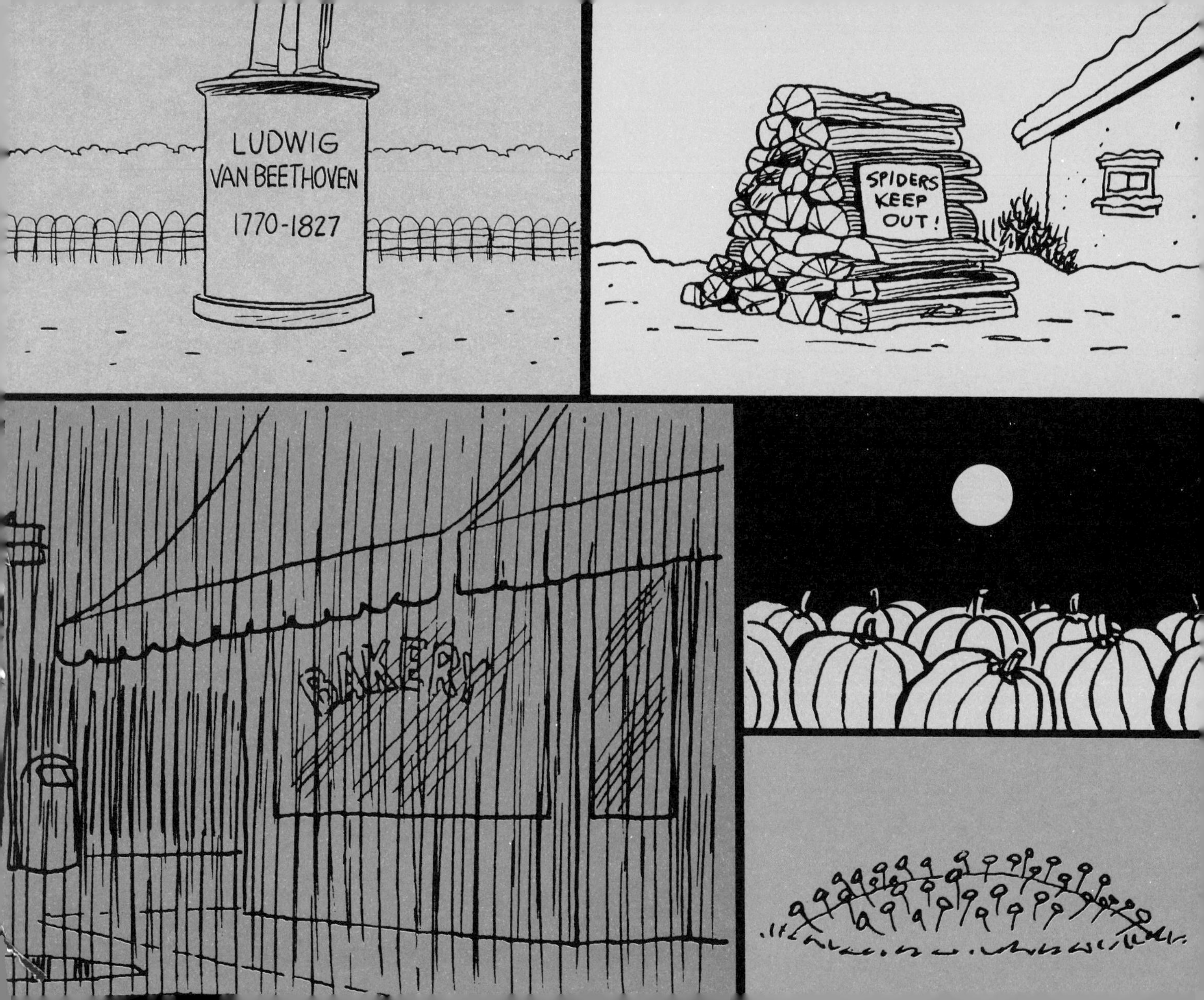
LUDWIG
VAN BEETHOVEN
1770-1827
SPIDERS
KEEP
OUT!
BAKERY

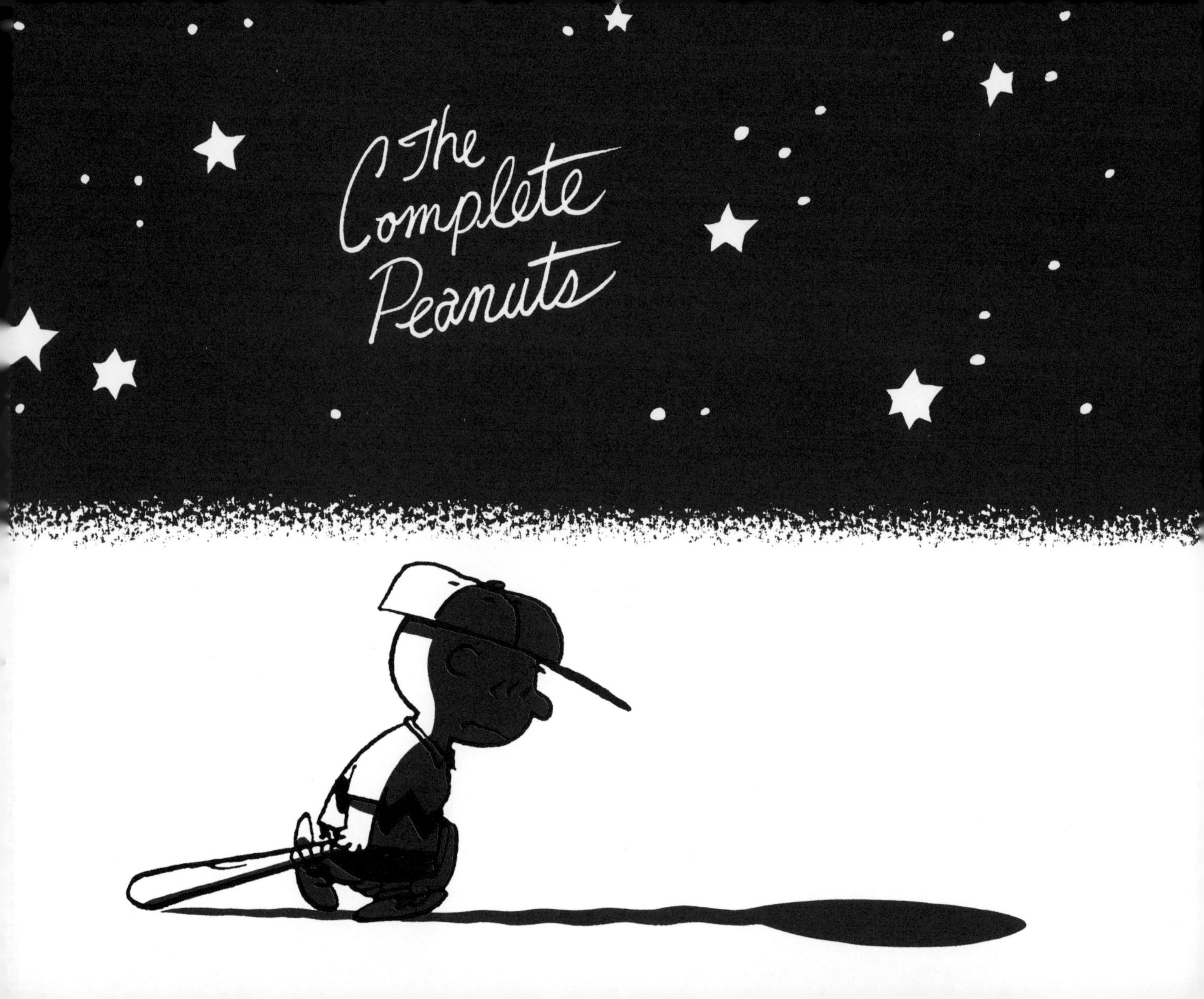
The Complete Peanuts

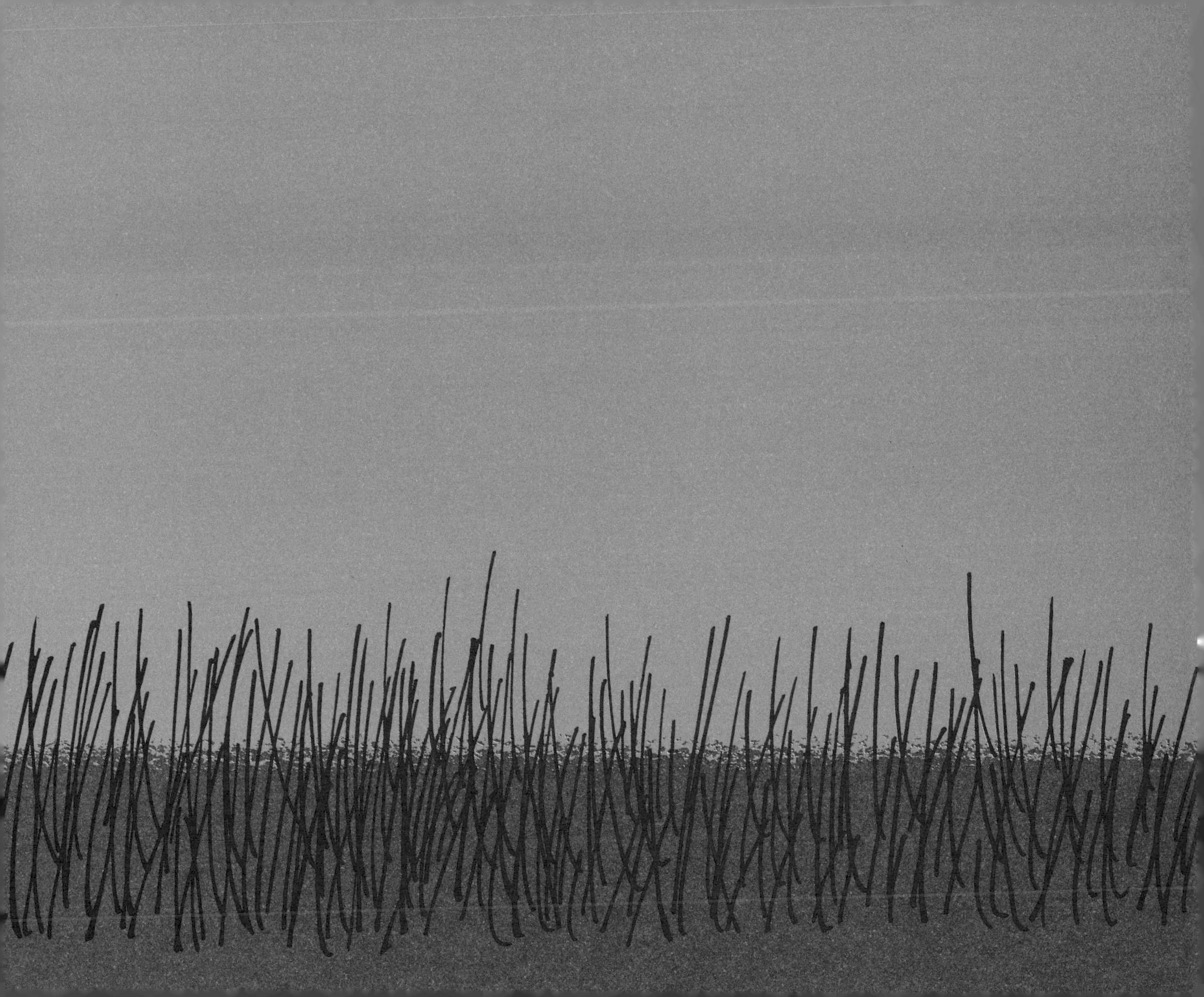

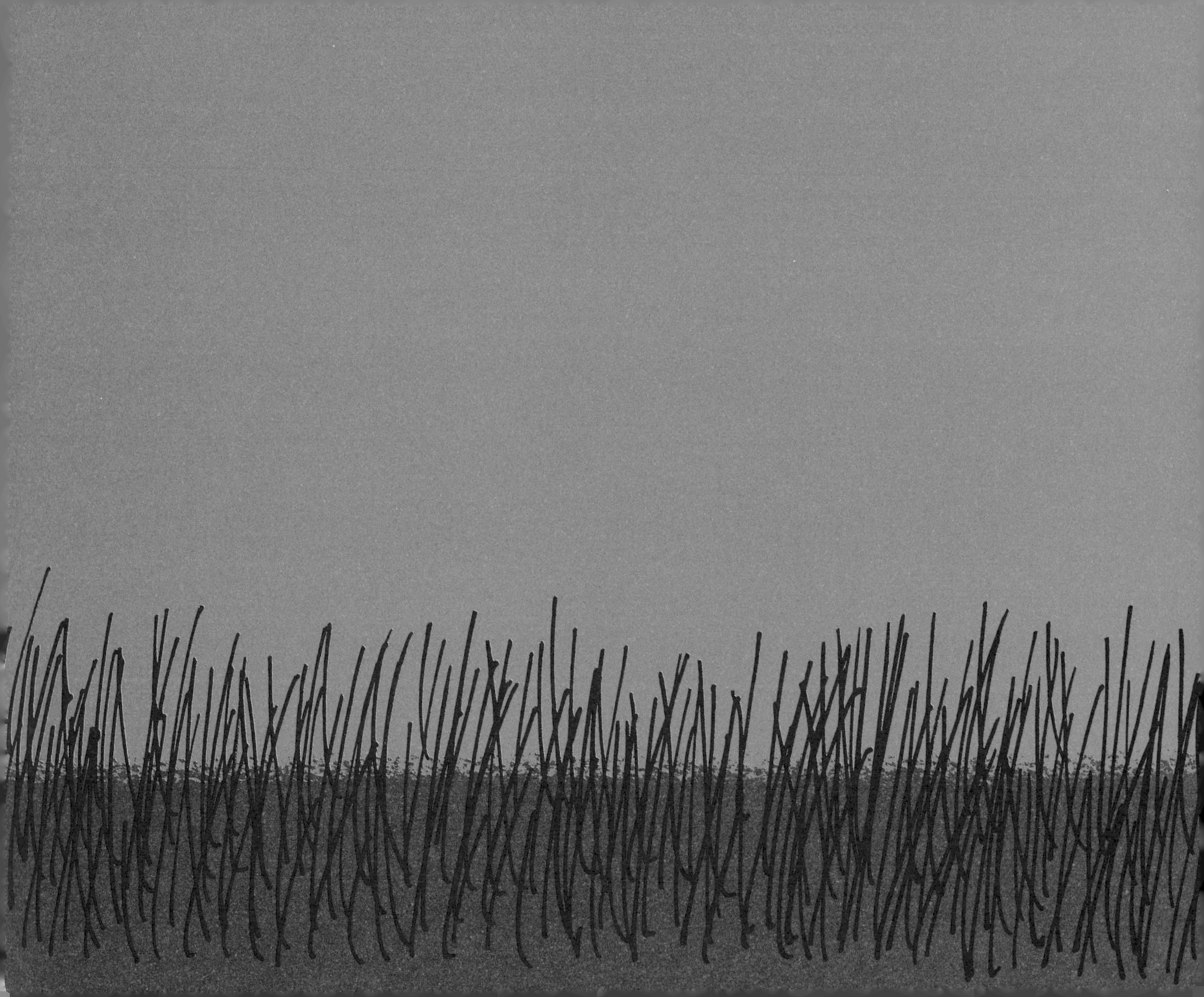

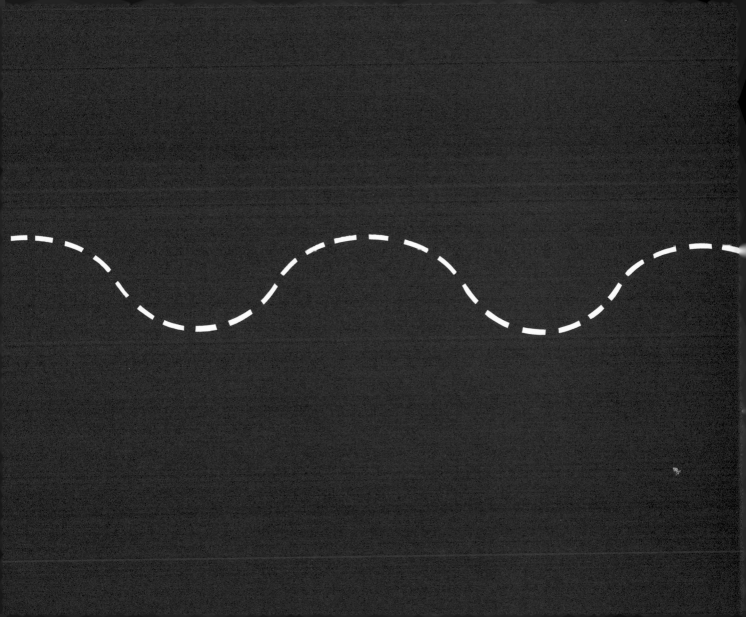

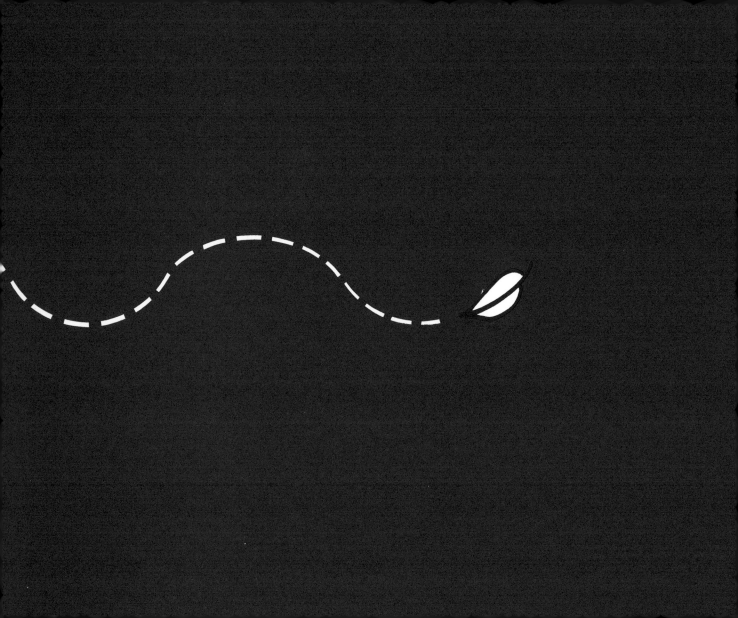

THE COMPLETE PEANUTS
by Charles M. Schulz

Publishers: Gary Groth & Kim Thompson
Designer: Seth

Special thanks to Jeannie Schulz, without whom this project would not have come to fruition.
Thanks to Charles M. Schulz Creative Associates, especially Paige Braddock and Kim Towner.
Thanks for special support from United Media.

First published in America in 2007 by Fantagraphics Books, 7563 Lake City Way, Seattle, WA 98115, USA

First published in Great Britain in 2010 by Canongate Books Ltd, 14 High Street, Edinburgh, EH1 1TE

5

British Library Cataloguing-in-Publication Data
A catalogue record for this book is available on request from the British Library

ISBN 978 1 84767 815 7

Printed and bound in Malaysia

canongate.co.uk

CHARLES M. SCHULZ

THE COMPLETE PEANUTS

1965 TO 1966

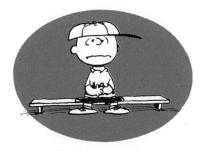

"I **MUST** BE A GOOD
MANAGER..MY STOMACH HURTS!"

CANONGATE BOOKS

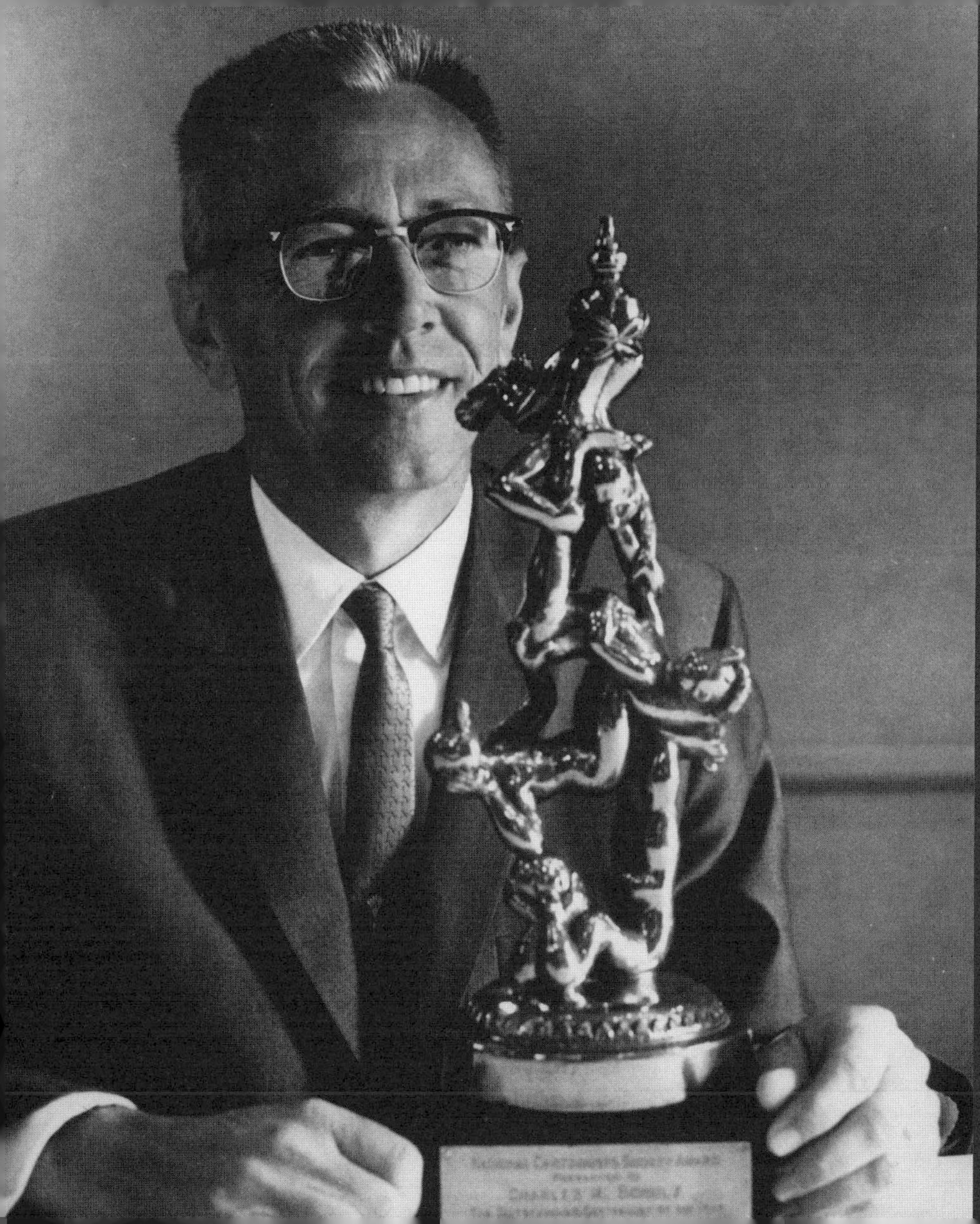

Charles Schulz with his second Reuben award, circa 1964.

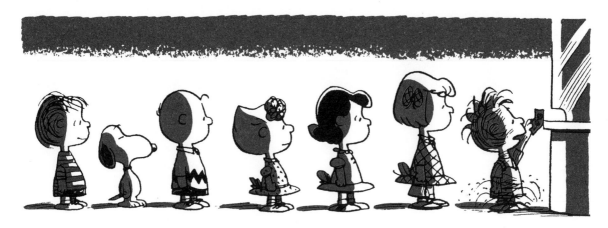

FOREWORD by HAL HARTLEY

I didn't grow up avidly reading comic books and don't remember being terribly preoccupied with the daily strips that appeared in the newspapers. But I liked to draw and I recall spending time trying to copy the drawings of certain comics rather than reading the dialogue balloons. I believe I must have read *Peanuts* — casually, as I guess comics are meant to be read. But that's all I remember of the strips at that time: sitting on the front steps in the warm months waiting for supper, flipping idly through the pages of the Long Island *Newsday* and, coming to the comics page, reading *Peanuts* and *Doonesbury*, then moving on.

When approached to consider writing an introduction for this volume of *The Complete Peanuts*, I asked

if I could have a collection of strips to ponder from the early-to-mid seventies; that is, from when I was an adolescent and young teenager. I wanted to see if there was evidence in those daily strips of the world I remember trying to get my bearings in.

There is. It's subtle, but it's there. Perhaps it's the very sparseness of the *Peanuts* world — the anywhere at anytime simplicity of its universe — that allows us to see the world we ourselves actually move through. It provides a mirror into which we can pour our preoccupations and memories. The characters are types at once perennial and contemporary. When I read these strips now, I sense the times in which they were written and drawn. I sense the characters to have been shaped by an awareness of

the real world that Charles Schulz moved through as well. I'm sure one can read through all of Peanuts and see nothing more than a continuing insight and feeling about kids and people of all times in all places. And that, in itself, would be fine. But I'm afraid I can't see them as simply that. These kids are American and the world that is palpably moving around just outside the frame of the panels affects and adjusts the things they say and do.

For instance, Lucy and Peppermint Patty are hanging around and Lucy suggests that they both go get their ears pierced. Patty turns to her friend and calmly explains that she has no doubts about her femininity — in just those words, that simply. The complete lack of an attempt to loosen up the language into something more natural is, for me, terribly funny. But maybe also there's a hint of exasperation, an honest fatigue with one's efforts to come to grips with the issues of the day — in this case the daily application of a feminism that was still new in the seventies. (I remember my own urgent conferences with my pals about whether we should call our new teacher "Miss" or the new "Ms" and what, after all was "Ms" an abbreviation for, if anything...)

I know little about Charles Schulz. But reading through these stacks of strips from the early and mid seventies now, in 2007, I definitely hear his voice. The author behind the scenes I hear seems a modest, hardworking, sharp-witted, observer of human nature, probably more conservative than not, but hard to pigeonhole. His is an independent sensibility; polite, but unflinching when it comes to illustrating our common foibles, quietly demonstrating the hollowness of much conventional wisdom, capable at times of what I can only call absurd realism and which I could easily convince myself I decided to steal and use for my own purposes fifteen or sixteen years later on.

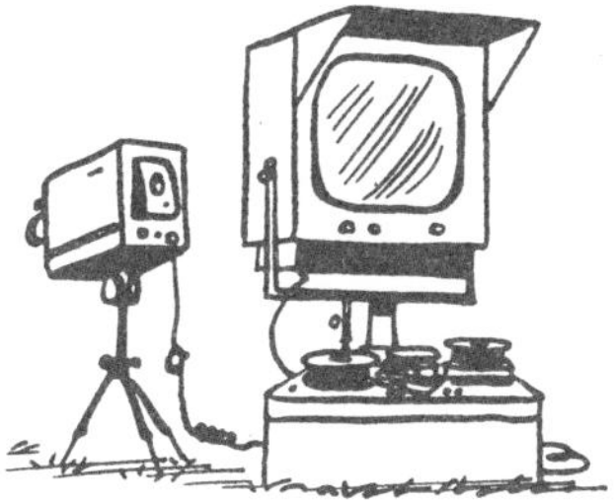

He is sometimes harsh. But then the victims are so durable.

I'm a filmmaker whose films are often referred to as funny, depressing, thought-provoking, poetic, shallow, stylish, or just plain bad. One learns to live with being categorized. But after twenty years at it, I'm still surprised that the mix of humor, critical thinking, dramatic structure, formal play, and philosophical musing that characterize films like mine is still seen to be so unusual or idiosyncratic. As if there were no precedent for it. But, there is: *Peanuts*.

I had a writing teacher in college, Howard Stein, who used to say that as we get older we acquire rust and that children see and feel everything more immediately before the rust sets in. He urged that in our writing we try to hold on to some of that childishness that allows for these unmediated impressions. This

made sense to me right away and I began writing in earnest for the first time in my life. And almost immediately I felt the excitement and potential of arranging childlike observance alongside mature, adult, consideration.

Because certainly, as a kid, I learned that people almost never say what they mean, at least, not exactly. We learn, if out of nothing else but kindness, to circumnavigate painful topics; divisive issues are flirted with by saying something seemingly unrelated that, however, when heard under the right circumstances, reveals its true meaning. All this I was taught to call irony and it was once considered the height of wit. These days it is often frowned upon and suspected of being anti-social and the disdainful expression of someone who thinks he or she knows more than anyone else. Personally, I still believe irony to be one of the most valuable and generous exercises of an engaged intelligence eager for a good laugh.

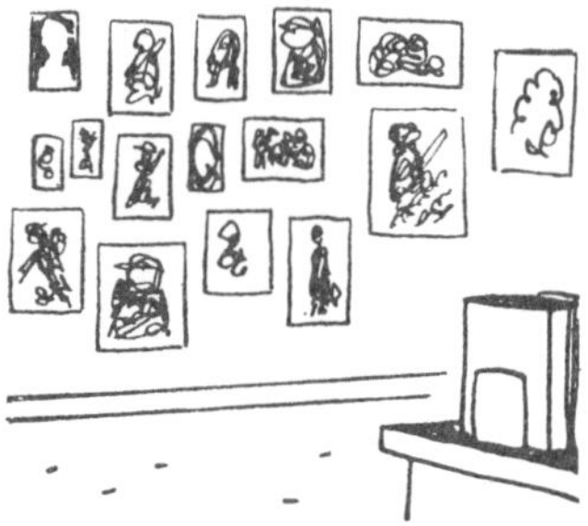

Peanuts was ironic and kind. And I knew this at thirteen.

Growing up in the seventies, I laughed and sighed a good deal at the cryptic, curiously ambiguous wisdom of the *Peanuts* comic strip. These little kids, who were somehow also *not* little kids, said what they meant, exactly. Charlie Brown so acutely expressed in words a self-esteem so low, I was often amazed Schulz left him standing at the end of the four panels. Frankly, I was often puzzled. I didn't know whether to laugh or sigh.

And so I wonder now to what extent my sense of humor, my thinking about life, and my storytelling inclinations might have been influenced by my regular and casual contact with Charlie Brown and his world at the age of thirteen or fourteen. The *Peanuts* gang were as regular a part of those days for me, sitting there on my front step with the newspaper, as were John Lennon and Yoko Ono being castigated for one thing or another, as much as Watergate or Nixon's trip to China. I was just as intrigued and confused by some of these strips as I was by Jane Fonda visiting North Vietnam and Salvador Allende's overthrow in Chile.

The world pours over a thirteen-year-old's head like so much water. The big picture is hard to see. But the details stick, and the questions remain. And the stark admission in *Peanuts* of not knowing really all that much at all was its own sort of wisdom.

It's hard to say exactly how *Peanuts* may have influenced me. No one had to explain to me why it was funny. I laughed without guidance. It came naturally.

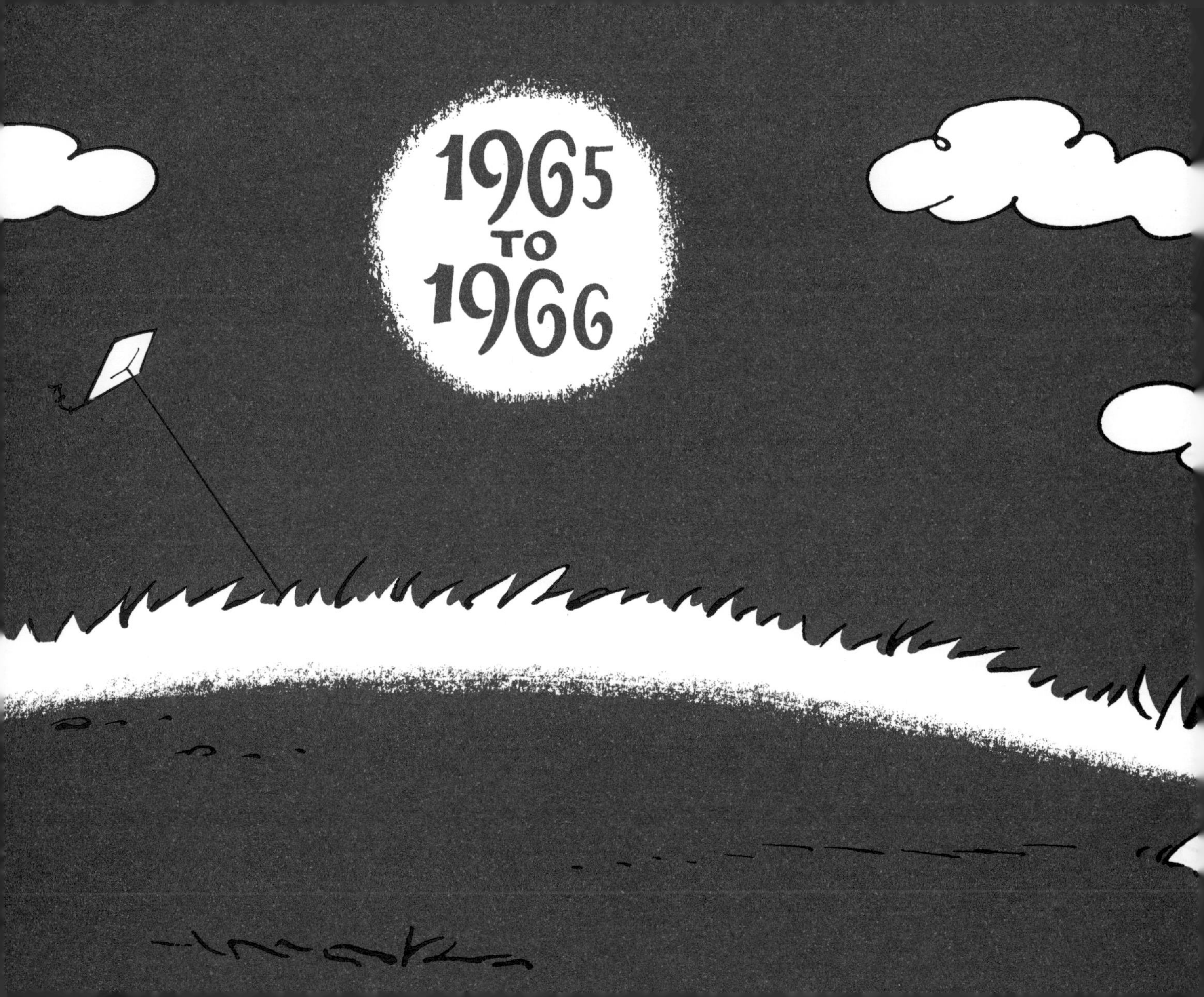
1965
TO
1966

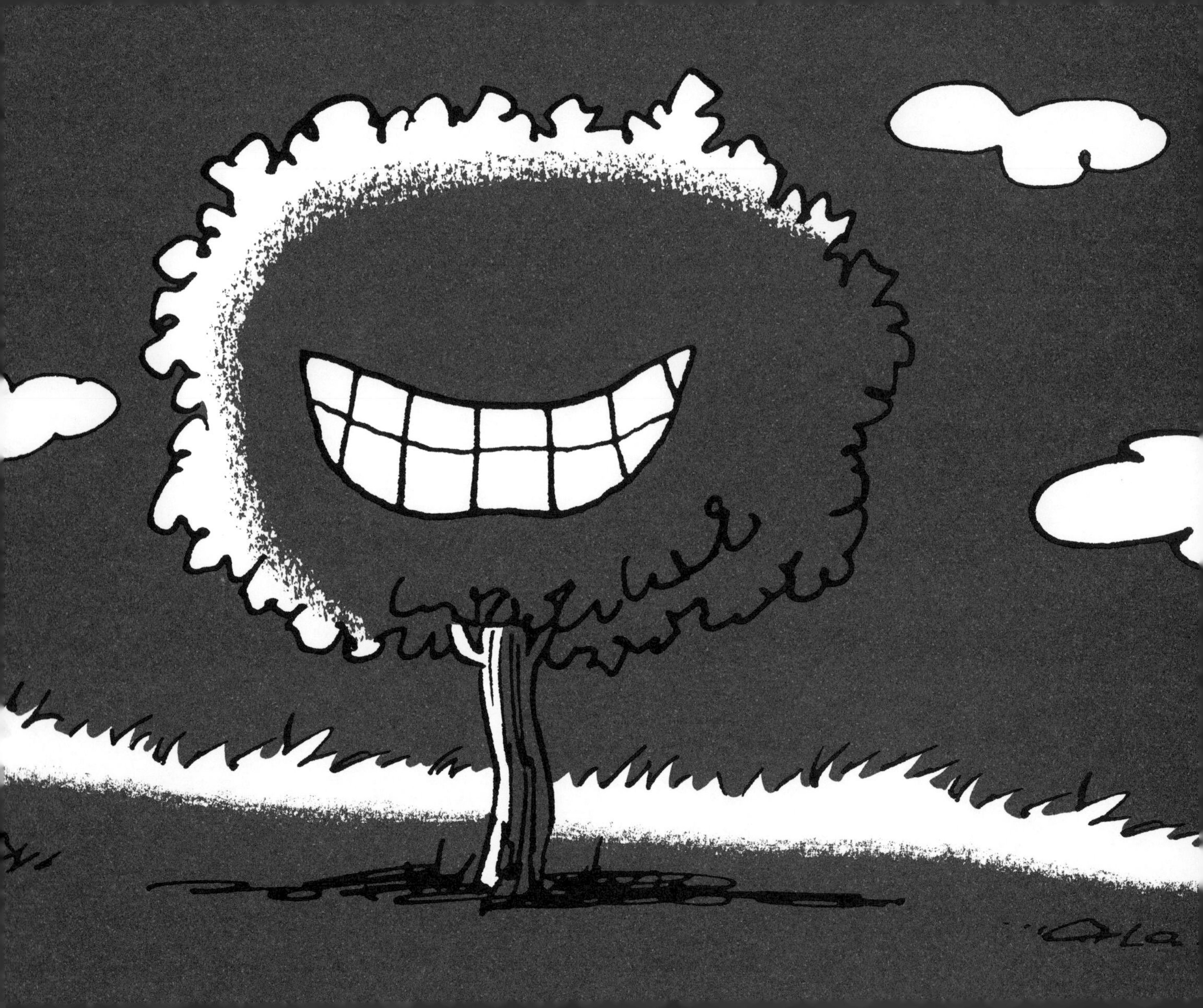

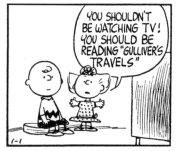

YOU SHOULDN'T BE WATCHING TV! YOU SHOULD BE READING "GULLIVER'S TRAVELS"

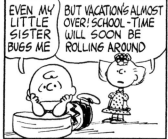

EVEN MY LITTLE SISTER BUGS ME

BUT VACATION'S ALMOST OVER! SCHOOL-TIME WILL SOON BE ROLLING AROUND

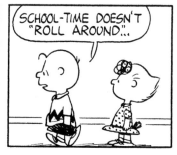

SCHOOL-TIME DOESN'T "ROLL AROUND"...

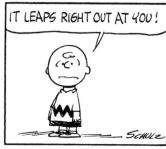

IT LEAPS RIGHT OUT AT YOU!

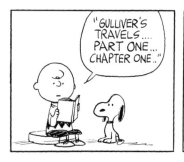

"GULLIVER'S TRAVELS.... PART ONE... CHAPTER ONE.."

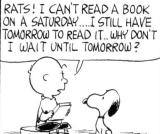

RATS! I CAN'T READ A BOOK ON A SATURDAY....I STILL HAVE TOMORROW TO READ IT.. WHY DON'T I WAIT UNTIL TOMORROW?

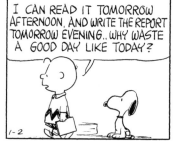

I CAN READ IT TOMORROW AFTERNOON, AND WRITE THE REPORT TOMORROW EVENING.. WHY WASTE A GOOD DAY LIKE TODAY?

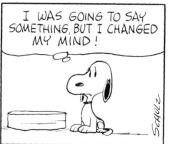

I WAS GOING TO SAY SOMETHING, BUT I CHANGED MY MIND!

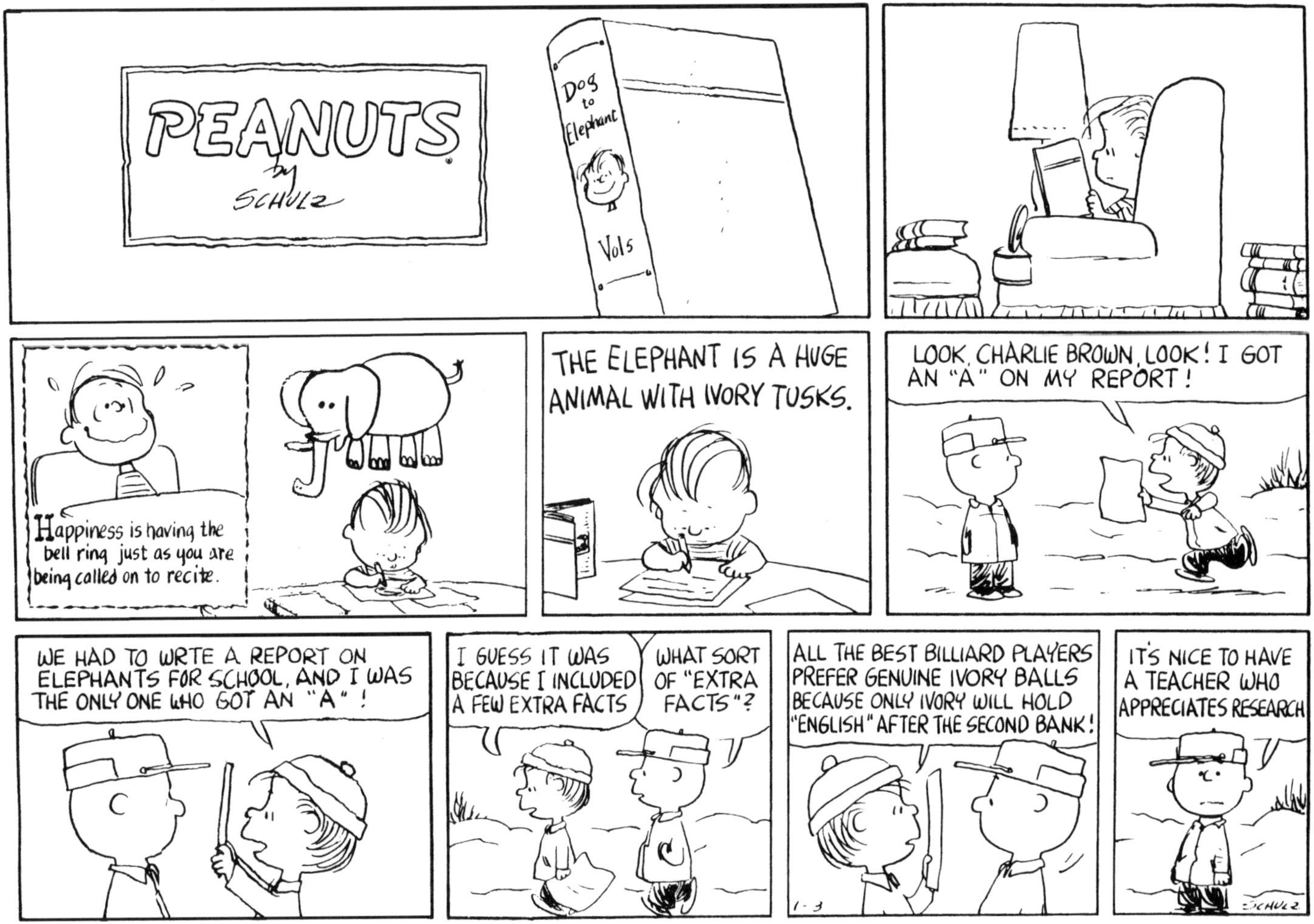
PEANUTS
by SCHULZ
Dog to Elephant
Vols
Happiness is having the bell ring just as you are being called on to recite.
THE ELEPHANT IS A HUGE ANIMAL WITH IVORY TUSKS.
LOOK, CHARLIE BROWN, LOOK! I GOT AN "A" ON MY REPORT!
WE HAD TO WRTE A REPORT ON ELEPHANTS FOR SCHOOL, AND I WAS THE ONLY ONE WHO GOT AN "A"!
I GUESS IT WAS BECAUSE I INCLUDED A FEW EXTRA FACTS
WHAT SORT OF "EXTRA FACTS"?
ALL THE BEST BILLIARD PLAYERS PREFER GENUINE IVORY BALLS BECAUSE ONLY IVORY WILL HOLD "ENGLISH" AFTER THE SECOND BANK!
1-3
IT'S NICE TO HAVE A TEACHER WHO APPRECIATES RESEARCH
SCHULZ

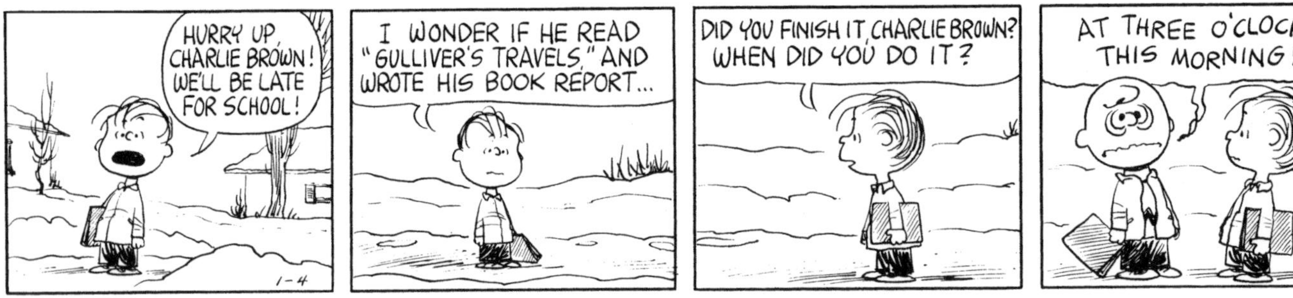
HURRY UP, CHARLIE BROWN! WE'LL BE LATE FOR SCHOOL!
I WONDER IF HE READ "GULLIVER'S TRAVELS," AND WROTE HIS BOOK REPORT...
DID YOU FINISH IT, CHARLIE BROWN? WHEN DID YOU DO IT?
AT THREE O'CLOCK THIS MORNING!!!

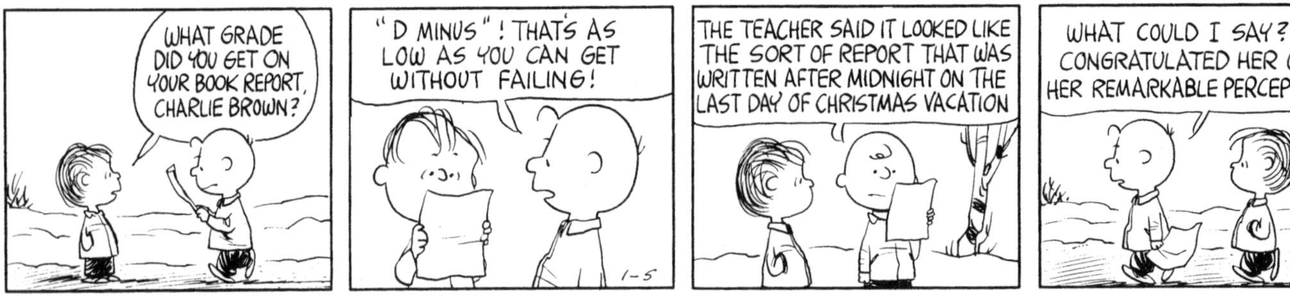
WHAT GRADE DID YOU GET ON YOUR BOOK REPORT, CHARLIE BROWN?
"D MINUS"! THAT'S AS LOW AS YOU CAN GET WITHOUT FAILING!
THE TEACHER SAID IT LOOKED LIKE THE SORT OF REPORT THAT WAS WRITTEN AFTER MIDNIGHT ON THE LAST DAY OF CHRISTMAS VACATION
WHAT COULD I SAY? I CONGRATULATED HER ON HER REMARKABLE PERCEPTIVITY!

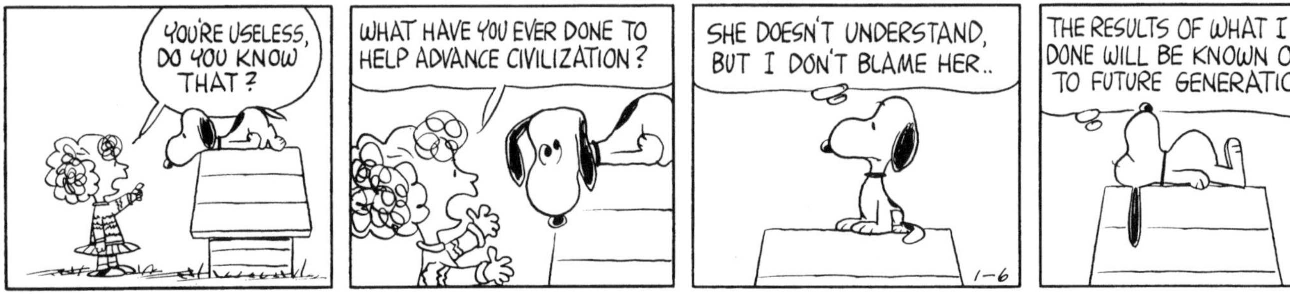
YOU'RE USELESS, DO YOU KNOW THAT?
WHAT HAVE YOU EVER DONE TO HELP ADVANCE CIVILIZATION?
SHE DOESN'T UNDERSTAND, BUT I DON'T BLAME HER..
THE RESULTS OF WHAT I HAVE DONE WILL BE KNOWN ONLY TO FUTURE GENERATIONS!

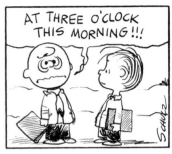

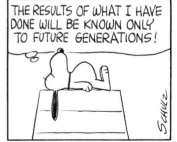

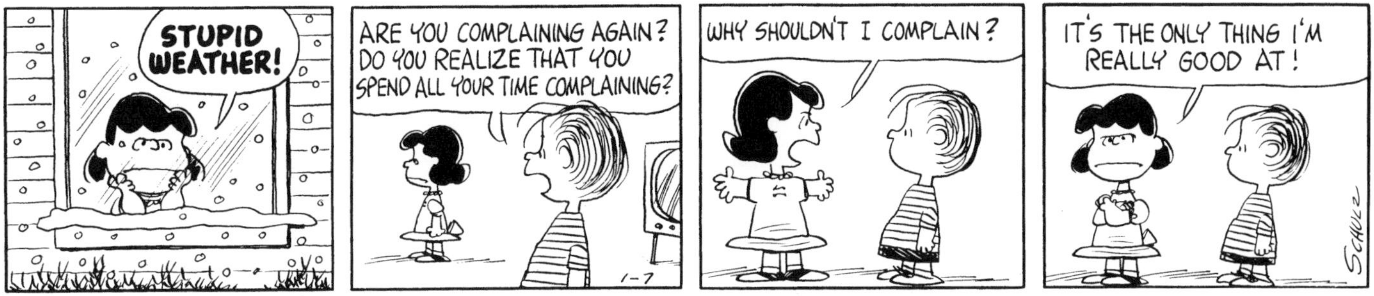
STUPID WEATHER!
ARE YOU COMPLAINING AGAIN? DO YOU REALIZE THAT YOU SPEND ALL YOUR TIME COMPLAINING?
WHY SHOULDN'T I COMPLAIN?
IT'S THE ONLY THING I'M REALLY GOOD AT!

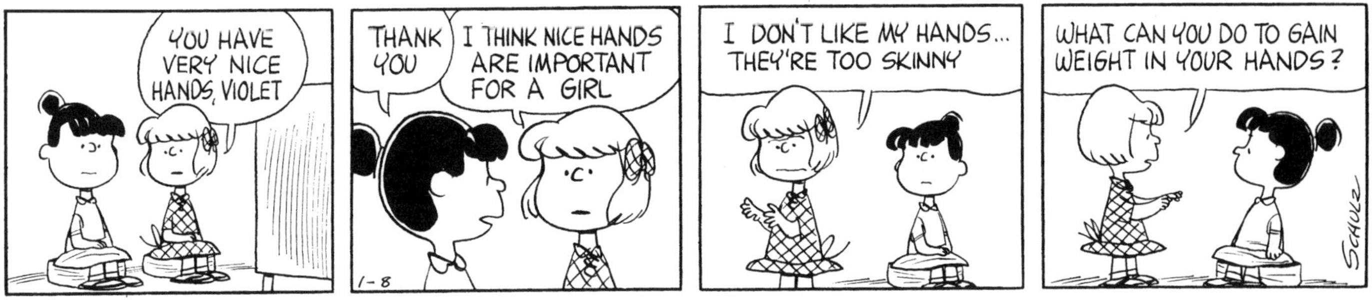
YOU HAVE VERY NICE HANDS, VIOLET
THANK YOU
I THINK NICE HANDS ARE IMPORTANT FOR A GIRL
I DON'T LIKE MY HANDS... THEY'RE TOO SKINNY
WHAT CAN YOU DO TO GAIN WEIGHT IN YOUR HANDS?

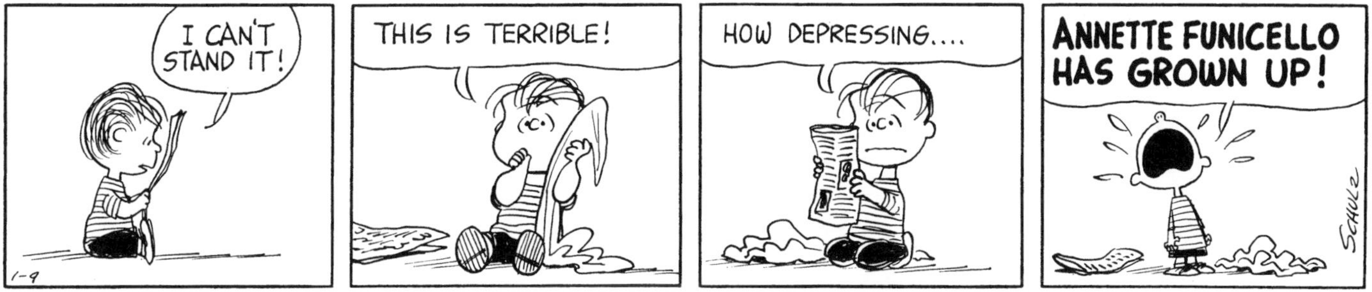
I CAN'T STAND IT!
THIS IS TERRIBLE!
HOW DEPRESSING....
ANNETTE FUNICELLO HAS GROWN UP!

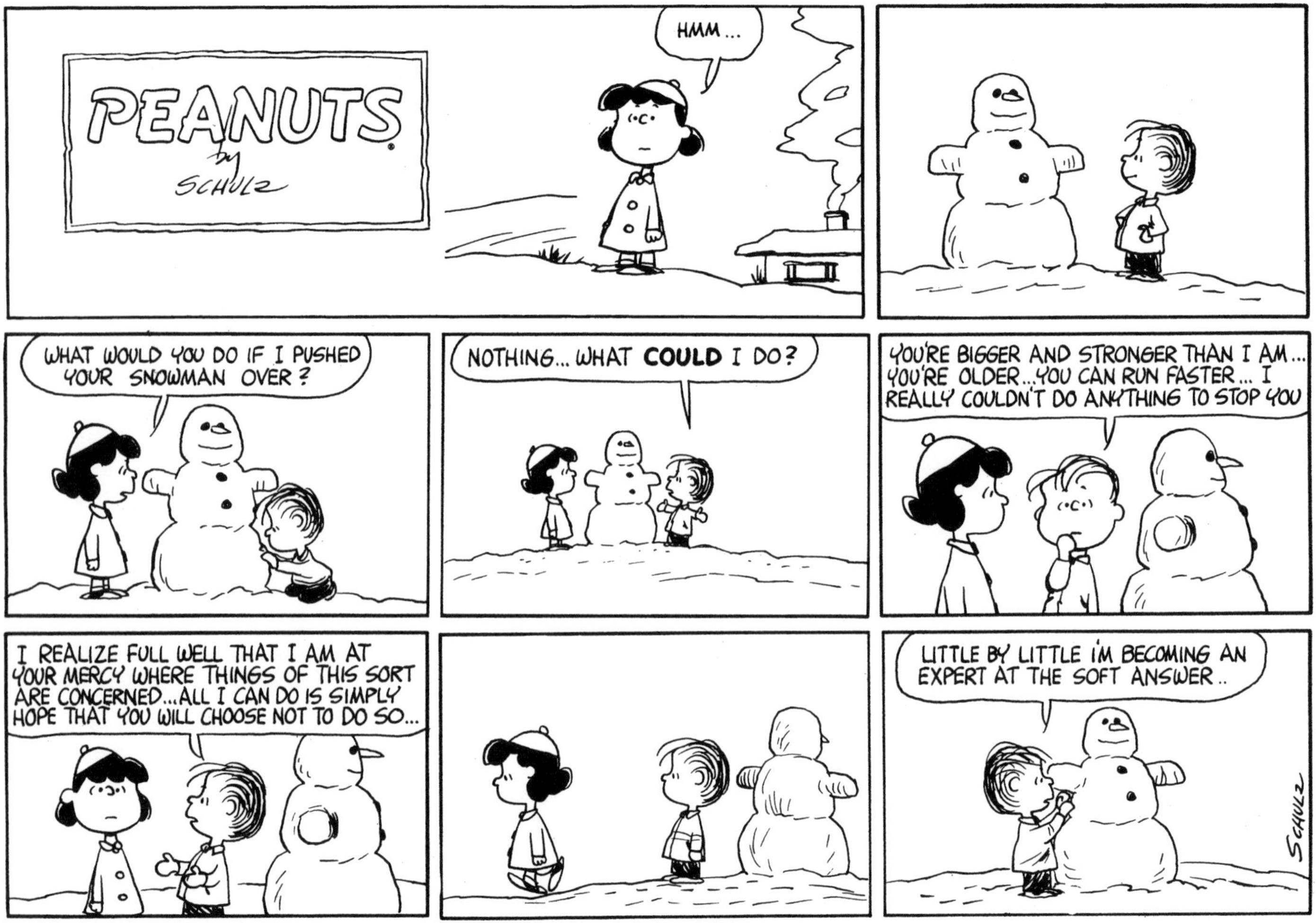
PEANUTS
by SCHULZ
HMM...
WHAT WOULD YOU DO IF I PUSHED YOUR SNOWMAN OVER?
NOTHING... WHAT **COULD** I DO?
YOU'RE BIGGER AND STRONGER THAN I AM... YOU'RE OLDER... YOU CAN RUN FASTER... I REALLY COULDN'T DO ANYTHING TO STOP YOU
I REALIZE FULL WELL THAT I AM AT YOUR MERCY WHERE THINGS OF THIS SORT ARE CONCERNED... ALL I CAN DO IS SIMPLY HOPE THAT YOU WILL CHOOSE NOT TO DO SO...
LITTLE BY LITTLE I'M BECOMING AN EXPERT AT THE SOFT ANSWER..
SCHULZ

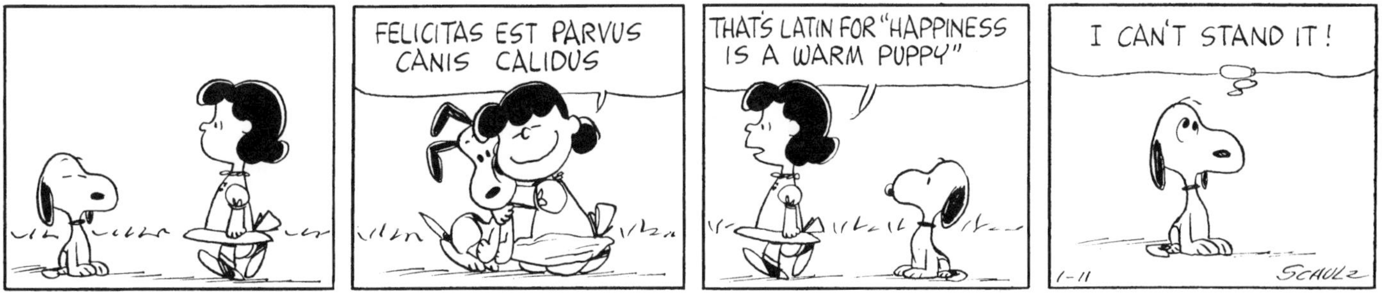
FELICITAS EST PARVUS CANIS CALIDUS
THAT'S LATIN FOR "HAPPINESS IS A WARM PUPPY"
I CAN'T STAND IT!
1-11
SCHULZ

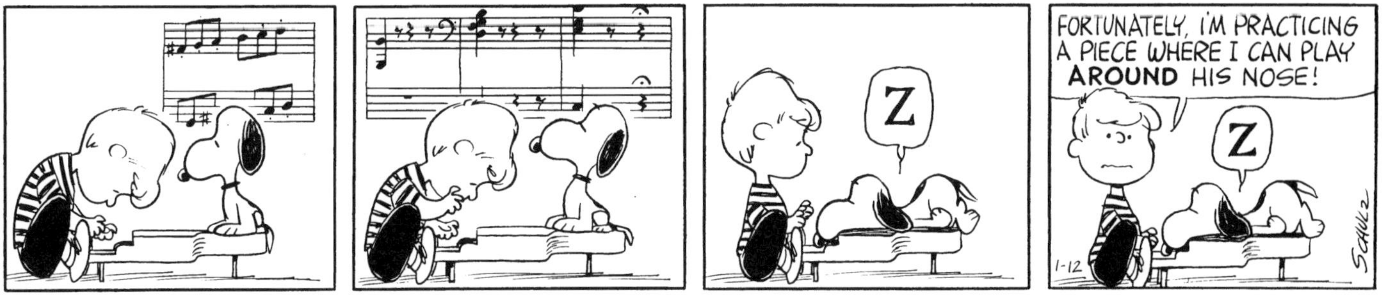
Z
FORTUNATELY, I'M PRACTICING A PIECE WHERE I CAN PLAY **AROUND** HIS NOSE!
Z
1-12
SCHULZ

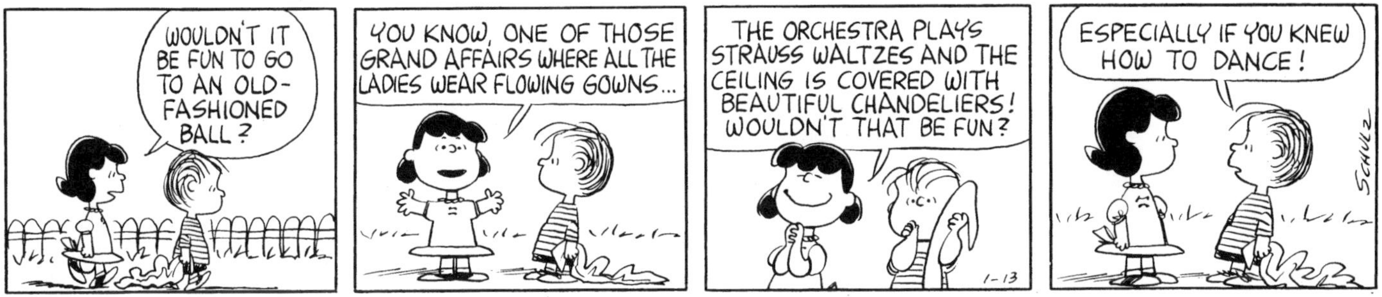
WOULDN'T IT BE FUN TO GO TO AN OLD-FASHIONED BALL?
YOU KNOW, ONE OF THOSE GRAND AFFAIRS WHERE ALL THE LADIES WEAR FLOWING GOWNS...
THE ORCHESTRA PLAYS STRAUSS WALTZES AND THE CEILING IS COVERED WITH BEAUTIFUL CHANDELIERS! WOULDN'T THAT BE FUN?
1-13
ESPECIALLY IF YOU KNEW HOW TO DANCE!
SCHULZ

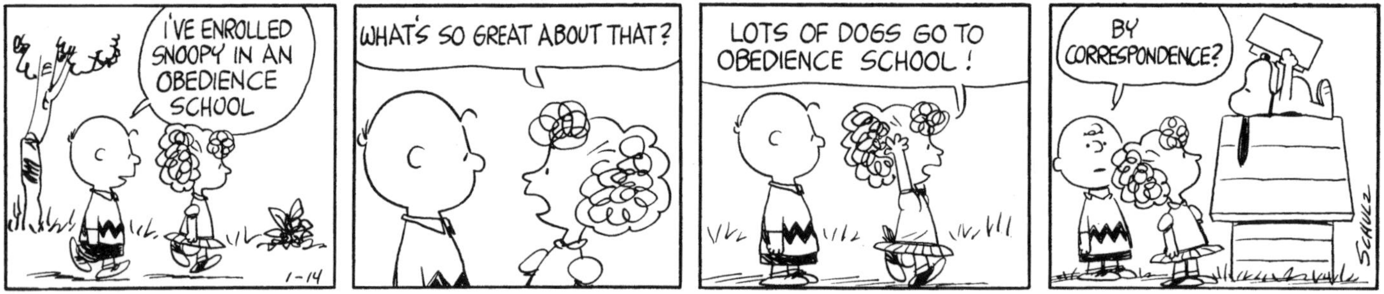
I'VE ENROLLED SNOOPY IN AN OBEDIENCE SCHOOL
1-14
WHAT'S SO GREAT ABOUT THAT?
LOTS OF DOGS GO TO OBEDIENCE SCHOOL!
BY CORRESPONDENCE?
SCHULZ

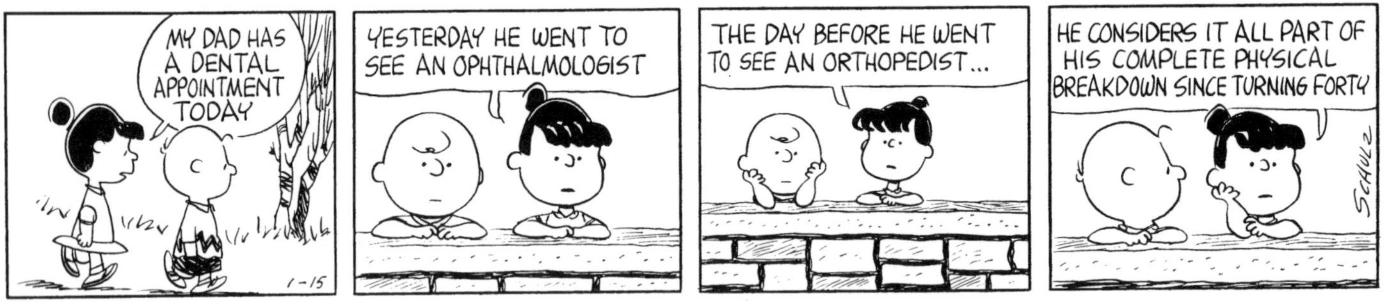
MY DAD HAS A DENTAL APPOINTMENT TODAY
1-15
YESTERDAY HE WENT TO SEE AN OPHTHALMOLOGIST
THE DAY BEFORE HE WENT TO SEE AN ORTHOPEDIST...
HE CONSIDERS IT ALL PART OF HIS COMPLETE PHYSICAL BREAKDOWN SINCE TURNING FORTY
SCHULZ

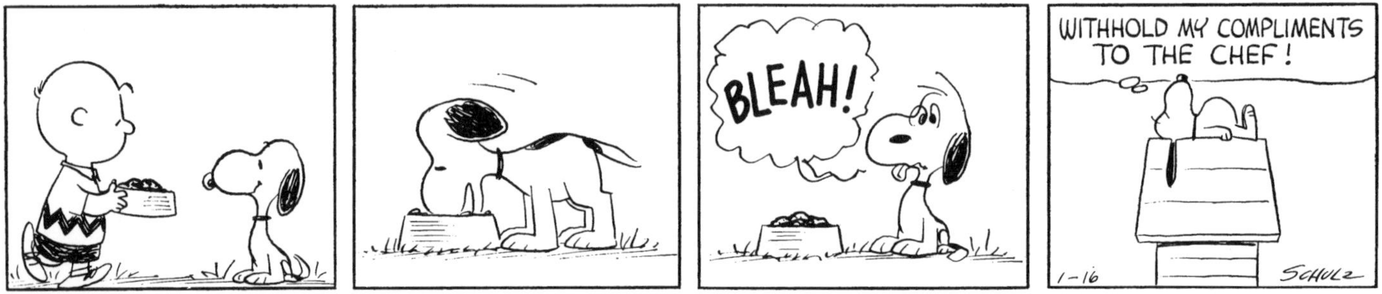
BLEAH!
WITHHOLD MY COMPLIMENTS TO THE CHEF!
1-16
SCHULZ

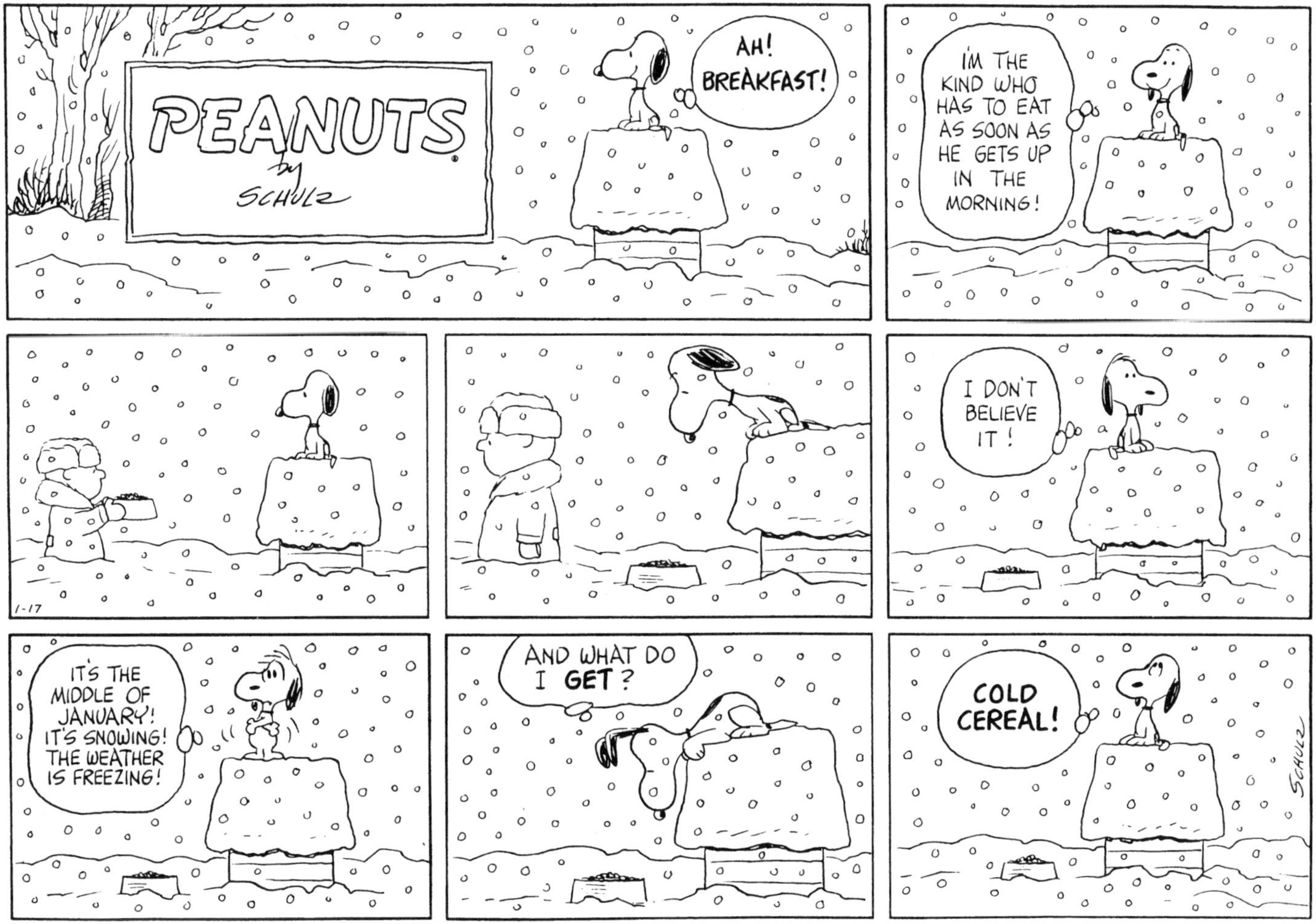
PEANUTS
by SCHULZ
AH! BREAKFAST!
I'M THE KIND WHO HAS TO EAT AS SOON AS HE GETS UP IN THE MORNING!
1-17
I DON'T BELIEVE IT!
IT'S THE MIDDLE OF JANUARY! IT'S SNOWING! THE WEATHER IS FREEZING!
AND WHAT DO I **GET**?
COLD CEREAL!
SCHULZ

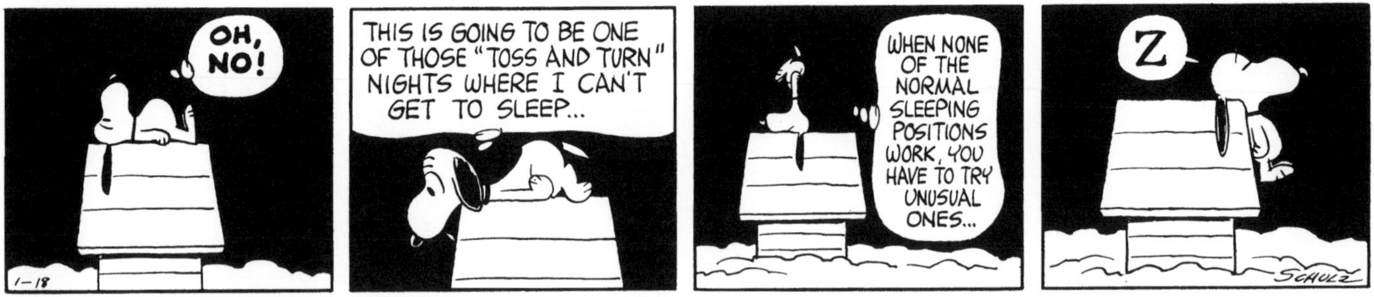
OH, NO!
THIS IS GOING TO BE ONE OF THOSE "TOSS AND TURN" NIGHTS WHERE I CAN'T GET TO SLEEP...
WHEN NONE OF THE NORMAL SLEEPING POSITIONS WORK, YOU HAVE TO TRY UNUSUAL ONES...
Z

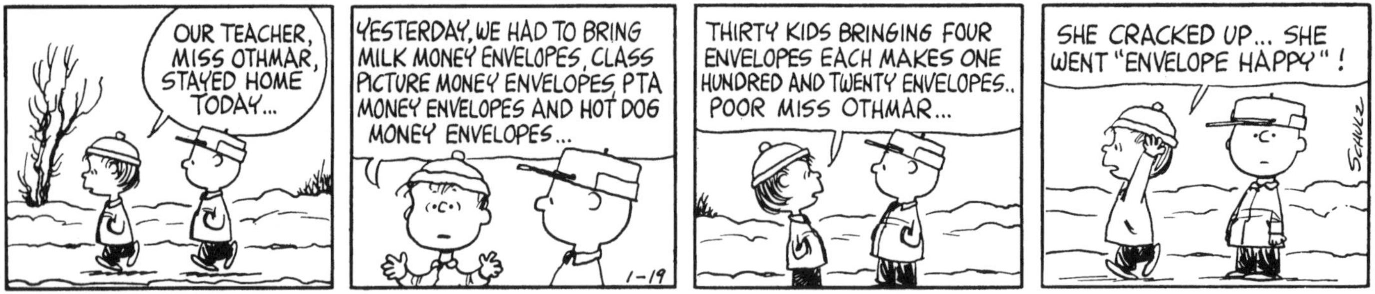
OUR TEACHER, MISS OTHMAR, STAYED HOME TODAY...
YESTERDAY, WE HAD TO BRING MILK MONEY ENVELOPES, CLASS PICTURE MONEY ENVELOPES, PTA MONEY ENVELOPES AND HOT DOG MONEY ENVELOPES...
THIRTY KIDS BRINGING FOUR ENVELOPES EACH MAKES ONE HUNDRED AND TWENTY ENVELOPES.. POOR MISS OTHMAR...
SHE CRACKED UP... SHE WENT "ENVELOPE HAPPY"!

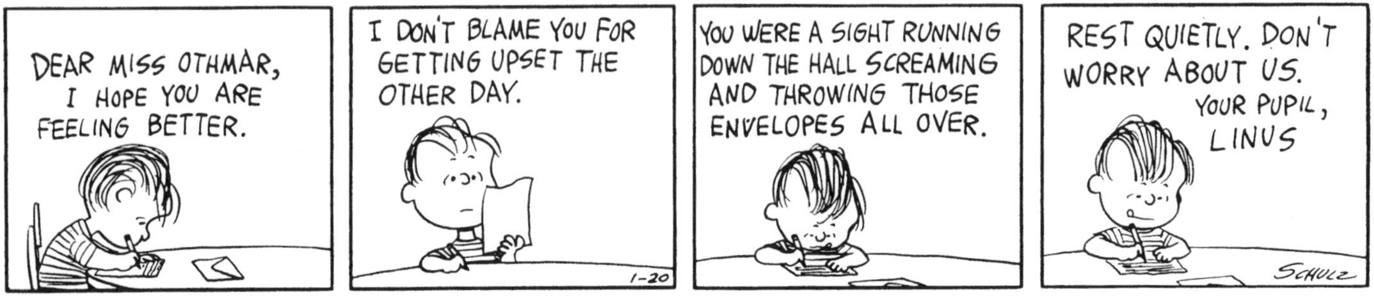
DEAR MISS OTHMAR, I HOPE YOU ARE FEELING BETTER.
I DON'T BLAME YOU FOR GETTING UPSET THE OTHER DAY.
YOU WERE A SIGHT RUNNING DOWN THE HALL SCREAMING AND THROWING THOSE ENVELOPES ALL OVER.
REST QUIETLY. DON'T WORRY ABOUT US. YOUR PUPIL, LINUS

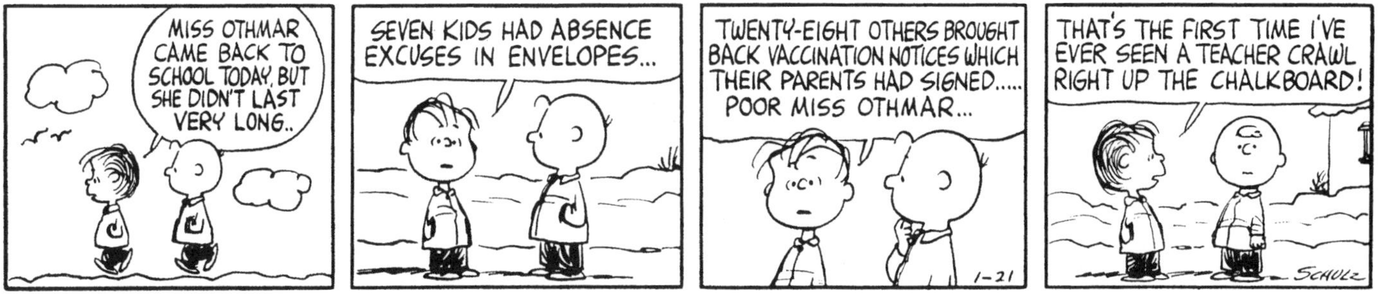
MISS OTHMAR CAME BACK TO SCHOOL TODAY, BUT SHE DIDN'T LAST VERY LONG..
SEVEN KIDS HAD ABSENCE EXCUSES IN ENVELOPES...
TWENTY-EIGHT OTHERS BROUGHT BACK VACCINATION NOTICES WHICH THEIR PARENTS HAD SIGNED..... POOR MISS OTHMAR...
1-21
THAT'S THE FIRST TIME I'VE EVER SEEN A TEACHER CRAWL RIGHT UP THE CHALKBOARD!
SCHULZ

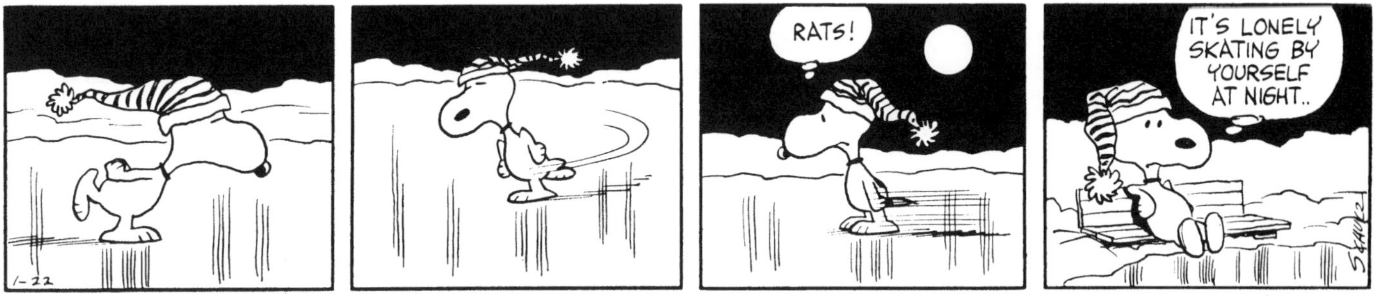
1-22
RATS!
IT'S LONELY SKATING BY YOURSELF AT NIGHT..
SCHULZ

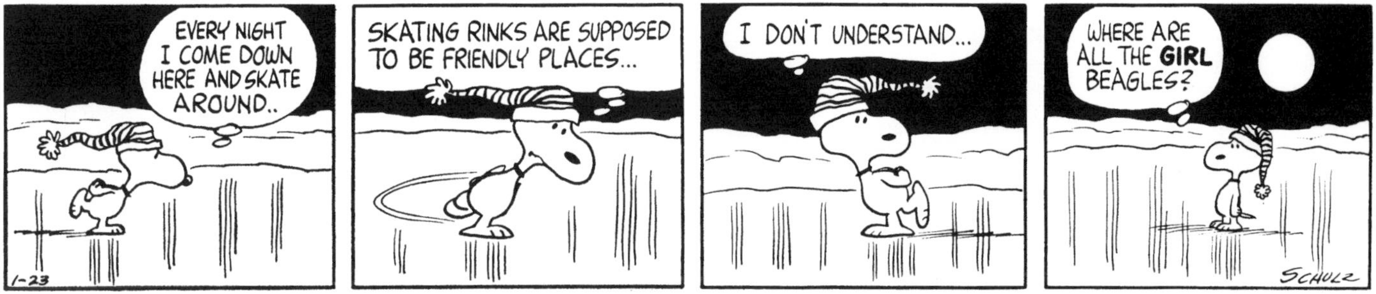
EVERY NIGHT I COME DOWN HERE AND SKATE AROUND..
1-23
SKATING RINKS ARE SUPPOSED TO BE FRIENDLY PLACES...
I DON'T UNDERSTAND...
WHERE ARE ALL THE GIRL BEAGLES?
SCHULZ

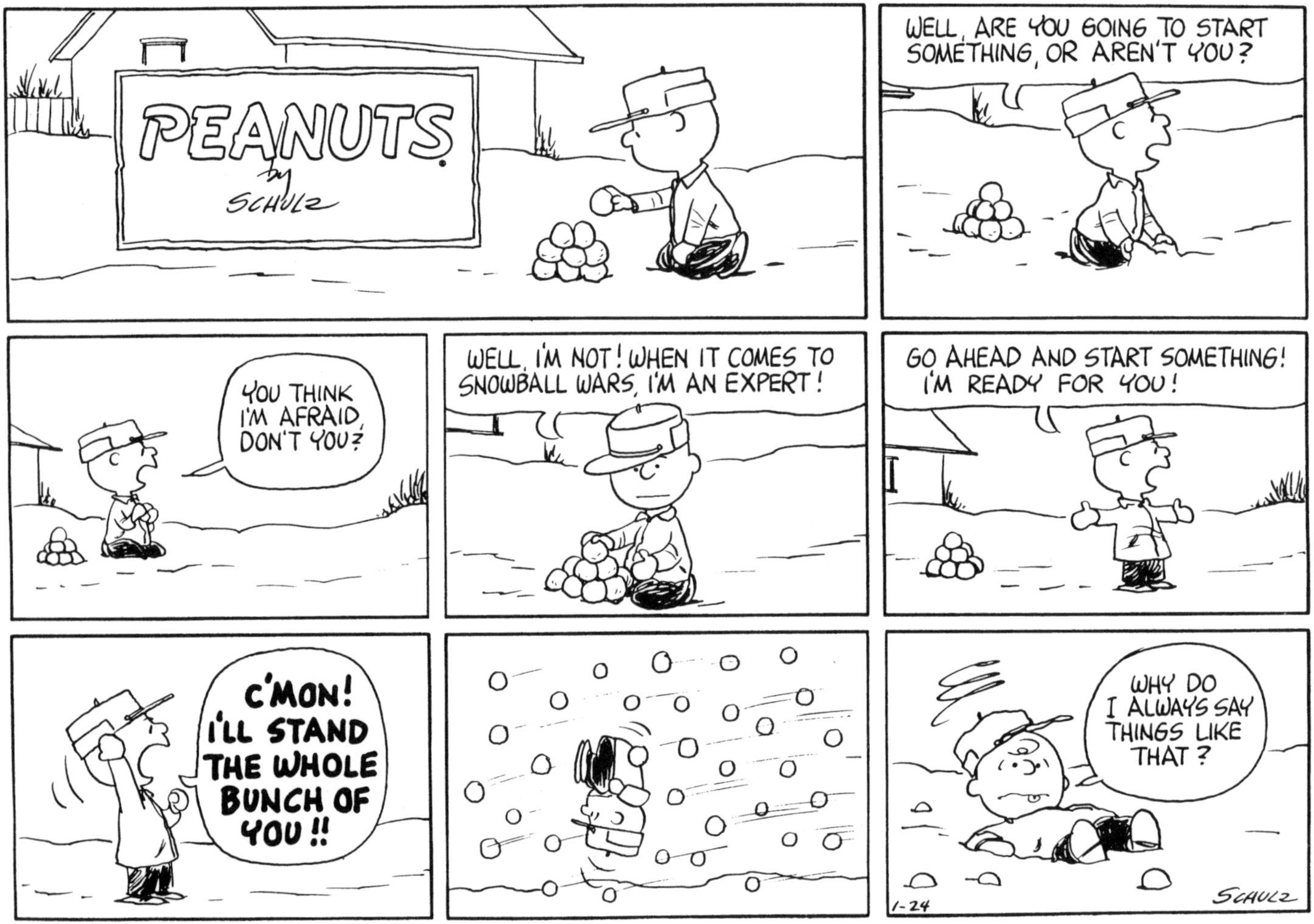
PEANUTS
by SCHULZ
WELL, ARE YOU GOING TO START SOMETHING, OR AREN'T YOU?
YOU THINK I'M AFRAID, DON'T YOU?
WELL, I'M NOT! WHEN IT COMES TO SNOWBALL WARS, I'M AN EXPERT!
GO AHEAD AND START SOMETHING! I'M READY FOR YOU!
C'MON! I'LL STAND THE WHOLE BUNCH OF YOU!!
WHY DO I ALWAYS SAY THINGS LIKE THAT?
1-24
SCHULZ

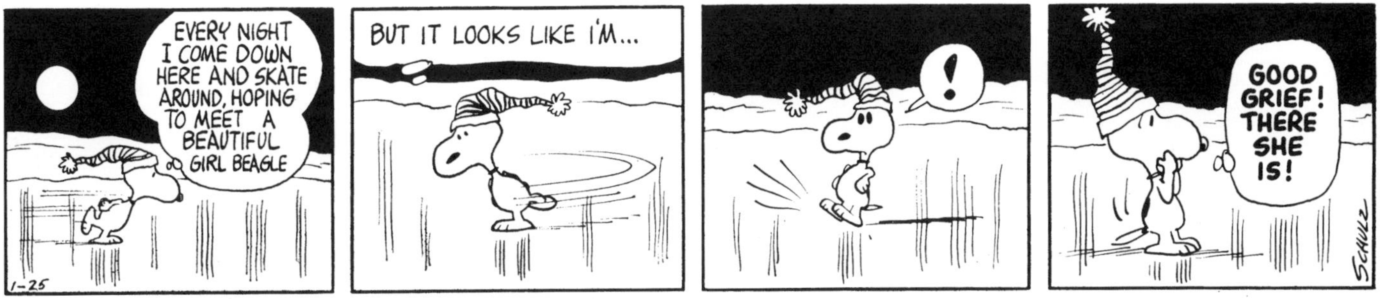
EVERY NIGHT I COME DOWN HERE AND SKATE AROUND, HOPING TO MEET A BEAUTIFUL GIRL BEAGLE
1-25
BUT IT LOOKS LIKE I'M...
!
GOOD GRIEF! THERE SHE IS!
SCHULZ

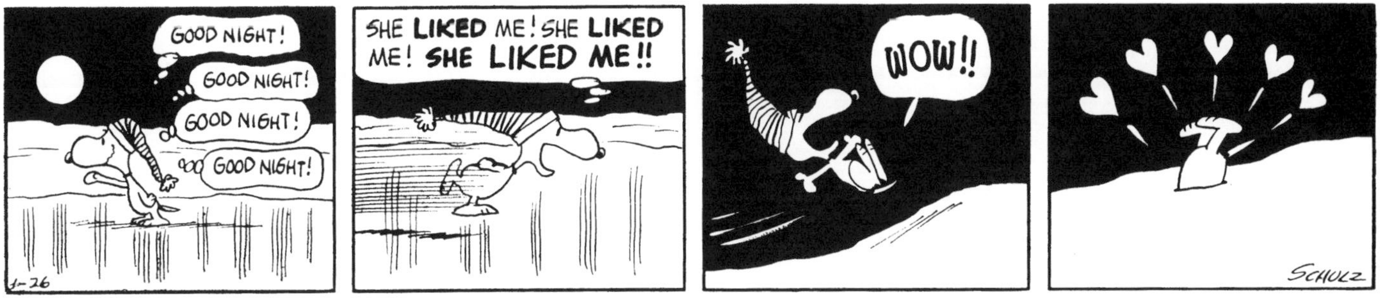
GOOD NIGHT!
GOOD NIGHT!
GOOD NIGHT!
GOOD NIGHT!
1-26
SHE **LIKED** ME! SHE **LIKED** ME! **SHE LIKED ME**!!
WOW!!
SCHULZ

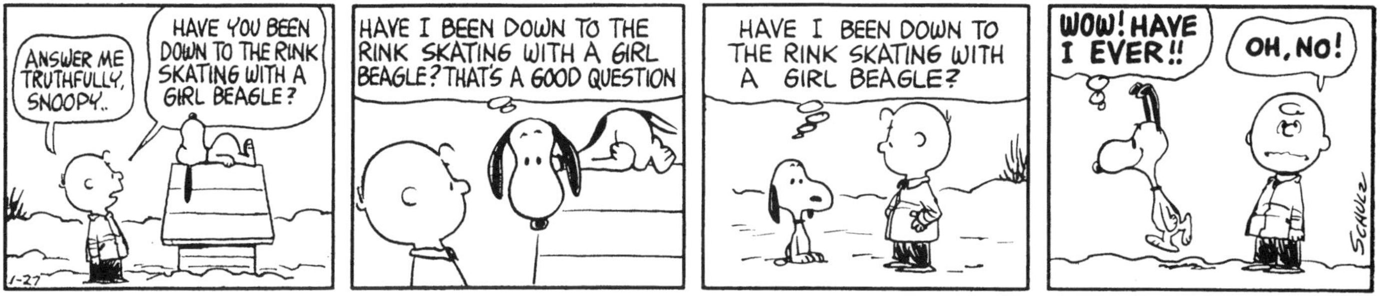
ANSWER ME TRUTHFULLY, SNOOPY..
HAVE YOU BEEN DOWN TO THE RINK SKATING WITH A GIRL BEAGLE?
1-27
HAVE I BEEN DOWN TO THE RINK SKATING WITH A GIRL BEAGLE? THAT'S A GOOD QUESTION
HAVE I BEEN DOWN TO THE RINK SKATING WITH A GIRL BEAGLE?
WOW! HAVE I EVER!!
OH, NO!
SCHULZ

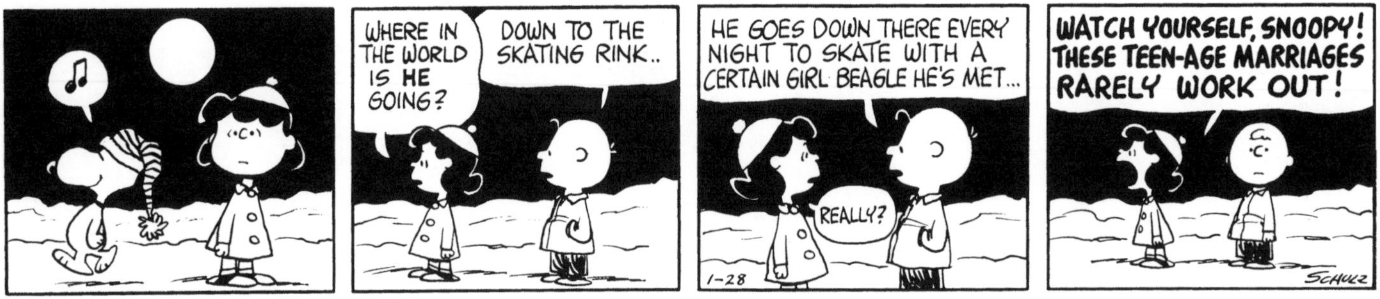
WHERE IN THE WORLD IS **HE** GOING?
DOWN TO THE SKATING RINK..
HE GOES DOWN THERE EVERY NIGHT TO SKATE WITH A CERTAIN GIRL BEAGLE HE'S MET...
REALLY?
1-28
WATCH YOURSELF, SNOOPY! THESE TEEN-AGE MARRIAGES RARELY WORK OUT!
SCHULZ

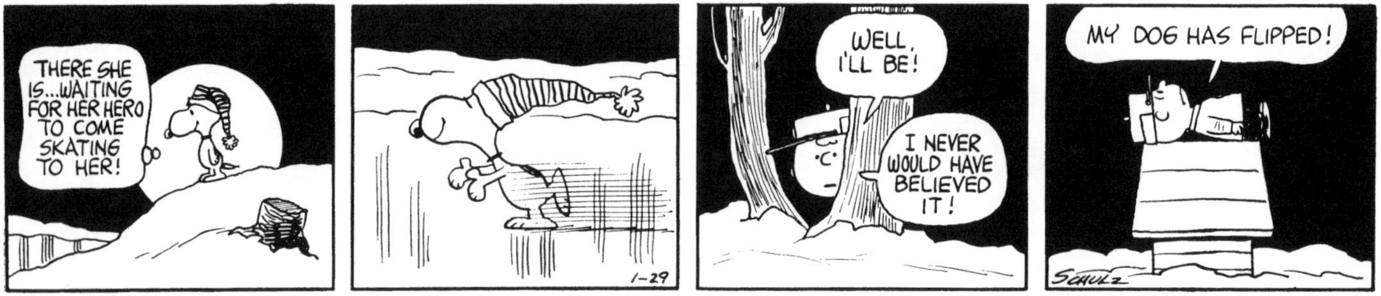
THERE SHE IS...WAITING FOR HER HERO TO COME SKATING TO HER!
1-29
WELL, I'LL BE!
I NEVER WOULD HAVE BELIEVED IT!
MY DOG HAS FLIPPED!
SCHULZ

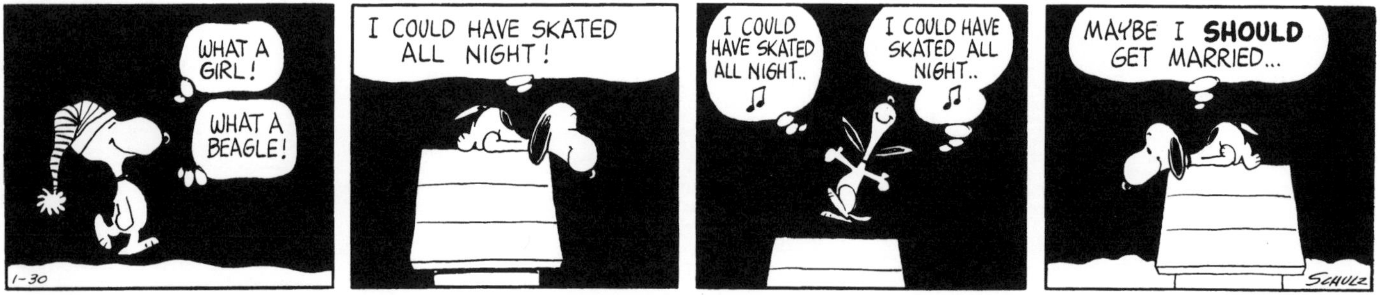
WHAT A GIRL!
WHAT A BEAGLE!
1-30
I COULD HAVE SKATED ALL NIGHT!
I COULD HAVE SKATED ALL NIGHT..
I COULD HAVE SKATED ALL NIGHT..
MAYBE I **SHOULD** GET MARRIED...
SCHULZ

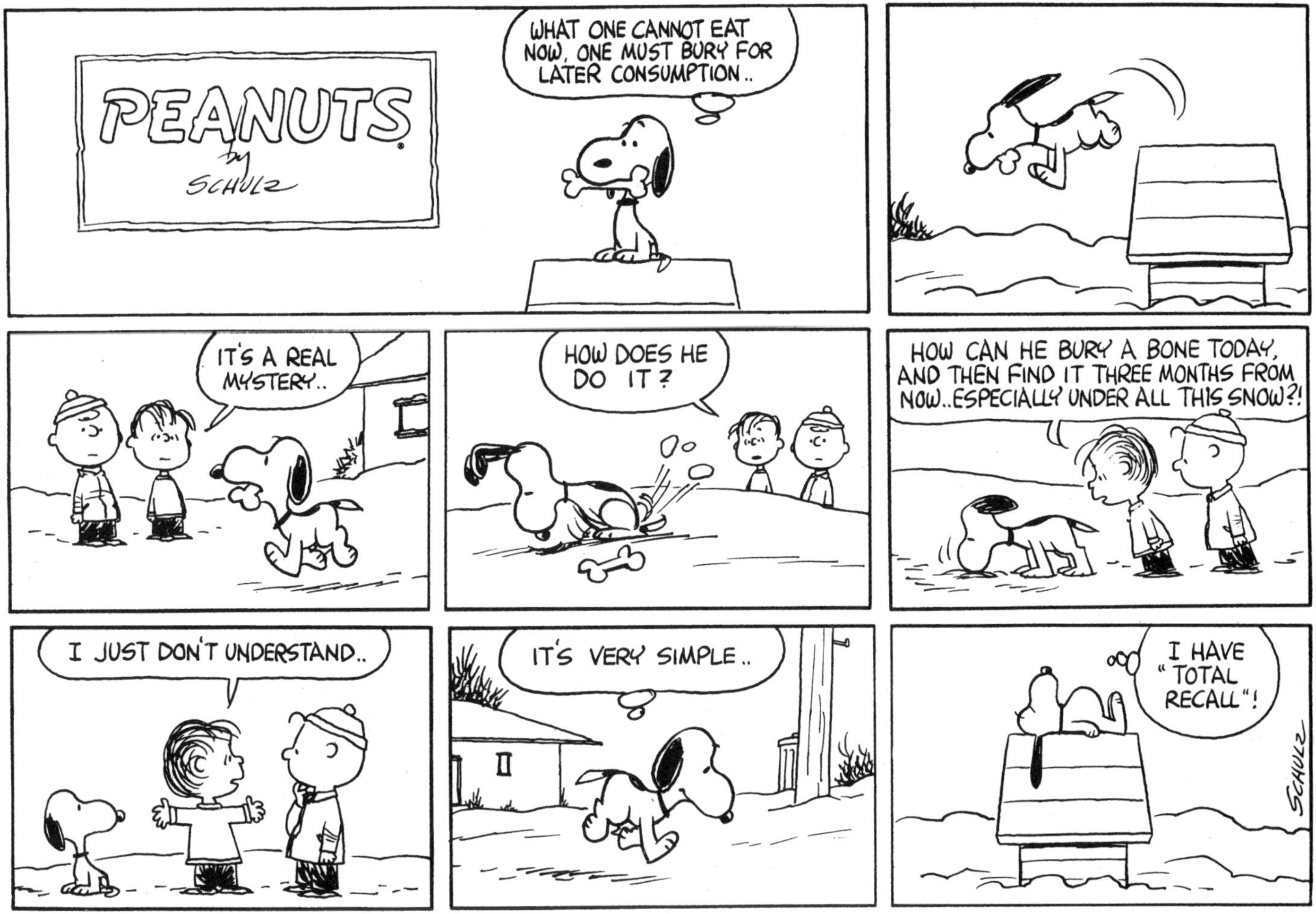
PEANUTS
by
SCHULZ
WHAT ONE CANNOT EAT NOW, ONE MUST BURY FOR LATER CONSUMPTION..
IT'S A REAL MYSTERY..
HOW DOES HE DO IT?
HOW CAN HE BURY A BONE TODAY, AND THEN FIND IT THREE MONTHS FROM NOW..ESPECIALLY UNDER ALL THIS SNOW?!
I JUST DON'T UNDERSTAND..
IT'S VERY SIMPLE..
I HAVE "TOTAL RECALL"!
SCHULZ

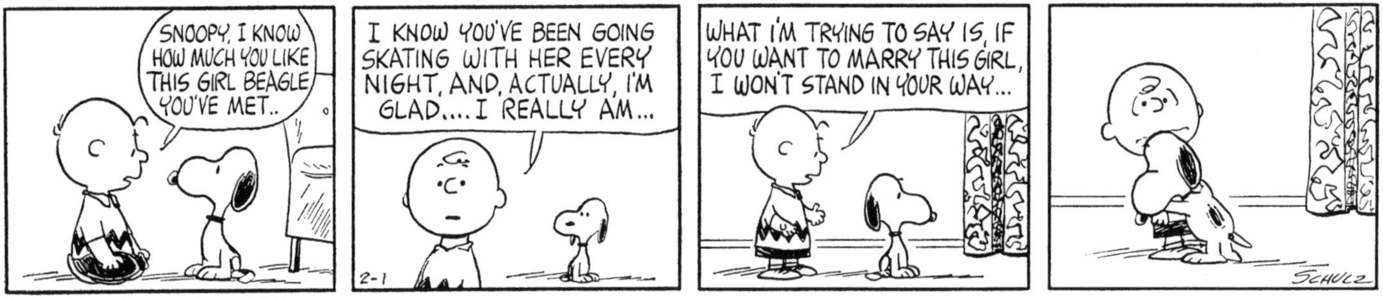
SNOOPY, I KNOW HOW MUCH YOU LIKE THIS GIRL BEAGLE YOU'VE MET..
I KNOW YOU'VE BEEN GOING SKATING WITH HER EVERY NIGHT, AND, ACTUALLY, I'M GLAD.... I REALLY AM...
2-1
WHAT I'M TRYING TO SAY IS, IF YOU WANT TO MARRY THIS GIRL, I WON'T STAND IN YOUR WAY...
SCHULZ

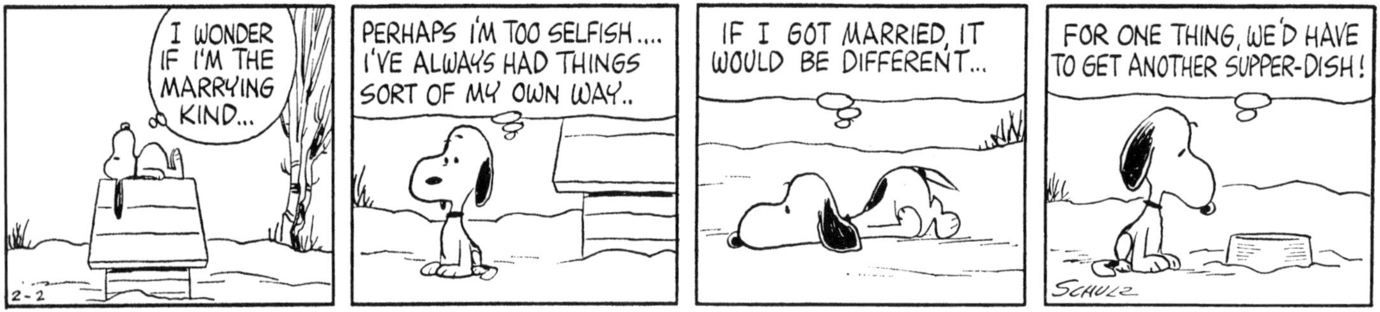
I WONDER IF I'M THE MARRYING KIND...
2-2
PERHAPS I'M TOO SELFISH.... I'VE ALWAYS HAD THINGS SORT OF MY OWN WAY..
IF I GOT MARRIED, IT WOULD BE DIFFERENT...
FOR ONE THING, WE'D HAVE TO GET ANOTHER SUPPER-DISH!
SCHULZ

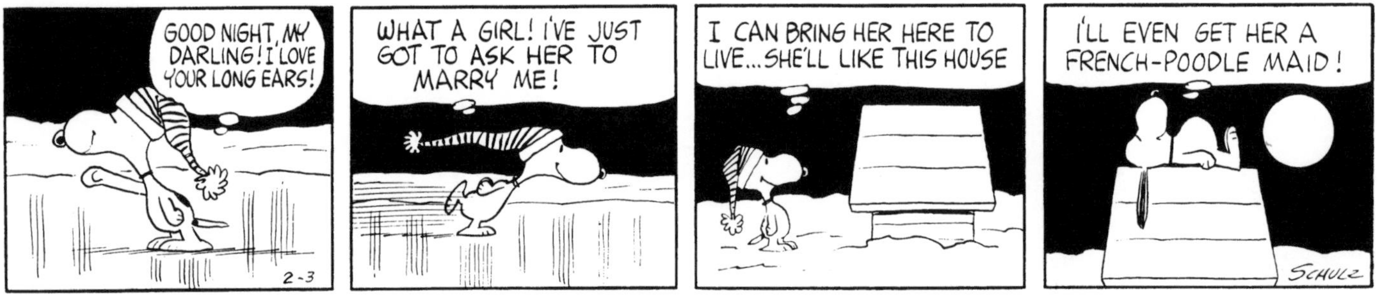
GOOD NIGHT, MY DARLING! I LOVE YOUR LONG EARS!
2-3
WHAT A GIRL! I'VE JUST GOT TO ASK HER TO MARRY ME!
I CAN BRING HER HERE TO LIVE...SHE'LL LIKE THIS HOUSE
I'LL EVEN GET HER A FRENCH-POODLE MAID!
SCHULZ

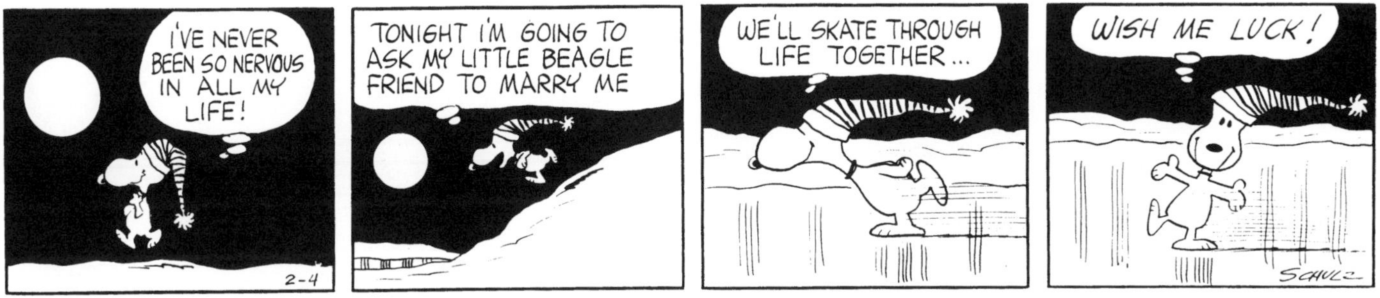
I'VE NEVER BEEN SO NERVOUS IN ALL MY LIFE!
2-4
TONIGHT I'M GOING TO ASK MY LITTLE BEAGLE FRIEND TO MARRY ME
WE'LL SKATE THROUGH LIFE TOGETHER...
WISH ME LUCK!
SCHULZ

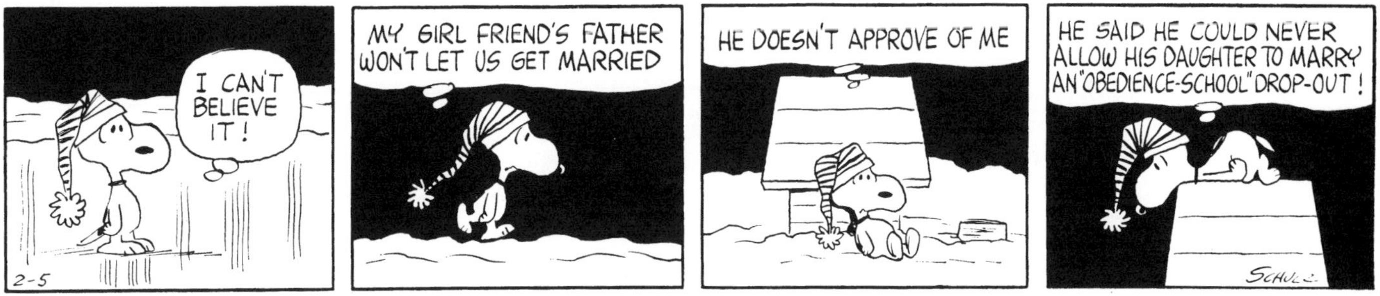
I CAN'T BELIEVE IT!
2-5
MY GIRL FRIEND'S FATHER WON'T LET US GET MARRIED
HE DOESN'T APPROVE OF ME
HE SAID HE COULD NEVER ALLOW HIS DAUGHTER TO MARRY AN "OBEDIENCE-SCHOOL" DROP-OUT!
SCHULZ

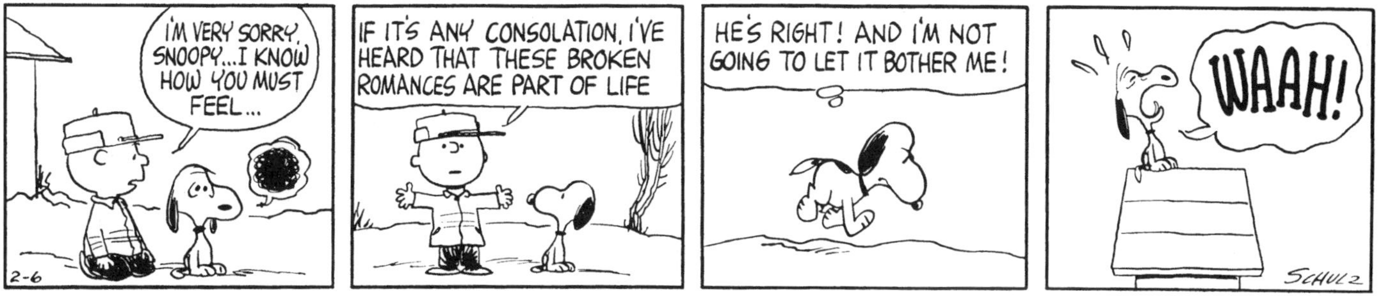
I'M VERY SORRY, SNOOPY...I KNOW HOW YOU MUST FEEL...
2-6
IF IT'S ANY CONSOLATION, I'VE HEARD THAT THESE BROKEN ROMANCES ARE PART OF LIFE
HE'S RIGHT! AND I'M NOT GOING TO LET IT BOTHER ME!
WAAH!
SCHULZ

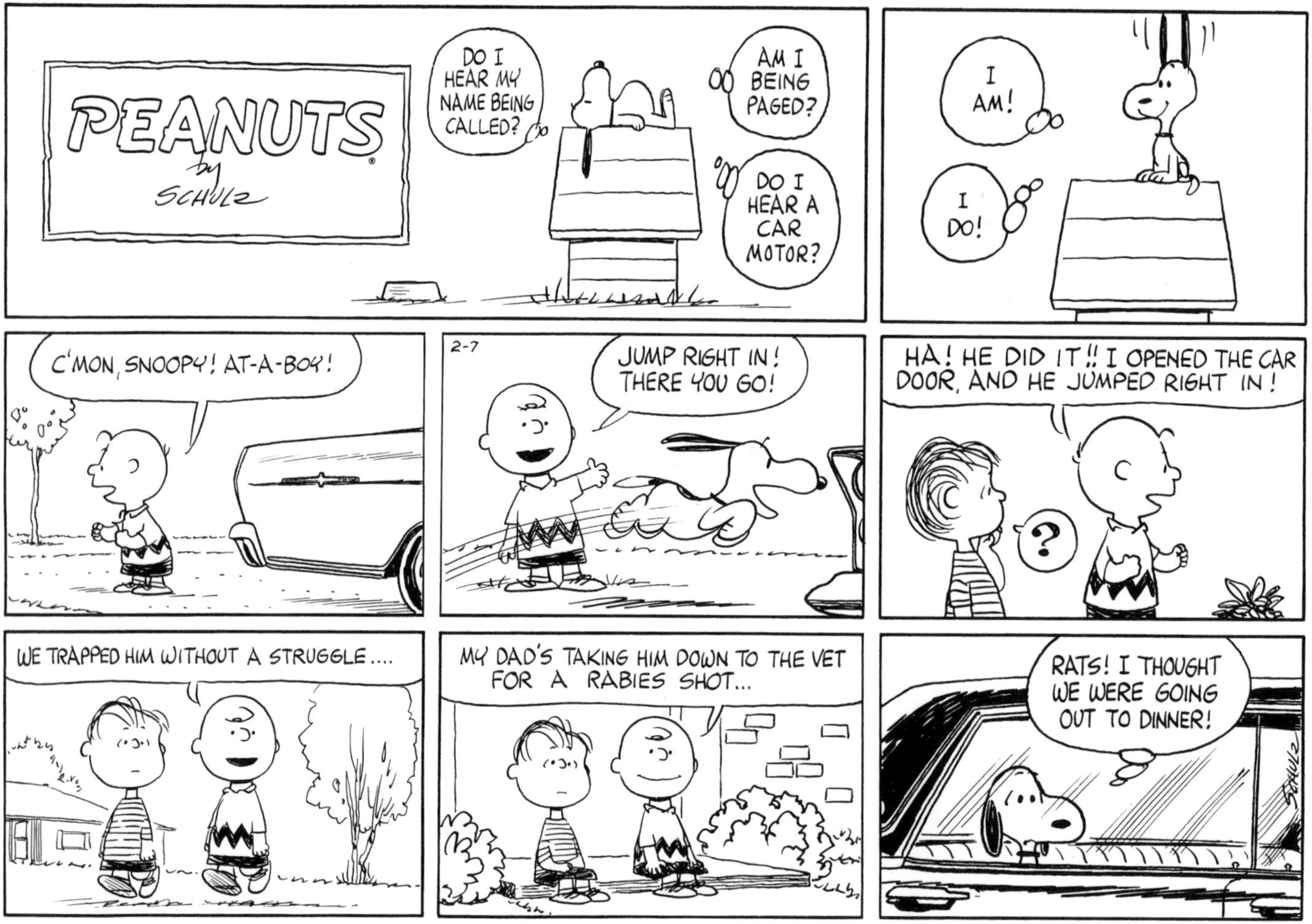
PEANUTS
by SCHULZ
DO I HEAR MY NAME BEING CALLED?
AM I BEING PAGED?
DO I HEAR A CAR MOTOR?
I AM!
I DO!
C'MON, SNOOPY! AT-A-BOY!
2-7
JUMP RIGHT IN! THERE YOU GO!
HA! HE DID IT!! I OPENED THE CAR DOOR, AND HE JUMPED RIGHT IN!
?
WE TRAPPED HIM WITHOUT A STRUGGLE....
MY DAD'S TAKING HIM DOWN TO THE VET FOR A RABIES SHOT...
RATS! I THOUGHT WE WERE GOING OUT TO DINNER!
SCHULZ

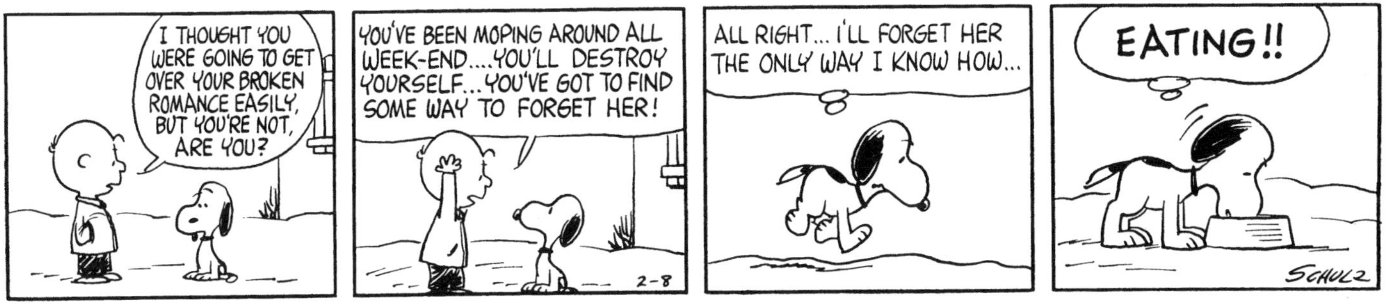
I THOUGHT YOU WERE GOING TO GET OVER YOUR BROKEN ROMANCE EASILY, BUT YOU'RE NOT, ARE YOU?
YOU'VE BEEN MOPING AROUND ALL WEEK-END....YOU'LL DESTROY YOURSELF...YOU'VE GOT TO FIND SOME WAY TO FORGET HER!
2-8
ALL RIGHT... I'LL FORGET HER THE ONLY WAY I KNOW HOW...
EATING!!
SCHULZ

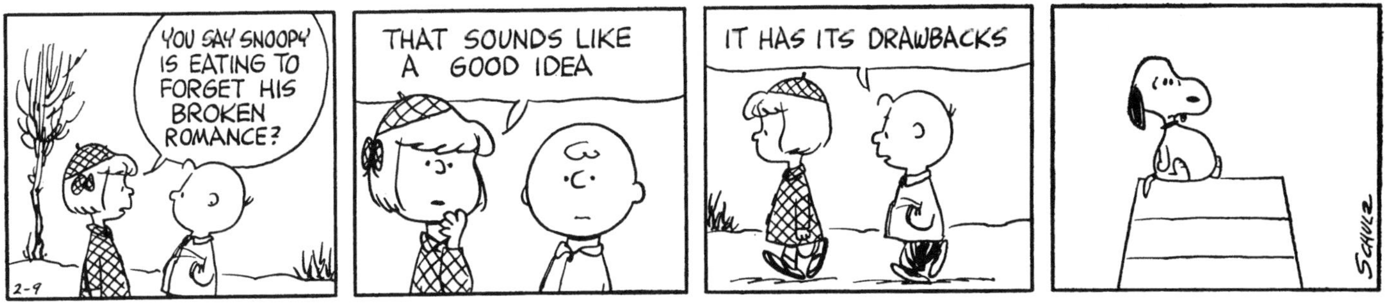
YOU SAY SNOOPY IS EATING TO FORGET HIS BROKEN ROMANCE?
2-9
THAT SOUNDS LIKE A GOOD IDEA
IT HAS ITS DRAWBACKS
SCHULZ

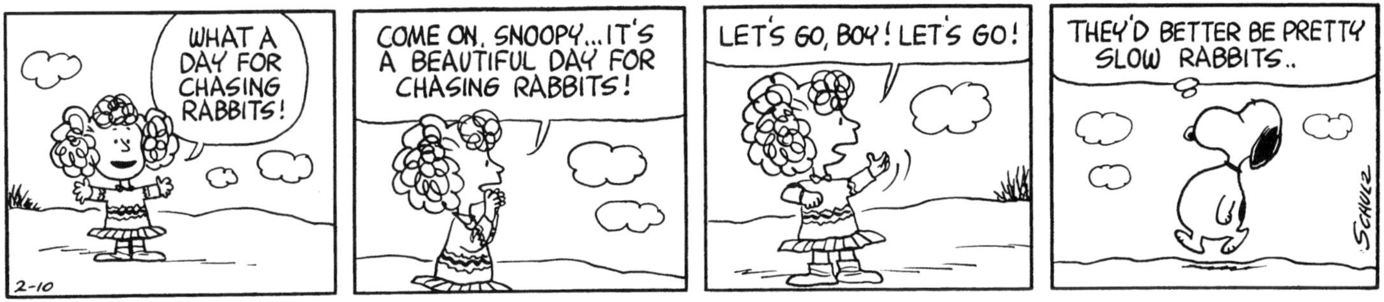
WHAT A DAY FOR CHASING RABBITS!
2-10
COME ON, SNOOPY...IT'S A BEAUTIFUL DAY FOR CHASING RABBITS!
LET'S GO, BOY! LET'S GO!
THEY'D BETTER BE PRETTY SLOW RABBITS..
SCHULZ

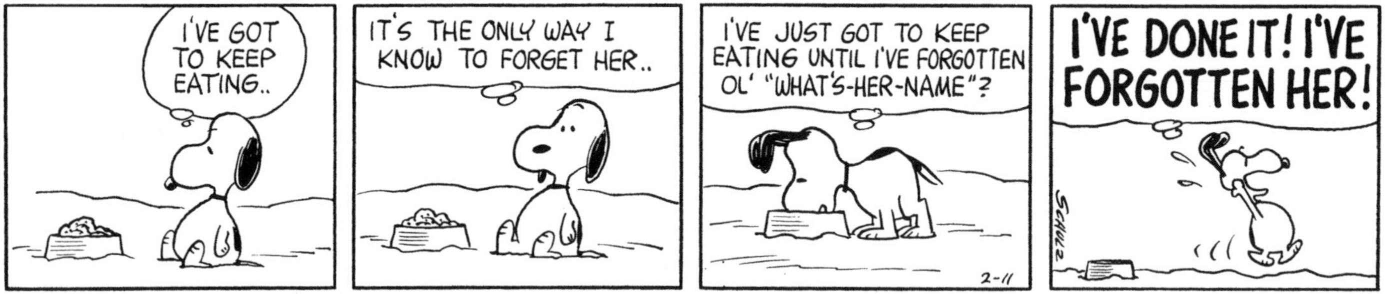
I'VE GOT TO KEEP EATING..
IT'S THE ONLY WAY I KNOW TO FORGET HER..
I'VE JUST GOT TO KEEP EATING UNTIL I'VE FORGOTTEN OL' "WHAT'S-HER-NAME"?
2-11
I'VE DONE IT! I'VE FORGOTTEN HER!

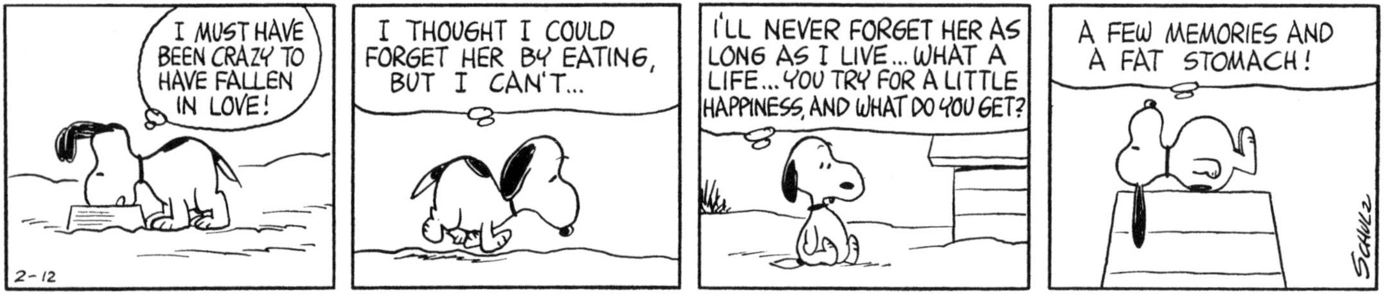
I MUST HAVE BEEN CRAZY TO HAVE FALLEN IN LOVE!
2-12
I THOUGHT I COULD FORGET HER BY EATING, BUT I CAN'T...
I'LL NEVER FORGET HER AS LONG AS I LIVE... WHAT A LIFE... YOU TRY FOR A LITTLE HAPPINESS, AND WHAT DO YOU GET?
A FEW MEMORIES AND A FAT STOMACH!

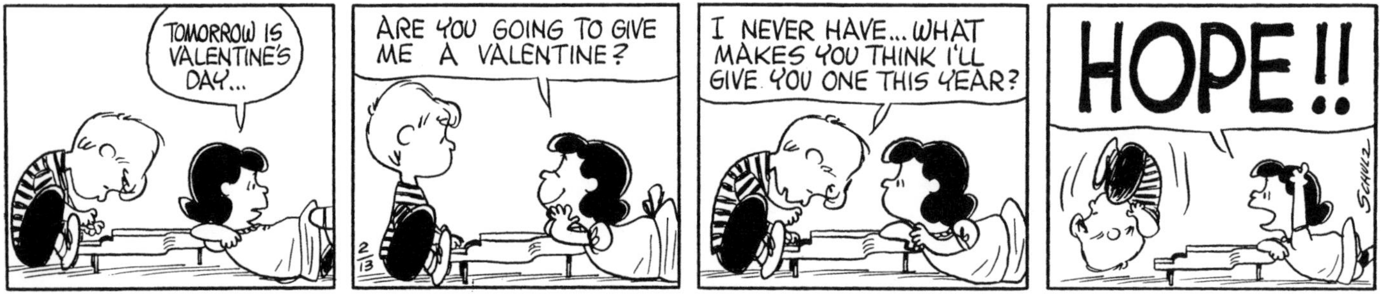
TOMORROW IS VALENTINE'S DAY...
ARE YOU GOING TO GIVE ME A VALENTINE?
2/13
I NEVER HAVE... WHAT MAKES YOU THINK I'LL GIVE YOU ONE THIS YEAR?
HOPE!!

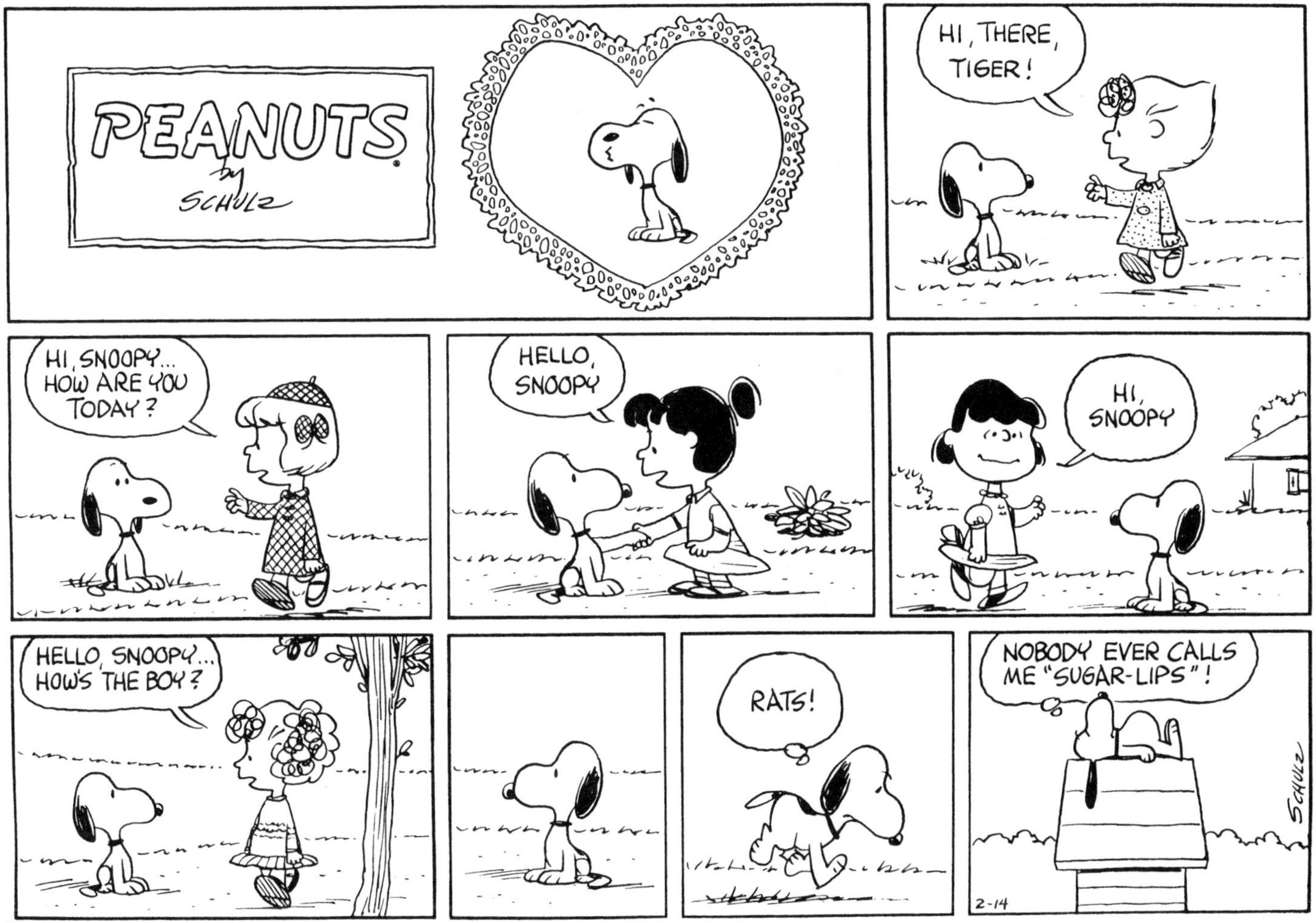
PEANUTS
by SCHULZ
HI, THERE, TIGER!
HI, SNOOPY... HOW ARE YOU TODAY?
HELLO, SNOOPY
HI, SNOOPY
HELLO, SNOOPY... HOW'S THE BOY?
RATS!
NOBODY EVER CALLS ME "SUGAR-LIPS"!
2-14
SCHULZ

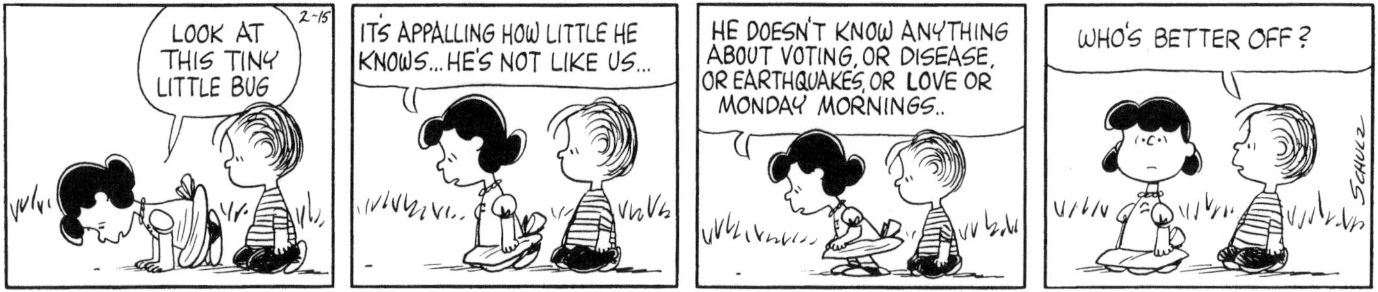
2-15
LOOK AT THIS TINY LITTLE BUG
IT'S APPALLING HOW LITTLE HE KNOWS... HE'S NOT LIKE US...
HE DOESN'T KNOW ANYTHING ABOUT VOTING, OR DISEASE, OR EARTHQUAKES, OR LOVE OR MONDAY MORNINGS..
WHO'S BETTER OFF?
SCHULZ

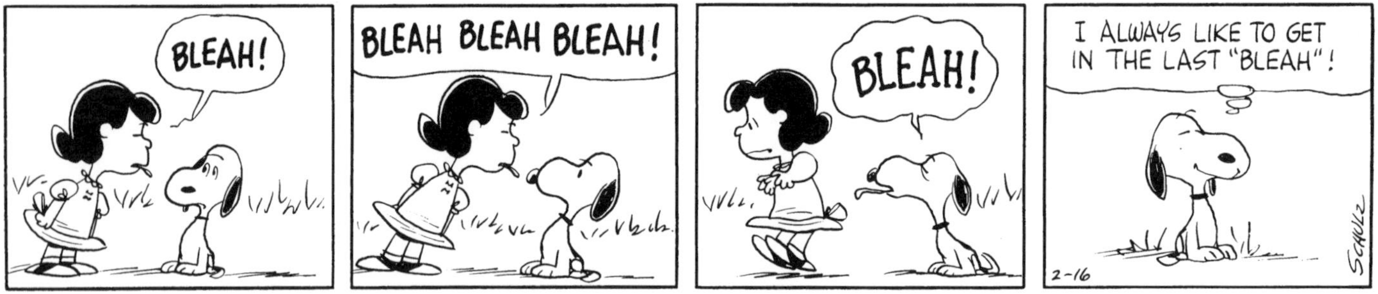
BLEAH!
BLEAH BLEAH BLEAH!
BLEAH!
I ALWAYS LIKE TO GET IN THE LAST "BLEAH"!
2-16
SCHULZ

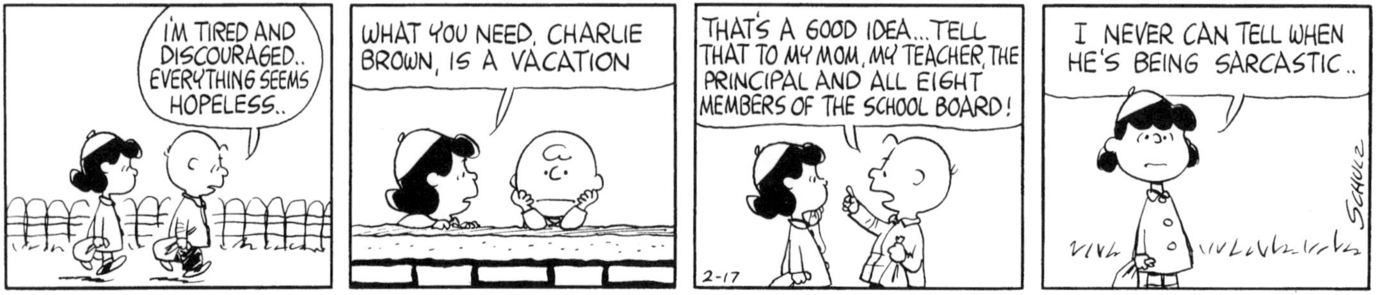
I'M TIRED AND DISCOURAGED.. EVERYTHING SEEMS HOPELESS..
WHAT YOU NEED, CHARLIE BROWN, IS A VACATION
THAT'S A GOOD IDEA... TELL THAT TO MY MOM, MY TEACHER, THE PRINCIPAL AND ALL EIGHT MEMBERS OF THE SCHOOL BOARD!
2-17
I NEVER CAN TELL WHEN HE'S BEING SARCASTIC..
SCHULZ

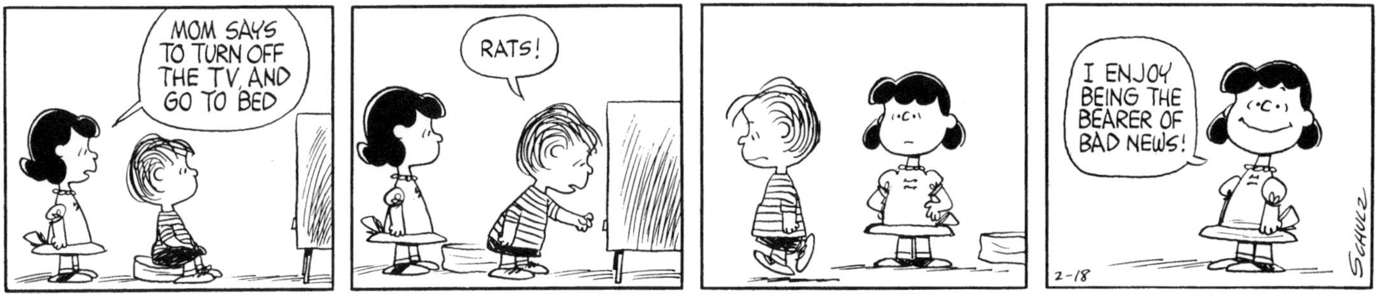
MOM SAYS TO TURN OFF THE TV AND GO TO BED
RATS!
I ENJOY BEING THE BEARER OF BAD NEWS!
2-18
SCHULZ

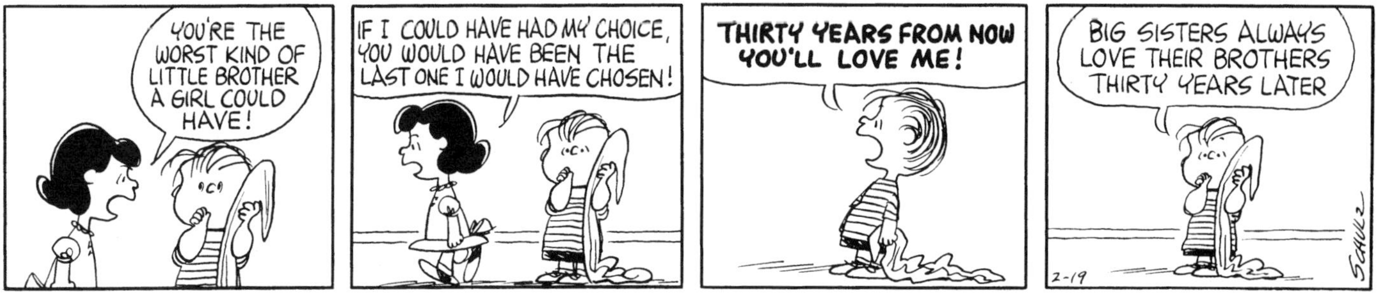
YOU'RE THE WORST KIND OF LITTLE BROTHER A GIRL COULD HAVE!
IF I COULD HAVE HAD MY CHOICE, YOU WOULD HAVE BEEN THE LAST ONE I WOULD HAVE CHOSEN!
THIRTY YEARS FROM NOW YOU'LL LOVE ME!
BIG SISTERS ALWAYS LOVE THEIR BROTHERS THIRTY YEARS LATER
2-19
SCHULZ

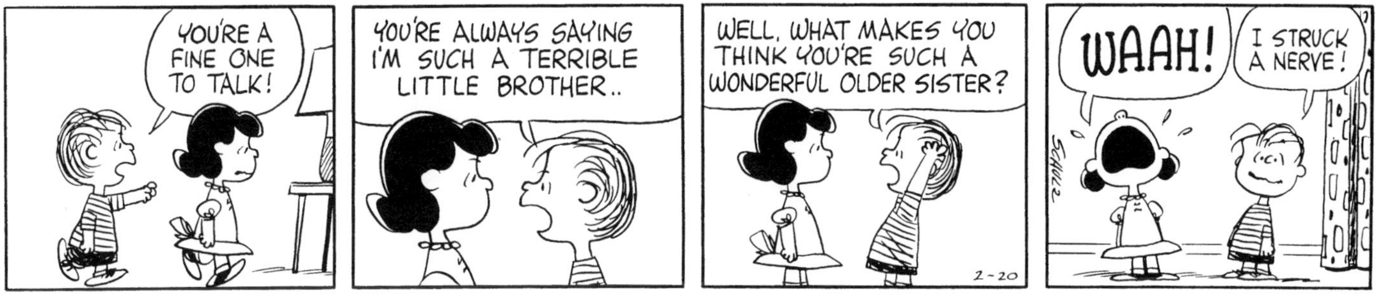
YOU'RE A FINE ONE TO TALK!
YOU'RE ALWAYS SAYING I'M SUCH A TERRIBLE LITTLE BROTHER..
WELL, WHAT MAKES YOU THINK YOU'RE SUCH A WONDERFUL OLDER SISTER?
2-20
SCHULZ
WAAH!
I STRUCK A NERVE!

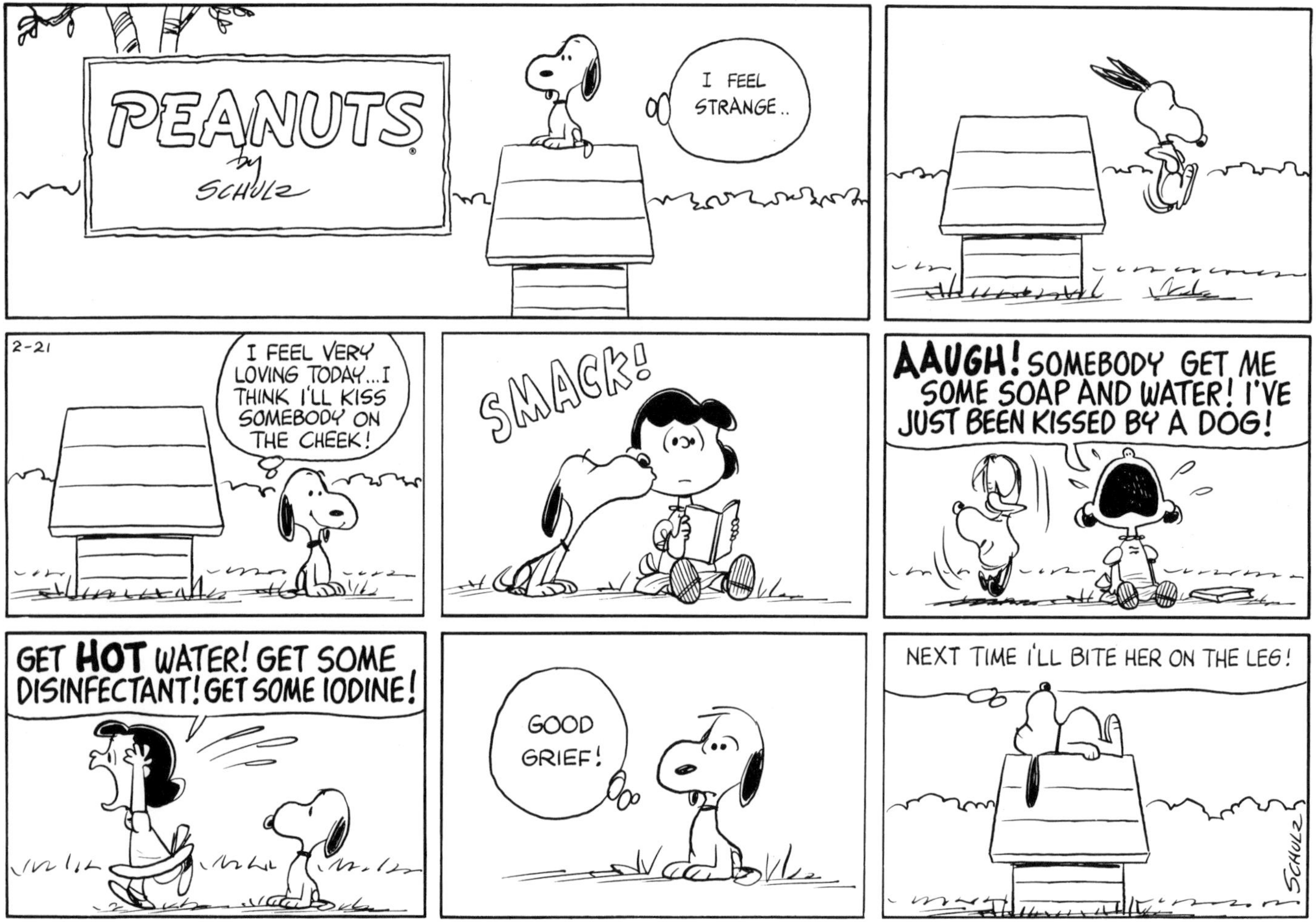
PEANUTS
by SCHULZ
I FEEL STRANGE..
2-21
I FEEL VERY LOVING TODAY...I THINK I'LL KISS SOMEBODY ON THE CHEEK!
SMACK!
AAUGH! SOMEBODY GET ME SOME SOAP AND WATER! I'VE JUST BEEN KISSED BY A DOG!
GET HOT WATER! GET SOME DISINFECTANT! GET SOME IODINE!
GOOD GRIEF!
NEXT TIME I'LL BITE HER ON THE LEG!
SCHULZ

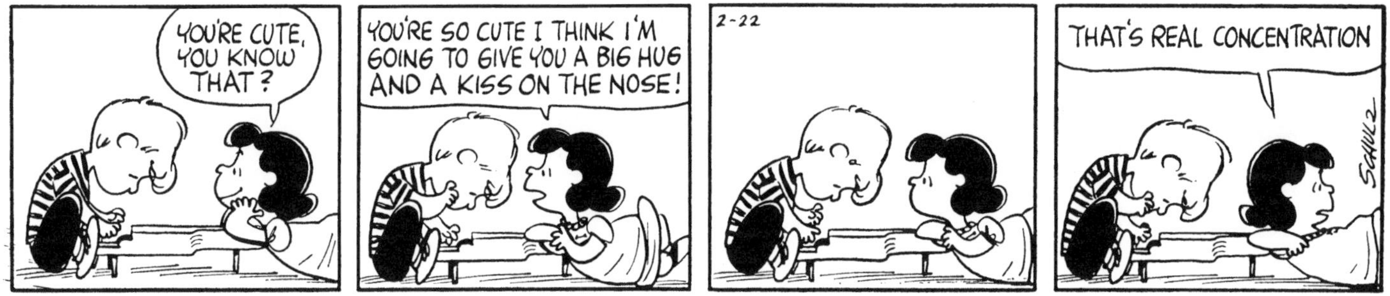
YOU'RE CUTE, YOU KNOW THAT?
YOU'RE SO CUTE I THINK I'M GOING TO GIVE YOU A BIG HUG AND A KISS ON THE NOSE!
2-22
THAT'S REAL CONCENTRATION
SCHULZ

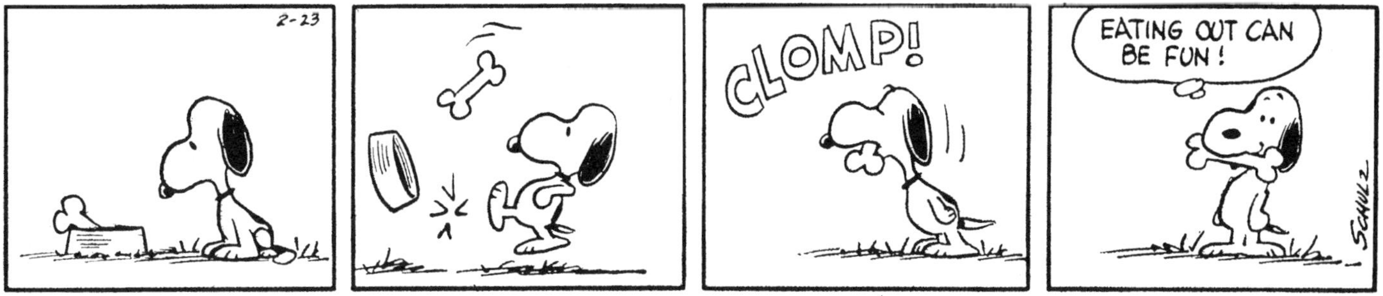
2-23
CLOMP!
EATING OUT CAN BE FUN!
SCHULZ

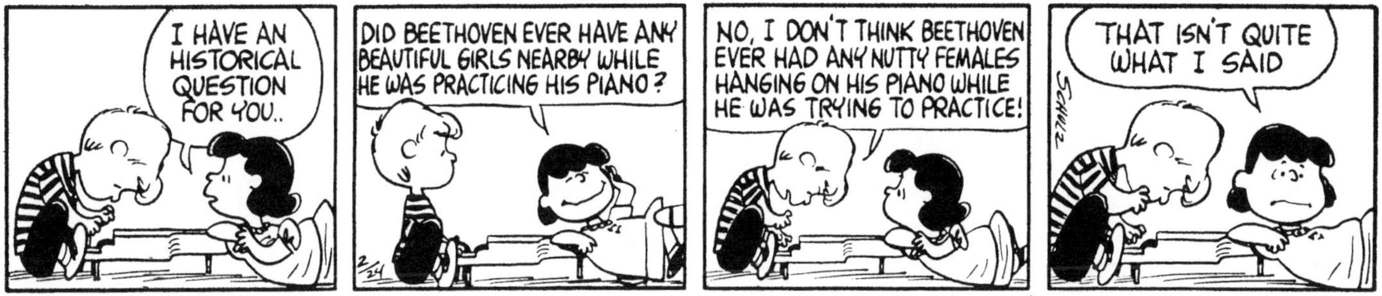
I HAVE AN HISTORICAL QUESTION FOR YOU..
DID BEETHOVEN EVER HAVE ANY BEAUTIFUL GIRLS NEARBY WHILE HE WAS PRACTICING HIS PIANO?
2/24
NO, I DON'T THINK BEETHOVEN EVER HAD ANY NUTTY FEMALES HANGING ON HIS PIANO WHILE HE WAS TRYING TO PRACTICE!
SCHULZ
THAT ISN'T QUITE WHAT I SAID

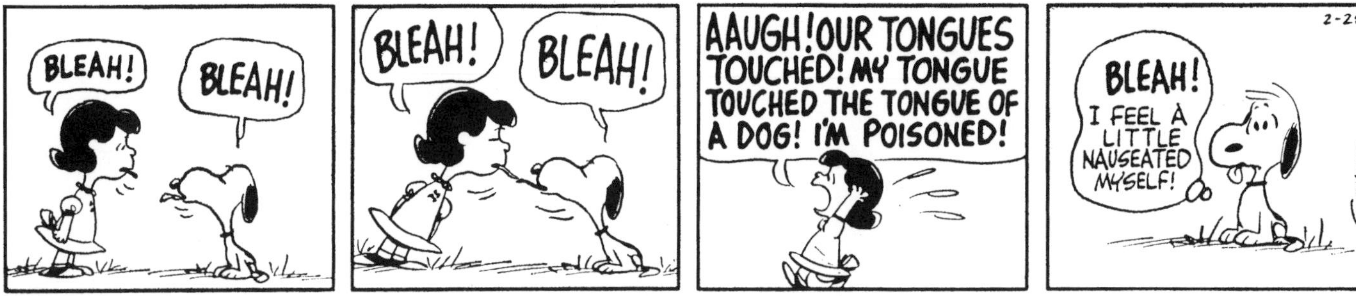
BLEAH!
BLEAH!
BLEAH!
BLEAH!
AAUGH! OUR TONGUES TOUCHED! MY TONGUE TOUCHED THE TONGUE OF A DOG! I'M POISONED!
2-25
BLEAH! I FEEL A LITTLE NAUSEATED MYSELF!
SCHULZ

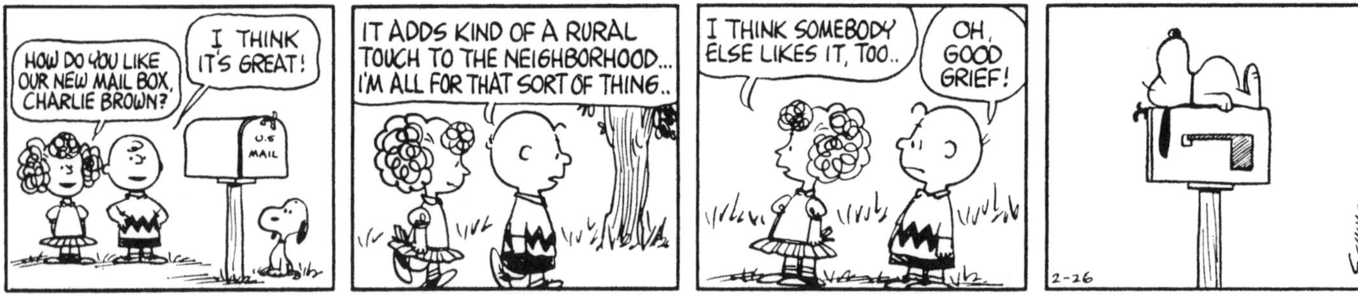
HOW DO YOU LIKE OUR NEW MAIL BOX, CHARLIE BROWN?
I THINK IT'S GREAT!
U.S MAIL
IT ADDS KIND OF A RURAL TOUCH TO THE NEIGHBORHOOD... I'M ALL FOR THAT SORT OF THING..
I THINK SOMEBODY ELSE LIKES IT, TOO..
OH, GOOD GRIEF!
SCHULZ
2-26

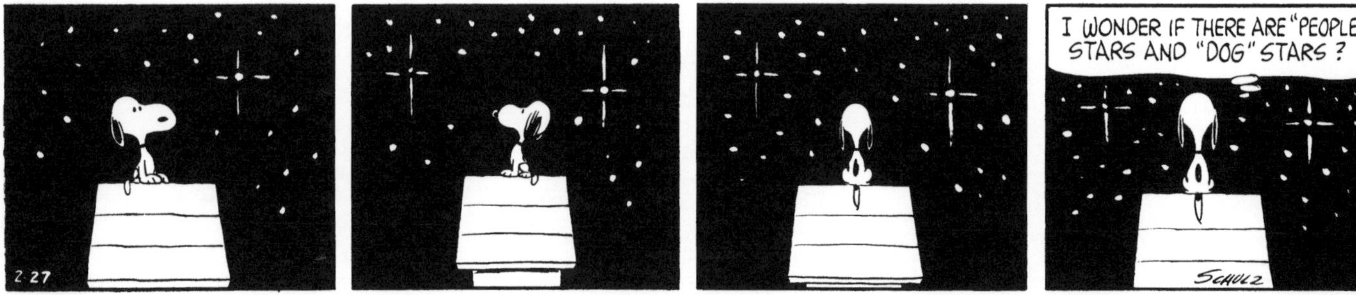
2-27
I WONDER IF THERE ARE "PEOPLE" STARS AND "DOG" STARS ?
SCHULZ

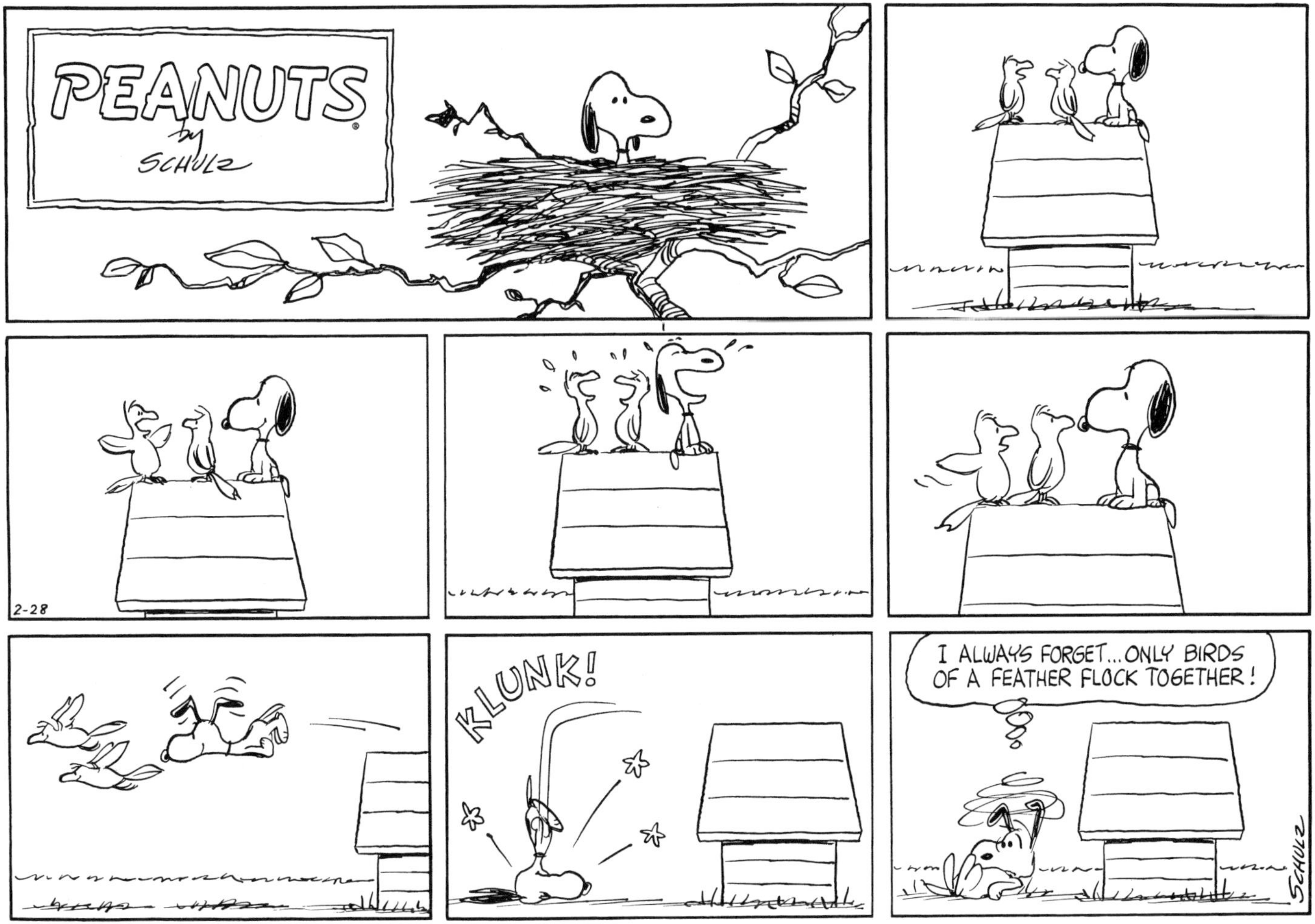
PEANUTS
by
SCHULZ
2-28
KLUNK!
I ALWAYS FORGET...ONLY BIRDS OF A FEATHER FLOCK TOGETHER!
SCHULZ

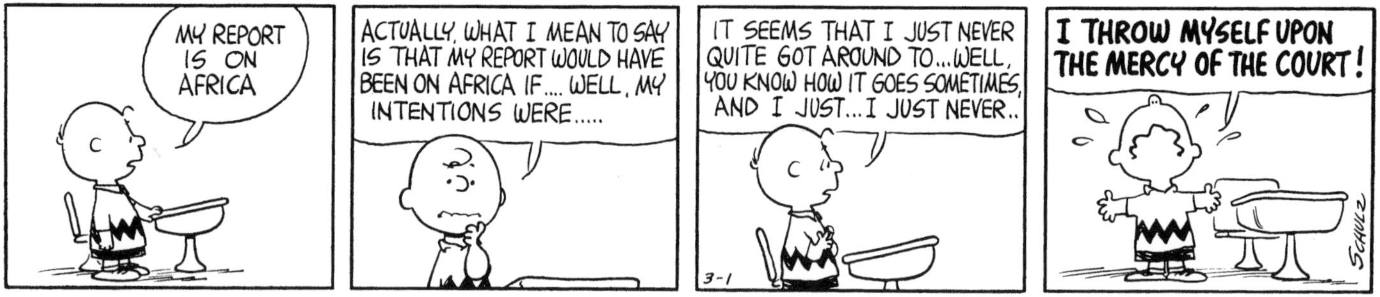
MY REPORT IS ON AFRICA
ACTUALLY, WHAT I MEAN TO SAY IS THAT MY REPORT WOULD HAVE BEEN ON AFRICA IF.... WELL, MY INTENTIONS WERE.....
IT SEEMS THAT I JUST NEVER QUITE GOT AROUND TO...WELL, YOU KNOW HOW IT GOES SOMETIMES, AND I JUST...I JUST NEVER..
3-1
I THROW MYSELF UPON THE MERCY OF THE COURT!
SCHULZ

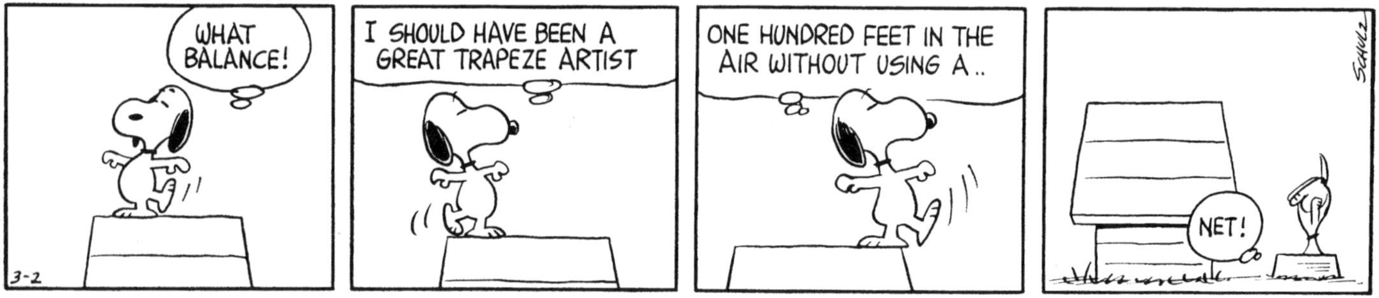
WHAT BALANCE!
3-2
I SHOULD HAVE BEEN A GREAT TRAPEZE ARTIST
ONE HUNDRED FEET IN THE AIR WITHOUT USING A..
SCHULZ
NET!

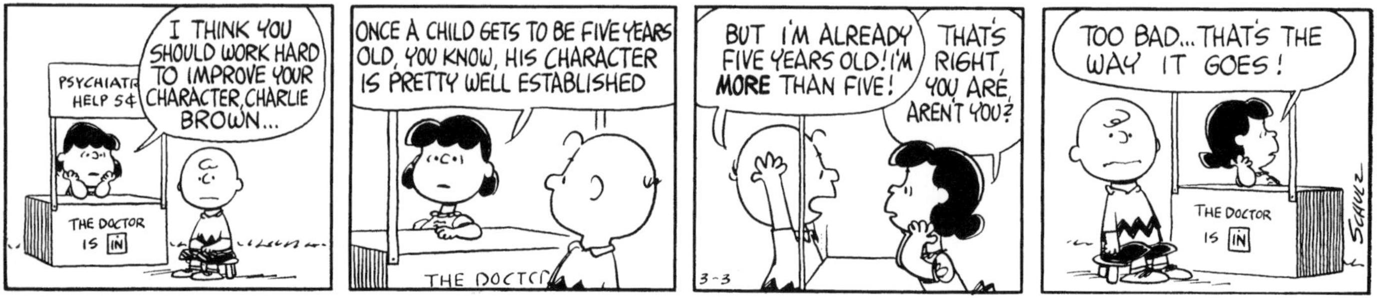
PSYCHIATR HELP 5¢
I THINK YOU SHOULD WORK HARD TO IMPROVE YOUR CHARACTER, CHARLIE BROWN...
THE DOCTOR IS IN
ONCE A CHILD GETS TO BE FIVE YEARS OLD, YOU KNOW, HIS CHARACTER IS PRETTY WELL ESTABLISHED
THE DOCTC
BUT I'M ALREADY FIVE YEARS OLD! I'M **MORE** THAN FIVE!
THAT'S RIGHT, YOU ARE, AREN'T YOU?
3-3
TOO BAD...THAT'S THE WAY IT GOES!
THE DOCTOR IS IN
SCHULZ

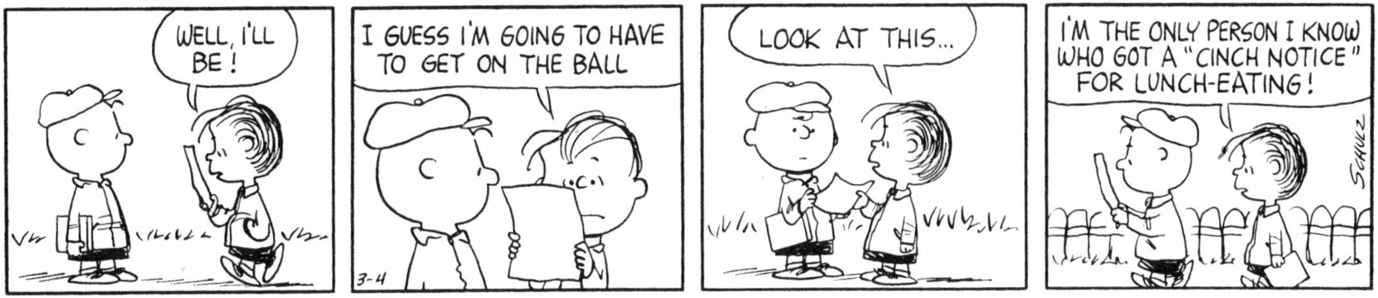
WELL, I'LL BE!
I GUESS I'M GOING TO HAVE TO GET ON THE BALL
3-4
LOOK AT THIS...
I'M THE ONLY PERSON I KNOW WHO GOT A "CINCH NOTICE" FOR LUNCH-EATING!
SCHULZ

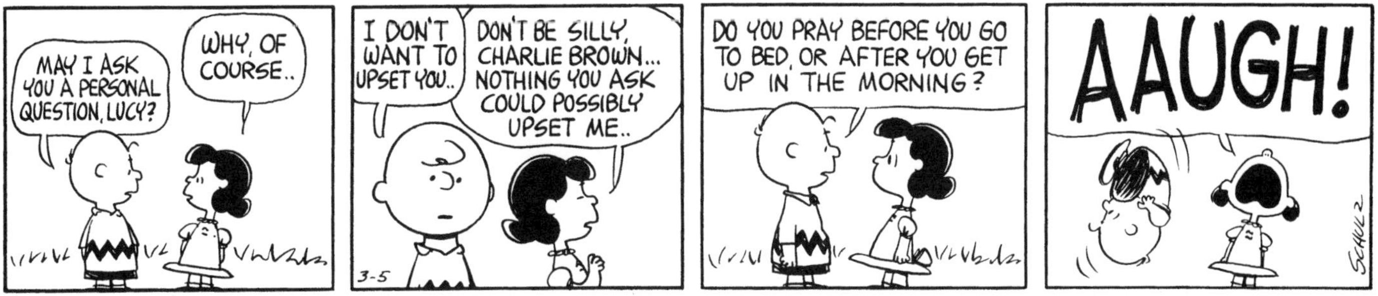
MAY I ASK YOU A PERSONAL QUESTION, LUCY?
WHY, OF COURSE..
I DON'T WANT TO UPSET YOU..
DON'T BE SILLY, CHARLIE BROWN... NOTHING YOU ASK COULD POSSIBLY UPSET ME..
3-5
DO YOU PRAY BEFORE YOU GO TO BED, OR AFTER YOU GET UP IN THE MORNING?
AAUGH!
SCHULZ

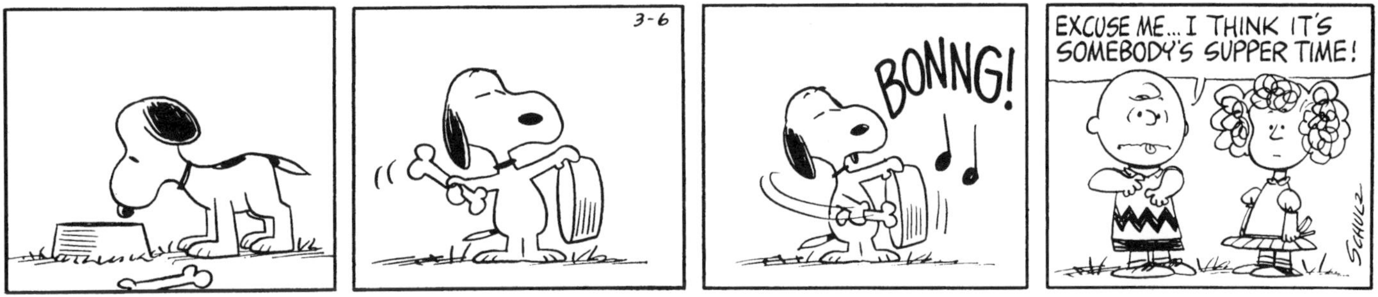
3-6
BONNG!
EXCUSE ME... I THINK IT'S SOMEBODY'S SUPPER TIME!
SCHULZ

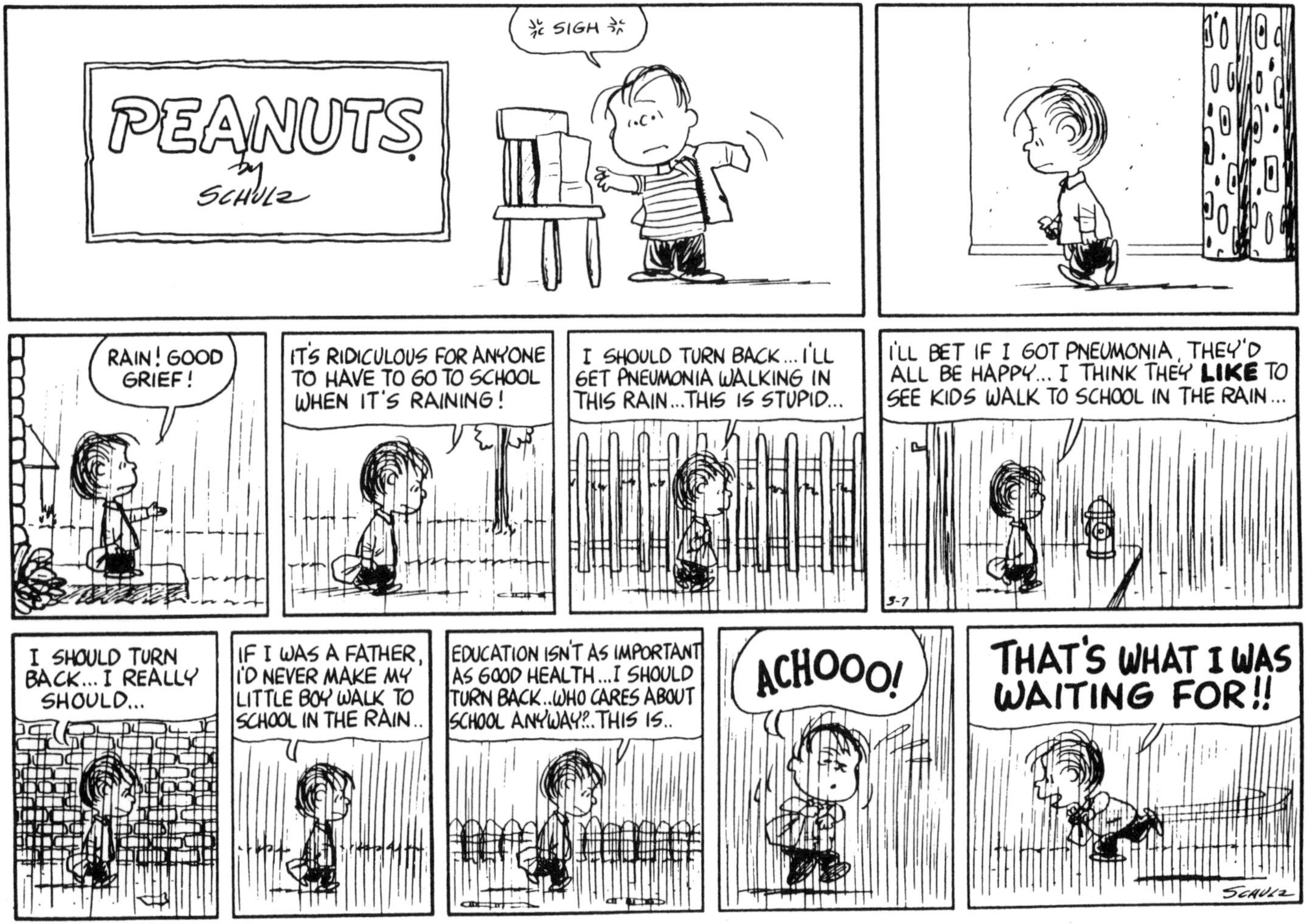
PEANUTS
by
SCHULZ
SIGH
RAIN! GOOD GRIEF!
IT'S RIDICULOUS FOR ANYONE TO HAVE TO GO TO SCHOOL WHEN IT'S RAINING!
I SHOULD TURN BACK... I'LL GET PNEUMONIA WALKING IN THIS RAIN... THIS IS STUPID...
I'LL BET IF I GOT PNEUMONIA, THEY'D ALL BE HAPPY... I THINK THEY **LIKE** TO SEE KIDS WALK TO SCHOOL IN THE RAIN...
3-7
I SHOULD TURN BACK... I REALLY SHOULD...
IF I WAS A FATHER, I'D NEVER MAKE MY LITTLE BOY WALK TO SCHOOL IN THE RAIN..
EDUCATION ISN'T AS IMPORTANT AS GOOD HEALTH... I SHOULD TURN BACK.. WHO CARES ABOUT SCHOOL ANYWAY?.. THIS IS..
ACHOOO!
THAT'S WHAT I WAS WAITING FOR!!
SCHULZ

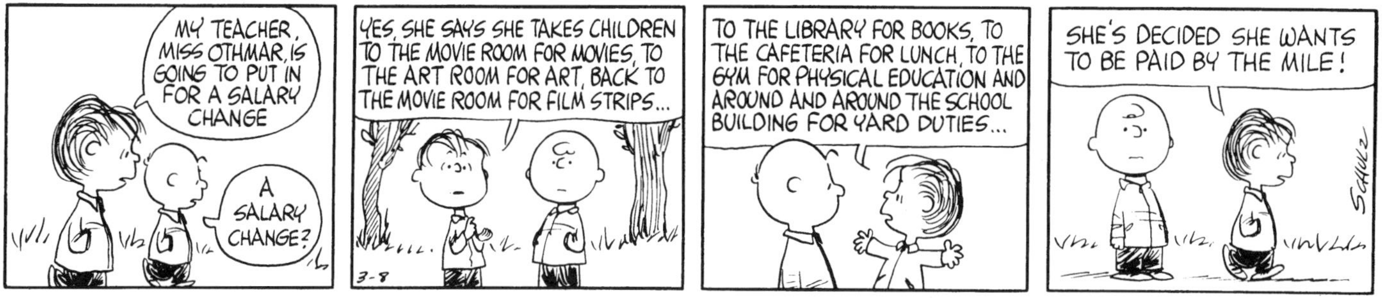
MY TEACHER, MISS OTHMAR, IS GOING TO PUT IN FOR A SALARY CHANGE
A SALARY CHANGE?
YES, SHE SAYS SHE TAKES CHILDREN TO THE MOVIE ROOM FOR MOVIES, TO THE ART ROOM FOR ART, BACK TO THE MOVIE ROOM FOR FILM STRIPS...
3-8
TO THE LIBRARY FOR BOOKS, TO THE CAFETERIA FOR LUNCH, TO THE GYM FOR PHYSICAL EDUCATION AND AROUND AND AROUND THE SCHOOL BUILDING FOR YARD DUTIES...
SHE'S DECIDED SHE WANTS TO BE PAID BY THE MILE!

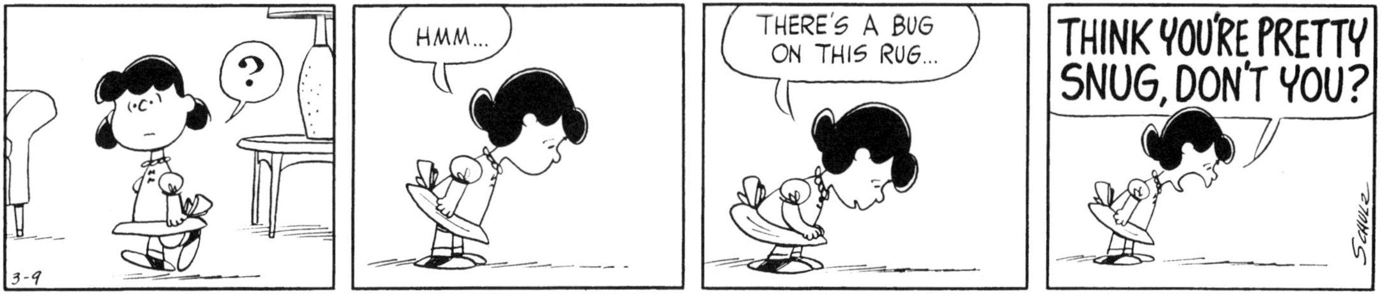
?
3-9
HMM...
THERE'S A BUG ON THIS RUG...
THINK YOU'RE PRETTY SNUG, DON'T YOU?

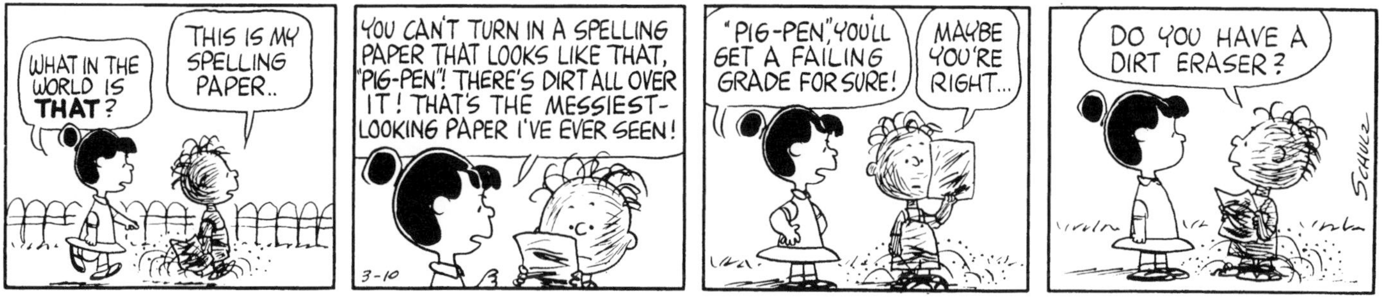
WHAT IN THE WORLD IS **THAT**?
THIS IS MY SPELLING PAPER..
YOU CAN'T TURN IN A SPELLING PAPER THAT LOOKS LIKE THAT, "PIG-PEN"! THERE'S DIRT ALL OVER IT! THAT'S THE MESSIEST-LOOKING PAPER I'VE EVER SEEN!
3-10
"PIG-PEN", YOU'LL GET A FAILING GRADE FOR SURE!
MAYBE YOU'RE RIGHT...
DO YOU HAVE A DIRT ERASER?

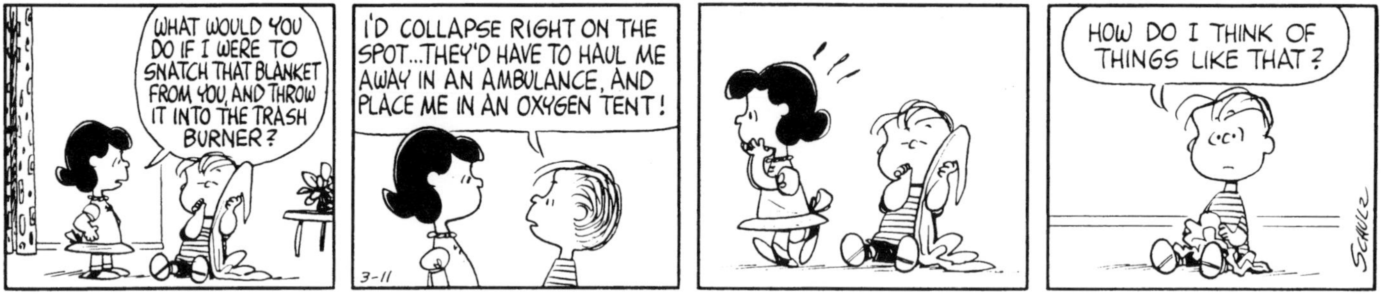
WHAT WOULD YOU DO IF I WERE TO SNATCH THAT BLANKET FROM YOU, AND THROW IT INTO THE TRASH BURNER?
I'D COLLAPSE RIGHT ON THE SPOT...THEY'D HAVE TO HAUL ME AWAY IN AN AMBULANCE, AND PLACE ME IN AN OXYGEN TENT!
3-11
HOW DO I THINK OF THINGS LIKE THAT?
SCHULZ

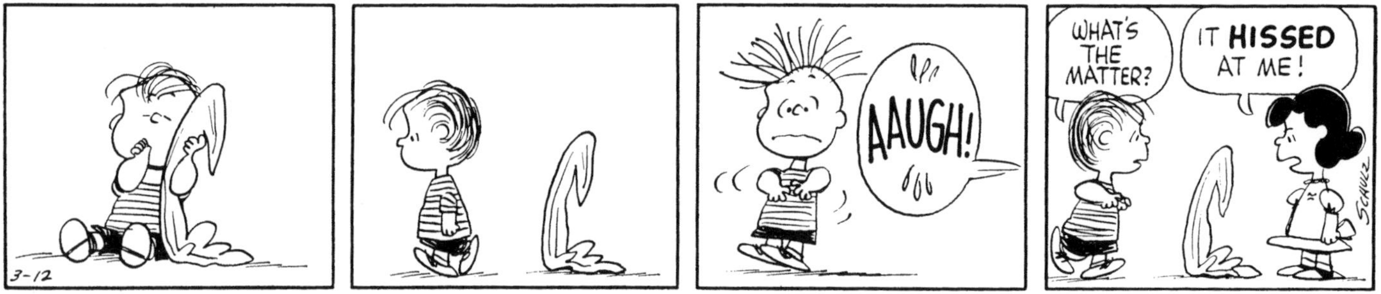
3-12
AAUGH!
WHAT'S THE MATTER?
IT **HISSED** AT ME!
SCHULZ

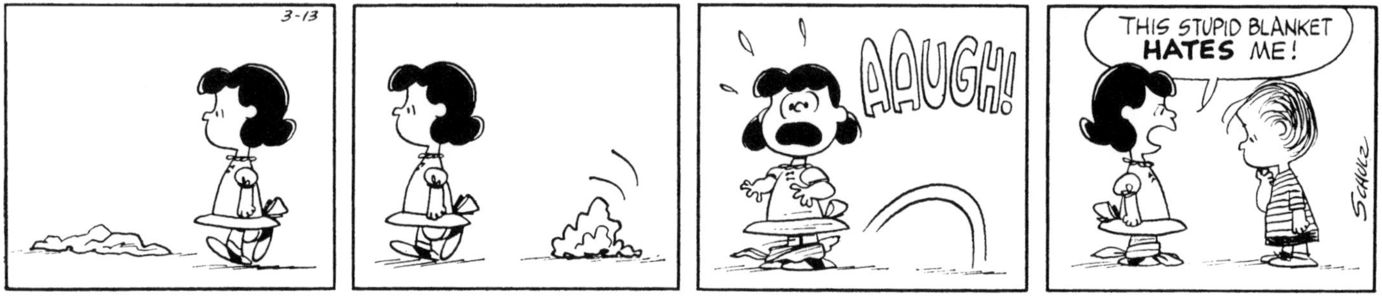
3-13
AAUGH!
THIS STUPID BLANKET **HATES** ME!
SCHULZ

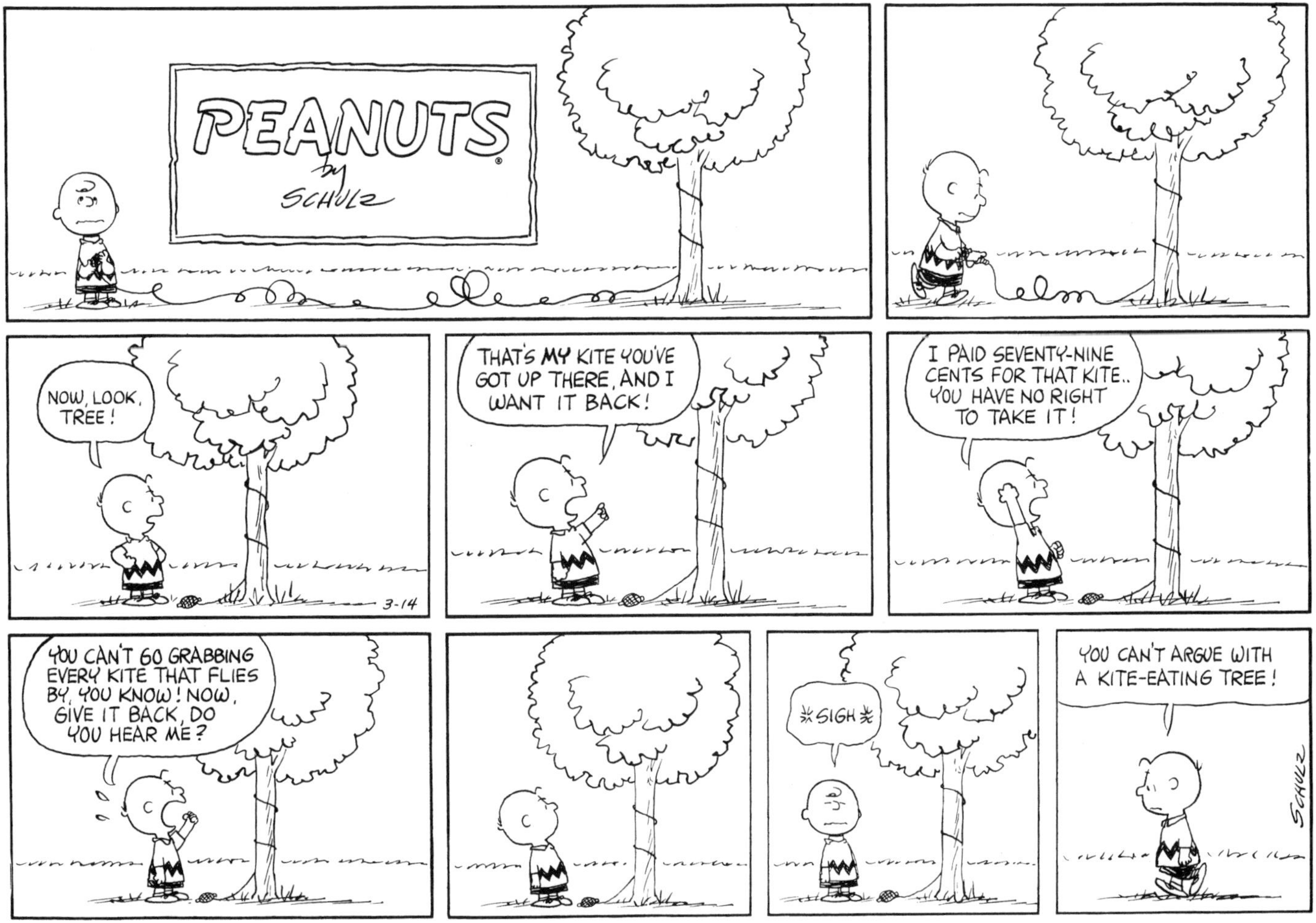
PEANUTS
by
SCHULZ
NOW, LOOK, TREE!
3-14
THAT'S MY KITE YOU'VE GOT UP THERE, AND I WANT IT BACK!
I PAID SEVENTY-NINE CENTS FOR THAT KITE.. YOU HAVE NO RIGHT TO TAKE IT!
YOU CAN'T GO GRABBING EVERY KITE THAT FLIES BY, YOU KNOW! NOW, GIVE IT BACK, DO YOU HEAR ME?
SIGH
YOU CAN'T ARGUE WITH A KITE-EATING TREE!
SCHULZ

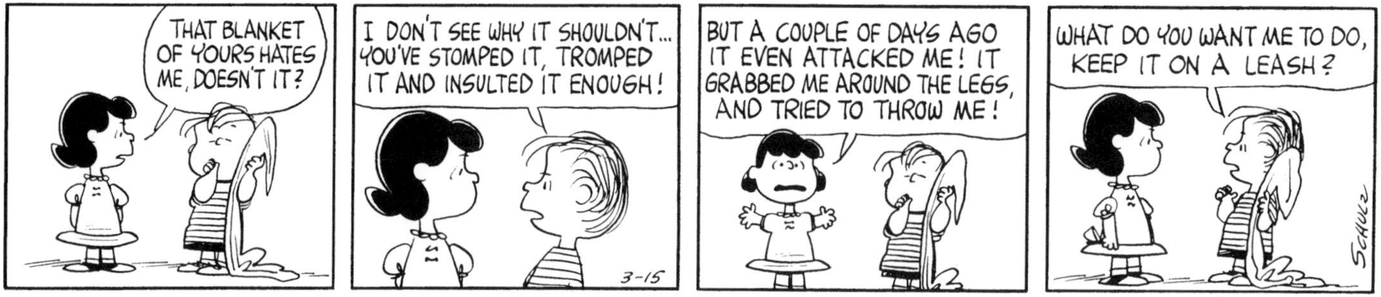
THAT BLANKET OF YOURS HATES ME, DOESN'T IT?
I DON'T SEE WHY IT SHOULDN'T... YOU'VE STOMPED IT, TROMPED IT AND INSULTED IT ENOUGH!
3-15
BUT A COUPLE OF DAYS AGO IT EVEN ATTACKED ME! IT GRABBED ME AROUND THE LEGS, AND TRIED TO THROW ME!
WHAT DO YOU WANT ME TO DO, KEEP IT ON A LEASH?
SCHULZ

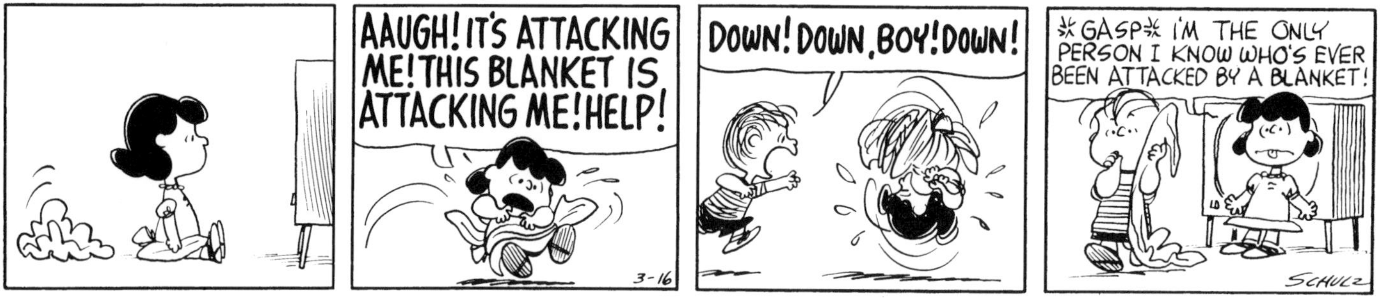
AAUGH! IT'S ATTACKING ME! THIS BLANKET IS ATTACKING ME! HELP!
3-16
DOWN! DOWN, BOY! DOWN!
GASP I'M THE ONLY PERSON I KNOW WHO'S EVER BEEN ATTACKED BY A BLANKET!
SCHULZ

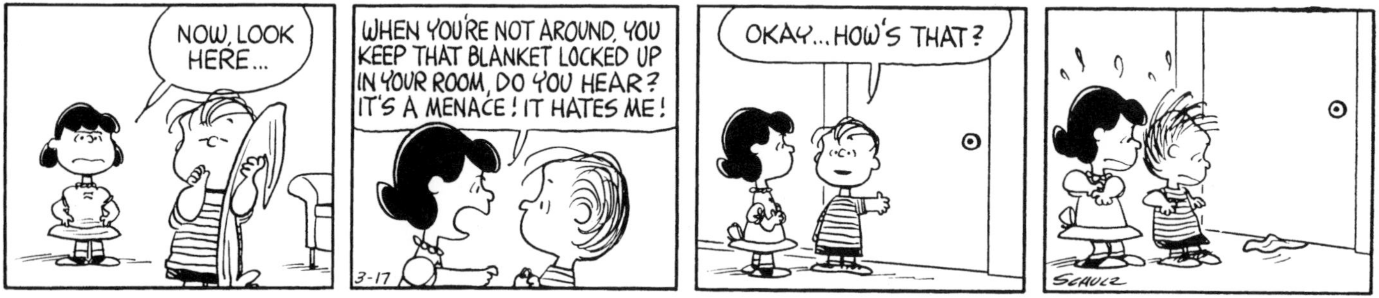
NOW, LOOK HERE...
WHEN YOU'RE NOT AROUND, YOU KEEP THAT BLANKET LOCKED UP IN YOUR ROOM, DO YOU HEAR? IT'S A MENACE! IT HATES ME!
3-17
OKAY... HOW'S THAT?
SCHULZ

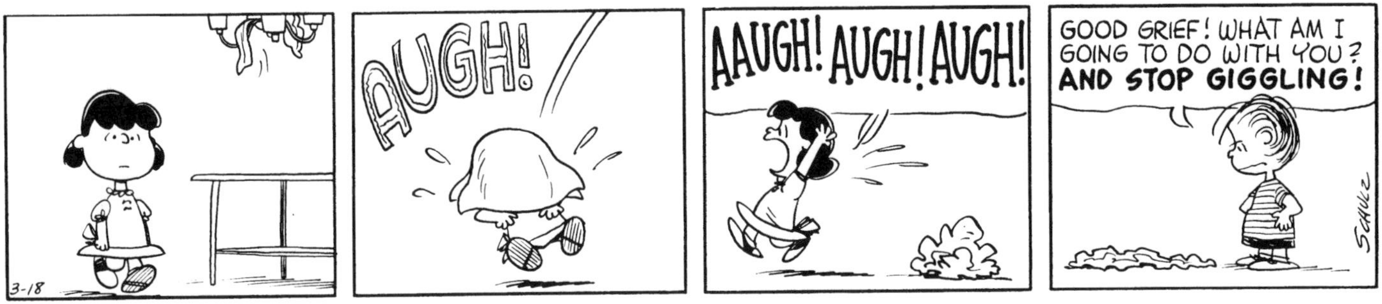
3-18
AUGH!
AAUGH! AUGH! AUGH!
GOOD GRIEF! WHAT AM I GOING TO DO WITH YOU? AND STOP GIGGLING!
SCHULZ

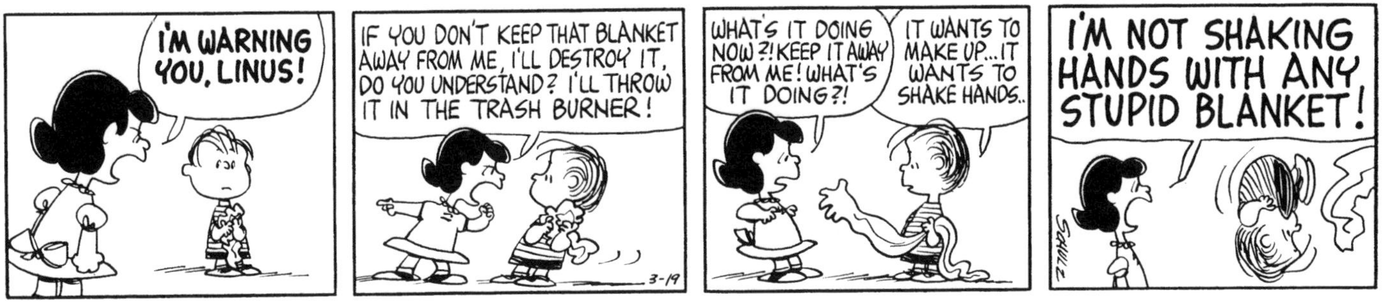
I'M WARNING YOU, LINUS!
IF YOU DON'T KEEP THAT BLANKET AWAY FROM ME, I'LL DESTROY IT, DO YOU UNDERSTAND? I'LL THROW IT IN THE TRASH BURNER!
3-19
WHAT'S IT DOING NOW?! KEEP IT AWAY FROM ME! WHAT'S IT DOING?!
IT WANTS TO MAKE UP... IT WANTS TO SHAKE HANDS..
I'M NOT SHAKING HANDS WITH ANY STUPID BLANKET!
SCHULZ

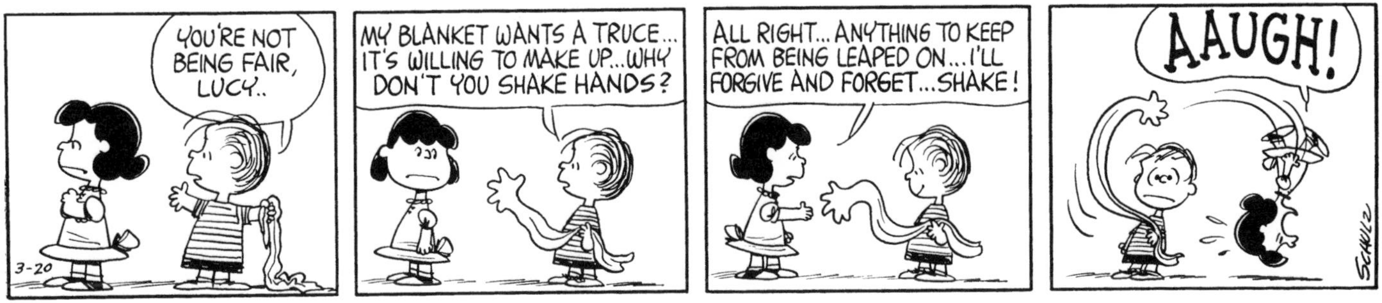
YOU'RE NOT BEING FAIR, LUCY..
3-20
MY BLANKET WANTS A TRUCE... IT'S WILLING TO MAKE UP... WHY DON'T YOU SHAKE HANDS?
ALL RIGHT... ANYTHING TO KEEP FROM BEING LEAPED ON... I'LL FORGIVE AND FORGET... SHAKE!
AAUGH!
SCHULZ

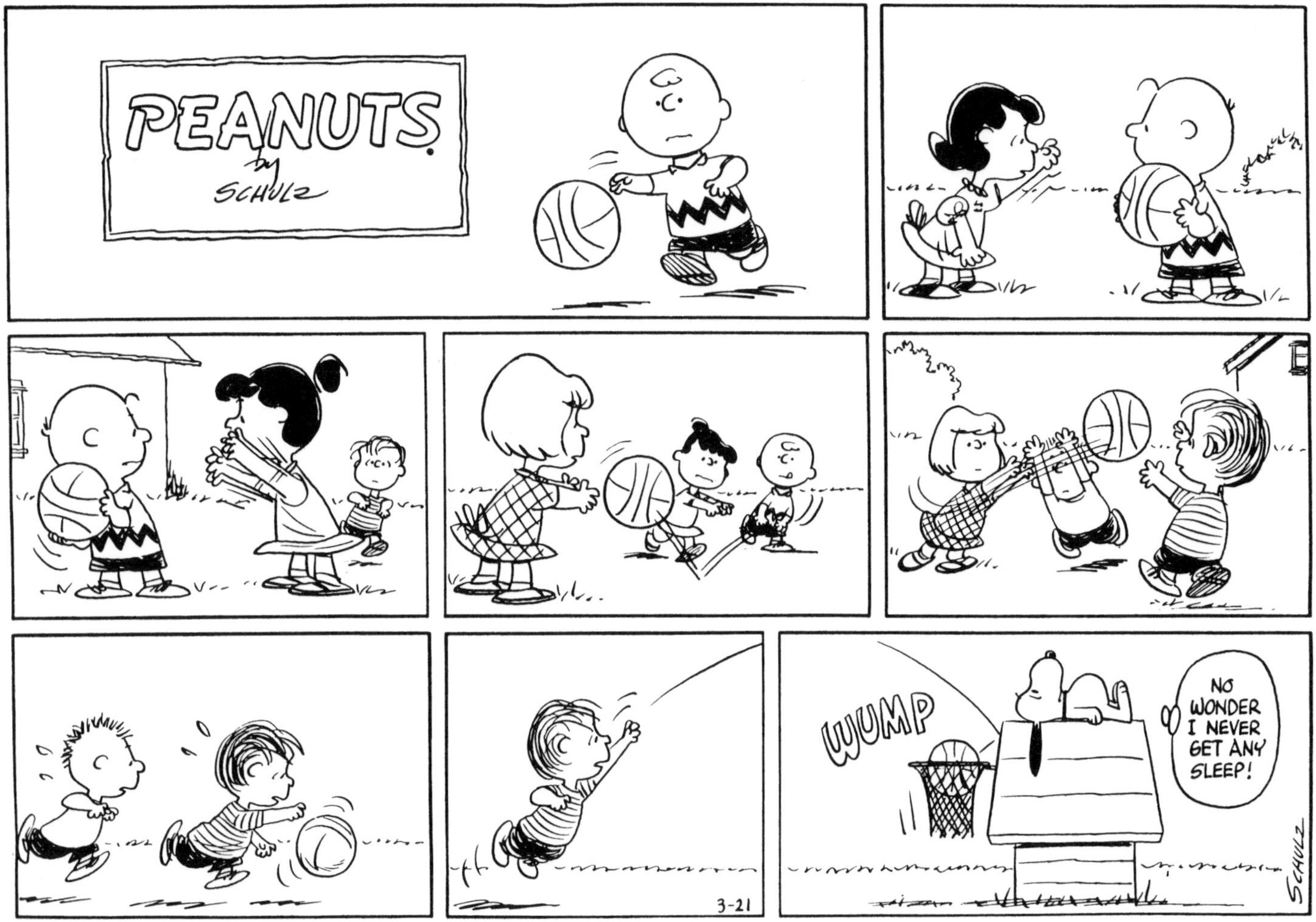
PEANUTS
by
SCHULZ
3-21
WUMP
NO WONDER I NEVER GET ANY SLEEP!
SCHULZ

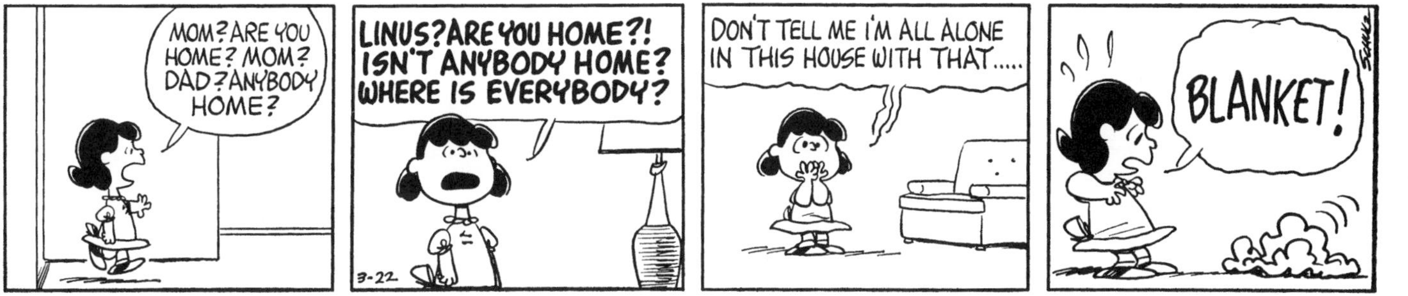
MOM? ARE YOU HOME? MOM? DAD? ANYBODY HOME?
LINUS? ARE YOU HOME?! ISN'T ANYBODY HOME? WHERE IS EVERYBODY?
DON'T TELL ME I'M ALL ALONE IN THIS HOUSE WITH THAT.....
BLANKET!

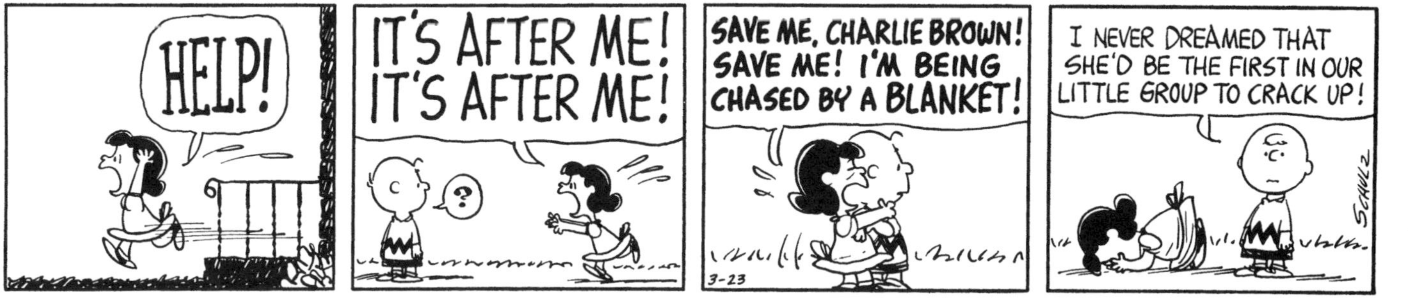
HELP!
IT'S AFTER ME! IT'S AFTER ME!
?
SAVE ME, CHARLIE BROWN! SAVE ME! I'M BEING CHASED BY A BLANKET!
I NEVER DREAMED THAT SHE'D BE THE FIRST IN OUR LITTLE GROUP TO CRACK UP!

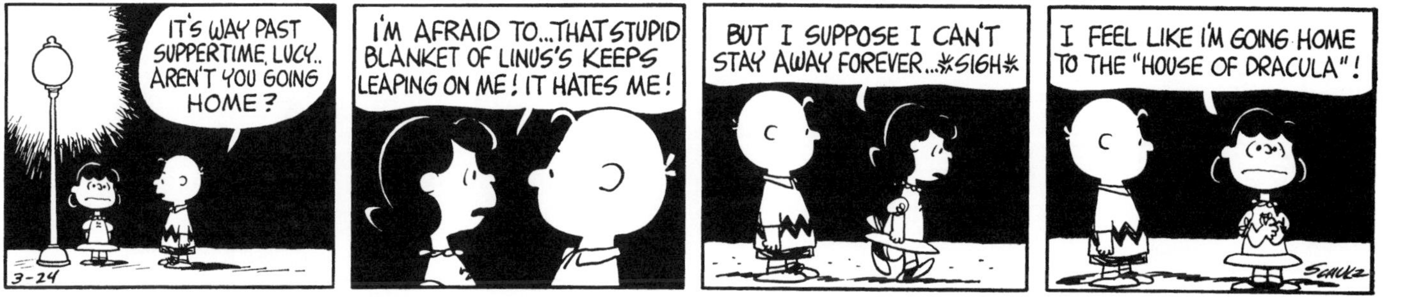
IT'S WAY PAST SUPPERTIME, LUCY.. AREN'T YOU GOING HOME?
I'M AFRAID TO...THAT STUPID BLANKET OF LINUS'S KEEPS LEAPING ON ME! IT HATES ME!
BUT I SUPPOSE I CAN'T STAY AWAY FOREVER...*SIGH*
I FEEL LIKE I'M GOING HOME TO THE "HOUSE OF DRACULA"!

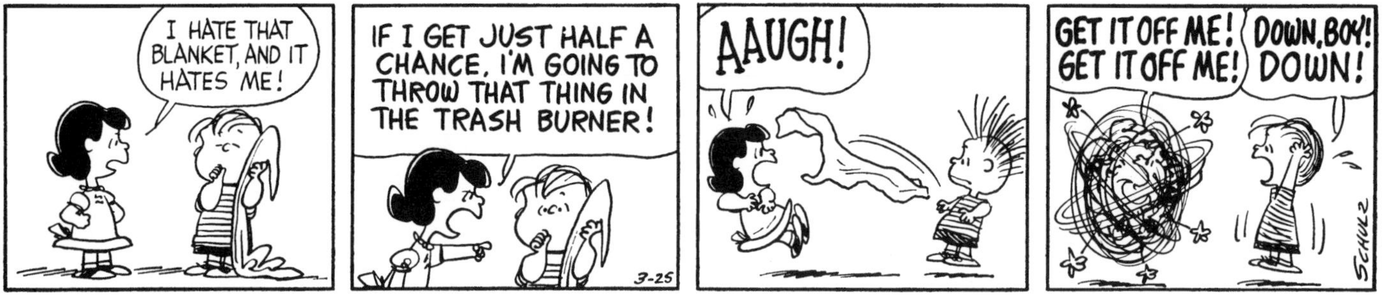
I HATE THAT BLANKET, AND IT HATES ME!
IF I GET JUST HALF A CHANCE, I'M GOING TO THROW THAT THING IN THE TRASH BURNER!
3-25
AAUGH!
GET IT OFF ME! GET IT OFF ME!
DOWN, BOY! DOWN!
SCHULZ

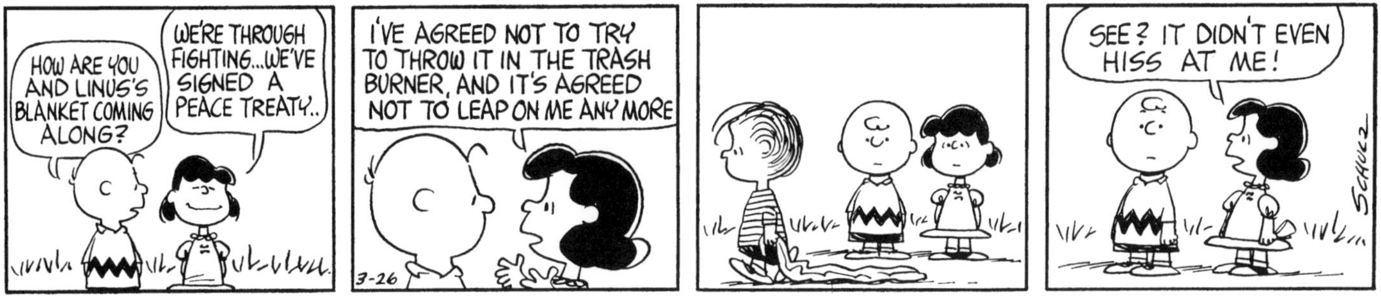
HOW ARE YOU AND LINUS'S BLANKET COMING ALONG?
WE'RE THROUGH FIGHTING...WE'VE SIGNED A PEACE TREATY..
I'VE AGREED NOT TO TRY TO THROW IT IN THE TRASH BURNER, AND IT'S AGREED NOT TO LEAP ON ME ANY MORE
3-26
SEE? IT DIDN'T EVEN HISS AT ME!
SCHULZ

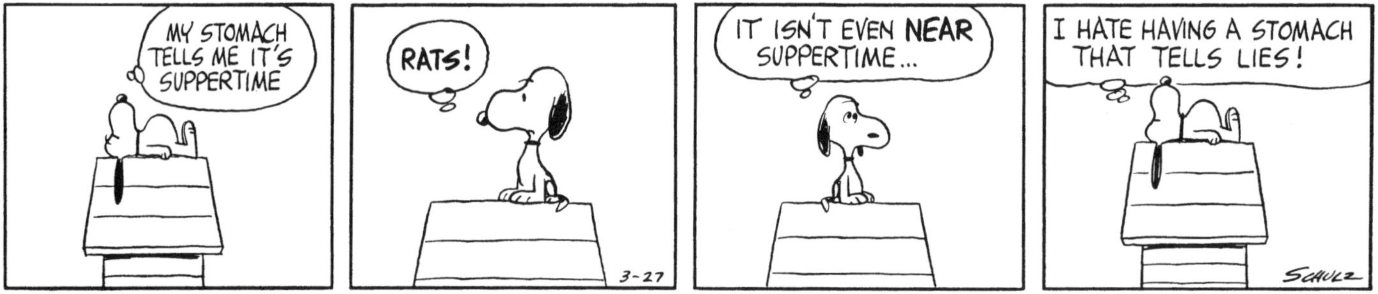
MY STOMACH TELLS ME IT'S SUPPERTIME
RATS!
3-27
IT ISN'T EVEN NEAR SUPPERTIME...
I HATE HAVING A STOMACH THAT TELLS LIES!
SCHULZ

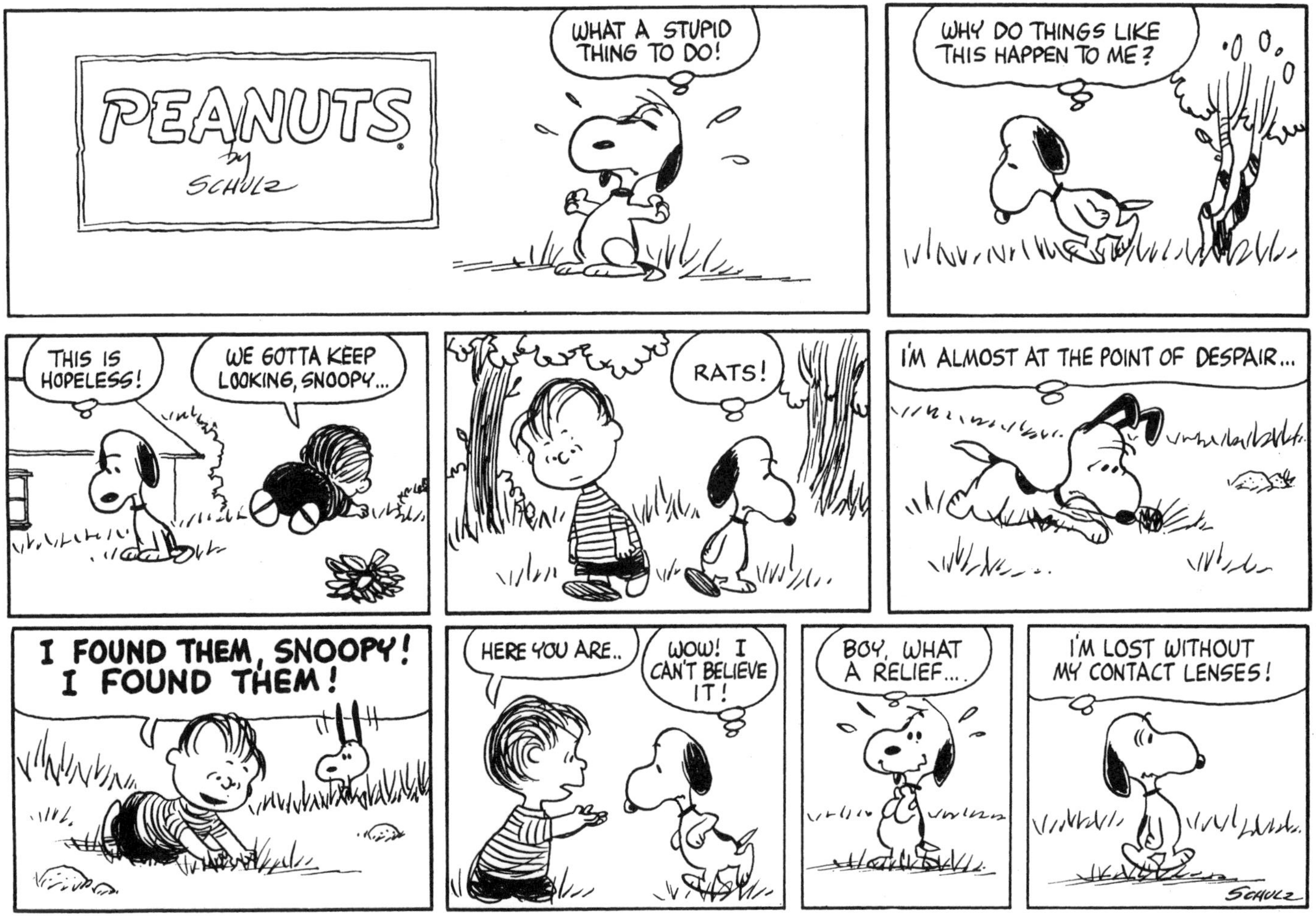
PEANUTS by SCHULZ
WHAT A STUPID THING TO DO!
WHY DO THINGS LIKE THIS HAPPEN TO ME?
THIS IS HOPELESS!
WE GOTTA KEEP LOOKING, SNOOPY...
RATS!
I'M ALMOST AT THE POINT OF DESPAIR...
I FOUND THEM, SNOOPY! I FOUND THEM!
HERE YOU ARE..
WOW! I CAN'T BELIEVE IT!
BOY, WHAT A RELIEF....
I'M LOST WITHOUT MY CONTACT LENSES!
SCHULZ

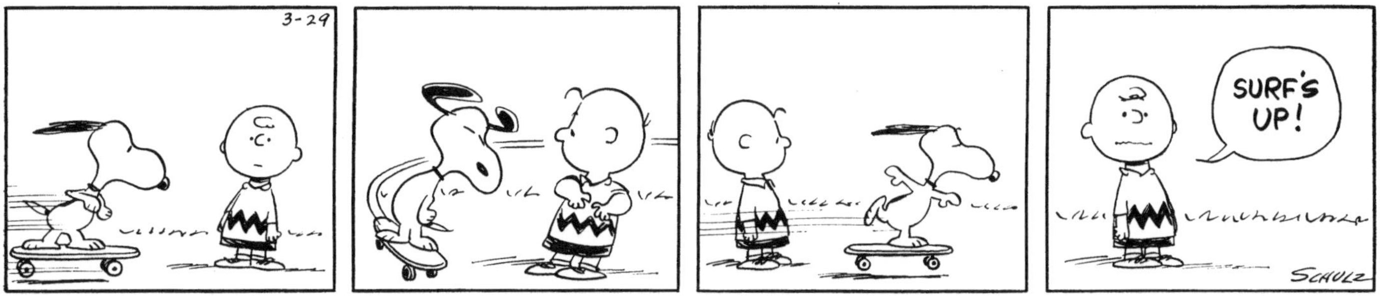
3-29
SURF'S UP!
SCHULZ

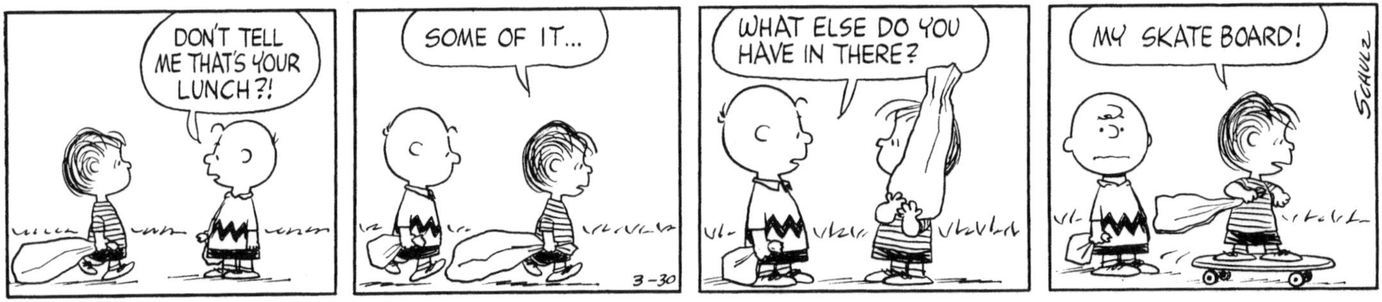
DON'T TELL ME THAT'S YOUR LUNCH?!
SOME OF IT...
3-30
WHAT ELSE DO YOU HAVE IN THERE?
MY SKATE BOARD!
SCHULZ

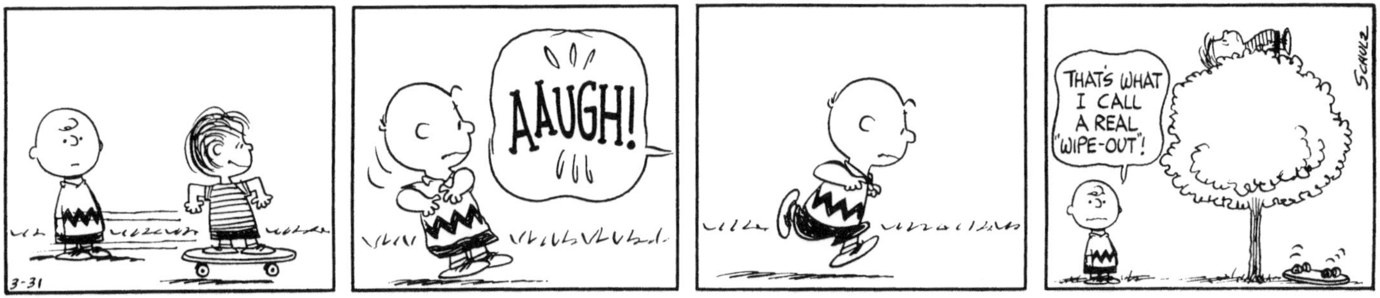
3-31
AAUGH!
SCHULZ
THAT'S WHAT I CALL A REAL "WIPE-OUT"!

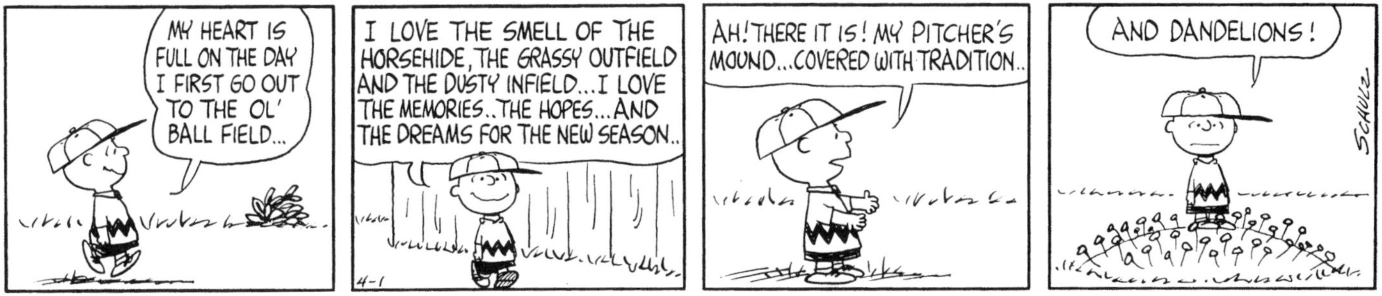
MY HEART IS FULL ON THE DAY I FIRST GO OUT TO THE OL' BALL FIELD...
I LOVE THE SMELL OF THE HORSEHIDE, THE GRASSY OUTFIELD AND THE DUSTY INFIELD...I LOVE THE MEMORIES..THE HOPES...AND THE DREAMS FOR THE NEW SEASON..
4-1
AH! THERE IT IS! MY PITCHER'S MOUND...COVERED WITH TRADITION..
AND DANDELIONS!
SCHULZ

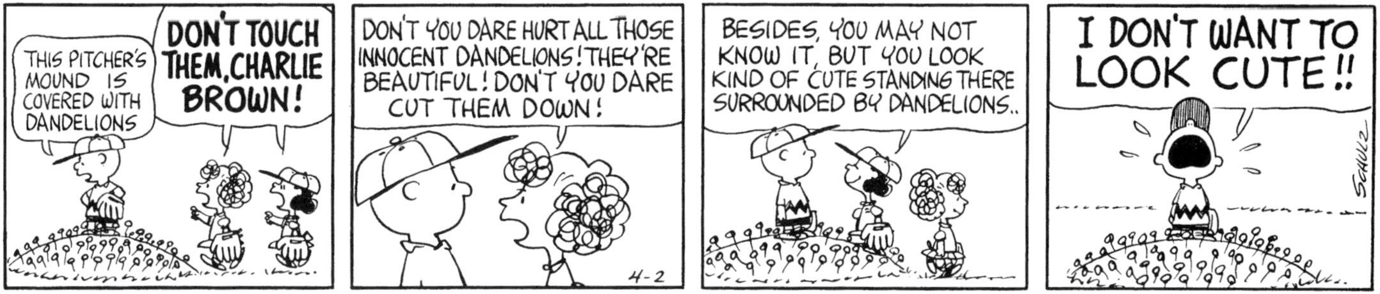
THIS PITCHER'S MOUND IS COVERED WITH DANDELIONS
DON'T TOUCH THEM, CHARLIE BROWN!
DON'T YOU DARE HURT ALL THOSE INNOCENT DANDELIONS! THEY'RE BEAUTIFUL! DON'T YOU DARE CUT THEM DOWN!
4-2
BESIDES, YOU MAY NOT KNOW IT, BUT YOU LOOK KIND OF CUTE STANDING THERE SURROUNDED BY DANDELIONS..
I DON'T WANT TO LOOK CUTE!!
SCHULZ

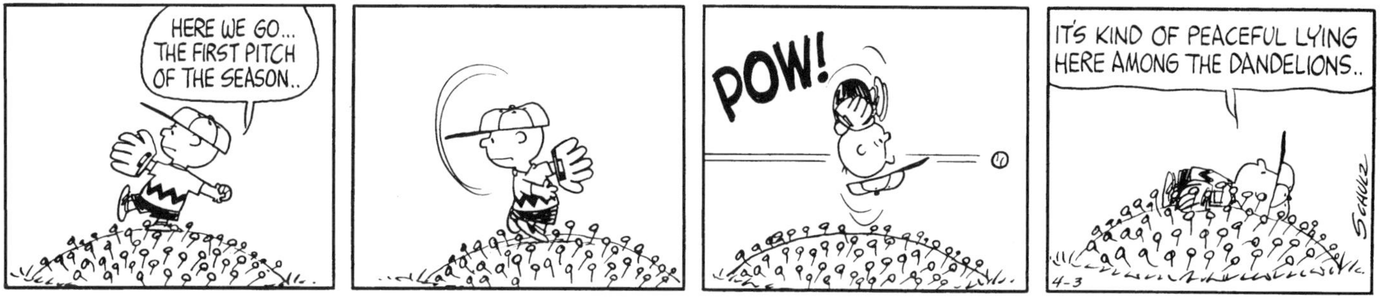
HERE WE GO... THE FIRST PITCH OF THE SEASON..
POW!
IT'S KIND OF PEACEFUL LYING HERE AMONG THE DANDELIONS..
SCHULZ
4-3

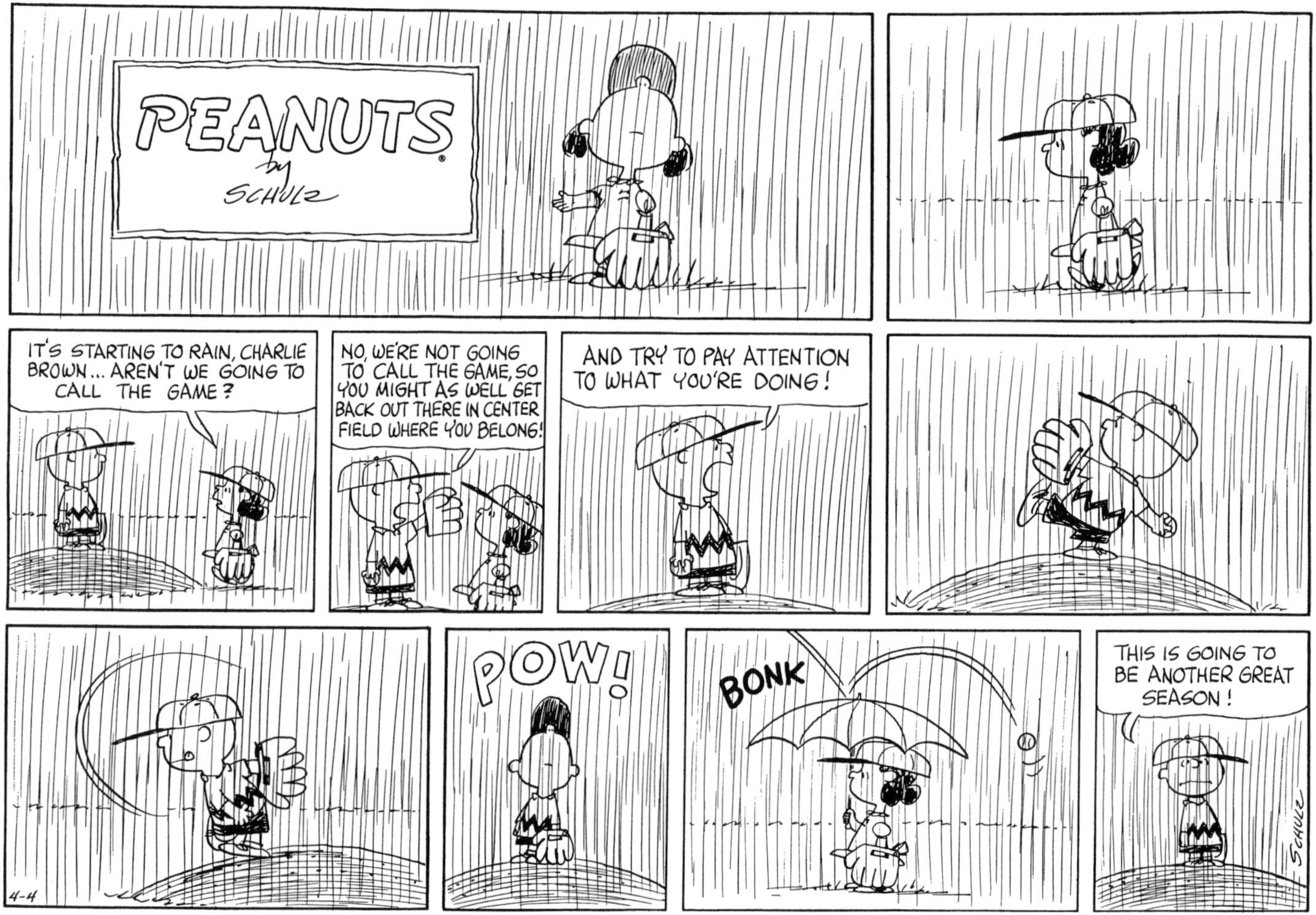
PEANUTS
by SCHULZ
IT'S STARTING TO RAIN, CHARLIE BROWN... AREN'T WE GOING TO CALL THE GAME?
NO, WE'RE NOT GOING TO CALL THE GAME, SO YOU MIGHT AS WELL GET BACK OUT THERE IN CENTER FIELD WHERE YOU BELONG!
AND TRY TO PAY ATTENTION TO WHAT YOU'RE DOING!
4-4
POW!
BONK
SCHULZ
THIS IS GOING TO BE ANOTHER GREAT SEASON!

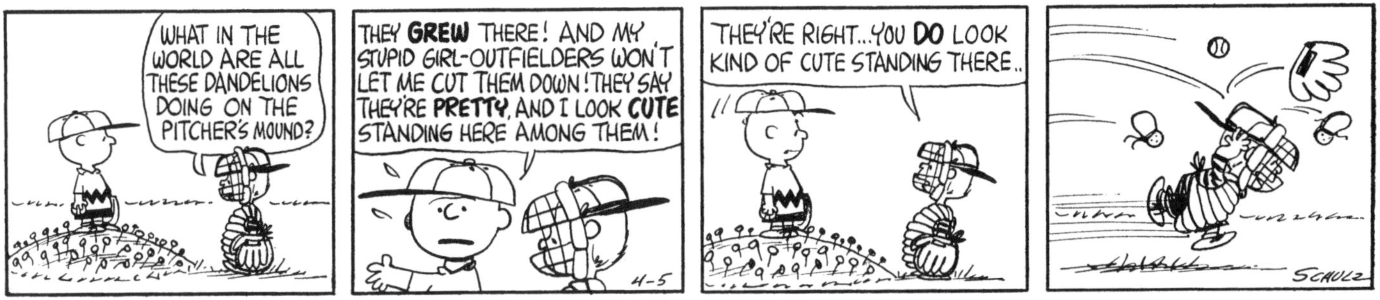
WHAT IN THE WORLD ARE ALL THESE DANDELIONS DOING ON THE PITCHER'S MOUND?
THEY GREW THERE! AND MY STUPID GIRL-OUTFIELDERS WON'T LET ME CUT THEM DOWN! THEY SAY THEY'RE PRETTY, AND I LOOK CUTE STANDING HERE AMONG THEM!
THEY'RE RIGHT...YOU DO LOOK KIND OF CUTE STANDING THERE..

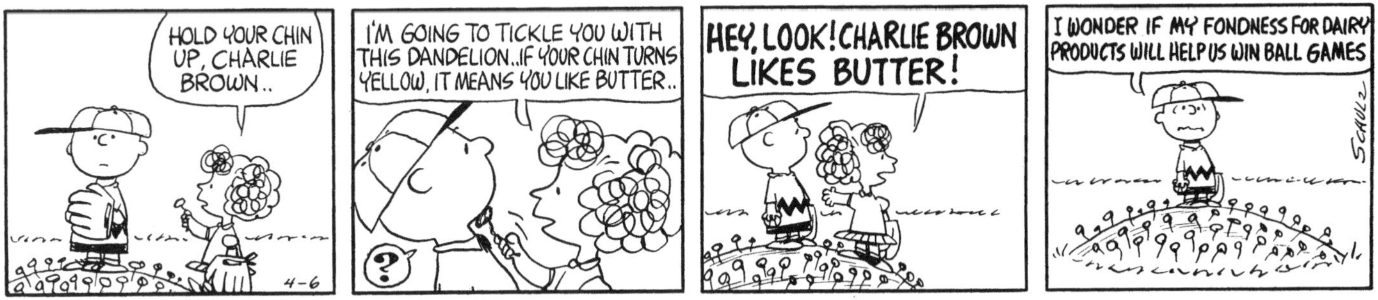
HOLD YOUR CHIN UP, CHARLIE BROWN..
I'M GOING TO TICKLE YOU WITH THIS DANDELION..IF YOUR CHIN TURNS YELLOW, IT MEANS YOU LIKE BUTTER..
?
HEY, LOOK! CHARLIE BROWN LIKES BUTTER!
I WONDER IF MY FONDNESS FOR DAIRY PRODUCTS WILL HELP US WIN BALL GAMES

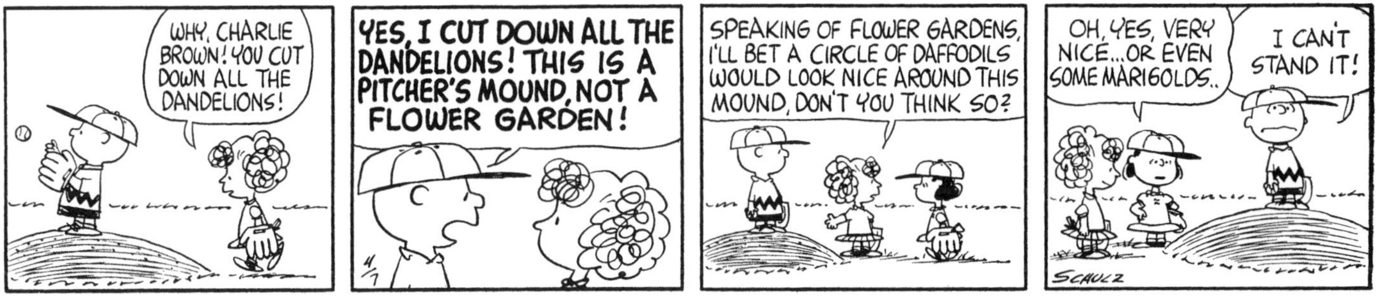
WHY, CHARLIE BROWN! YOU CUT DOWN ALL THE DANDELIONS!
YES, I CUT DOWN ALL THE DANDELIONS! THIS IS A PITCHER'S MOUND, NOT A FLOWER GARDEN!
SPEAKING OF FLOWER GARDENS, I'LL BET A CIRCLE OF DAFFODILS WOULD LOOK NICE AROUND THIS MOUND, DON'T YOU THINK SO?
OH, YES, VERY NICE...OR EVEN SOME MARIGOLDS..
I CAN'T STAND IT!

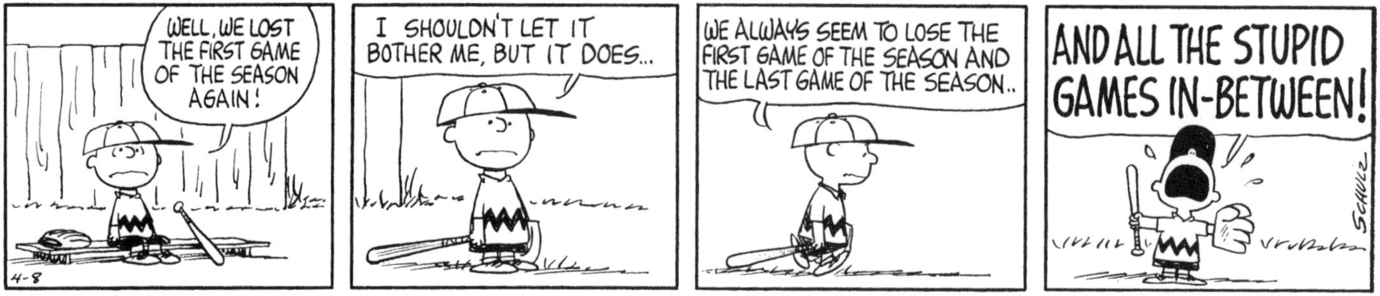
WELL, WE LOST THE FIRST GAME OF THE SEASON AGAIN!
I SHOULDN'T LET IT BOTHER ME, BUT IT DOES...
WE ALWAYS SEEM TO LOSE THE FIRST GAME OF THE SEASON AND THE LAST GAME OF THE SEASON..
AND ALL THE STUPID GAMES IN-BETWEEN!

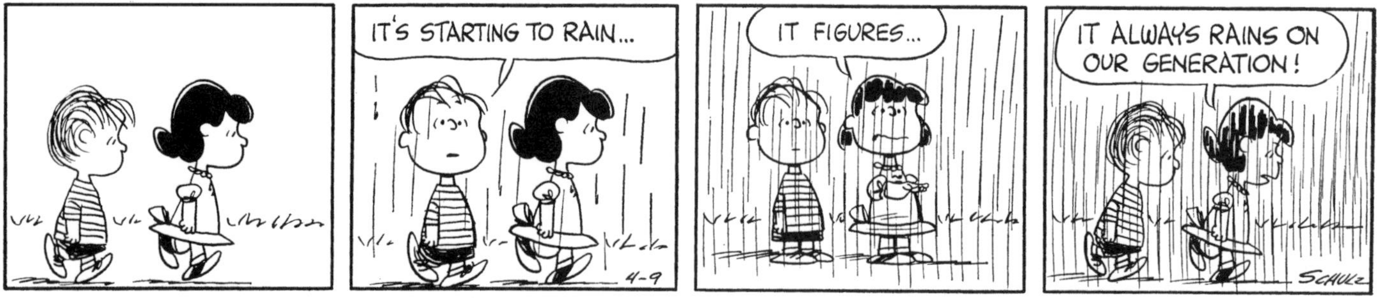
IT'S STARTING TO RAIN...
IT FIGURES...
IT ALWAYS RAINS ON OUR GENERATION!

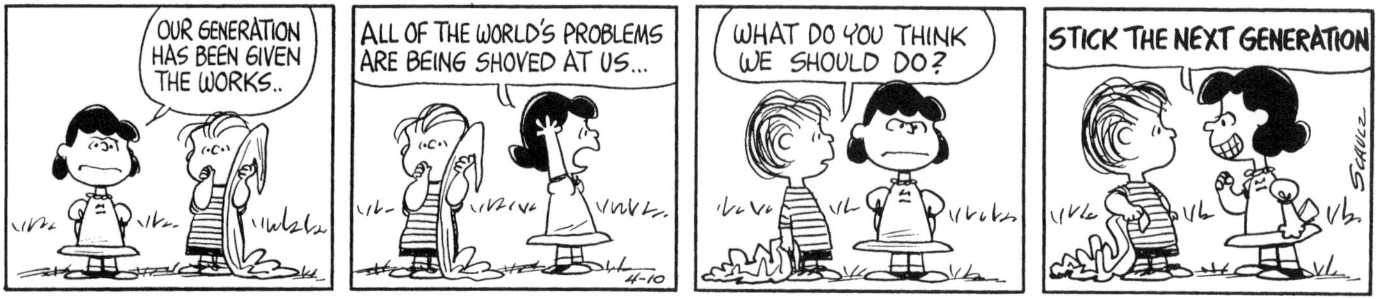
OUR GENERATION HAS BEEN GIVEN THE WORKS..
ALL OF THE WORLD'S PROBLEMS ARE BEING SHOVED AT US...
WHAT DO YOU THINK WE SHOULD DO?
STICK THE NEXT GENERATION

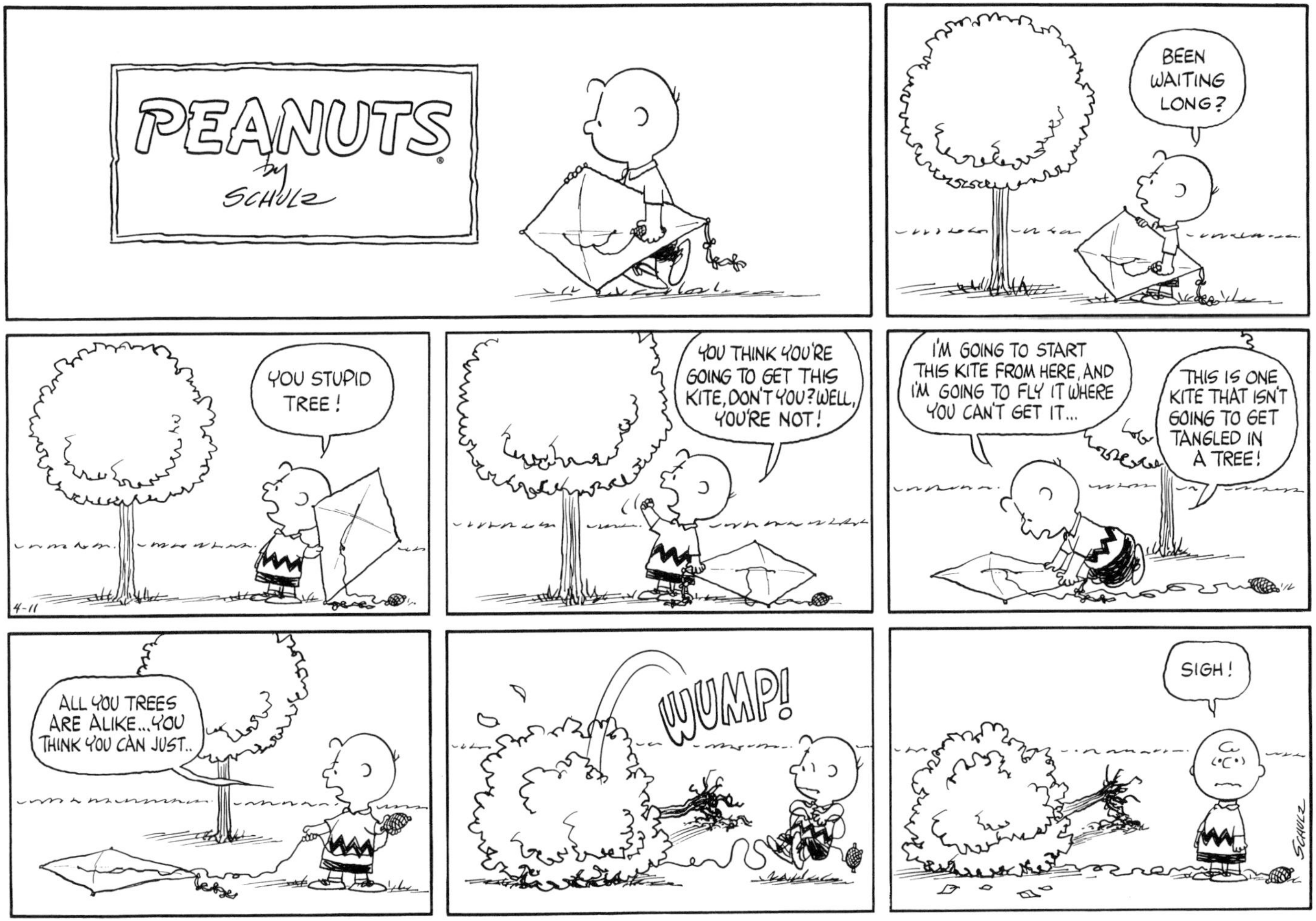
PEANUTS
by SCHULZ
BEEN WAITING LONG?
YOU STUPID TREE!
4-11
YOU THINK YOU'RE GOING TO GET THIS KITE, DON'T YOU? WELL, YOU'RE NOT!
I'M GOING TO START THIS KITE FROM HERE, AND I'M GOING TO FLY IT WHERE YOU CAN'T GET IT...
THIS IS ONE KITE THAT ISN'T GOING TO GET TANGLED IN A TREE!
ALL YOU TREES ARE ALIKE... YOU THINK YOU CAN JUST..
WUMP!
SIGH!
SCHULZ

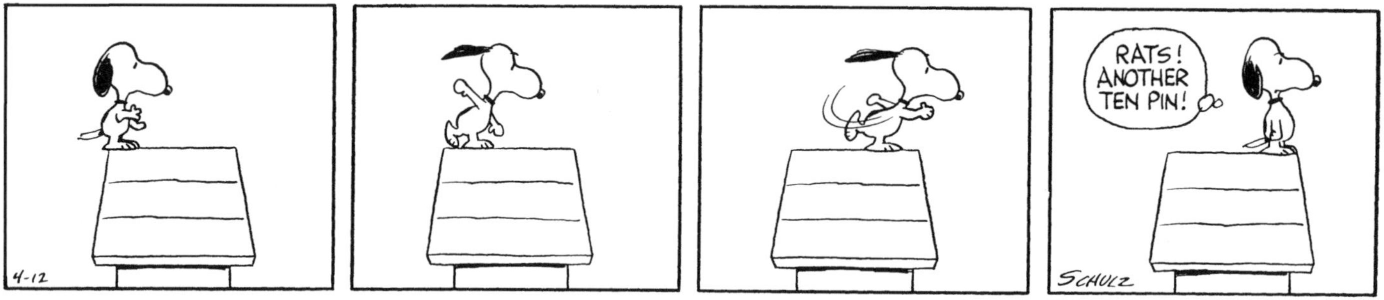
4-12
RATS! ANOTHER TEN PIN!
SCHULZ

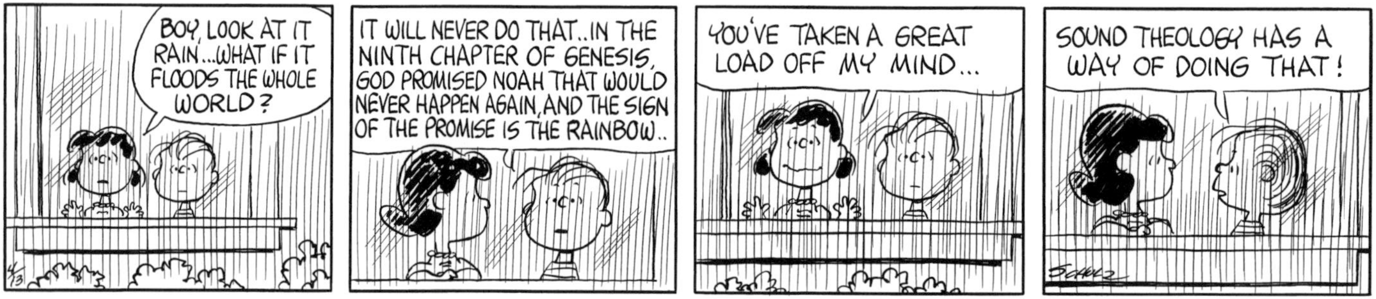
BOY, LOOK AT IT RAIN...WHAT IF IT FLOODS THE WHOLE WORLD?
4/13
IT WILL NEVER DO THAT..IN THE NINTH CHAPTER OF GENESIS, GOD PROMISED NOAH THAT WOULD NEVER HAPPEN AGAIN, AND THE SIGN OF THE PROMISE IS THE RAINBOW..
YOU'VE TAKEN A GREAT LOAD OFF MY MIND...
SOUND THEOLOGY HAS A WAY OF DOING THAT!
SCHULZ

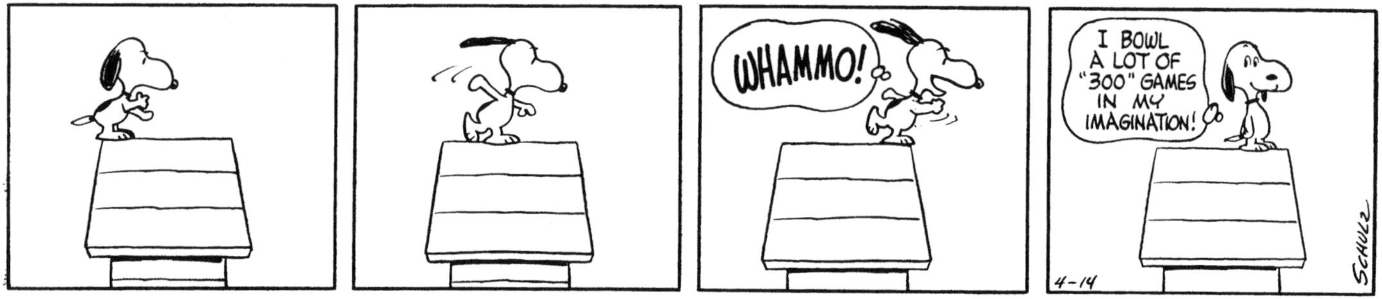
WHAMMO!
I BOWL A LOT OF "300" GAMES IN MY IMAGINATION!
4-14
SCHULZ

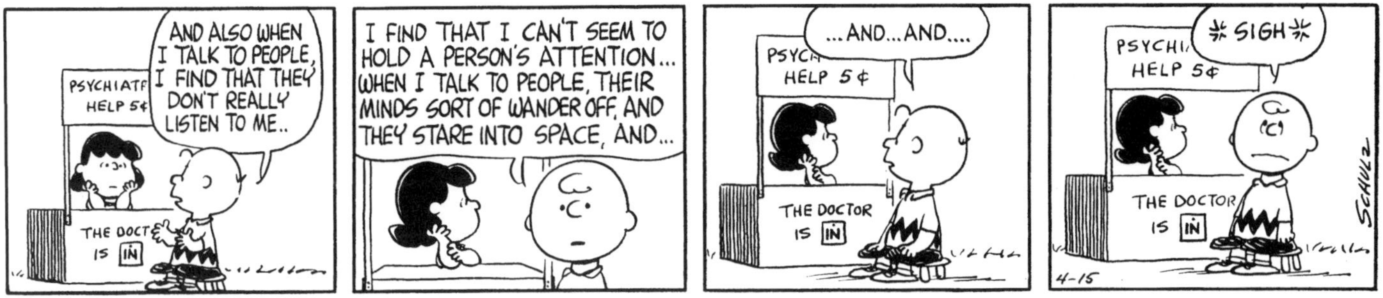
AND ALSO WHEN I TALK TO PEOPLE, I FIND THAT THEY DON'T REALLY LISTEN TO ME..
I FIND THAT I CAN'T SEEM TO HOLD A PERSON'S ATTENTION... WHEN I TALK TO PEOPLE, THEIR MINDS SORT OF WANDER OFF, AND THEY STARE INTO SPACE, AND...
HELP 5¢
...AND...AND....
THE DOCTOR IS IN
HELP 5¢
SIGH
THE DOCTOR IS IN
SCHULZ
4-15

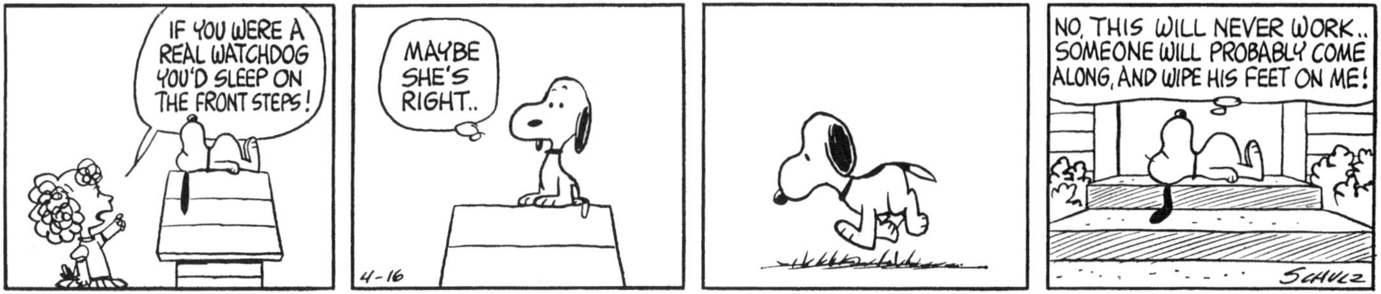
IF YOU WERE A REAL WATCHDOG YOU'D SLEEP ON THE FRONT STEPS!
MAYBE SHE'S RIGHT..
4-16
NO, THIS WILL NEVER WORK.. SOMEONE WILL PROBABLY COME ALONG, AND WIPE HIS FEET ON ME!
SCHULZ

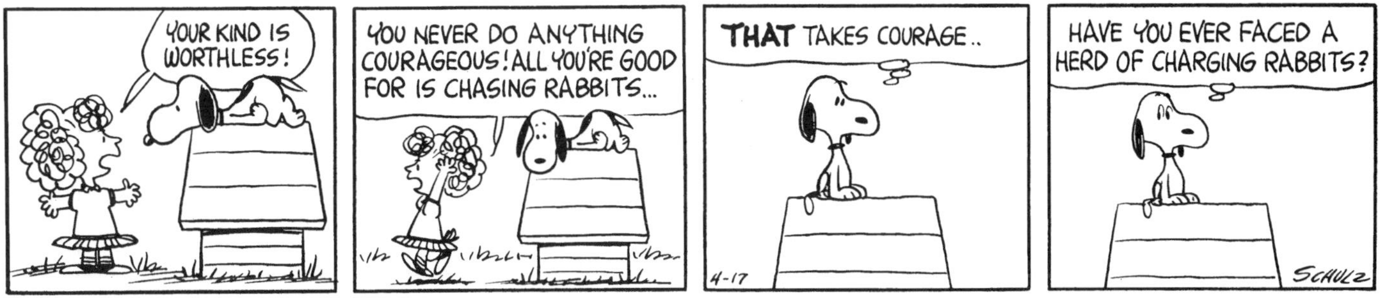
YOUR KIND IS WORTHLESS!
YOU NEVER DO ANYTHING COURAGEOUS! ALL YOU'RE GOOD FOR IS CHASING RABBITS...
THAT TAKES COURAGE..
4-17
HAVE YOU EVER FACED A HERD OF CHARGING RABBITS?
SCHULZ

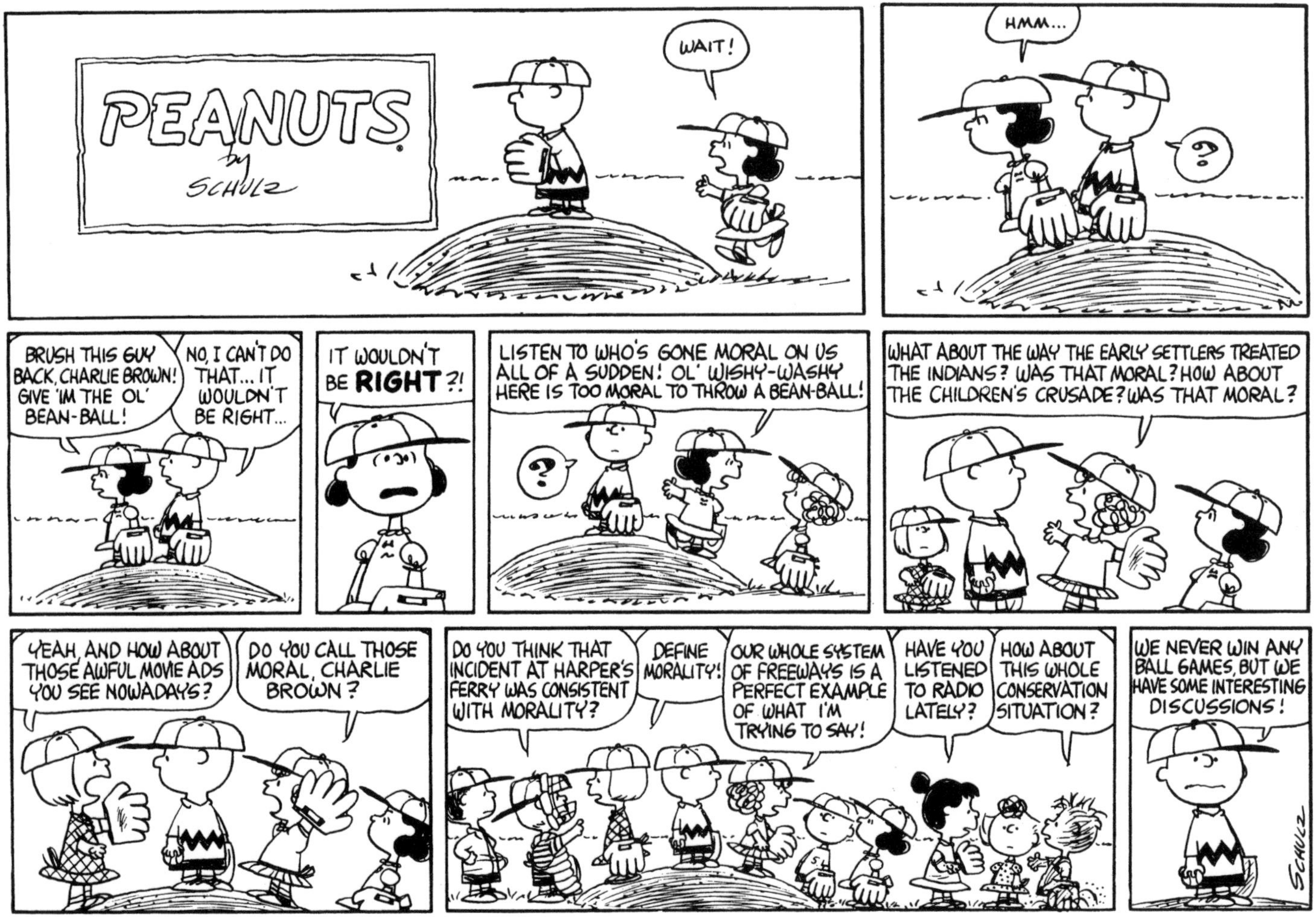
PEANUTS
by SCHULZ
WAIT!
HMM...
?
BRUSH THIS GUY BACK, CHARLIE BROWN! GIVE 'IM THE OL' BEAN-BALL!
NO, I CAN'T DO THAT... IT WOULDN'T BE RIGHT...
IT WOULDN'T BE **RIGHT** ?!
LISTEN TO WHO'S GONE MORAL ON US ALL OF A SUDDEN! OL' WISHY-WASHY HERE IS TOO MORAL TO THROW A BEAN-BALL!
?
WHAT ABOUT THE WAY THE EARLY SETTLERS TREATED THE INDIANS? WAS THAT MORAL? HOW ABOUT THE CHILDREN'S CRUSADE? WAS THAT MORAL?
YEAH, AND HOW ABOUT THOSE AWFUL MOVIE ADS YOU SEE NOWADAYS?
DO YOU CALL THOSE MORAL, CHARLIE BROWN?
DO YOU THINK THAT INCIDENT AT HARPER'S FERRY WAS CONSISTENT WITH MORALITY?
DEFINE MORALITY!
OUR WHOLE SYSTEM OF FREEWAYS IS A PERFECT EXAMPLE OF WHAT I'M TRYING TO SAY!
HAVE YOU LISTENED TO RADIO LATELY?
HOW ABOUT THIS WHOLE CONSERVATION SITUATION?
WE NEVER WIN ANY BALL GAMES, BUT WE HAVE SOME INTERESTING DISCUSSIONS!
SCHULZ

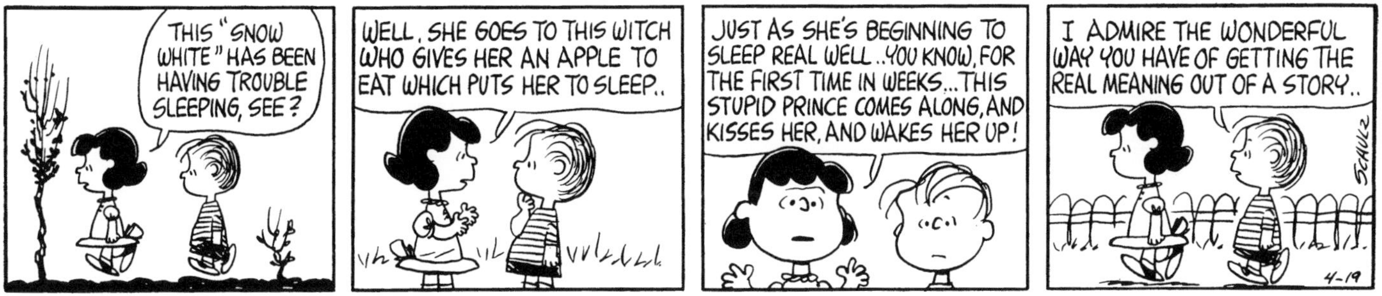
THIS "SNOW WHITE" HAS BEEN HAVING TROUBLE SLEEPING, SEE?
WELL, SHE GOES TO THIS WITCH WHO GIVES HER AN APPLE TO EAT WHICH PUTS HER TO SLEEP..
JUST AS SHE'S BEGINNING TO SLEEP REAL WELL..YOU KNOW, FOR THE FIRST TIME IN WEEKS...THIS STUPID PRINCE COMES ALONG, AND KISSES HER, AND WAKES HER UP!
I ADMIRE THE WONDERFUL WAY YOU HAVE OF GETTING THE REAL MEANING OUT OF A STORY..
SCHULZ
4-19

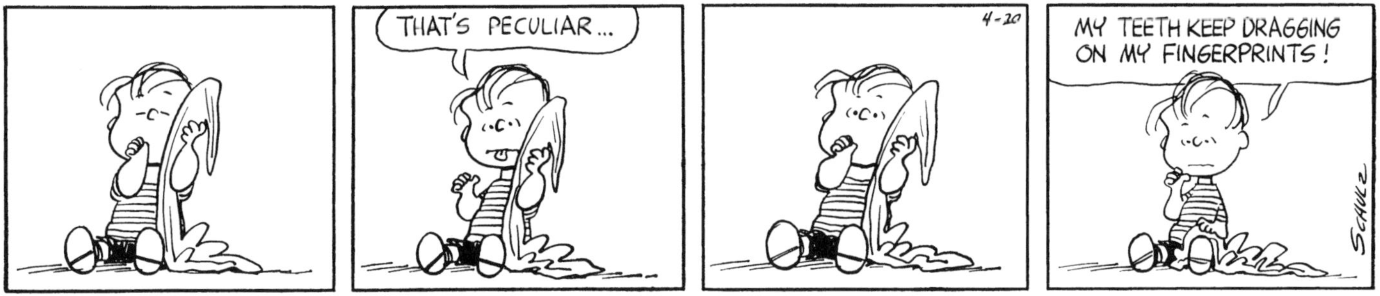
THAT'S PECULIAR...
4-20
MY TEETH KEEP DRAGGING ON MY FINGERPRINTS!
SCHULZ

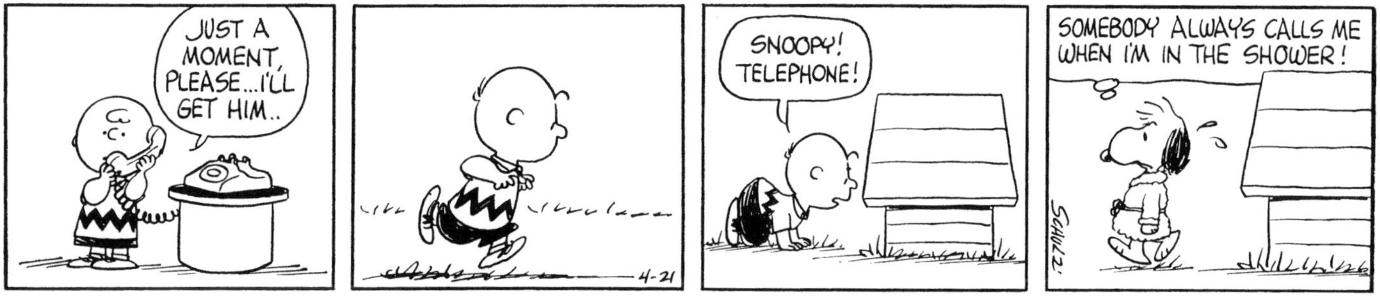
JUST A MOMENT, PLEASE...I'LL GET HIM..
4-21
SNOOPY! TELEPHONE!
SOMEBODY ALWAYS CALLS ME WHEN I'M IN THE SHOWER!
SCHULZ

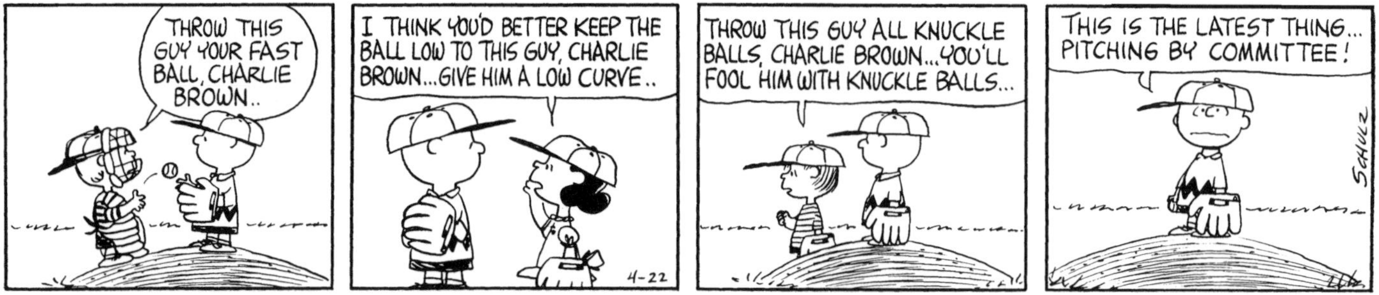
THROW THIS GUY YOUR FAST BALL, CHARLIE BROWN..
I THINK YOU'D BETTER KEEP THE BALL LOW TO THIS GUY, CHARLIE BROWN...GIVE HIM A LOW CURVE..
4-22
THROW THIS GUY ALL KNUCKLE BALLS, CHARLIE BROWN...YOU'LL FOOL HIM WITH KNUCKLE BALLS...
THIS IS THE LATEST THING... PITCHING BY COMMITTEE!
SCHULZ

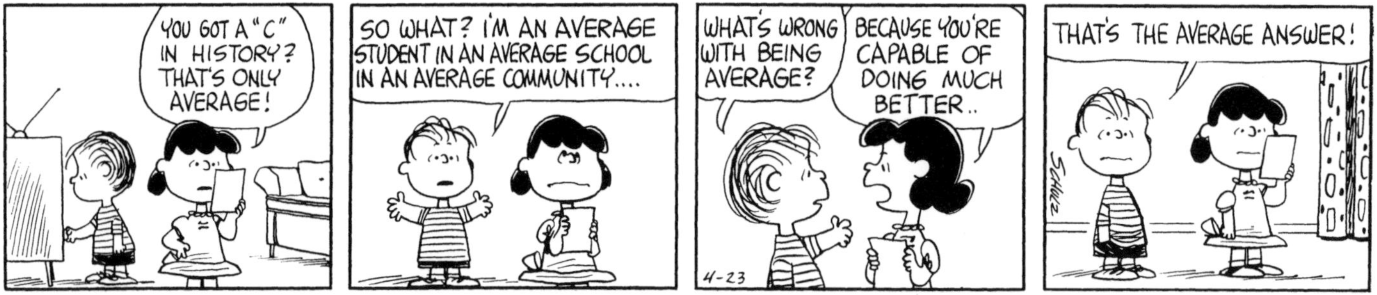
YOU GOT A "C" IN HISTORY? THAT'S ONLY AVERAGE!
SO WHAT? I'M AN AVERAGE STUDENT IN AN AVERAGE SCHOOL IN AN AVERAGE COMMUNITY....
WHAT'S WRONG WITH BEING AVERAGE?
BECAUSE YOU'RE CAPABLE OF DOING MUCH BETTER..
4-23
THAT'S THE AVERAGE ANSWER!
SCHULZ

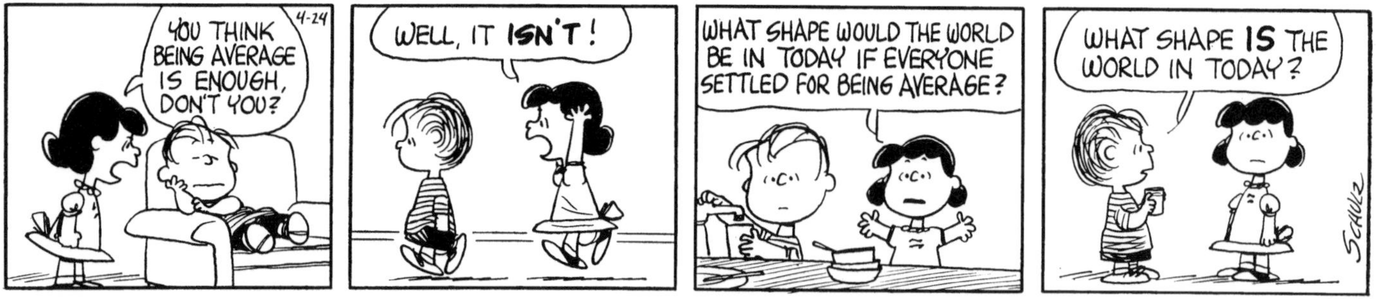
4-24
YOU THINK BEING AVERAGE IS ENOUGH, DON'T YOU?
WELL, IT **ISN'T**!
WHAT SHAPE WOULD THE WORLD BE IN TODAY IF EVERYONE SETTLED FOR BEING AVERAGE?
WHAT SHAPE **IS** THE WORLD IN TODAY?
SCHULZ

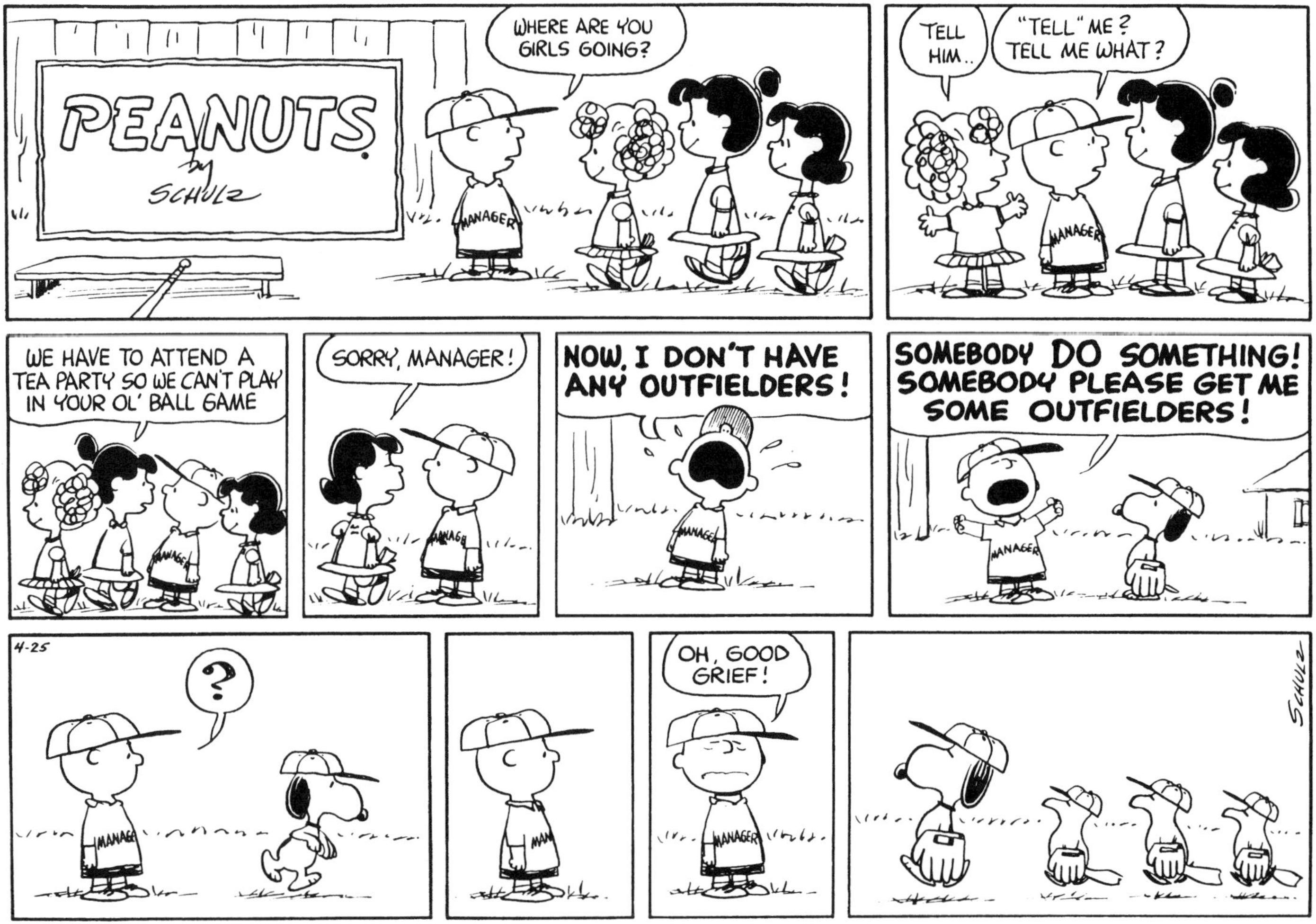
PEANUTS
by SCHULZ
WHERE ARE YOU GIRLS GOING?
TELL HIM..
"TELL" ME? TELL ME WHAT?
WE HAVE TO ATTEND A TEA PARTY SO WE CAN'T PLAY IN YOUR OL' BALL GAME
SORRY, MANAGER!
NOW, I DON'T HAVE ANY OUTFIELDERS!
SOMEBODY DO SOMETHING! SOMEBODY PLEASE GET ME SOME OUTFIELDERS!
4-25
?
OH, GOOD GRIEF!
SCHULZ

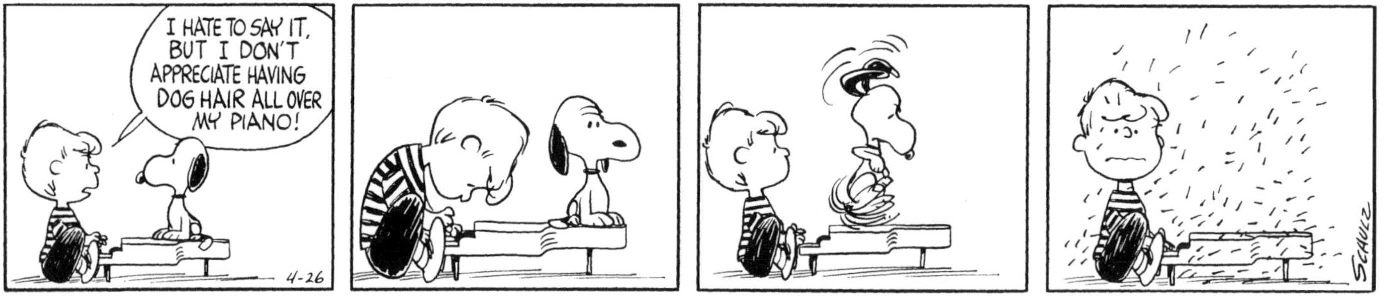
I HATE TO SAY IT, BUT I DON'T APPRECIATE HAVING DOG HAIR ALL OVER MY PIANO!
4-26

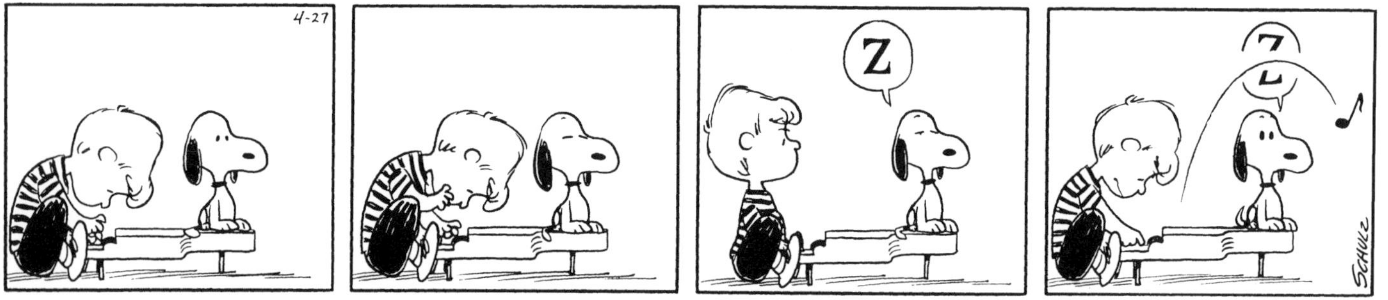
4-27
Z
Z

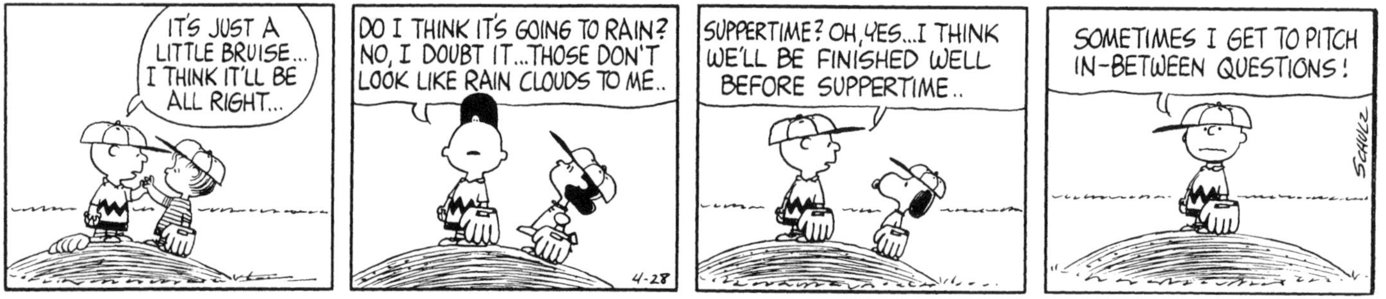
IT'S JUST A LITTLE BRUISE... I THINK IT'LL BE ALL RIGHT...
DO I THINK IT'S GOING TO RAIN? NO, I DOUBT IT...THOSE DON'T LOOK LIKE RAIN CLOUDS TO ME..
4-28
SUPPERTIME? OH, YES...I THINK WE'LL BE FINISHED WELL BEFORE SUPPERTIME..
SOMETIMES I GET TO PITCH IN-BETWEEN QUESTIONS!

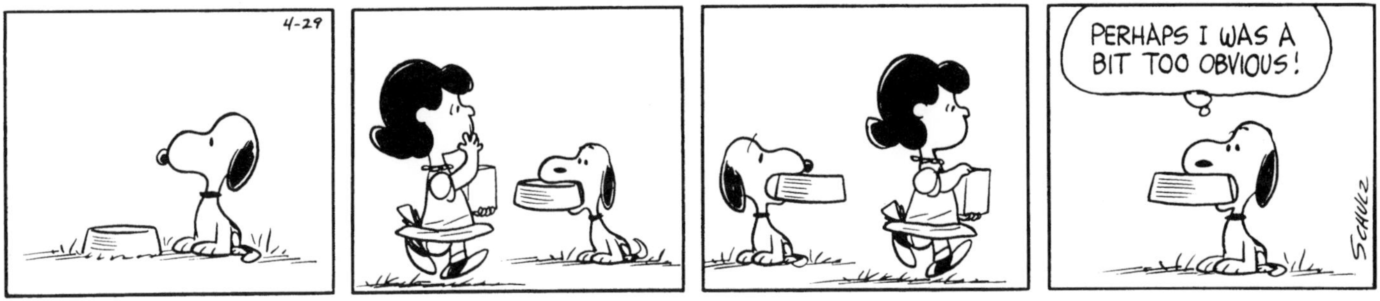
4-29
PERHAPS I WAS A BIT TOO OBVIOUS!
SCHULZ

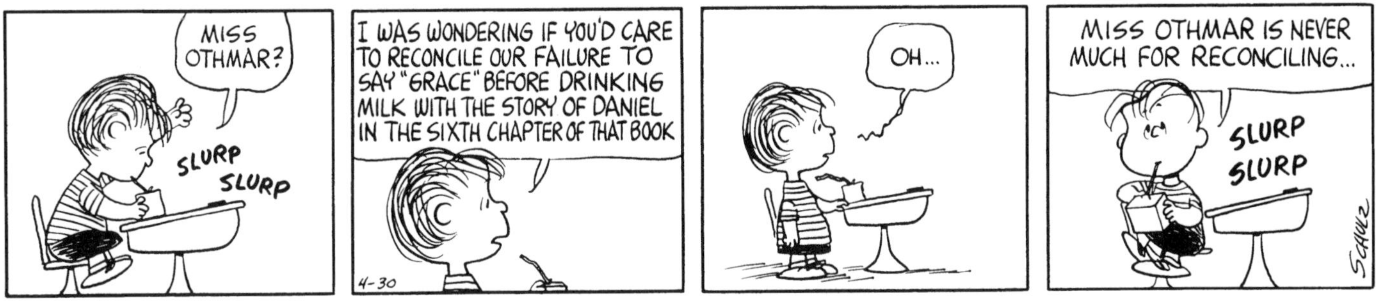
MISS OTHMAR?
SLURP
SLURP
I WAS WONDERING IF YOU'D CARE TO RECONCILE OUR FAILURE TO SAY "GRACE" BEFORE DRINKING MILK WITH THE STORY OF DANIEL IN THE SIXTH CHAPTER OF THAT BOOK
4-30
OH...
MISS OTHMAR IS NEVER MUCH FOR RECONCILING...
SLURP
SLURP
SCHULZ

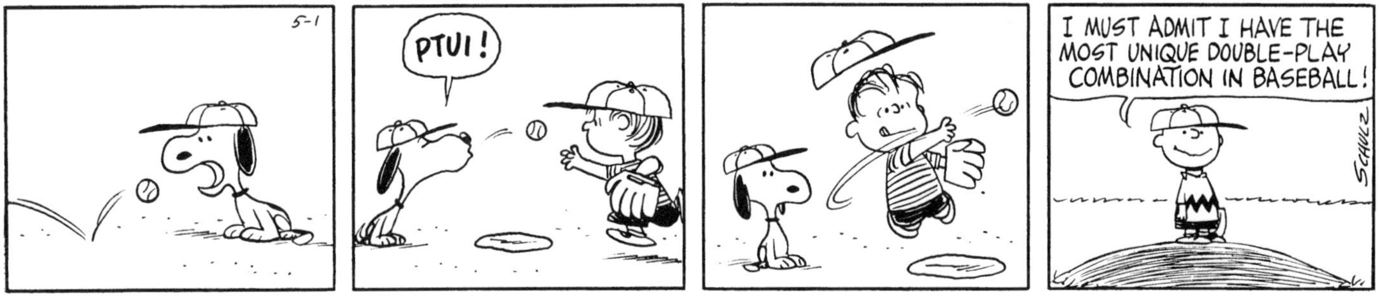
5-1
PTUI!
SCHULZ
I MUST ADMIT I HAVE THE MOST UNIQUE DOUBLE-PLAY COMBINATION IN BASEBALL!

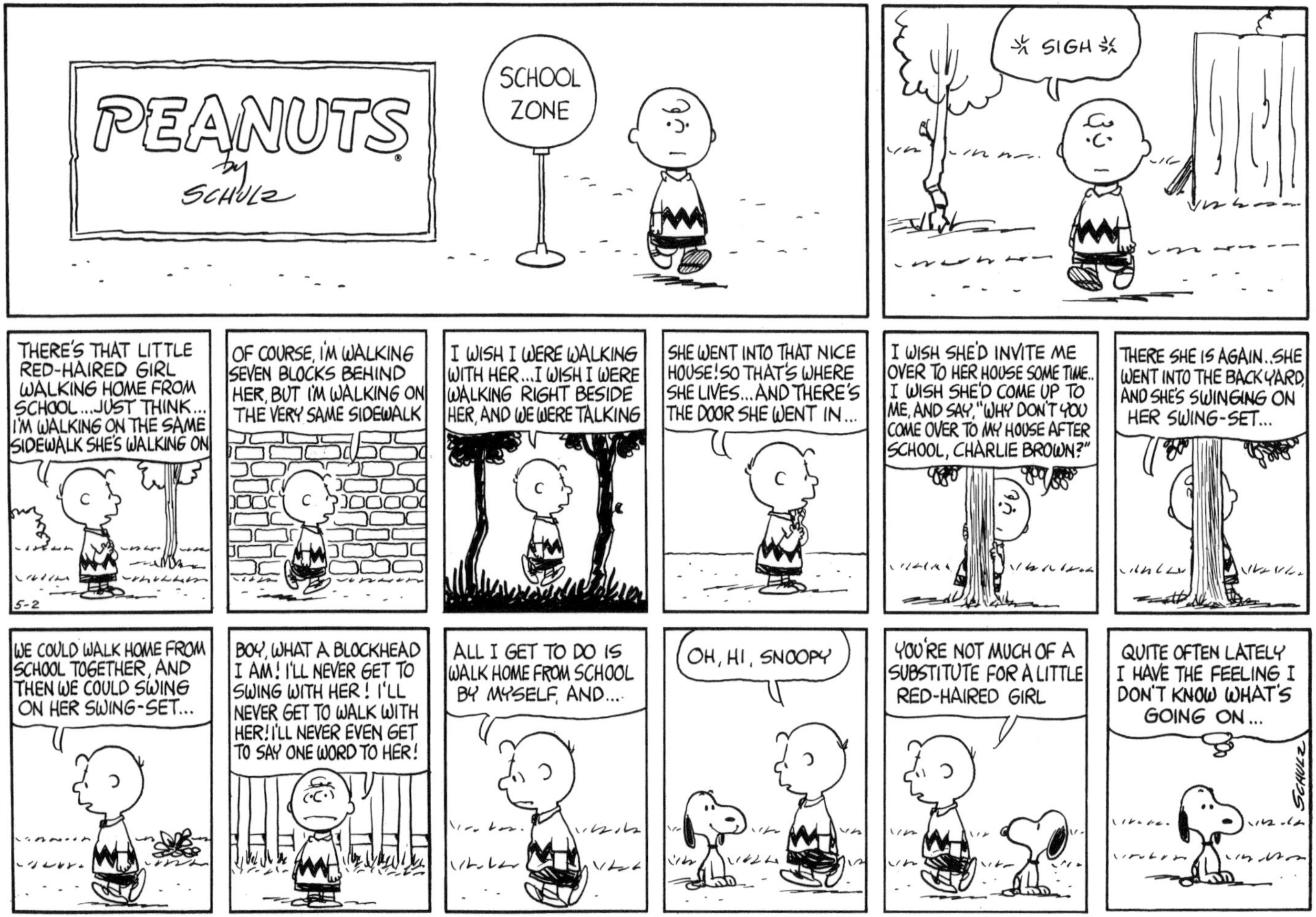
PEANUTS
by SCHULZ
SCHOOL ZONE
SIGH
THERE'S THAT LITTLE RED-HAIRED GIRL WALKING HOME FROM SCHOOL...JUST THINK... I'M WALKING ON THE SAME SIDEWALK SHE'S WALKING ON
5-2
OF COURSE, I'M WALKING SEVEN BLOCKS BEHIND HER, BUT I'M WALKING ON THE VERY SAME SIDEWALK
I WISH I WERE WALKING WITH HER...I WISH I WERE WALKING RIGHT BESIDE HER, AND WE WERE TALKING
SHE WENT INTO THAT NICE HOUSE! SO THAT'S WHERE SHE LIVES...AND THERE'S THE DOOR SHE WENT IN...
I WISH SHE'D INVITE ME OVER TO HER HOUSE SOME TIME.. I WISH SHE'D COME UP TO ME, AND SAY, "WHY DON'T YOU COME OVER TO MY HOUSE AFTER SCHOOL, CHARLIE BROWN?"
THERE SHE IS AGAIN..SHE WENT INTO THE BACK YARD, AND SHE'S SWINGING ON HER SWING-SET...
WE COULD WALK HOME FROM SCHOOL TOGETHER, AND THEN WE COULD SWING ON HER SWING-SET...
BOY, WHAT A BLOCKHEAD I AM! I'LL NEVER GET TO SWING WITH HER! I'LL NEVER GET TO WALK WITH HER! I'LL NEVER EVEN GET TO SAY ONE WORD TO HER!
ALL I GET TO DO IS WALK HOME FROM SCHOOL BY MYSELF, AND...
OH, HI, SNOOPY
YOU'RE NOT MUCH OF A SUBSTITUTE FOR A LITTLE RED-HAIRED GIRL
QUITE OFTEN LATELY I HAVE THE FEELING I DON'T KNOW WHAT'S GOING ON...
SCHULZ

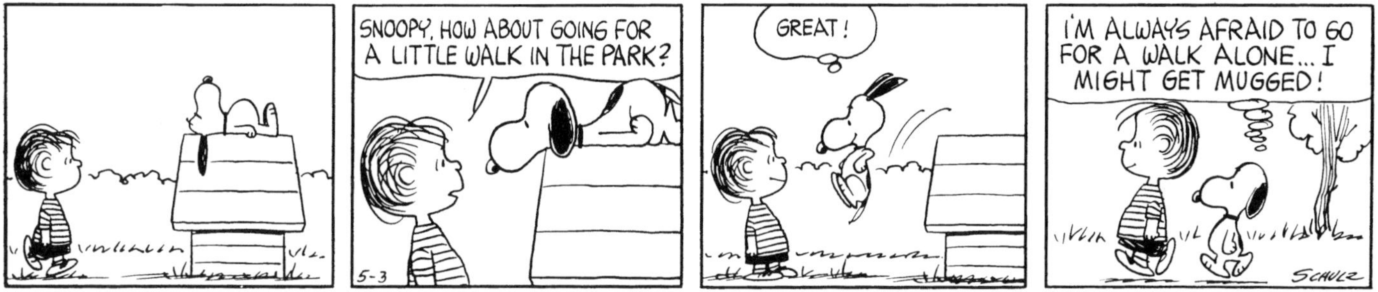
SNOOPY, HOW ABOUT GOING FOR A LITTLE WALK IN THE PARK?
5-3
GREAT!
I'M ALWAYS AFRAID TO GO FOR A WALK ALONE... I MIGHT GET MUGGED!
SCHULZ

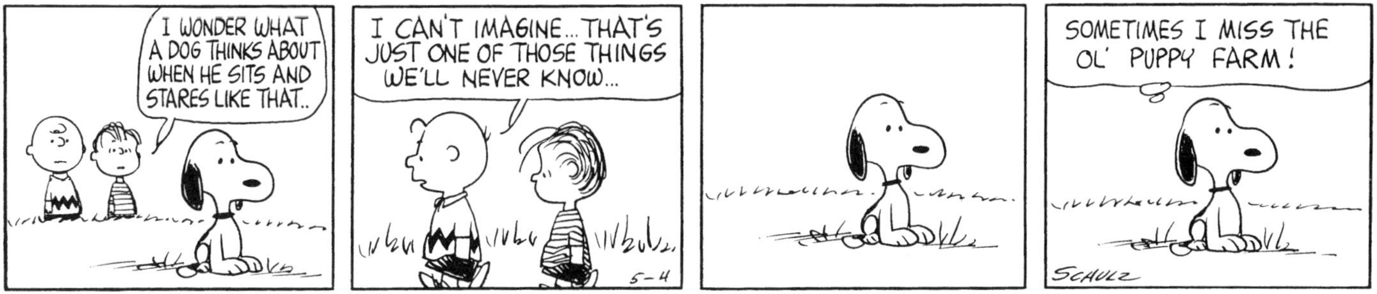
I WONDER WHAT A DOG THINKS ABOUT WHEN HE SITS AND STARES LIKE THAT..
I CAN'T IMAGINE... THAT'S JUST ONE OF THOSE THINGS WE'LL NEVER KNOW...
5-4
SOMETIMES I MISS THE OL' PUPPY FARM!
SCHULZ

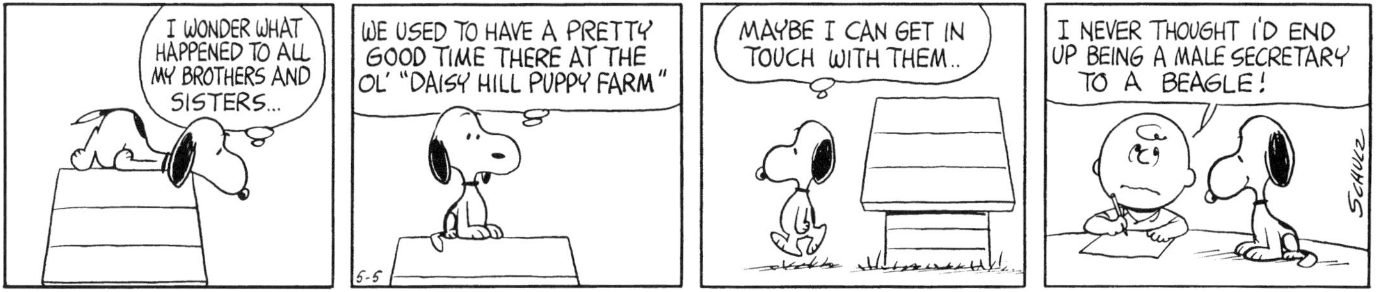
I WONDER WHAT HAPPENED TO ALL MY BROTHERS AND SISTERS...
WE USED TO HAVE A PRETTY GOOD TIME THERE AT THE OL' "DAISY HILL PUPPY FARM"
5-5
MAYBE I CAN GET IN TOUCH WITH THEM..
I NEVER THOUGHT I'D END UP BEING A MALE SECRETARY TO A BEAGLE!
SCHULZ

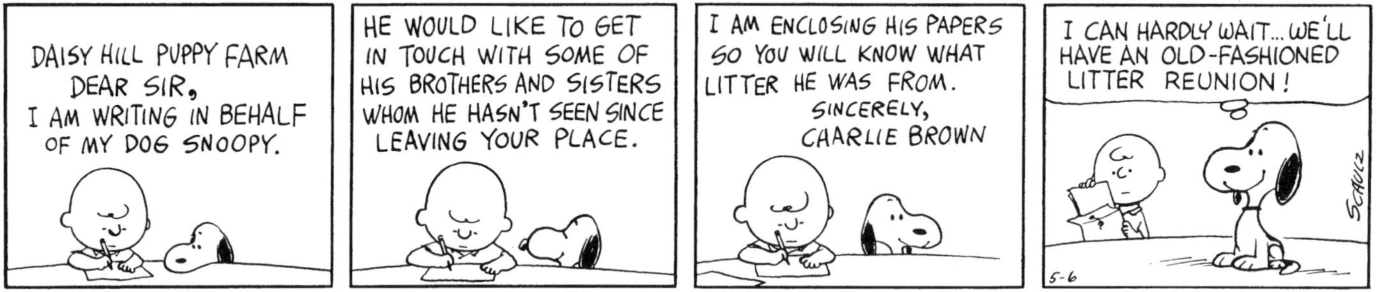
DAISY HILL PUPPY FARM
DEAR SIR,
I AM WRITING IN BEHALF OF MY DOG SNOOPY.
HE WOULD LIKE TO GET IN TOUCH WITH SOME OF HIS BROTHERS AND SISTERS WHOM HE HASN'T SEEN SINCE LEAVING YOUR PLACE.
I AM ENCLOSING HIS PAPERS SO YOU WILL KNOW WHAT LITTER HE WAS FROM.
SINCERELY,
CHARLIE BROWN
I CAN HARDLY WAIT... WE'LL HAVE AN OLD-FASHIONED LITTER REUNION!

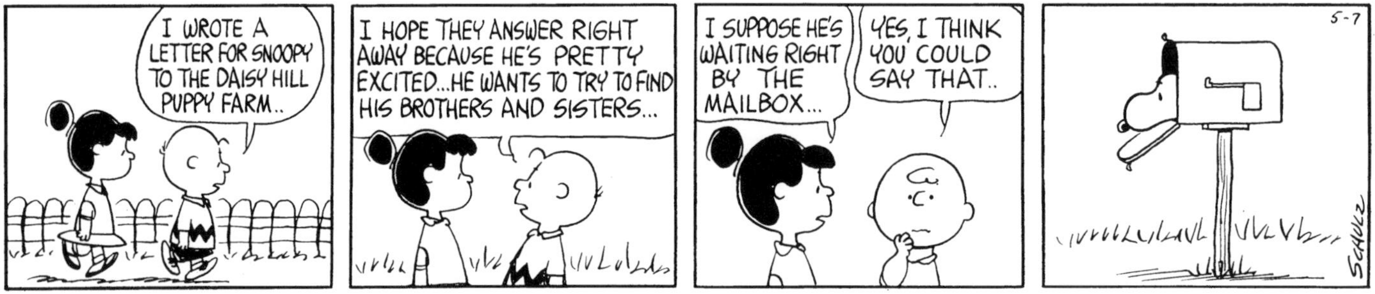
I WROTE A LETTER FOR SNOOPY TO THE DAISY HILL PUPPY FARM..
I HOPE THEY ANSWER RIGHT AWAY BECAUSE HE'S PRETTY EXCITED...HE WANTS TO TRY TO FIND HIS BROTHERS AND SISTERS...
I SUPPOSE HE'S WAITING RIGHT BY THE MAILBOX...
YES, I THINK YOU COULD SAY THAT..

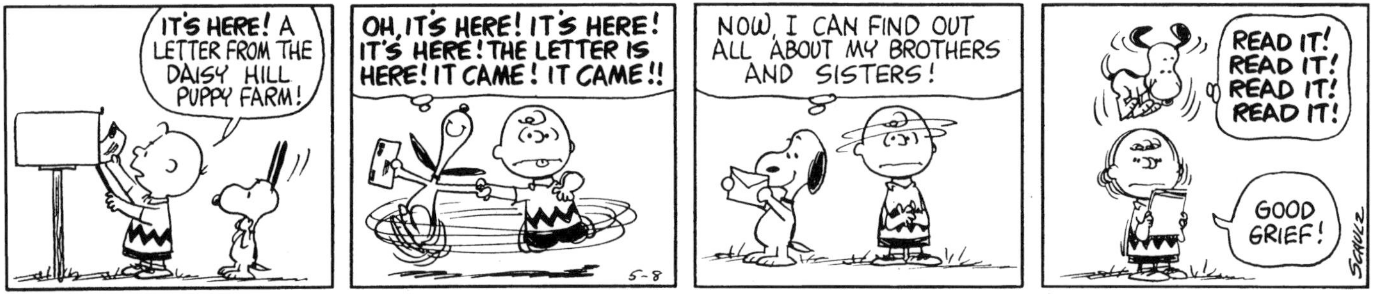
IT'S HERE! A LETTER FROM THE DAISY HILL PUPPY FARM!
OH, IT'S HERE! IT'S HERE! IT'S HERE! THE LETTER IS HERE! IT CAME! IT CAME!!
NOW, I CAN FIND OUT ALL ABOUT MY BROTHERS AND SISTERS!
READ IT! READ IT! READ IT! READ IT!
GOOD GRIEF!

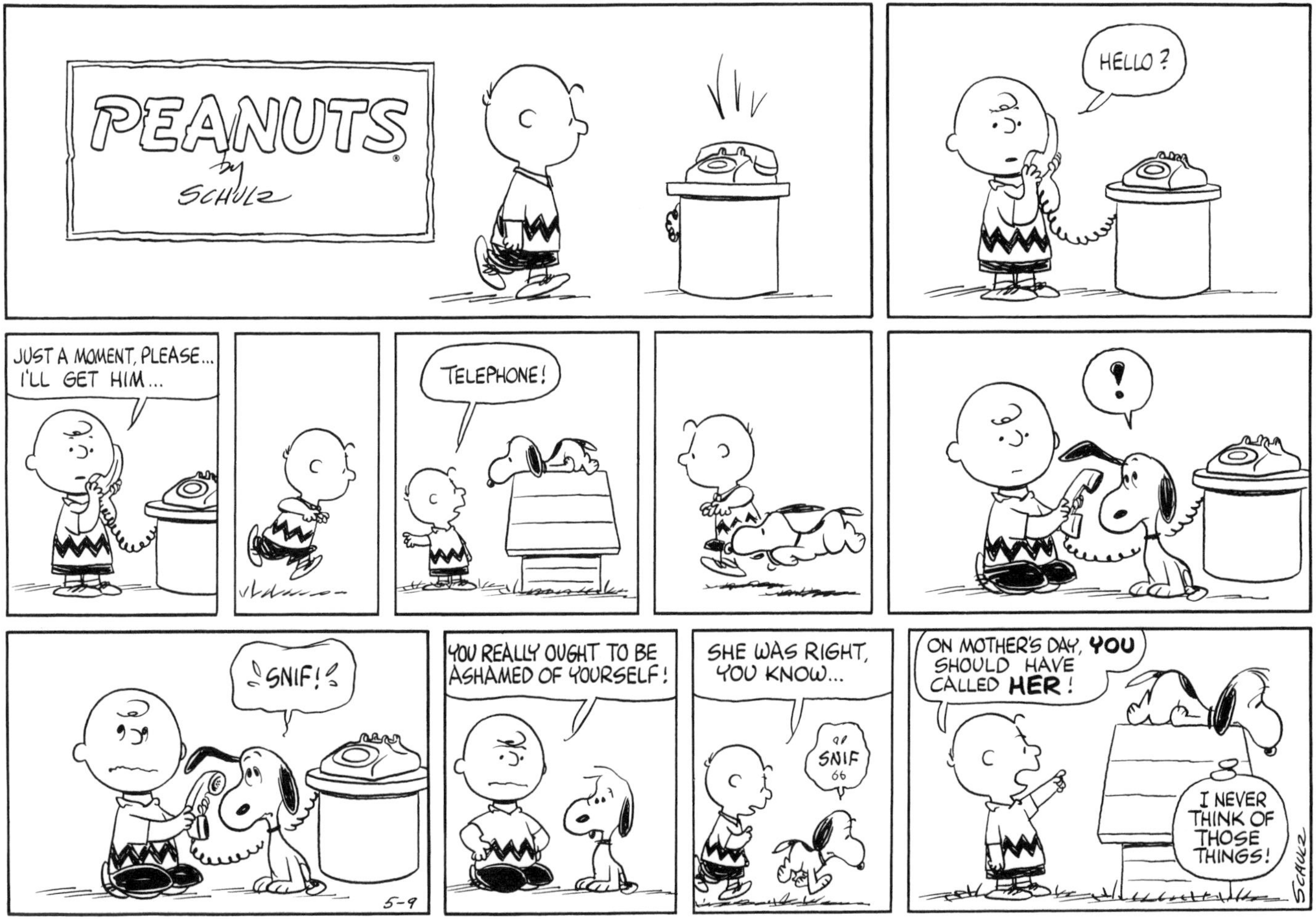
PEANUTS
by SCHULZ
HELLO ?
JUST A MOMENT, PLEASE... I'LL GET HIM...
TELEPHONE!
!
SNIF!
5-9
YOU REALLY OUGHT TO BE ASHAMED OF YOURSELF!
SHE WAS RIGHT, YOU KNOW...
SNIF
ON MOTHER'S DAY, YOU SHOULD HAVE CALLED HER!
I NEVER THINK OF THOSE THINGS!
SCHULZ

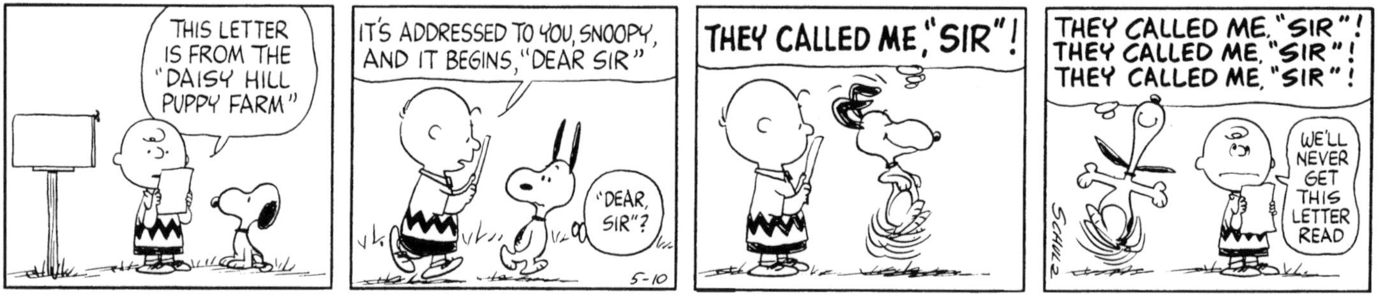
THIS LETTER IS FROM THE "DAISY HILL PUPPY FARM"
IT'S ADDRESSED TO YOU, SNOOPY, AND IT BEGINS, "DEAR SIR"
"DEAR, SIR"?
5-10
THEY CALLED ME, "SIR"!
THEY CALLED ME, "SIR"! THEY CALLED ME, "SIR"! THEY CALLED ME, "SIR"!
WE'LL NEVER GET THIS LETTER READ
SCHULZ

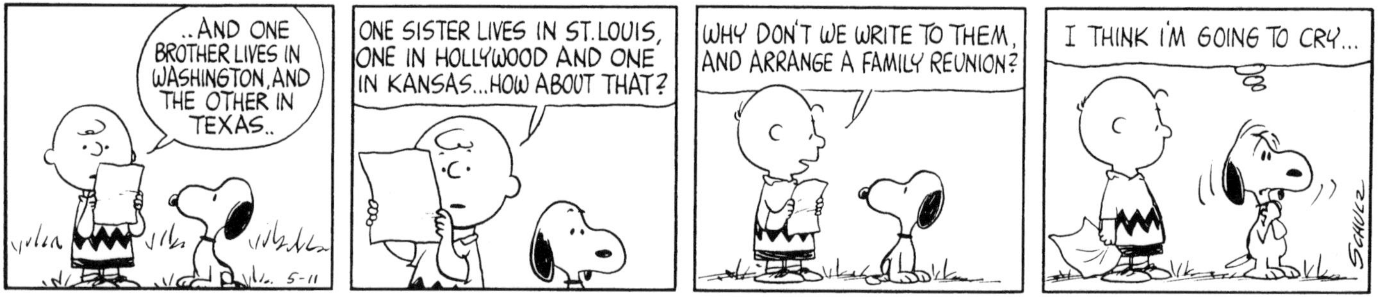
..AND ONE BROTHER LIVES IN WASHINGTON, AND THE OTHER IN TEXAS..
5-11
ONE SISTER LIVES IN ST. LOUIS, ONE IN HOLLYWOOD AND ONE IN KANSAS...HOW ABOUT THAT?
WHY DON'T WE WRITE TO THEM, AND ARRANGE A FAMILY REUNION?
I THINK I'M GOING TO CRY...
SCHULZ

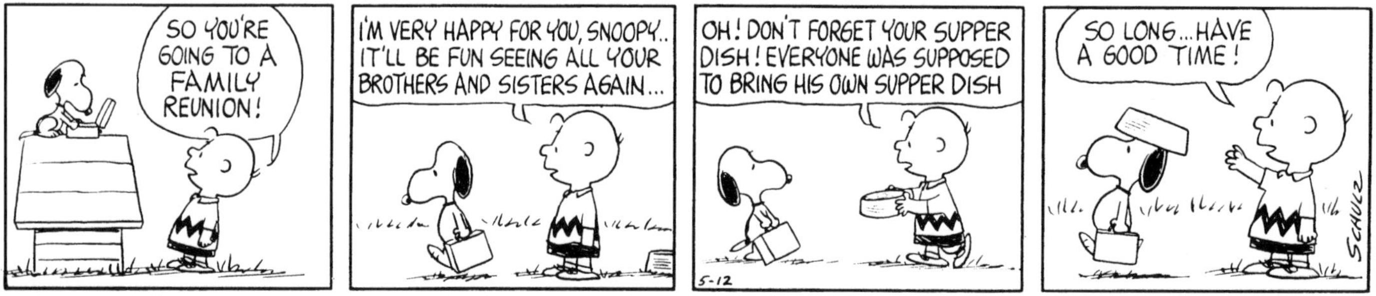
SO YOU'RE GOING TO A FAMILY REUNION!
I'M VERY HAPPY FOR YOU, SNOOPY.. IT'LL BE FUN SEEING ALL YOUR BROTHERS AND SISTERS AGAIN...
OH! DON'T FORGET YOUR SUPPER DISH! EVERYONE WAS SUPPOSED TO BRING HIS OWN SUPPER DISH
5-12
SO LONG...HAVE A GOOD TIME!
SCHULZ

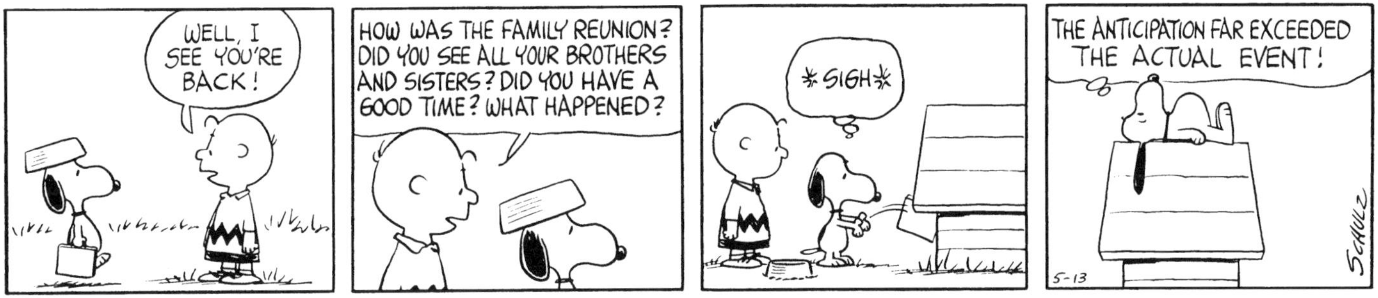
WELL, I SEE YOU'RE BACK!
HOW WAS THE FAMILY REUNION? DID YOU SEE ALL YOUR BROTHERS AND SISTERS? DID YOU HAVE A GOOD TIME? WHAT HAPPENED?
SIGH
THE ANTICIPATION FAR EXCEEDED THE ACTUAL EVENT!
5-13
SCHULZ

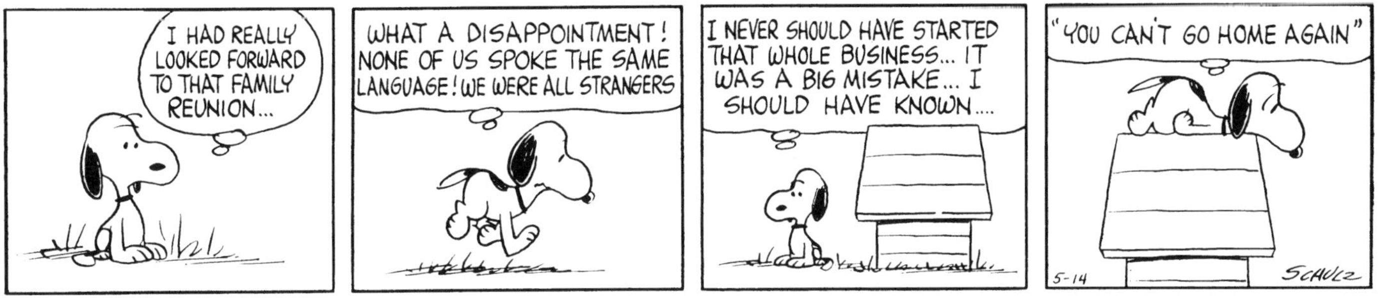
I HAD REALLY LOOKED FORWARD TO THAT FAMILY REUNION...
WHAT A DISAPPOINTMENT! NONE OF US SPOKE THE SAME LANGUAGE! WE WERE ALL STRANGERS
I NEVER SHOULD HAVE STARTED THAT WHOLE BUSINESS... IT WAS A BIG MISTAKE... I SHOULD HAVE KNOWN....
"YOU CAN'T GO HOME AGAIN"
5-14
SCHULZ

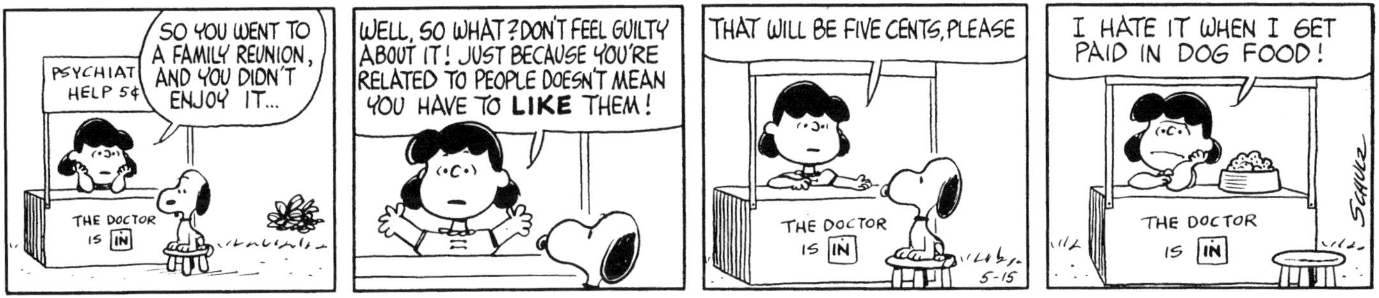
PSYCHIAT
HELP 5¢
SO YOU WENT TO A FAMILY REUNION, AND YOU DIDN'T ENJOY IT...
THE DOCTOR IS IN
WELL, SO WHAT? DON'T FEEL GUILTY ABOUT IT! JUST BECAUSE YOU'RE RELATED TO PEOPLE DOESN'T MEAN YOU HAVE TO **LIKE** THEM!
THAT WILL BE FIVE CENTS, PLEASE
THE DOCTOR IS IN
5-15
I HATE IT WHEN I GET PAID IN DOG FOOD!
THE DOCTOR IS IN
SCHULZ

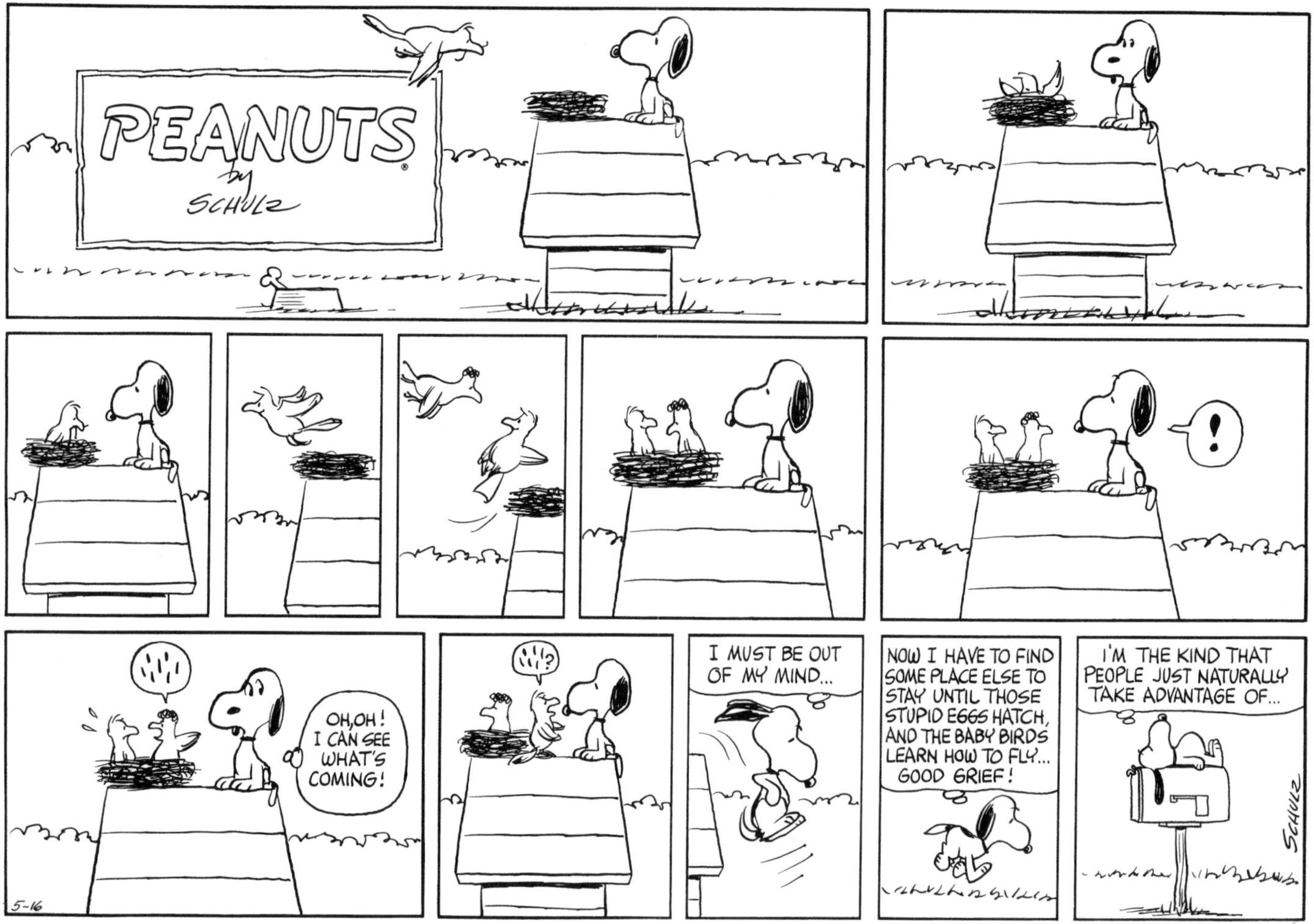
PEANUTS
by SCHULZ
5-16
!
OH,OH! I CAN SEE WHAT'S COMING!
I MUST BE OUT OF MY MIND...
NOW I HAVE TO FIND SOME PLACE ELSE TO STAY UNTIL THOSE STUPID EGGS HATCH, AND THE BABY BIRDS LEARN HOW TO FLY... GOOD GRIEF!
I'M THE KIND THAT PEOPLE JUST NATURALLY TAKE ADVANTAGE OF...
SCHULZ

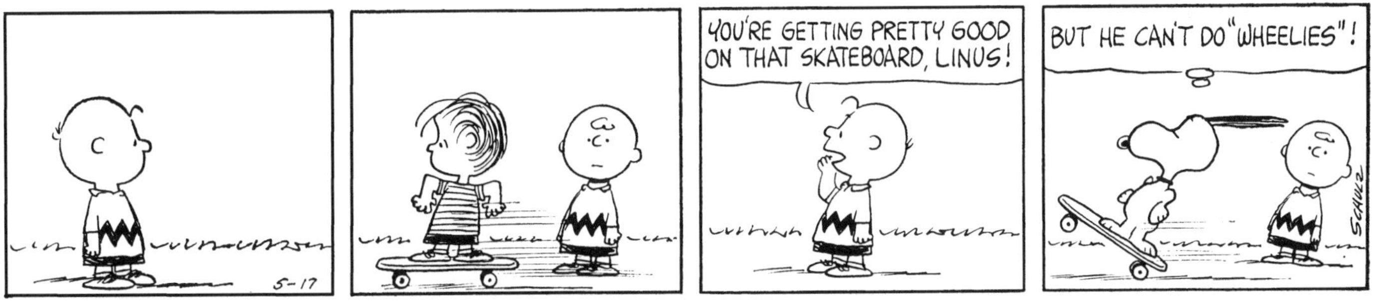
5-17
YOU'RE GETTING PRETTY GOOD ON THAT SKATEBOARD, LINUS!
BUT HE CAN'T DO "WHEELIES"!
SCHULZ

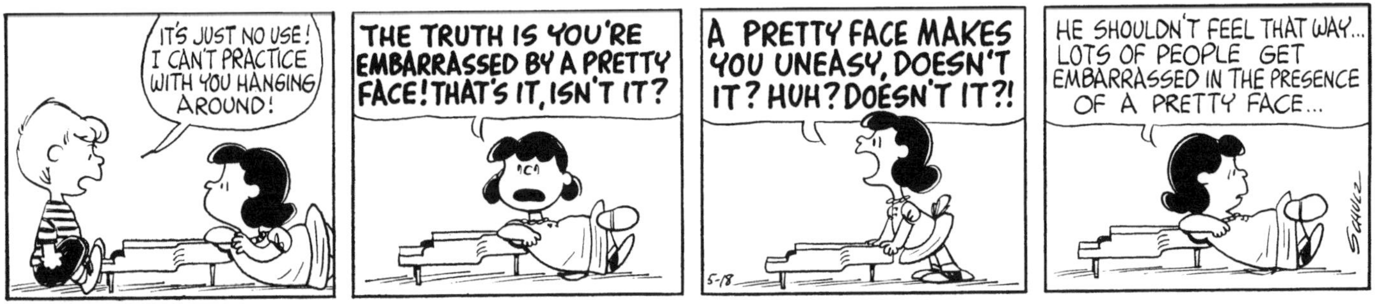
IT'S JUST NO USE! I CAN'T PRACTICE WITH YOU HANGING AROUND!
THE TRUTH IS YOU'RE EMBARRASSED BY A PRETTY FACE! THAT'S IT, ISN'T IT?
A PRETTY FACE MAKES YOU UNEASY, DOESN'T IT? HUH? DOESN'T IT?!
5-18
HE SHOULDN'T FEEL THAT WAY... LOTS OF PEOPLE GET EMBARRASSED IN THE PRESENCE OF A PRETTY FACE...
SCHULZ

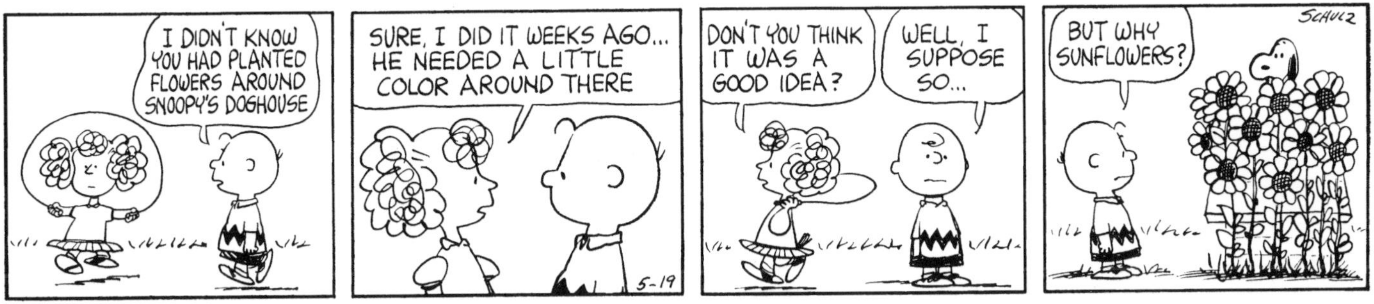
I DIDN'T KNOW YOU HAD PLANTED FLOWERS AROUND SNOOPY'S DOGHOUSE
SURE, I DID IT WEEKS AGO... HE NEEDED A LITTLE COLOR AROUND THERE
5-19
DON'T YOU THINK IT WAS A GOOD IDEA?
WELL, I SUPPOSE SO...
SCHULZ
BUT WHY SUNFLOWERS?

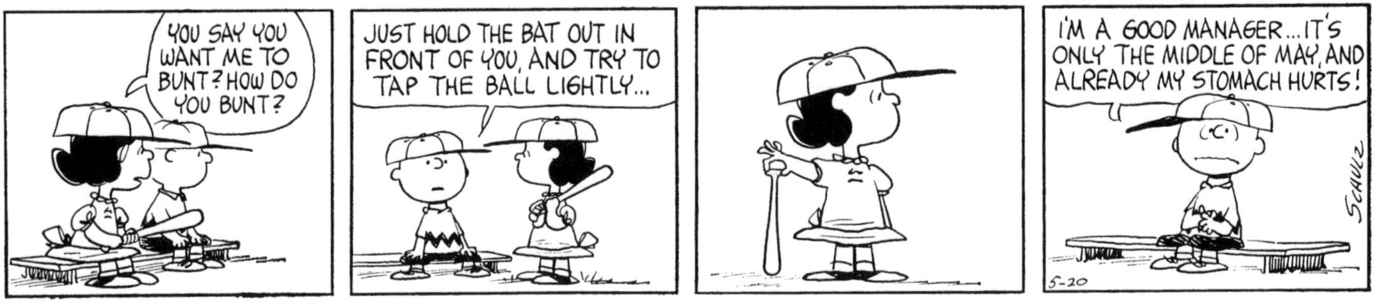
YOU SAY YOU WANT ME TO BUNT? HOW DO YOU BUNT?
JUST HOLD THE BAT OUT IN FRONT OF YOU, AND TRY TO TAP THE BALL LIGHTLY...
I'M A GOOD MANAGER...IT'S ONLY THE MIDDLE OF MAY, AND ALREADY MY STOMACH HURTS!
SCHULZ
5-20

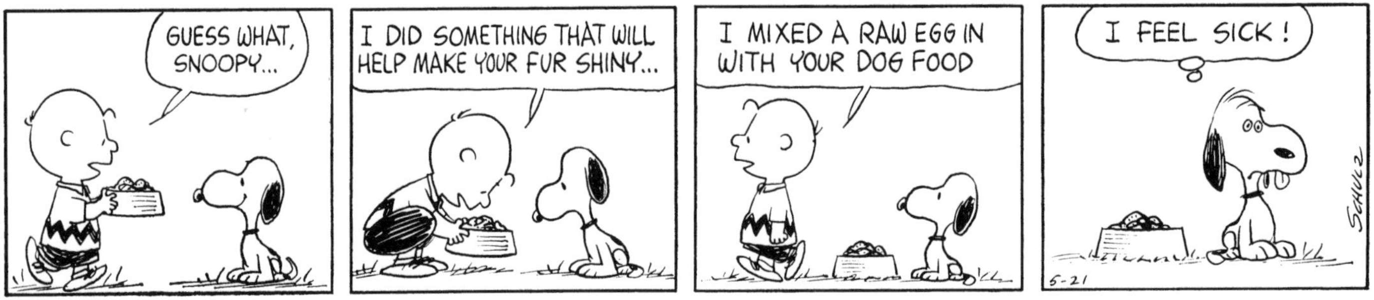
GUESS WHAT, SNOOPY...
I DID SOMETHING THAT WILL HELP MAKE YOUR FUR SHINY...
I MIXED A RAW EGG IN WITH YOUR DOG FOOD
I FEEL SICK!
SCHULZ
5-21

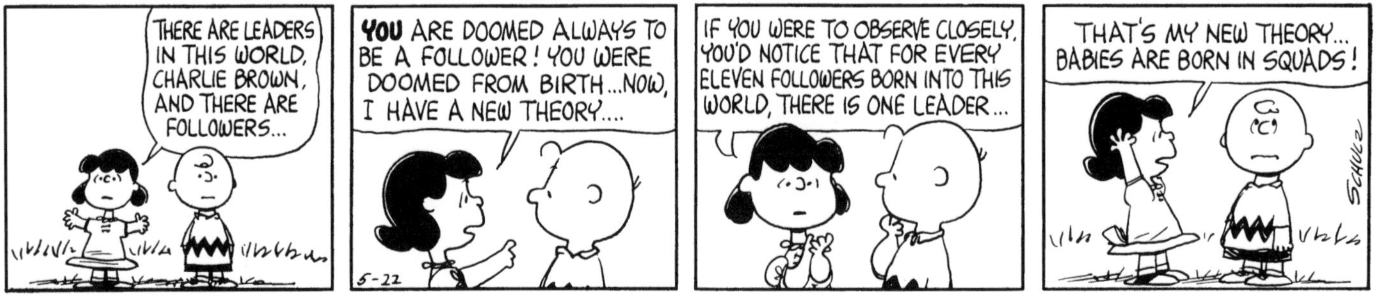
THERE ARE LEADERS IN THIS WORLD, CHARLIE BROWN, AND THERE ARE FOLLOWERS...
YOU ARE DOOMED ALWAYS TO BE A FOLLOWER! YOU WERE DOOMED FROM BIRTH...NOW, I HAVE A NEW THEORY....
5-22
IF YOU WERE TO OBSERVE CLOSELY, YOU'D NOTICE THAT FOR EVERY ELEVEN FOLLOWERS BORN INTO THIS WORLD, THERE IS ONE LEADER...
THAT'S MY NEW THEORY... BABIES ARE BORN IN SQUADS!
SCHULZ

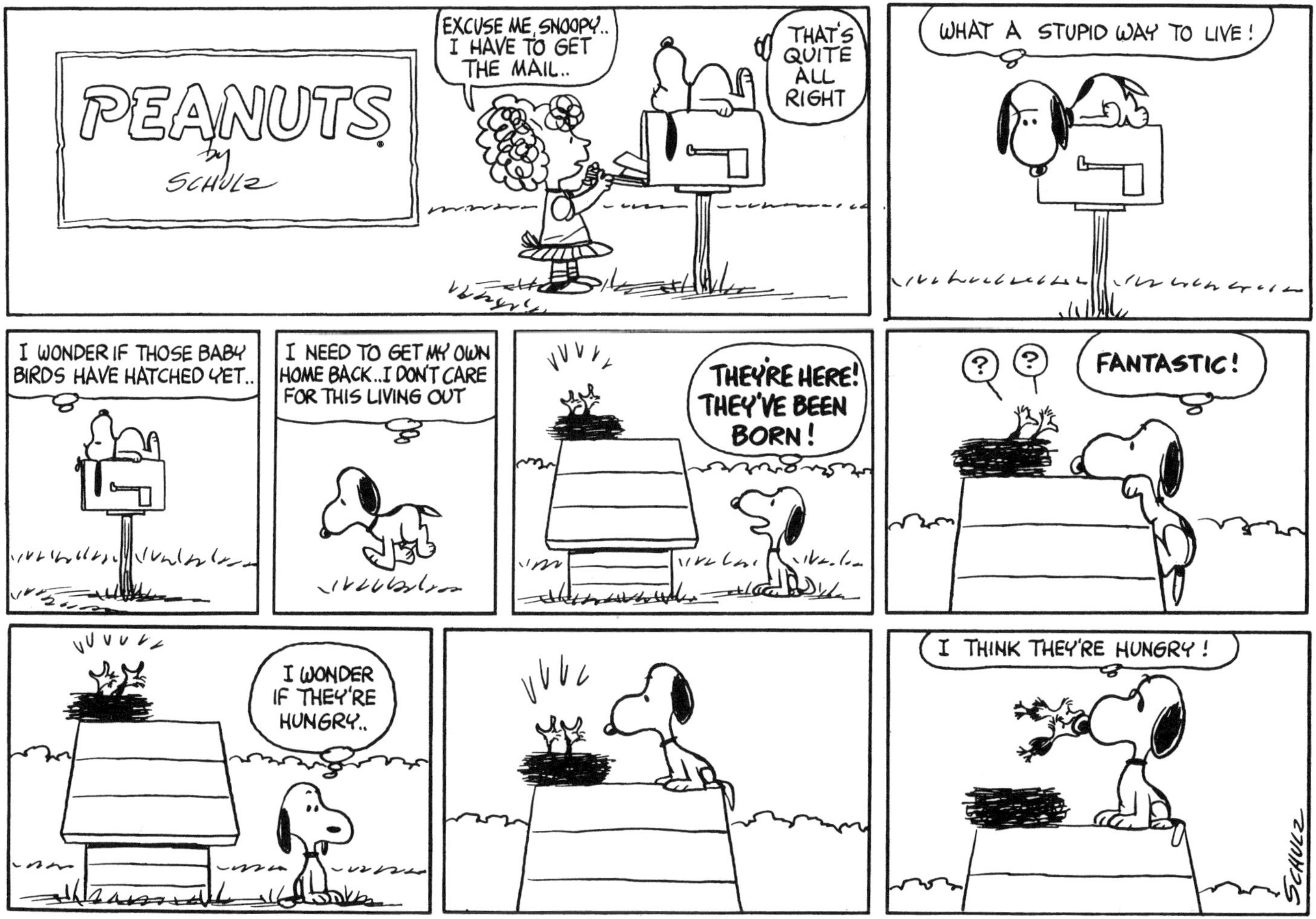
PEANUTS
by SCHULZ
EXCUSE ME, SNOOPY.. I HAVE TO GET THE MAIL..
THAT'S QUITE ALL RIGHT
WHAT A STUPID WAY TO LIVE!
I WONDER IF THOSE BABY BIRDS HAVE HATCHED YET..
I NEED TO GET MY OWN HOME BACK..I DON'T CARE FOR THIS LIVING OUT
THEY'RE HERE! THEY'VE BEEN BORN!
?
?
FANTASTIC!
I WONDER IF THEY'RE HUNGRY..
I THINK THEY'RE HUNGRY!
SCHULZ

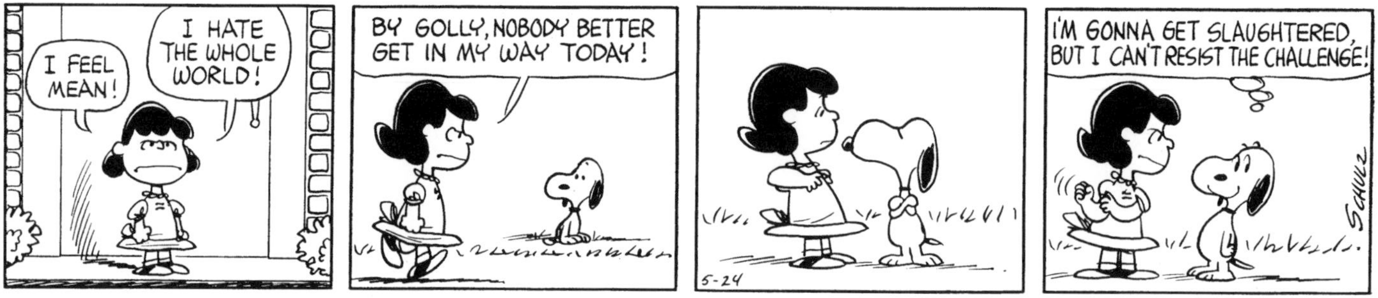
I FEEL MEAN!
I HATE THE WHOLE WORLD!
BY GOLLY, NOBODY BETTER GET IN MY WAY TODAY!
5-24
I'M GONNA GET SLAUGHTERED, BUT I CAN'T RESIST THE CHALLENGE!
SCHULZ

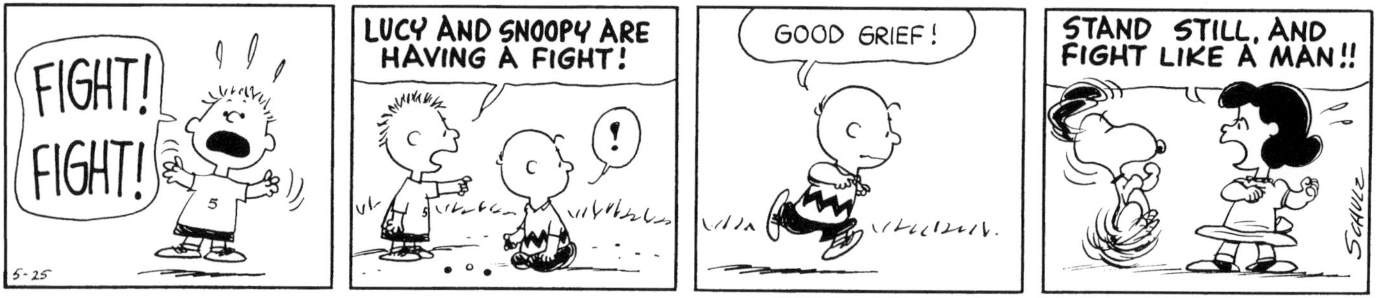
FIGHT! FIGHT!
5
5-25
LUCY AND SNOOPY ARE HAVING A FIGHT!
5
!
GOOD GRIEF!
STAND STILL, AND FIGHT LIKE A MAN!!
SCHULZ

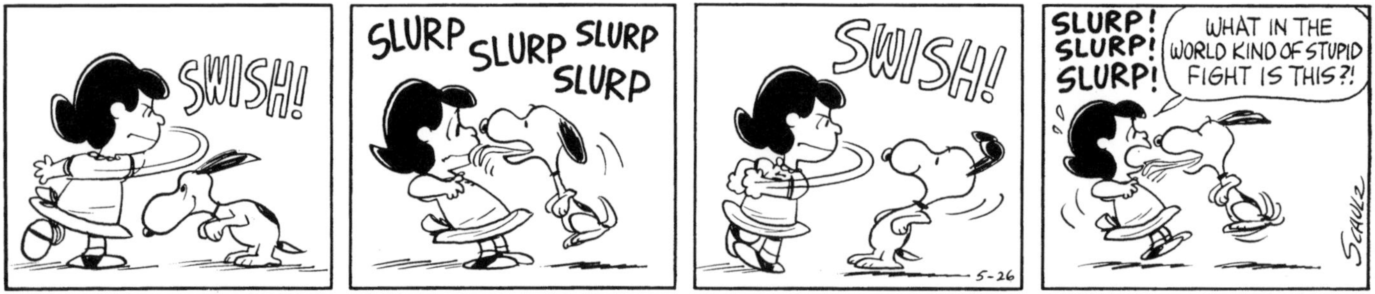
SWISH!
SLURP SLURP SLURP SLURP
SWISH!
5-26
SLURP! SLURP! SLURP!
WHAT IN THE WORLD KIND OF STUPID FIGHT IS THIS?!
SCHULZ

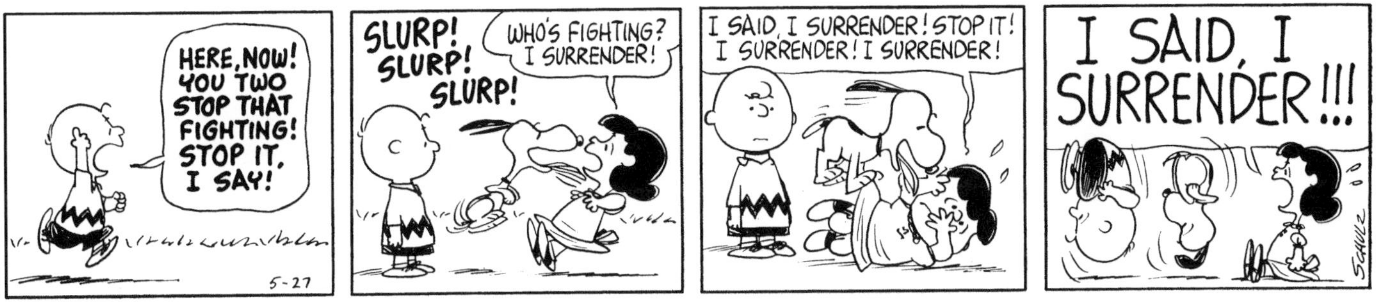
HERE, NOW! YOU TWO STOP THAT FIGHTING! STOP IT, I SAY!
SLURP! SLURP! SLURP!
WHO'S FIGHTING? I SURRENDER!
I SAID, I SURRENDER! STOP IT! I SURRENDER! I SURRENDER!
I SAID, I SURRENDER!!!

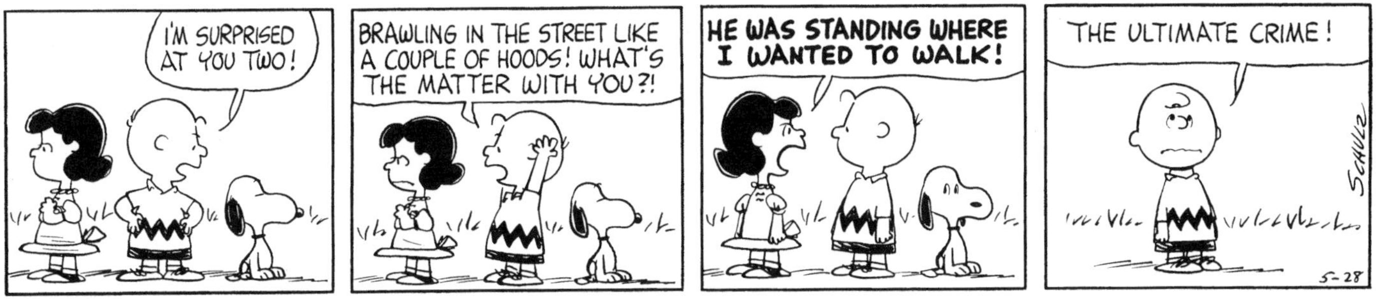
I'M SURPRISED AT YOU TWO!
BRAWLING IN THE STREET LIKE A COUPLE OF HOODS! WHAT'S THE MATTER WITH YOU?!
HE WAS STANDING WHERE I WANTED TO WALK!
THE ULTIMATE CRIME!

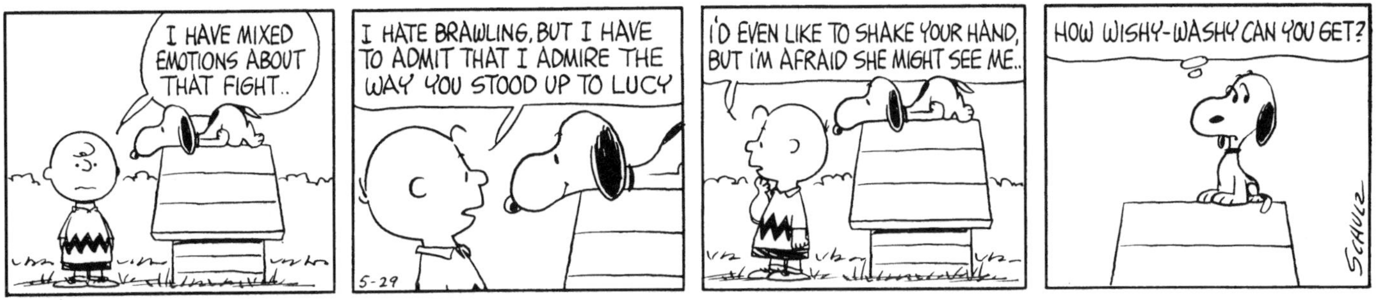
I HAVE MIXED EMOTIONS ABOUT THAT FIGHT..
I HATE BRAWLING, BUT I HAVE TO ADMIT THAT I ADMIRE THE WAY YOU STOOD UP TO LUCY
I'D EVEN LIKE TO SHAKE YOUR HAND, BUT I'M AFRAID SHE MIGHT SEE ME..
HOW WISHY-WASHY CAN YOU GET?

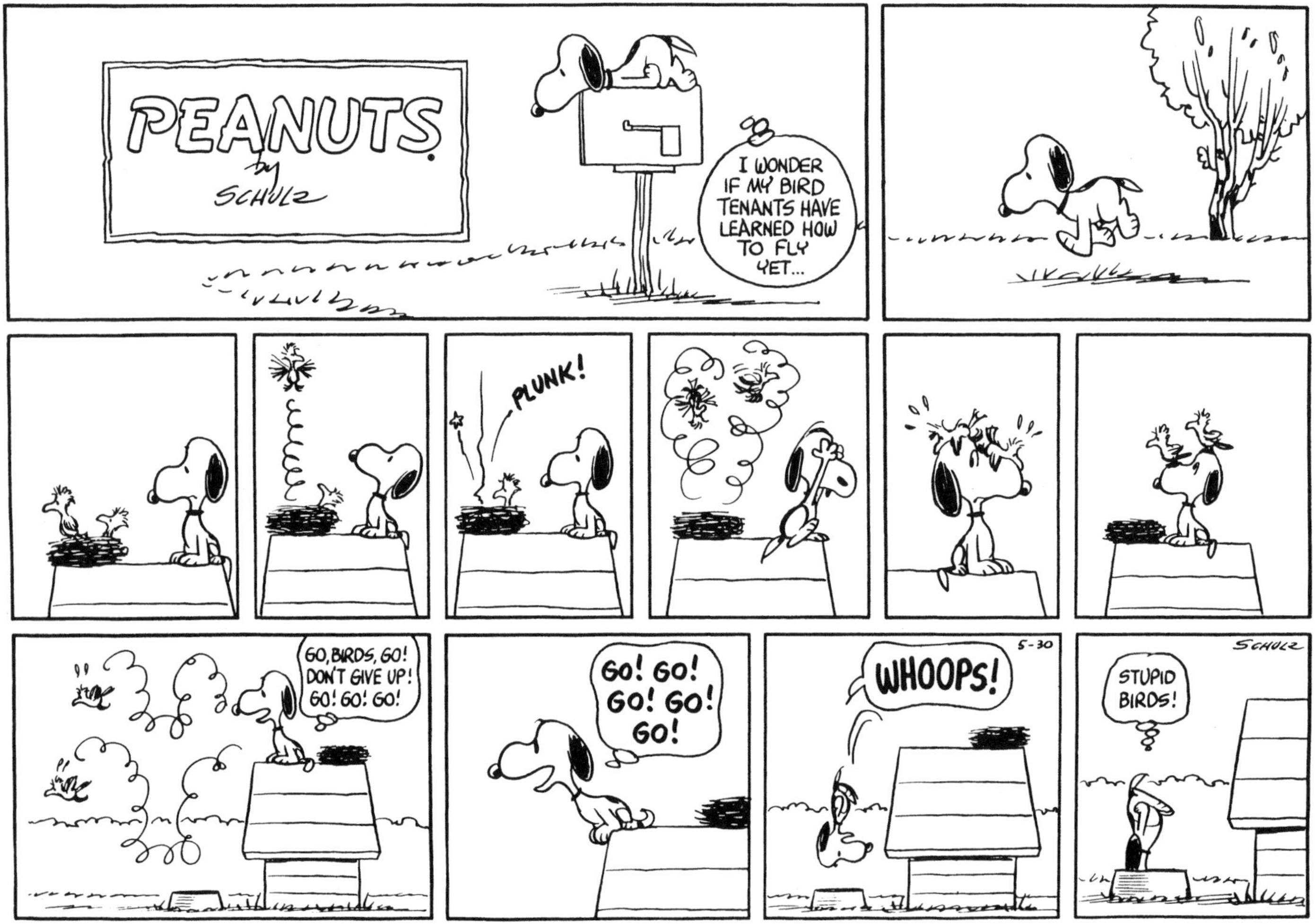
PEANUTS
by SCHULZ
I WONDER IF MY BIRD TENANTS HAVE LEARNED HOW TO FLY YET...
PLUNK!
GO, BIRDS, GO! DON'T GIVE UP! GO! GO! GO!
GO! GO! GO! GO! GO!
5-30
WHOOPS!
SCHULZ
STUPID BIRDS!

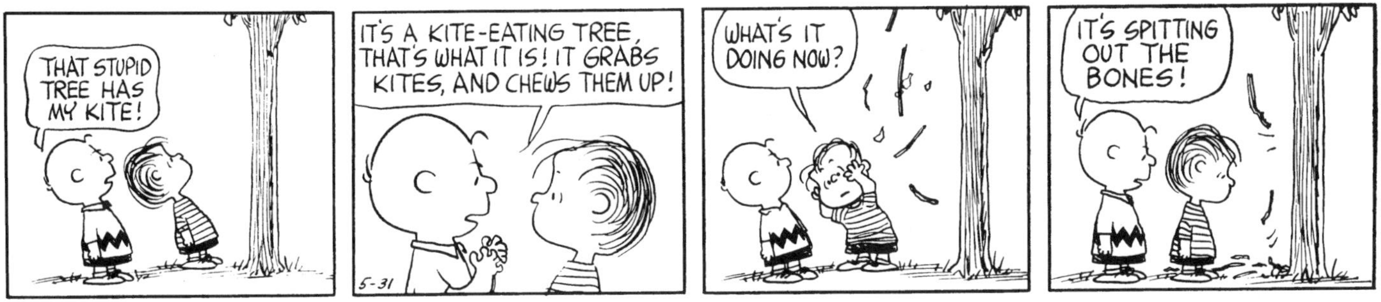
THAT STUPID TREE HAS MY KITE!
IT'S A KITE-EATING TREE, THAT'S WHAT IT IS! IT GRABS KITES, AND CHEWS THEM UP!
5-31
WHAT'S IT DOING NOW?
IT'S SPITTING OUT THE BONES!

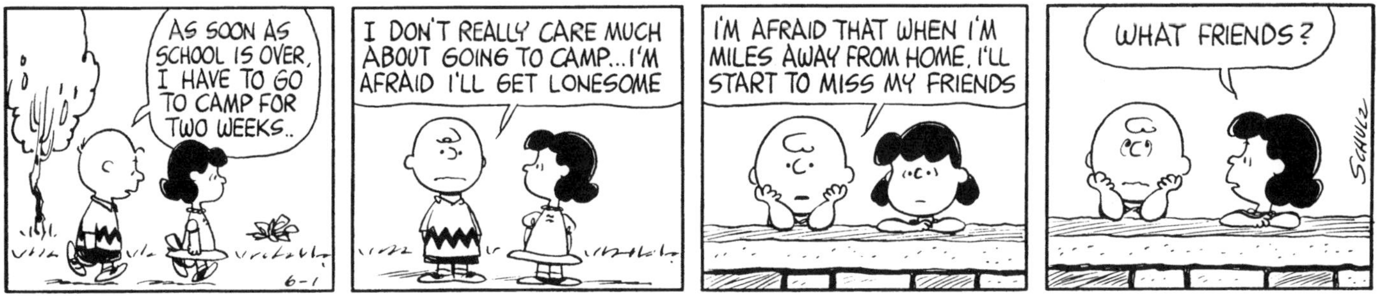
AS SOON AS SCHOOL IS OVER, I HAVE TO GO TO CAMP FOR TWO WEEKS..
6-1
I DON'T REALLY CARE MUCH ABOUT GOING TO CAMP...I'M AFRAID I'LL GET LONESOME
I'M AFRAID THAT WHEN I'M MILES AWAY FROM HOME, I'LL START TO MISS MY FRIENDS
WHAT FRIENDS?
SCHULZ

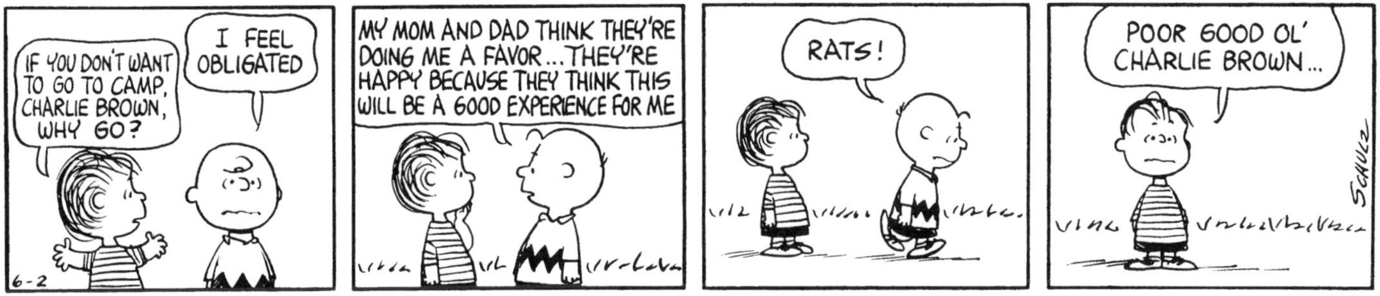
IF YOU DON'T WANT TO GO TO CAMP, CHARLIE BROWN, WHY GO?
I FEEL OBLIGATED
6-2
MY MOM AND DAD THINK THEY'RE DOING ME A FAVOR...THEY'RE HAPPY BECAUSE THEY THINK THIS WILL BE A GOOD EXPERIENCE FOR ME
RATS!
POOR GOOD OL' CHARLIE BROWN...
SCHULZ

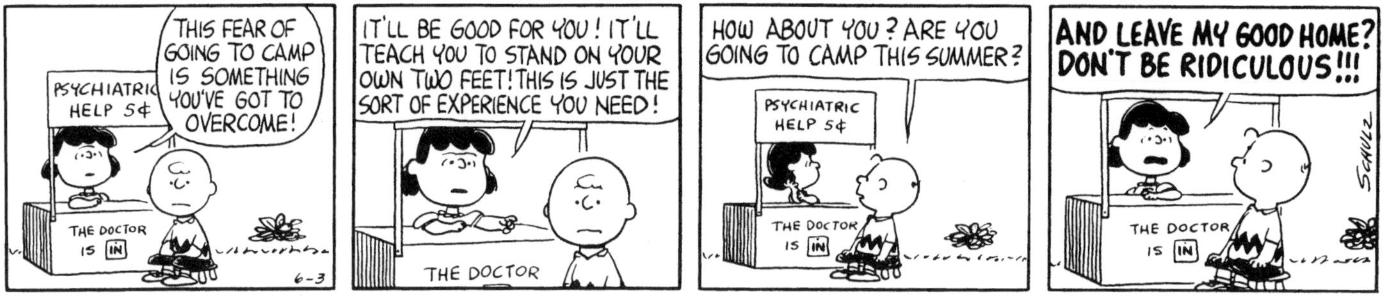
PSYCHIATRIC HELP 5¢
THIS FEAR OF GOING TO CAMP IS SOMETHING YOU'VE GOT TO OVERCOME!
THE DOCTOR IS IN
6-3
IT'LL BE GOOD FOR YOU! IT'LL TEACH YOU TO STAND ON YOUR OWN TWO FEET! THIS IS JUST THE SORT OF EXPERIENCE YOU NEED!
THE DOCTOR
HOW ABOUT YOU? ARE YOU GOING TO CAMP THIS SUMMER?
PSYCHIATRIC HELP 5¢
THE DOCTOR IS IN
AND LEAVE MY GOOD HOME? DON'T BE RIDICULOUS!!!
SCHULZ
THE DOCTOR IS IN

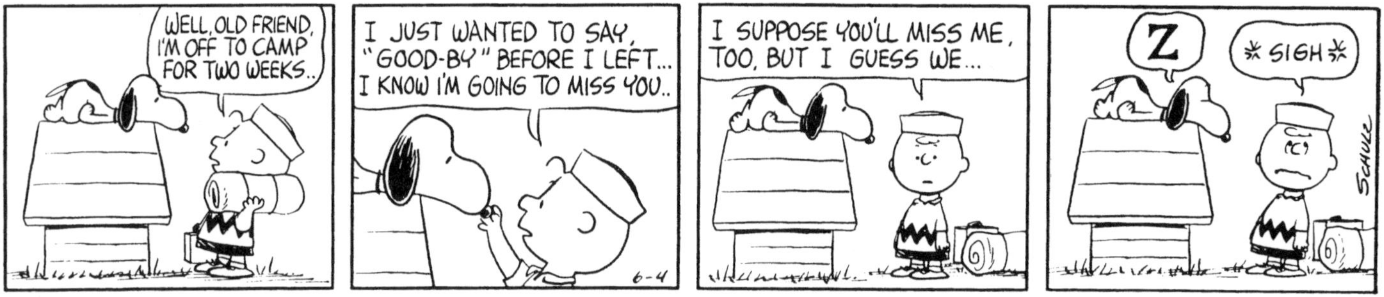
WELL, OLD FRIEND, I'M OFF TO CAMP FOR TWO WEEKS..
I JUST WANTED TO SAY, "GOOD-BY" BEFORE I LEFT... I KNOW I'M GOING TO MISS YOU..
6-4
I SUPPOSE YOU'LL MISS ME, TOO, BUT I GUESS WE...
Z
SIGH
SCHULZ

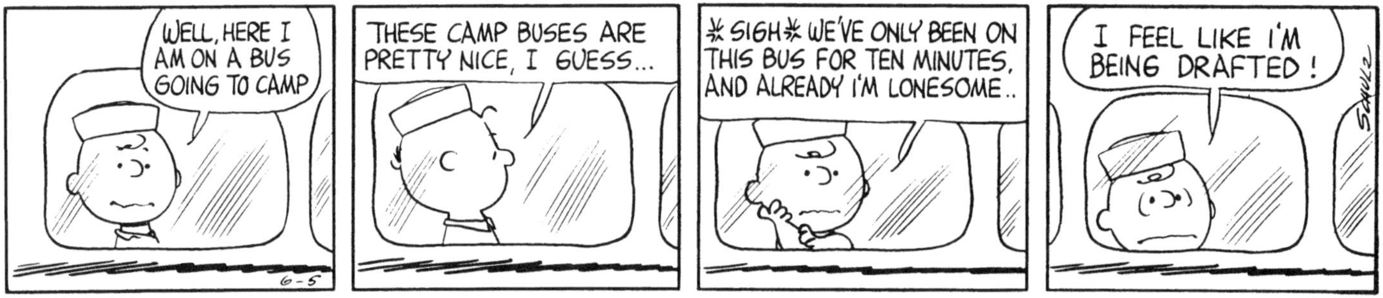
WELL, HERE I AM ON A BUS GOING TO CAMP
6-5
THESE CAMP BUSES ARE PRETTY NICE, I GUESS...
SIGH WE'VE ONLY BEEN ON THIS BUS FOR TEN MINUTES, AND ALREADY I'M LONESOME..
I FEEL LIKE I'M BEING DRAFTED!
SCHULZ

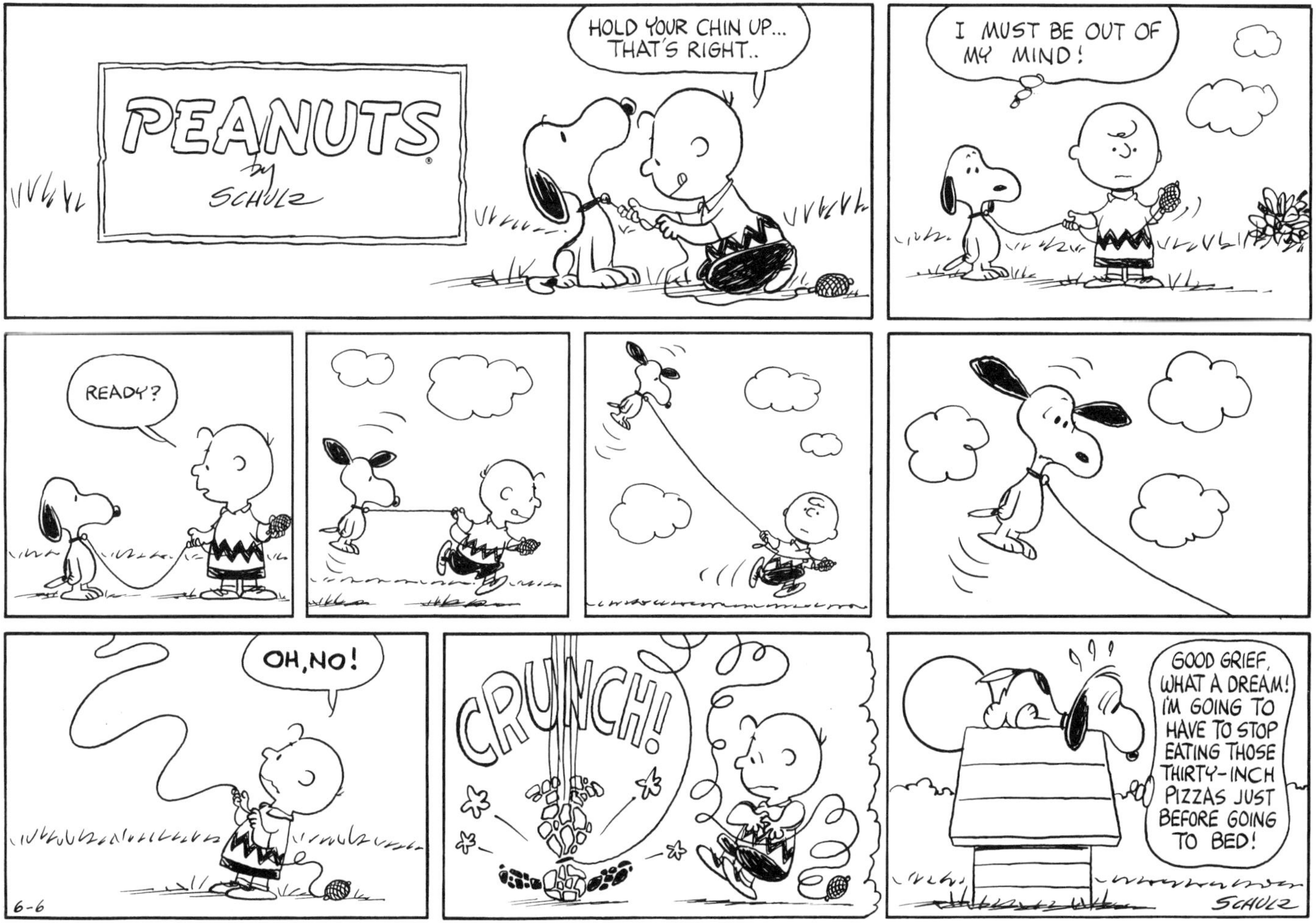
PEANUTS
by SCHULZ
HOLD YOUR CHIN UP... THAT'S RIGHT..
I MUST BE OUT OF MY MIND!
READY?
OH, NO!
CRUNCH!
GOOD GRIEF, WHAT A DREAM! I'M GOING TO HAVE TO STOP EATING THOSE THIRTY-INCH PIZZAS JUST BEFORE GOING TO BED!
6-6
SCHULZ

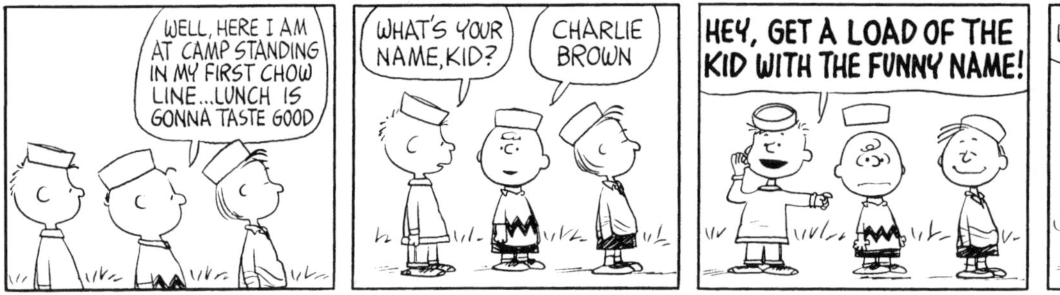
WELL, HERE I AM AT CAMP STANDING IN MY FIRST CHOW LINE...LUNCH IS GONNA TASTE GOOD
WHAT'S YOUR NAME, KID?
CHARLIE BROWN
HEY, GET A LOAD OF THE KID WITH THE FUNNY NAME!
LUNCH IS GONNA TASTE AWFUL!
SCHULZ
6-7

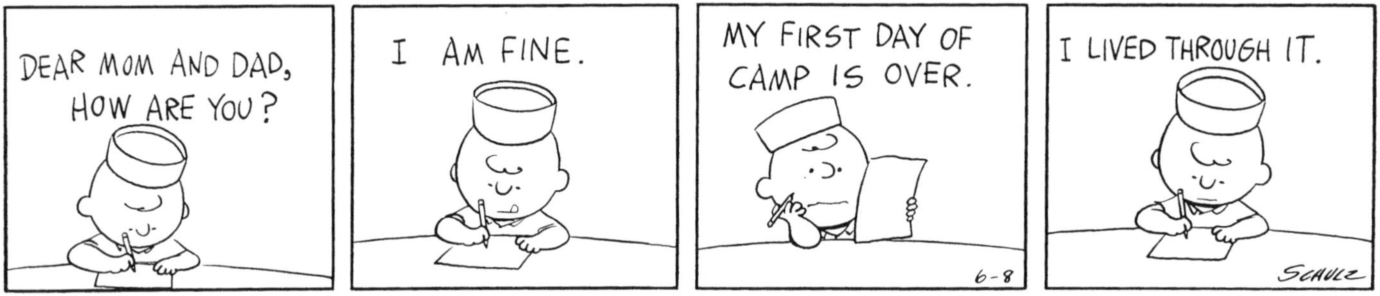
DEAR MOM AND DAD, HOW ARE YOU?
I AM FINE.
MY FIRST DAY OF CAMP IS OVER.
6-8
I LIVED THROUGH IT.
SCHULZ

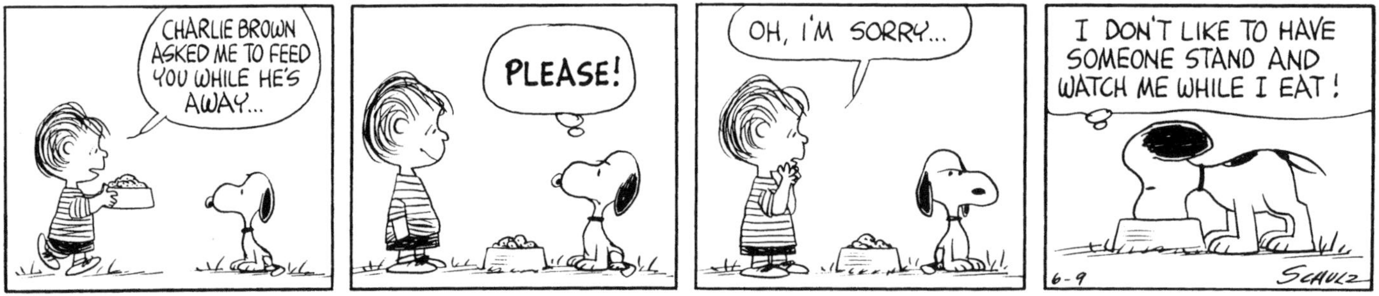
CHARLIE BROWN ASKED ME TO FEED YOU WHILE HE'S AWAY...
PLEASE!
OH, I'M SORRY...
I DON'T LIKE TO HAVE SOMEONE STAND AND WATCH ME WHILE I EAT!
6-9
SCHULZ

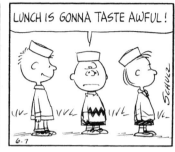

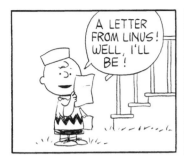

A LETTER FROM LINUS! WELL, I'LL BE!

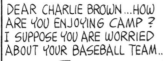
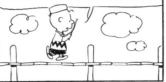

DEAR CHARLIE BROWN...HOW ARE YOU ENJOYING CAMP? I SUPPOSE YOU ARE WORRIED ABOUT YOUR BASEBALL TEAM..

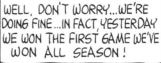
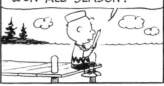

WELL, DON'T WORRY...WE'RE DOING FINE...IN FACT, YESTERDAY WE WON THE FIRST GAME WE'VE WON ALL SEASON!

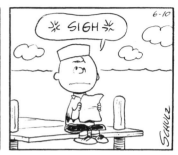

6-10

⁂ SIGH ⁂

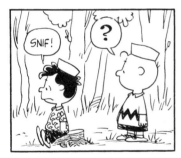

SNIF!   ?

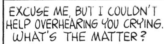
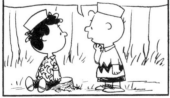

EXCUSE ME, BUT I COULDN'T HELP OVERHEARING YOU CRYING.. WHAT'S THE MATTER?

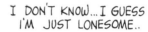
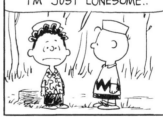

I DON'T KNOW... I GUESS I'M JUST LONESOME..

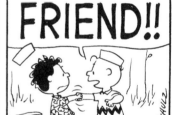

FRIEND!!

6-11

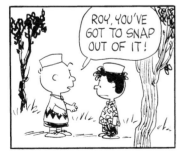

ROY, YOU'VE GOT TO SNAP OUT OF IT!

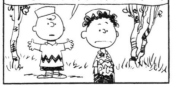

A CAMP LIKE THIS IS THE BEST PLACE FOR SOMEONE LIKE YOU...IT HELPS YOU TO BREAK THOSE OLD APRON STRINGS!

6-12

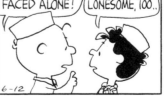

LIFE IS FULL OF EXPERIENCES THAT HAVE TO BE FACED ALONE!   BUT YOU SAID YOU WERE LONESOME, TOO..

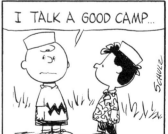

I TALK A GOOD CAMP...

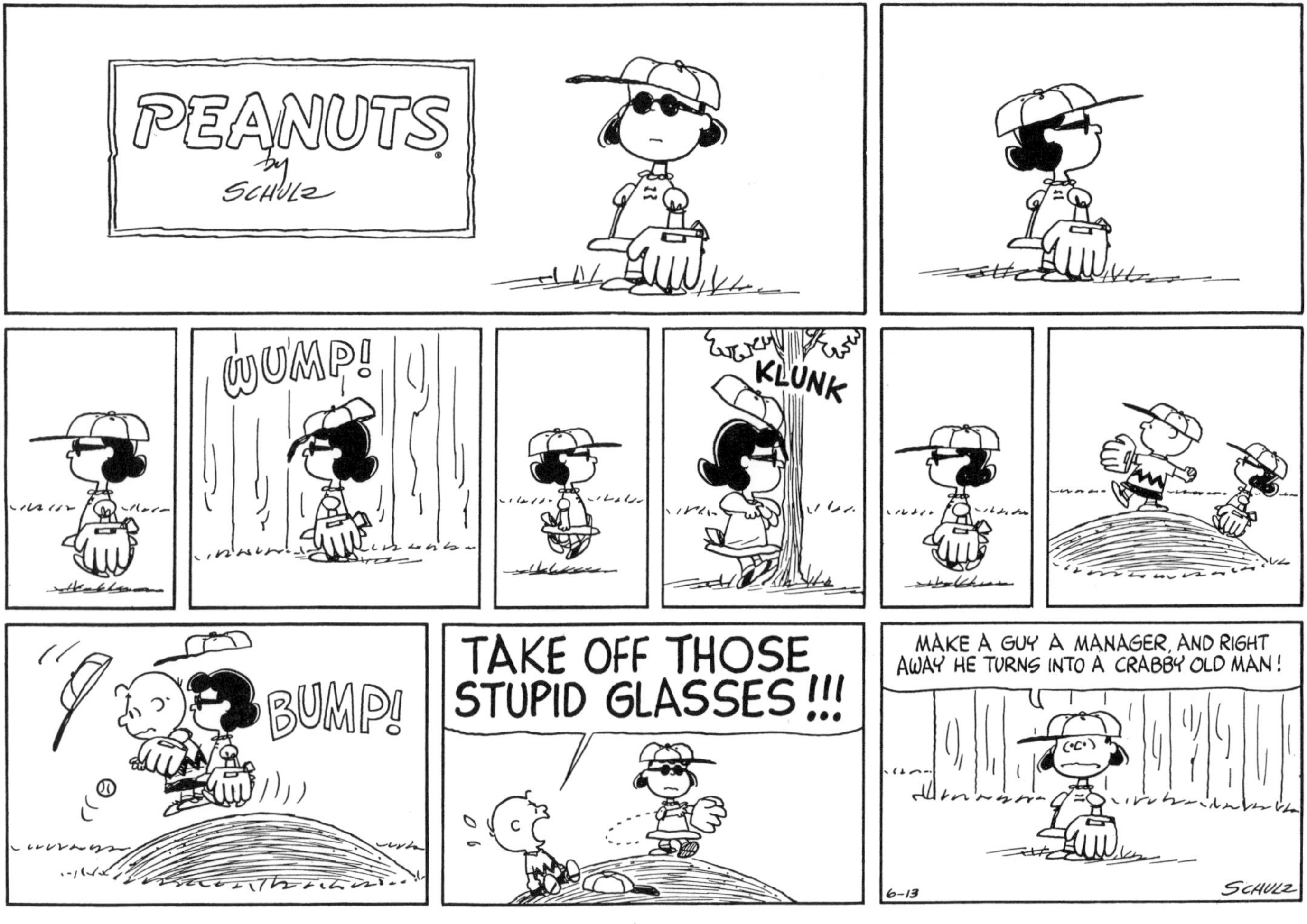
PEANUTS
by SCHULZ
WUMP!
KLUNK
BUMP!
TAKE OFF THOSE STUPID GLASSES!!!
MAKE A GUY A MANAGER, AND RIGHT AWAY HE TURNS INTO A CRABBY OLD MAN!
6-13
SCHULZ

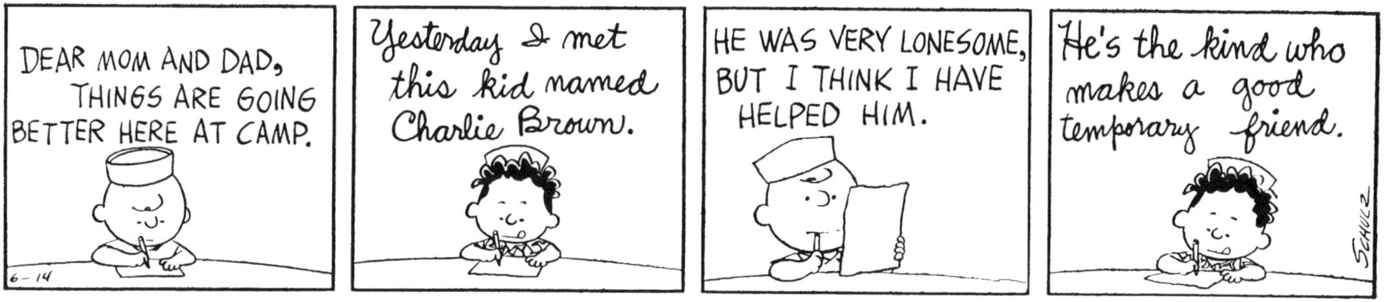
DEAR MOM AND DAD,
THINGS ARE GOING BETTER HERE AT CAMP.
Yesterday I met this kid named Charlie Brown.
HE WAS VERY LONESOME, BUT I THINK I HAVE HELPED HIM.
He's the kind who makes a good temporary friend.

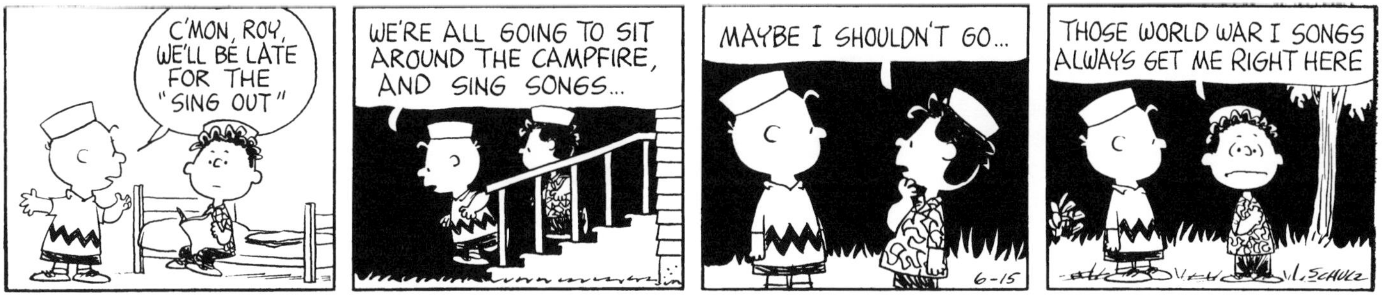
C'MON, ROY, WE'LL BE LATE FOR THE "SING OUT"
WE'RE ALL GOING TO SIT AROUND THE CAMPFIRE, AND SING SONGS...
MAYBE I SHOULDN'T GO...
THOSE WORLD WAR I SONGS ALWAYS GET ME RIGHT HERE

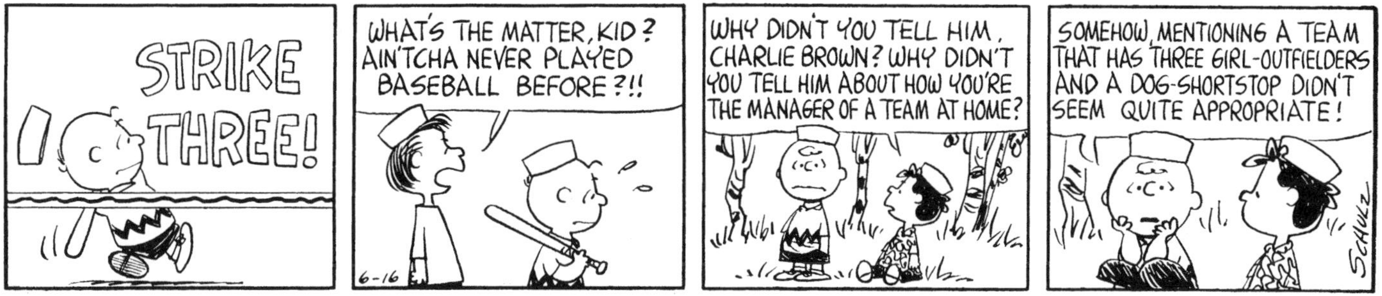
STRIKE THREE!
WHAT'S THE MATTER, KID? AIN'TCHA NEVER PLAYED BASEBALL BEFORE?!!
WHY DIDN'T YOU TELL HIM, CHARLIE BROWN? WHY DIDN'T YOU TELL HIM ABOUT HOW YOU'RE THE MANAGER OF A TEAM AT HOME?
SOMEHOW, MENTIONING A TEAM THAT HAS THREE GIRL-OUTFIELDERS AND A DOG-SHORTSTOP DIDN'T SEEM QUITE APPROPRIATE!

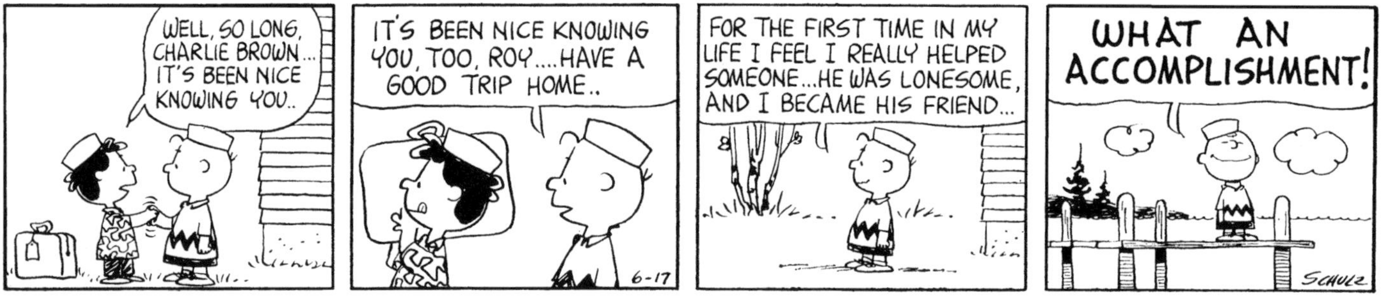
WELL, SO LONG, CHARLIE BROWN... IT'S BEEN NICE KNOWING YOU..
IT'S BEEN NICE KNOWING YOU, TOO, ROY....HAVE A GOOD TRIP HOME..
6-17
FOR THE FIRST TIME IN MY LIFE I FEEL I REALLY HELPED SOMEONE...HE WAS LONESOME, AND I BECAME HIS FRIEND...
WHAT AN ACCOMPLISHMENT!
SCHULZ

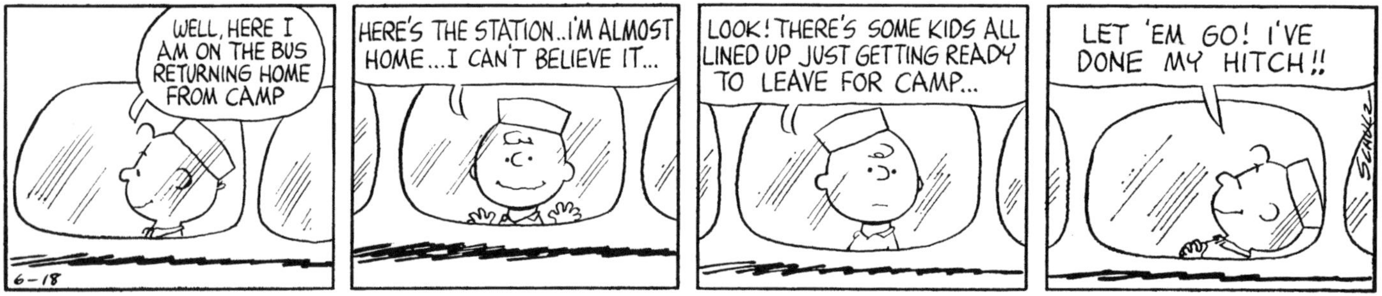
WELL, HERE I AM ON THE BUS RETURNING HOME FROM CAMP
6-18
HERE'S THE STATION..I'M ALMOST HOME...I CAN'T BELIEVE IT...
LOOK! THERE'S SOME KIDS ALL LINED UP JUST GETTING READY TO LEAVE FOR CAMP...
LET 'EM GO! I'VE DONE MY HITCH!!
SCHULZ

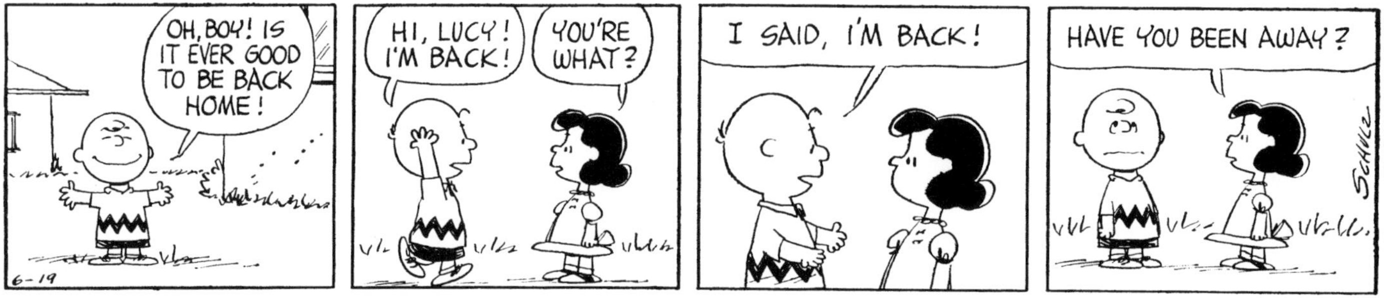
OH, BOY! IS IT EVER GOOD TO BE BACK HOME!
6-19
HI, LUCY! I'M BACK!
YOU'RE WHAT?
I SAID, I'M BACK!
HAVE YOU BEEN AWAY?
SCHULZ

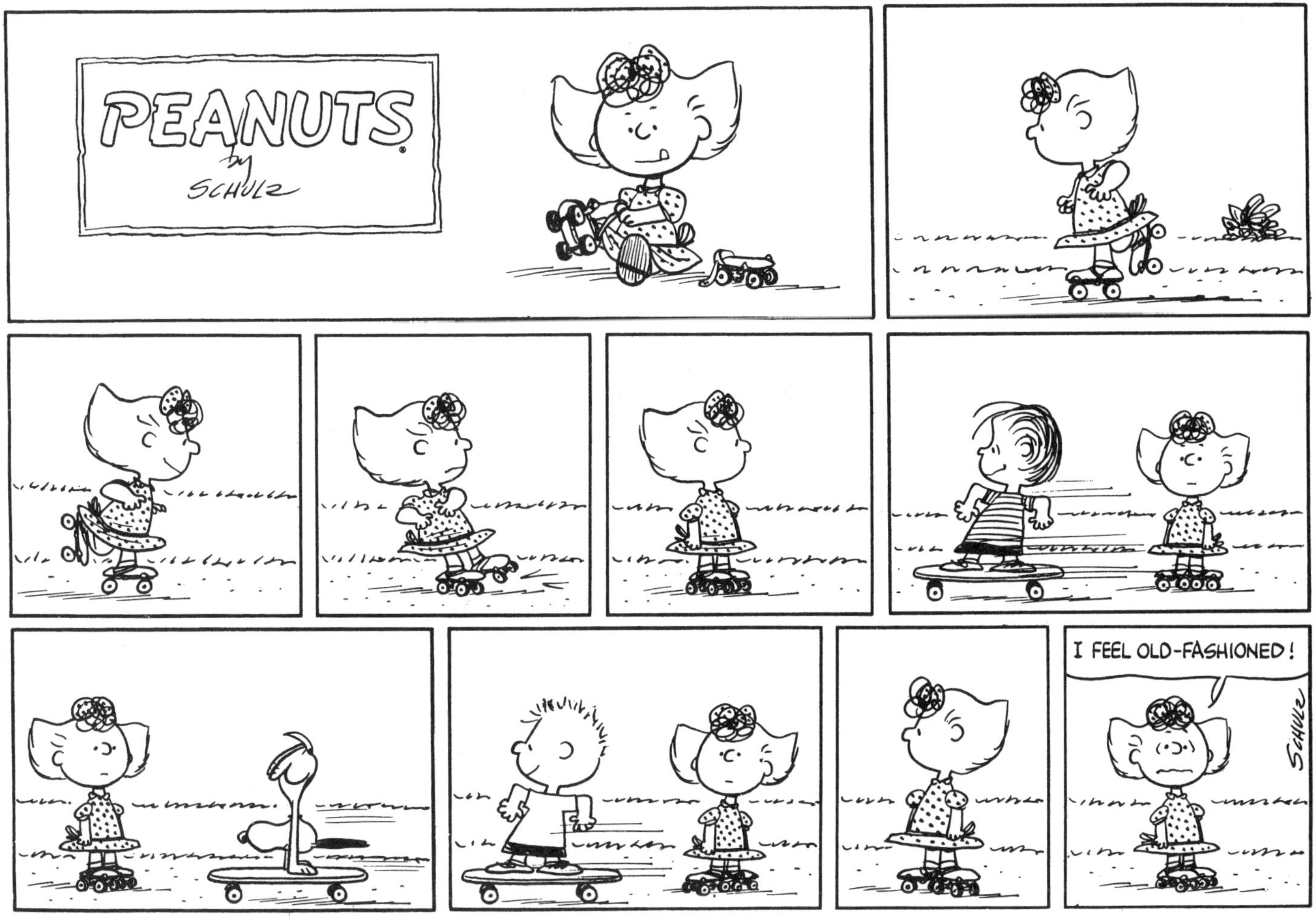
PEANUTS
by
SCHULZ
I FEEL OLD-FASHIONED!
SCHULZ

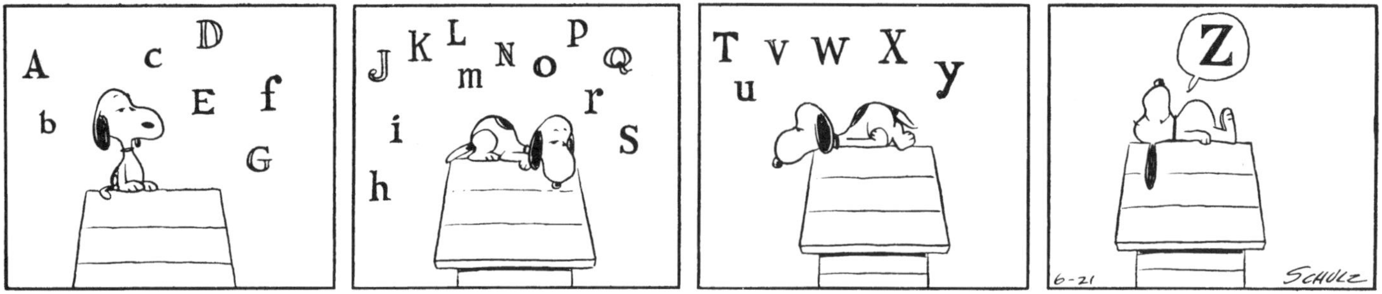
A b c D E f G
h i J K L m N o P Q r S
T u V W X y
Z
6-21
SCHULZ

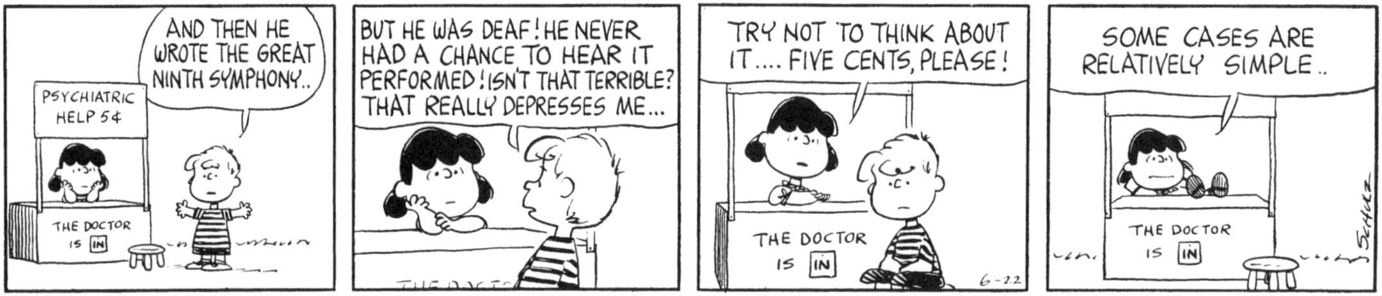
PSYCHIATRIC HELP 5¢
AND THEN HE WROTE THE GREAT NINTH SYMPHONY..
THE DOCTOR IS IN
BUT HE WAS DEAF! HE NEVER HAD A CHANCE TO HEAR IT PERFORMED! ISN'T THAT TERRIBLE? THAT REALLY DEPRESSES ME...
TRY NOT TO THINK ABOUT IT.... FIVE CENTS, PLEASE!
THE DOCTOR IS IN
6-22
SOME CASES ARE RELATIVELY SIMPLE..
THE DOCTOR IS IN
SCHULZ

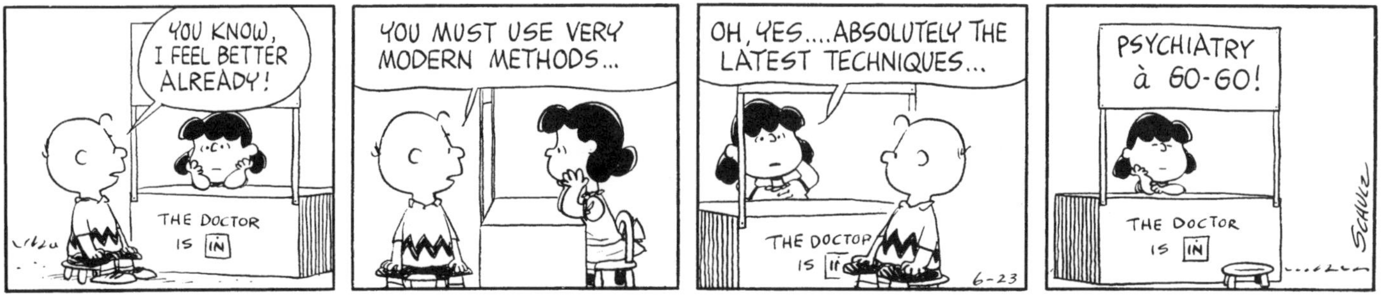
YOU KNOW, I FEEL BETTER ALREADY!
THE DOCTOR IS IN
YOU MUST USE VERY MODERN METHODS...
OH, YES....ABSOLUTELY THE LATEST TECHNIQUES...
6-23
PSYCHIATRY à GO-GO!
THE DOCTOR IS IN
SCHULZ

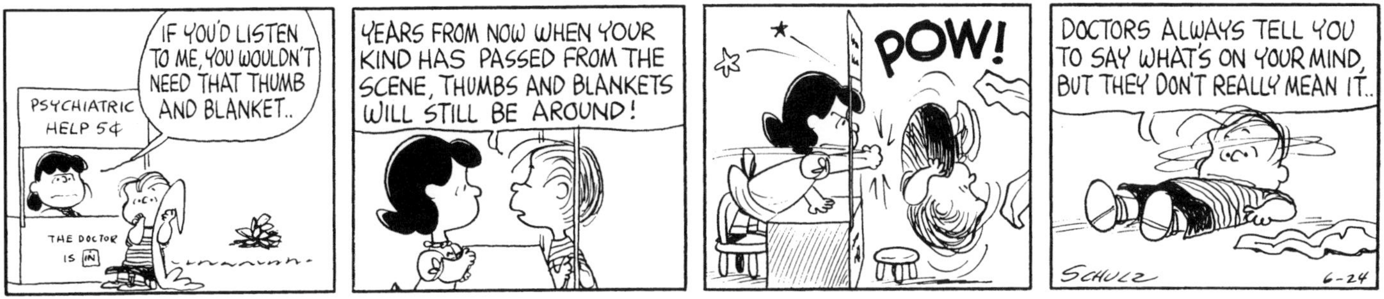
IF YOU'D LISTEN TO ME, YOU WOULDN'T NEED THAT THUMB AND BLANKET..
PSYCHIATRIC HELP 5¢
THE DOCTOR IS IN
YEARS FROM NOW WHEN YOUR KIND HAS PASSED FROM THE SCENE, THUMBS AND BLANKETS WILL STILL BE AROUND!
POW!
DOCTORS ALWAYS TELL YOU TO SAY WHAT'S ON YOUR MIND, BUT THEY DON'T REALLY MEAN IT..
SCHULZ
6-24

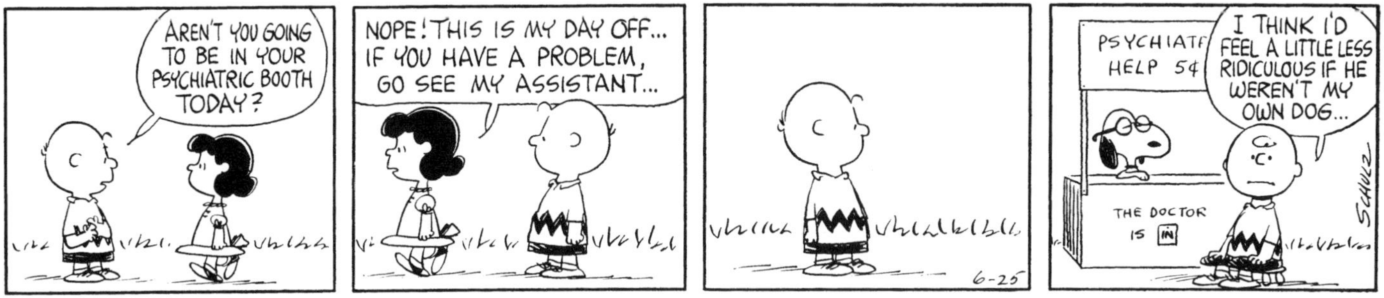
AREN'T YOU GOING TO BE IN YOUR PSYCHIATRIC BOOTH TODAY?
NOPE! THIS IS MY DAY OFF... IF YOU HAVE A PROBLEM, GO SEE MY ASSISTANT...
6-25
PSYCHIAT
HELP 5¢
I THINK I'D FEEL A LITTLE LESS RIDICULOUS IF HE WEREN'T MY OWN DOG...
THE DOCTOR IS IN
SCHULZ

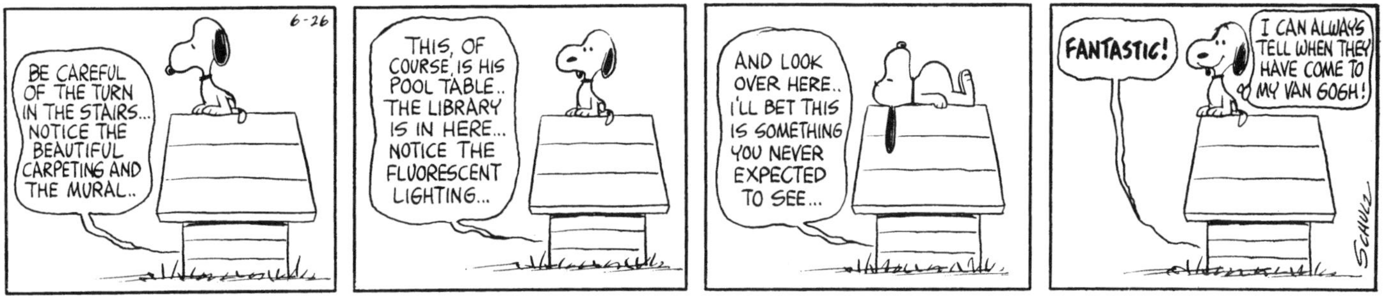
6-26
BE CAREFUL OF THE TURN IN THE STAIRS... NOTICE THE BEAUTIFUL CARPETING AND THE MURAL..
THIS, OF COURSE, IS HIS POOL TABLE.. THE LIBRARY IS IN HERE... NOTICE THE FLUORESCENT LIGHTING...
AND LOOK OVER HERE.. I'LL BET THIS IS SOMETHING YOU NEVER EXPECTED TO SEE...
FANTASTIC!
I CAN ALWAYS TELL WHEN THEY HAVE COME TO MY VAN GOGH!
SCHULZ

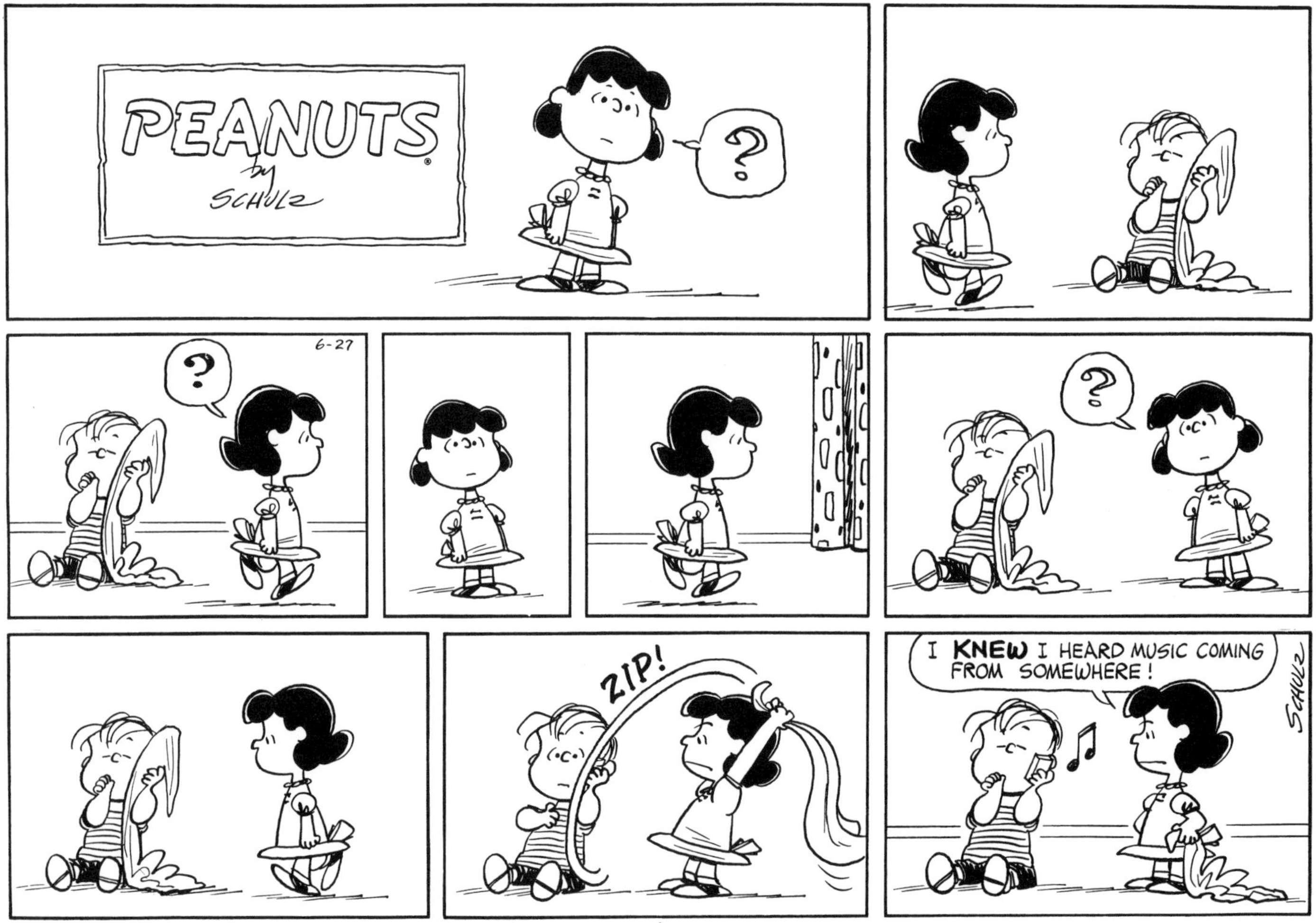
PEANUTS
by
SCHULZ
?
6-27
?
?
ZIP!
I KNEW I HEARD MUSIC COMING FROM SOMEWHERE!
SCHULZ

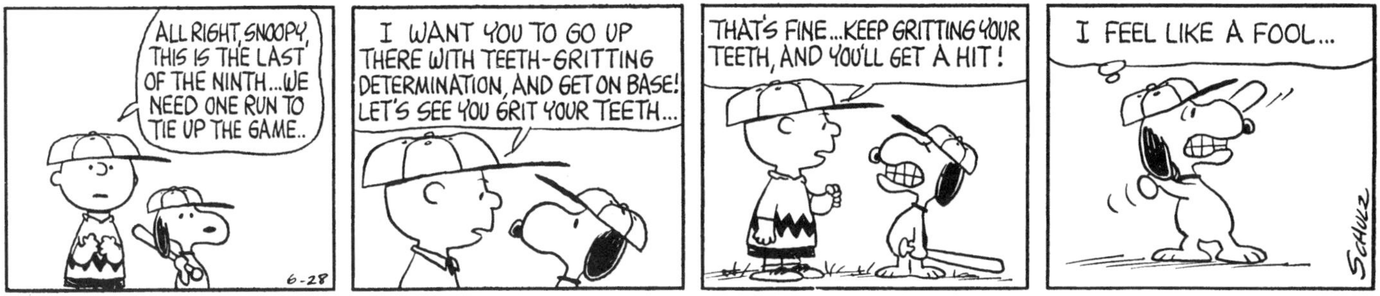
ALL RIGHT, SNOOPY, THIS IS THE LAST OF THE NINTH...WE NEED ONE RUN TO TIE UP THE GAME..
6-28
I WANT YOU TO GO UP THERE WITH TEETH-GRITTING DETERMINATION, AND GET ON BASE! LET'S SEE YOU GRIT YOUR TEETH...
THAT'S FINE...KEEP GRITTING YOUR TEETH, AND YOU'LL GET A HIT!
I FEEL LIKE A FOOL...
SCHULZ

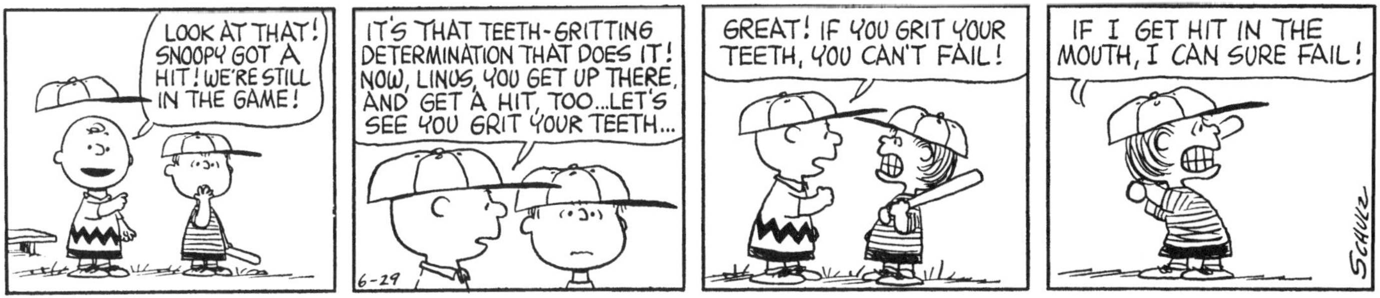
LOOK AT THAT! SNOOPY GOT A HIT! WE'RE STILL IN THE GAME!
IT'S THAT TEETH-GRITTING DETERMINATION THAT DOES IT! NOW, LINUS, YOU GET UP THERE, AND GET A HIT, TOO...LET'S SEE YOU GRIT YOUR TEETH...
6-29
GREAT! IF YOU GRIT YOUR TEETH, YOU CAN'T FAIL!
IF I GET HIT IN THE MOUTH, I CAN SURE FAIL!
SCHULZ

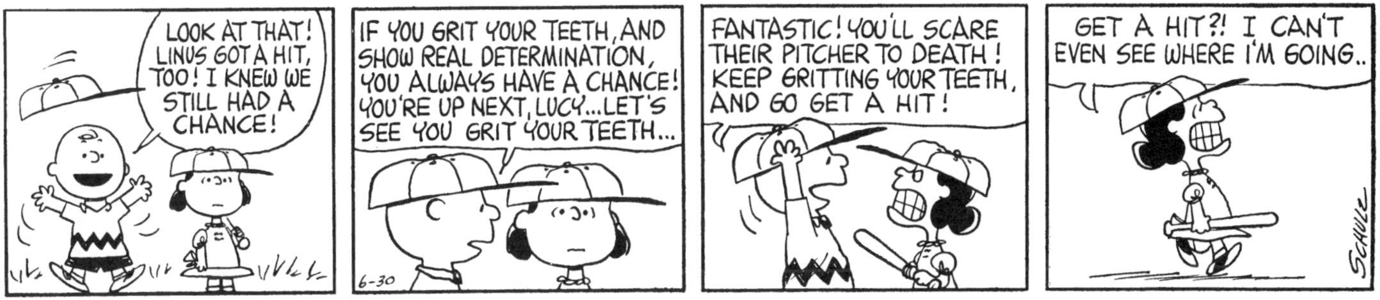
LOOK AT THAT! LINUS GOT A HIT, TOO! I KNEW WE STILL HAD A CHANCE!
IF YOU GRIT YOUR TEETH, AND SHOW REAL DETERMINATION, YOU ALWAYS HAVE A CHANCE! YOU'RE UP NEXT, LUCY...LET'S SEE YOU GRIT YOUR TEETH...
6-30
FANTASTIC! YOU'LL SCARE THEIR PITCHER TO DEATH! KEEP GRITTING YOUR TEETH, AND GO GET A HIT!
GET A HIT?! I CAN'T EVEN SEE WHERE I'M GOING..
SCHULZ

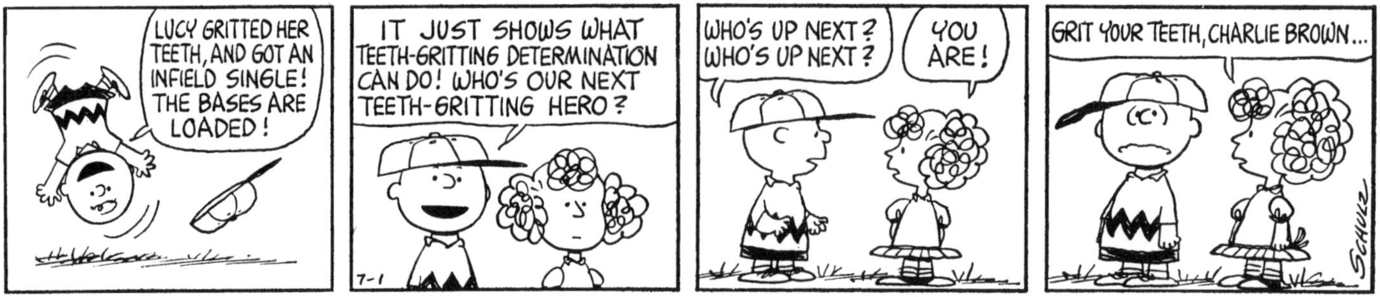
LUCY GRITTED HER TEETH, AND GOT AN INFIELD SINGLE! THE BASES ARE LOADED!
IT JUST SHOWS WHAT TEETH-GRITTING DETERMINATION CAN DO! WHO'S OUR NEXT TEETH-GRITTING HERO?
7-1
WHO'S UP NEXT? WHO'S UP NEXT?
YOU ARE!
GRIT YOUR TEETH, CHARLIE BROWN...
SCHULZ

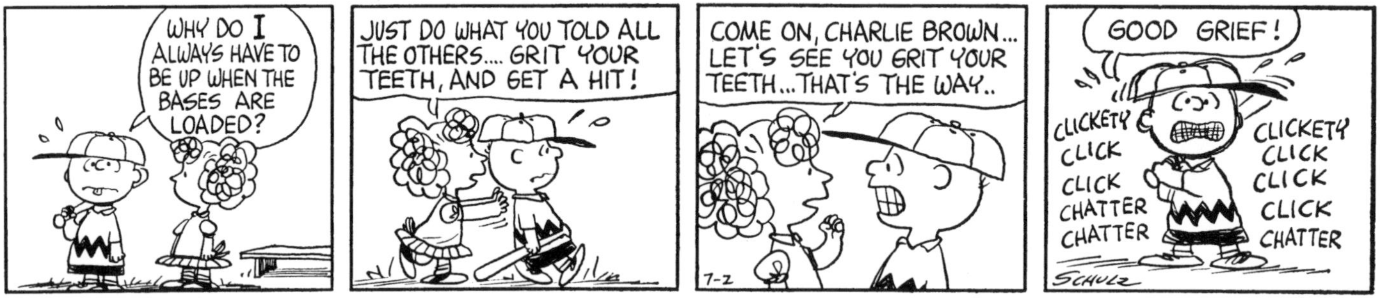
WHY DO I ALWAYS HAVE TO BE UP WHEN THE BASES ARE LOADED?
JUST DO WHAT YOU TOLD ALL THE OTHERS.... GRIT YOUR TEETH, AND GET A HIT!
COME ON, CHARLIE BROWN... LET'S SEE YOU GRIT YOUR TEETH...THAT'S THE WAY..
7-2
GOOD GRIEF!
CLICKETY CLICK CLICK CHATTER CHATTER
CLICKETY CLICK CLICK CLICK CHATTER
SCHULZ

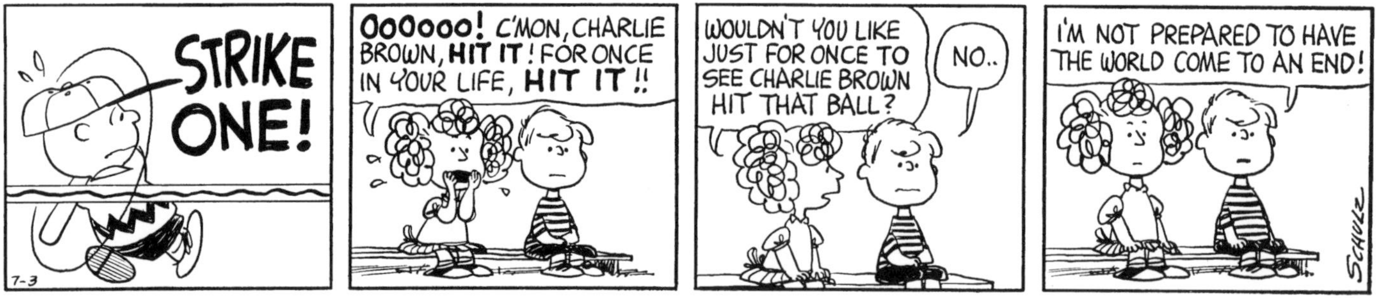
STRIKE ONE!
7-3
OOOOOO! C'MON, CHARLIE BROWN, HIT IT! FOR ONCE IN YOUR LIFE, HIT IT!!
WOULDN'T YOU LIKE JUST FOR ONCE TO SEE CHARLIE BROWN HIT THAT BALL?
NO..
I'M NOT PREPARED TO HAVE THE WORLD COME TO AN END!
SCHULZ

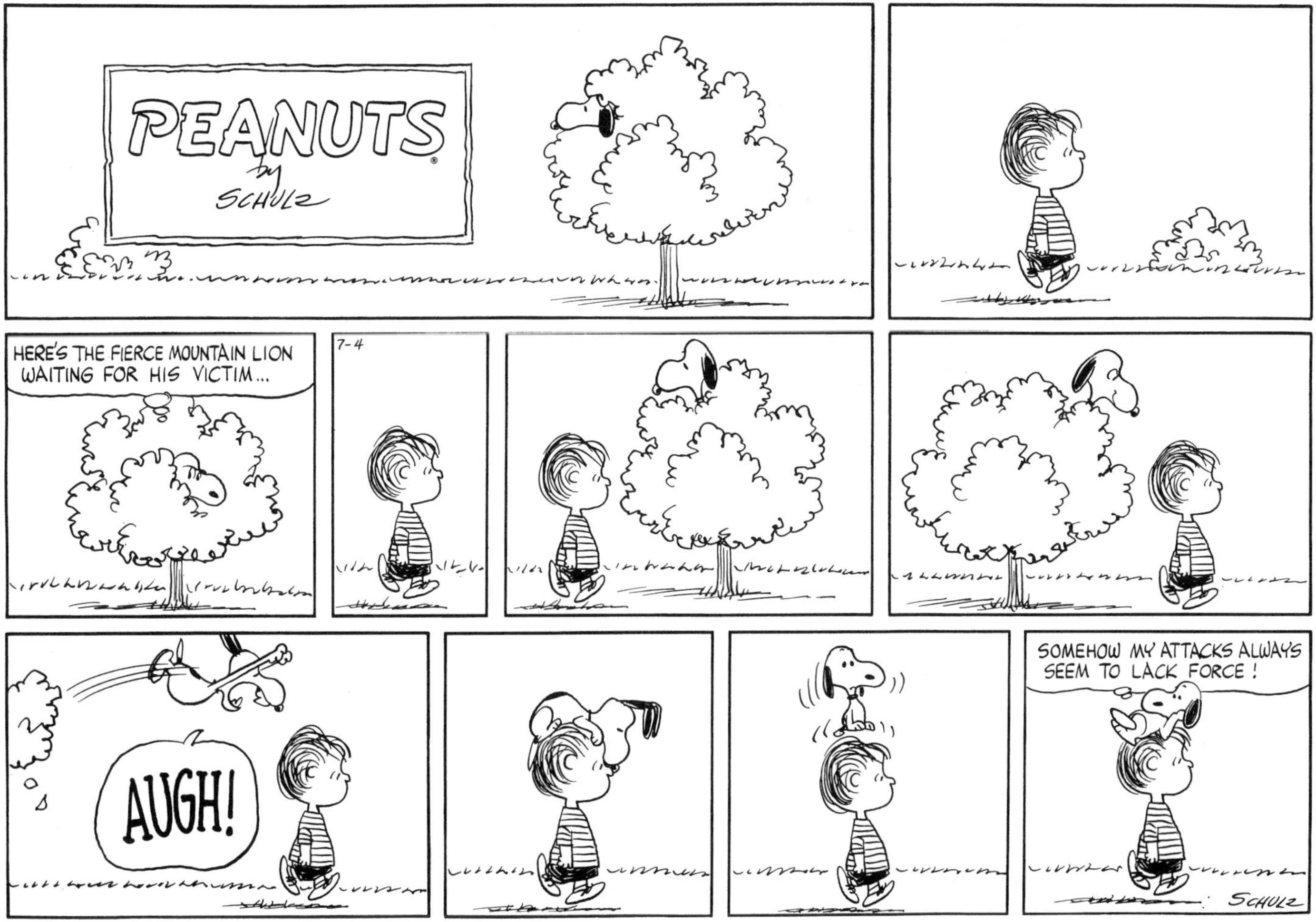
PEANUTS
by
SCHULZ
HERE'S THE FIERCE MOUNTAIN LION WAITING FOR HIS VICTIM...
7-4
AUGH!
SOMEHOW MY ATTACKS ALWAYS SEEM TO LACK FORCE!
SCHULZ

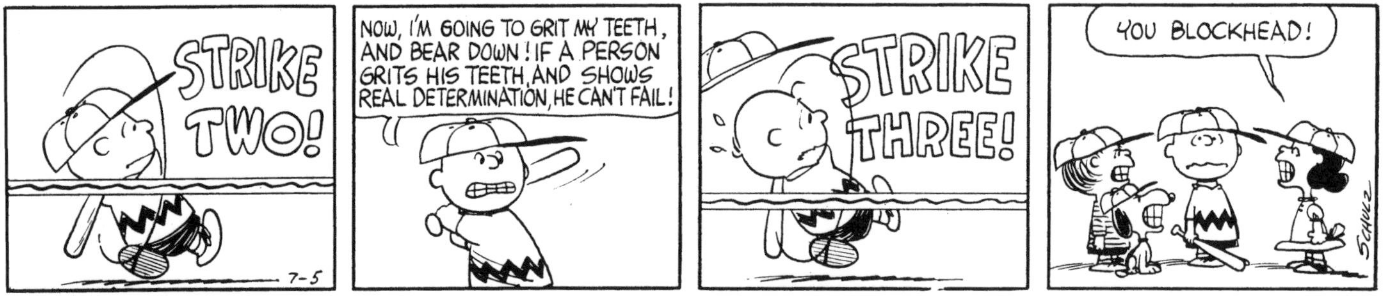
STRIKE TWO!
7-5
NOW, I'M GOING TO GRIT MY TEETH, AND BEAR DOWN! IF A PERSON GRITS HIS TEETH, AND SHOWS REAL DETERMINATION, HE CAN'T FAIL!
STRIKE THREE!
YOU BLOCKHEAD!
SCHULZ

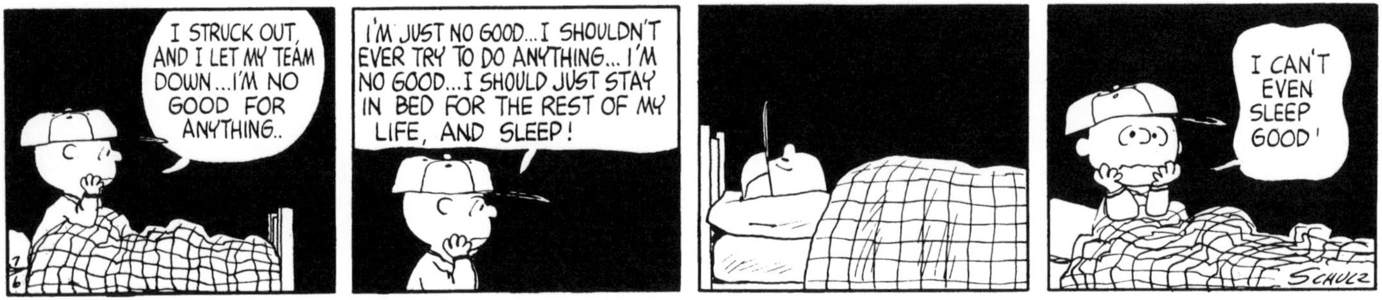
I STRUCK OUT, AND I LET MY TEAM DOWN...I'M NO GOOD FOR ANYTHING..
7 6
I'M JUST NO GOOD...I SHOULDN'T EVER TRY TO DO ANYTHING... I'M NO GOOD...I SHOULD JUST STAY IN BED FOR THE REST OF MY LIFE, AND SLEEP!
I CAN'T EVEN SLEEP GOOD!
SCHULZ

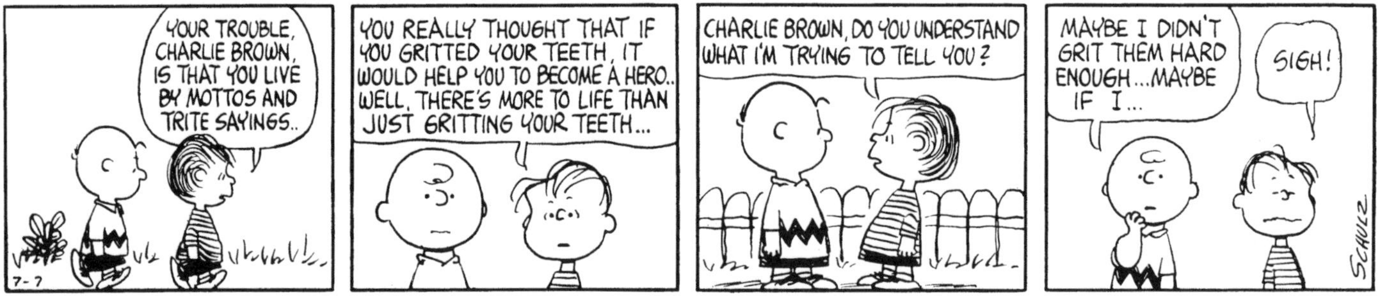
YOUR TROUBLE, CHARLIE BROWN, IS THAT YOU LIVE BY MOTTOS AND TRITE SAYINGS..
7-7
YOU REALLY THOUGHT THAT IF YOU GRITTED YOUR TEETH, IT WOULD HELP YOU TO BECOME A HERO.. WELL, THERE'S MORE TO LIFE THAN JUST GRITTING YOUR TEETH...
CHARLIE BROWN, DO YOU UNDERSTAND WHAT I'M TRYING TO TELL YOU?
MAYBE I DIDN'T GRIT THEM HARD ENOUGH...MAYBE IF I...
SIGH!
SCHULZ

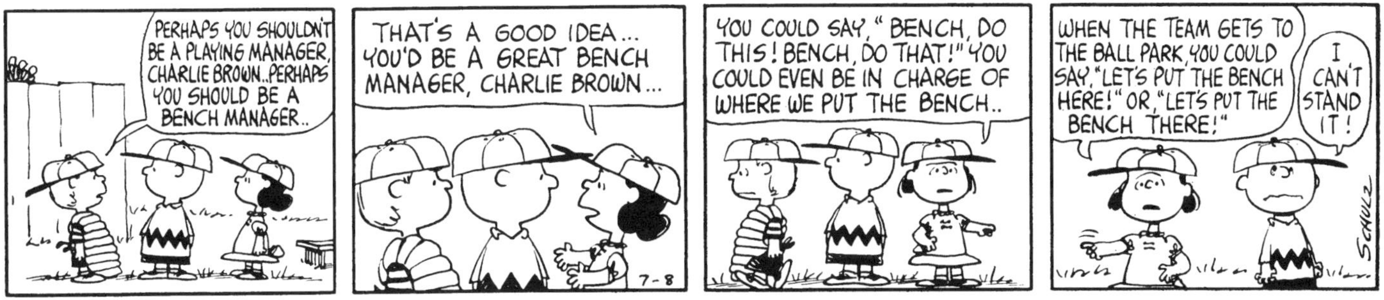
PERHAPS YOU SHOULDN'T BE A PLAYING MANAGER, CHARLIE BROWN..PERHAPS YOU SHOULD BE A BENCH MANAGER..
THAT'S A GOOD IDEA... YOU'D BE A GREAT BENCH MANAGER, CHARLIE BROWN...
7-8
YOU COULD SAY, "BENCH, DO THIS! BENCH, DO THAT!" YOU COULD EVEN BE IN CHARGE OF WHERE WE PUT THE BENCH..
WHEN THE TEAM GETS TO THE BALL PARK, YOU COULD SAY, "LET'S PUT THE BENCH HERE!" OR, "LET'S PUT THE BENCH THERE!"
I CAN'T STAND IT!
SCHULZ

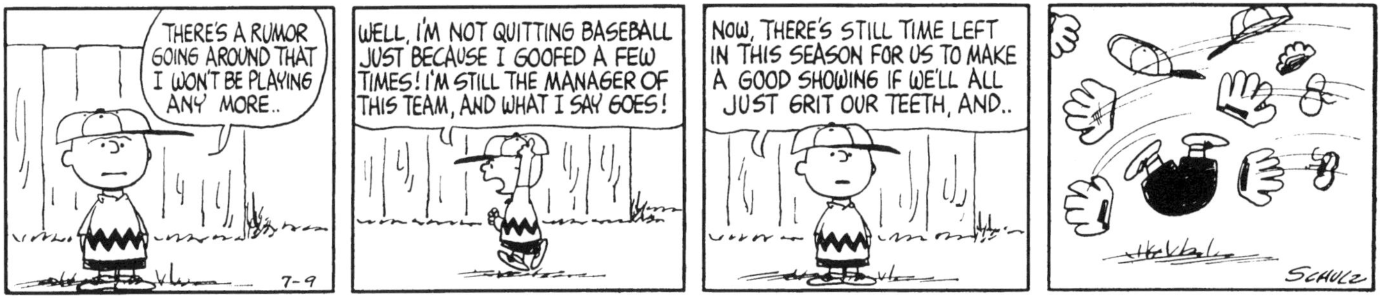
THERE'S A RUMOR GOING AROUND THAT I WON'T BE PLAYING ANY MORE..
7-9
WELL, I'M NOT QUITTING BASEBALL JUST BECAUSE I GOOFED A FEW TIMES! I'M STILL THE MANAGER OF THIS TEAM, AND WHAT I SAY GOES!
NOW, THERE'S STILL TIME LEFT IN THIS SEASON FOR US TO MAKE A GOOD SHOWING IF WE'LL ALL JUST GRIT OUR TEETH, AND..
SCHULZ

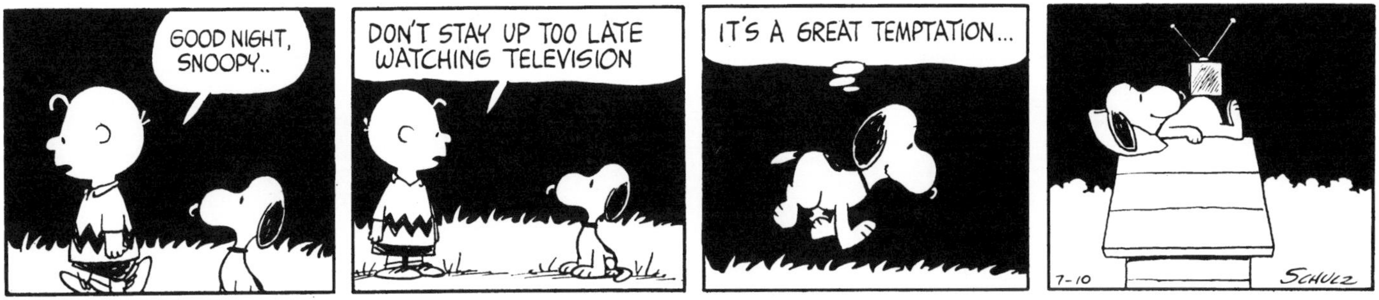
GOOD NIGHT, SNOOPY..
DON'T STAY UP TOO LATE WATCHING TELEVISION
IT'S A GREAT TEMPTATION...
7-10
SCHULZ

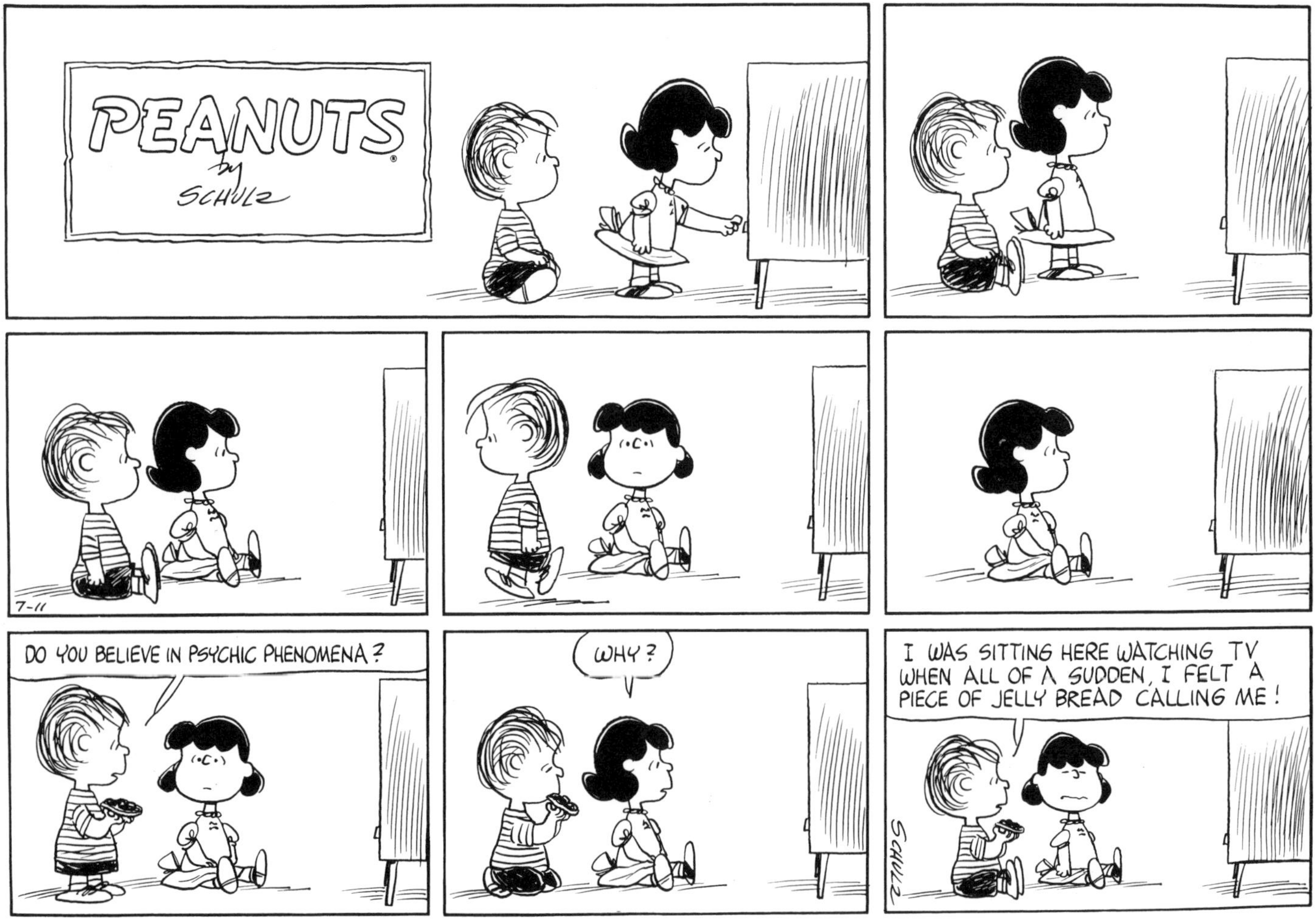
PEANUTS
by SCHULZ
7-11
DO YOU BELIEVE IN PSYCHIC PHENOMENA?
WHY?
I WAS SITTING HERE WATCHING TV WHEN ALL OF A SUDDEN, I FELT A PIECE OF JELLY BREAD CALLING ME!
SCHULZ

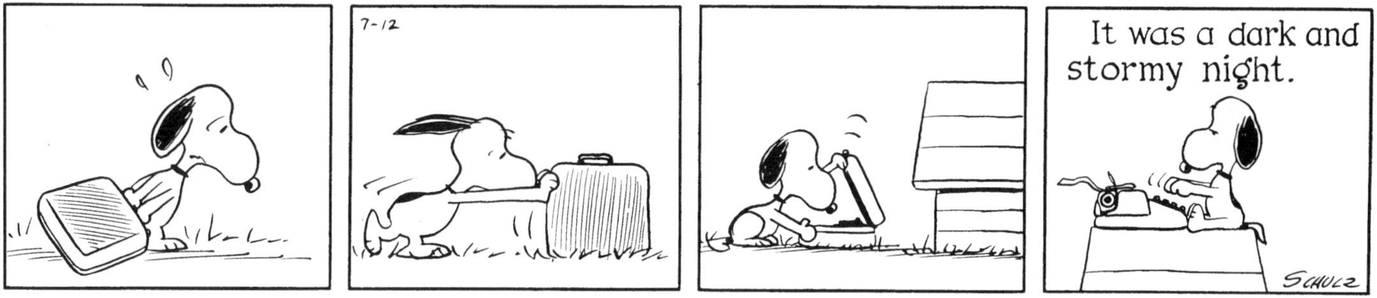
It was a dark and stormy night.

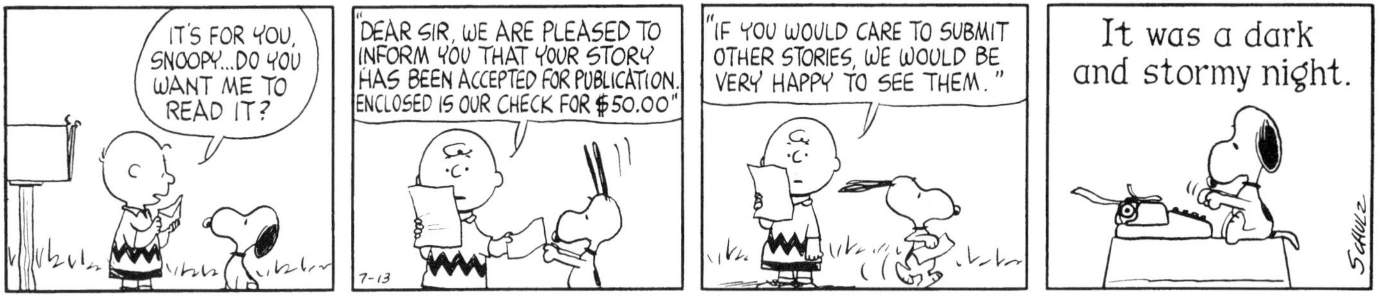
IT'S FOR YOU, SNOOPY...DO YOU WANT ME TO READ IT?
"DEAR SIR, WE ARE PLEASED TO INFORM YOU THAT YOUR STORY HAS BEEN ACCEPTED FOR PUBLICATION. ENCLOSED IS OUR CHECK FOR $50.00"
"IF YOU WOULD CARE TO SUBMIT OTHER STORIES, WE WOULD BE VERY HAPPY TO SEE THEM."
It was a dark and stormy night.

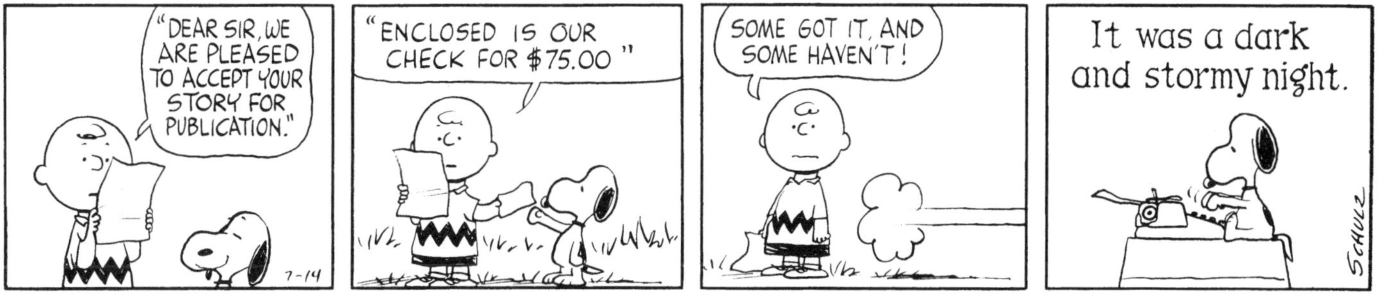
"DEAR SIR, WE ARE PLEASED TO ACCEPT YOUR STORY FOR PUBLICATION."
"ENCLOSED IS OUR CHECK FOR $75.00"
SOME GOT IT, AND SOME HAVEN'T!
It was a dark and stormy night.

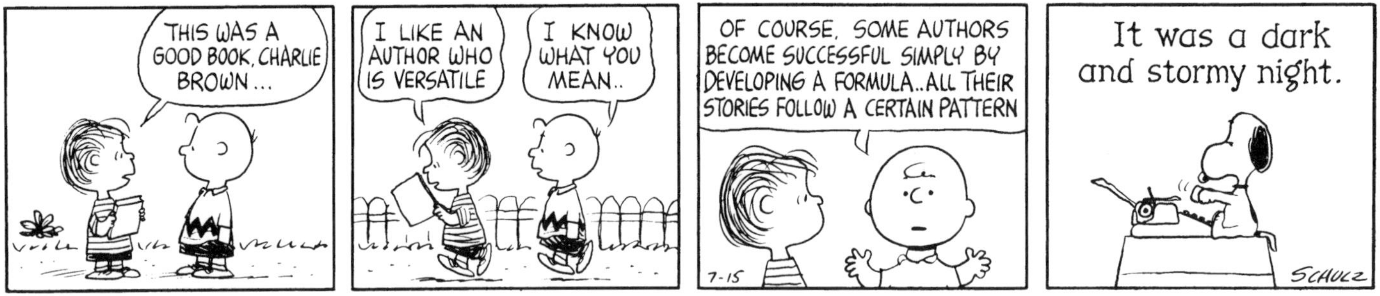
THIS WAS A GOOD BOOK, CHARLIE BROWN...
I LIKE AN AUTHOR WHO IS VERSATILE
I KNOW WHAT YOU MEAN..
OF COURSE, SOME AUTHORS BECOME SUCCESSFUL SIMPLY BY DEVELOPING A FORMULA..ALL THEIR STORIES FOLLOW A CERTAIN PATTERN
7-15
It was a dark and stormy night.
SCHULZ

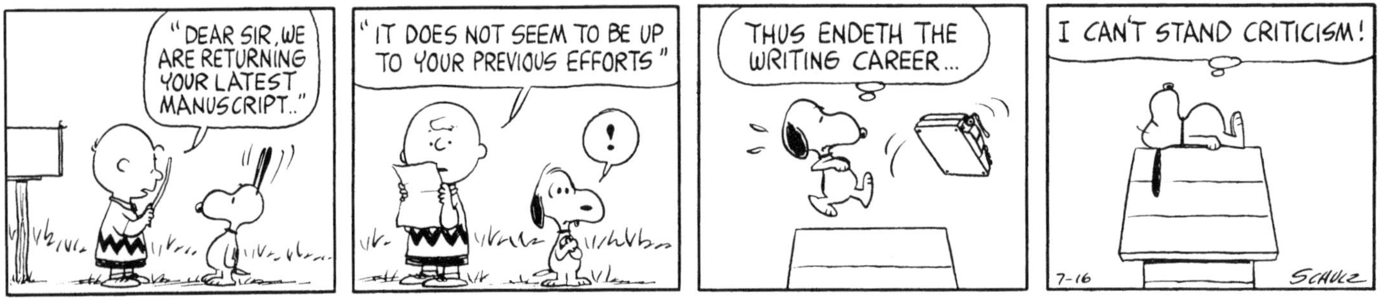
"DEAR SIR, WE ARE RETURNING YOUR LATEST MANUSCRIPT.."
"IT DOES NOT SEEM TO BE UP TO YOUR PREVIOUS EFFORTS"
!
THUS ENDETH THE WRITING CAREER...
I CAN'T STAND CRITICISM!
7-16
SCHULZ

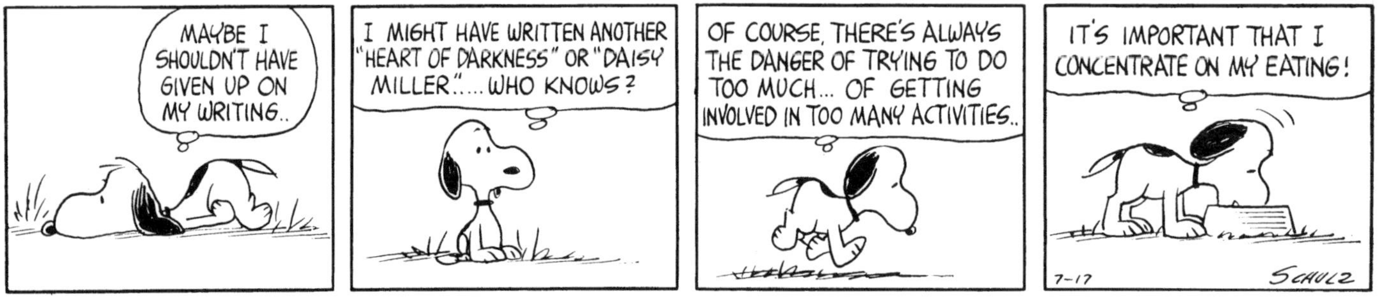
MAYBE I SHOULDN'T HAVE GIVEN UP ON MY WRITING..
I MIGHT HAVE WRITTEN ANOTHER "HEART OF DARKNESS" OR "DAISY MILLER".... WHO KNOWS?
OF COURSE, THERE'S ALWAYS THE DANGER OF TRYING TO DO TOO MUCH... OF GETTING INVOLVED IN TOO MANY ACTIVITIES..
IT'S IMPORTANT THAT I CONCENTRATE ON MY EATING!
7-17
SCHULZ

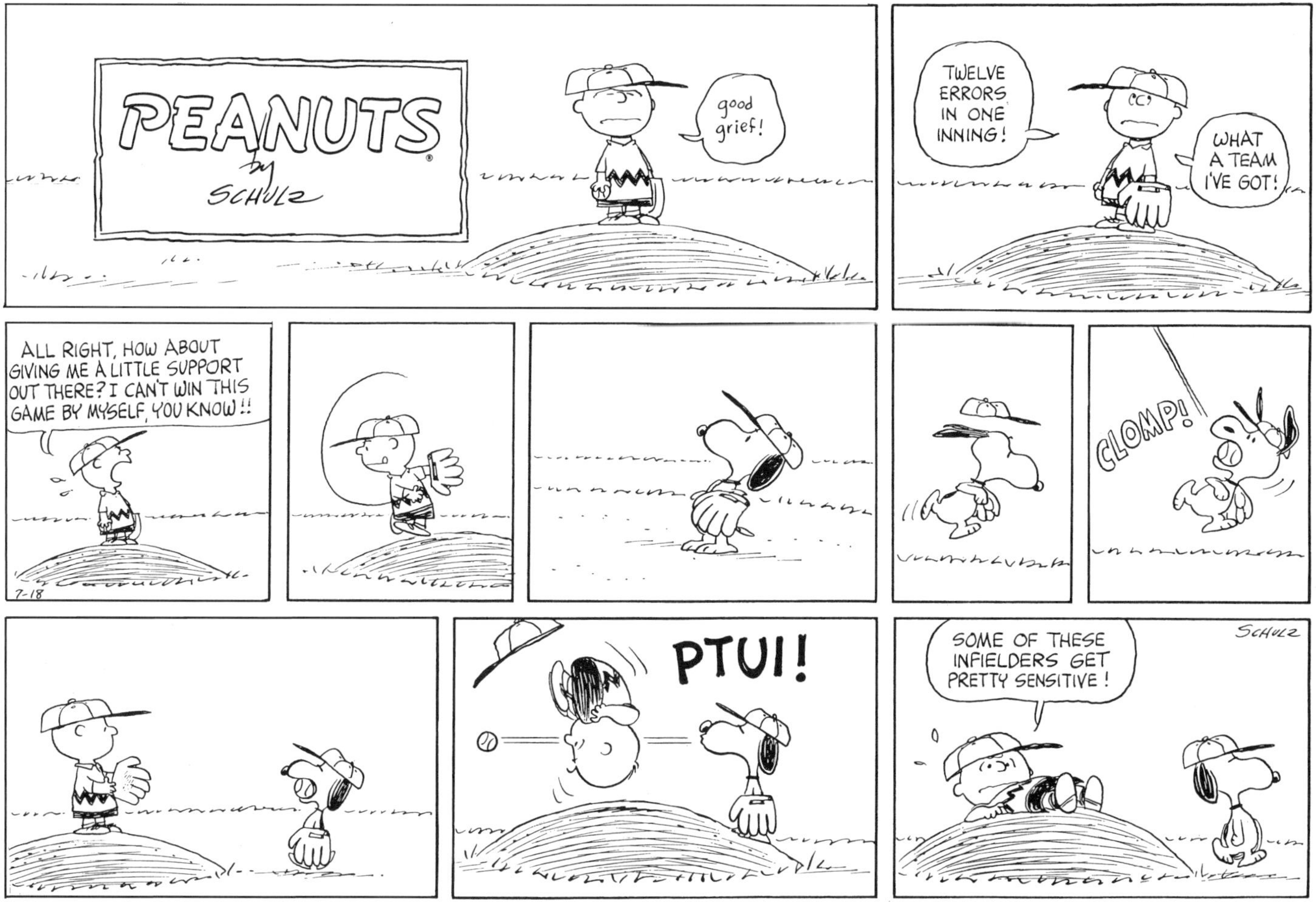
PEANUTS
by
SCHULZ
good grief!
TWELVE ERRORS IN ONE INNING!
WHAT A TEAM I'VE GOT!
ALL RIGHT, HOW ABOUT GIVING ME A LITTLE SUPPORT OUT THERE? I CAN'T WIN THIS GAME BY MYSELF, YOU KNOW!!
7-18
CLOMP!
PTUI!
SOME OF THESE INFIELDERS GET PRETTY SENSITIVE!
SCHULZ

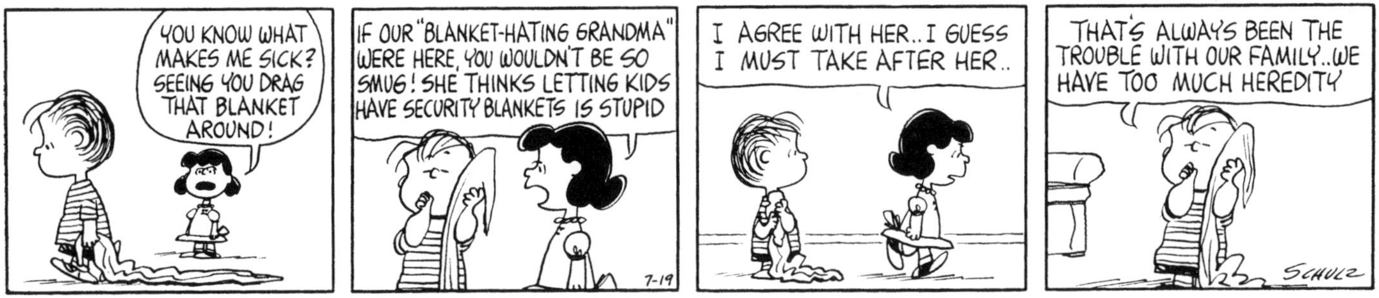
YOU KNOW WHAT MAKES ME SICK? SEEING YOU DRAG THAT BLANKET AROUND!
IF OUR "BLANKET-HATING GRANDMA" WERE HERE, YOU WOULDN'T BE SO SMUG! SHE THINKS LETTING KIDS HAVE SECURITY BLANKETS IS STUPID
7-19
I AGREE WITH HER.. I GUESS I MUST TAKE AFTER HER..
THAT'S ALWAYS BEEN THE TROUBLE WITH OUR FAMILY..WE HAVE TOO MUCH HEREDITY
SCHULZ

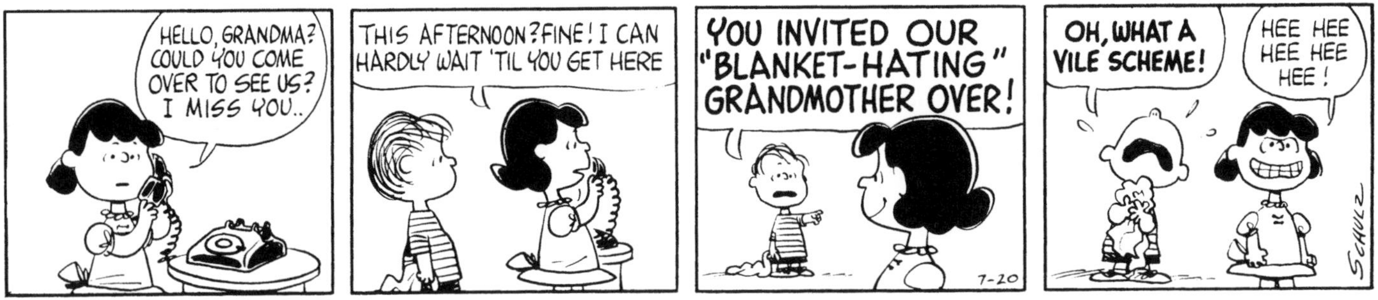
HELLO, GRANDMA? COULD YOU COME OVER TO SEE US? I MISS YOU..
THIS AFTERNOON? FINE! I CAN HARDLY WAIT 'TIL YOU GET HERE
YOU INVITED OUR "BLANKET-HATING" GRANDMOTHER OVER!
7-20
OH, WHAT A VILE SCHEME!
HEE HEE HEE HEE HEE!
SCHULZ

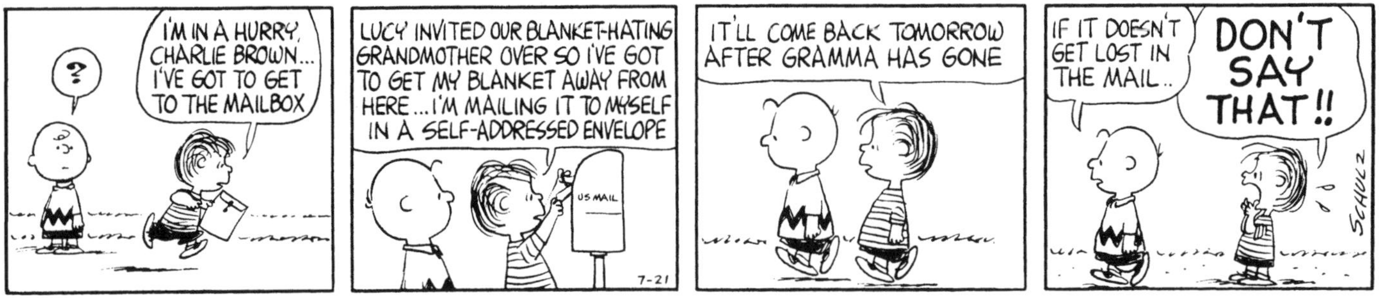
?
I'M IN A HURRY, CHARLIE BROWN... I'VE GOT TO GET TO THE MAILBOX
LUCY INVITED OUR BLANKET-HATING GRANDMOTHER OVER SO I'VE GOT TO GET MY BLANKET AWAY FROM HERE... I'M MAILING IT TO MYSELF IN A SELF-ADDRESSED ENVELOPE
US MAIL
7-21
IT'LL COME BACK TOMORROW AFTER GRAMMA HAS GONE
IF IT DOESN'T GET LOST IN THE MAIL..
DON'T SAY THAT!!
SCHULZ

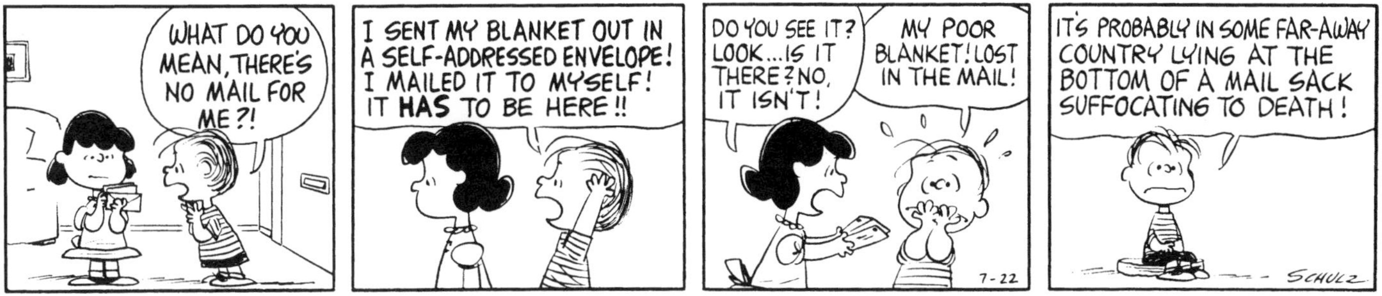
WHAT DO YOU MEAN, THERE'S NO MAIL FOR ME?!
I SENT MY BLANKET OUT IN A SELF-ADDRESSED ENVELOPE! I MAILED IT TO MYSELF! IT **HAS** TO BE HERE!!
DO YOU SEE IT? LOOK...IS IT THERE? NO, IT ISN'T!
MY POOR BLANKET! LOST IN THE MAIL!
7-22
IT'S PROBABLY IN SOME FAR-AWAY COUNTRY LYING AT THE BOTTOM OF A MAIL SACK SUFFOCATING TO DEATH!
SCHULZ

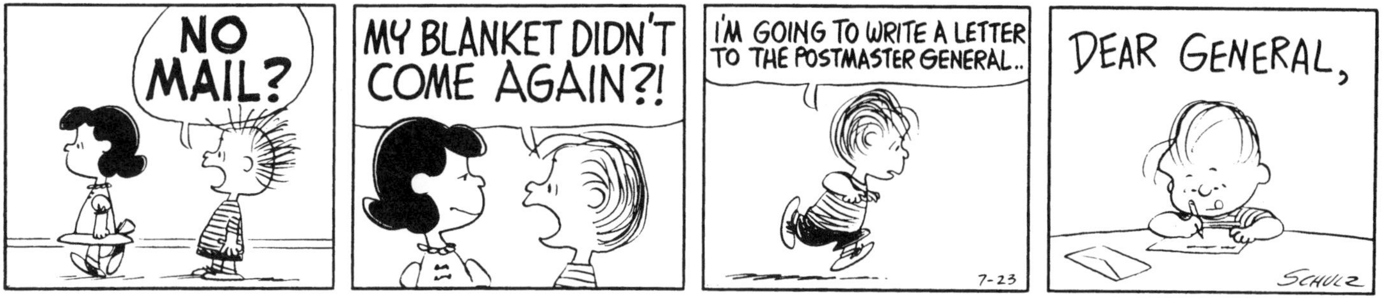
NO MAIL?
MY BLANKET DIDN'T COME AGAIN?!
I'M GOING TO WRITE A LETTER TO THE POSTMASTER GENERAL..
7-23
DEAR GENERAL,
SCHULZ

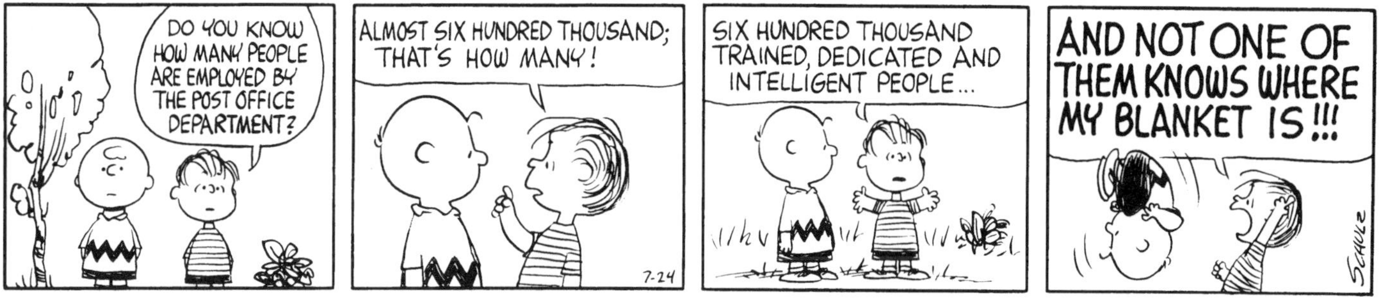
DO YOU KNOW HOW MANY PEOPLE ARE EMPLOYED BY THE POST OFFICE DEPARTMENT?
ALMOST SIX HUNDRED THOUSAND; THAT'S HOW MANY!
7-24
SIX HUNDRED THOUSAND TRAINED, DEDICATED AND INTELLIGENT PEOPLE...
AND NOT ONE OF THEM KNOWS WHERE MY BLANKET IS!!!
SCHULZ

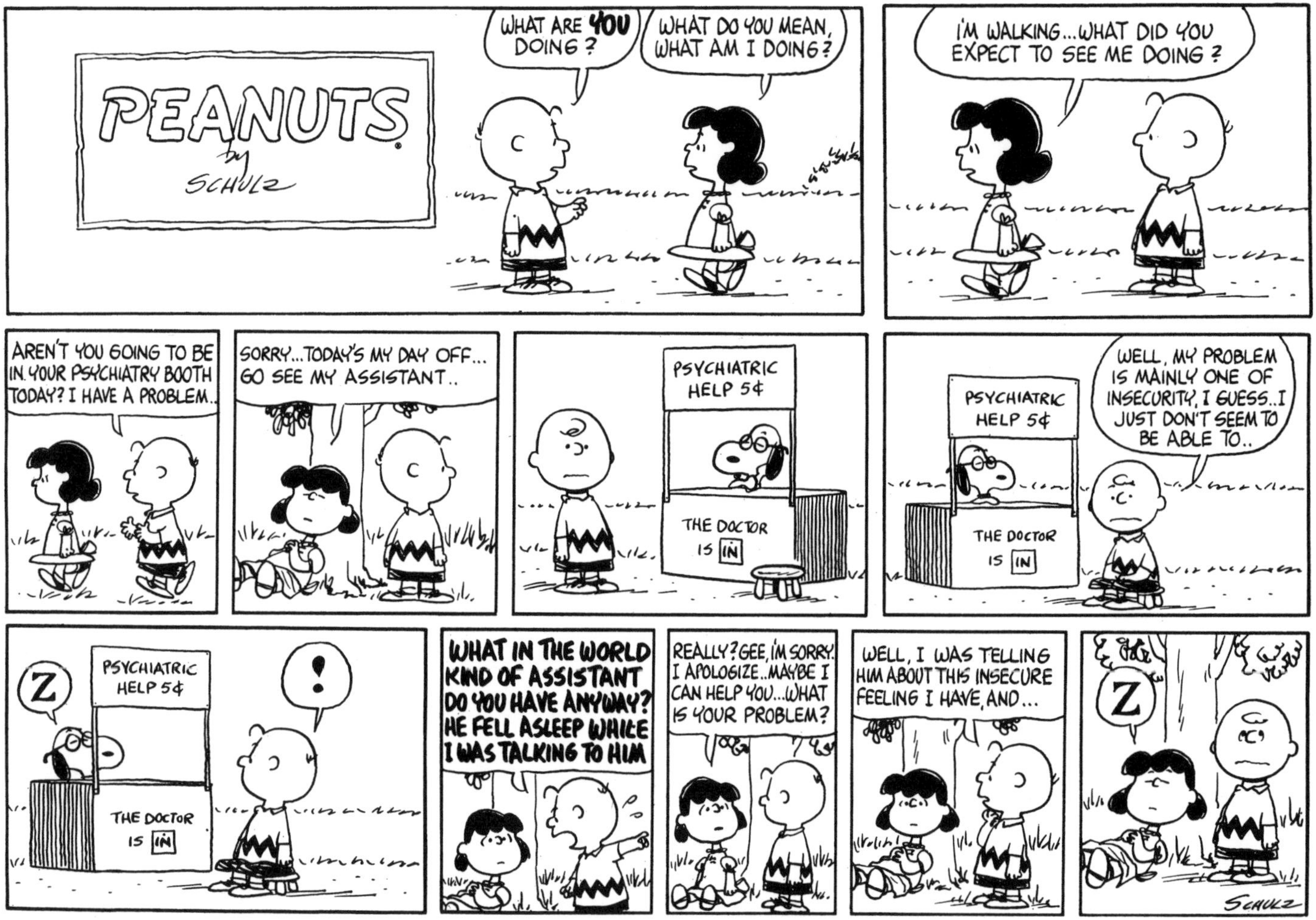
PEANUTS
by SCHULZ
WHAT ARE YOU DOING?
WHAT DO YOU MEAN, WHAT AM I DOING?
I'M WALKING...WHAT DID YOU EXPECT TO SEE ME DOING?
AREN'T YOU GOING TO BE IN YOUR PSYCHIATRY BOOTH TODAY? I HAVE A PROBLEM..
SORRY...TODAY'S MY DAY OFF...GO SEE MY ASSISTANT..
PSYCHIATRIC HELP 5¢
THE DOCTOR IS IN
PSYCHIATRIC HELP 5¢
THE DOCTOR IS IN
WELL, MY PROBLEM IS MAINLY ONE OF INSECURITY, I GUESS..I JUST DON'T SEEM TO BE ABLE TO..
Z
PSYCHIATRIC HELP 5¢
THE DOCTOR IS IN
!
WHAT IN THE WORLD KIND OF ASSISTANT DO YOU HAVE ANYWAY? HE FELL ASLEEP WHILE I WAS TALKING TO HIM
REALLY? GEE, I'M SORRY. I APOLOGIZE..MAYBE I CAN HELP YOU...WHAT IS YOUR PROBLEM?
WELL, I WAS TELLING HIM ABOUT THIS INSECURE FEELING I HAVE, AND...
Z
SCHULZ

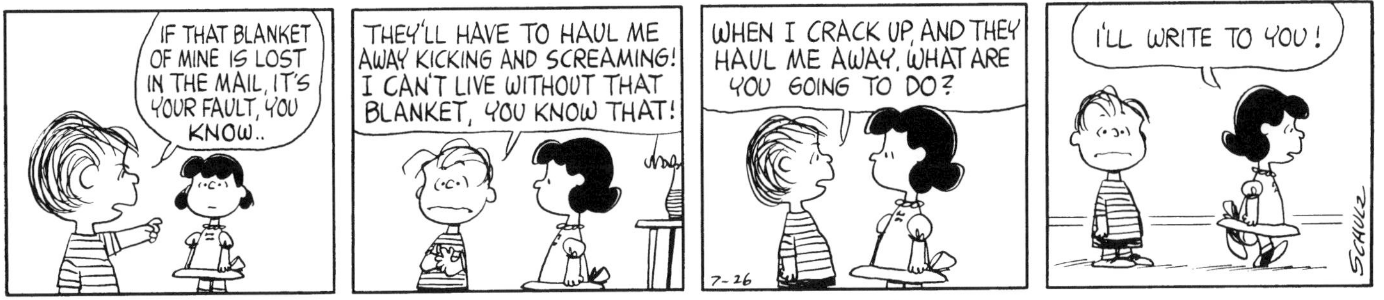
IF THAT BLANKET OF MINE IS LOST IN THE MAIL, IT'S YOUR FAULT, YOU KNOW..
THEY'LL HAVE TO HAUL ME AWAY KICKING AND SCREAMING! I CAN'T LIVE WITHOUT THAT BLANKET, YOU KNOW THAT!
WHEN I CRACK UP, AND THEY HAUL ME AWAY, WHAT ARE YOU GOING TO DO?
7-26
I'LL WRITE TO YOU!
SCHULZ

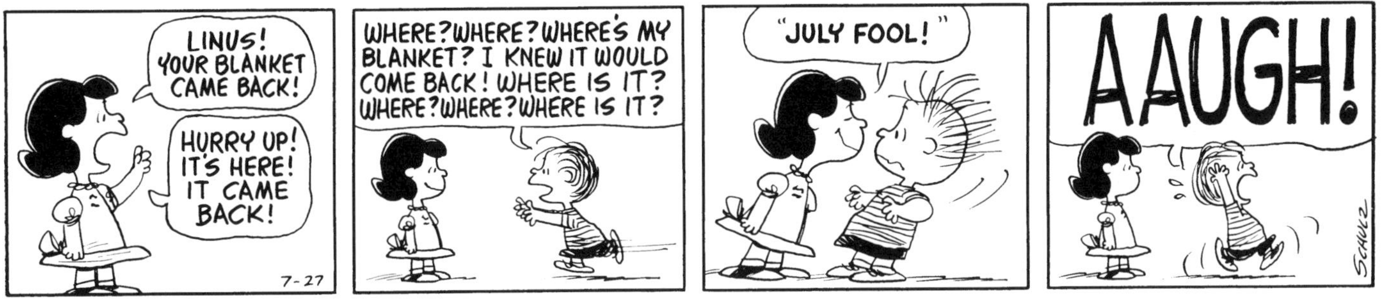
LINUS! YOUR BLANKET CAME BACK!
HURRY UP! IT'S HERE! IT CAME BACK!
7-27
WHERE? WHERE? WHERE'S MY BLANKET? I KNEW IT WOULD COME BACK! WHERE IS IT? WHERE? WHERE? WHERE IS IT?
"JULY FOOL!"
AAUGH!
SCHULZ

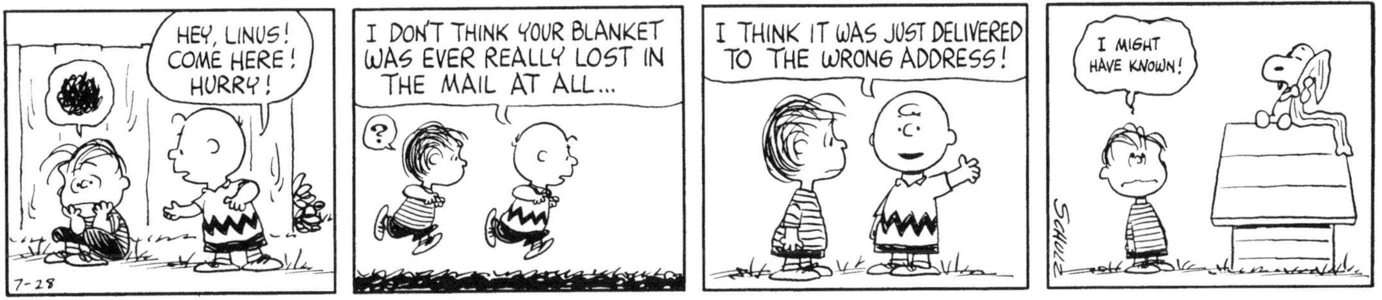
HEY, LINUS! COME HERE! HURRY!
7-28
I DON'T THINK YOUR BLANKET WAS EVER REALLY LOST IN THE MAIL AT ALL...
?
I THINK IT WAS JUST DELIVERED TO THE WRONG ADDRESS!
I MIGHT HAVE KNOWN!
SCHULZ

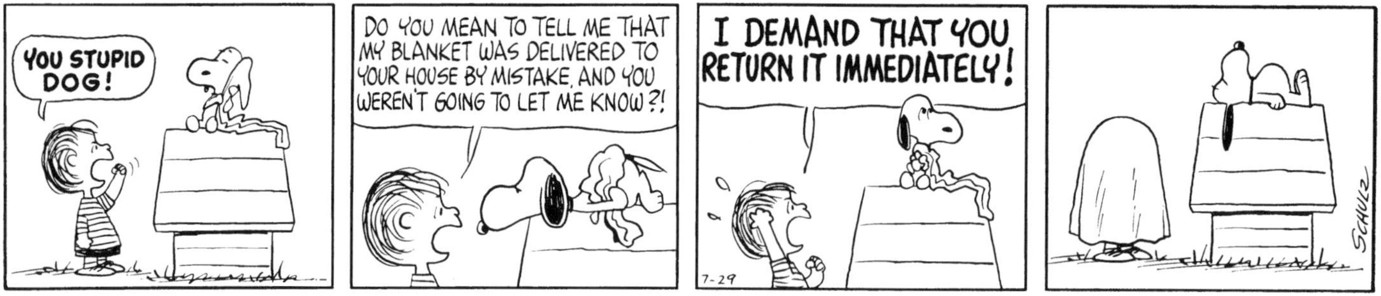
YOU STUPID DOG!
DO YOU MEAN TO TELL ME THAT MY BLANKET WAS DELIVERED TO YOUR HOUSE BY MISTAKE, AND YOU WEREN'T GOING TO LET ME KNOW?!
I DEMAND THAT YOU RETURN IT IMMEDIATELY!
7-29
SCHULZ

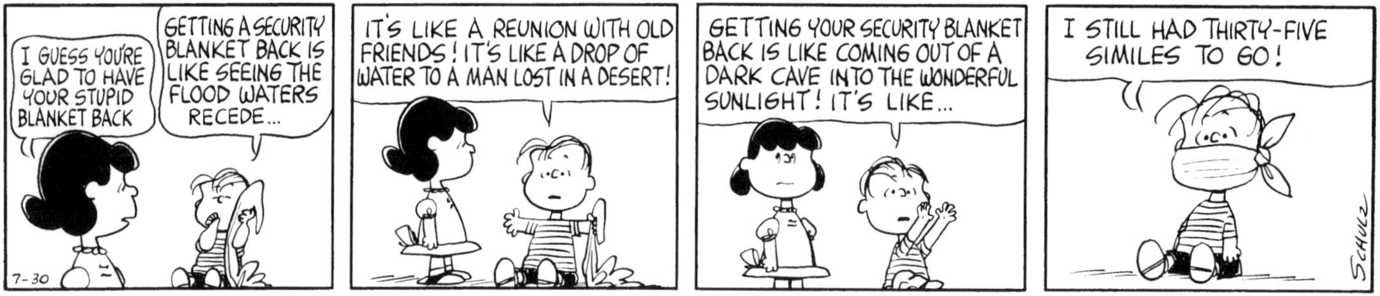
I GUESS YOU'RE GLAD TO HAVE YOUR STUPID BLANKET BACK
GETTING A SECURITY BLANKET BACK IS LIKE SEEING THE FLOOD WATERS RECEDE...
7-30
IT'S LIKE A REUNION WITH OLD FRIENDS! IT'S LIKE A DROP OF WATER TO A MAN LOST IN A DESERT!
GETTING YOUR SECURITY BLANKET BACK IS LIKE COMING OUT OF A DARK CAVE INTO THE WONDERFUL SUNLIGHT! IT'S LIKE...
I STILL HAD THIRTY-FIVE SIMILES TO GO!
SCHULZ

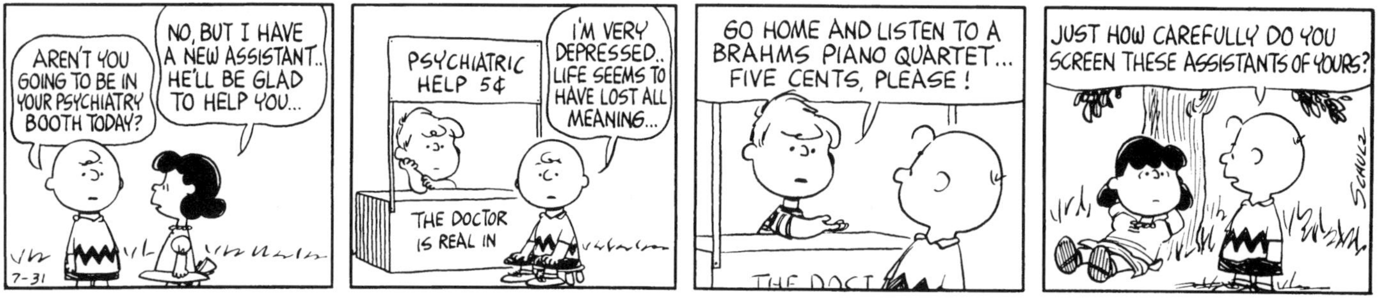
AREN'T YOU GOING TO BE IN YOUR PSYCHIATRY BOOTH TODAY?
NO, BUT I HAVE A NEW ASSISTANT.. HE'LL BE GLAD TO HELP YOU...
7-31
PSYCHIATRIC HELP 5¢
THE DOCTOR IS REAL IN
I'M VERY DEPRESSED.. LIFE SEEMS TO HAVE LOST ALL MEANING...
GO HOME AND LISTEN TO A BRAHMS PIANO QUARTET... FIVE CENTS, PLEASE!
THE DOCT
JUST HOW CAREFULLY DO YOU SCREEN THESE ASSISTANTS OF YOURS?
SCHULZ

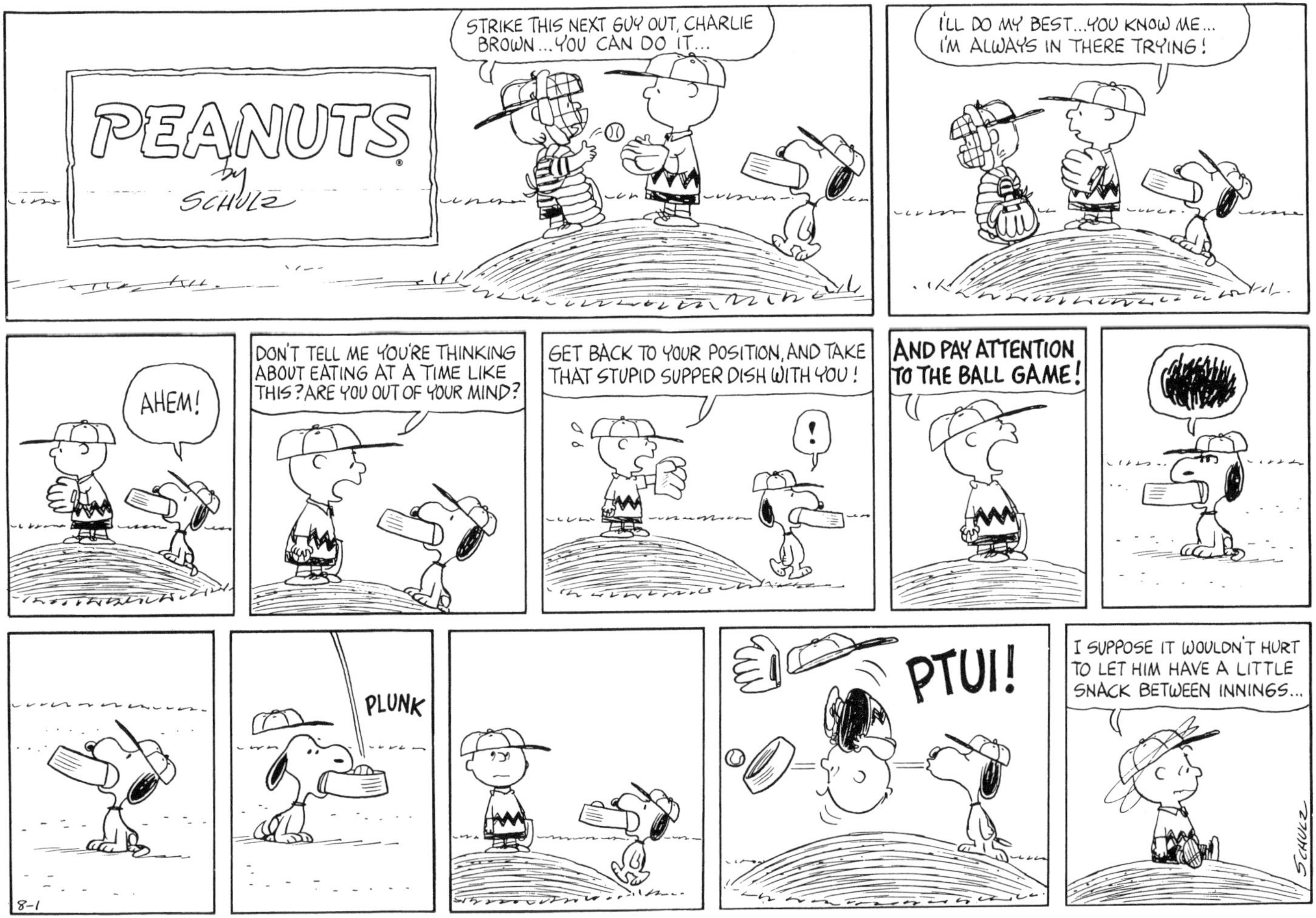
PEANUTS
by SCHULZ
STRIKE THIS NEXT GUY OUT, CHARLIE BROWN...YOU CAN DO IT...
I'LL DO MY BEST...YOU KNOW ME... I'M ALWAYS IN THERE TRYING!
AHEM!
DON'T TELL ME YOU'RE THINKING ABOUT EATING AT A TIME LIKE THIS? ARE YOU OUT OF YOUR MIND?
GET BACK TO YOUR POSITION, AND TAKE THAT STUPID SUPPER DISH WITH YOU!
!
AND PAY ATTENTION TO THE BALL GAME!
8-1
PLUNK
PTUI!
I SUPPOSE IT WOULDN'T HURT TO LET HIM HAVE A LITTLE SNACK BETWEEN INNINGS...
SCHULZ

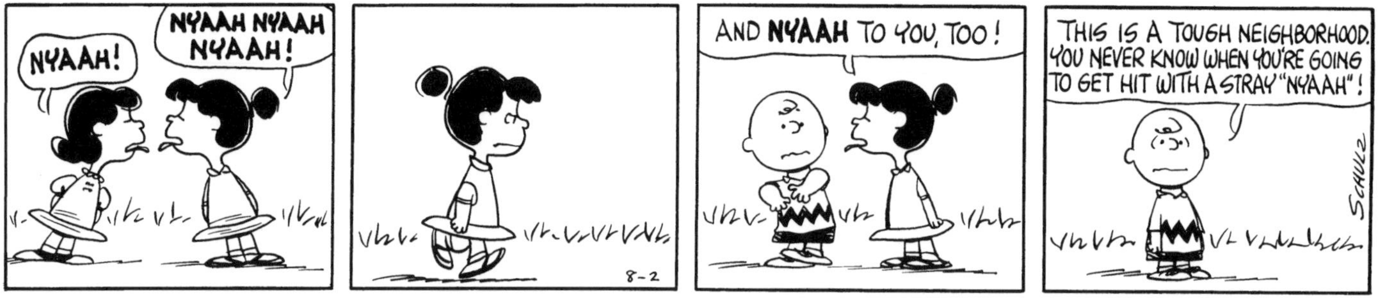
NYAAH!
NYAAH NYAAH NYAAH!
8-2
AND **NYAAH** TO YOU, TOO!
THIS IS A TOUGH NEIGHBORHOOD. YOU NEVER KNOW WHEN YOU'RE GOING TO GET HIT WITH A STRAY "NYAAH"!
SCHULZ

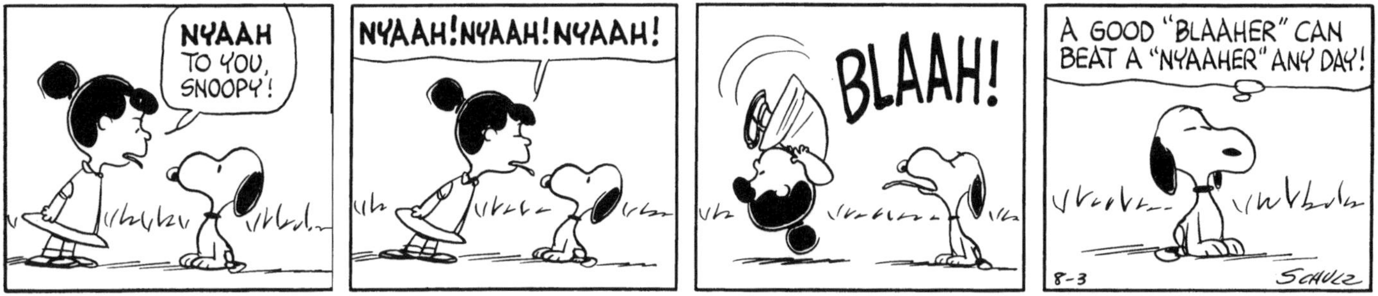
NYAAH TO YOU, SNOOPY!
NYAAH! NYAAH! NYAAH!
BLAAH!
A GOOD "BLAAHER" CAN BEAT A "NYAAHER" ANY DAY!
8-3
SCHULZ

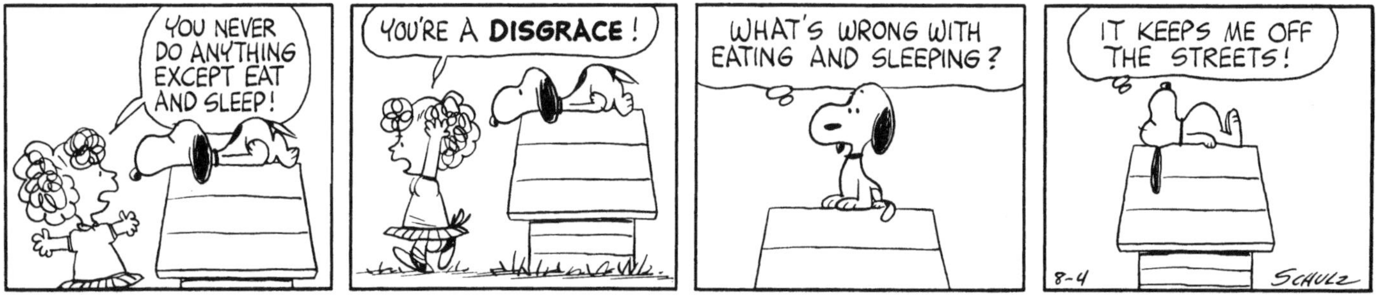
YOU NEVER DO ANYTHING EXCEPT EAT AND SLEEP!
YOU'RE A **DISGRACE**!
WHAT'S WRONG WITH EATING AND SLEEPING?
IT KEEPS ME OFF THE STREETS!
8-4
SCHULZ

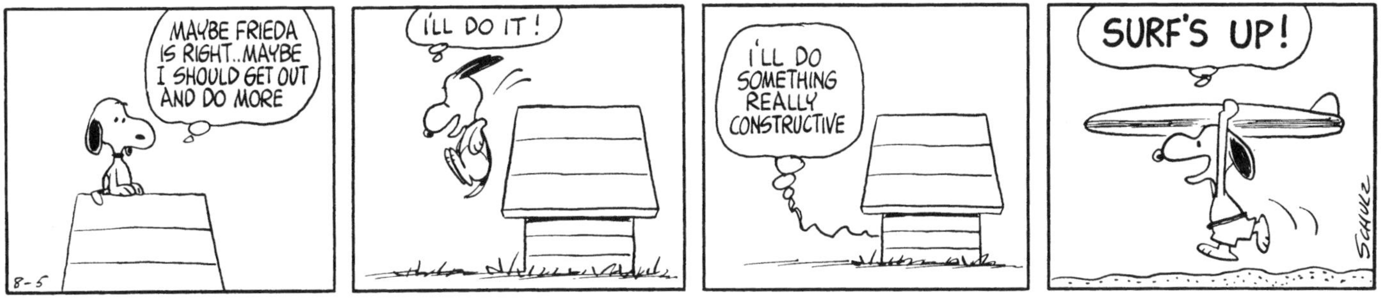
MAYBE FRIEDA IS RIGHT..MAYBE I SHOULD GET OUT AND DO MORE
8-5
I'LL DO IT!
I'LL DO SOMETHING REALLY CONSTRUCTIVE
SURF'S UP!
SCHULZ

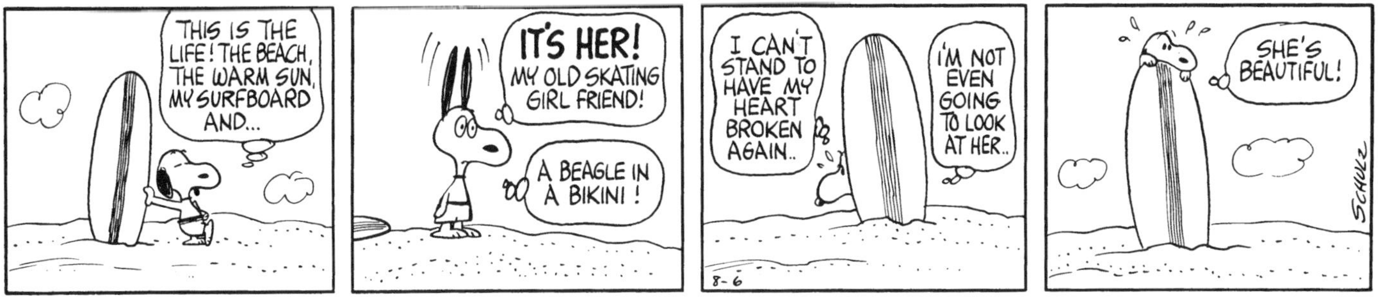
THIS IS THE LIFE! THE BEACH, THE WARM SUN, MY SURFBOARD AND...
IT'S HER! MY OLD SKATING GIRL FRIEND!
A BEAGLE IN A BIKINI!
I CAN'T STAND TO HAVE MY HEART BROKEN AGAIN..
I'M NOT EVEN GOING TO LOOK AT HER..
8-6
SHE'S BEAUTIFUL!
SCHULZ

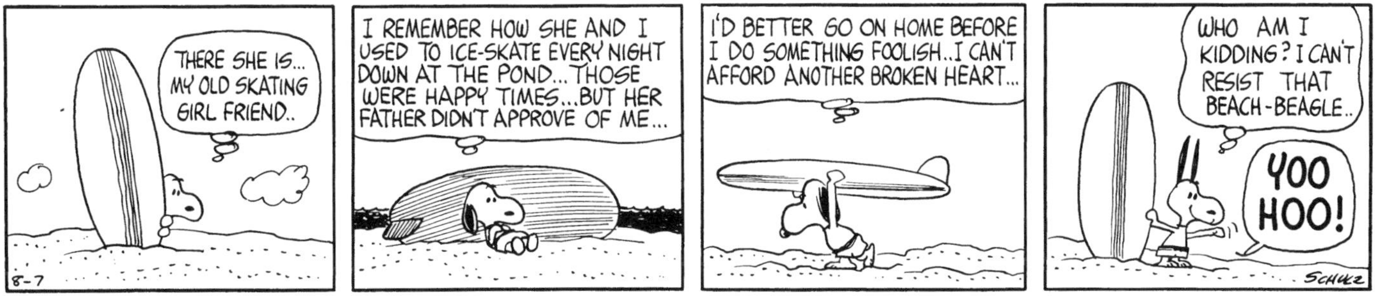
THERE SHE IS... MY OLD SKATING GIRL FRIEND..
8-7
I REMEMBER HOW SHE AND I USED TO ICE-SKATE EVERY NIGHT DOWN AT THE POND... THOSE WERE HAPPY TIMES...BUT HER FATHER DIDN'T APPROVE OF ME...
I'D BETTER GO ON HOME BEFORE I DO SOMETHING FOOLISH..I CAN'T AFFORD ANOTHER BROKEN HEART...
WHO AM I KIDDING? I CAN'T RESIST THAT BEACH-BEAGLE..
YOO HOO!
SCHULZ

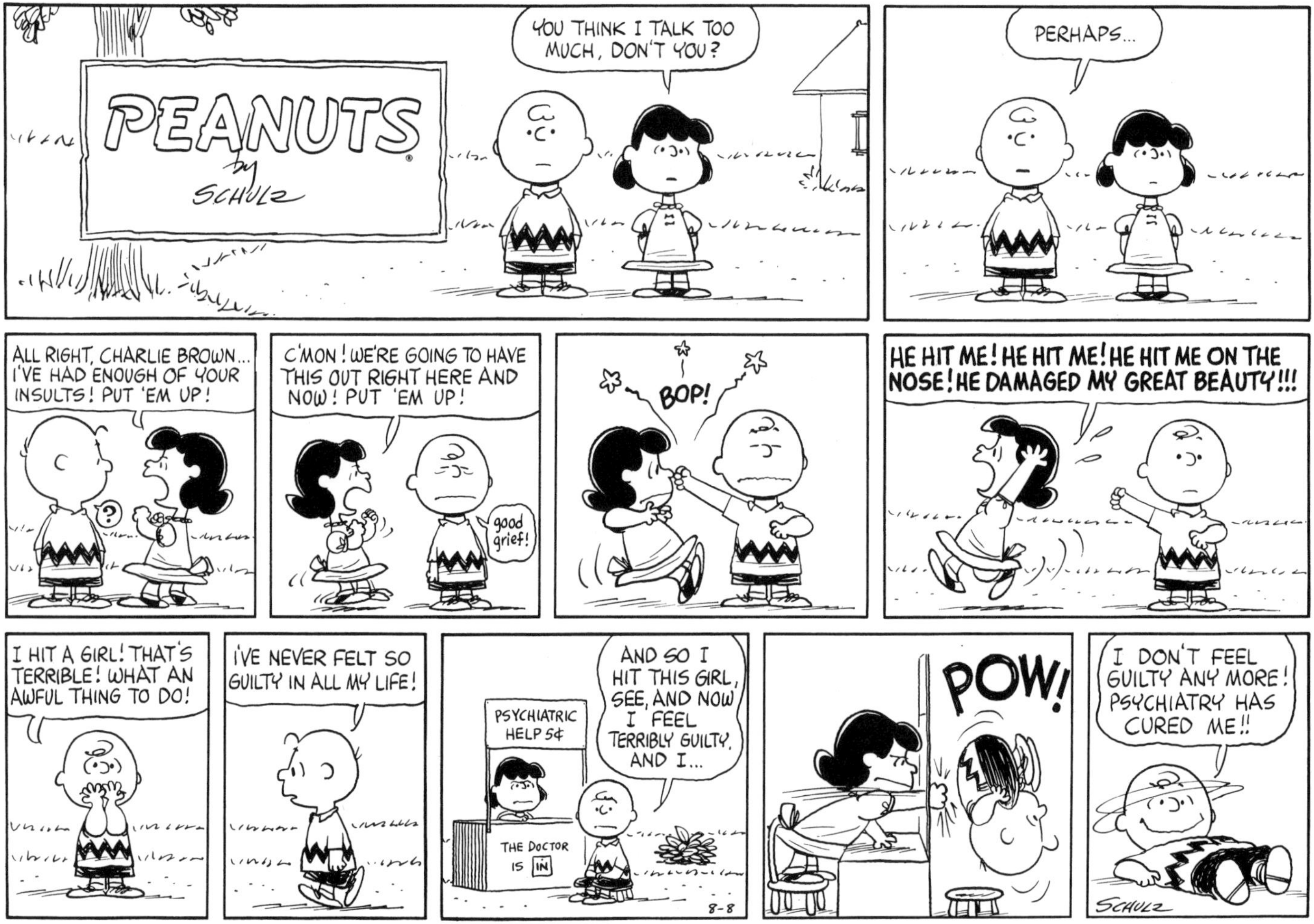
PEANUTS
by SCHULZ
YOU THINK I TALK TOO MUCH, DON'T YOU?
PERHAPS...
ALL RIGHT, CHARLIE BROWN... I'VE HAD ENOUGH OF YOUR INSULTS! PUT 'EM UP!
?
C'MON! WE'RE GOING TO HAVE THIS OUT RIGHT HERE AND NOW! PUT 'EM UP!
good grief!
BOP!
HE HIT ME! HE HIT ME! HE HIT ME ON THE NOSE! HE DAMAGED MY GREAT BEAUTY!!!
I HIT A GIRL! THAT'S TERRIBLE! WHAT AN AWFUL THING TO DO!
I'VE NEVER FELT SO GUILTY IN ALL MY LIFE!
PSYCHIATRIC HELP 5¢
THE DOCTOR IS IN
AND SO I HIT THIS GIRL, SEE, AND NOW I FEEL TERRIBLY GUILTY, AND I...
8-8
POW!
I DON'T FEEL GUILTY ANY MORE! PSYCHIATRY HAS CURED ME!!
SCHULZ

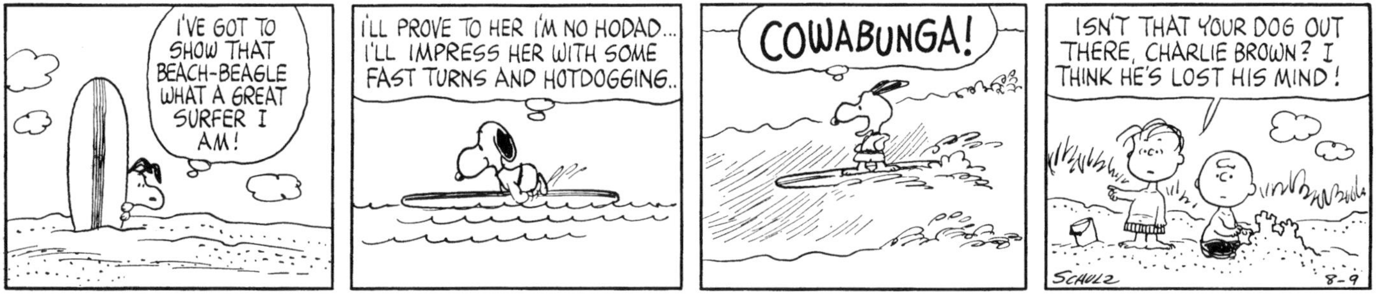
I'VE GOT TO SHOW THAT BEACH-BEAGLE WHAT A GREAT SURFER I AM!
I'LL PROVE TO HER I'M NO HODAD... I'LL IMPRESS HER WITH SOME FAST TURNS AND HOTDOGGING..
COWABUNGA!
ISN'T THAT YOUR DOG OUT THERE, CHARLIE BROWN? I THINK HE'S LOST HIS MIND!
SCHULZ
8-9

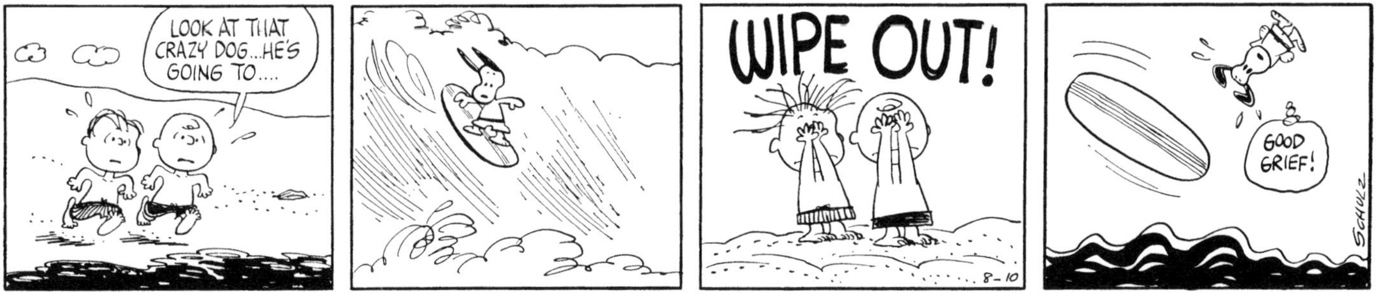
LOOK AT THAT CRAZY DOG...HE'S GOING TO....
WIPE OUT!
8-10
GOOD GRIEF!
SCHULZ

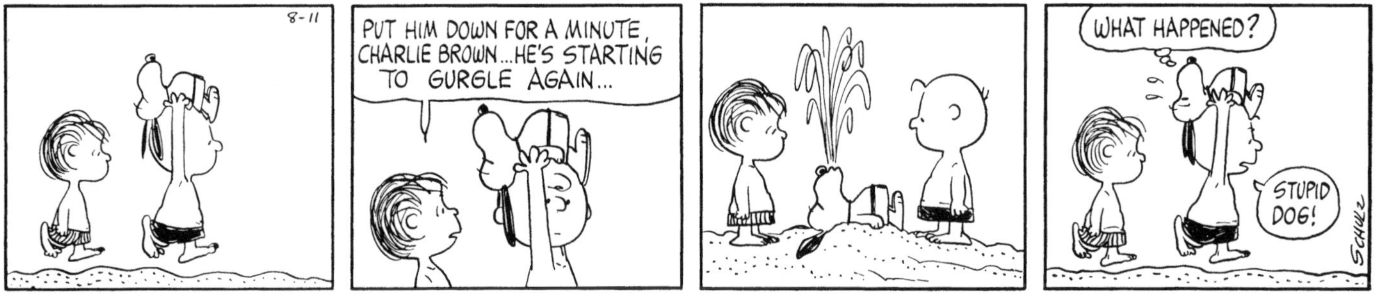
8-11
PUT HIM DOWN FOR A MINUTE, CHARLIE BROWN...HE'S STARTING TO GURGLE AGAIN...
WHAT HAPPENED?
STUPID DOG!
SCHULZ

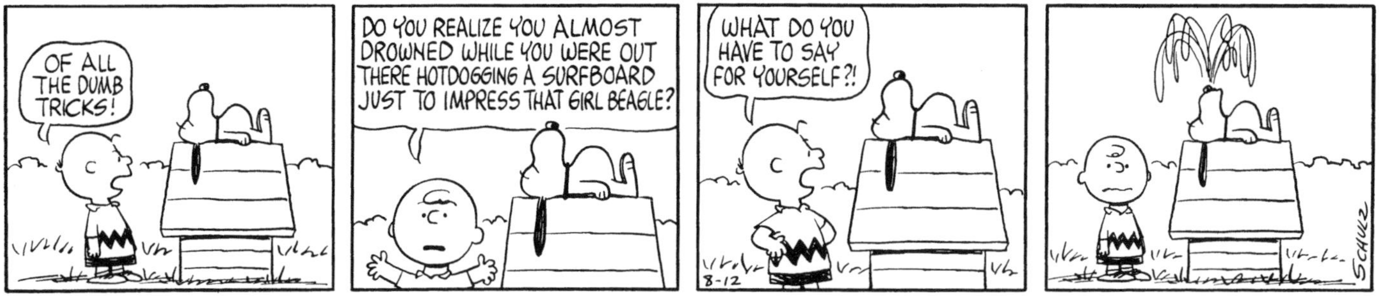
OF ALL THE DUMB TRICKS!
DO YOU REALIZE YOU ALMOST DROWNED WHILE YOU WERE OUT THERE HOTDOGGING A SURFBOARD JUST TO IMPRESS THAT GIRL BEAGLE?
WHAT DO YOU HAVE TO SAY FOR YOURSELF?!

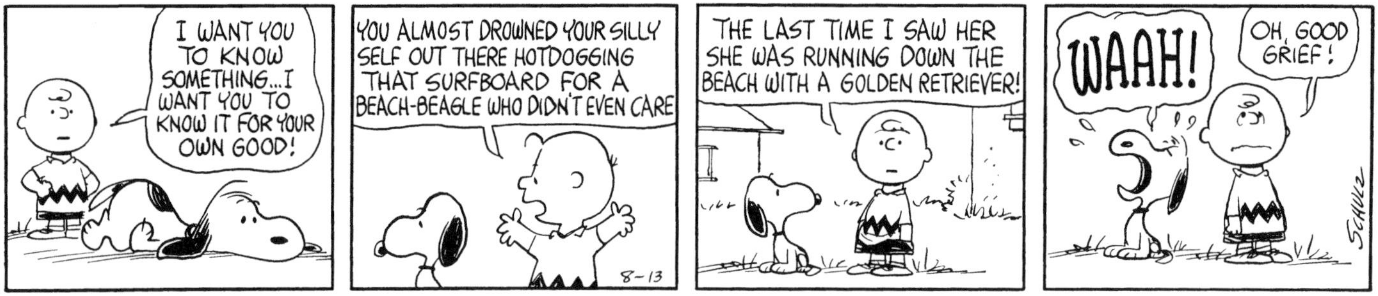
I WANT YOU TO KNOW SOMETHING...I WANT YOU TO KNOW IT FOR YOUR OWN GOOD!
YOU ALMOST DROWNED YOUR SILLY SELF OUT THERE HOTDOGGING THAT SURFBOARD FOR A BEACH-BEAGLE WHO DIDN'T EVEN CARE
THE LAST TIME I SAW HER SHE WAS RUNNING DOWN THE BEACH WITH A GOLDEN RETRIEVER!
WAAH!
OH, GOOD GRIEF!

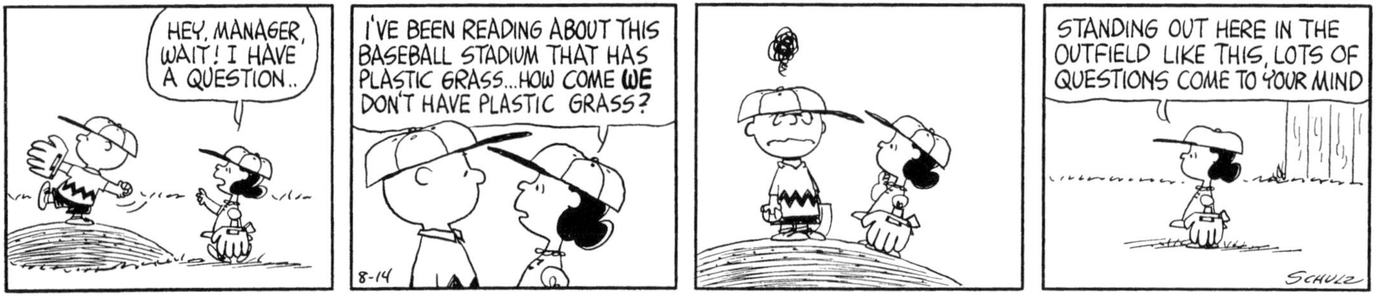
HEY, MANAGER, WAIT! I HAVE A QUESTION..
I'VE BEEN READING ABOUT THIS BASEBALL STADIUM THAT HAS PLASTIC GRASS...HOW COME **WE** DON'T HAVE PLASTIC GRASS?
STANDING OUT HERE IN THE OUTFIELD LIKE THIS, LOTS OF QUESTIONS COME TO YOUR MIND

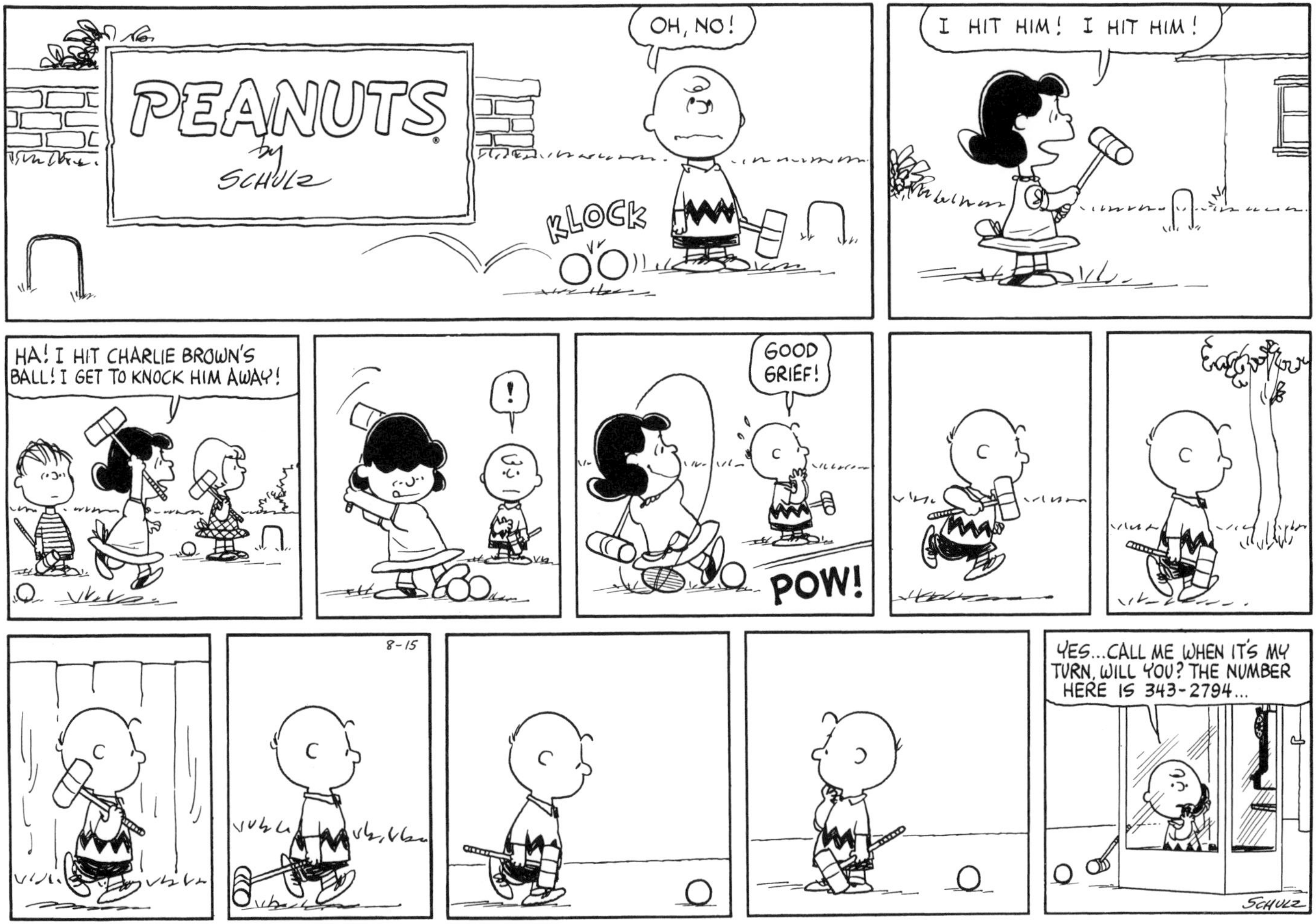
PEANUTS
by SCHULZ
OH, NO!
KLOCK
I HIT HIM! I HIT HIM!
HA! I HIT CHARLIE BROWN'S BALL! I GET TO KNOCK HIM AWAY!
!
GOOD GRIEF!
POW!
8-15
YES...CALL ME WHEN IT'S MY TURN, WILL YOU? THE NUMBER HERE IS 343-2794...
SCHULZ

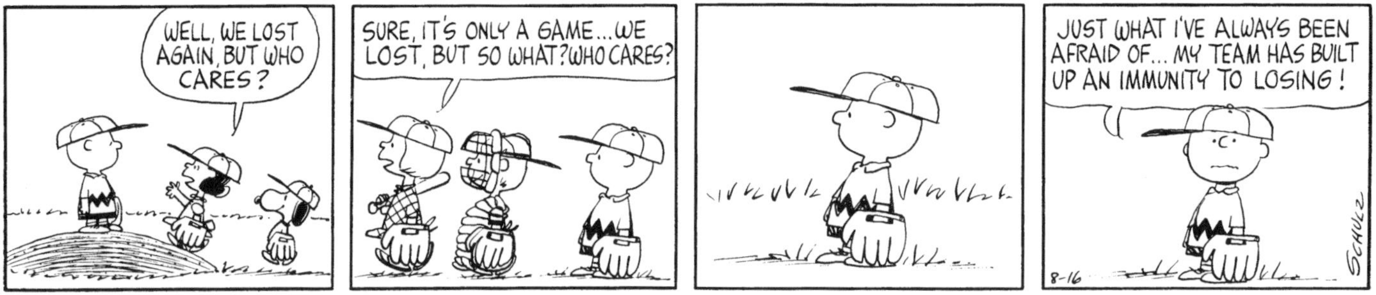
WELL, WE LOST AGAIN, BUT WHO CARES?
SURE, IT'S ONLY A GAME... WE LOST, BUT SO WHAT? WHO CARES?
JUST WHAT I'VE ALWAYS BEEN AFRAID OF... MY TEAM HAS BUILT UP AN IMMUNITY TO LOSING!
8-16
SCHULZ

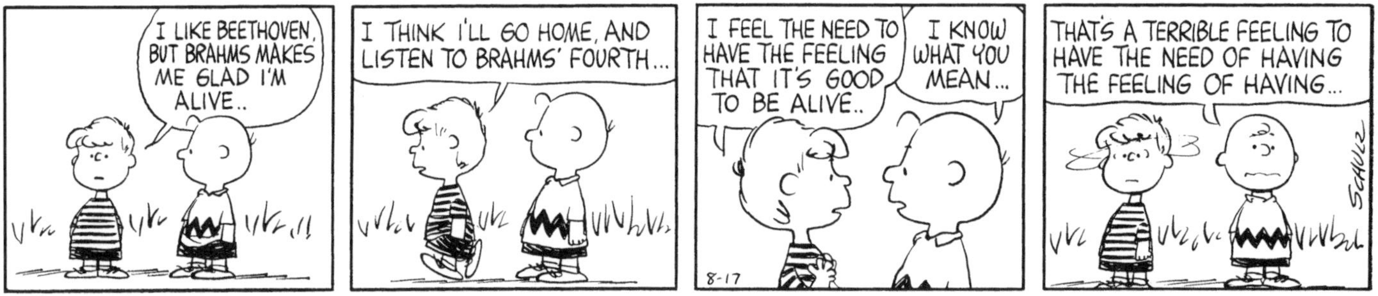
I LIKE BEETHOVEN, BUT BRAHMS MAKES ME GLAD I'M ALIVE..
I THINK I'LL GO HOME, AND LISTEN TO BRAHMS' FOURTH...
I FEEL THE NEED TO HAVE THE FEELING THAT IT'S GOOD TO BE ALIVE..
I KNOW WHAT YOU MEAN...
8-17
THAT'S A TERRIBLE FEELING TO HAVE THE NEED OF HAVING THE FEELING OF HAVING...
SCHULZ

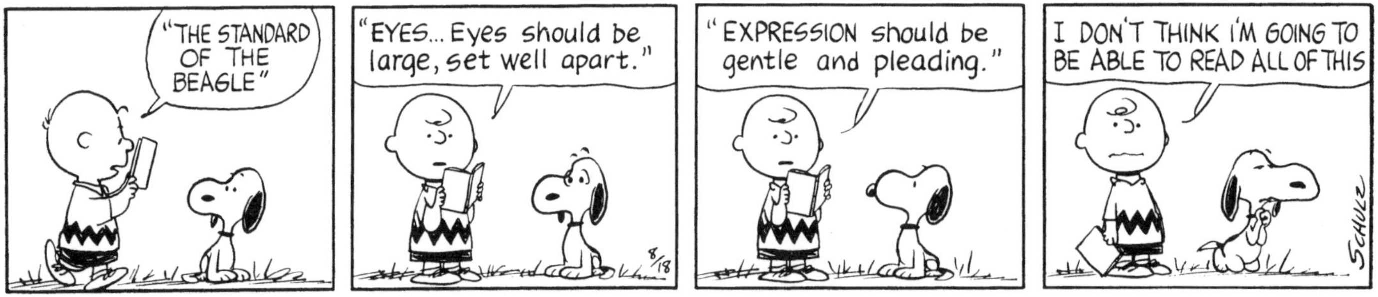
"THE STANDARD OF THE BEAGLE"
"EYES... Eyes should be large, set well apart."
8/18
"EXPRESSION should be gentle and pleading."
I DON'T THINK I'M GOING TO BE ABLE TO READ ALL OF THIS
SCHULZ

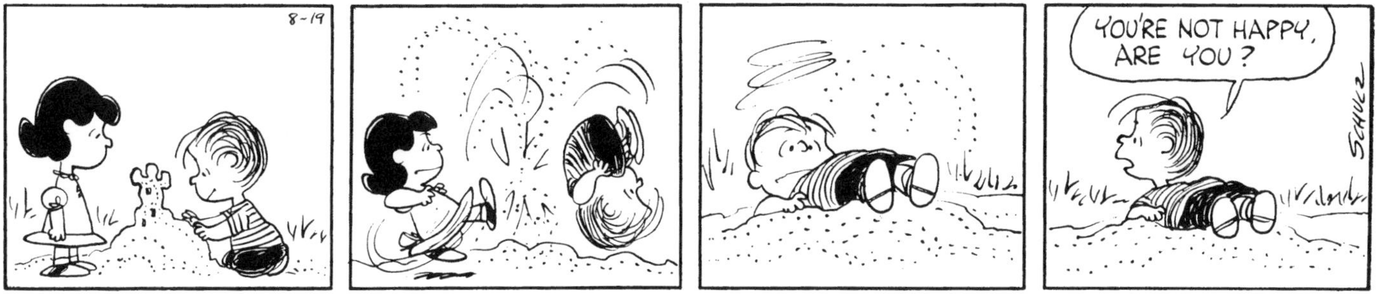
8-19
YOU'RE NOT HAPPY, ARE YOU?
SCHULZ

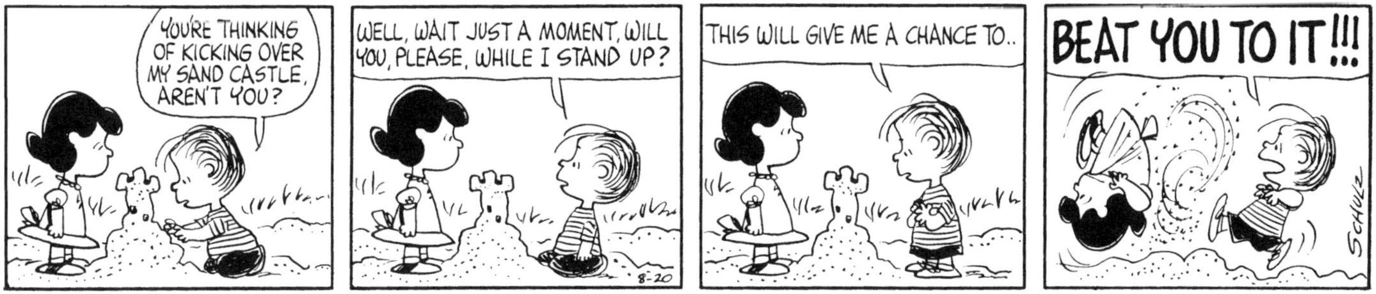
YOU'RE THINKING OF KICKING OVER MY SAND CASTLE, AREN'T YOU?
WELL, WAIT JUST A MOMENT, WILL YOU, PLEASE, WHILE I STAND UP?
8-20
THIS WILL GIVE ME A CHANCE TO..
BEAT YOU TO IT!!!
SCHULZ

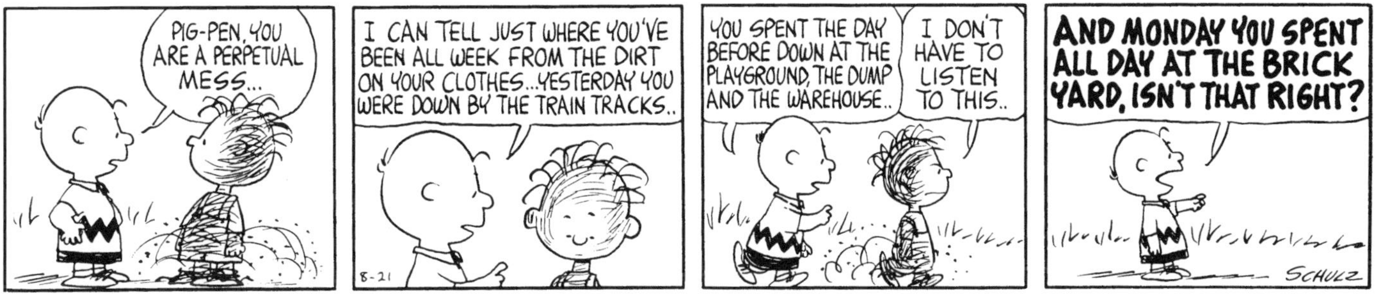
PIG-PEN, YOU ARE A PERPETUAL MESS...
I CAN TELL JUST WHERE YOU'VE BEEN ALL WEEK FROM THE DIRT ON YOUR CLOTHES...YESTERDAY YOU WERE DOWN BY THE TRAIN TRACKS..
8-21
YOU SPENT THE DAY BEFORE DOWN AT THE PLAYGROUND, THE DUMP AND THE WAREHOUSE..
I DON'T HAVE TO LISTEN TO THIS..
AND MONDAY YOU SPENT ALL DAY AT THE BRICK YARD, ISN'T THAT RIGHT?
SCHULZ

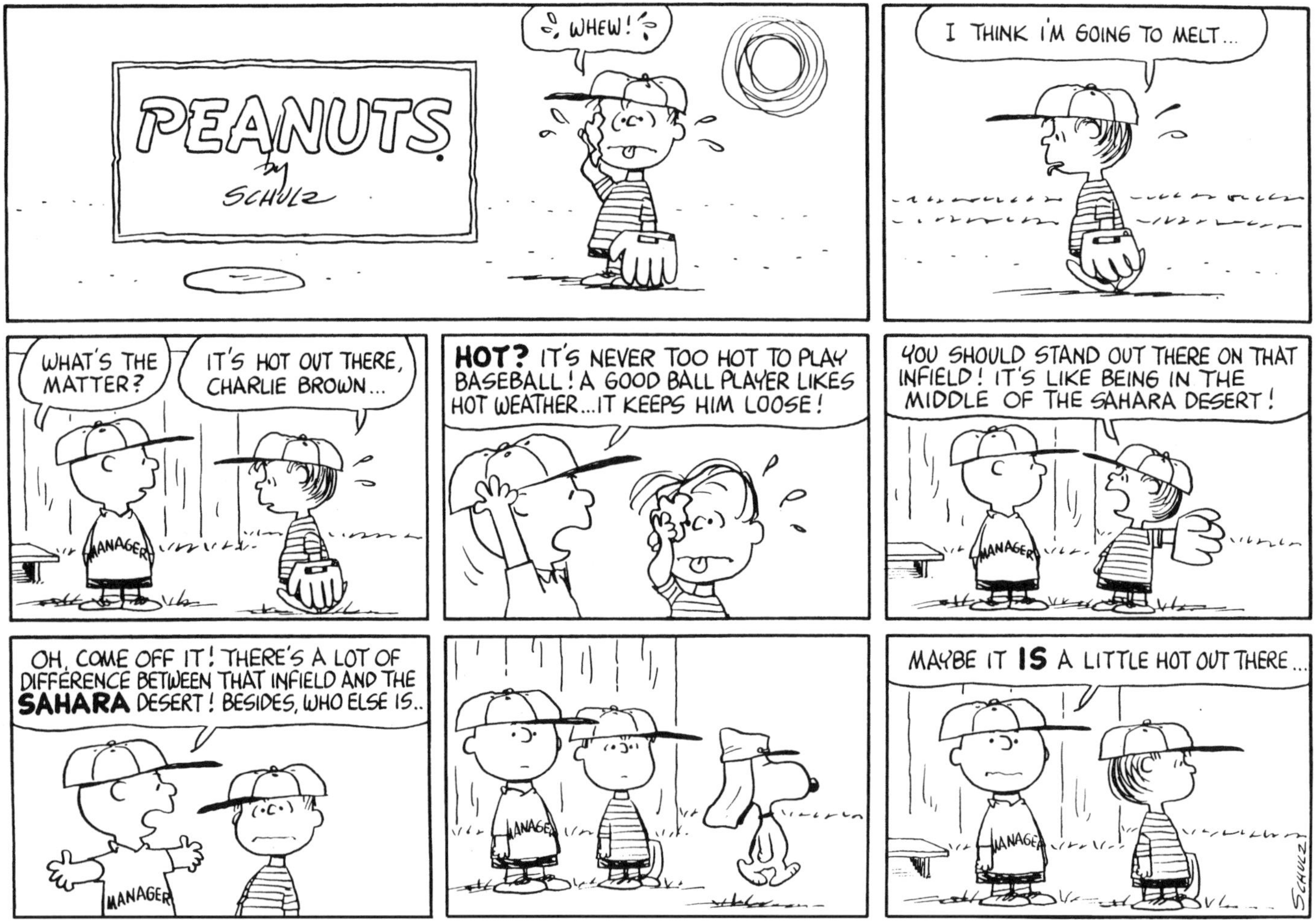
PEANUTS
by
SCHULZ
WHEW!
I THINK I'M GOING TO MELT...
WHAT'S THE MATTER?
IT'S HOT OUT THERE, CHARLIE BROWN...
MANAGER
HOT? IT'S NEVER TOO HOT TO PLAY BASEBALL! A GOOD BALL PLAYER LIKES HOT WEATHER...IT KEEPS HIM LOOSE!
YOU SHOULD STAND OUT THERE ON THAT INFIELD! IT'S LIKE BEING IN THE MIDDLE OF THE SAHARA DESERT!
MANAGER
OH, COME OFF IT! THERE'S A LOT OF DIFFERENCE BETWEEN THAT INFIELD AND THE SAHARA DESERT! BESIDES, WHO ELSE IS..
MANAGER
MAYBE IT IS A LITTLE HOT OUT THERE...
SCHULZ

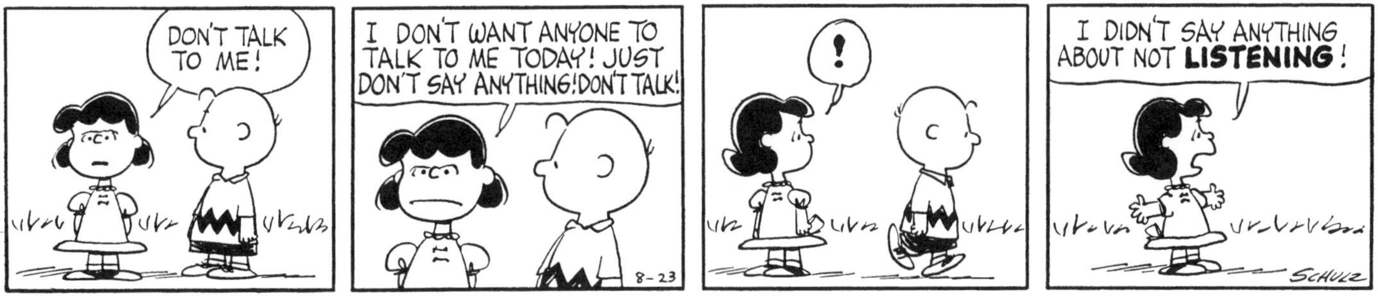
DON'T TALK TO ME!
I DON'T WANT ANYONE TO TALK TO ME TODAY! JUST DON'T SAY ANYTHING! DON'T TALK!
8-23
!
I DIDN'T SAY ANYTHING ABOUT NOT **LISTENING**!
SCHULZ

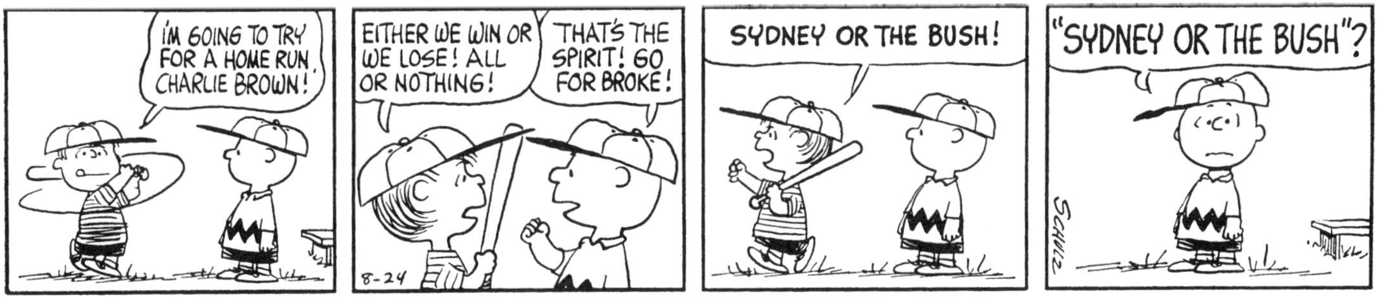
I'M GOING TO TRY FOR A HOME RUN, CHARLIE BROWN!
EITHER WE WIN OR WE LOSE! ALL OR NOTHING!
THAT'S THE SPIRIT! GO FOR BROKE!
8-24
SYDNEY OR THE BUSH!
"SYDNEY OR THE BUSH"?
SCHULZ

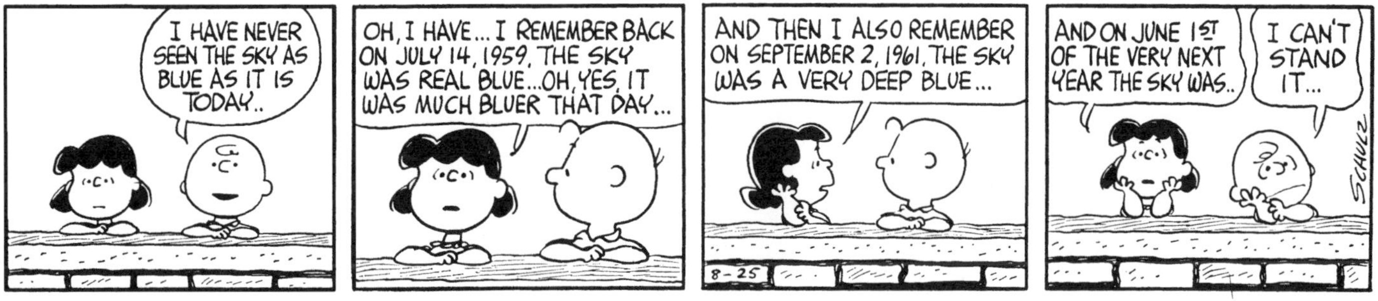
I HAVE NEVER SEEN THE SKY AS BLUE AS IT IS TODAY..
OH, I HAVE... I REMEMBER BACK ON JULY 14, 1959, THE SKY WAS REAL BLUE...OH, YES, IT WAS MUCH BLUER THAT DAY...
AND THEN I ALSO REMEMBER ON SEPTEMBER 2, 1961, THE SKY WAS A VERY DEEP BLUE...
8-25
AND ON JUNE 1ST OF THE VERY NEXT YEAR THE SKY WAS..
I CAN'T STAND IT...
SCHULZ

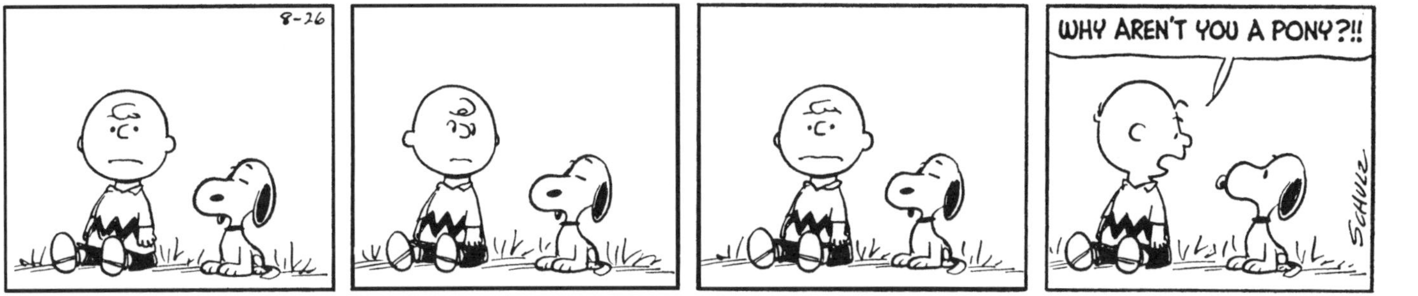
8-26
WHY AREN'T YOU A PONY?!!
SCHULZ

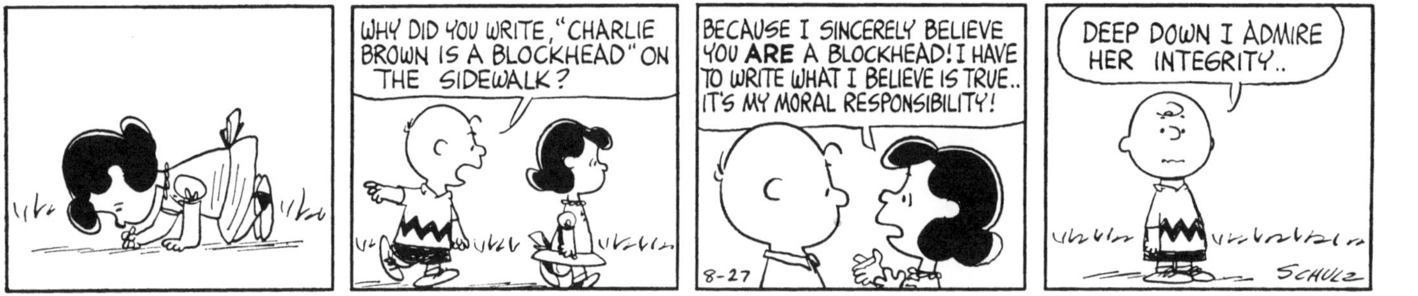
WHY DID YOU WRITE, "CHARLIE BROWN IS A BLOCKHEAD" ON THE SIDEWALK?
BECAUSE I SINCERELY BELIEVE YOU ARE A BLOCKHEAD! I HAVE TO WRITE WHAT I BELIEVE IS TRUE.. IT'S MY MORAL RESPONSIBILITY!
8-27
DEEP DOWN I ADMIRE HER INTEGRITY..
SCHULZ

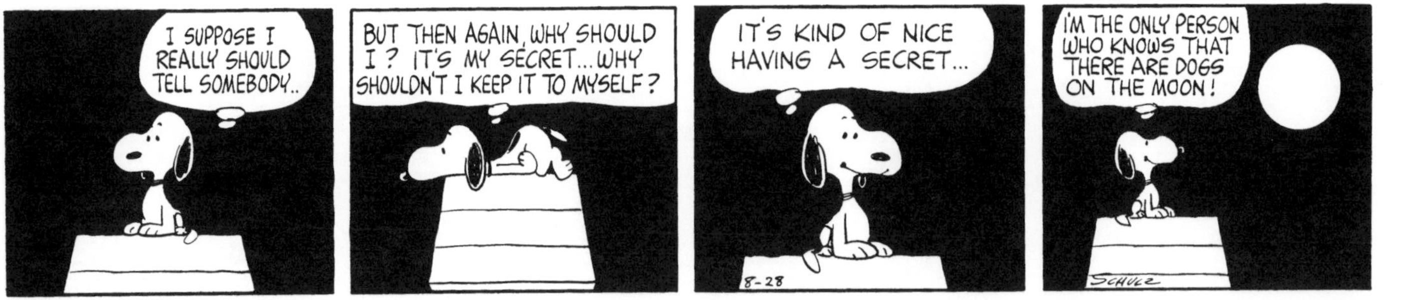
I SUPPOSE I REALLY SHOULD TELL SOMEBODY..
BUT THEN AGAIN, WHY SHOULD I? IT'S MY SECRET... WHY SHOULDN'T I KEEP IT TO MYSELF?
IT'S KIND OF NICE HAVING A SECRET...
8-28
I'M THE ONLY PERSON WHO KNOWS THAT THERE ARE DOGS ON THE MOON!
SCHULZ

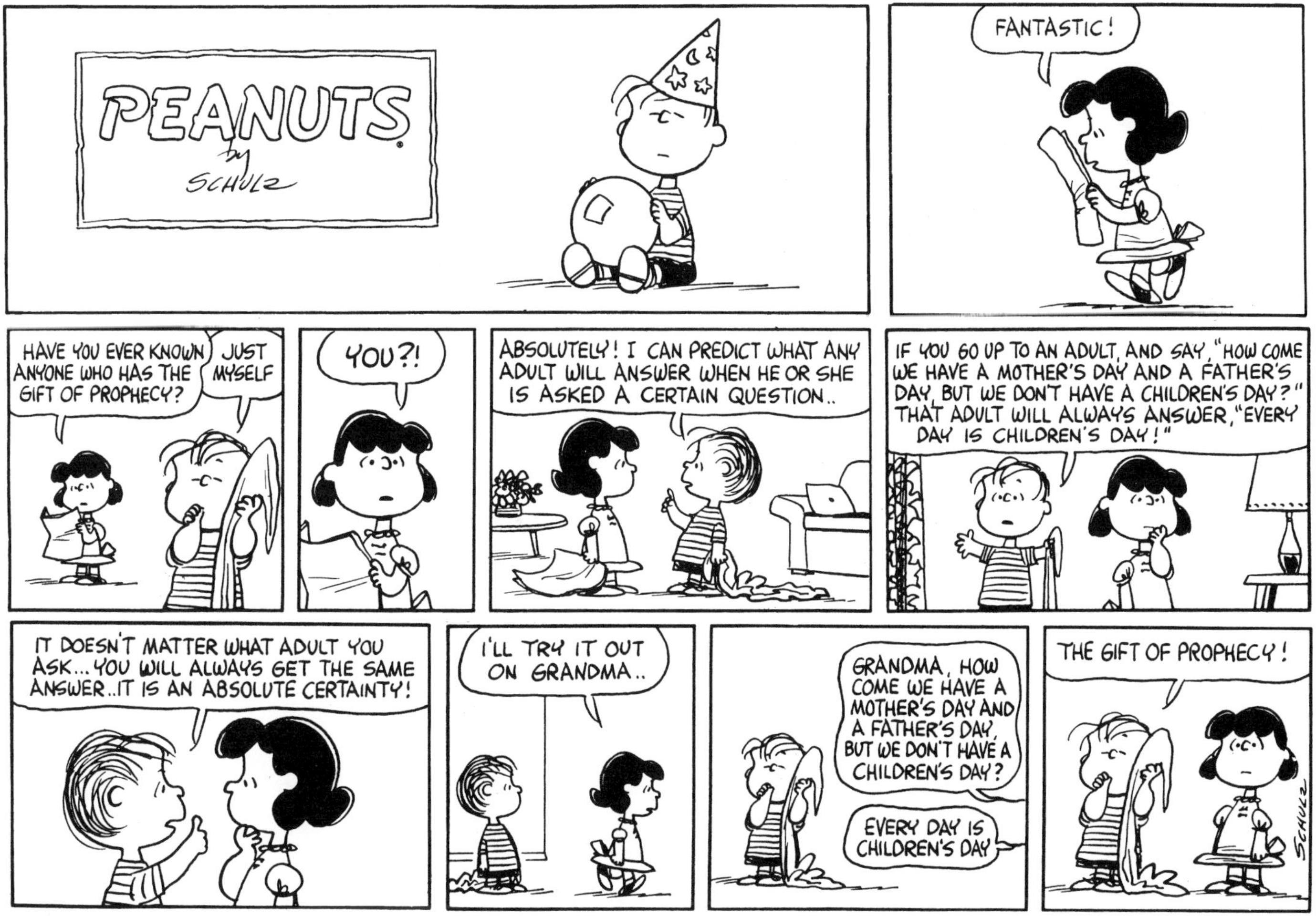
PEANUTS
by SCHULZ
FANTASTIC!
HAVE YOU EVER KNOWN ANYONE WHO HAS THE GIFT OF PROPHECY?
JUST MYSELF
YOU?!
ABSOLUTELY! I CAN PREDICT WHAT ANY ADULT WILL ANSWER WHEN HE OR SHE IS ASKED A CERTAIN QUESTION..
IF YOU GO UP TO AN ADULT, AND SAY, "HOW COME WE HAVE A MOTHER'S DAY AND A FATHER'S DAY, BUT WE DON'T HAVE A CHILDREN'S DAY?" THAT ADULT WILL ALWAYS ANSWER, "EVERY DAY IS CHILDREN'S DAY!"
IT DOESN'T MATTER WHAT ADULT YOU ASK... YOU WILL ALWAYS GET THE SAME ANSWER..IT IS AN ABSOLUTE CERTAINTY!
I'LL TRY IT OUT ON GRANDMA..
GRANDMA, HOW COME WE HAVE A MOTHER'S DAY AND A FATHER'S DAY, BUT WE DON'T HAVE A CHILDREN'S DAY?
EVERY DAY IS CHILDREN'S DAY
THE GIFT OF PROPHECY!
SCHULZ

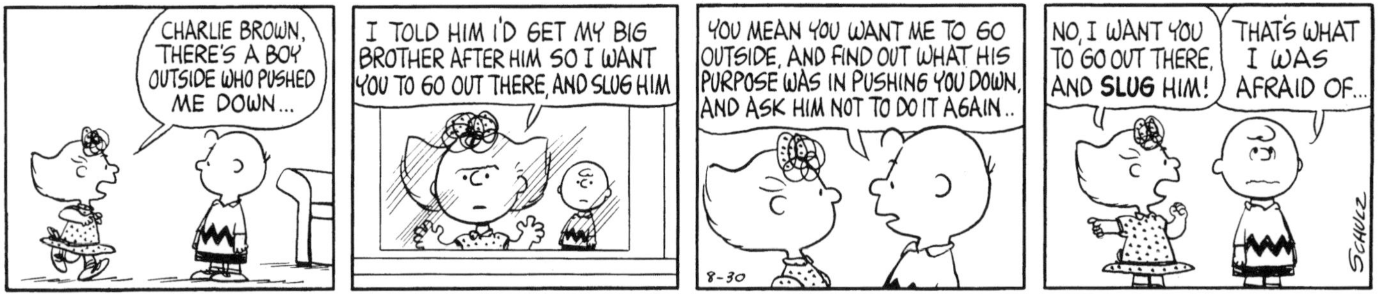
CHARLIE BROWN, THERE'S A BOY OUTSIDE WHO PUSHED ME DOWN...
I TOLD HIM I'D GET MY BIG BROTHER AFTER HIM SO I WANT YOU TO GO OUT THERE, AND SLUG HIM
YOU MEAN YOU WANT ME TO GO OUTSIDE, AND FIND OUT WHAT HIS PURPOSE WAS IN PUSHING YOU DOWN, AND ASK HIM NOT TO DO IT AGAIN..
8-30
NO, I WANT YOU TO GO OUT THERE, AND **SLUG** HIM!
THAT'S WHAT I WAS AFRAID OF...
SCHULZ

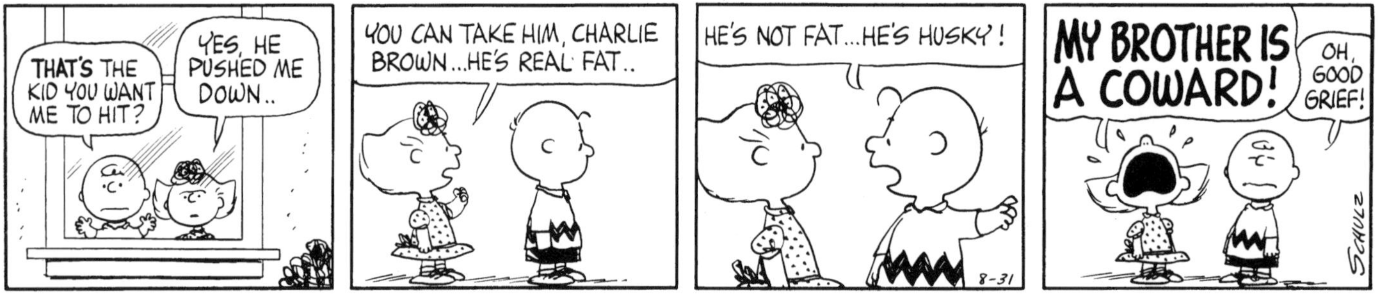
THAT'S THE KID YOU WANT ME TO HIT?
YES, HE PUSHED ME DOWN..
YOU CAN TAKE HIM, CHARLIE BROWN...HE'S REAL FAT..
HE'S NOT FAT...HE'S HUSKY!
8-31
MY BROTHER IS A COWARD!
OH, GOOD GRIEF!
SCHULZ

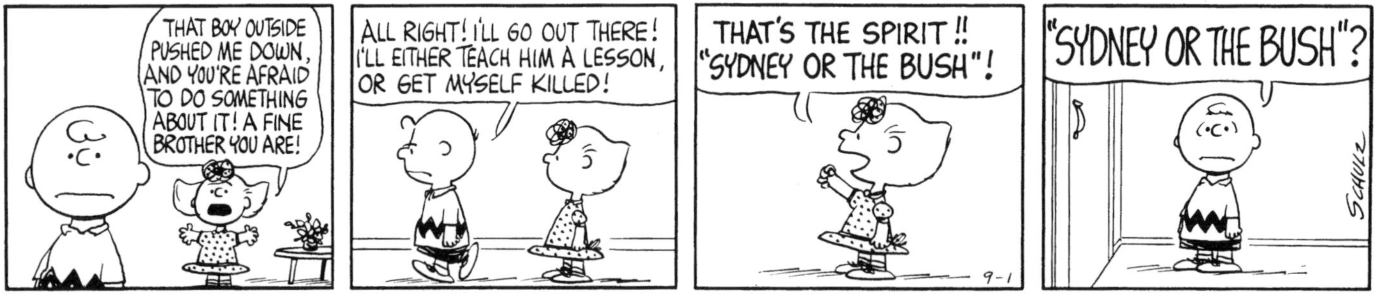
THAT BOY OUTSIDE PUSHED ME DOWN, AND YOU'RE AFRAID TO DO SOMETHING ABOUT IT! A FINE BROTHER YOU ARE!
ALL RIGHT! I'LL GO OUT THERE! I'LL EITHER TEACH HIM A LESSON, OR GET MYSELF KILLED!
THAT'S THE SPIRIT!! "SYDNEY OR THE BUSH"!
9-1
"SYDNEY OR THE BUSH"?
SCHULZ

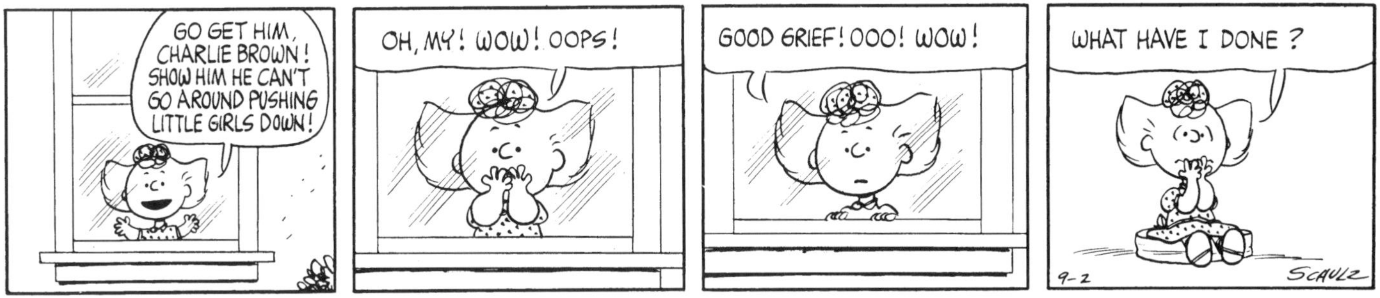
GO GET HIM, CHARLIE BROWN! SHOW HIM HE CAN'T GO AROUND PUSHING LITTLE GIRLS DOWN!
OH, MY! WOW! OOPS!
GOOD GRIEF! OOO! WOW!
WHAT HAVE I DONE?

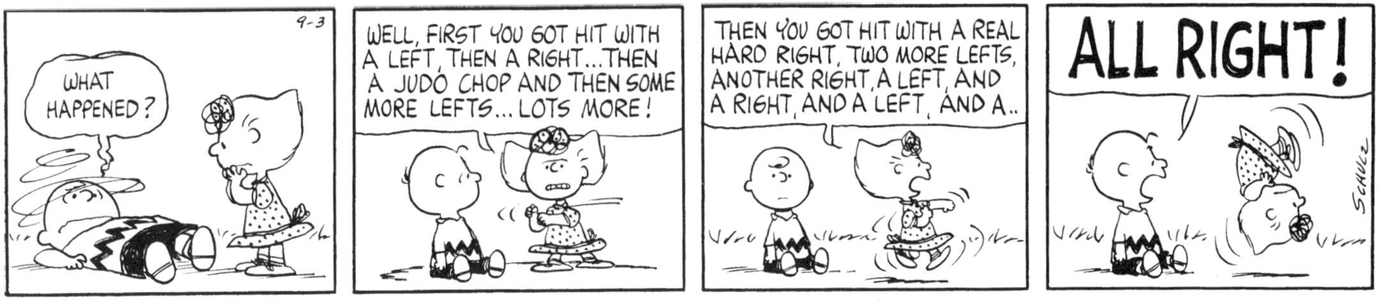
WHAT HAPPENED?
WELL, FIRST YOU GOT HIT WITH A LEFT, THEN A RIGHT...THEN A JUDO CHOP AND THEN SOME MORE LEFTS... LOTS MORE!
THEN YOU GOT HIT WITH A REAL HARD RIGHT, TWO MORE LEFTS, ANOTHER RIGHT, A LEFT, AND A RIGHT, AND A LEFT, AND A..
ALL RIGHT!

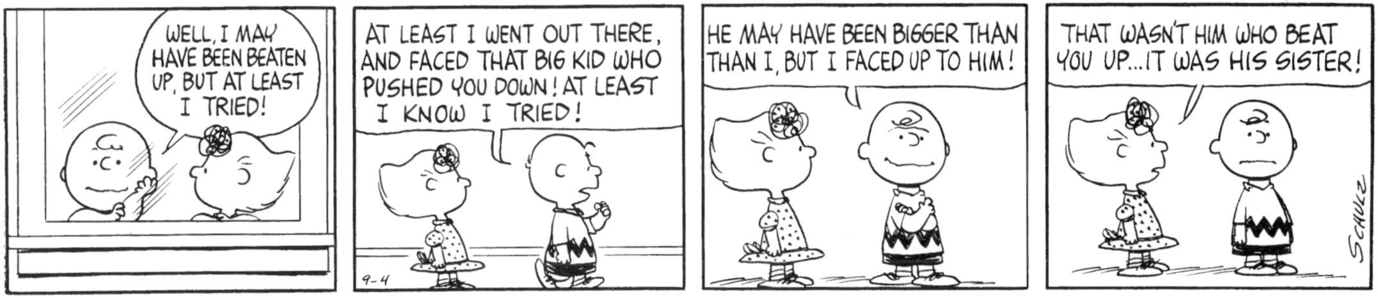
WELL, I MAY HAVE BEEN BEATEN UP, BUT AT LEAST I TRIED!
AT LEAST I WENT OUT THERE, AND FACED THAT BIG KID WHO PUSHED YOU DOWN! AT LEAST I KNOW I TRIED!
HE MAY HAVE BEEN BIGGER THAN THAN I, BUT I FACED UP TO HIM!
THAT WASN'T HIM WHO BEAT YOU UP...IT WAS HIS SISTER!

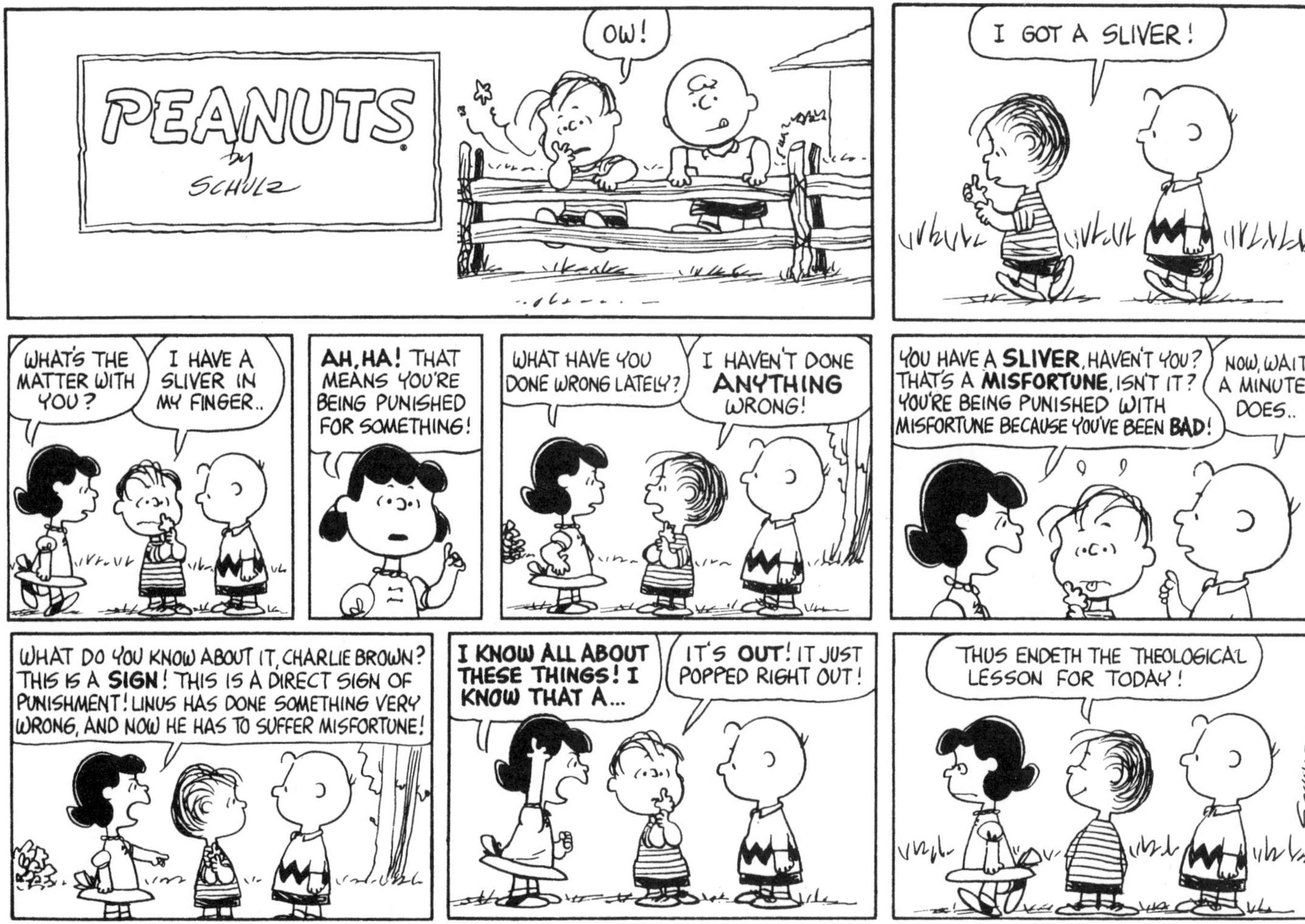
PEANUTS
by
SCHULZ
OW!
I GOT A SLIVER!
WHAT'S THE MATTER WITH YOU?
I HAVE A SLIVER IN MY FINGER..
AH, HA! THAT MEANS YOU'RE BEING PUNISHED FOR SOMETHING!
WHAT HAVE YOU DONE WRONG LATELY?
I HAVEN'T DONE ANYTHING WRONG!
YOU HAVE A SLIVER, HAVEN'T YOU? THAT'S A MISFORTUNE, ISN'T IT? YOU'RE BEING PUNISHED WITH MISFORTUNE BECAUSE YOU'VE BEEN BAD!
NOW, WAIT A MINUTE.. DOES..
WHAT DO YOU KNOW ABOUT IT, CHARLIE BROWN? THIS IS A SIGN! THIS IS A DIRECT SIGN OF PUNISHMENT! LINUS HAS DONE SOMETHING VERY WRONG, AND NOW HE HAS TO SUFFER MISFORTUNE!
I KNOW ALL ABOUT THESE THINGS! I KNOW THAT A...
IT'S OUT! IT JUST POPPED RIGHT OUT!
THUS ENDETH THE THEOLOGICAL LESSON FOR TODAY!
SCHULZ

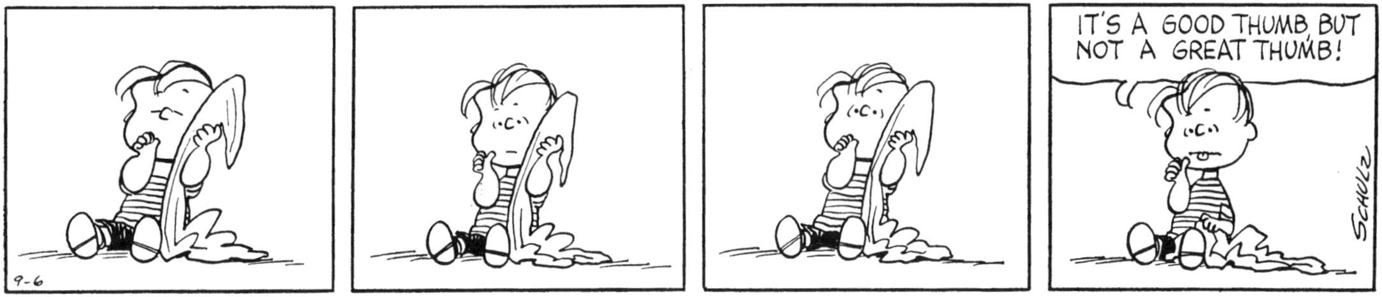
9-6
IT'S A GOOD THUMB, BUT NOT A GREAT THUMB!
SCHULZ

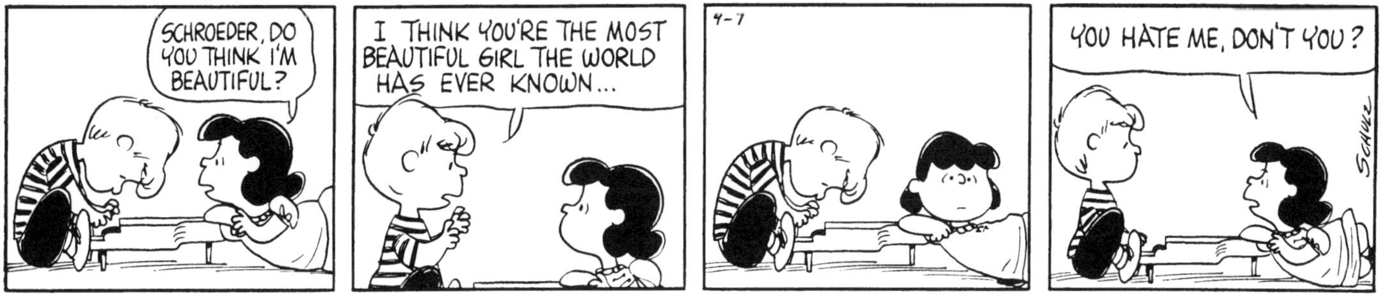
SCHROEDER, DO YOU THINK I'M BEAUTIFUL?
I THINK YOU'RE THE MOST BEAUTIFUL GIRL THE WORLD HAS EVER KNOWN...
9-7
YOU HATE ME, DON'T YOU?
SCHULZ

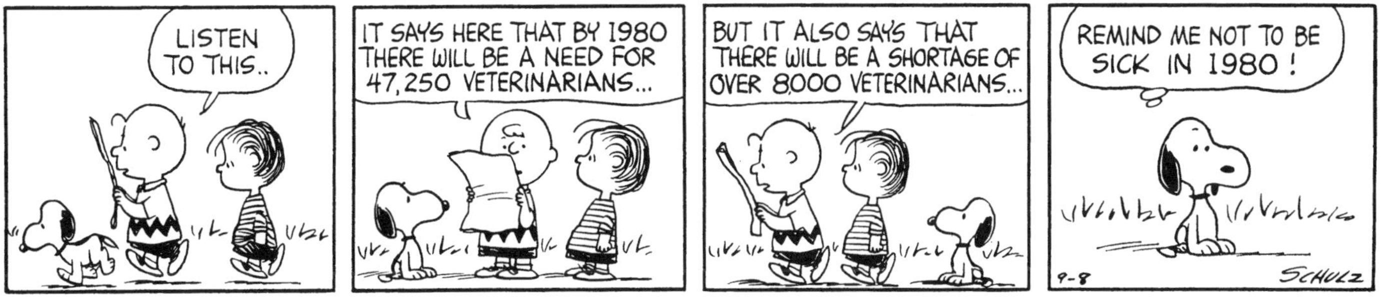
LISTEN TO THIS..
IT SAYS HERE THAT BY 1980 THERE WILL BE A NEED FOR 47,250 VETERINARIANS...
BUT IT ALSO SAYS THAT THERE WILL BE A SHORTAGE OF OVER 8,000 VETERINARIANS...
REMIND ME NOT TO BE SICK IN 1980!
9-8
SCHULZ

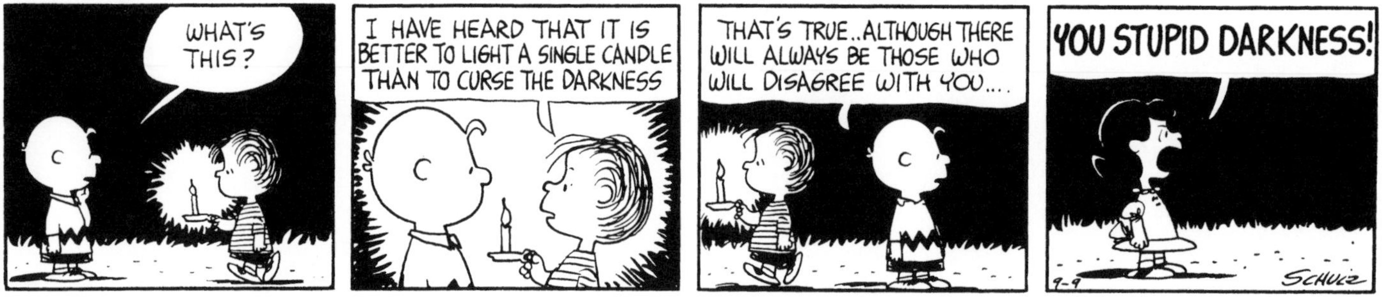
WHAT'S THIS?
I HAVE HEARD THAT IT IS BETTER TO LIGHT A SINGLE CANDLE THAN TO CURSE THE DARKNESS
THAT'S TRUE..ALTHOUGH THERE WILL ALWAYS BE THOSE WHO WILL DISAGREE WITH YOU....
YOU STUPID DARKNESS!

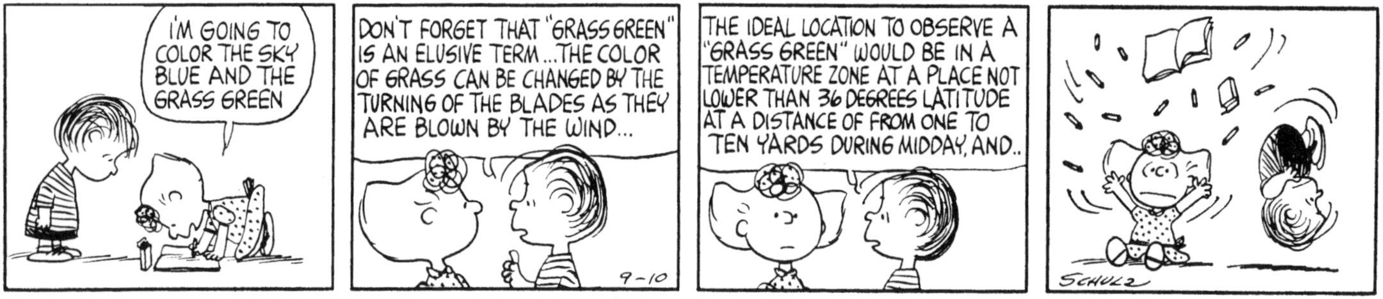
I'M GOING TO COLOR THE SKY BLUE AND THE GRASS GREEN
DON'T FORGET THAT "GRASS GREEN" IS AN ELUSIVE TERM...THE COLOR OF GRASS CAN BE CHANGED BY THE TURNING OF THE BLADES AS THEY ARE BLOWN BY THE WIND...
THE IDEAL LOCATION TO OBSERVE A "GRASS GREEN" WOULD BE IN A TEMPERATURE ZONE AT A PLACE NOT LOWER THAN 36 DEGREES LATITUDE AT A DISTANCE OF FROM ONE TO TEN YARDS DURING MIDDAY, AND..

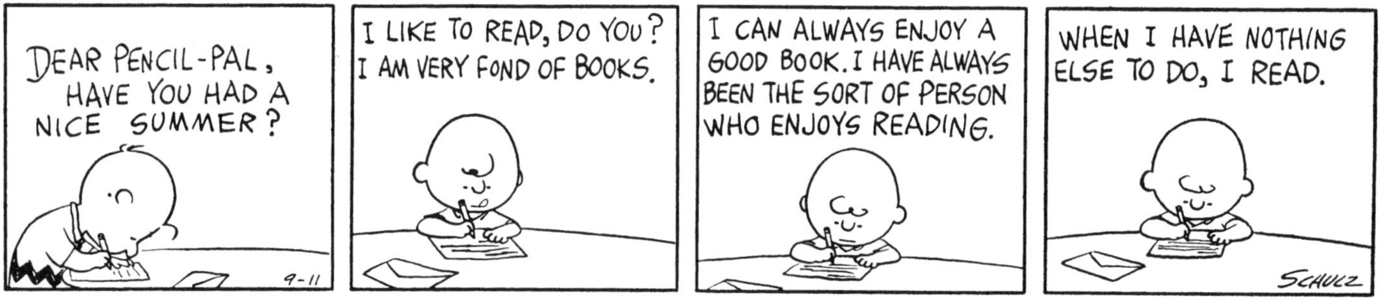
DEAR PENCIL-PAL, HAVE YOU HAD A NICE SUMMER?
I LIKE TO READ, DO YOU? I AM VERY FOND OF BOOKS.
I CAN ALWAYS ENJOY A GOOD BOOK. I HAVE ALWAYS BEEN THE SORT OF PERSON WHO ENJOYS READING.
WHEN I HAVE NOTHING ELSE TO DO, I READ.

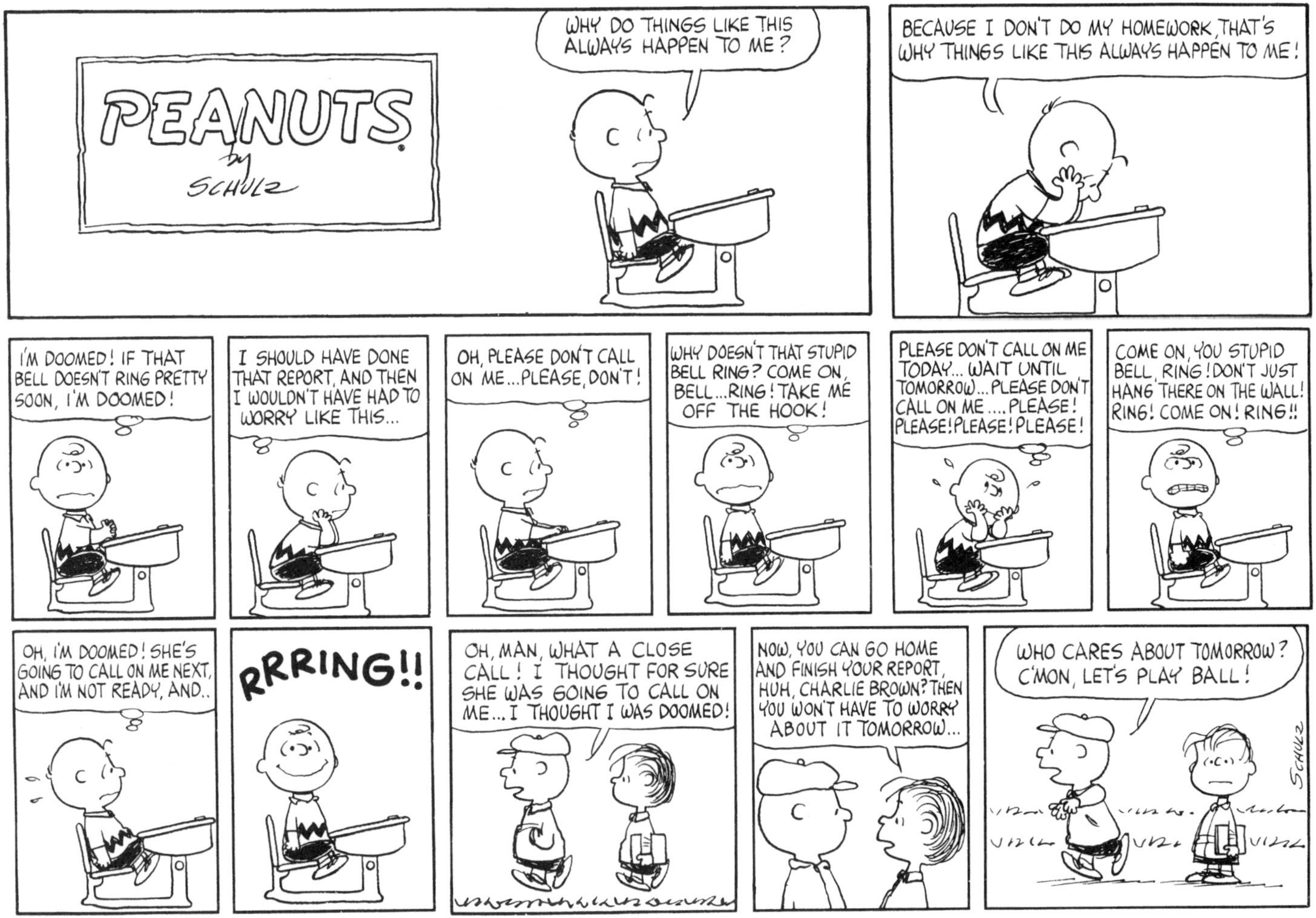
PEANUTS
by SCHULZ
WHY DO THINGS LIKE THIS ALWAYS HAPPEN TO ME?
BECAUSE I DON'T DO MY HOMEWORK, THAT'S WHY THINGS LIKE THIS ALWAYS HAPPEN TO ME!
I'M DOOMED! IF THAT BELL DOESN'T RING PRETTY SOON, I'M DOOMED!
I SHOULD HAVE DONE THAT REPORT, AND THEN I WOULDN'T HAVE HAD TO WORRY LIKE THIS...
OH, PLEASE DON'T CALL ON ME...PLEASE, DON'T!
WHY DOESN'T THAT STUPID BELL RING? COME ON, BELL...RING! TAKE ME OFF THE HOOK!
PLEASE DON'T CALL ON ME TODAY... WAIT UNTIL TOMORROW... PLEASE DON'T CALL ON ME .... PLEASE! PLEASE! PLEASE! PLEASE!
COME ON, YOU STUPID BELL, RING! DON'T JUST HANG THERE ON THE WALL! RING! COME ON! RING!!
OH, I'M DOOMED! SHE'S GOING TO CALL ON ME NEXT, AND I'M NOT READY, AND..
RRRING!!
OH, MAN, WHAT A CLOSE CALL! I THOUGHT FOR SURE SHE WAS GOING TO CALL ON ME... I THOUGHT I WAS DOOMED!
NOW, YOU CAN GO HOME AND FINISH YOUR REPORT, HUH, CHARLIE BROWN? THEN YOU WON'T HAVE TO WORRY ABOUT IT TOMORROW...
WHO CARES ABOUT TOMORROW? C'MON, LET'S PLAY BALL!
SCHULZ

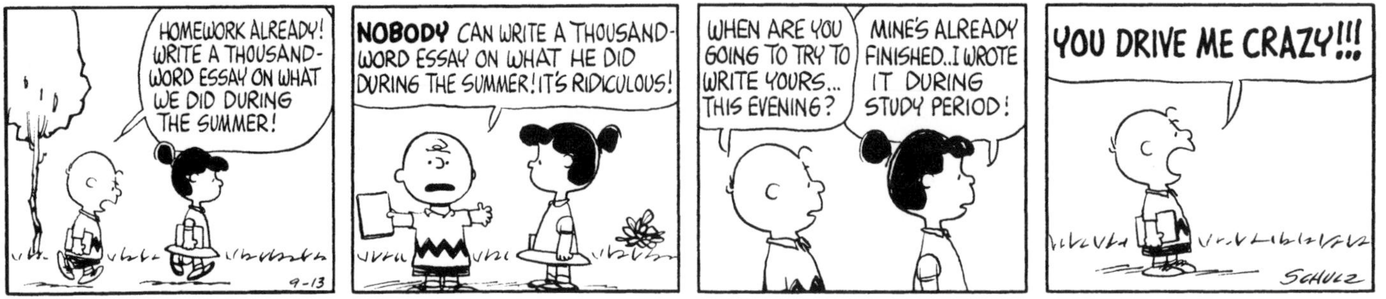
HOMEWORK ALREADY! WRITE A THOUSAND-WORD ESSAY ON WHAT WE DID DURING THE SUMMER!
9-13
NOBODY CAN WRITE A THOUSAND-WORD ESSAY ON WHAT HE DID DURING THE SUMMER! IT'S RIDICULOUS!
WHEN ARE YOU GOING TO TRY TO WRITE YOURS... THIS EVENING?
MINE'S ALREADY FINISHED..I WROTE IT DURING STUDY PERIOD!
YOU DRIVE ME CRAZY!!!
SCHULZ

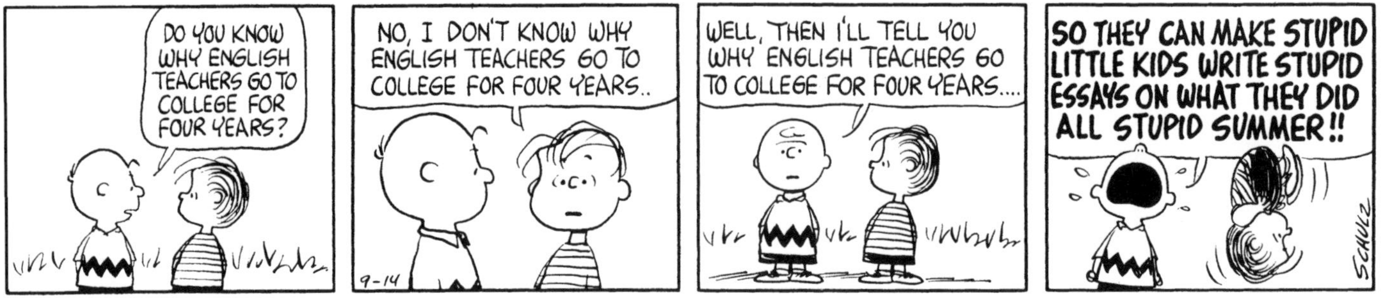
DO YOU KNOW WHY ENGLISH TEACHERS GO TO COLLEGE FOR FOUR YEARS?
NO, I DON'T KNOW WHY ENGLISH TEACHERS GO TO COLLEGE FOR FOUR YEARS..
9-14
WELL, THEN I'LL TELL YOU WHY ENGLISH TEACHERS GO TO COLLEGE FOR FOUR YEARS....
SO THEY CAN MAKE STUPID LITTLE KIDS WRITE STUPID ESSAYS ON WHAT THEY DID ALL STUPID SUMMER!!
SCHULZ

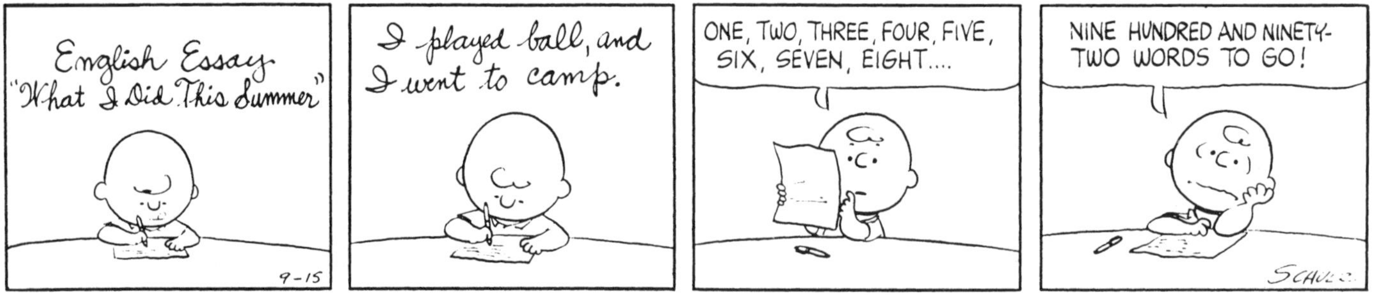
English Essay "What I Did This Summer"
9-15
I played ball, and I went to camp.
ONE, TWO, THREE, FOUR, FIVE, SIX, SEVEN, EIGHT....
NINE HUNDRED AND NINETY-TWO WORDS TO GO!

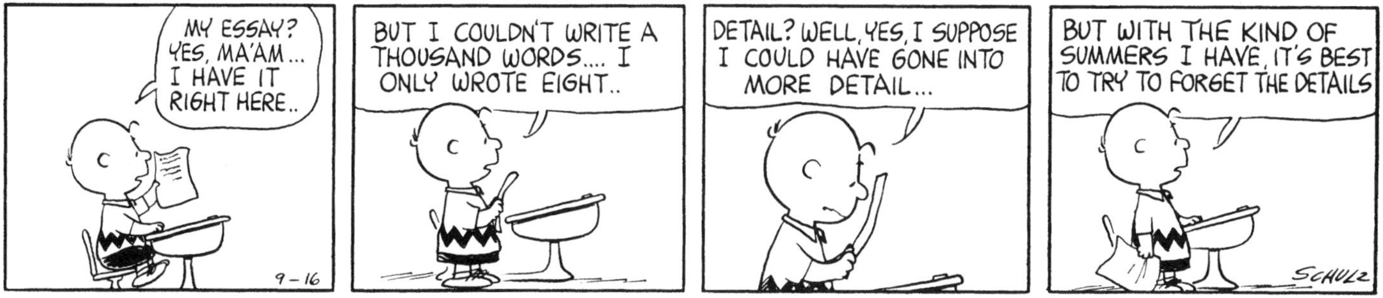
MY ESSAY? YES, MA'AM... I HAVE IT RIGHT HERE..
9-16
BUT I COULDN'T WRITE A THOUSAND WORDS.... I ONLY WROTE EIGHT..
DETAIL? WELL, YES, I SUPPOSE I COULD HAVE GONE INTO MORE DETAIL...
BUT WITH THE KIND OF SUMMERS I HAVE, IT'S BEST TO TRY TO FORGET THE DETAILS
SCHULZ

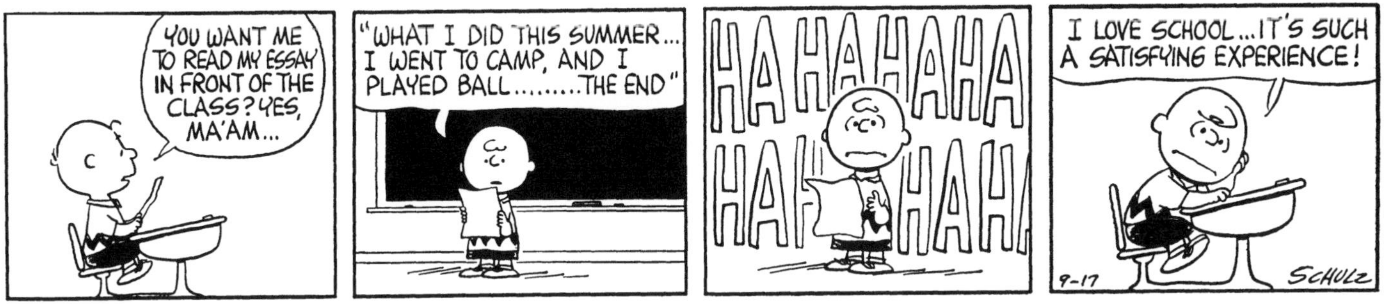
YOU WANT ME TO READ MY ESSAY IN FRONT OF THE CLASS? YES, MA'AM...
"WHAT I DID THIS SUMMER... I WENT TO CAMP, AND I PLAYED BALL.........THE END"
HA HA HA HA HA HA
I LOVE SCHOOL...IT'S SUCH A SATISFYING EXPERIENCE!
9-17
SCHULZ

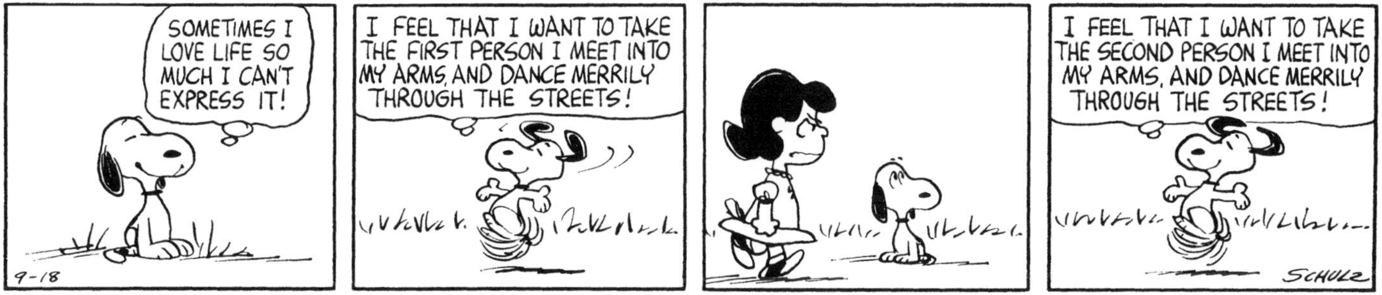
SOMETIMES I LOVE LIFE SO MUCH I CAN'T EXPRESS IT!
9-18
I FEEL THAT I WANT TO TAKE THE FIRST PERSON I MEET INTO MY ARMS, AND DANCE MERRILY THROUGH THE STREETS!
I FEEL THAT I WANT TO TAKE THE SECOND PERSON I MEET INTO MY ARMS, AND DANCE MERRILY THROUGH THE STREETS!
SCHULZ

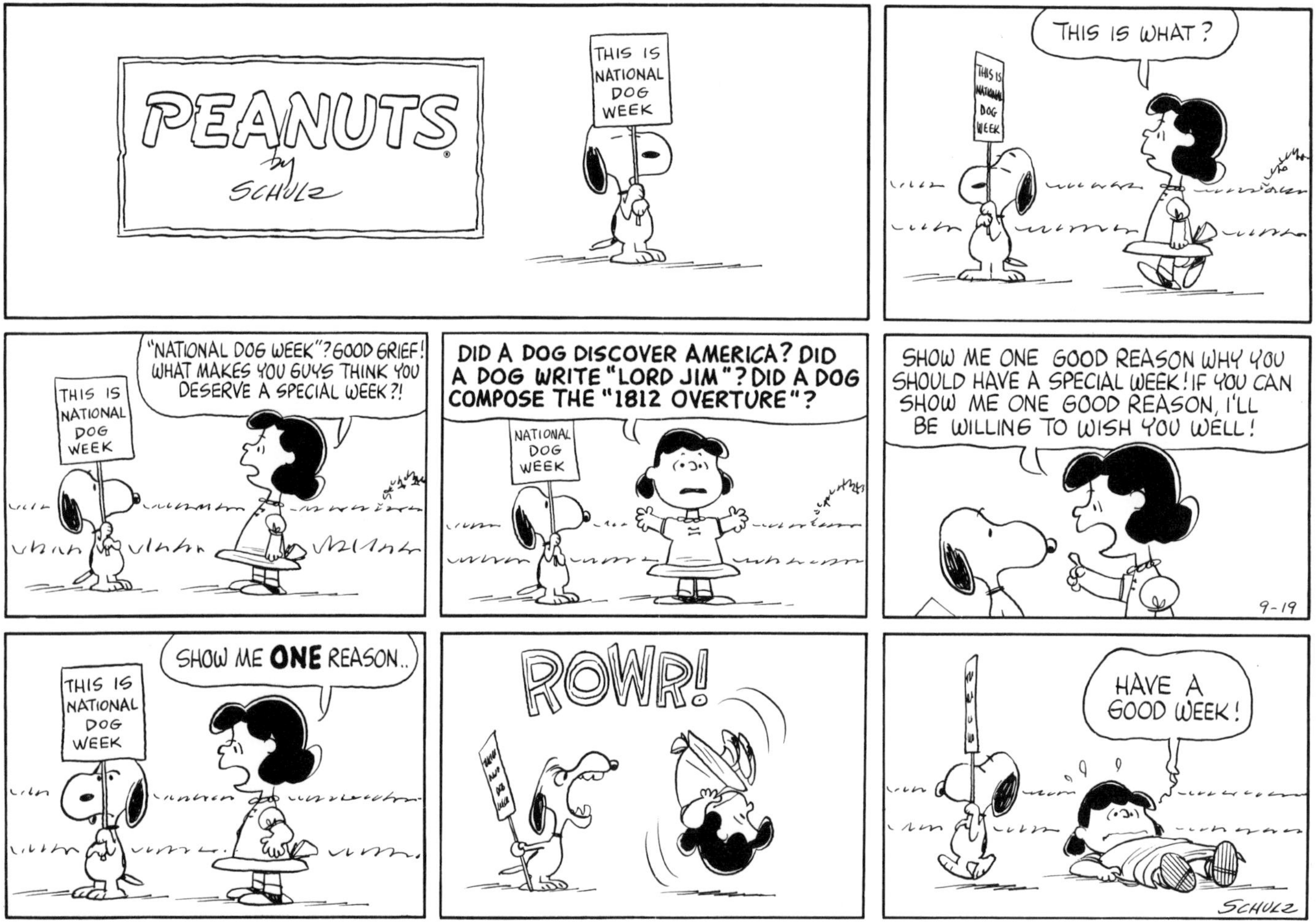
PEANUTS
by SCHULZ
THIS IS NATIONAL DOG WEEK
THIS IS WHAT?
THIS IS NATIONAL DOG WEEK
THIS IS NATIONAL DOG WEEK
"NATIONAL DOG WEEK"? GOOD GRIEF! WHAT MAKES YOU GUYS THINK YOU DESERVE A SPECIAL WEEK?!
NATIONAL DOG WEEK
DID A DOG DISCOVER AMERICA? DID A DOG WRITE "LORD JIM"? DID A DOG COMPOSE THE "1812 OVERTURE"?
SHOW ME ONE GOOD REASON WHY YOU SHOULD HAVE A SPECIAL WEEK! IF YOU CAN SHOW ME ONE GOOD REASON, I'LL BE WILLING TO WISH YOU WELL!
9-19
THIS IS NATIONAL DOG WEEK
SHOW ME **ONE** REASON..
ROWR!
HAVE A GOOD WEEK!
SCHULZ

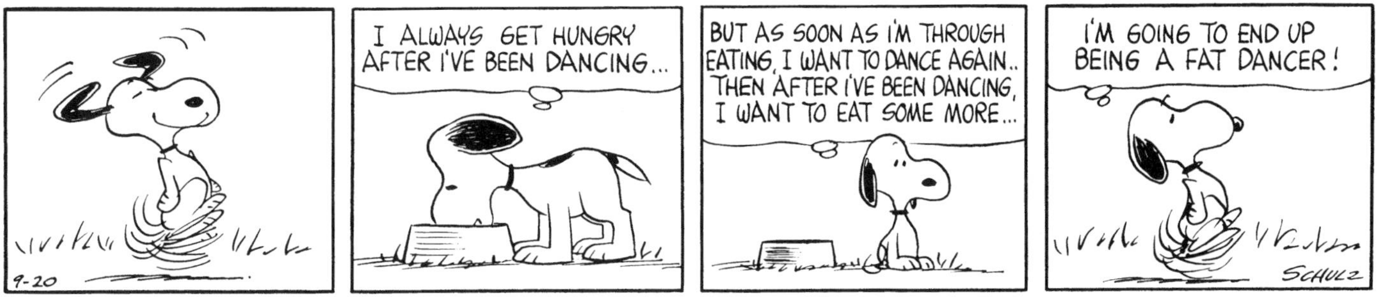
9-20
I ALWAYS GET HUNGRY AFTER I'VE BEEN DANCING...
BUT AS SOON AS I'M THROUGH EATING, I WANT TO DANCE AGAIN.. THEN AFTER I'VE BEEN DANCING, I WANT TO EAT SOME MORE...
I'M GOING TO END UP BEING A FAT DANCER!
SCHULZ

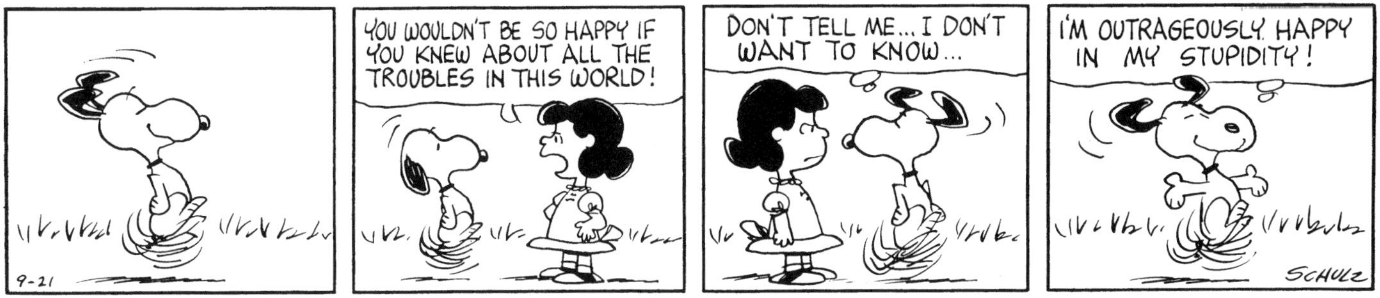
9-21
YOU WOULDN'T BE SO HAPPY IF YOU KNEW ABOUT ALL THE TROUBLES IN THIS WORLD!
DON'T TELL ME... I DON'T WANT TO KNOW...
I'M OUTRAGEOUSLY HAPPY IN MY STUPIDITY!
SCHULZ

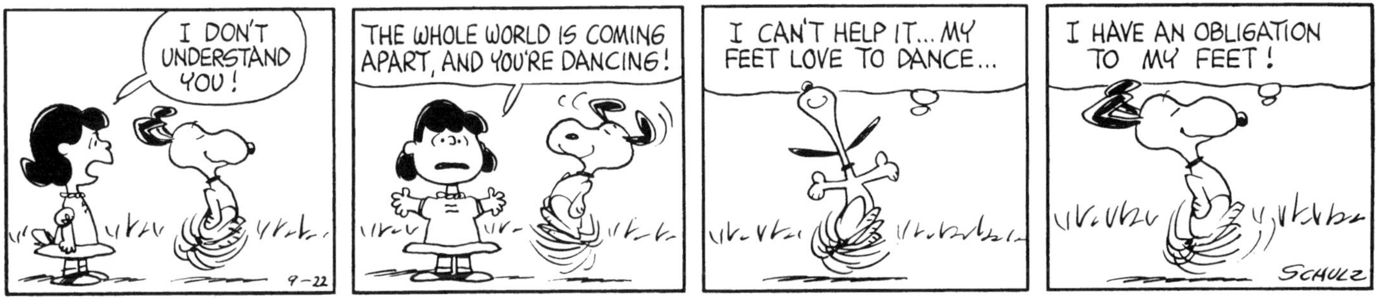
I DON'T UNDERSTAND YOU!
9-22
THE WHOLE WORLD IS COMING APART, AND YOU'RE DANCING!
I CAN'T HELP IT... MY FEET LOVE TO DANCE...
I HAVE AN OBLIGATION TO MY FEET!
SCHULZ

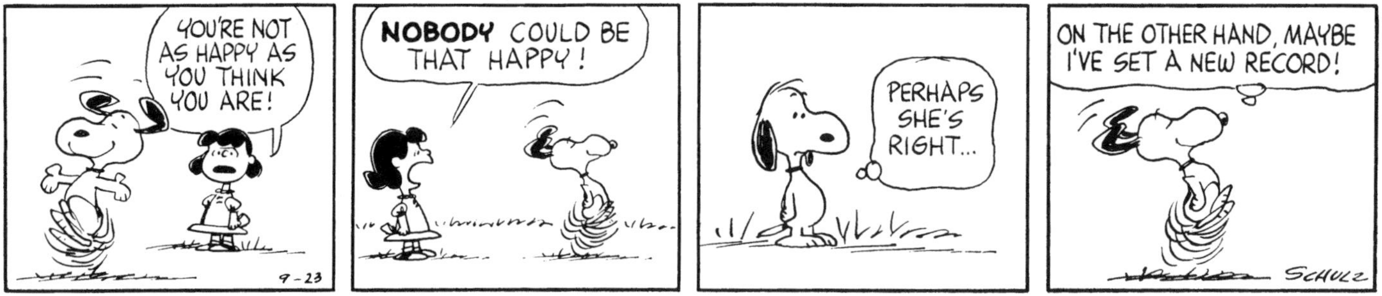
YOU'RE NOT AS HAPPY AS YOU THINK YOU ARE!
9-23
NOBODY COULD BE THAT HAPPY!
PERHAPS SHE'S RIGHT...
ON THE OTHER HAND, MAYBE I'VE SET A NEW RECORD!
SCHULZ

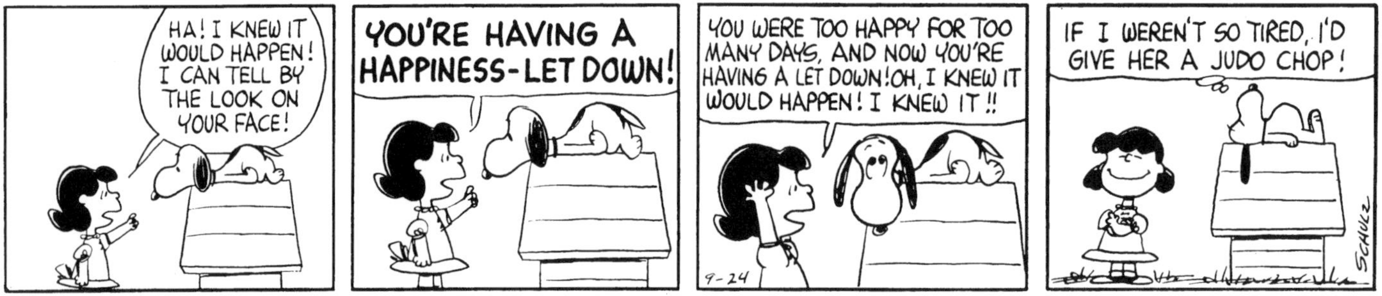
HA! I KNEW IT WOULD HAPPEN! I CAN TELL BY THE LOOK ON YOUR FACE!
YOU'RE HAVING A HAPPINESS-LET DOWN!
YOU WERE TOO HAPPY FOR TOO MANY DAYS, AND NOW YOU'RE HAVING A LET DOWN! OH, I KNEW IT WOULD HAPPEN! I KNEW IT!!
9-24
IF I WEREN'T SO TIRED, I'D GIVE HER A JUDO CHOP!
SCHULZ

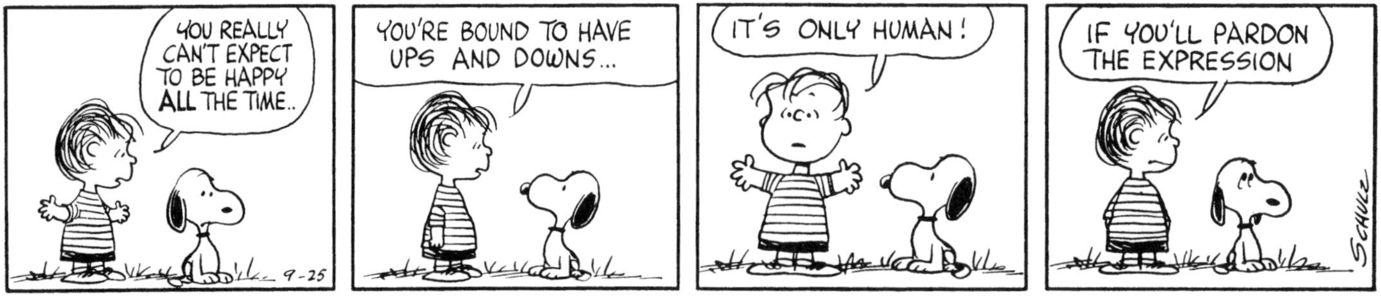
YOU REALLY CAN'T EXPECT TO BE HAPPY ALL THE TIME..
9-25
YOU'RE BOUND TO HAVE UPS AND DOWNS...
IT'S ONLY HUMAN!
IF YOU'LL PARDON THE EXPRESSION
SCHULZ

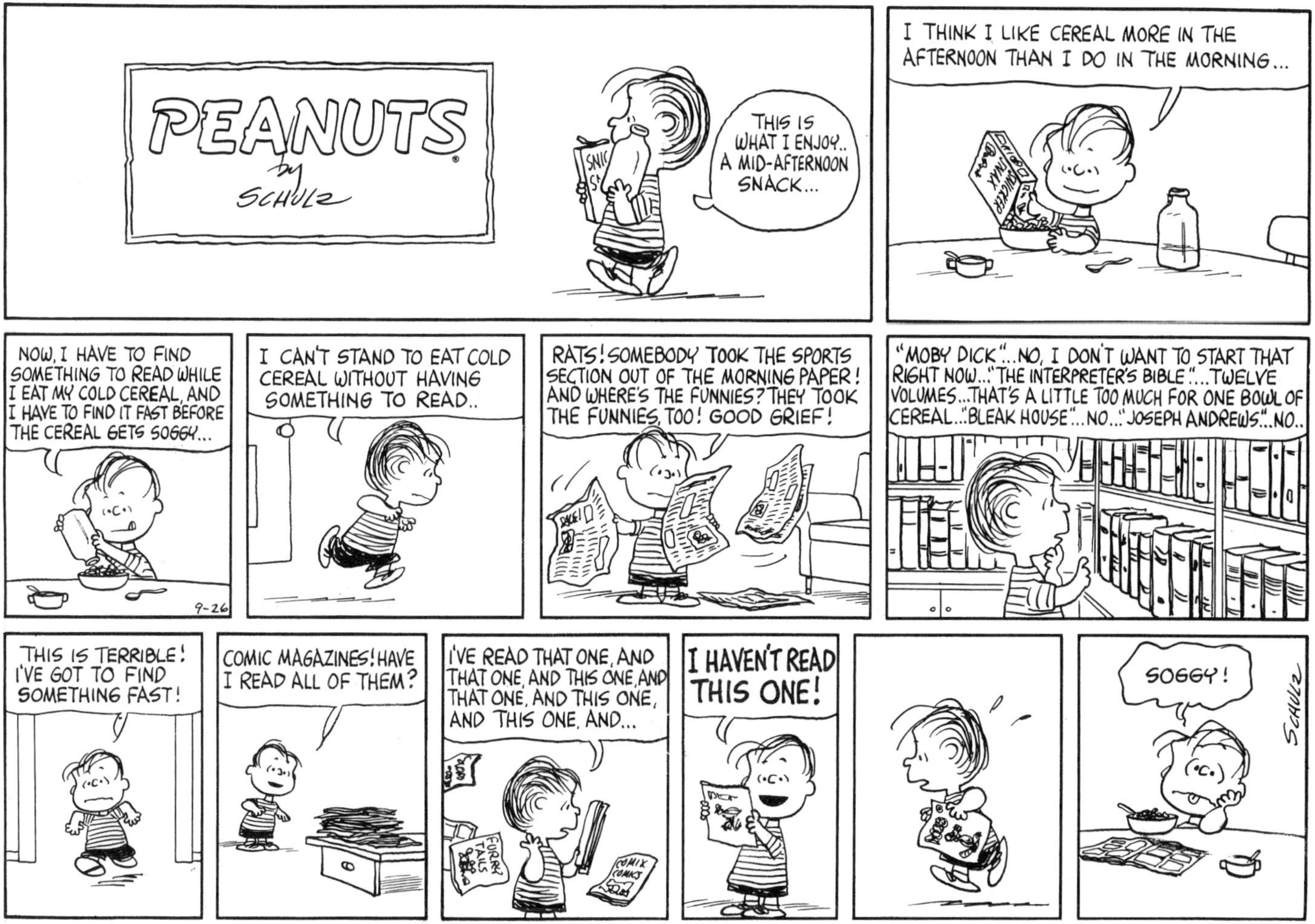
PEANUTS
by SCHULZ
THIS IS WHAT I ENJOY.. A MID-AFTERNOON SNACK...
I THINK I LIKE CEREAL MORE IN THE AFTERNOON THAN I DO IN THE MORNING...
NOW, I HAVE TO FIND SOMETHING TO READ WHILE I EAT MY COLD CEREAL, AND I HAVE TO FIND IT FAST BEFORE THE CEREAL GETS SOGGY...
9-26
I CAN'T STAND TO EAT COLD CEREAL WITHOUT HAVING SOMETHING TO READ..
RATS! SOMEBODY TOOK THE SPORTS SECTION OUT OF THE MORNING PAPER! AND WHERE'S THE FUNNIES? THEY TOOK THE FUNNIES, TOO! GOOD GRIEF!
"MOBY DICK"...NO, I DON'T WANT TO START THAT RIGHT NOW..."THE INTERPRETER'S BIBLE"...TWELVE VOLUMES...THAT'S A LITTLE TOO MUCH FOR ONE BOWL OF CEREAL..."BLEAK HOUSE"...NO..."JOSEPH ANDREWS"...NO..
THIS IS TERRIBLE! I'VE GOT TO FIND SOMETHING FAST!
COMIC MAGAZINES! HAVE I READ ALL OF THEM?
I'VE READ THAT ONE, AND THAT ONE, AND THIS ONE, AND THAT ONE, AND THIS ONE, AND THIS ONE, AND...
FURRY TAILS
COMIX COMICS
I HAVEN'T READ THIS ONE!
SOGGY!
SCHULZ

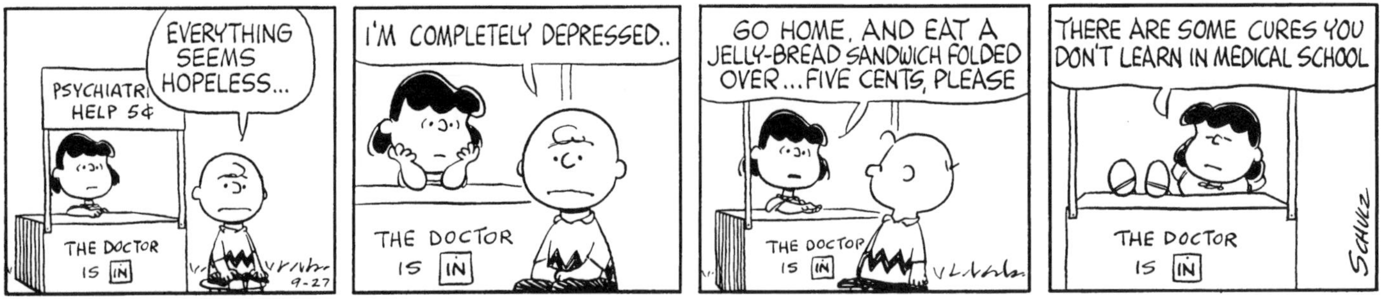
PSYCHIATRI HELP 5¢
EVERYTHING SEEMS HOPELESS...
THE DOCTOR IS IN
9-27
I'M COMPLETELY DEPRESSED..
THE DOCTOR IS IN
GO HOME, AND EAT A JELLY-BREAD SANDWICH FOLDED OVER...FIVE CENTS, PLEASE
THE DOCTOR IS IN
THERE ARE SOME CURES YOU DON'T LEARN IN MEDICAL SCHOOL
THE DOCTOR IS IN
SCHULZ

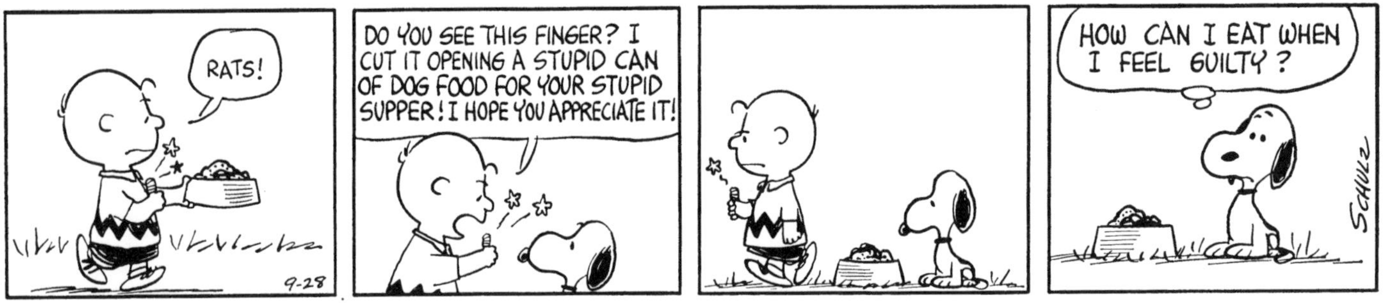
RATS!
9-28
DO YOU SEE THIS FINGER? I CUT IT OPENING A STUPID CAN OF DOG FOOD FOR YOUR STUPID SUPPER! I HOPE YOU APPRECIATE IT!
HOW CAN I EAT WHEN I FEEL GUILTY?
SCHULZ

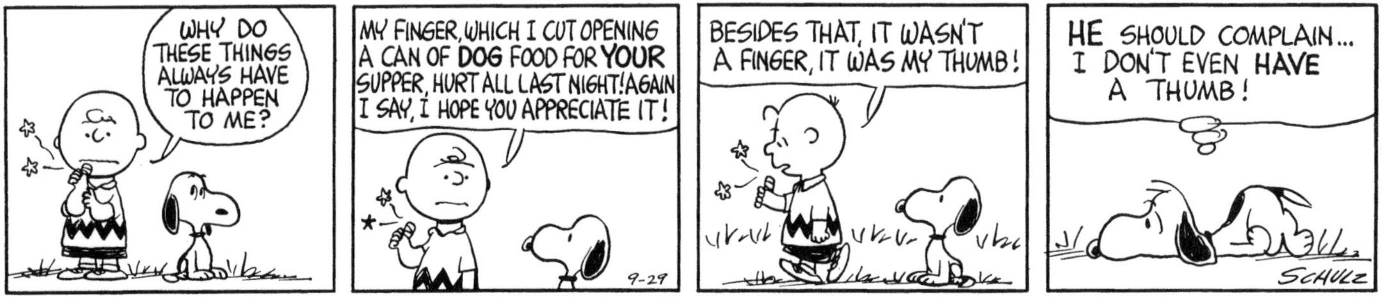
WHY DO THESE THINGS ALWAYS HAVE TO HAPPEN TO ME?
MY FINGER, WHICH I CUT OPENING A CAN OF DOG FOOD FOR YOUR SUPPER, HURT ALL LAST NIGHT! AGAIN I SAY, I HOPE YOU APPRECIATE IT!
9-29
BESIDES THAT, IT WASN'T A FINGER, IT WAS MY THUMB!
HE SHOULD COMPLAIN... I DON'T EVEN HAVE A THUMB!
SCHULZ

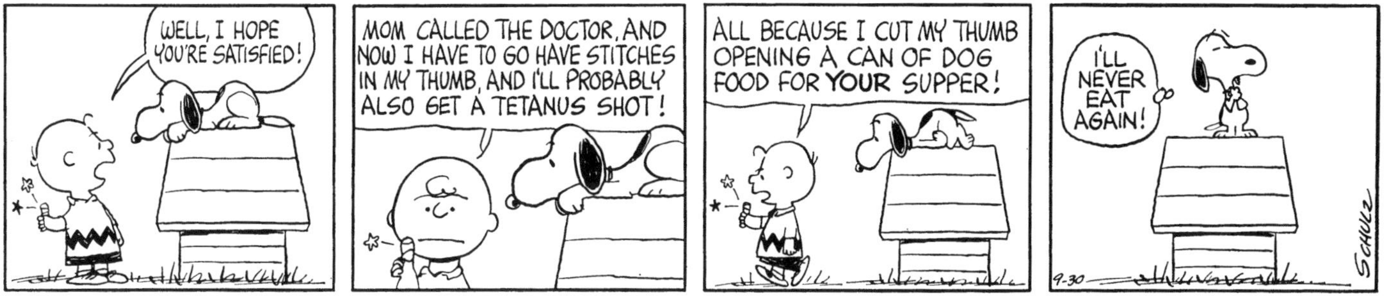
WELL, I HOPE YOU'RE SATISFIED!
MOM CALLED THE DOCTOR, AND NOW I HAVE TO GO HAVE STITCHES IN MY THUMB, AND I'LL PROBABLY ALSO GET A TETANUS SHOT!
ALL BECAUSE I CUT MY THUMB OPENING A CAN OF DOG FOOD FOR **YOUR** SUPPER!
I'LL NEVER EAT AGAIN!

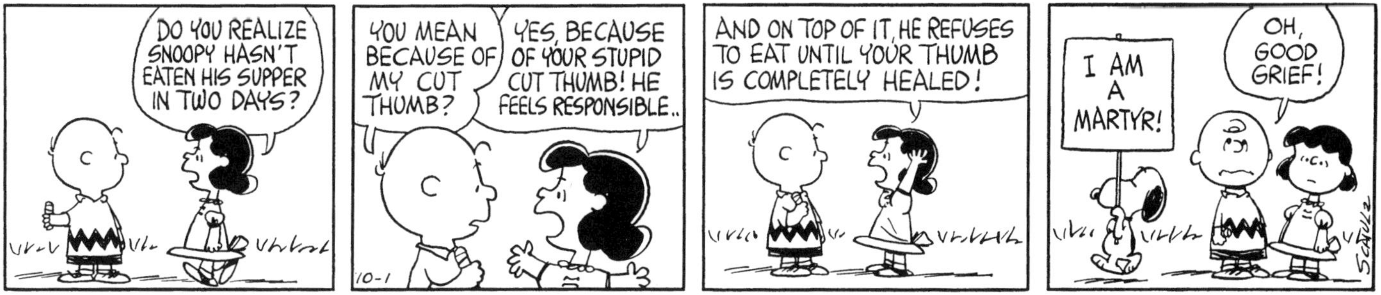
DO YOU REALIZE SNOOPY HASN'T EATEN HIS SUPPER IN TWO DAYS?
YOU MEAN BECAUSE OF MY CUT THUMB?
YES, BECAUSE OF YOUR STUPID CUT THUMB! HE FEELS RESPONSIBLE..
AND ON TOP OF IT, HE REFUSES TO EAT UNTIL YOUR THUMB IS COMPLETELY HEALED!
I AM A MARTYR!
OH, GOOD GRIEF!

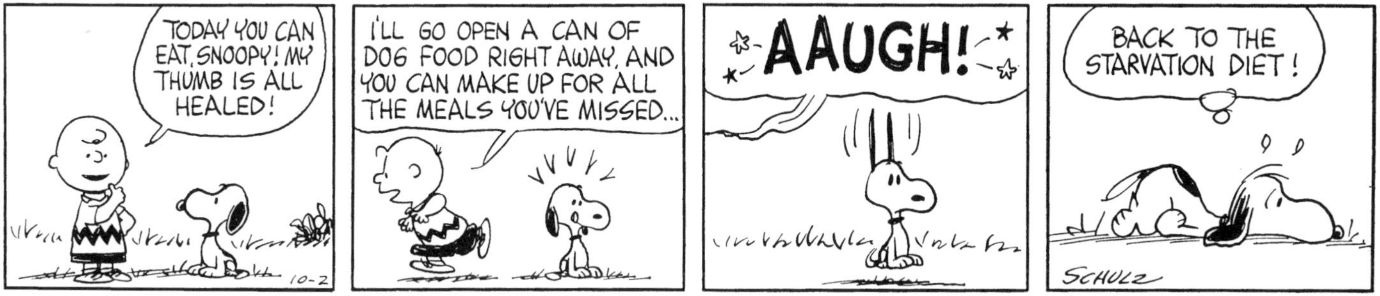
TODAY YOU CAN EAT, SNOOPY! MY THUMB IS ALL HEALED!
I'LL GO OPEN A CAN OF DOG FOOD RIGHT AWAY, AND YOU CAN MAKE UP FOR ALL THE MEALS YOU'VE MISSED...
AAUGH!
BACK TO THE STARVATION DIET!

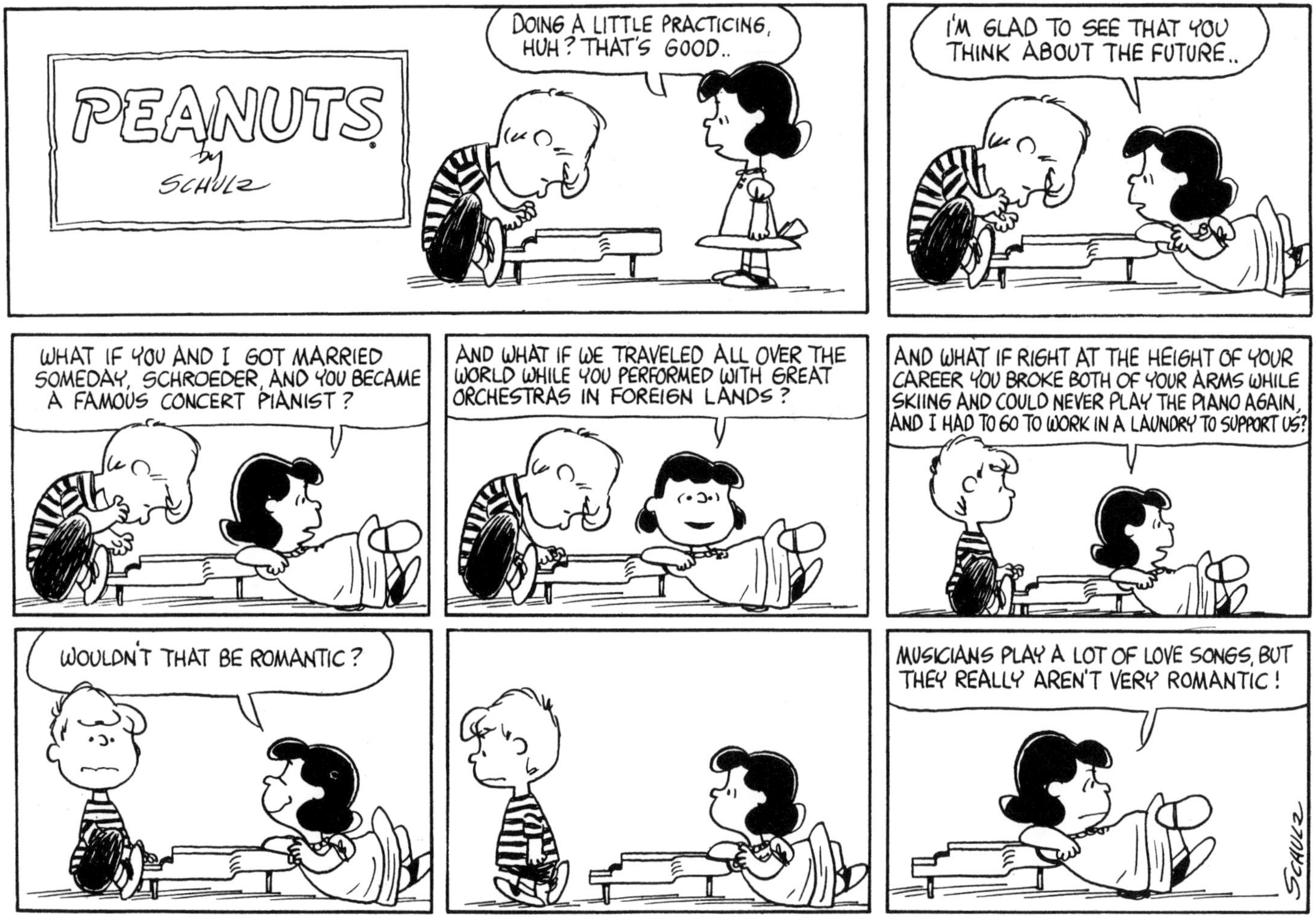
PEANUTS
by SCHULZ
DOING A LITTLE PRACTICING, HUH? THAT'S GOOD..
I'M GLAD TO SEE THAT YOU THINK ABOUT THE FUTURE..
WHAT IF YOU AND I GOT MARRIED SOMEDAY, SCHROEDER, AND YOU BECAME A FAMOUS CONCERT PIANIST?
AND WHAT IF WE TRAVELED ALL OVER THE WORLD WHILE YOU PERFORMED WITH GREAT ORCHESTRAS IN FOREIGN LANDS?
AND WHAT IF RIGHT AT THE HEIGHT OF YOUR CAREER YOU BROKE BOTH OF YOUR ARMS WHILE SKIING AND COULD NEVER PLAY THE PIANO AGAIN, AND I HAD TO GO TO WORK IN A LAUNDRY TO SUPPORT US?
WOULDN'T THAT BE ROMANTIC?
MUSICIANS PLAY A LOT OF LOVE SONGS, BUT THEY REALLY AREN'T VERY ROMANTIC!
SCHULZ

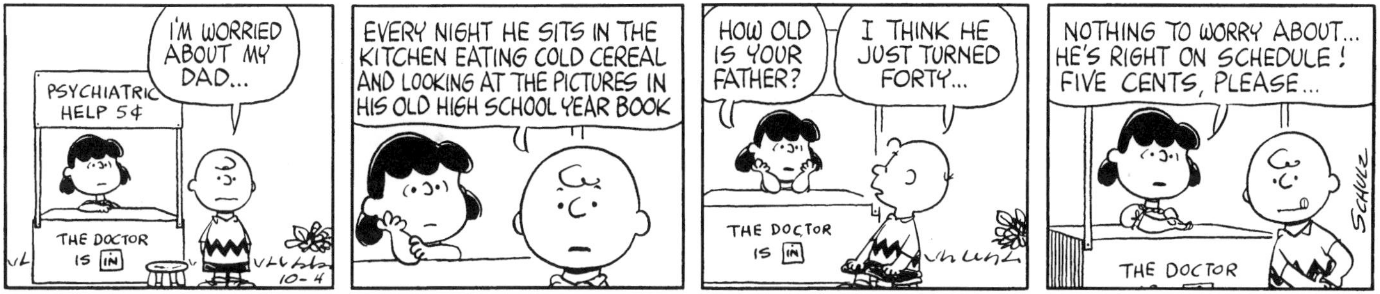
PSYCHIATRIC HELP 5¢
THE DOCTOR IS IN
I'M WORRIED ABOUT MY DAD...
EVERY NIGHT HE SITS IN THE KITCHEN EATING COLD CEREAL AND LOOKING AT THE PICTURES IN HIS OLD HIGH SCHOOL YEAR BOOK
HOW OLD IS YOUR FATHER?
I THINK HE JUST TURNED FORTY...
THE DOCTOR IS IN
NOTHING TO WORRY ABOUT... HE'S RIGHT ON SCHEDULE! FIVE CENTS, PLEASE...
THE DOCTOR

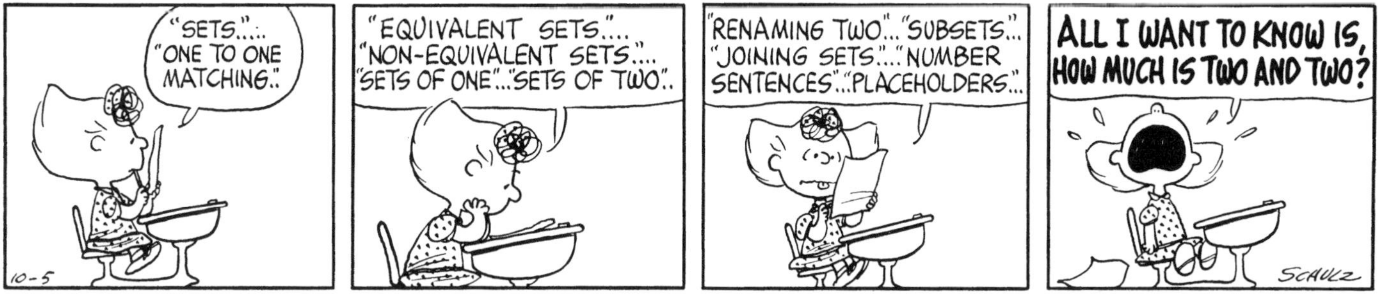
"SETS."... "ONE TO ONE MATCHING."
"EQUIVALENT SETS."... "NON-EQUIVALENT SETS."... "SETS OF ONE"..."SETS OF TWO"..
"RENAMING TWO"..."SUBSETS"... "JOINING SETS"..."NUMBER SENTENCES"..."PLACEHOLDERS"..
ALL I WANT TO KNOW IS, HOW MUCH IS TWO AND TWO?

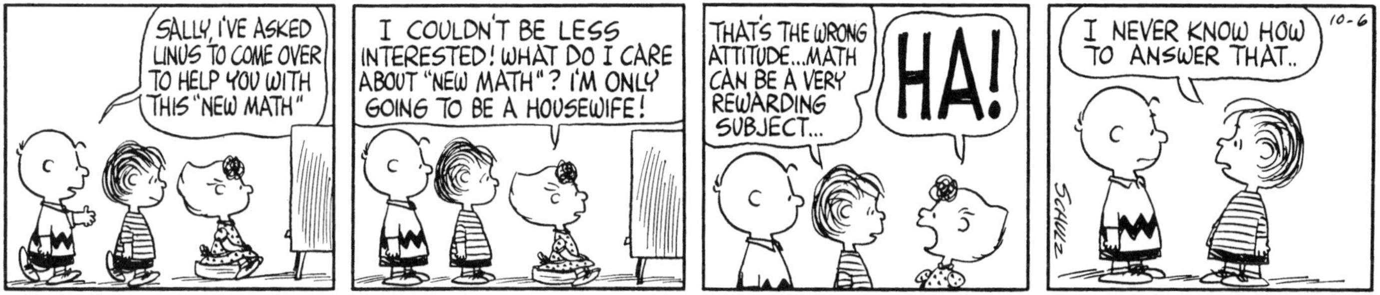
SALLY, I'VE ASKED LINUS TO COME OVER TO HELP YOU WITH THIS "NEW MATH"
I COULDN'T BE LESS INTERESTED! WHAT DO I CARE ABOUT "NEW MATH"? I'M ONLY GOING TO BE A HOUSEWIFE!
THAT'S THE WRONG ATTITUDE...MATH CAN BE A VERY REWARDING SUBJECT...
HA!
I NEVER KNOW HOW TO ANSWER THAT..

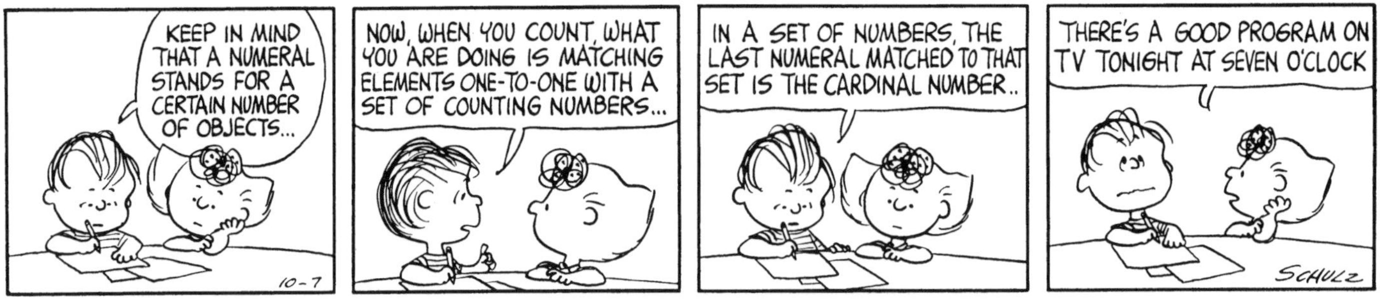
KEEP IN MIND THAT A NUMERAL STANDS FOR A CERTAIN NUMBER OF OBJECTS...
10-7
NOW, WHEN YOU COUNT, WHAT YOU ARE DOING IS MATCHING ELEMENTS ONE-TO-ONE WITH A SET OF COUNTING NUMBERS...
IN A SET OF NUMBERS, THE LAST NUMERAL MATCHED TO THAT SET IS THE CARDINAL NUMBER..
THERE'S A GOOD PROGRAM ON TV TONIGHT AT SEVEN O'CLOCK
SCHULZ

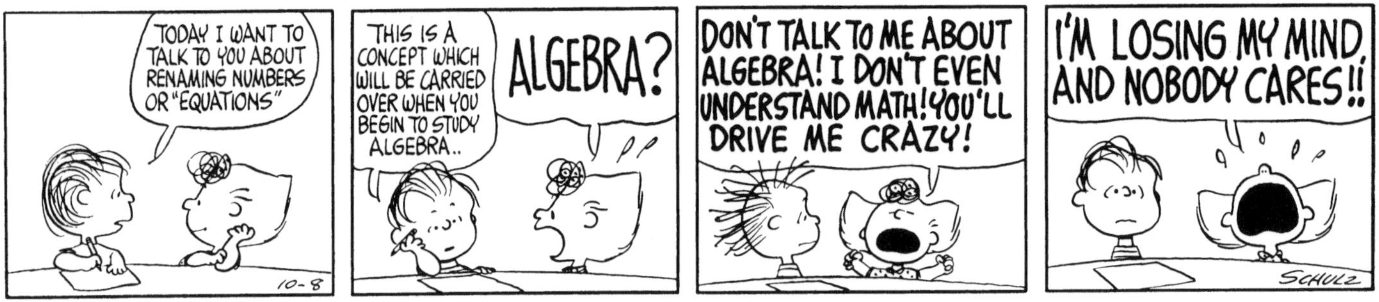
TODAY I WANT TO TALK TO YOU ABOUT RENAMING NUMBERS OR "EQUATIONS"
10-8
THIS IS A CONCEPT WHICH WILL BE CARRIED OVER WHEN YOU BEGIN TO STUDY ALGEBRA..
ALGEBRA?
DON'T TALK TO ME ABOUT ALGEBRA! I DON'T EVEN UNDERSTAND MATH! YOU'LL DRIVE ME CRAZY!
I'M LOSING MY MIND, AND NOBODY CARES!!
SCHULZ

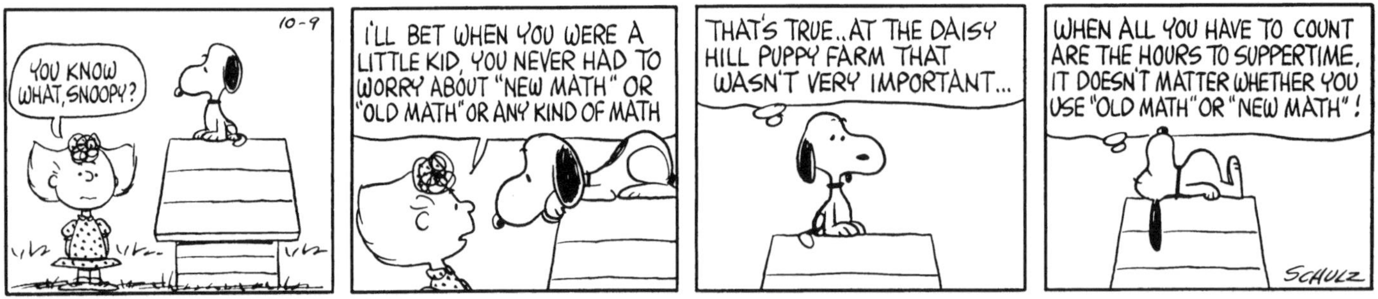
10-9
YOU KNOW WHAT, SNOOPY?
I'LL BET WHEN YOU WERE A LITTLE KID, YOU NEVER HAD TO WORRY ABOUT "NEW MATH" OR "OLD MATH" OR ANY KIND OF MATH
THAT'S TRUE.. AT THE DAISY HILL PUPPY FARM THAT WASN'T VERY IMPORTANT...
WHEN ALL YOU HAVE TO COUNT ARE THE HOURS TO SUPPERTIME, IT DOESN'T MATTER WHETHER YOU USE "OLD MATH" OR "NEW MATH"!
SCHULZ

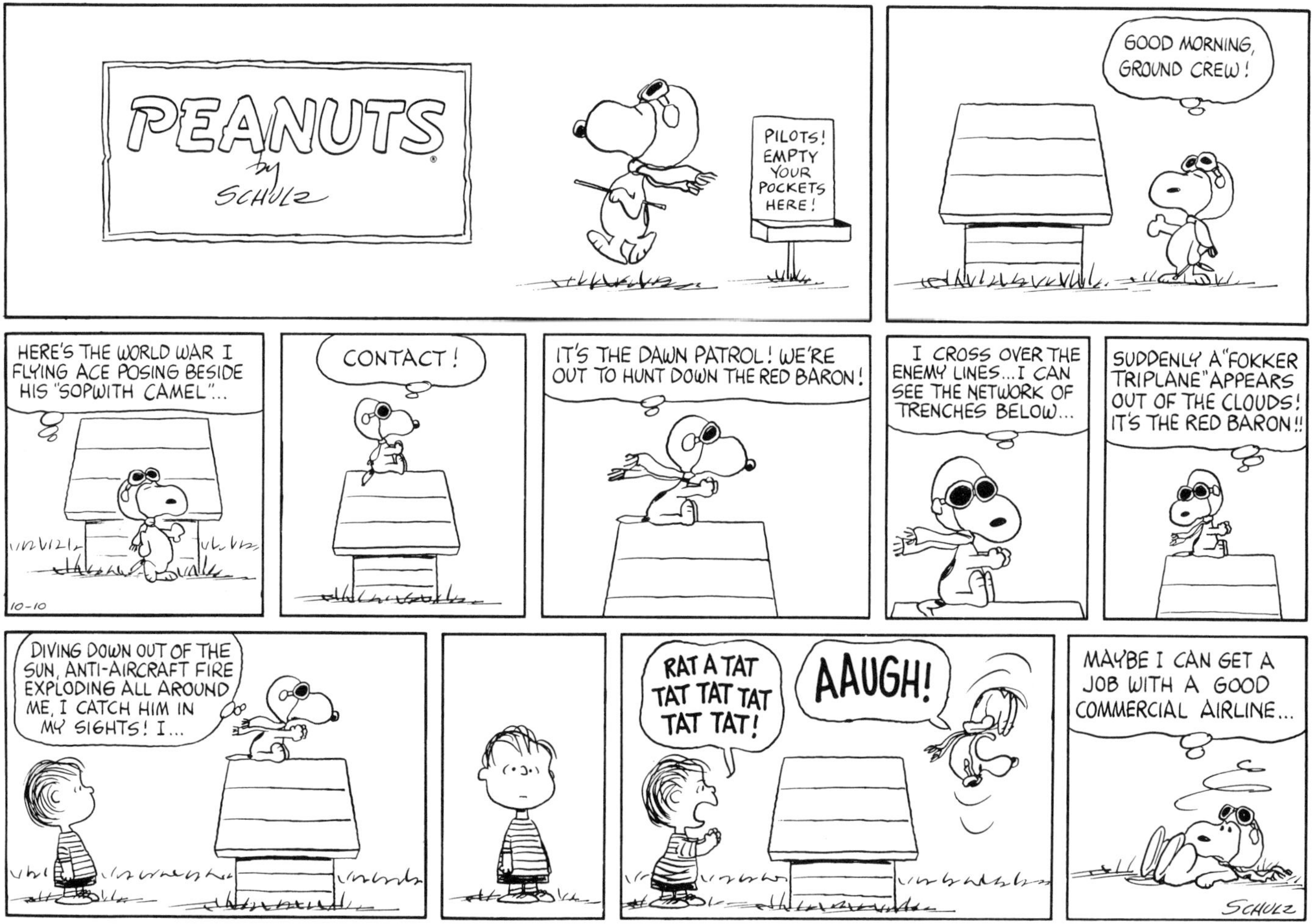
PEANUTS
by SCHULZ
PILOTS! EMPTY YOUR POCKETS HERE!
GOOD MORNING, GROUND CREW!
HERE'S THE WORLD WAR I FLYING ACE POSING BESIDE HIS "SOPWITH CAMEL"...
10-10
CONTACT!
IT'S THE DAWN PATROL! WE'RE OUT TO HUNT DOWN THE RED BARON!
I CROSS OVER THE ENEMY LINES...I CAN SEE THE NETWORK OF TRENCHES BELOW...
SUDDENLY A "FOKKER TRIPLANE" APPEARS OUT OF THE CLOUDS! IT'S THE RED BARON!!
DIVING DOWN OUT OF THE SUN, ANTI-AIRCRAFT FIRE EXPLODING ALL AROUND ME, I CATCH HIM IN MY SIGHTS! I...
RAT A TAT TAT TAT TAT TAT TAT!
AAUGH!
MAYBE I CAN GET A JOB WITH A GOOD COMMERCIAL AIRLINE...
SCHULZ

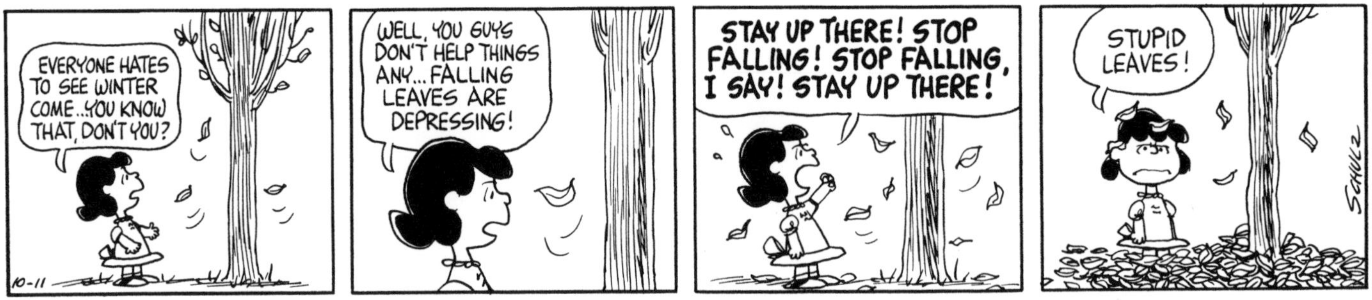
EVERYONE HATES TO SEE WINTER COME...YOU KNOW THAT, DON'T YOU?
10-11
WELL, YOU GUYS DON'T HELP THINGS ANY... FALLING LEAVES ARE DEPRESSING!
STAY UP THERE! STOP FALLING! STOP FALLING, I SAY! STAY UP THERE!
STUPID LEAVES!
SCHULZ

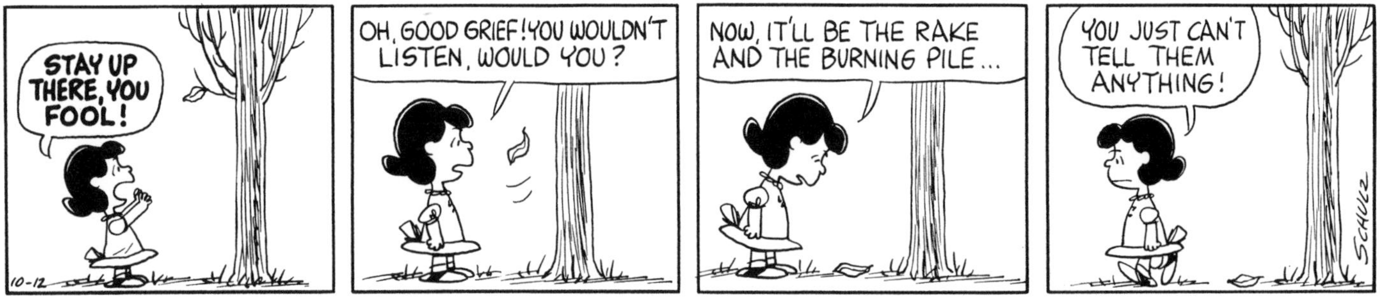
STAY UP THERE, YOU FOOL!
10-12
OH, GOOD GRIEF! YOU WOULDN'T LISTEN, WOULD YOU?
NOW, IT'LL BE THE RAKE AND THE BURNING PILE...
YOU JUST CAN'T TELL THEM ANYTHING!
SCHULZ

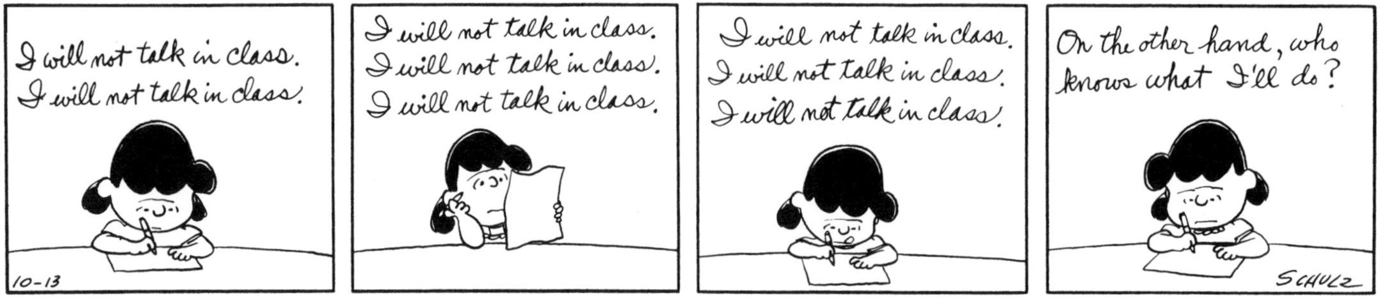
I will not talk in class.
I will not talk in class.
10-13
I will not talk in class.
I will not talk in class.
I will not talk in class.
I will not talk in class.
I will not talk in class.
I will not talk in class.
On the other hand, who knows what I'll do?
SCHULZ

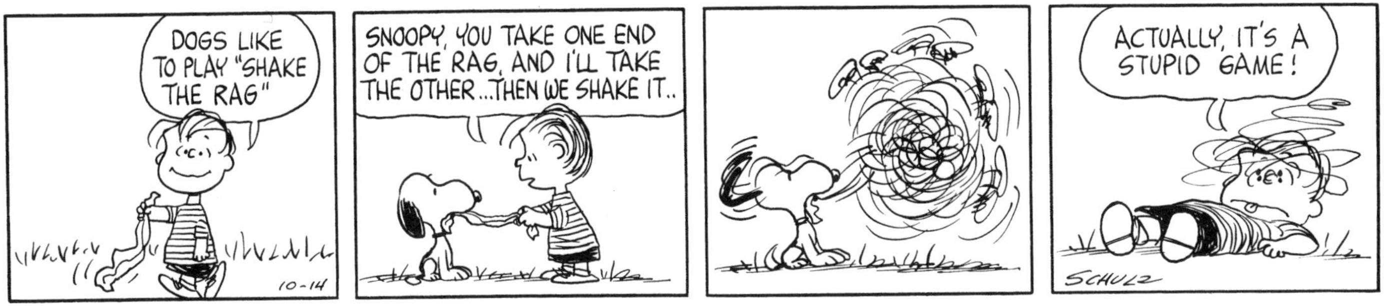
DOGS LIKE TO PLAY "SHAKE THE RAG"
SNOOPY, YOU TAKE ONE END OF THE RAG, AND I'LL TAKE THE OTHER...THEN WE SHAKE IT..
ACTUALLY, IT'S A STUPID GAME!

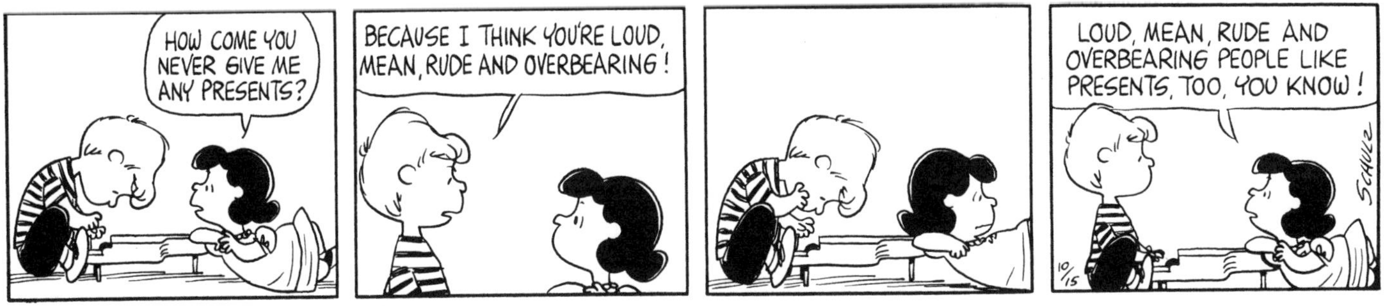
HOW COME YOU NEVER GIVE ME ANY PRESENTS?
BECAUSE I THINK YOU'RE LOUD, MEAN, RUDE AND OVERBEARING!
LOUD, MEAN, RUDE AND OVERBEARING PEOPLE LIKE PRESENTS, TOO, YOU KNOW!

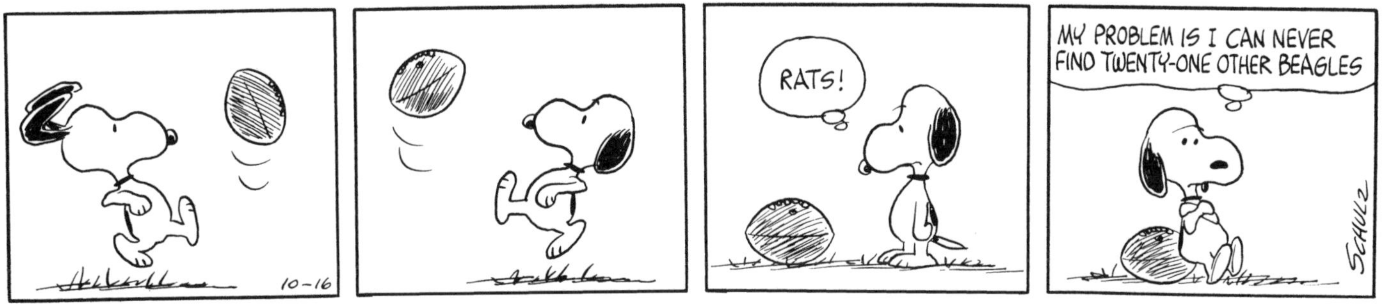
RATS!
MY PROBLEM IS I CAN NEVER FIND TWENTY-ONE OTHER BEAGLES

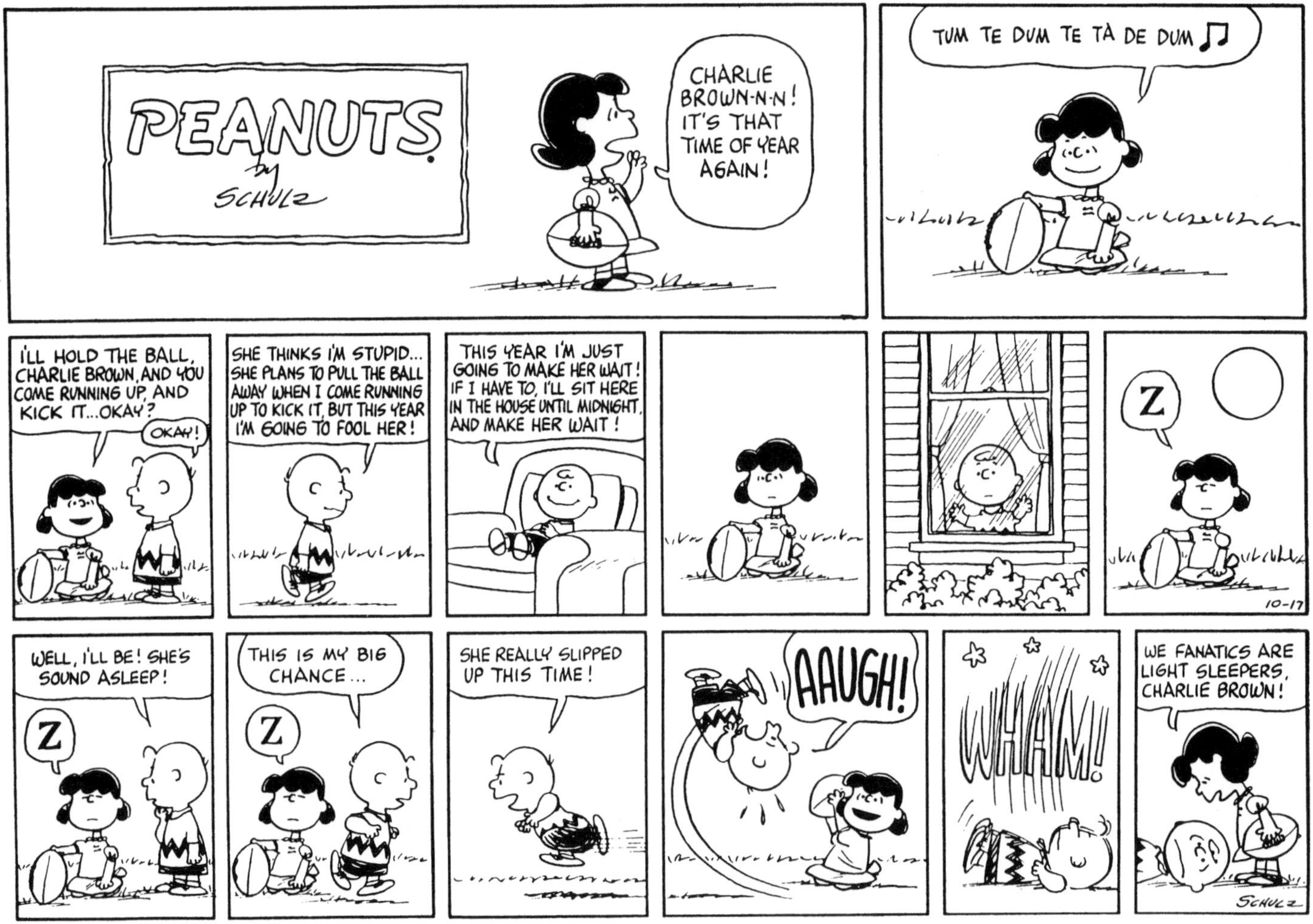
PEANUTS
by SCHULZ
CHARLIE BROWN-N-N! IT'S THAT TIME OF YEAR AGAIN!
TUM TE DUM TE TA DE DUM
I'LL HOLD THE BALL, CHARLIE BROWN, AND YOU COME RUNNING UP, AND KICK IT...OKAY?
OKAY!
SHE THINKS I'M STUPID... SHE PLANS TO PULL THE BALL AWAY WHEN I COME RUNNING UP TO KICK IT, BUT THIS YEAR I'M GOING TO FOOL HER!
THIS YEAR I'M JUST GOING TO MAKE HER WAIT! IF I HAVE TO, I'LL SIT HERE IN THE HOUSE UNTIL MIDNIGHT, AND MAKE HER WAIT!
Z
10-17
WELL, I'LL BE! SHE'S SOUND ASLEEP!
Z
THIS IS MY BIG CHANCE...
Z
SHE REALLY SLIPPED UP THIS TIME!
AAUGH!
WHAM!
WE FANATICS ARE LIGHT SLEEPERS, CHARLIE BROWN!
SCHULZ

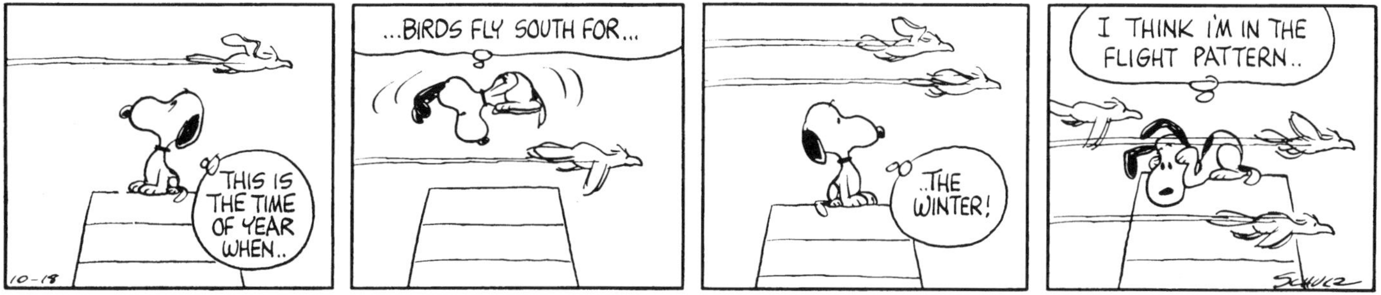
THIS IS THE TIME OF YEAR WHEN..
...BIRDS FLY SOUTH FOR...
..THE WINTER!
I THINK I'M IN THE FLIGHT PATTERN..

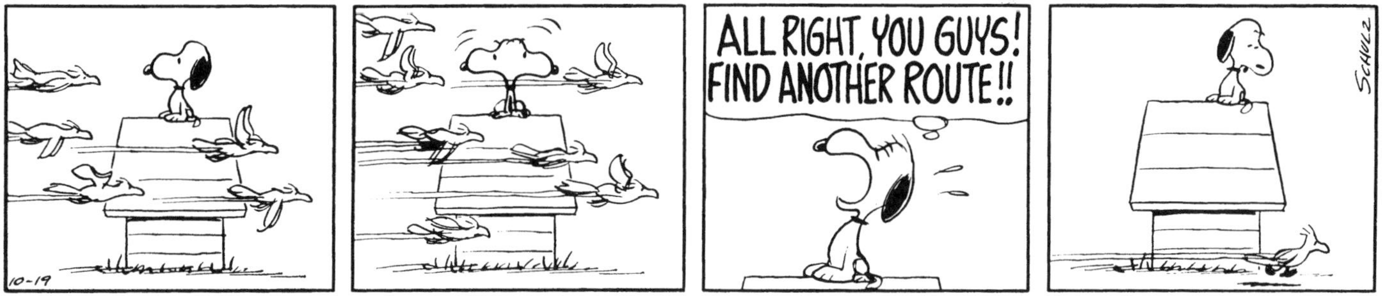
ALL RIGHT, YOU GUYS! FIND ANOTHER ROUTE!!

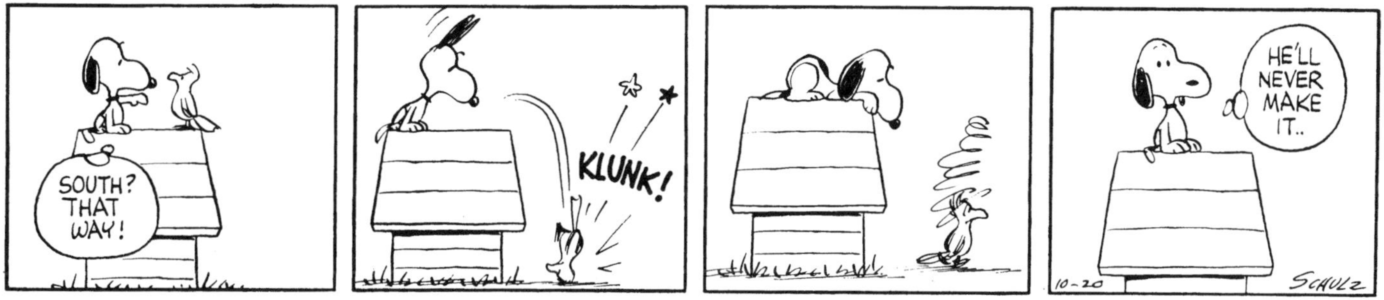
SOUTH? THAT WAY!
KLUNK!
HE'LL NEVER MAKE IT..

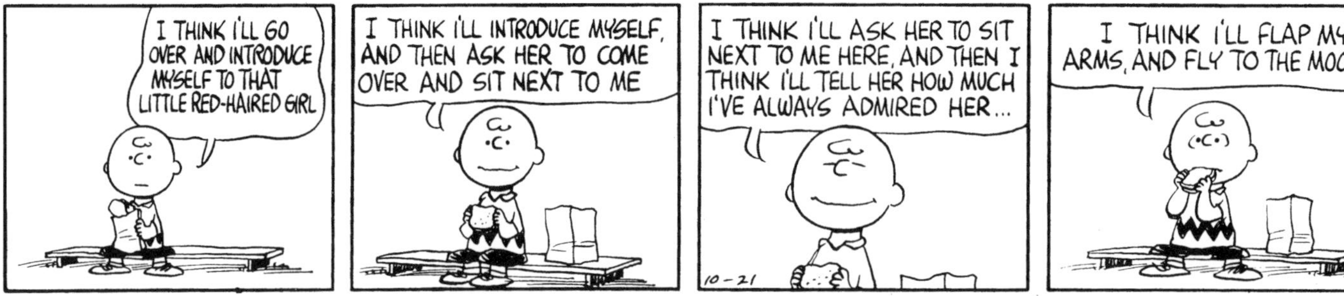
I THINK I'LL GO OVER AND INTRODUCE MYSELF TO THAT LITTLE RED-HAIRED GIRL
I THINK I'LL INTRODUCE MYSELF, AND THEN ASK HER TO COME OVER AND SIT NEXT TO ME
I THINK I'LL ASK HER TO SIT NEXT TO ME HERE, AND THEN I THINK I'LL TELL HER HOW MUCH I'VE ALWAYS ADMIRED HER...
10-21
I THINK I'LL FLAP MY ARMS, AND FLY TO THE MOON
SCHULZ

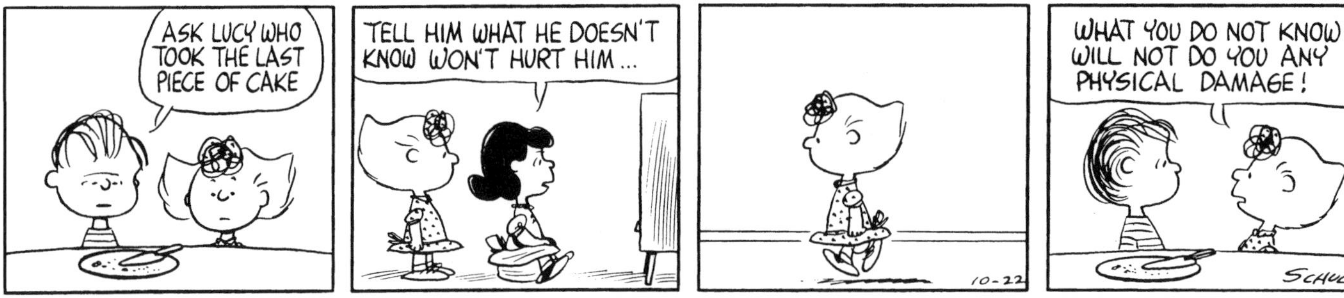
ASK LUCY WHO TOOK THE LAST PIECE OF CAKE
TELL HIM WHAT HE DOESN'T KNOW WON'T HURT HIM...
10-22
WHAT YOU DO NOT KNOW WILL NOT DO YOU ANY PHYSICAL DAMAGE!
SCHULZ

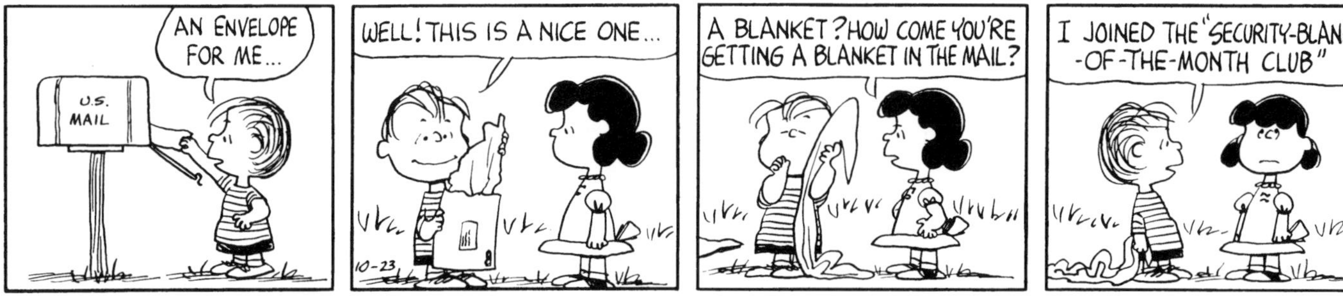
AN ENVELOPE FOR ME...
U.S. MAIL
WELL! THIS IS A NICE ONE...
10-23
A BLANKET? HOW COME YOU'RE GETTING A BLANKET IN THE MAIL?
I JOINED THE "SECURITY-BLANKET-OF-THE-MONTH CLUB"
SCHULZ

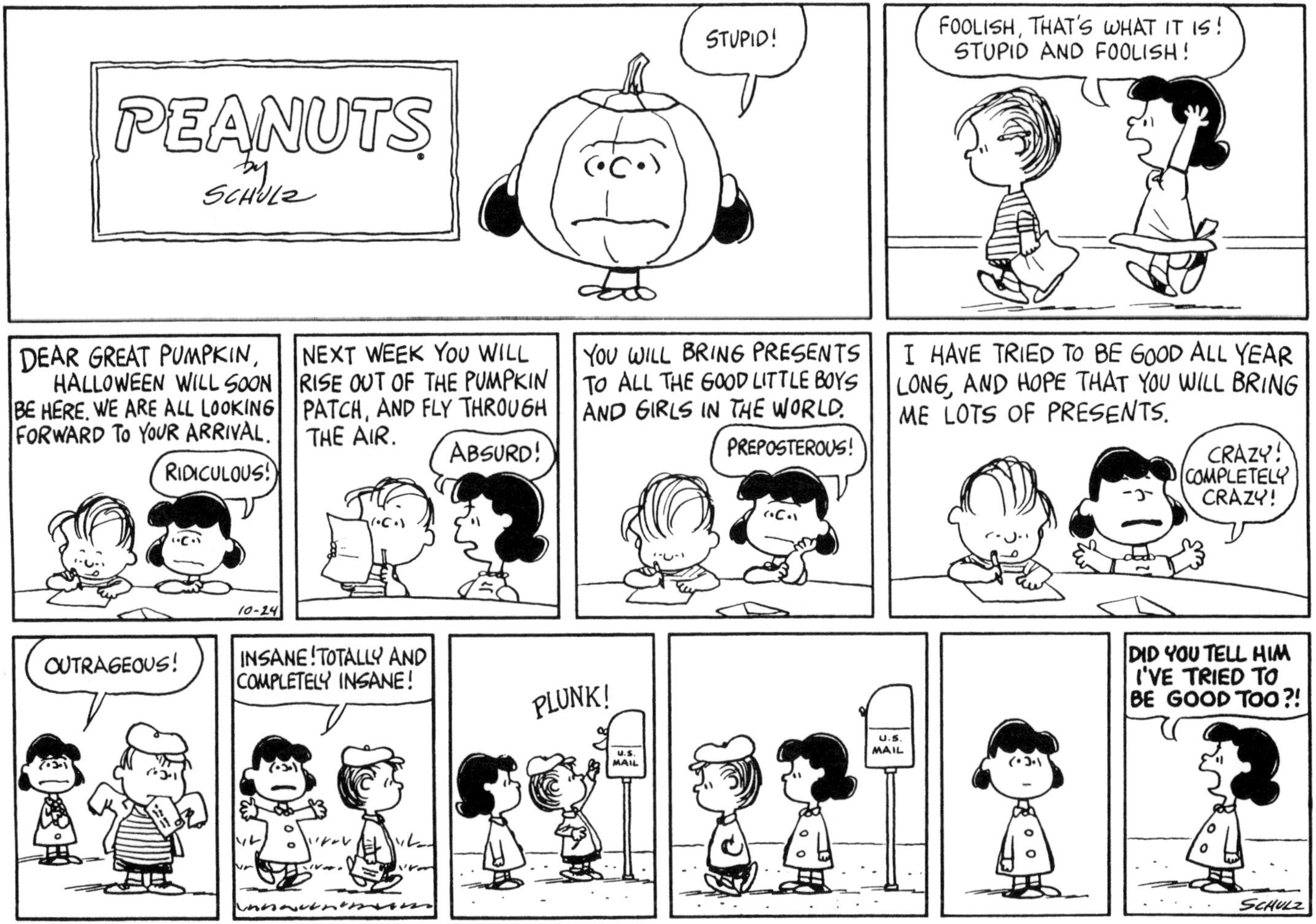
PEANUTS
by SCHULZ
STUPID!
FOOLISH, THAT'S WHAT IT IS! STUPID AND FOOLISH!
DEAR GREAT PUMPKIN, HALLOWEEN WILL SOON BE HERE. WE ARE ALL LOOKING FORWARD TO YOUR ARRIVAL.
RIDICULOUS!
10-24
NEXT WEEK YOU WILL RISE OUT OF THE PUMPKIN PATCH, AND FLY THROUGH THE AIR.
ABSURD!
YOU WILL BRING PRESENTS TO ALL THE GOOD LITTLE BOYS AND GIRLS IN THE WORLD.
PREPOSTEROUS!
I HAVE TRIED TO BE GOOD ALL YEAR LONG, AND HOPE THAT YOU WILL BRING ME LOTS OF PRESENTS.
CRAZY! COMPLETELY CRAZY!
OUTRAGEOUS!
INSANE! TOTALLY AND COMPLETELY INSANE!
PLUNK!
U.S. MAIL
U.S. MAIL
DID YOU TELL HIM I'VE TRIED TO BE GOOD TOO?!
SCHULZ

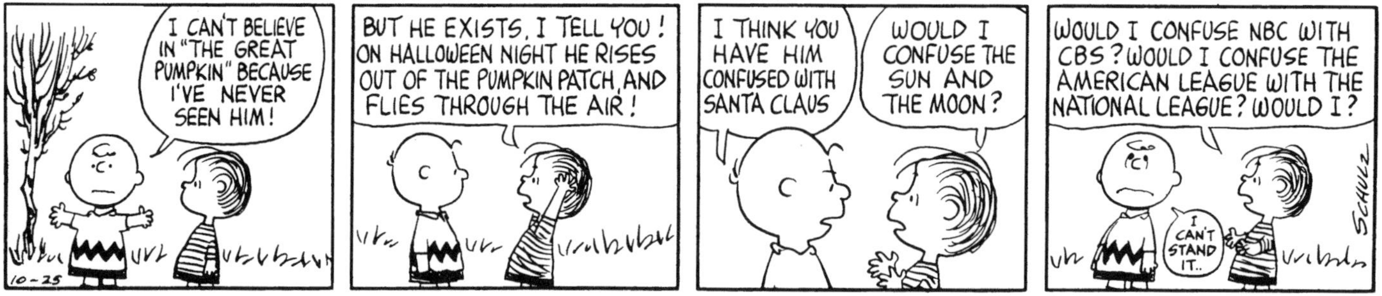
I CAN'T BELIEVE IN "THE GREAT PUMPKIN" BECAUSE I'VE NEVER SEEN HIM!
10-25
BUT HE EXISTS, I TELL YOU! ON HALLOWEEN NIGHT HE RISES OUT OF THE PUMPKIN PATCH, AND FLIES THROUGH THE AIR!
I THINK YOU HAVE HIM CONFUSED WITH SANTA CLAUS
WOULD I CONFUSE THE SUN AND THE MOON?
WOULD I CONFUSE NBC WITH CBS? WOULD I CONFUSE THE AMERICAN LEAGUE WITH THE NATIONAL LEAGUE? WOULD I?
I CAN'T STAND IT..
SCHULZ

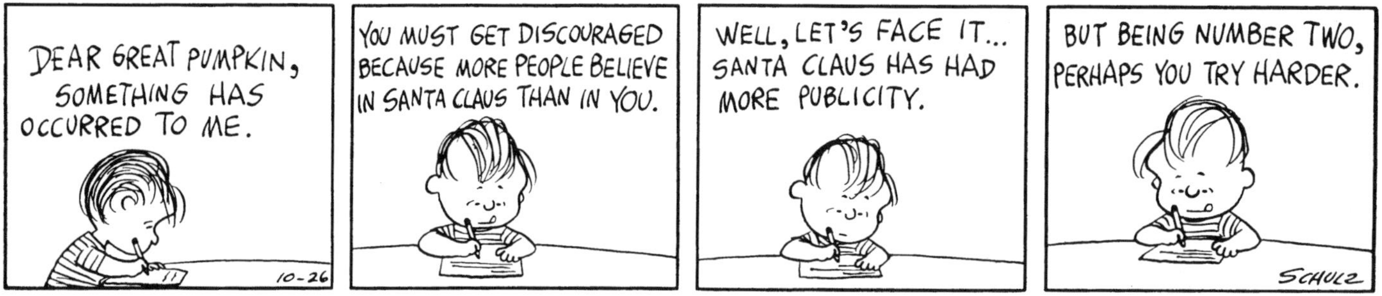
DEAR GREAT PUMPKIN, SOMETHING HAS OCCURRED TO ME.
10-26
YOU MUST GET DISCOURAGED BECAUSE MORE PEOPLE BELIEVE IN SANTA CLAUS THAN IN YOU.
WELL, LET'S FACE IT... SANTA CLAUS HAS HAD MORE PUBLICITY.
BUT BEING NUMBER TWO, PERHAPS YOU TRY HARDER.
SCHULZ

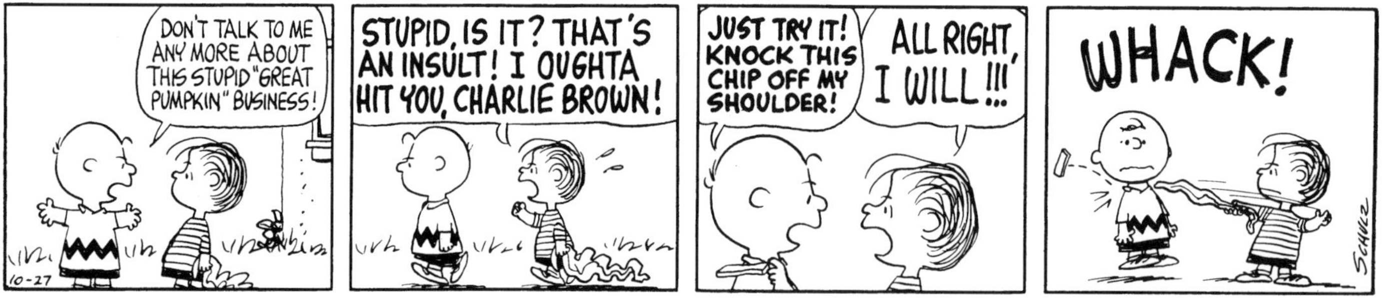
DON'T TALK TO ME ANY MORE ABOUT THIS STUPID "GREAT PUMPKIN" BUSINESS!
10-27
STUPID, IS IT? THAT'S AN INSULT! I OUGHTA HIT YOU, CHARLIE BROWN!
JUST TRY IT! KNOCK THIS CHIP OFF MY SHOULDER!
ALL RIGHT, I WILL!!!
WHACK!
SCHULZ

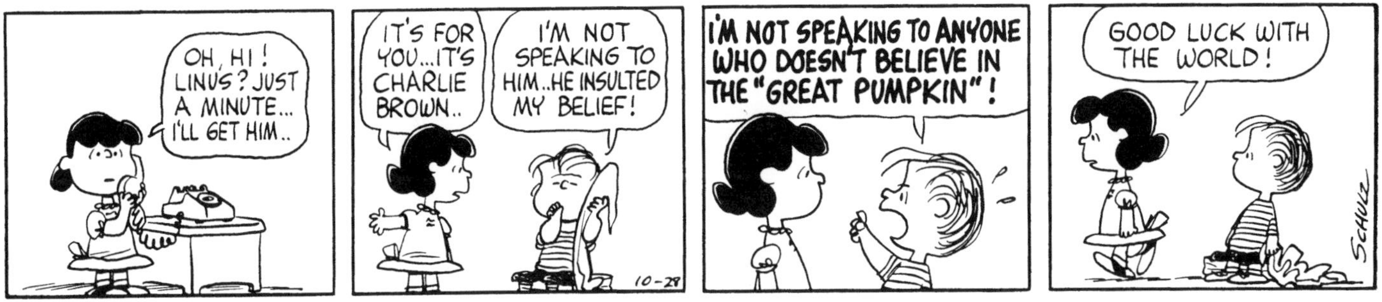
OH, HI! LINUS? JUST A MINUTE... I'LL GET HIM..
IT'S FOR YOU...IT'S CHARLIE BROWN..
I'M NOT SPEAKING TO HIM..HE INSULTED MY BELIEF!
10-28
I'M NOT SPEAKING TO ANYONE WHO DOESN'T BELIEVE IN THE "GREAT PUMPKIN"!
GOOD LUCK WITH THE WORLD!
SCHULZ

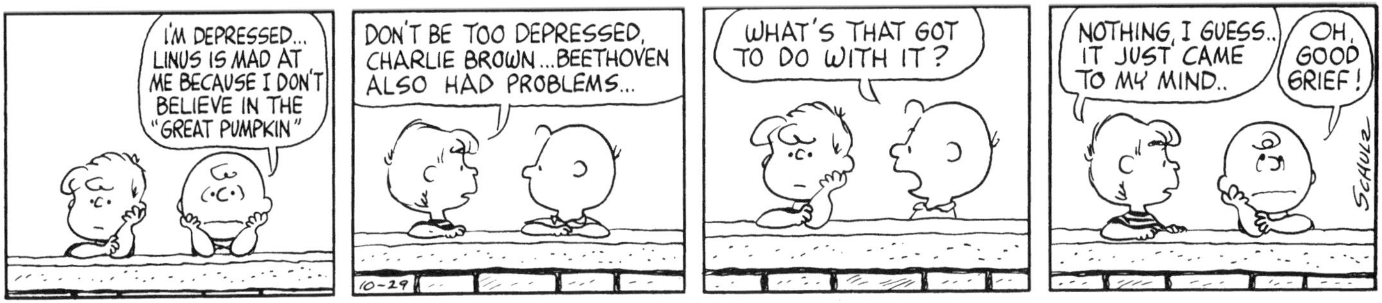
I'M DEPRESSED... LINUS IS MAD AT ME BECAUSE I DON'T BELIEVE IN THE "GREAT PUMPKIN"
DON'T BE TOO DEPRESSED, CHARLIE BROWN...BEETHOVEN ALSO HAD PROBLEMS...
10-29
WHAT'S THAT GOT TO DO WITH IT?
NOTHING, I GUESS.. IT JUST CAME TO MY MIND..
OH, GOOD GRIEF!
SCHULZ

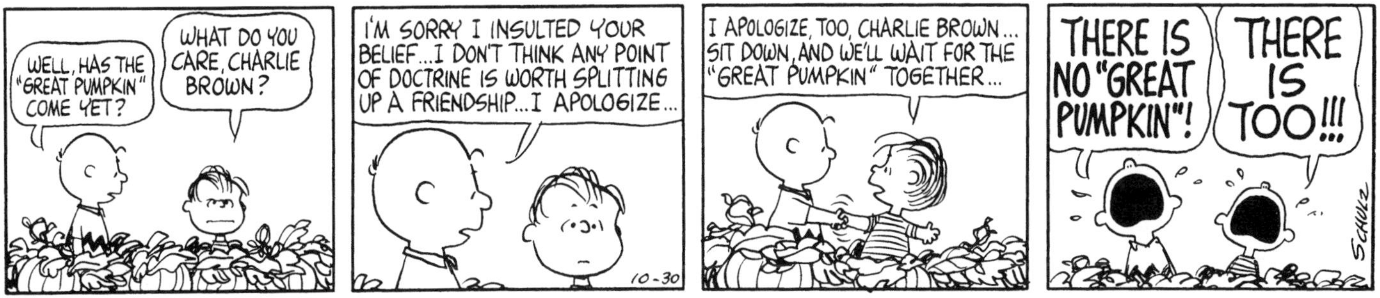
WELL, HAS THE "GREAT PUMPKIN" COME YET?
WHAT DO YOU CARE, CHARLIE BROWN?
I'M SORRY I INSULTED YOUR BELIEF...I DON'T THINK ANY POINT OF DOCTRINE IS WORTH SPLITTING UP A FRIENDSHIP...I APOLOGIZE...
10-30
I APOLOGIZE, TOO, CHARLIE BROWN... SIT DOWN, AND WE'LL WAIT FOR THE "GREAT PUMPKIN" TOGETHER...
THERE IS NO "GREAT PUMPKIN"!
THERE IS TOO!!!
SCHULZ

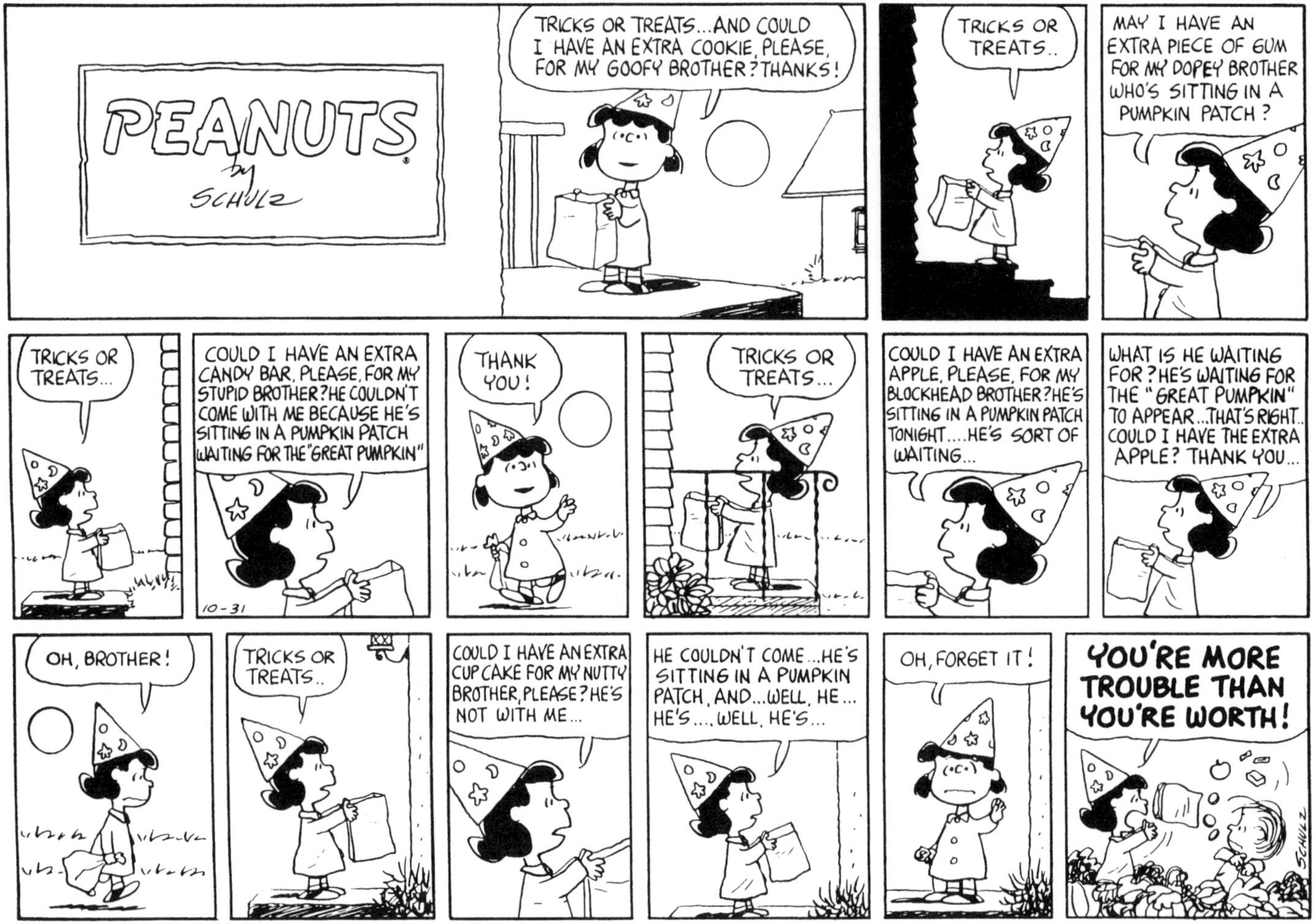
PEANUTS
by SCHULZ
TRICKS OR TREATS...AND COULD I HAVE AN EXTRA COOKIE, PLEASE, FOR MY GOOFY BROTHER? THANKS!
TRICKS OR TREATS..
MAY I HAVE AN EXTRA PIECE OF GUM FOR MY DOPEY BROTHER WHO'S SITTING IN A PUMPKIN PATCH?
TRICKS OR TREATS...
COULD I HAVE AN EXTRA CANDY BAR, PLEASE, FOR MY STUPID BROTHER? HE COULDN'T COME WITH ME BECAUSE HE'S SITTING IN A PUMPKIN PATCH WAITING FOR THE "GREAT PUMPKIN"
10-31
THANK YOU!
TRICKS OR TREATS...
COULD I HAVE AN EXTRA APPLE, PLEASE, FOR MY BLOCKHEAD BROTHER? HE'S SITTING IN A PUMPKIN PATCH TONIGHT....HE'S SORT OF WAITING...
WHAT IS HE WAITING FOR? HE'S WAITING FOR THE "GREAT PUMPKIN" TO APPEAR...THAT'S RIGHT.. COULD I HAVE THE EXTRA APPLE? THANK YOU...
OH, BROTHER!
TRICKS OR TREATS..
COULD I HAVE AN EXTRA CUP CAKE FOR MY NUTTY BROTHER, PLEASE? HE'S NOT WITH ME...
HE COULDN'T COME...HE'S SITTING IN A PUMPKIN PATCH, AND...WELL, HE... HE'S....WELL, HE'S...
OH, FORGET IT!
YOU'RE MORE TROUBLE THAN YOU'RE WORTH!
SCHULZ

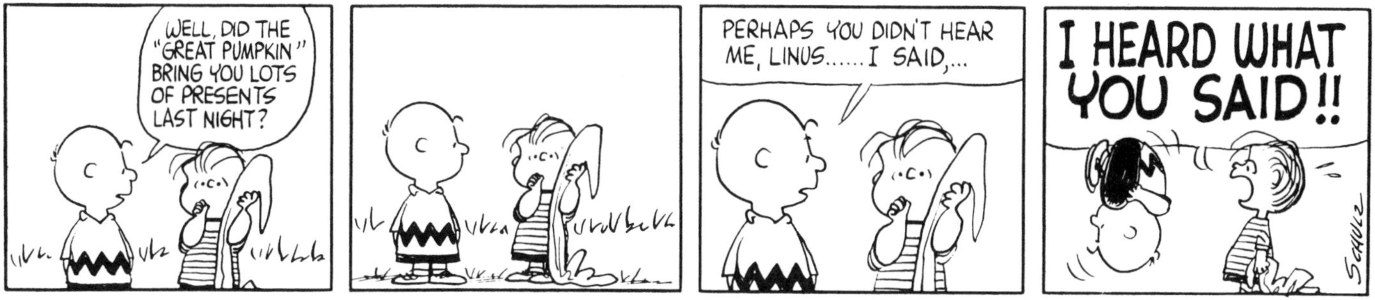
WELL, DID THE "GREAT PUMPKIN" BRING YOU LOTS OF PRESENTS LAST NIGHT?
PERHAPS YOU DIDN'T HEAR ME, LINUS......I SAID,...
I HEARD WHAT YOU SAID!!
SCHULZ

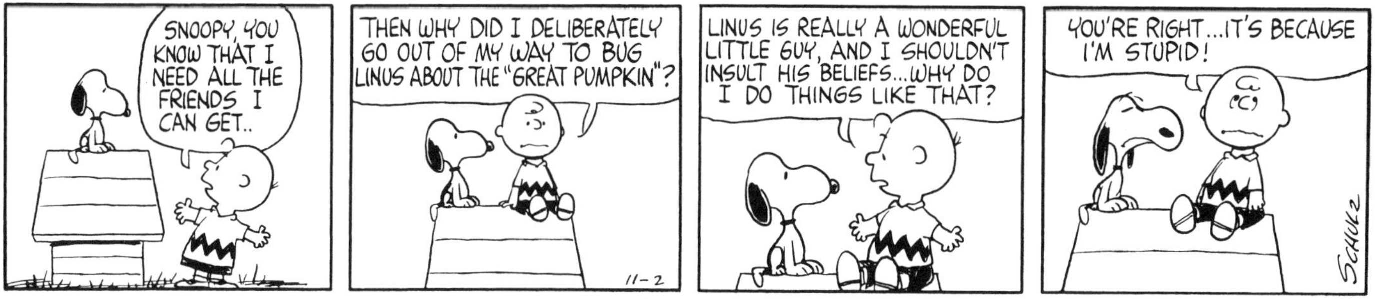
SNOOPY, YOU KNOW THAT I NEED ALL THE FRIENDS I CAN GET..
THEN WHY DID I DELIBERATELY GO OUT OF MY WAY TO BUG LINUS ABOUT THE "GREAT PUMPKIN"?
11-2
LINUS IS REALLY A WONDERFUL LITTLE GUY, AND I SHOULDN'T INSULT HIS BELIEFS...WHY DO I DO THINGS LIKE THAT?
YOU'RE RIGHT...IT'S BECAUSE I'M STUPID!
SCHULZ

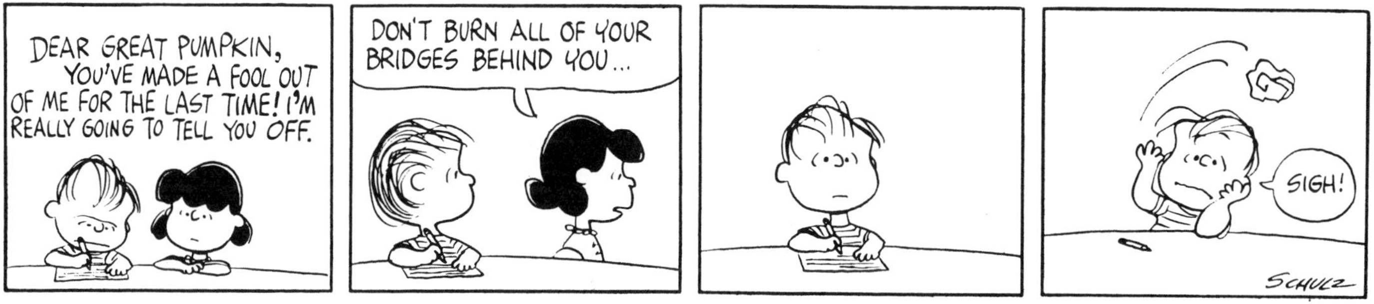
DEAR GREAT PUMPKIN, YOU'VE MADE A FOOL OUT OF ME FOR THE LAST TIME! I'M REALLY GOING TO TELL YOU OFF.
DON'T BURN ALL OF YOUR BRIDGES BEHIND YOU...
SIGH!
SCHULZ

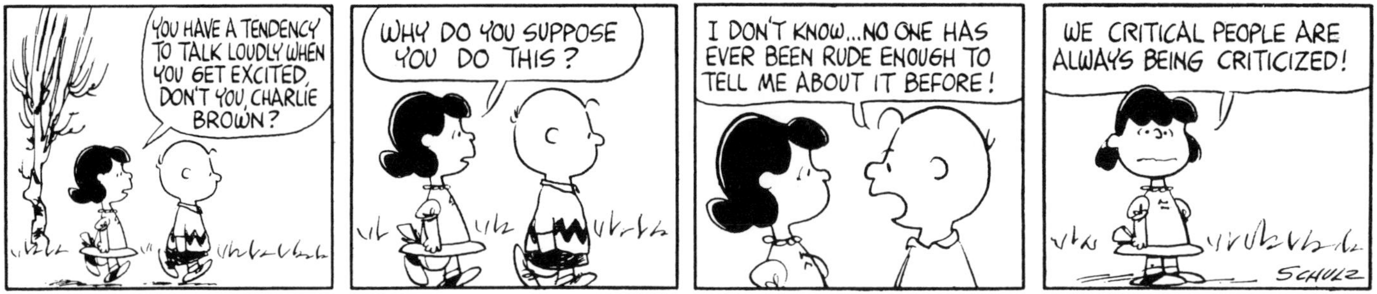
YOU HAVE A TENDENCY TO TALK LOUDLY WHEN YOU GET EXCITED, DON'T YOU, CHARLIE BROWN?
WHY DO YOU SUPPOSE YOU DO THIS?
I DON'T KNOW...NO ONE HAS EVER BEEN RUDE ENOUGH TO TELL ME ABOUT IT BEFORE!
WE CRITICAL PEOPLE ARE ALWAYS BEING CRITICIZED!
SCHULZ

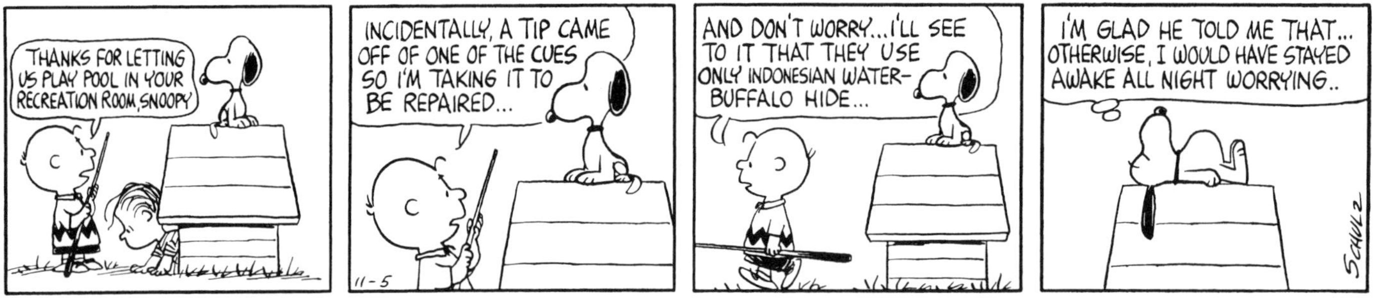
THANKS FOR LETTING US PLAY POOL IN YOUR RECREATION ROOM, SNOOPY
INCIDENTALLY, A TIP CAME OFF OF ONE OF THE CUES SO I'M TAKING IT TO BE REPAIRED...
11-5
AND DON'T WORRY...I'LL SEE TO IT THAT THEY USE ONLY INDONESIAN WATER-BUFFALO HIDE...
I'M GLAD HE TOLD ME THAT... OTHERWISE, I WOULD HAVE STAYED AWAKE ALL NIGHT WORRYING..
SCHULZ

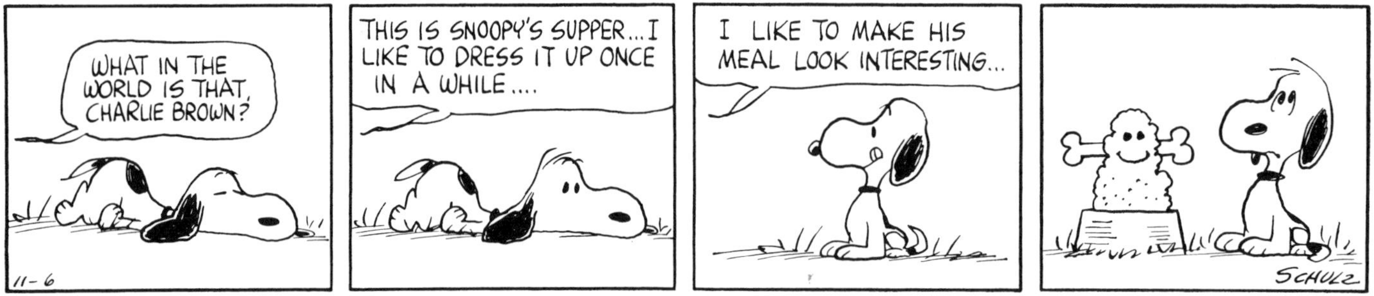
WHAT IN THE WORLD IS THAT, CHARLIE BROWN?
11-6
THIS IS SNOOPY'S SUPPER...I LIKE TO DRESS IT UP ONCE IN A WHILE....
I LIKE TO MAKE HIS MEAL LOOK INTERESTING...
SCHULZ

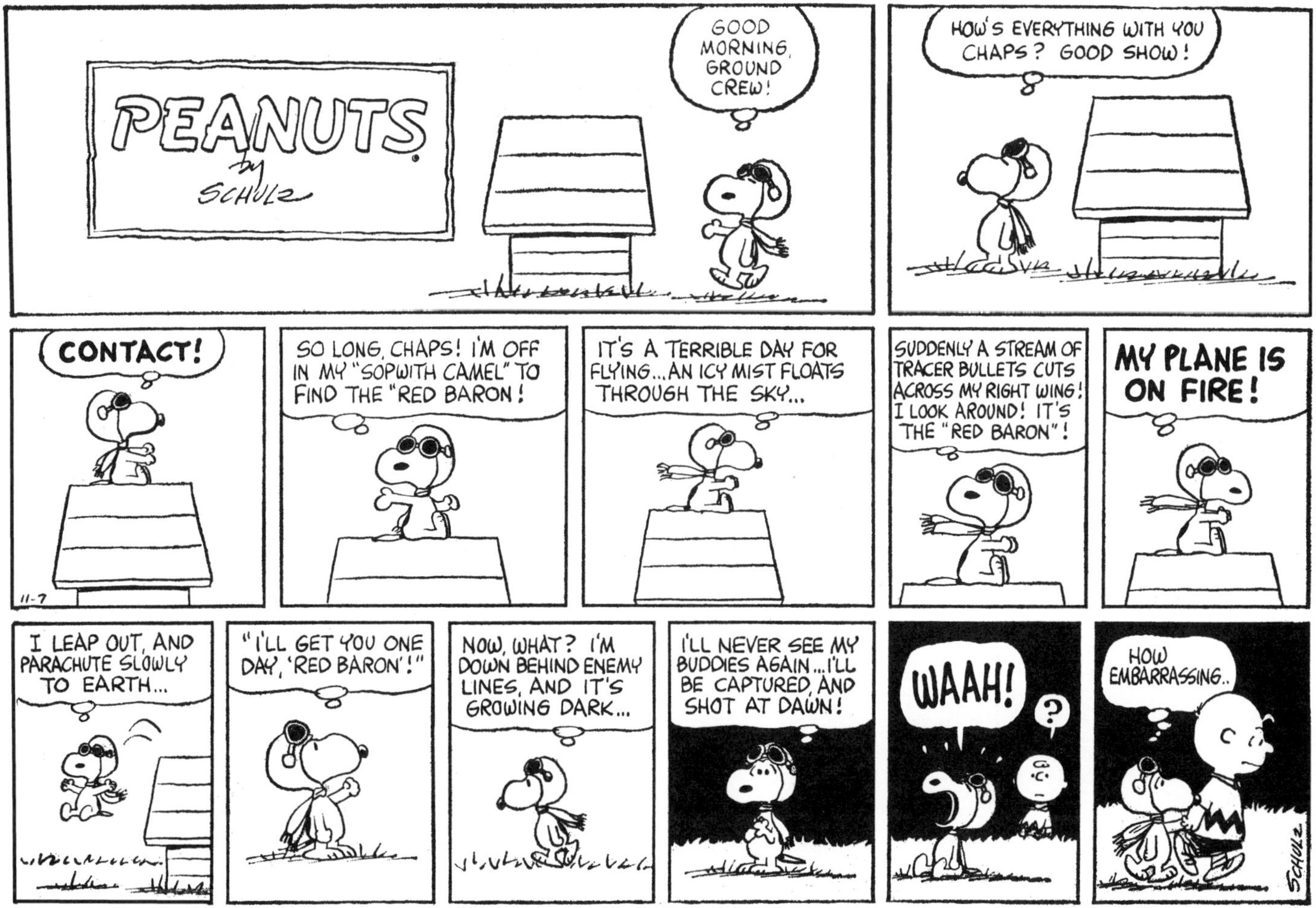
PEANUTS
by SCHULZ
GOOD MORNING, GROUND CREW!
HOW'S EVERYTHING WITH YOU CHAPS? GOOD SHOW!
CONTACT!
11-7
SO LONG, CHAPS! I'M OFF IN MY "SOPWITH CAMEL" TO FIND THE "RED BARON!
IT'S A TERRIBLE DAY FOR FLYING...AN ICY MIST FLOATS THROUGH THE SKY...
SUDDENLY A STREAM OF TRACER BULLETS CUTS ACROSS MY RIGHT WING! I LOOK AROUND! IT'S THE "RED BARON"!
MY PLANE IS ON FIRE!
I LEAP OUT, AND PARACHUTE SLOWLY TO EARTH...
"I'LL GET YOU ONE DAY, 'RED BARON'!"
NOW, WHAT? I'M DOWN BEHIND ENEMY LINES, AND IT'S GROWING DARK...
I'LL NEVER SEE MY BUDDIES AGAIN...I'LL BE CAPTURED, AND SHOT AT DAWN!
WAAH!
?
HOW EMBARRASSING..
SCHULZ

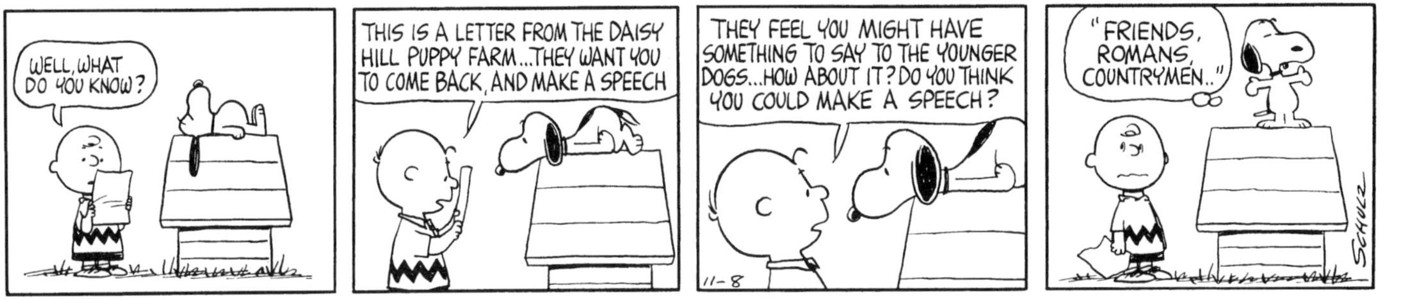
WELL, WHAT DO YOU KNOW?
THIS IS A LETTER FROM THE DAISY HILL PUPPY FARM...THEY WANT YOU TO COME BACK, AND MAKE A SPEECH
THEY FEEL YOU MIGHT HAVE SOMETHING TO SAY TO THE YOUNGER DOGS...HOW ABOUT IT? DO YOU THINK YOU COULD MAKE A SPEECH?
11-8
"FRIENDS, ROMANS, COUNTRYMEN.."
SCHULZ
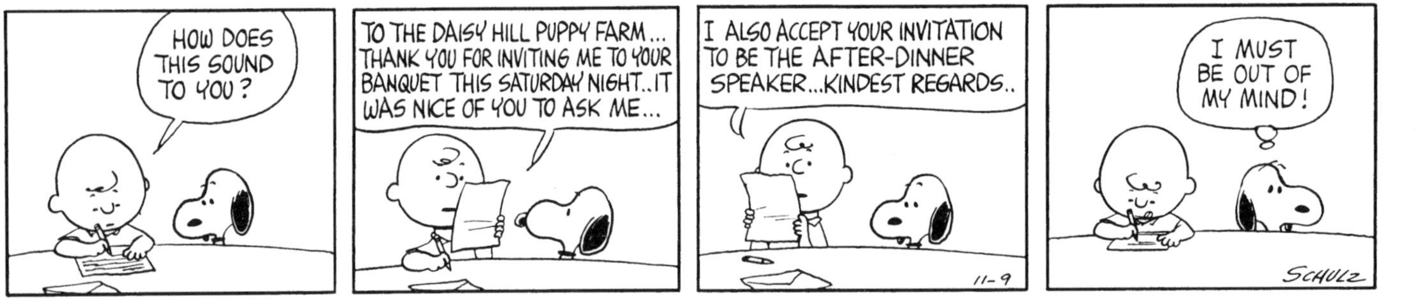
HOW DOES THIS SOUND TO YOU?
TO THE DAISY HILL PUPPY FARM... THANK YOU FOR INVITING ME TO YOUR BANQUET THIS SATURDAY NIGHT..IT WAS NICE OF YOU TO ASK ME...
I ALSO ACCEPT YOUR INVITATION TO BE THE AFTER-DINNER SPEAKER...KINDEST REGARDS..
11-9
I MUST BE OUT OF MY MIND!
SCHULZ
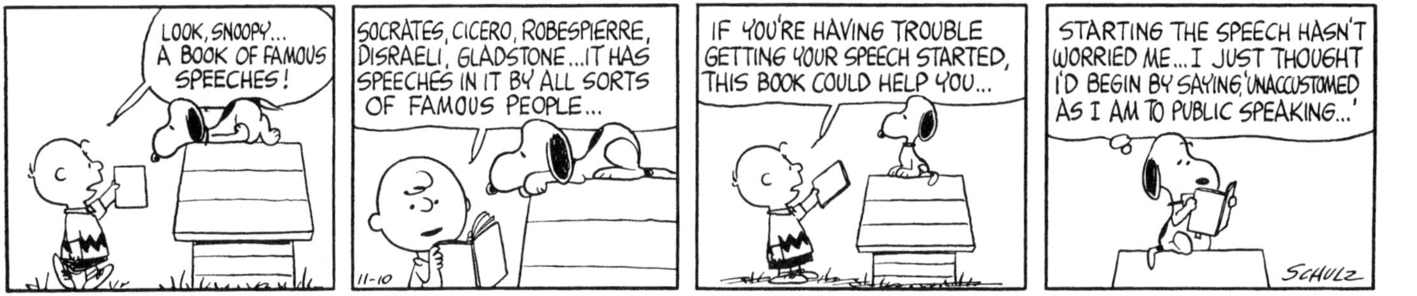
LOOK, SNOOPY... A BOOK OF FAMOUS SPEECHES!
SOCRATES, CICERO, ROBESPIERRE, DISRAELI, GLADSTONE...IT HAS SPEECHES IN IT BY ALL SORTS OF FAMOUS PEOPLE...
11-10
IF YOU'RE HAVING TROUBLE GETTING YOUR SPEECH STARTED, THIS BOOK COULD HELP YOU...
STARTING THE SPEECH HASN'T WORRIED ME...I JUST THOUGHT I'D BEGIN BY SAYING, 'UNACCUSTOMED AS I AM TO PUBLIC SPEAKING...'
SCHULZ

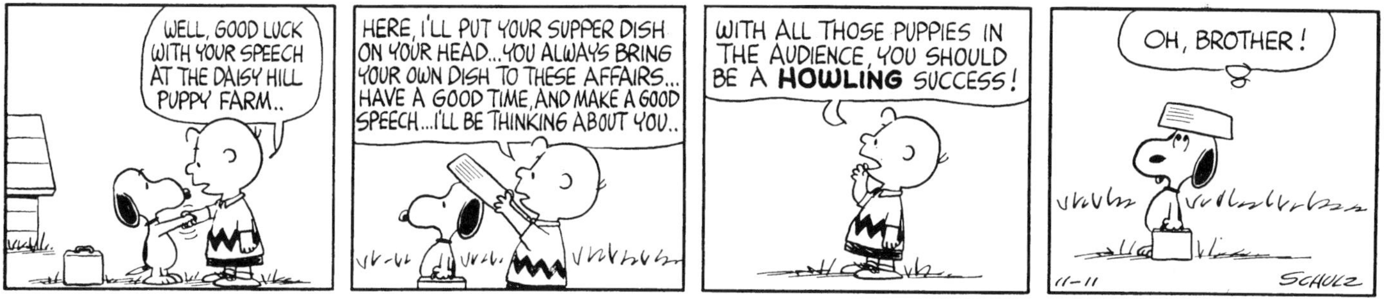
WELL, GOOD LUCK WITH YOUR SPEECH AT THE DAISY HILL PUPPY FARM..
HERE, I'LL PUT YOUR SUPPER DISH ON YOUR HEAD...YOU ALWAYS BRING YOUR OWN DISH TO THESE AFFAIRS...HAVE A GOOD TIME, AND MAKE A GOOD SPEECH...I'LL BE THINKING ABOUT YOU..
WITH ALL THOSE PUPPIES IN THE AUDIENCE, YOU SHOULD BE A **HOWLING** SUCCESS!
OH, BROTHER!
11-11
SCHULZ

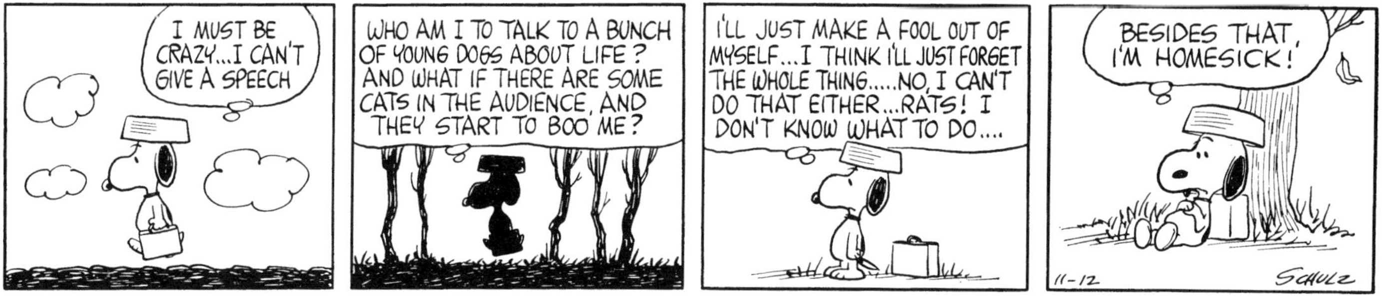
I MUST BE CRAZY...I CAN'T GIVE A SPEECH
WHO AM I TO TALK TO A BUNCH OF YOUNG DOGS ABOUT LIFE? AND WHAT IF THERE ARE SOME CATS IN THE AUDIENCE, AND THEY START TO BOO ME?
I'LL JUST MAKE A FOOL OUT OF MYSELF...I THINK I'LL JUST FORGET THE WHOLE THING.....NO, I CAN'T DO THAT EITHER...RATS! I DON'T KNOW WHAT TO DO....
BESIDES THAT, I'M HOMESICK!
11-12
SCHULZ

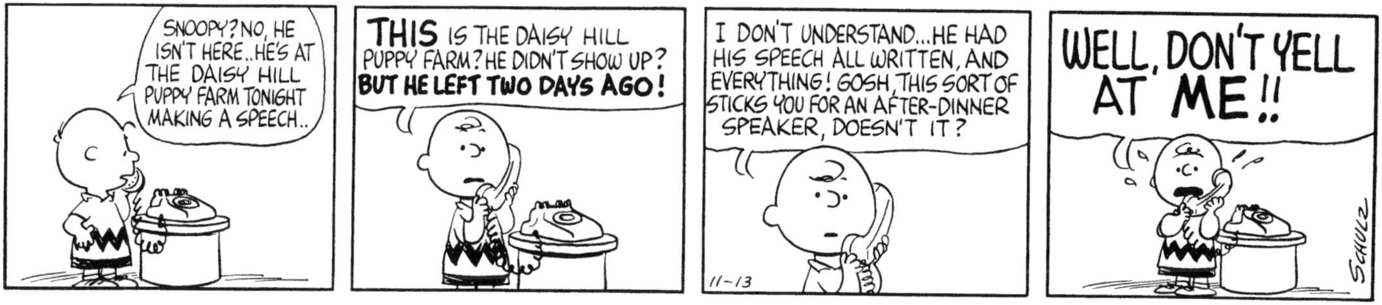
SNOOPY? NO, HE ISN'T HERE..HE'S AT THE DAISY HILL PUPPY FARM TONIGHT MAKING A SPEECH..
THIS IS THE DAISY HILL PUPPY FARM? HE DIDN'T SHOW UP? **BUT HE LEFT TWO DAYS AGO!**
I DON'T UNDERSTAND...HE HAD HIS SPEECH ALL WRITTEN, AND EVERYTHING! GOSH, THIS SORT OF STICKS YOU FOR AN AFTER-DINNER SPEAKER, DOESN'T IT?
11-13
WELL, DON'T YELL AT **ME**!!
SCHULZ

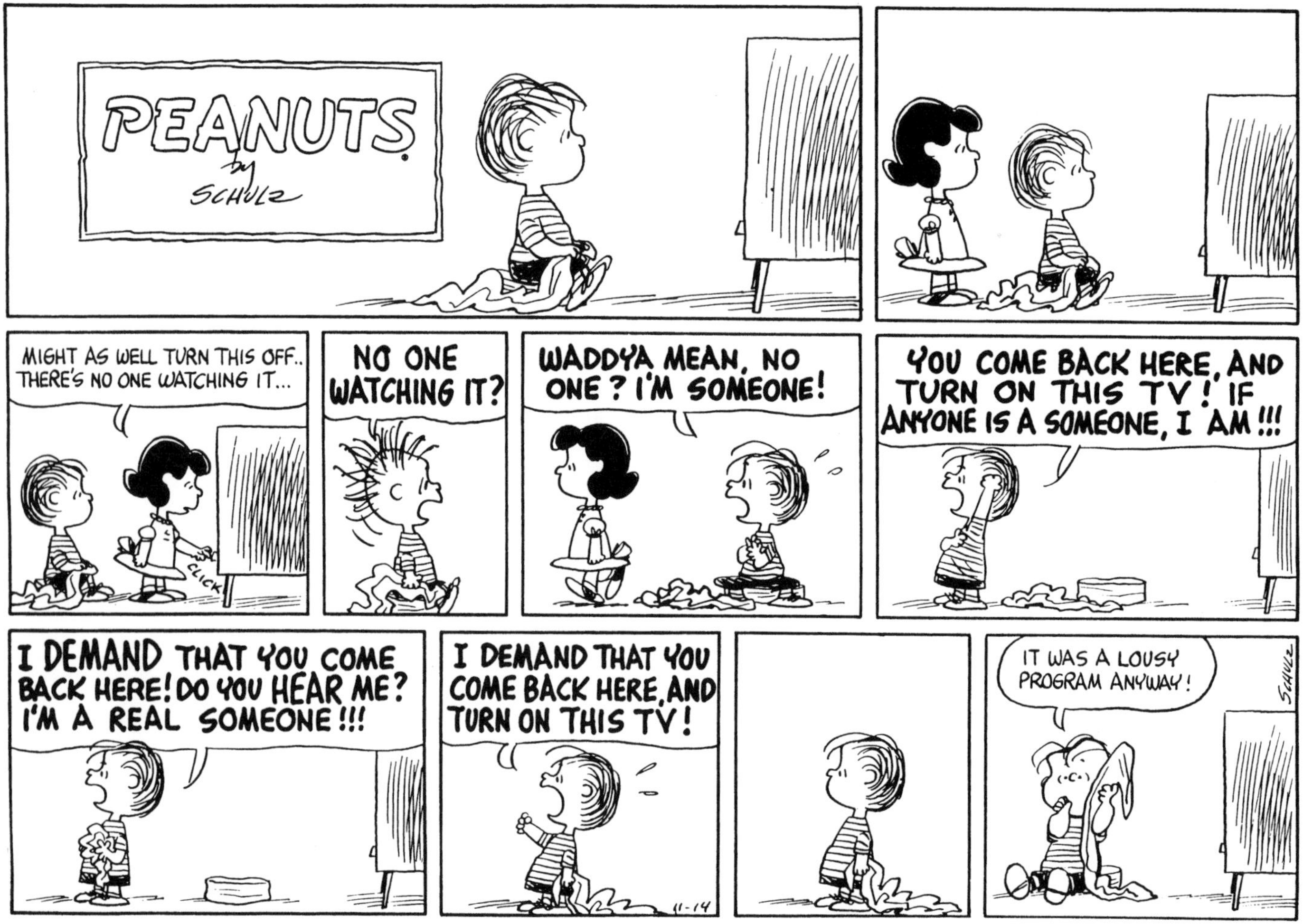
PEANUTS
by SCHULZ
MIGHT AS WELL TURN THIS OFF.. THERE'S NO ONE WATCHING IT...
CLICK
NO ONE WATCHING IT?
WADDYA MEAN, NO ONE? I'M SOMEONE!
YOU COME BACK HERE, AND TURN ON THIS TV! IF ANYONE IS A SOMEONE, I AM!!!
I DEMAND THAT YOU COME BACK HERE! DO YOU HEAR ME? I'M A REAL SOMEONE!!!
I DEMAND THAT YOU COME BACK HERE, AND TURN ON THIS TV!
11-14
IT WAS A LOUSY PROGRAM ANYWAY!
SCHULZ

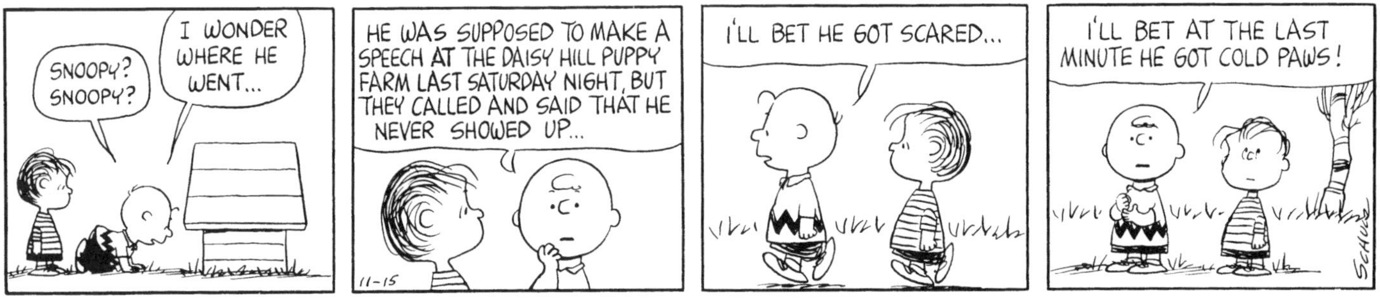
SNOOPY? SNOOPY?
I WONDER WHERE HE WENT...
HE WAS SUPPOSED TO MAKE A SPEECH AT THE DAISY HILL PUPPY FARM LAST SATURDAY NIGHT, BUT THEY CALLED AND SAID THAT HE NEVER SHOWED UP...
I'LL BET HE GOT SCARED...
I'LL BET AT THE LAST MINUTE HE GOT COLD PAWS!

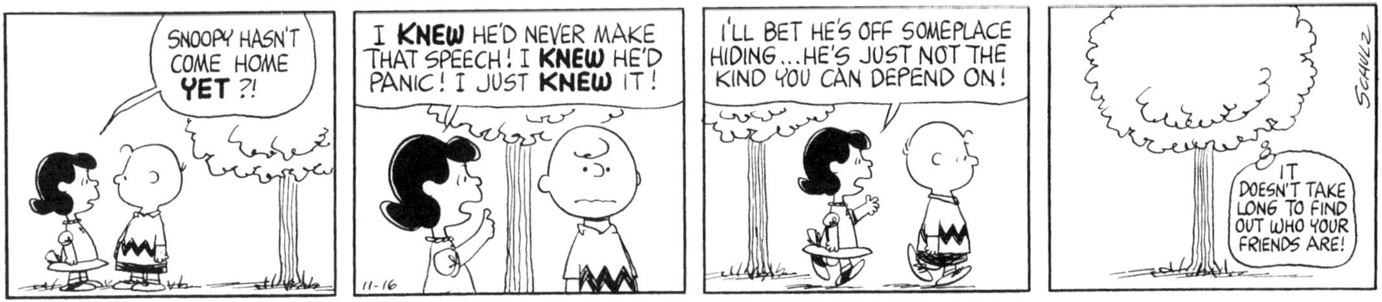
SNOOPY HASN'T COME HOME **YET** ?!
I **KNEW** HE'D NEVER MAKE THAT SPEECH! I **KNEW** HE'D PANIC! I JUST **KNEW** IT!
I'LL BET HE'S OFF SOMEPLACE HIDING...HE'S JUST NOT THE KIND YOU CAN DEPEND ON!
IT DOESN'T TAKE LONG TO FIND OUT WHO YOUR FRIENDS ARE!

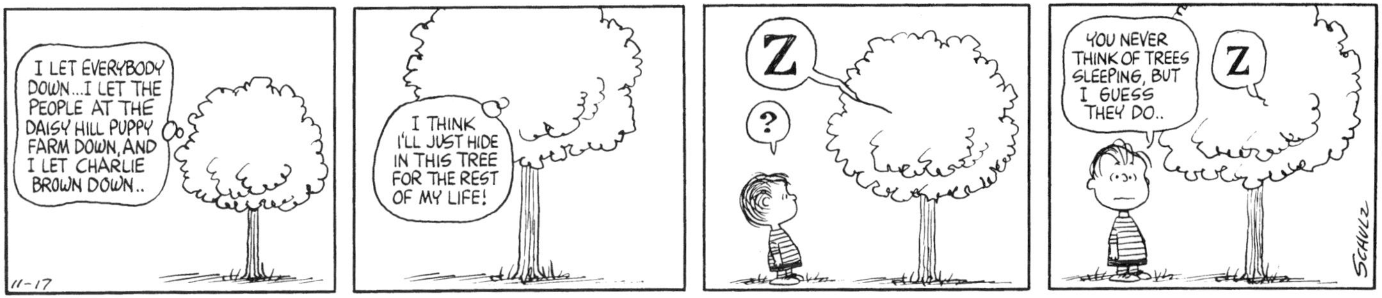
I LET EVERYBODY DOWN...I LET THE PEOPLE AT THE DAISY HILL PUPPY FARM DOWN, AND I LET CHARLIE BROWN DOWN..
I THINK I'LL JUST HIDE IN THIS TREE FOR THE REST OF MY LIFE!
Z
?
YOU NEVER THINK OF TREES SLEEPING, BUT I GUESS THEY DO..
Z

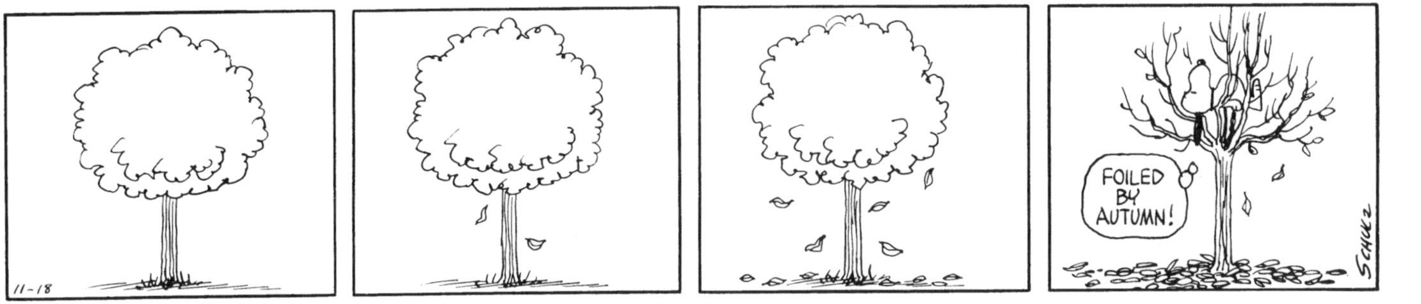
11-18
FOILED BY AUTUMN!
SCHULZ

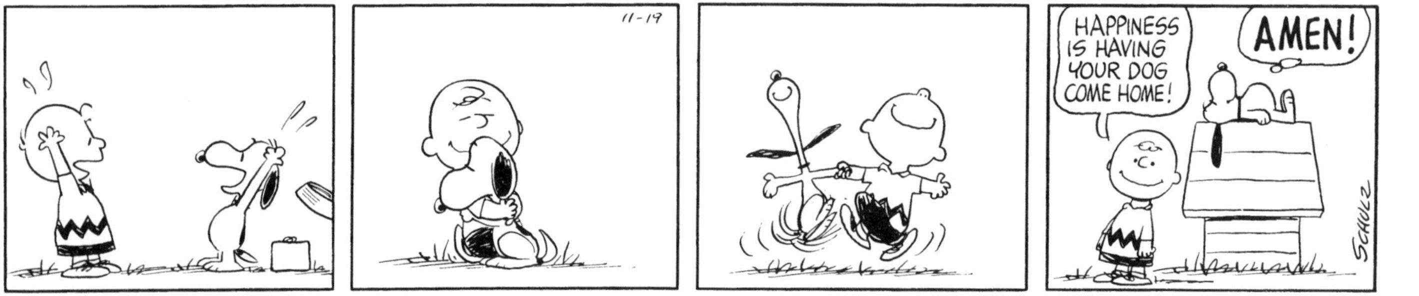
11-19
HAPPINESS IS HAVING YOUR DOG COME HOME!
AMEN!
SCHULZ

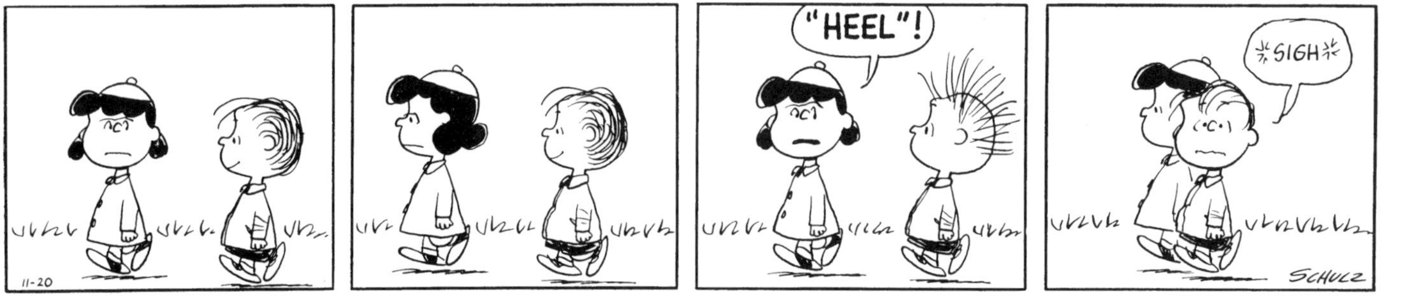
11-20
"HEEL"!
SIGH
SCHULZ

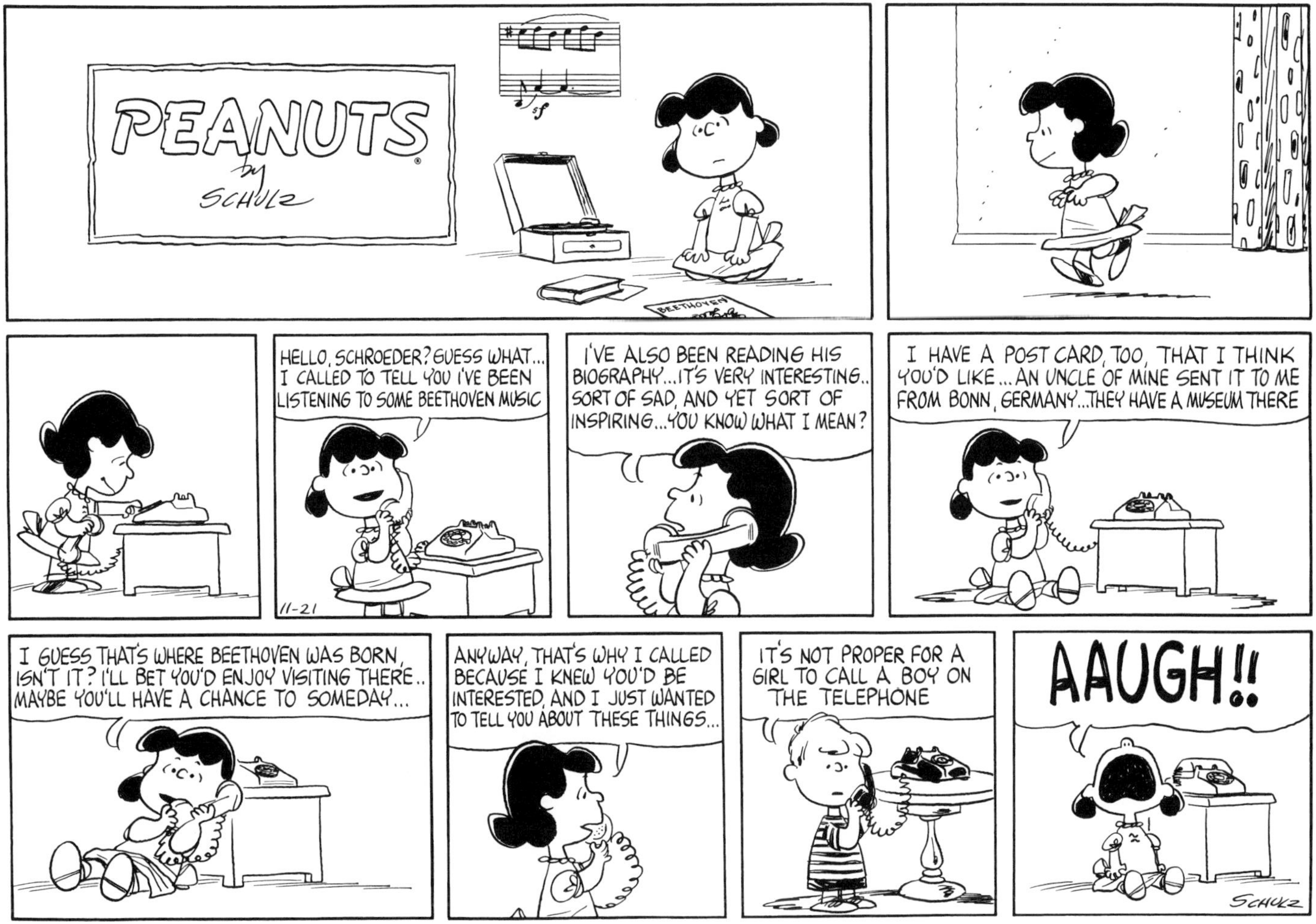
PEANUTS
by
SCHULZ
sf
BEETHOVEN
HELLO, SCHROEDER? GUESS WHAT... I CALLED TO TELL YOU I'VE BEEN LISTENING TO SOME BEETHOVEN MUSIC
11-21
I'VE ALSO BEEN READING HIS BIOGRAPHY...IT'S VERY INTERESTING.. SORT OF SAD, AND YET SORT OF INSPIRING...YOU KNOW WHAT I MEAN?
I HAVE A POST CARD, TOO, THAT I THINK YOU'D LIKE... AN UNCLE OF MINE SENT IT TO ME FROM BONN, GERMANY...THEY HAVE A MUSEUM THERE
I GUESS THAT'S WHERE BEETHOVEN WAS BORN, ISN'T IT? I'LL BET YOU'D ENJOY VISITING THERE.. MAYBE YOU'LL HAVE A CHANCE TO SOMEDAY...
ANYWAY, THAT'S WHY I CALLED BECAUSE I KNEW YOU'D BE INTERESTED, AND I JUST WANTED TO TELL YOU ABOUT THESE THINGS...
IT'S NOT PROPER FOR A GIRL TO CALL A BOY ON THE TELEPHONE
AAUGH!!
SCHULZ

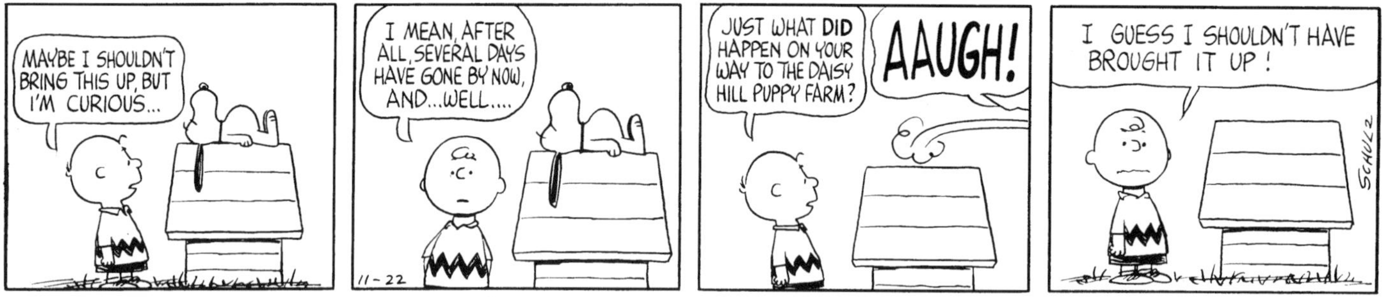
MAYBE I SHOULDN'T BRING THIS UP, BUT I'M CURIOUS...
I MEAN, AFTER ALL, SEVERAL DAYS HAVE GONE BY NOW, AND...WELL....
11-22
JUST WHAT DID HAPPEN ON YOUR WAY TO THE DAISY HILL PUPPY FARM?
AAUGH!
I GUESS I SHOULDN'T HAVE BROUGHT IT UP!
SCHULZ

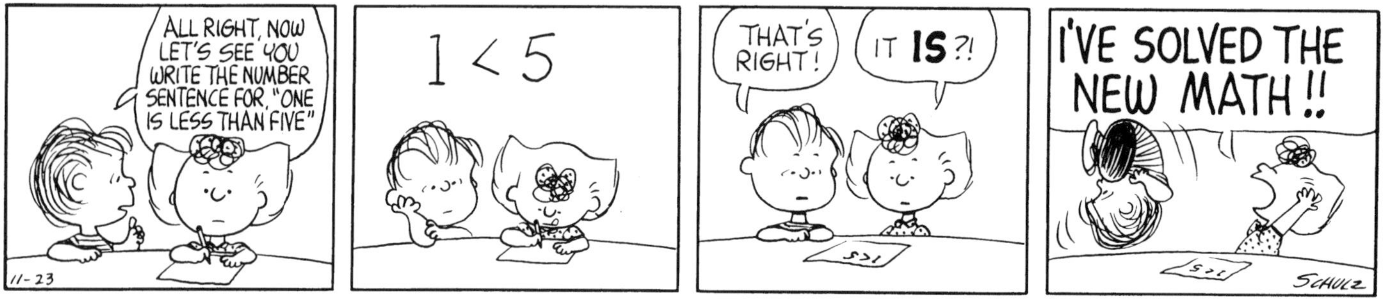
ALL RIGHT, NOW LET'S SEE YOU WRITE THE NUMBER SENTENCE FOR, "ONE IS LESS THAN FIVE"
11-23
1 < 5
THAT'S RIGHT!
IT IS?!
I'VE SOLVED THE NEW MATH!!
SCHULZ

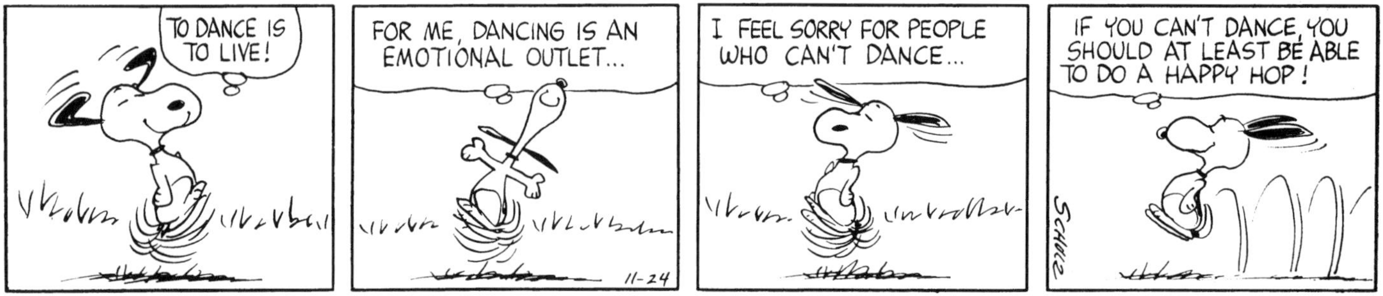
TO DANCE IS TO LIVE!
FOR ME, DANCING IS AN EMOTIONAL OUTLET...
11-24
I FEEL SORRY FOR PEOPLE WHO CAN'T DANCE...
IF YOU CAN'T DANCE, YOU SHOULD AT LEAST BE ABLE TO DO A HAPPY HOP!
SCHULZ

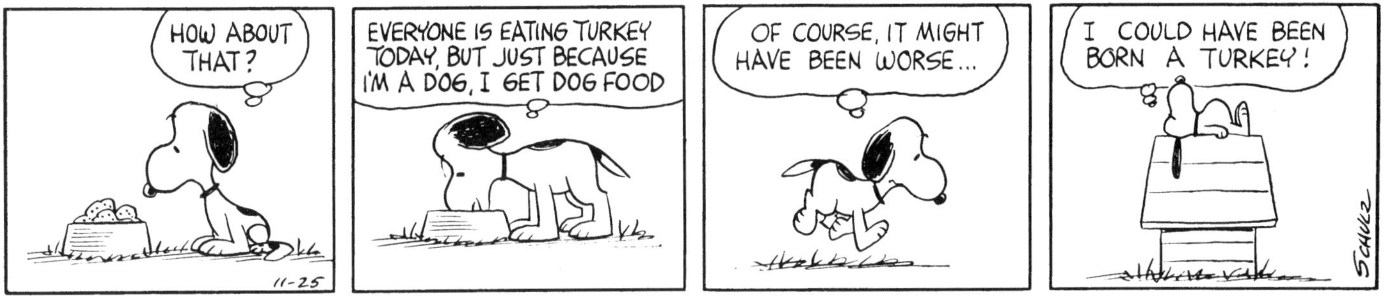
HOW ABOUT THAT?
11-25
EVERYONE IS EATING TURKEY TODAY, BUT JUST BECAUSE I'M A DOG, I GET DOG FOOD
OF COURSE, IT MIGHT HAVE BEEN WORSE...
I COULD HAVE BEEN BORN A TURKEY!
SCHULZ

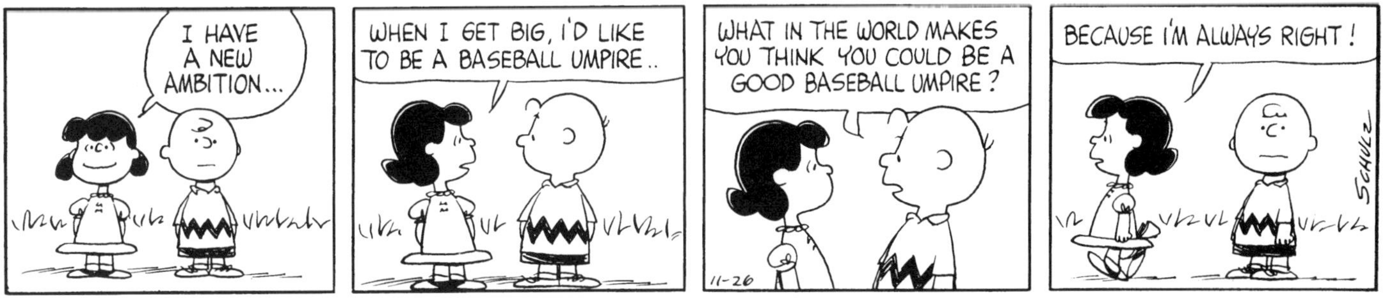
I HAVE A NEW AMBITION...
WHEN I GET BIG, I'D LIKE TO BE A BASEBALL UMPIRE..
WHAT IN THE WORLD MAKES YOU THINK YOU COULD BE A GOOD BASEBALL UMPIRE?
11-26
BECAUSE I'M ALWAYS RIGHT!
SCHULZ

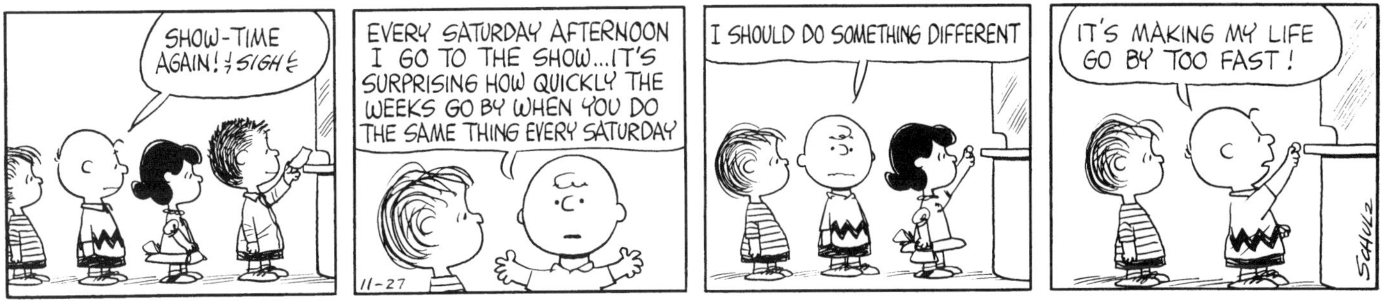
SHOW-TIME AGAIN! SIGH
EVERY SATURDAY AFTERNOON I GO TO THE SHOW...IT'S SURPRISING HOW QUICKLY THE WEEKS GO BY WHEN YOU DO THE SAME THING EVERY SATURDAY
11-27
I SHOULD DO SOMETHING DIFFERENT
IT'S MAKING MY LIFE GO BY TOO FAST!
SCHULZ

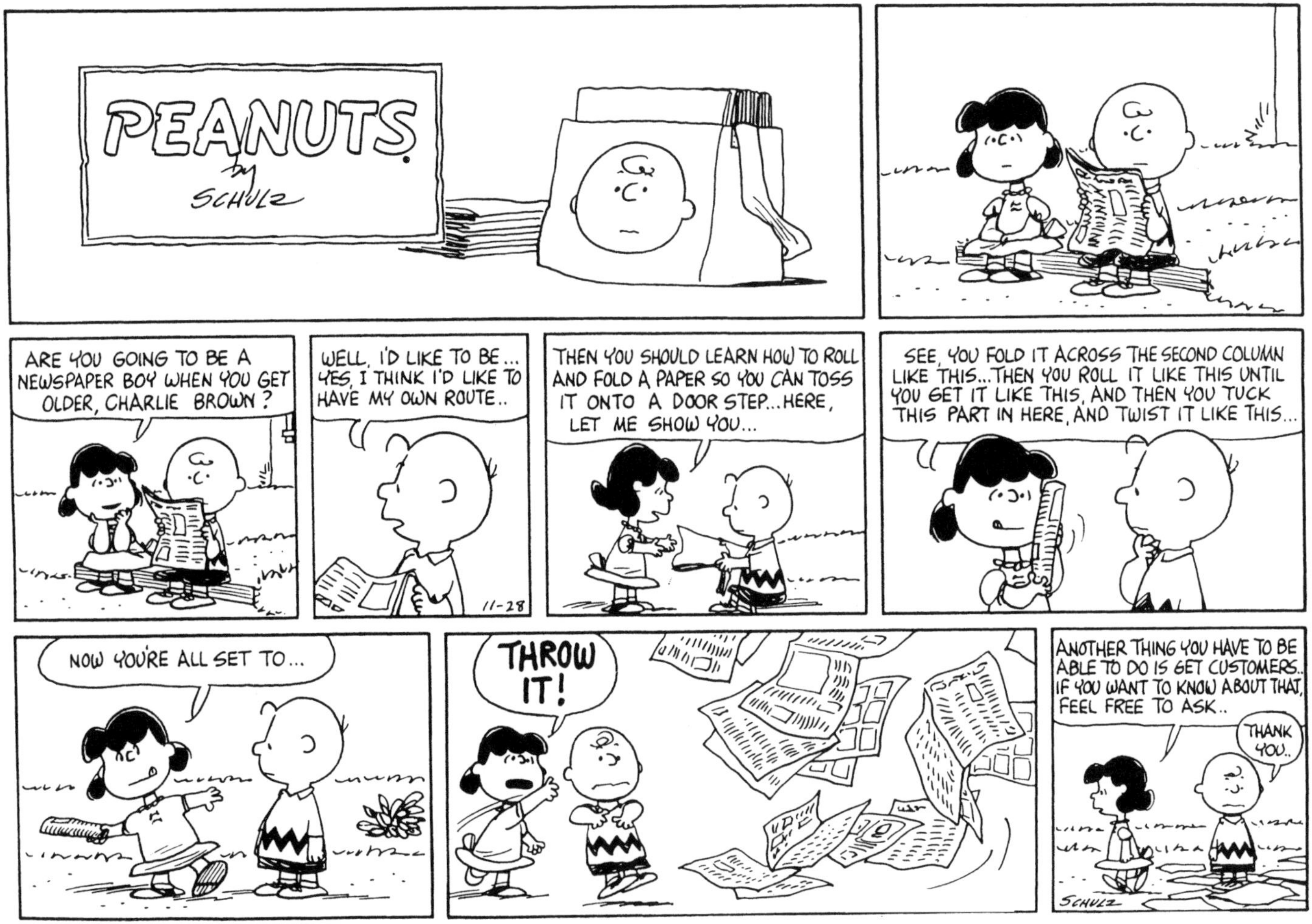
PEANUTS
by SCHULZ
ARE YOU GOING TO BE A NEWSPAPER BOY WHEN YOU GET OLDER, CHARLIE BROWN?
WELL, I'D LIKE TO BE... YES, I THINK I'D LIKE TO HAVE MY OWN ROUTE..
11-28
THEN YOU SHOULD LEARN HOW TO ROLL AND FOLD A PAPER SO YOU CAN TOSS IT ONTO A DOOR STEP...HERE, LET ME SHOW YOU...
SEE, YOU FOLD IT ACROSS THE SECOND COLUMN LIKE THIS...THEN YOU ROLL IT LIKE THIS UNTIL YOU GET IT LIKE THIS, AND THEN YOU TUCK THIS PART IN HERE, AND TWIST IT LIKE THIS...
NOW YOU'RE ALL SET TO...
THROW IT!
ANOTHER THING YOU HAVE TO BE ABLE TO DO IS GET CUSTOMERS.. IF YOU WANT TO KNOW ABOUT THAT, FEEL FREE TO ASK..
THANK YOU..
SCHULZ

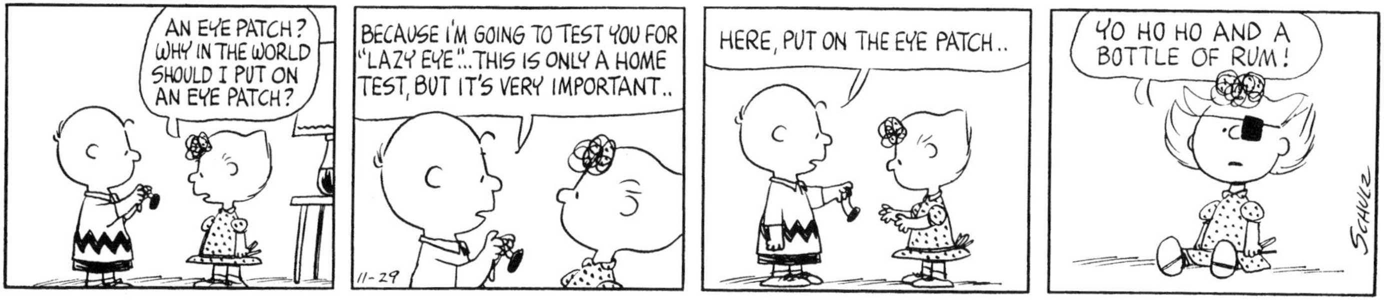
AN EYE PATCH? WHY IN THE WORLD SHOULD I PUT ON AN EYE PATCH?
BECAUSE I'M GOING TO TEST YOU FOR "LAZY EYE"... THIS IS ONLY A HOME TEST, BUT IT'S VERY IMPORTANT..
11-29
HERE, PUT ON THE EYE PATCH..
YO HO HO AND A BOTTLE OF RUM!
SCHULZ

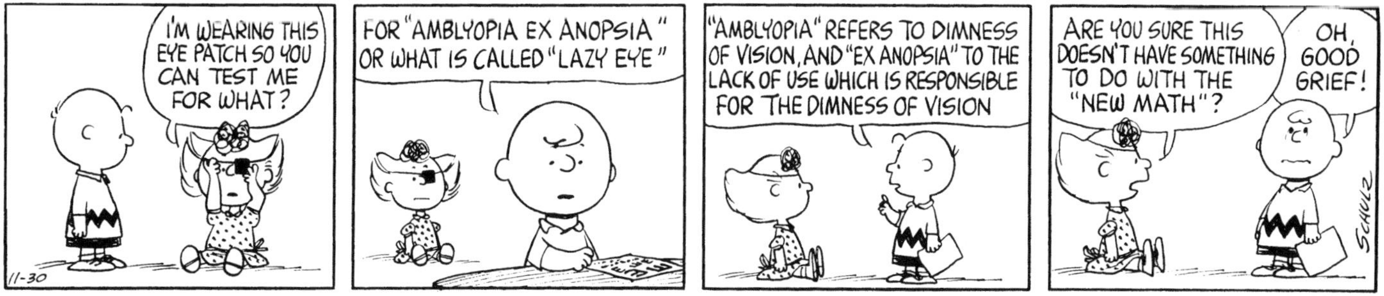
I'M WEARING THIS EYE PATCH SO YOU CAN TEST ME FOR WHAT?
11-30
FOR "AMBLYOPIA EX ANOPSIA" OR WHAT IS CALLED "LAZY EYE"
"AMBLYOPIA" REFERS TO DIMNESS OF VISION, AND "EX ANOPSIA" TO THE LACK OF USE WHICH IS RESPONSIBLE FOR THE DIMNESS OF VISION
ARE YOU SURE THIS DOESN'T HAVE SOMETHING TO DO WITH THE "NEW MATH"?
OH, GOOD GRIEF!
SCHULZ

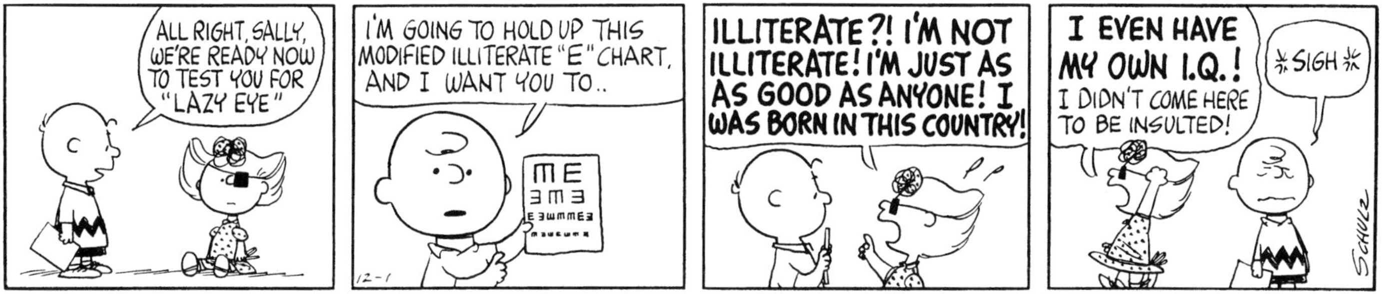
ALL RIGHT, SALLY, WE'RE READY NOW TO TEST YOU FOR "LAZY EYE"
I'M GOING TO HOLD UP THIS MODIFIED ILLITERATE "E" CHART, AND I WANT YOU TO..
12-1
ILLITERATE?! I'M NOT ILLITERATE! I'M JUST AS AS GOOD AS ANYONE! I WAS BORN IN THIS COUNTRY!
I EVEN HAVE MY OWN I.Q.! I DIDN'T COME HERE TO BE INSULTED!
SIGH
SCHULZ

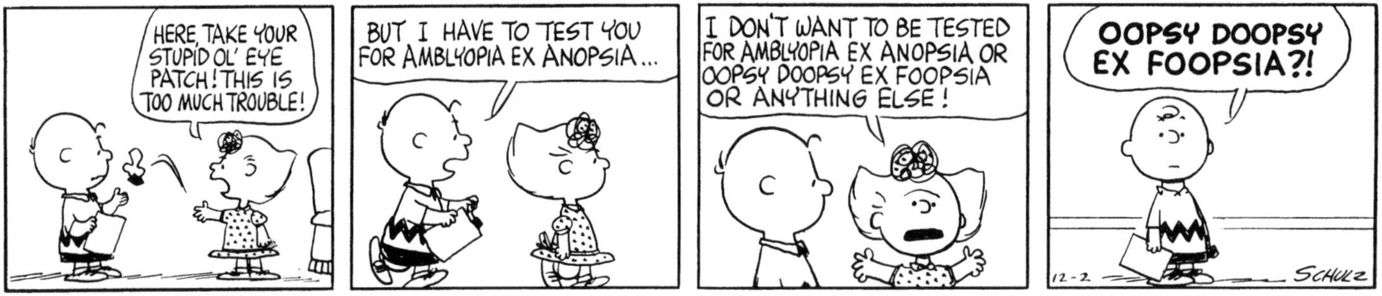
HERE, TAKE YOUR STUPID OL' EYE PATCH! THIS IS TOO MUCH TROUBLE!
BUT I HAVE TO TEST YOU FOR AMBLYOPIA EX ANOPSIA...
I DON'T WANT TO BE TESTED FOR AMBLYOPIA EX ANOPSIA OR OOPSY DOOPSY EX FOOPSIA OR ANYTHING ELSE!
OOPSY DOOPSY EX FOOPSIA?!
12-2
SCHULZ

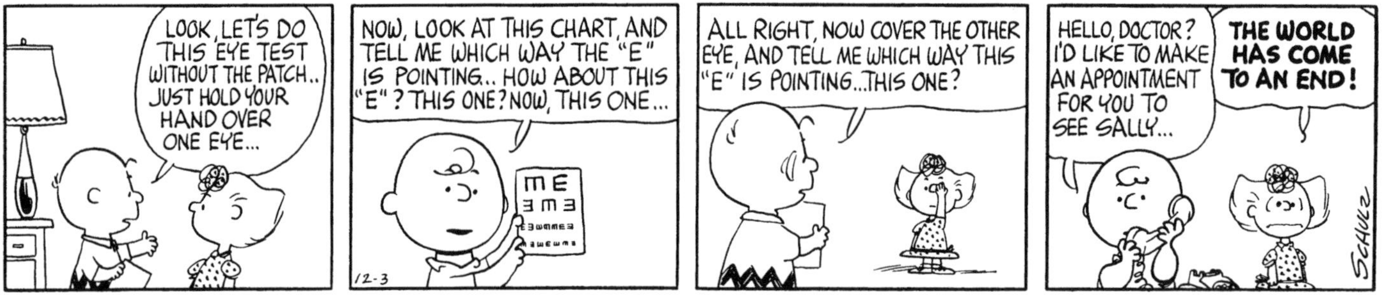
LOOK, LET'S DO THIS EYE TEST WITHOUT THE PATCH.. JUST HOLD YOUR HAND OVER ONE EYE...
NOW, LOOK AT THIS CHART, AND TELL ME WHICH WAY THE "E" IS POINTING.. HOW ABOUT THIS "E"? THIS ONE? NOW, THIS ONE...
12-3
ALL RIGHT, NOW COVER THE OTHER EYE, AND TELL ME WHICH WAY THIS "E" IS POINTING...THIS ONE?
HELLO, DOCTOR? I'D LIKE TO MAKE AN APPOINTMENT FOR YOU TO SEE SALLY...
THE WORLD HAS COME TO AN END!
SCHULZ

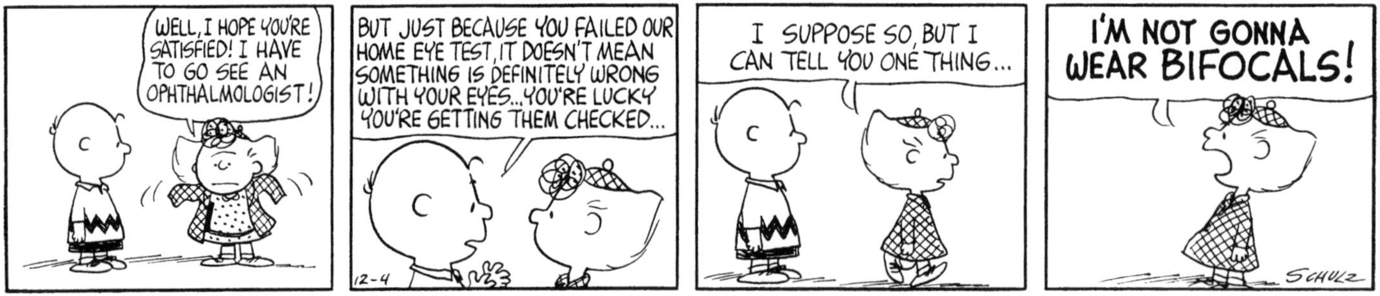
WELL, I HOPE YOU'RE SATISFIED! I HAVE TO GO SEE AN OPHTHALMOLOGIST!
BUT JUST BECAUSE YOU FAILED OUR HOME EYE TEST, IT DOESN'T MEAN SOMETHING IS DEFINITELY WRONG WITH YOUR EYES...YOU'RE LUCKY YOU'RE GETTING THEM CHECKED...
12-4
I SUPPOSE SO, BUT I CAN TELL YOU ONE THING...
I'M NOT GONNA WEAR BIFOCALS!
SCHULZ

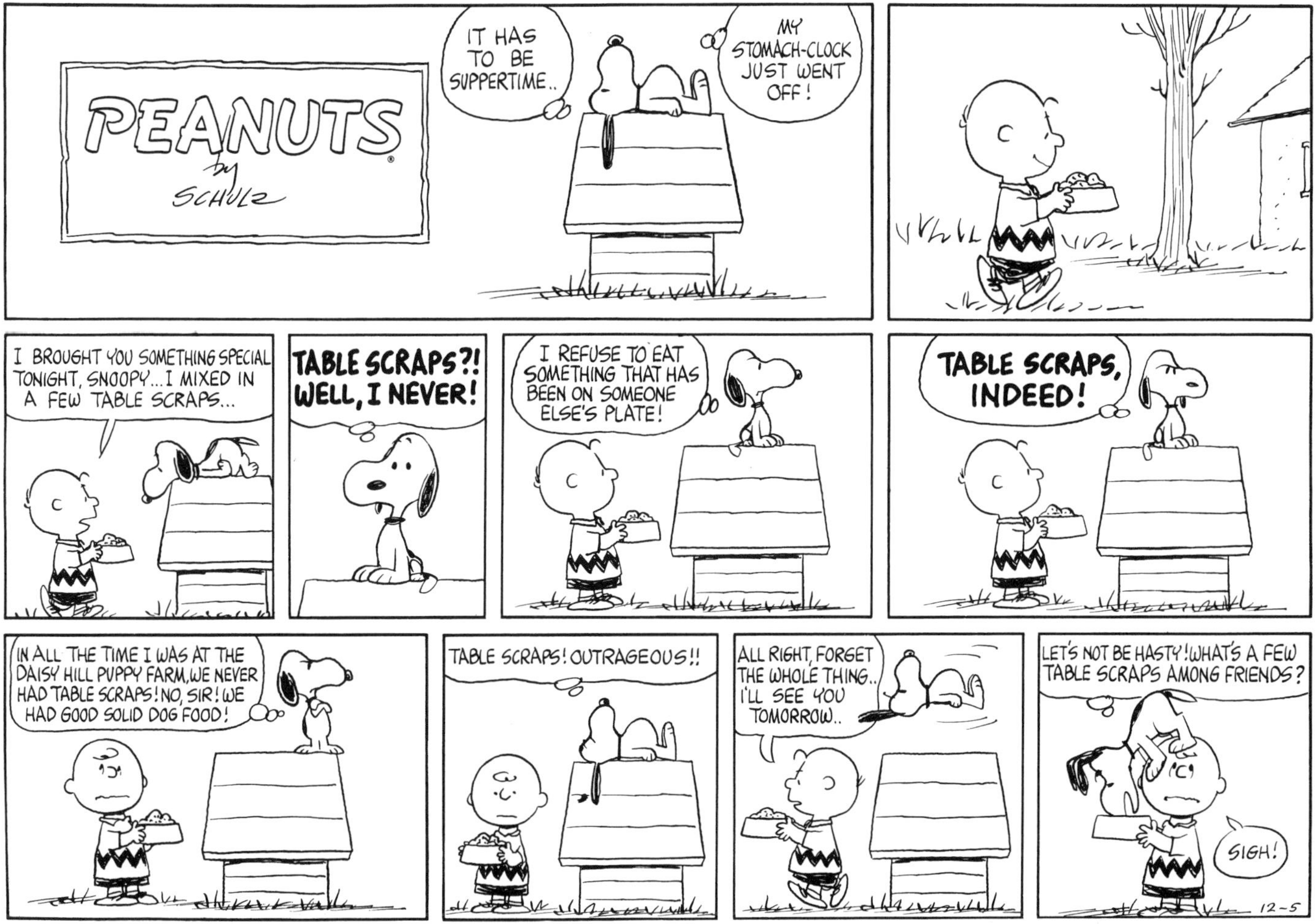
PEANUTS
by SCHULZ
IT HAS TO BE SUPPERTIME..
MY STOMACH-CLOCK JUST WENT OFF!
I BROUGHT YOU SOMETHING SPECIAL TONIGHT, SNOOPY...I MIXED IN A FEW TABLE SCRAPS...
TABLE SCRAPS?! WELL, I NEVER!
I REFUSE TO EAT SOMETHING THAT HAS BEEN ON SOMEONE ELSE'S PLATE!
TABLE SCRAPS, INDEED!
IN ALL THE TIME I WAS AT THE DAISY HILL PUPPY FARM, WE NEVER HAD TABLE SCRAPS! NO, SIR! WE HAD GOOD SOLID DOG FOOD!
TABLE SCRAPS! OUTRAGEOUS!!
ALL RIGHT, FORGET THE WHOLE THING.. I'LL SEE YOU TOMORROW..
LET'S NOT BE HASTY! WHAT'S A FEW TABLE SCRAPS AMONG FRIENDS?
SIGH!
12-5

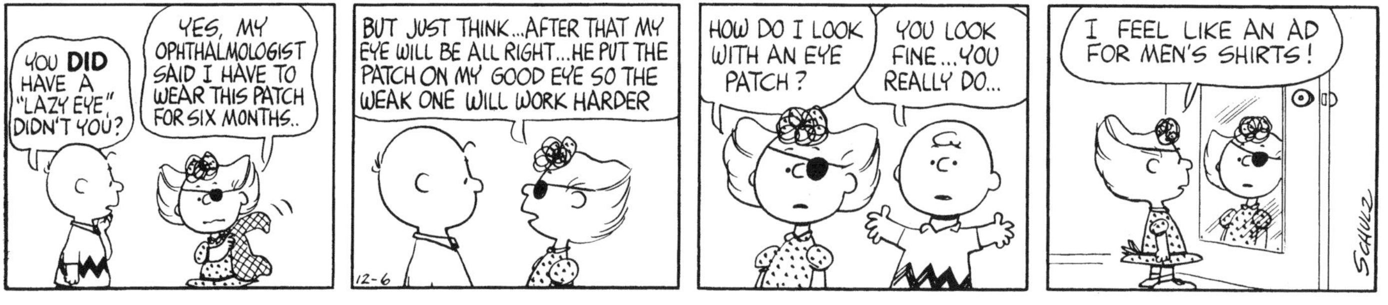
YOU **DID** HAVE A "LAZY EYE" DIDN'T YOU?
YES, MY OPHTHALMOLOGIST SAID I HAVE TO WEAR THIS PATCH FOR SIX MONTHS..
BUT JUST THINK...AFTER THAT MY EYE WILL BE ALL RIGHT...HE PUT THE PATCH ON MY GOOD EYE SO THE WEAK ONE WILL WORK HARDER
12-6
HOW DO I LOOK WITH AN EYE PATCH?
YOU LOOK FINE...YOU REALLY DO...
I FEEL LIKE AN AD FOR MEN'S SHIRTS!
SCHULZ

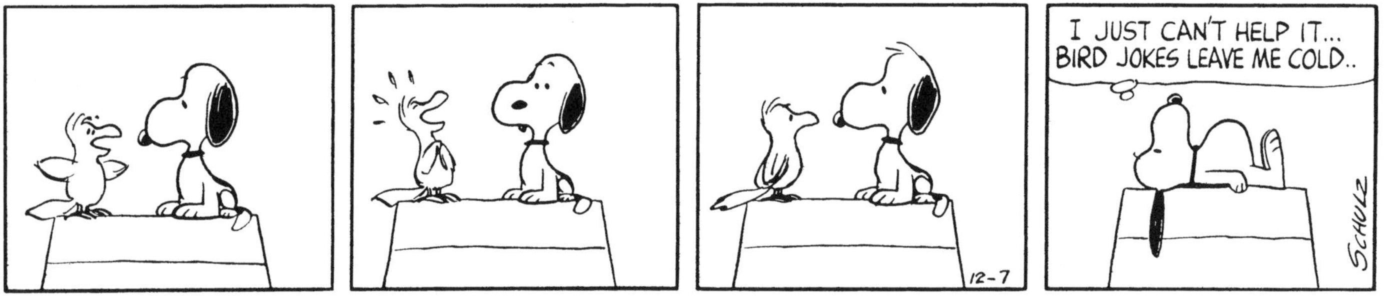
12-7
I JUST CAN'T HELP IT... BIRD JOKES LEAVE ME COLD..
SCHULZ

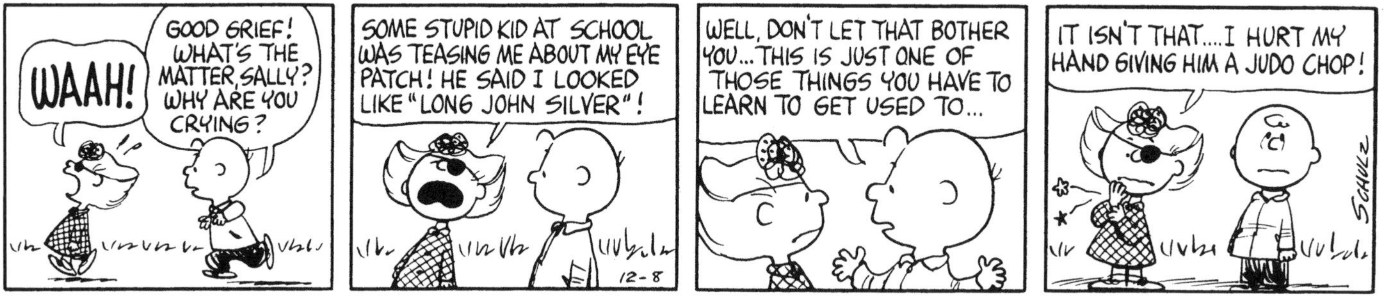
WAAH!
GOOD GRIEF! WHAT'S THE MATTER, SALLY? WHY ARE YOU CRYING?
SOME STUPID KID AT SCHOOL WAS TEASING ME ABOUT MY EYE PATCH! HE SAID I LOOKED LIKE "LONG JOHN SILVER"!
12-8
WELL, DON'T LET THAT BOTHER YOU...THIS IS JUST ONE OF THOSE THINGS YOU HAVE TO LEARN TO GET USED TO...
IT ISN'T THAT....I HURT MY HAND GIVING HIM A JUDO CHOP!
SCHULZ

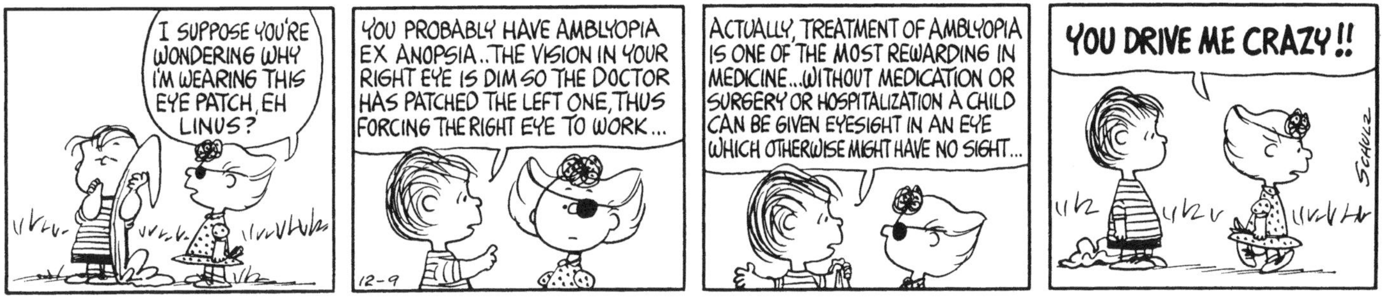
I SUPPOSE YOU'RE WONDERING WHY I'M WEARING THIS EYE PATCH, EH LINUS?
YOU PROBABLY HAVE AMBLYOPIA EX ANOPSIA..THE VISION IN YOUR RIGHT EYE IS DIM SO THE DOCTOR HAS PATCHED THE LEFT ONE, THUS FORCING THE RIGHT EYE TO WORK...
12-9
ACTUALLY, TREATMENT OF AMBLYOPIA IS ONE OF THE MOST REWARDING IN MEDICINE...WITHOUT MEDICATION OR SURGERY OR HOSPITALIZATION A CHILD CAN BE GIVEN EYESIGHT IN AN EYE WHICH OTHERWISE MIGHT HAVE NO SIGHT...
YOU DRIVE ME CRAZY!!
SCHULZ

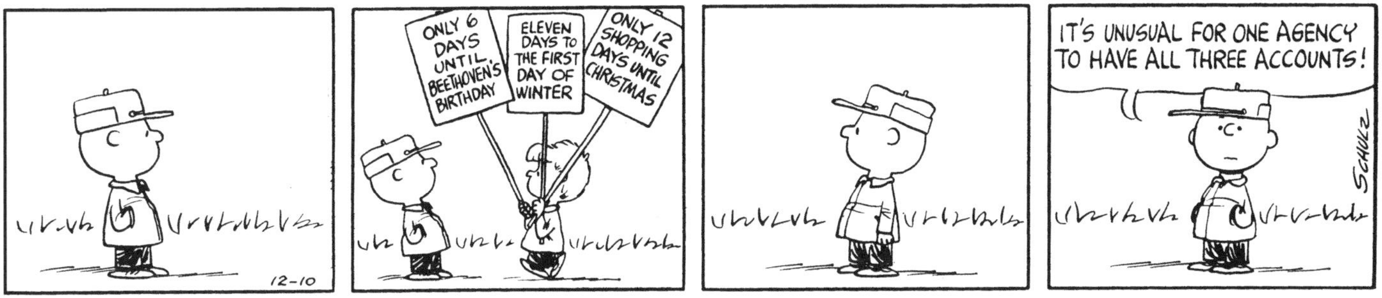
12-10
ONLY 6 DAYS UNTIL BEETHOVEN'S BIRTHDAY
ELEVEN DAYS TO THE FIRST DAY OF WINTER
ONLY 12 SHOPPING DAYS UNTIL CHRISTMAS
IT'S UNUSUAL FOR ONE AGENCY TO HAVE ALL THREE ACCOUNTS!
SCHULZ

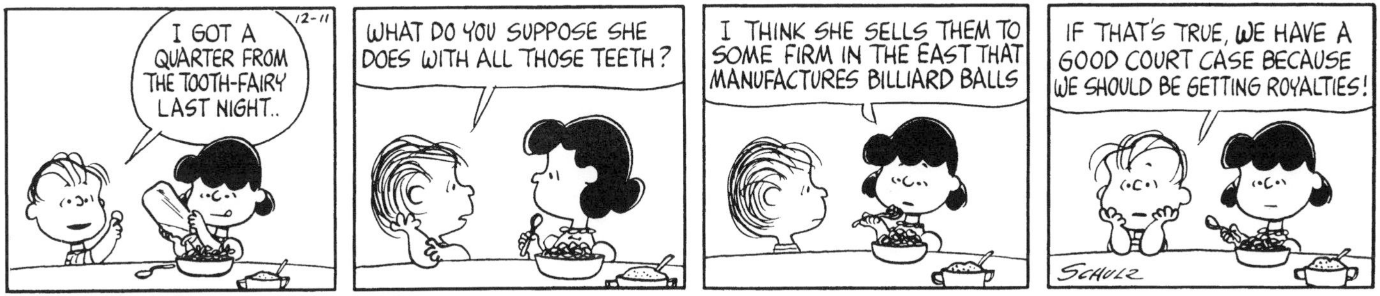
12-11
I GOT A QUARTER FROM THE TOOTH-FAIRY LAST NIGHT..
WHAT DO YOU SUPPOSE SHE DOES WITH ALL THOSE TEETH?
I THINK SHE SELLS THEM TO SOME FIRM IN THE EAST THAT MANUFACTURES BILLIARD BALLS
IF THAT'S TRUE, WE HAVE A GOOD COURT CASE BECAUSE WE SHOULD BE GETTING ROYALTIES!
SCHULZ

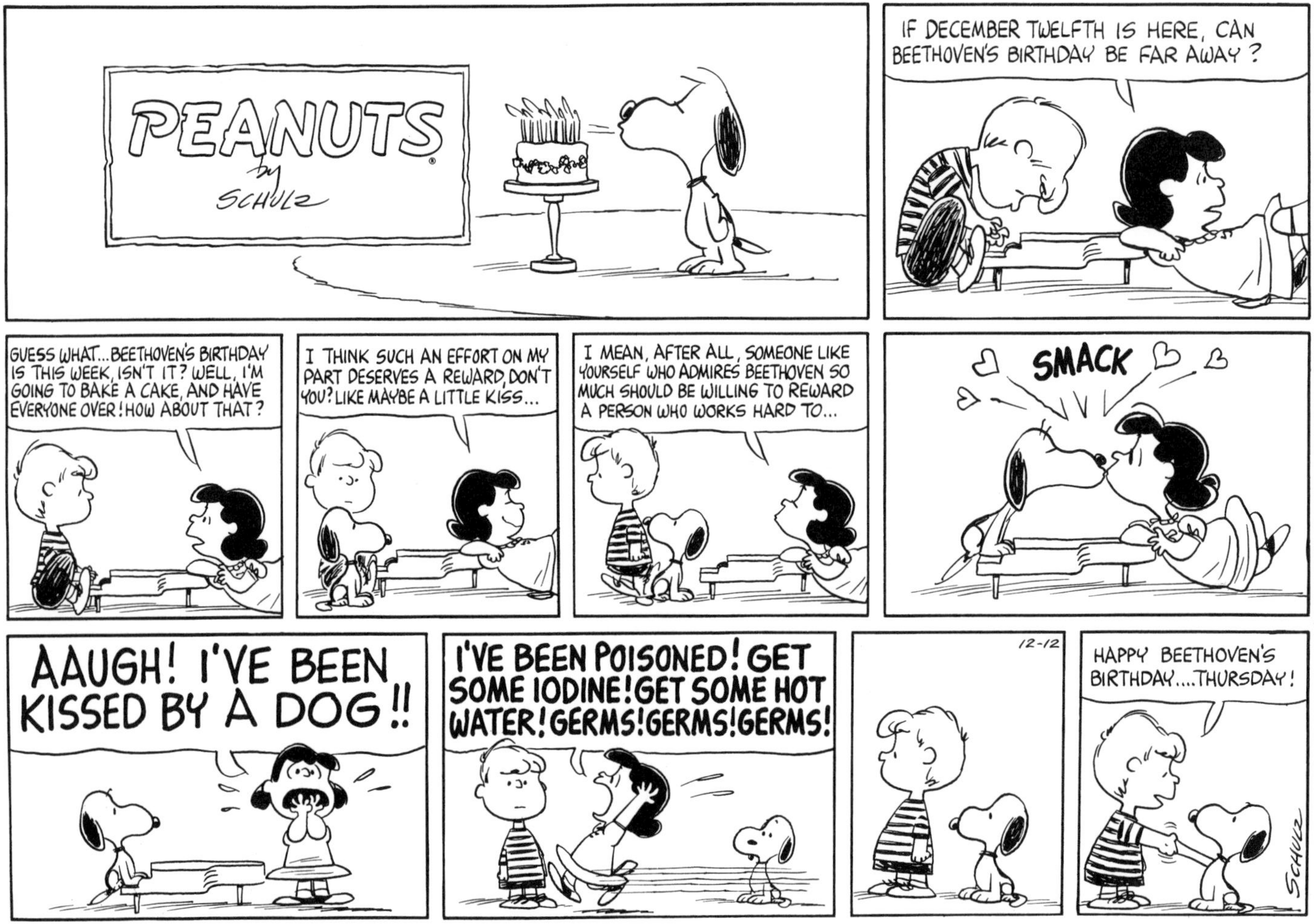
PEANUTS
by SCHULZ
IF DECEMBER TWELFTH IS HERE, CAN BEETHOVEN'S BIRTHDAY BE FAR AWAY?
GUESS WHAT...BEETHOVEN'S BIRTHDAY IS THIS WEEK, ISN'T IT? WELL, I'M GOING TO BAKE A CAKE, AND HAVE EVERYONE OVER! HOW ABOUT THAT?
I THINK SUCH AN EFFORT ON MY PART DESERVES A REWARD, DON'T YOU? LIKE MAYBE A LITTLE KISS...
I MEAN, AFTER ALL, SOMEONE LIKE YOURSELF WHO ADMIRES BEETHOVEN SO MUCH SHOULD BE WILLING TO REWARD A PERSON WHO WORKS HARD TO...
SMACK
AAUGH! I'VE BEEN KISSED BY A DOG!!
I'VE BEEN POISONED! GET SOME IODINE! GET SOME HOT WATER! GERMS! GERMS! GERMS!
12-12
HAPPY BEETHOVEN'S BIRTHDAY....THURSDAY!
SCHULZ

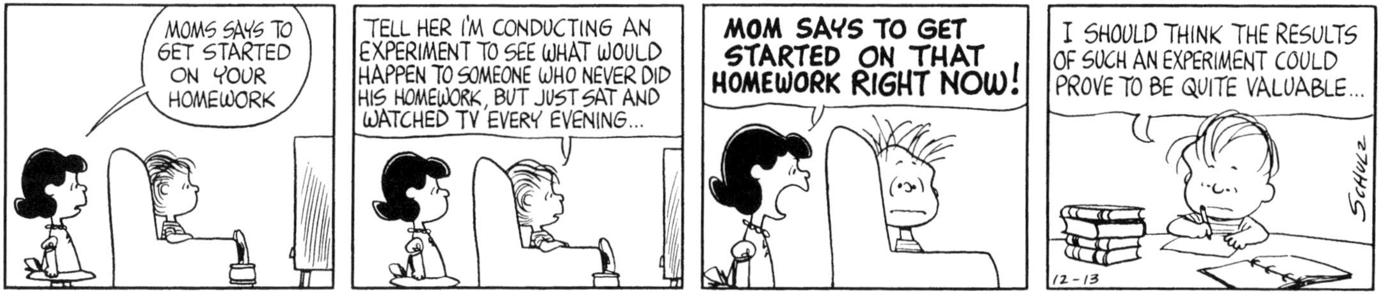
MOMS SAYS TO GET STARTED ON YOUR HOMEWORK
TELL HER I'M CONDUCTING AN EXPERIMENT TO SEE WHAT WOULD HAPPEN TO SOMEONE WHO NEVER DID HIS HOMEWORK, BUT JUST SAT AND WATCHED TV EVERY EVENING...
MOM SAYS TO GET STARTED ON THAT HOMEWORK RIGHT NOW!
I SHOULD THINK THE RESULTS OF SUCH AN EXPERIMENT COULD PROVE TO BE QUITE VALUABLE...
SCHULZ
12-13

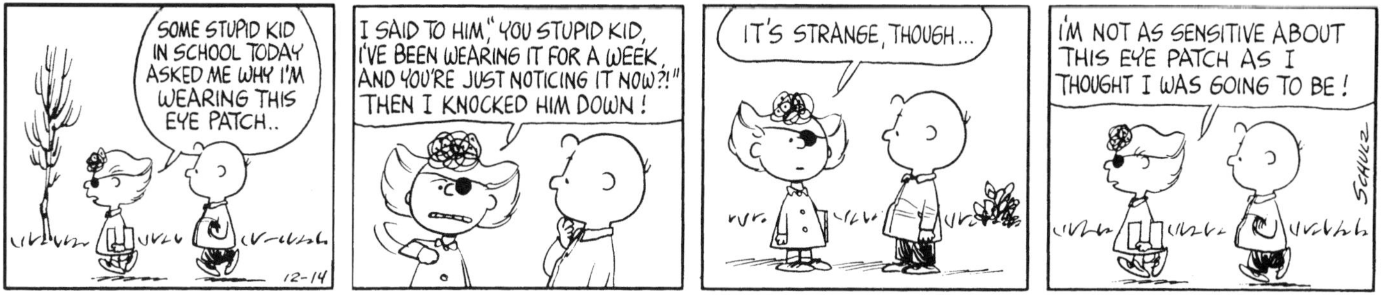
SOME STUPID KID IN SCHOOL TODAY ASKED ME WHY I'M WEARING THIS EYE PATCH..
12-14
I SAID TO HIM, "YOU STUPID KID, I'VE BEEN WEARING IT FOR A WEEK, AND YOU'RE JUST NOTICING IT NOW?!" THEN I KNOCKED HIM DOWN!
IT'S STRANGE, THOUGH...
I'M NOT AS SENSITIVE ABOUT THIS EYE PATCH AS I THOUGHT I WAS GOING TO BE!
SCHULZ

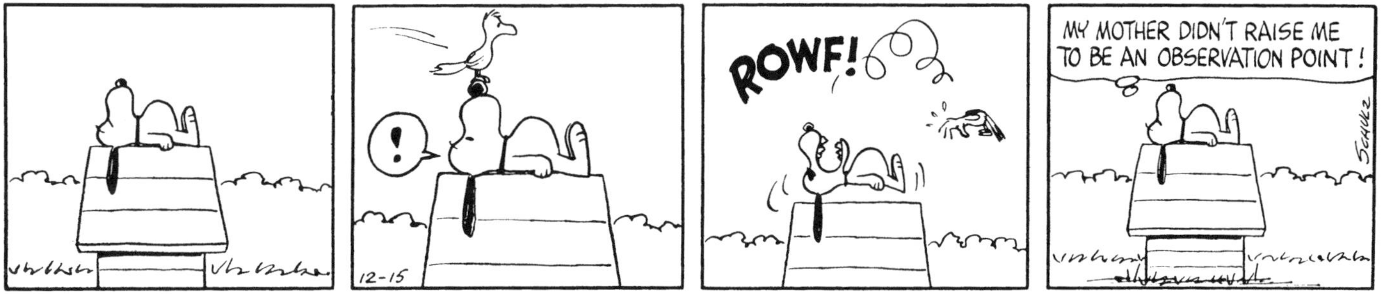
!
12-15
ROWF!
MY MOTHER DIDN'T RAISE ME TO BE AN OBSERVATION POINT!
SCHULZ

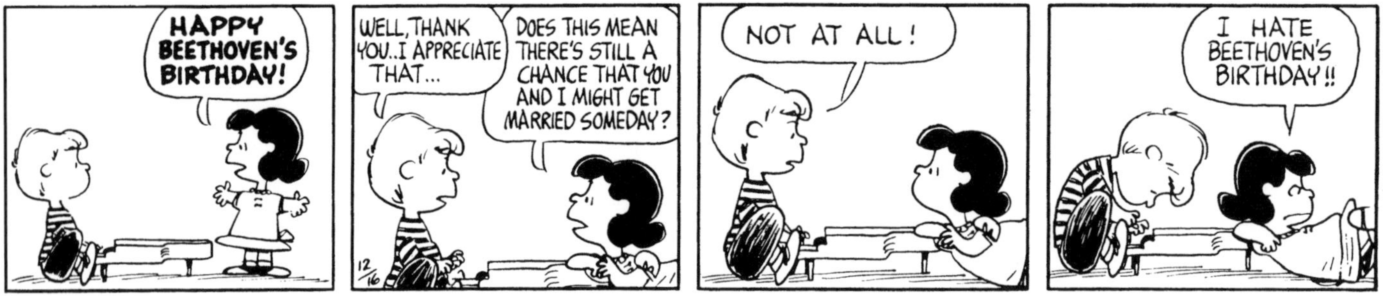
HAPPY BEETHOVEN'S BIRTHDAY!
WELL, THANK YOU..I APPRECIATE THAT...
DOES THIS MEAN THERE'S STILL A CHANCE THAT YOU AND I MIGHT GET MARRIED SOMEDAY?
NOT AT ALL!
I HATE BEETHOVEN'S BIRTHDAY!!

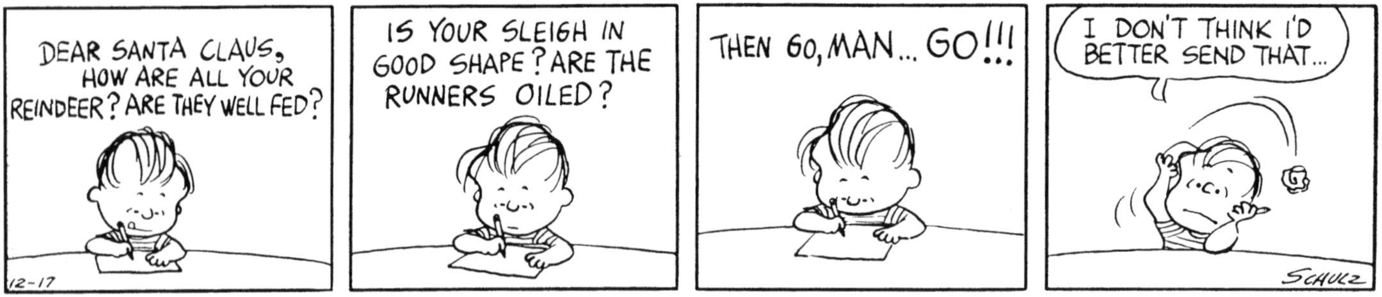
DEAR SANTA CLAUS, HOW ARE ALL YOUR REINDEER? ARE THEY WELL FED?
IS YOUR SLEIGH IN GOOD SHAPE? ARE THE RUNNERS OILED?
THEN GO, MAN... GO!!!
I DON'T THINK I'D BETTER SEND THAT...

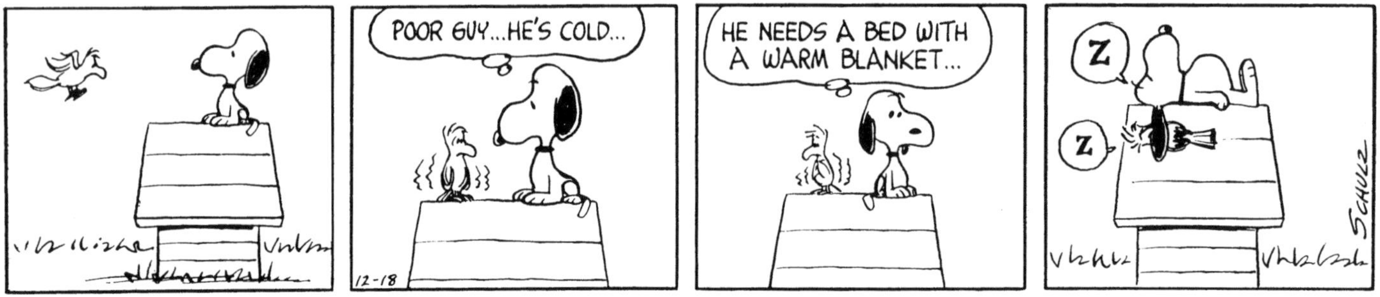
POOR GUY...HE'S COLD...
HE NEEDS A BED WITH A WARM BLANKET...
Z
Z

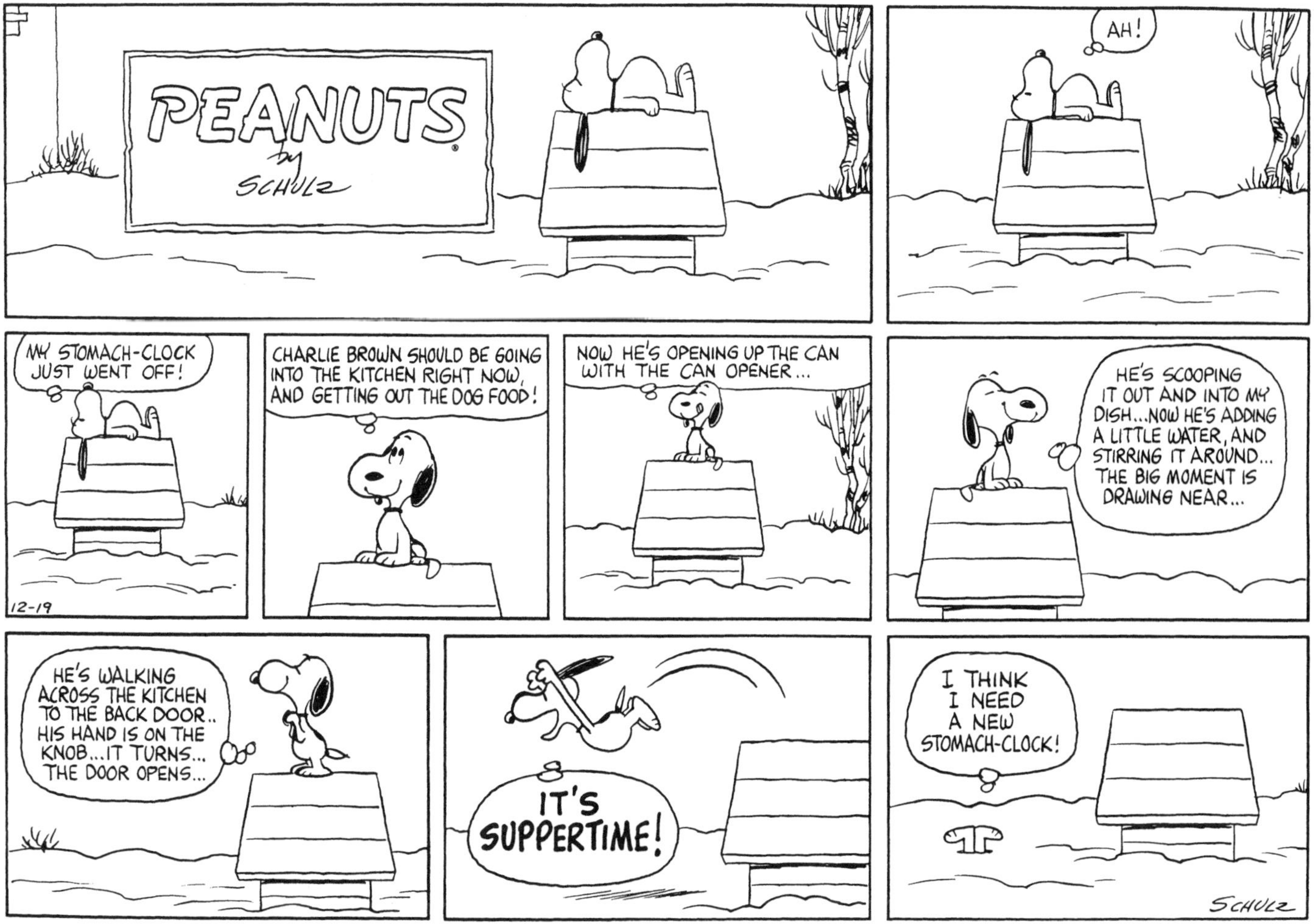
PEANUTS
by SCHULZ
AH!
MY STOMACH-CLOCK JUST WENT OFF!
12-19
CHARLIE BROWN SHOULD BE GOING INTO THE KITCHEN RIGHT NOW, AND GETTING OUT THE DOG FOOD!
NOW HE'S OPENING UP THE CAN WITH THE CAN OPENER...
HE'S SCOOPING IT OUT AND INTO MY DISH...NOW HE'S ADDING A LITTLE WATER, AND STIRRING IT AROUND... THE BIG MOMENT IS DRAWING NEAR...
HE'S WALKING ACROSS THE KITCHEN TO THE BACK DOOR.. HIS HAND IS ON THE KNOB...IT TURNS... THE DOOR OPENS...
IT'S SUPPERTIME!
I THINK I NEED A NEW STOMACH-CLOCK!
SCHULZ

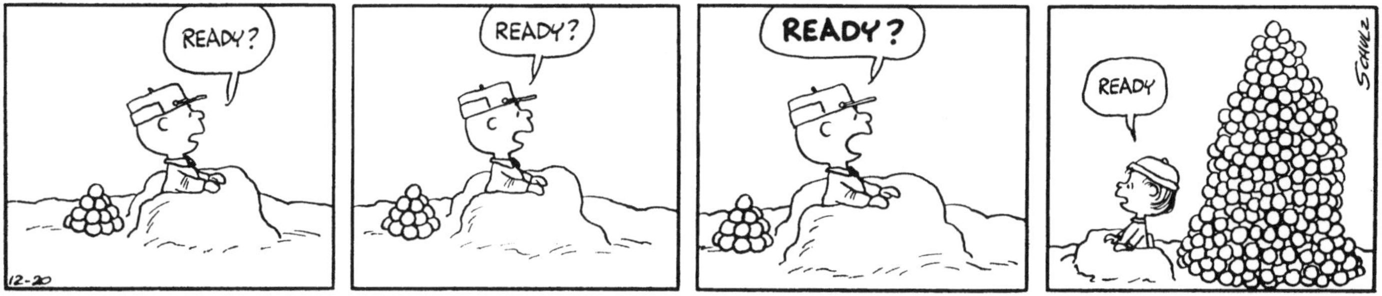
READY?
12-20
READY?
READY?
READY
SCHULZ

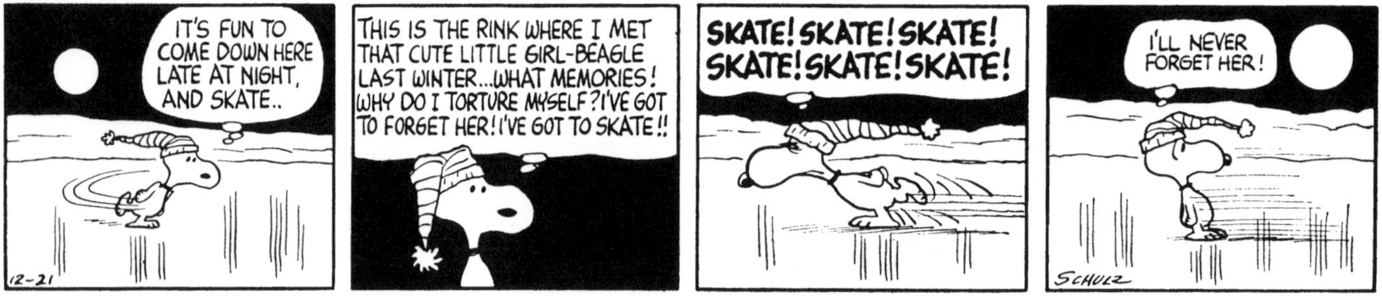
IT'S FUN TO COME DOWN HERE LATE AT NIGHT, AND SKATE..
12-21
THIS IS THE RINK WHERE I MET THAT CUTE LITTLE GIRL-BEAGLE LAST WINTER...WHAT MEMORIES! WHY DO I TORTURE MYSELF? I'VE GOT TO FORGET HER! I'VE GOT TO SKATE!!
SKATE! SKATE! SKATE! SKATE! SKATE! SKATE!
I'LL NEVER FORGET HER!
SCHULZ

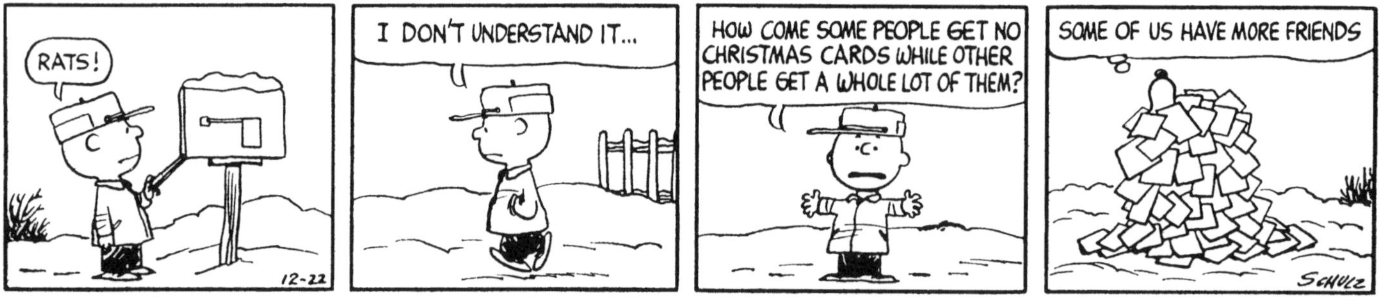
RATS!
12-22
I DON'T UNDERSTAND IT...
HOW COME SOME PEOPLE GET NO CHRISTMAS CARDS WHILE OTHER PEOPLE GET A WHOLE LOT OF THEM?
SOME OF US HAVE MORE FRIENDS
SCHULZ

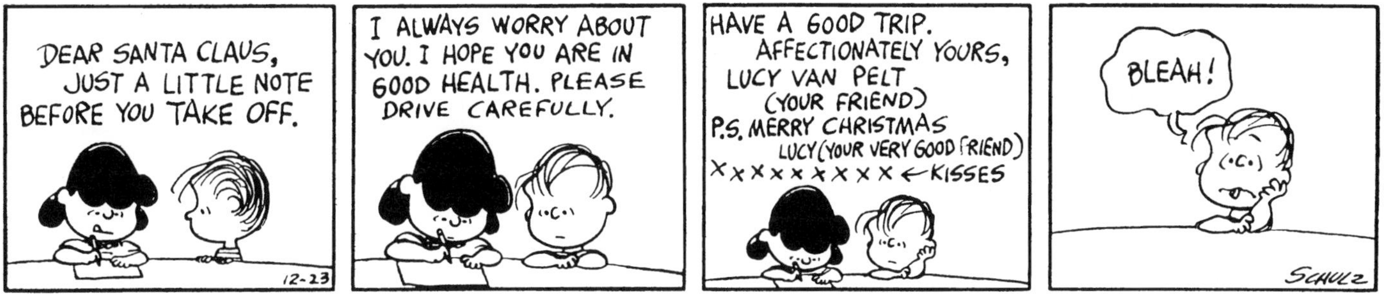
DEAR SANTA CLAUS,
JUST A LITTLE NOTE BEFORE YOU TAKE OFF.
12-23
I ALWAYS WORRY ABOUT YOU. I HOPE YOU ARE IN GOOD HEALTH. PLEASE DRIVE CAREFULLY.
HAVE A GOOD TRIP.
AFFECTIONATELY YOURS,
LUCY VAN PELT
(YOUR FRIEND)
P.S. MERRY CHRISTMAS
LUCY (YOUR VERY GOOD FRIEND)
XXXXXXXXXX ← KISSES
BLEAH!
SCHULZ

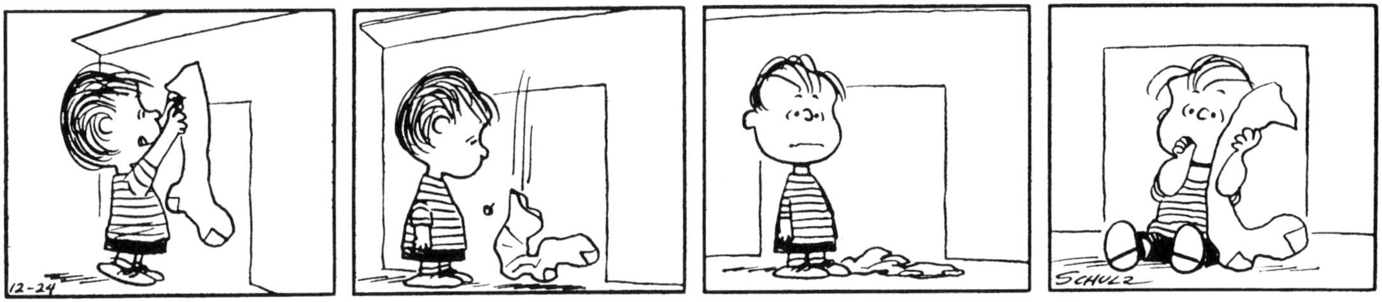
12-24
SCHULZ

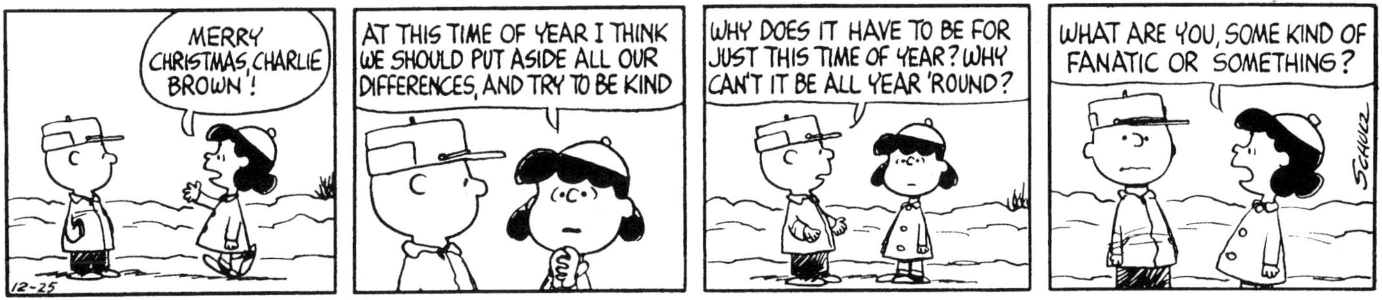
MERRY CHRISTMAS, CHARLIE BROWN!
12-25
AT THIS TIME OF YEAR I THINK WE SHOULD PUT ASIDE ALL OUR DIFFERENCES, AND TRY TO BE KIND
WHY DOES IT HAVE TO BE FOR JUST THIS TIME OF YEAR? WHY CAN'T IT BE ALL YEAR 'ROUND?
WHAT ARE YOU, SOME KIND OF FANATIC OR SOMETHING?
SCHULZ

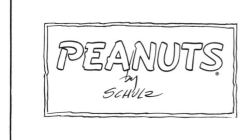

PSYCHIATRIC
HELP 5¢

HOLIDAY
RATES

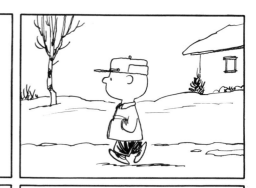

PSYCHIATRIC
HELP 5¢

HOLIDAY
RATES

12-26

WELL, WHAT
DO YOU WANT?!

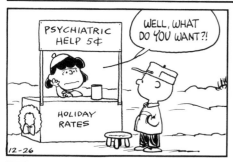

WHO, ME? WHY..AH...WHY, NOTHING MUCH
REALLY...I JUST FELT A LITTLE BLUE, AND...

HOLIDAY
RATES

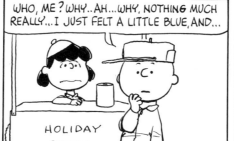

PUT YOUR STUPID NICKEL IN HERE AND
SIT DOWN! AND STOP LOOKING SO DEPRESSED!

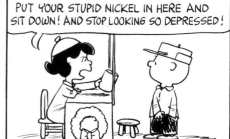

YOU JUST BETTER GET HOLD OF YOURSELF
BEFORE IT'S TOO LATE! THERE'S NO SENSE
IN GOING AROUND MOPING ALL THE TIME!

HOLIDAY
RATES

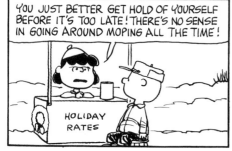

NOW, GET OUT OF HERE
AND LEAVE ME ALONE!

HOLIDAY
RATES

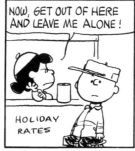

BOY, WHAT A CRABBY
PSYCHIATRIST!

CHIATRIC
HELP 5¢

HOLIDAY
RATES

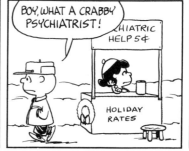

WELL, WE DOCTORS HAVE OUR
POST-CHRISTMAS LETDOWNS
TOO, YOU KNOW !!!

HOLIDAY
RATES

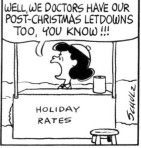

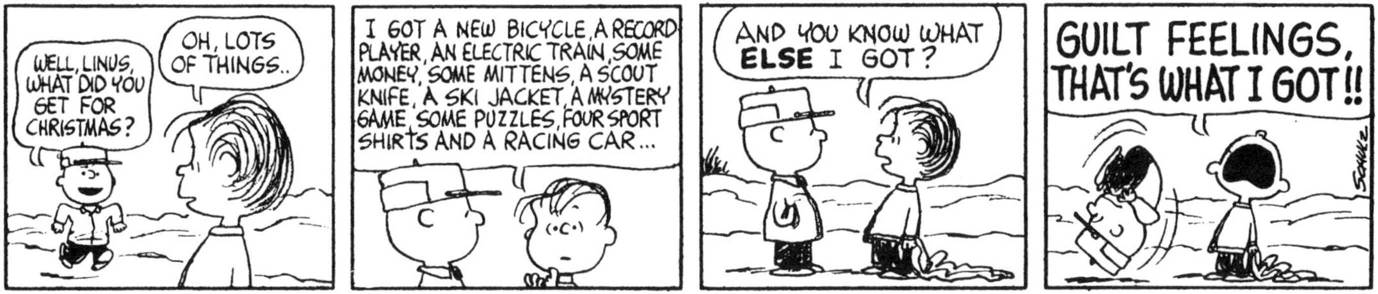
WELL, LINUS, WHAT DID YOU GET FOR CHRISTMAS?
OH, LOTS OF THINGS..
I GOT A NEW BICYCLE, A RECORD PLAYER, AN ELECTRIC TRAIN, SOME MONEY, SOME MITTENS, A SCOUT KNIFE, A SKI JACKET, A MYSTERY GAME, SOME PUZZLES, FOUR SPORT SHIRTS AND A RACING CAR...
AND YOU KNOW WHAT ELSE I GOT?
GUILT FEELINGS, THAT'S WHAT I GOT!!
SCHULZ

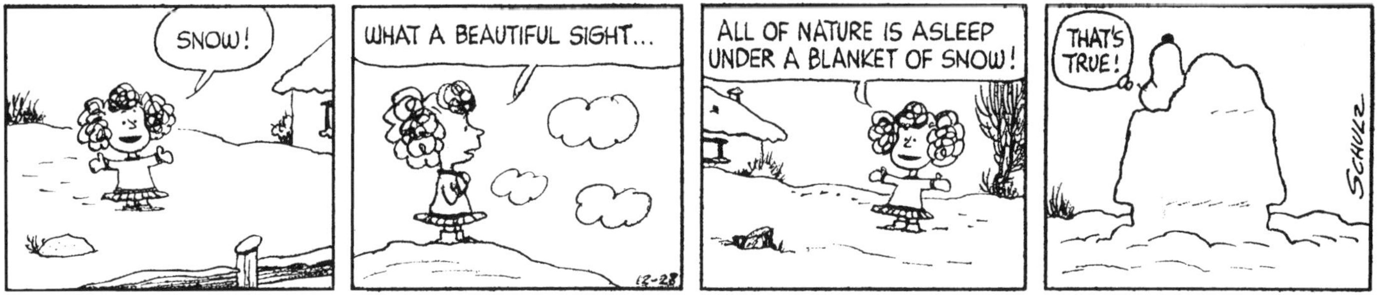
SNOW!
WHAT A BEAUTIFUL SIGHT...
12-28
ALL OF NATURE IS ASLEEP UNDER A BLANKET OF SNOW!
THAT'S TRUE!
SCHULZ

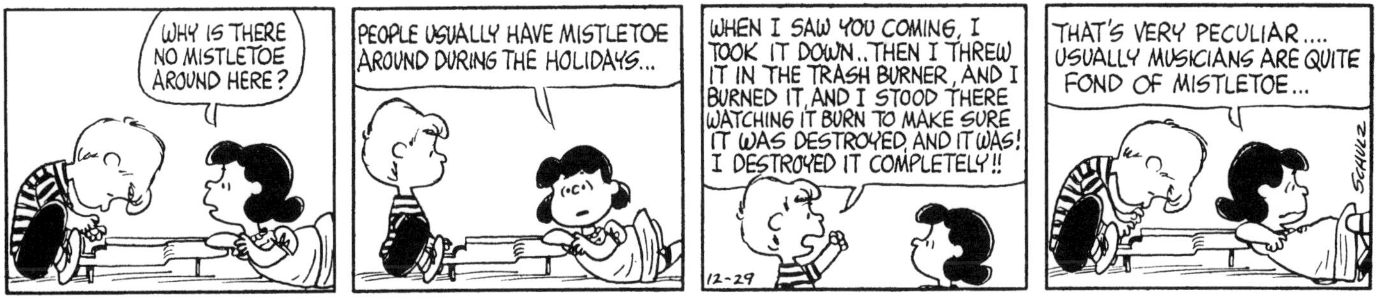
WHY IS THERE NO MISTLETOE AROUND HERE?
PEOPLE USUALLY HAVE MISTLETOE AROUND DURING THE HOLIDAYS...
WHEN I SAW YOU COMING, I TOOK IT DOWN..THEN I THREW IT IN THE TRASH BURNER, AND I BURNED IT, AND I STOOD THERE WATCHING IT BURN TO MAKE SURE IT WAS DESTROYED, AND IT WAS! I DESTROYED IT COMPLETELY!!
12-29
THAT'S VERY PECULIAR.... USUALLY MUSICIANS ARE QUITE FOND OF MISTLETOE...
SCHULZ

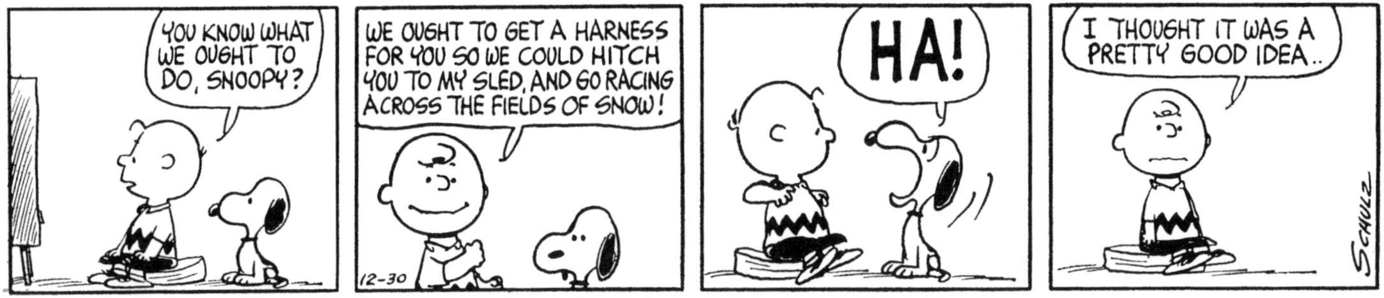
YOU KNOW WHAT WE OUGHT TO DO, SNOOPY?
WE OUGHT TO GET A HARNESS FOR YOU SO WE COULD HITCH YOU TO MY SLED, AND GO RACING ACROSS THE FIELDS OF SNOW!
HA!
I THOUGHT IT WAS A PRETTY GOOD IDEA..

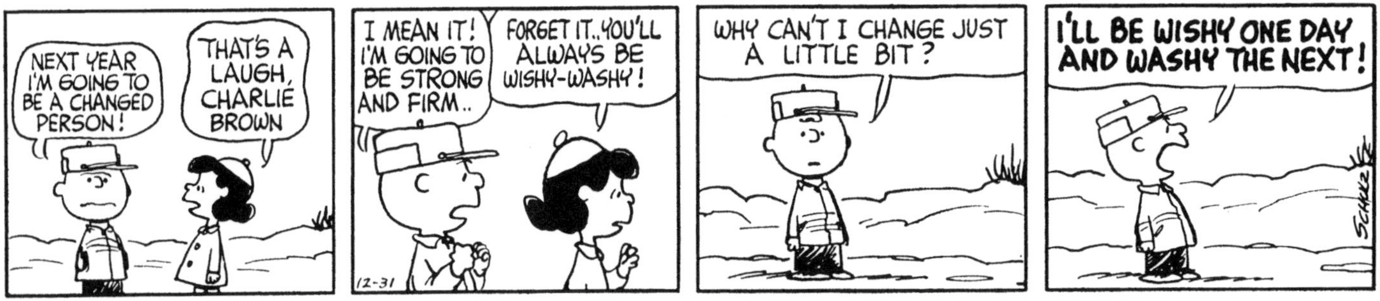
NEXT YEAR I'M GOING TO BE A CHANGED PERSON!
THAT'S A LAUGH, CHARLIE BROWN
I MEAN IT! I'M GOING TO BE STRONG AND FIRM..
FORGET IT..YOU'LL ALWAYS BE WISHY-WASHY!
WHY CAN'T I CHANGE JUST A LITTLE BIT?
I'LL BE WISHY ONE DAY AND WASHY THE NEXT!

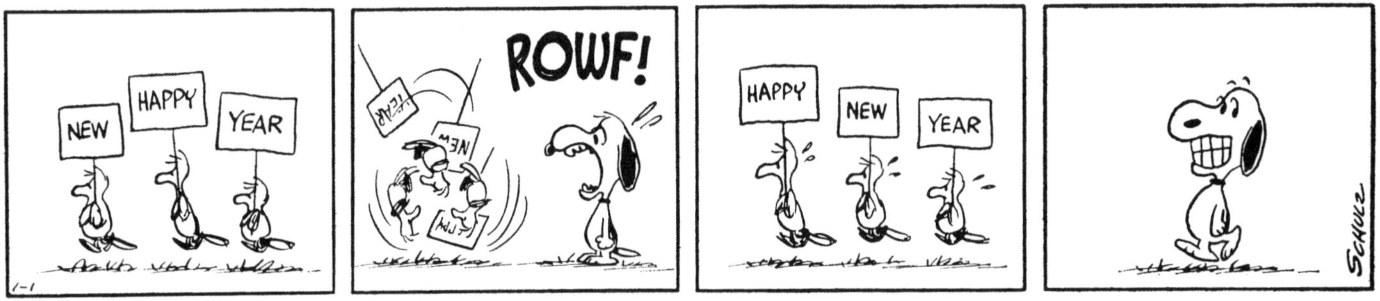
NEW
HAPPY
YEAR
ROWF!
HAPPY
NEW
YEAR

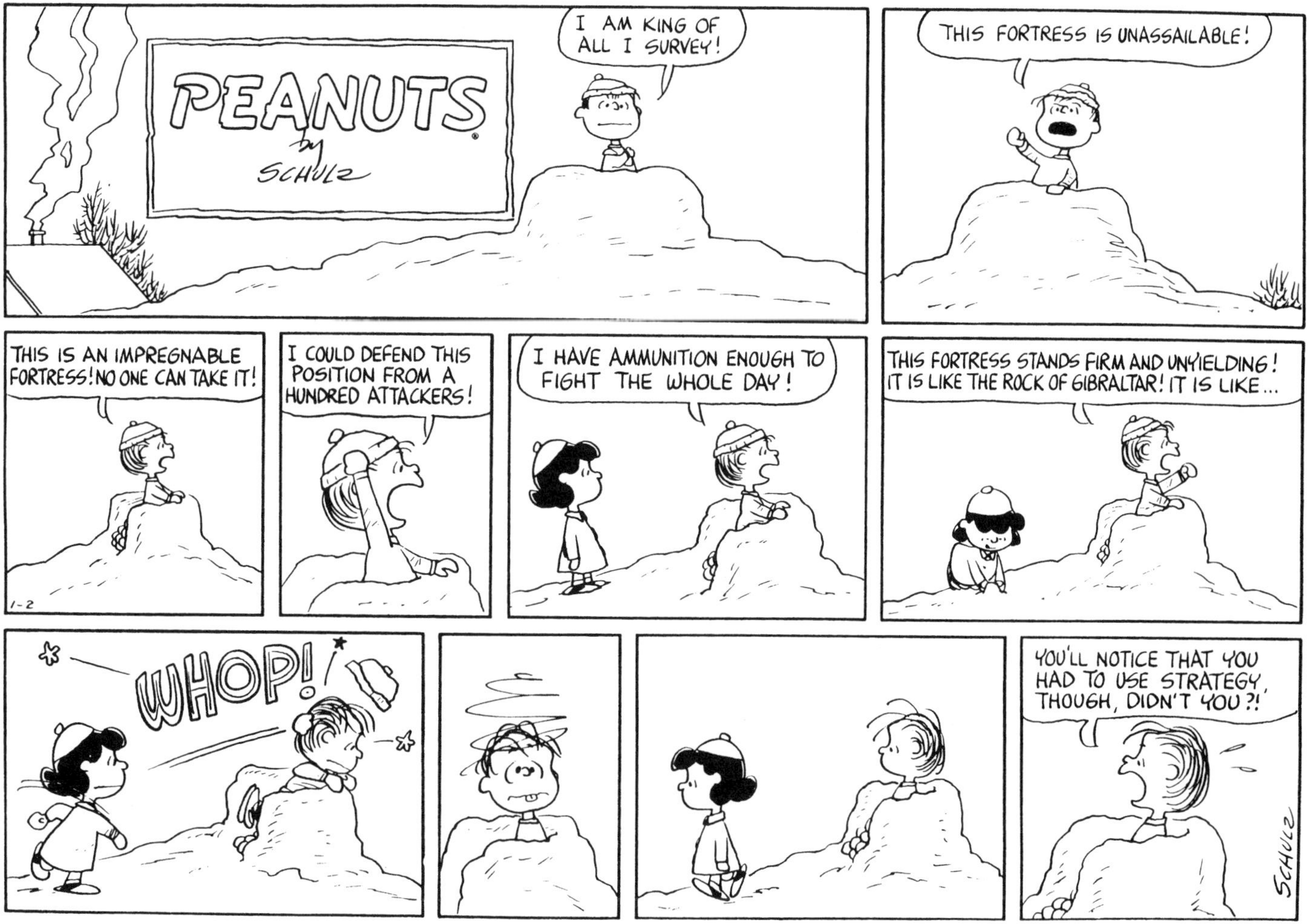
PEANUTS
by SCHULZ
I AM KING OF ALL I SURVEY!
THIS FORTRESS IS UNASSAILABLE!
THIS IS AN IMPREGNABLE FORTRESS! NO ONE CAN TAKE IT!
1-2
I COULD DEFEND THIS POSITION FROM A HUNDRED ATTACKERS!
I HAVE AMMUNITION ENOUGH TO FIGHT THE WHOLE DAY!
THIS FORTRESS STANDS FIRM AND UNYIELDING! IT IS LIKE THE ROCK OF GIBRALTAR! IT IS LIKE...
WHOP!
YOU'LL NOTICE THAT YOU HAD TO USE STRATEGY, THOUGH, DIDN'T YOU?!
SCHULZ

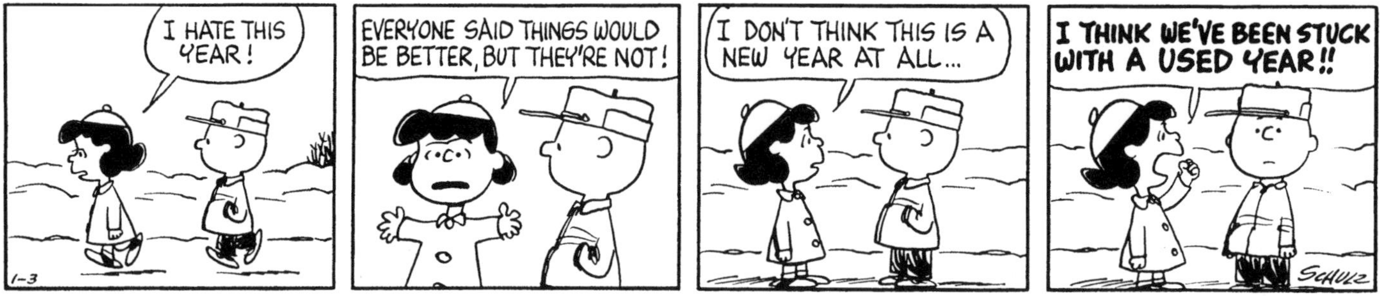
I HATE THIS YEAR!
EVERYONE SAID THINGS WOULD BE BETTER, BUT THEY'RE NOT!
I DON'T THINK THIS IS A NEW YEAR AT ALL...
I THINK WE'VE BEEN STUCK WITH A USED YEAR!!

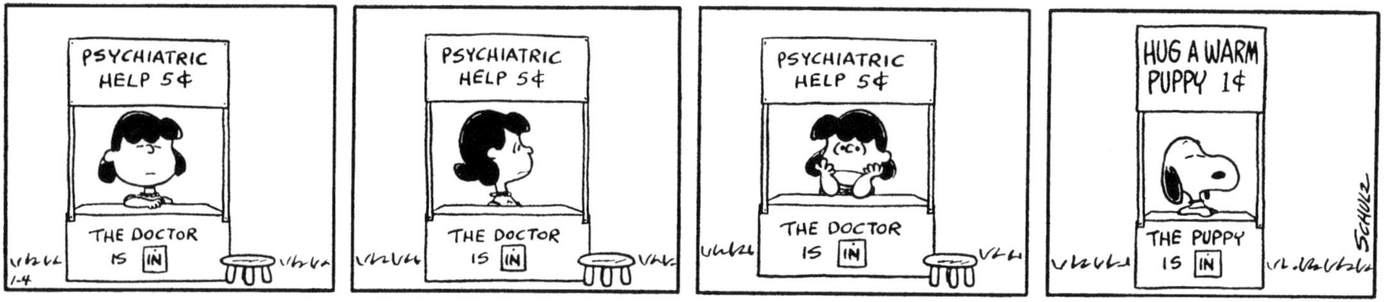
PSYCHIATRIC HELP 5¢
THE DOCTOR IS IN
PSYCHIATRIC HELP 5¢
THE DOCTOR IS IN
PSYCHIATRIC HELP 5¢
THE DOCTOR IS IN
HUG A WARM PUPPY 1¢
THE PUPPY IS IN

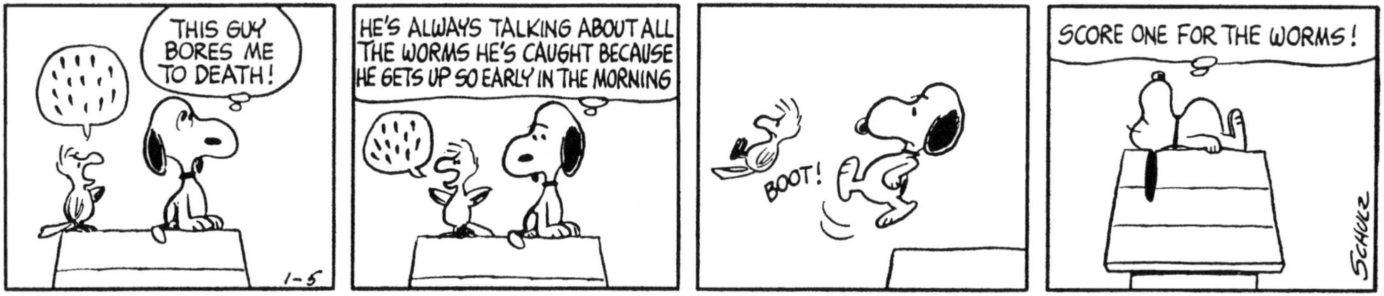
THIS GUY BORES ME TO DEATH!
HE'S ALWAYS TALKING ABOUT ALL THE WORMS HE'S CAUGHT BECAUSE HE GETS UP SO EARLY IN THE MORNING
BOOT!
SCORE ONE FOR THE WORMS!

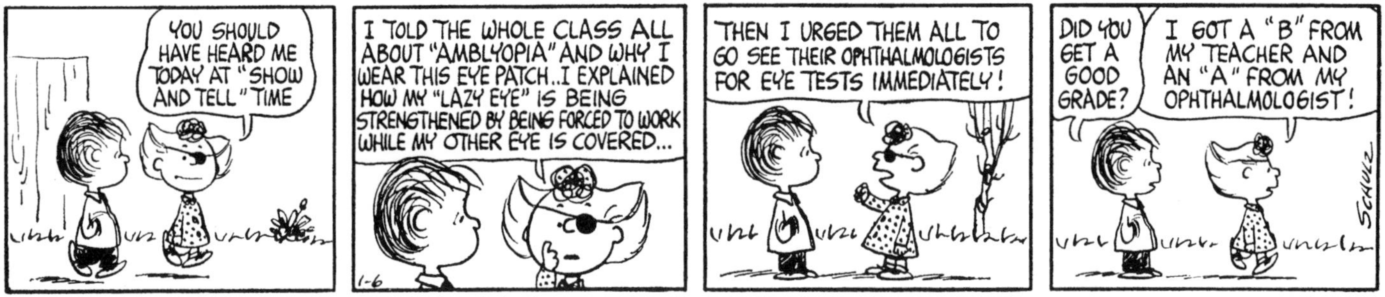
YOU SHOULD HAVE HEARD ME TODAY AT "SHOW AND TELL" TIME
I TOLD THE WHOLE CLASS ALL ABOUT "AMBLYOPIA" AND WHY I WEAR THIS EYE PATCH..I EXPLAINED HOW MY "LAZY EYE" IS BEING STRENGTHENED BY BEING FORCED TO WORK WHILE MY OTHER EYE IS COVERED...
THEN I URGED THEM ALL TO GO SEE THEIR OPHTHALMOLOGISTS FOR EYE TESTS IMMEDIATELY!
DID YOU GET A GOOD GRADE?
I GOT A "B" FROM MY TEACHER AND AN "A" FROM MY OPHTHALMOLOGIST!

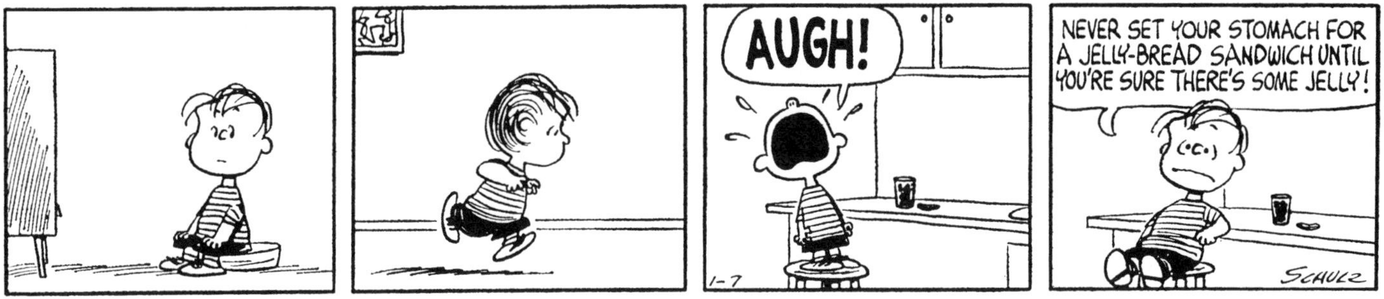
AUGH!
NEVER SET YOUR STOMACH FOR A JELLY-BREAD SANDWICH UNTIL YOU'RE SURE THERE'S SOME JELLY!

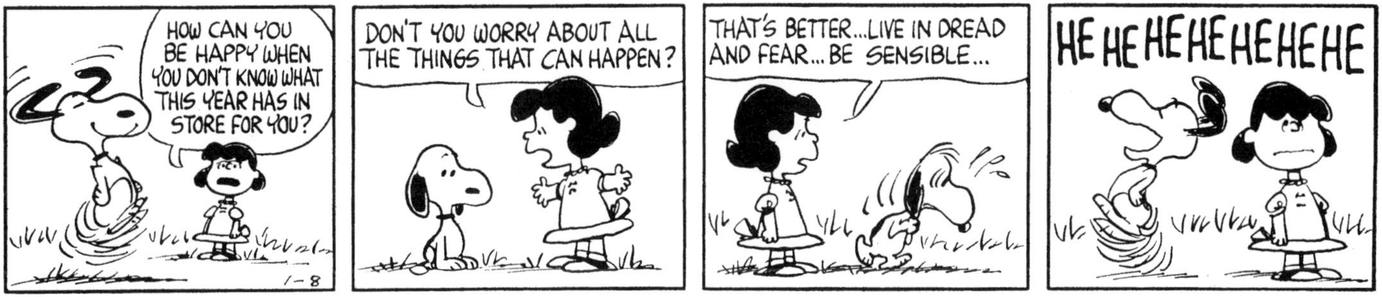
HOW CAN YOU BE HAPPY WHEN YOU DON'T KNOW WHAT THIS YEAR HAS IN STORE FOR YOU?
DON'T YOU WORRY ABOUT ALL THE THINGS THAT CAN HAPPEN?
THAT'S BETTER...LIVE IN DREAD AND FEAR... BE SENSIBLE...
HE HE HE HE HE HE HE HE HE

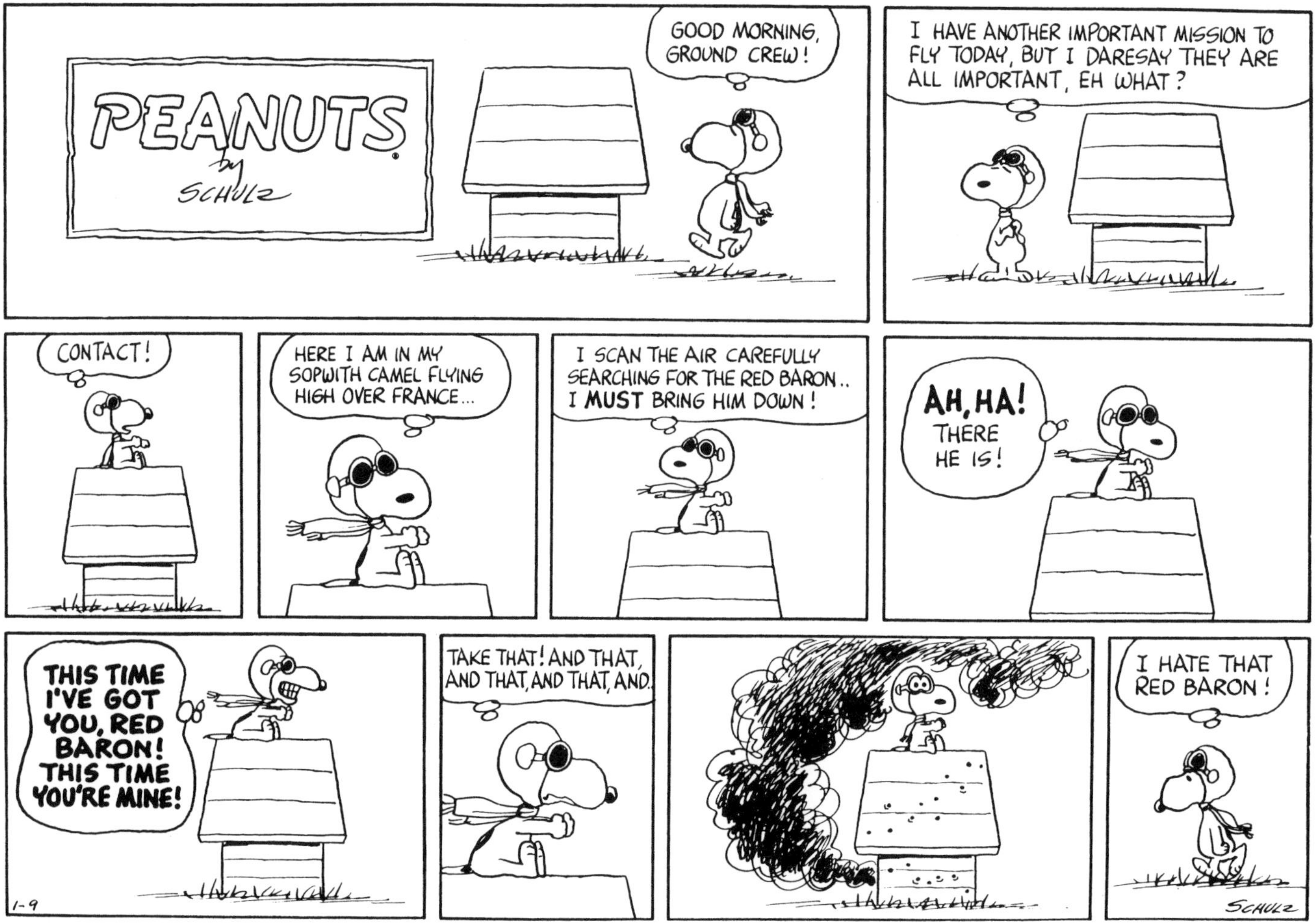
PEANUTS
by SCHULZ
GOOD MORNING, GROUND CREW!
I HAVE ANOTHER IMPORTANT MISSION TO FLY TODAY, BUT I DARESAY THEY ARE ALL IMPORTANT, EH WHAT?
CONTACT!
HERE I AM IN MY SOPWITH CAMEL FLYING HIGH OVER FRANCE...
I SCAN THE AIR CAREFULLY SEARCHING FOR THE RED BARON.. I MUST BRING HIM DOWN!
AH, HA! THERE HE IS!
THIS TIME I'VE GOT YOU, RED BARON! THIS TIME YOU'RE MINE!
1-9
TAKE THAT! AND THAT, AND THAT, AND THAT, AND
I HATE THAT RED BARON!
SCHULZ

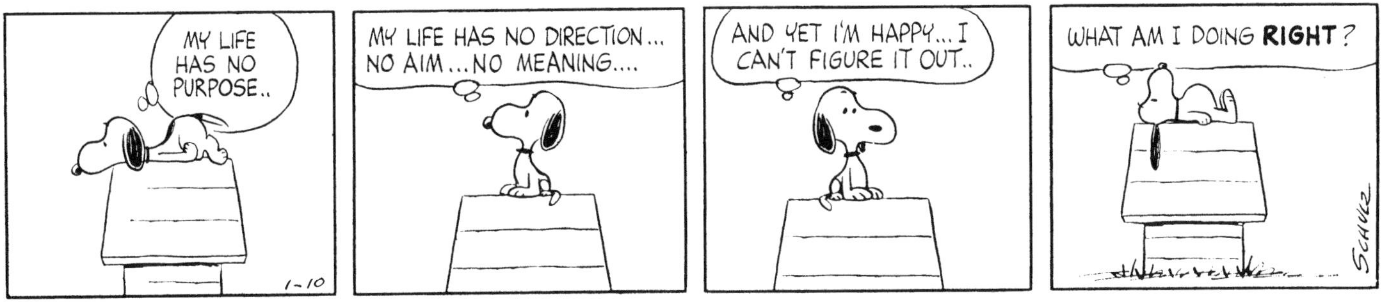
MY LIFE HAS NO PURPOSE..
1-10
MY LIFE HAS NO DIRECTION... NO AIM...NO MEANING....
AND YET I'M HAPPY... I CAN'T FIGURE IT OUT..
WHAT AM I DOING **RIGHT**?
SCHULZ

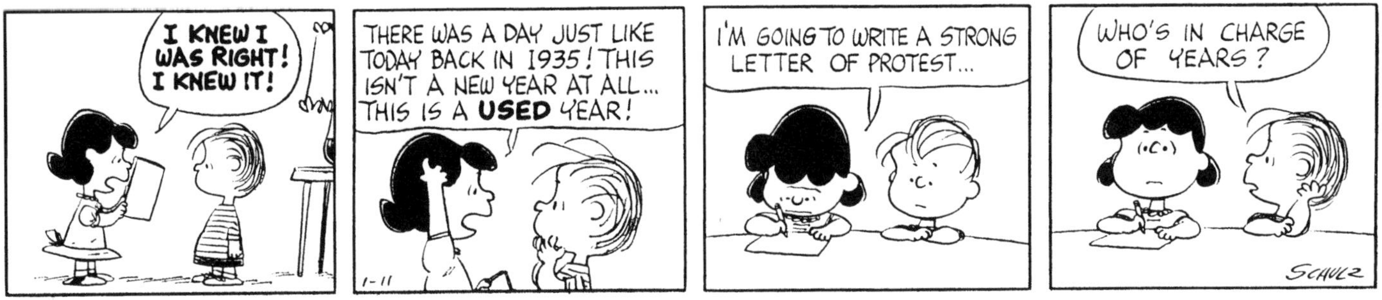
I KNEW I WAS RIGHT! I KNEW IT!
THERE WAS A DAY JUST LIKE TODAY BACK IN 1935! THIS ISN'T A NEW YEAR AT ALL... THIS IS A **USED** YEAR!
1-11
I'M GOING TO WRITE A STRONG LETTER OF PROTEST...
WHO'S IN CHARGE OF YEARS?
SCHULZ

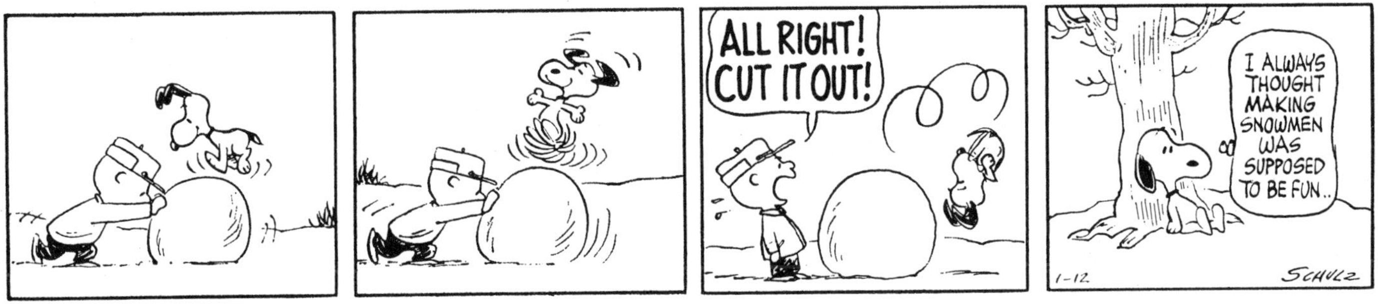
ALL RIGHT! CUT IT OUT!
I ALWAYS THOUGHT MAKING SNOWMEN WAS SUPPOSED TO BE FUN..
1-12
SCHULZ

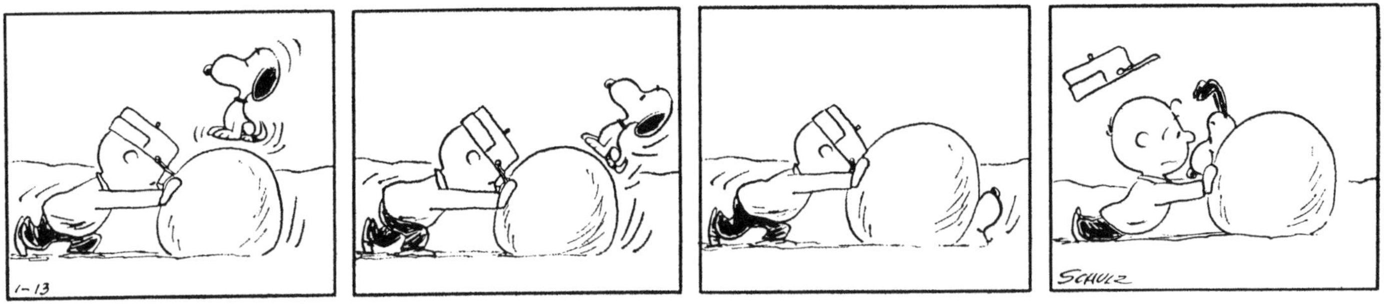
1-13
SCHULZ

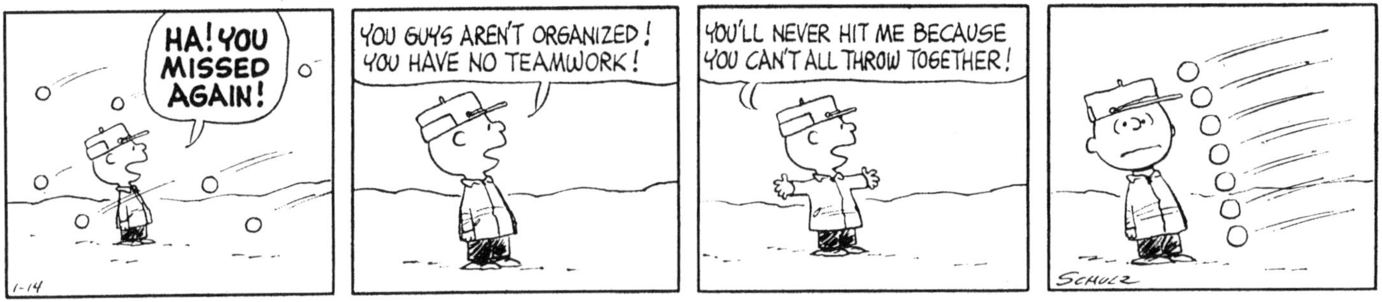
HA! YOU MISSED AGAIN!
1-14
YOU GUYS AREN'T ORGANIZED! YOU HAVE NO TEAMWORK!
YOU'LL NEVER HIT ME BECAUSE YOU CAN'T ALL THROW TOGETHER!
SCHULZ

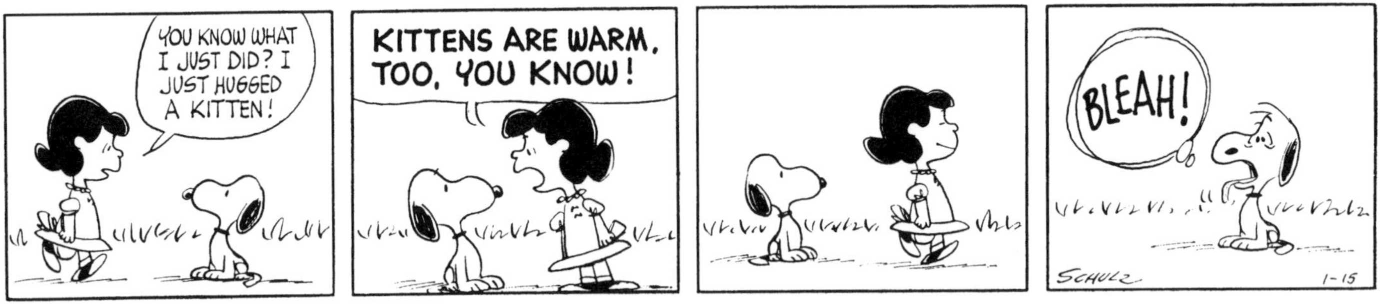
YOU KNOW WHAT I JUST DID? I JUST HUGGED A KITTEN!
KITTENS ARE WARM, TOO, YOU KNOW!
BLEAH!
SCHULZ
1-15

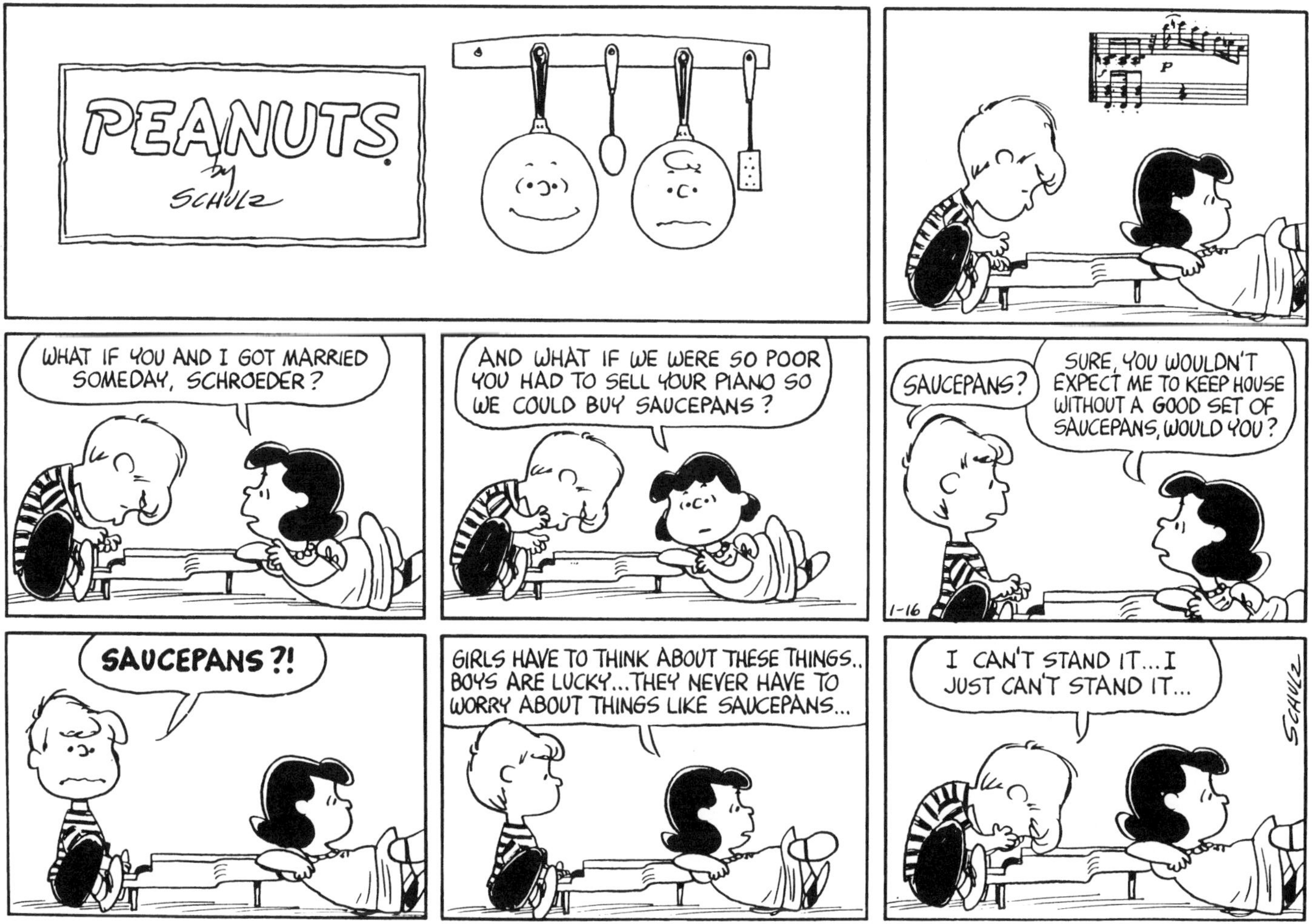
PEANUTS
by SCHULZ
WHAT IF YOU AND I GOT MARRIED SOMEDAY, SCHROEDER?
AND WHAT IF WE WERE SO POOR YOU HAD TO SELL YOUR PIANO SO WE COULD BUY SAUCEPANS?
SAUCEPANS?
SURE, YOU WOULDN'T EXPECT ME TO KEEP HOUSE WITHOUT A GOOD SET OF SAUCEPANS, WOULD YOU?
1-16
SAUCEPANS?!
GIRLS HAVE TO THINK ABOUT THESE THINGS.. BOYS ARE LUCKY...THEY NEVER HAVE TO WORRY ABOUT THINGS LIKE SAUCEPANS...
I CAN'T STAND IT...I JUST CAN'T STAND IT...
SCHULZ

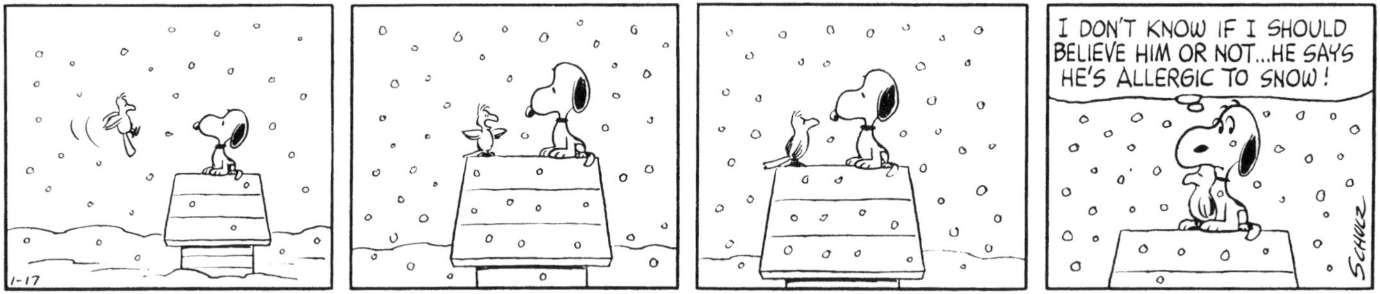
I DON'T KNOW IF I SHOULD BELIEVE HIM OR NOT...HE SAYS HE'S ALLERGIC TO SNOW!

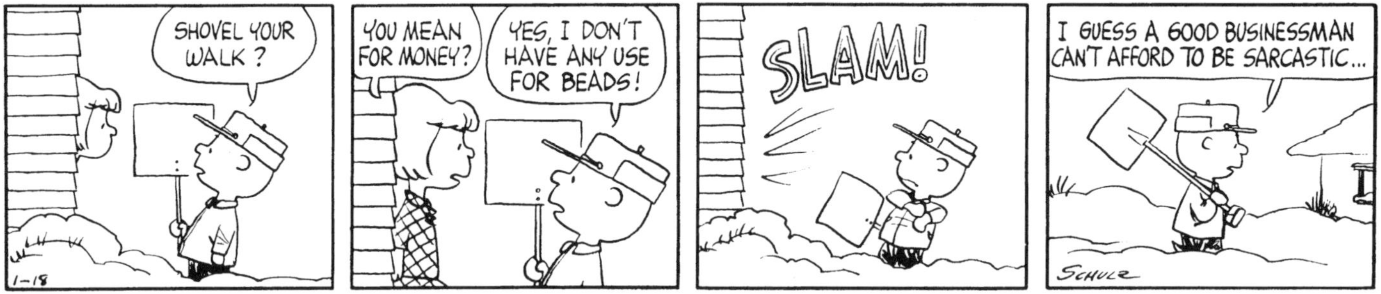
SHOVEL YOUR WALK?
YOU MEAN FOR MONEY?
YES, I DON'T HAVE ANY USE FOR BEADS!
SLAM!
I GUESS A GOOD BUSINESSMAN CAN'T AFFORD TO BE SARCASTIC...

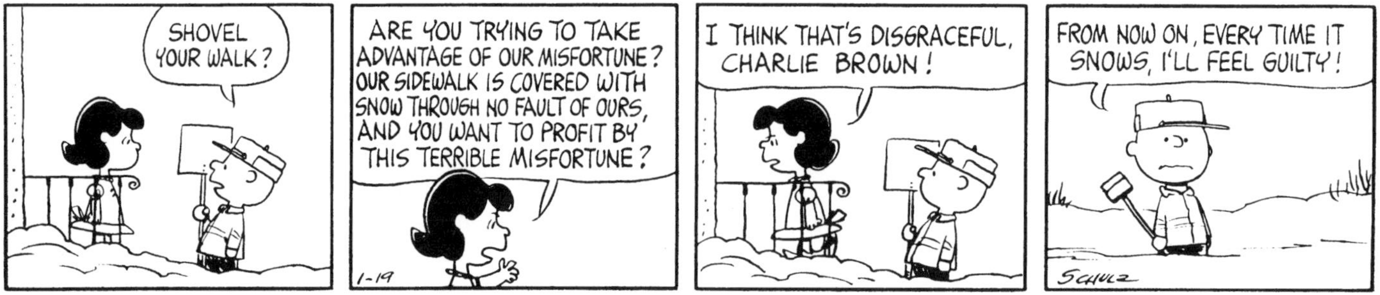
SHOVEL YOUR WALK?
ARE YOU TRYING TO TAKE ADVANTAGE OF OUR MISFORTUNE? OUR SIDEWALK IS COVERED WITH SNOW THROUGH NO FAULT OF OURS, AND YOU WANT TO PROFIT BY THIS TERRIBLE MISFORTUNE?
I THINK THAT'S DISGRACEFUL, CHARLIE BROWN!
FROM NOW ON, EVERY TIME IT SNOWS, I'LL FEEL GUILTY!

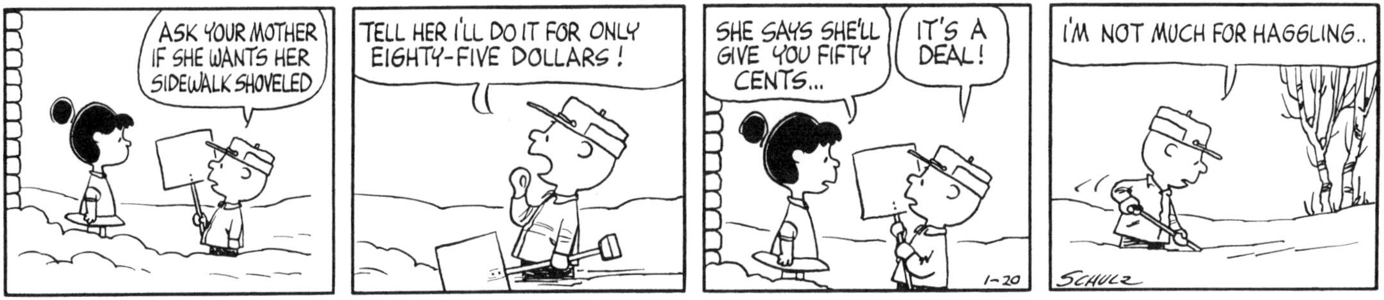
ASK YOUR MOTHER IF SHE WANTS HER SIDEWALK SHOVELED
TELL HER I'LL DO IT FOR ONLY EIGHTY-FIVE DOLLARS !
SHE SAYS SHE'LL GIVE YOU FIFTY CENTS...
IT'S A DEAL!
I'M NOT MUCH FOR HAGGLING..

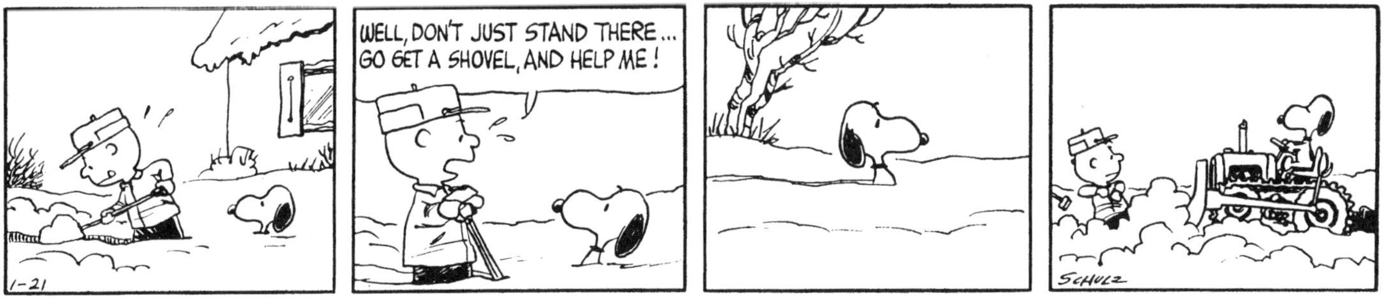
WELL, DON'T JUST STAND THERE... GO GET A SHOVEL, AND HELP ME !

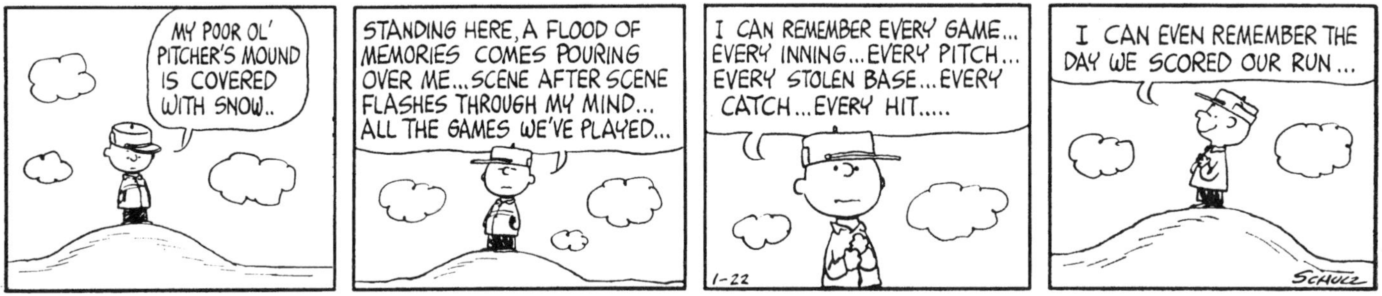
MY POOR OL' PITCHER'S MOUND IS COVERED WITH SNOW..
STANDING HERE, A FLOOD OF MEMORIES COMES POURING OVER ME...SCENE AFTER SCENE FLASHES THROUGH MY MIND... ALL THE GAMES WE'VE PLAYED...
I CAN REMEMBER EVERY GAME... EVERY INNING...EVERY PITCH... EVERY STOLEN BASE...EVERY CATCH...EVERY HIT.....
I CAN EVEN REMEMBER THE DAY WE SCORED OUR RUN...

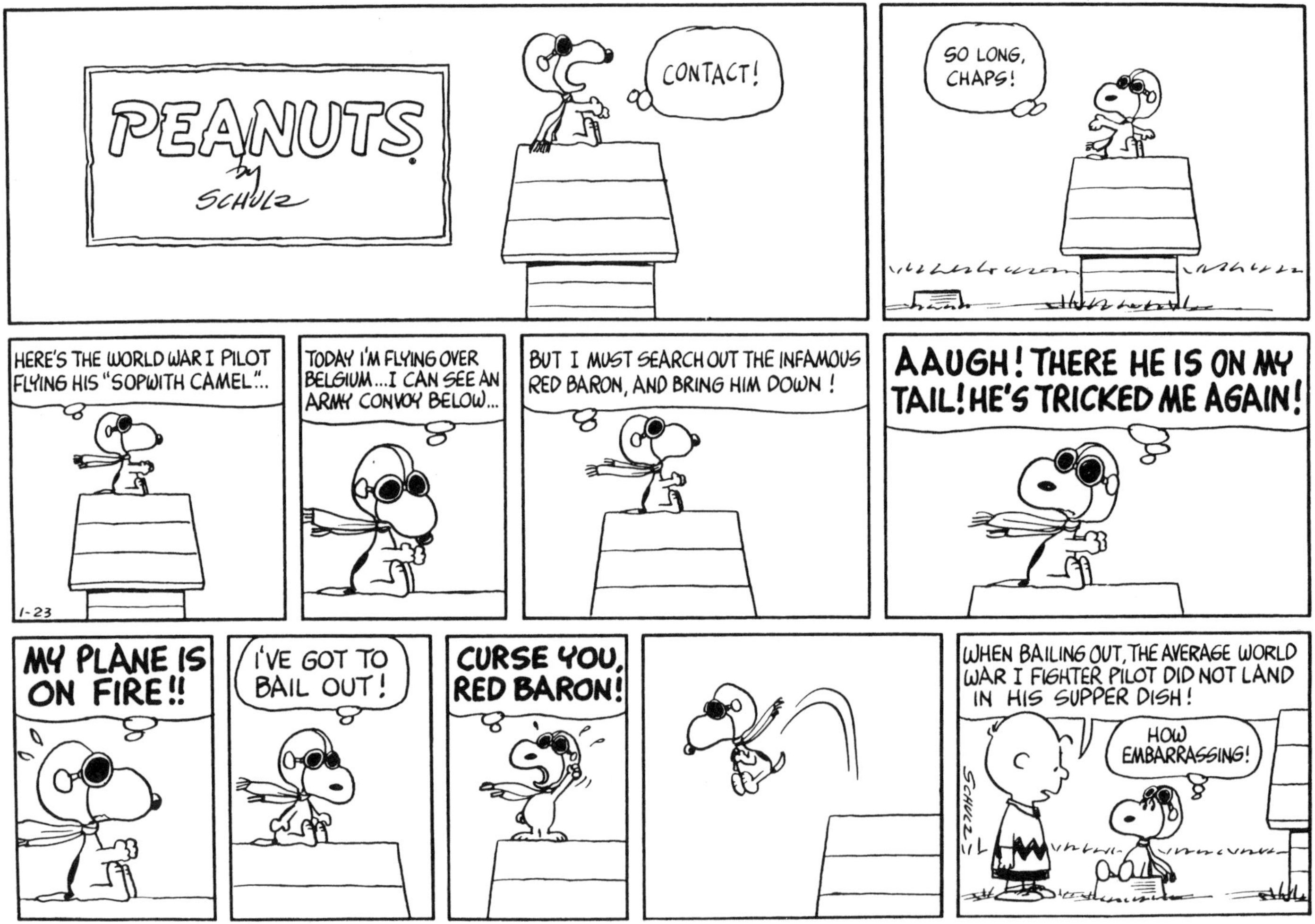
PEANUTS
by SCHULZ
CONTACT!
SO LONG, CHAPS!
HERE'S THE WORLD WAR I PILOT FLYING HIS "SOPWITH CAMEL"...
1-23
TODAY I'M FLYING OVER BELGIUM...I CAN SEE AN ARMY CONVOY BELOW...
BUT I MUST SEARCH OUT THE INFAMOUS RED BARON, AND BRING HIM DOWN!
AAUGH! THERE HE IS ON MY TAIL! HE'S TRICKED ME AGAIN!
MY PLANE IS ON FIRE!!
I'VE GOT TO BAIL OUT!
CURSE YOU, RED BARON!
WHEN BAILING OUT, THE AVERAGE WORLD WAR I FIGHTER PILOT DID NOT LAND IN HIS SUPPER DISH!
HOW EMBARRASSING!
SCHULZ

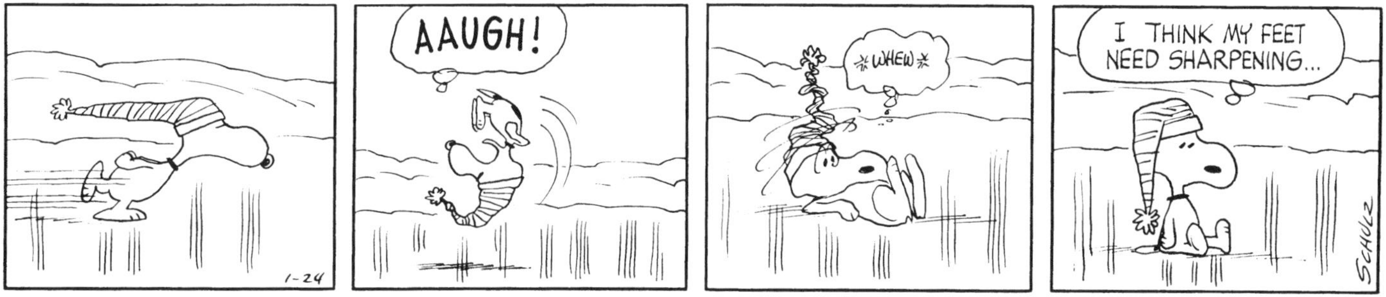
1-24
AAUGH!
WHEW
I THINK MY FEET NEED SHARPENING...
SCHULZ

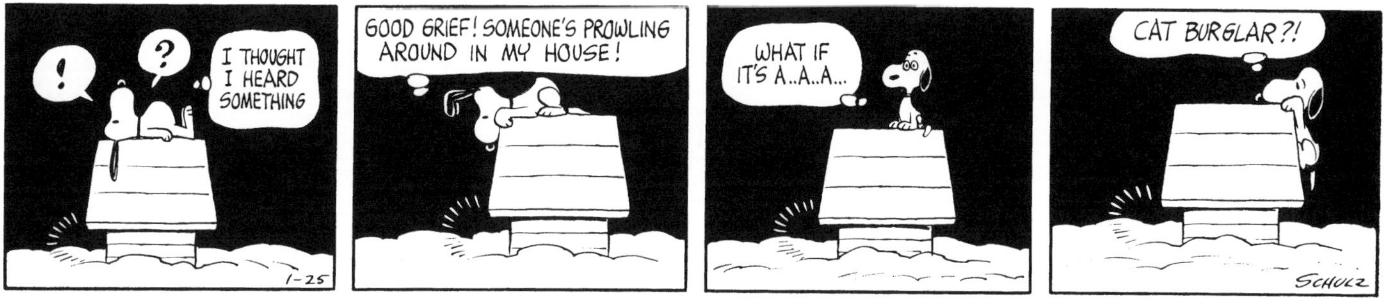
!
?
I THOUGHT I HEARD SOMETHING
1-25
GOOD GRIEF! SOMEONE'S PROWLING AROUND IN MY HOUSE!
WHAT IF IT'S A..A..A...
CAT BURGLAR?!
SCHULZ

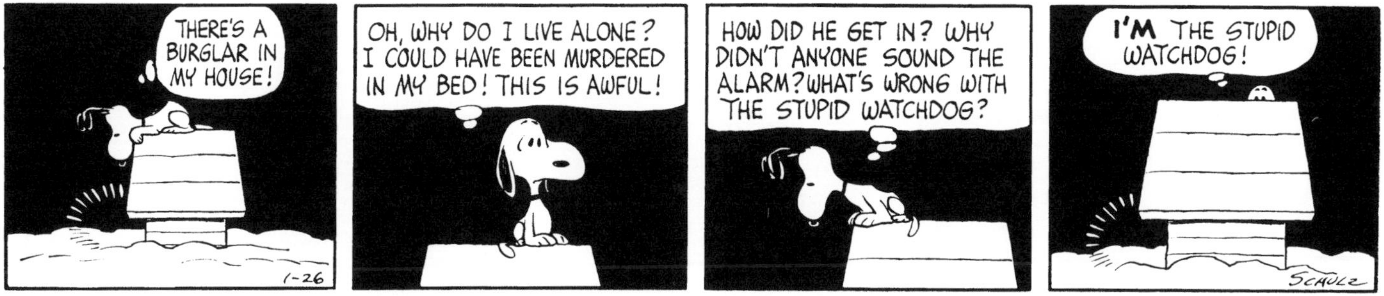
THERE'S A BURGLAR IN MY HOUSE!
1-26
OH, WHY DO I LIVE ALONE? I COULD HAVE BEEN MURDERED IN MY BED! THIS IS AWFUL!
HOW DID HE GET IN? WHY DIDN'T ANYONE SOUND THE ALARM? WHAT'S WRONG WITH THE STUPID WATCHDOG?
I'M THE STUPID WATCHDOG!
SCHULZ

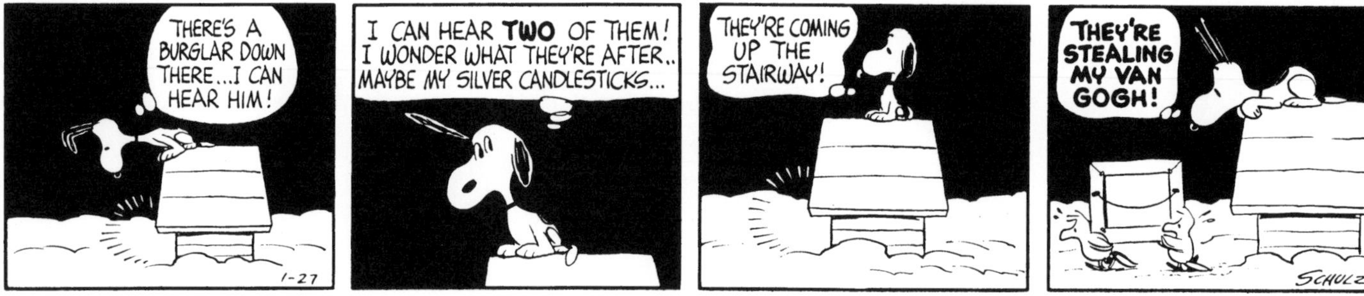
THERE'S A BURGLAR DOWN THERE...I CAN HEAR HIM!
1-27
I CAN HEAR **TWO** OF THEM! I WONDER WHAT THEY'RE AFTER.. MAYBE MY SILVER CANDLESTICKS...
THEY'RE COMING UP THE STAIRWAY!
THEY'RE STEALING MY VAN GOGH!
SCHULZ

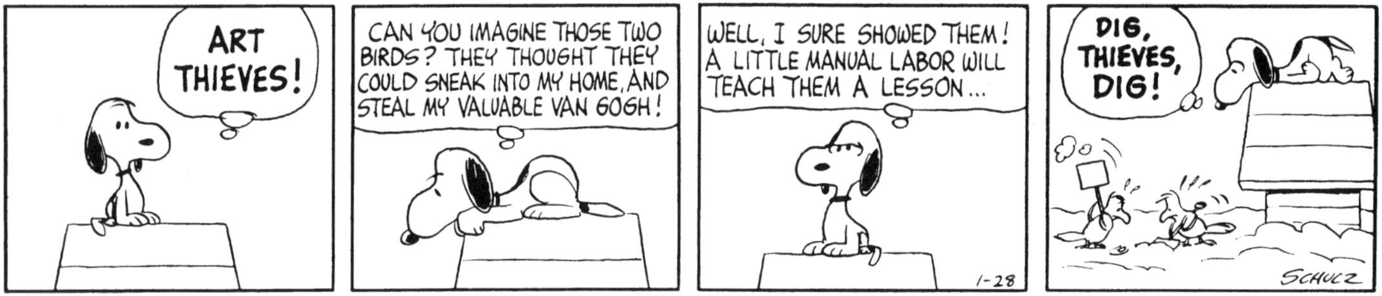
ART THIEVES!
CAN YOU IMAGINE THOSE TWO BIRDS? THEY THOUGHT THEY COULD SNEAK INTO MY HOME, AND STEAL MY VALUABLE VAN GOGH!
WELL, I SURE SHOWED THEM! A LITTLE MANUAL LABOR WILL TEACH THEM A LESSON...
1-28
DIG, THIEVES, DIG!
SCHULZ

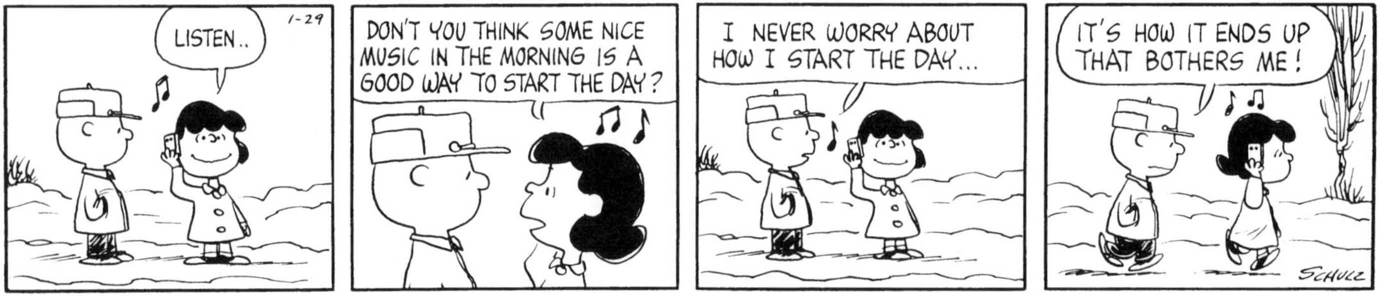
LISTEN..
1-29
DON'T YOU THINK SOME NICE MUSIC IN THE MORNING IS A GOOD WAY TO START THE DAY?
I NEVER WORRY ABOUT HOW I START THE DAY...
IT'S HOW IT ENDS UP THAT BOTHERS ME!
SCHULZ

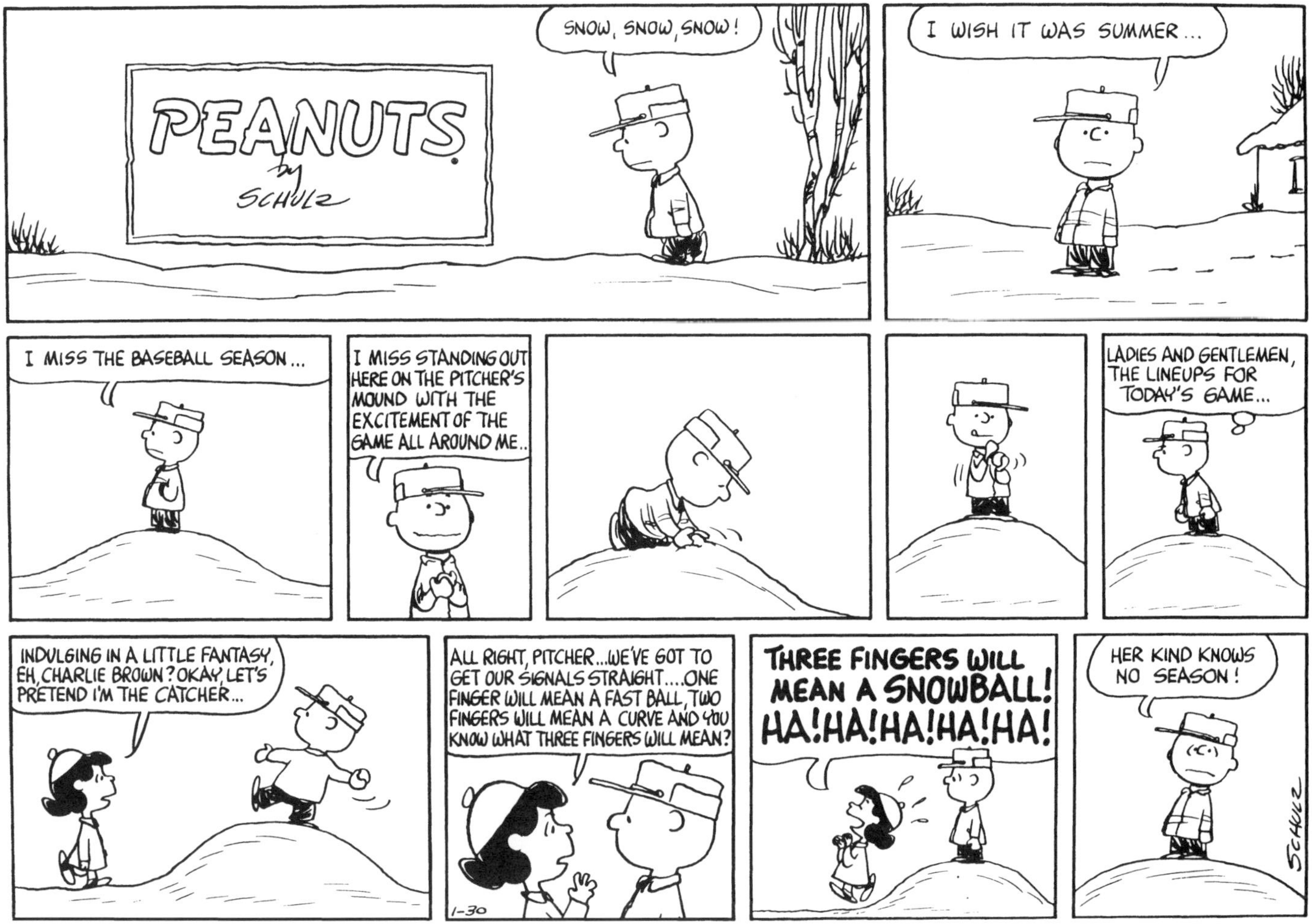
PEANUTS
by SCHULZ
SNOW, SNOW, SNOW!
I WISH IT WAS SUMMER...
I MISS THE BASEBALL SEASON...
I MISS STANDING OUT HERE ON THE PITCHER'S MOUND WITH THE EXCITEMENT OF THE GAME ALL AROUND ME..
LADIES AND GENTLEMEN, THE LINEUPS FOR TODAY'S GAME...
INDULGING IN A LITTLE FANTASY, EH, CHARLIE BROWN? OKAY, LET'S PRETEND I'M THE CATCHER...
ALL RIGHT, PITCHER...WE'VE GOT TO GET OUR SIGNALS STRAIGHT....ONE FINGER WILL MEAN A FAST BALL, TWO FINGERS WILL MEAN A CURVE AND YOU KNOW WHAT THREE FINGERS WILL MEAN?
1-30
THREE FINGERS WILL MEAN A SNOWBALL! HA!HA!HA!HA!HA!
HER KIND KNOWS NO SEASON!
SCHULZ

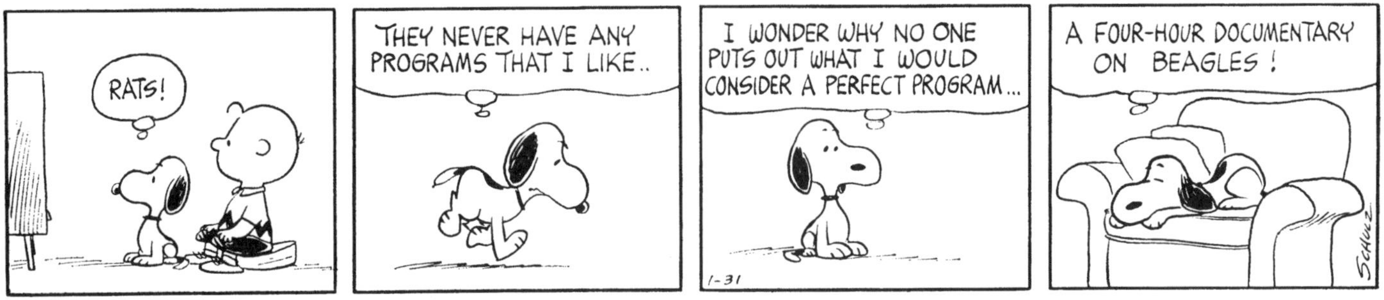
RATS!
THEY NEVER HAVE ANY PROGRAMS THAT I LIKE..
I WONDER WHY NO ONE PUTS OUT WHAT I WOULD CONSIDER A PERFECT PROGRAM...
1-31
A FOUR-HOUR DOCUMENTARY ON BEAGLES!
SCHULZ

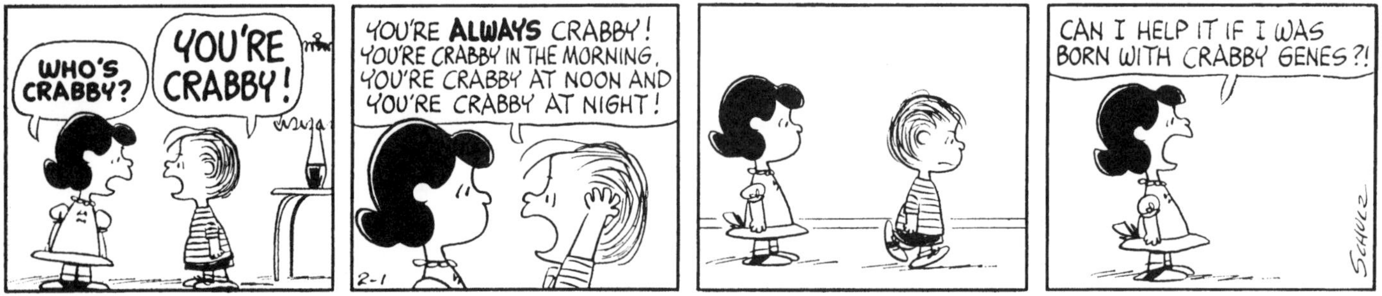
WHO'S CRABBY?
YOU'RE CRABBY!
YOU'RE ALWAYS CRABBY! YOU'RE CRABBY IN THE MORNING, YOU'RE CRABBY AT NOON AND YOU'RE CRABBY AT NIGHT!
2-1
CAN I HELP IT IF I WAS BORN WITH CRABBY GENES?!
SCHULZ

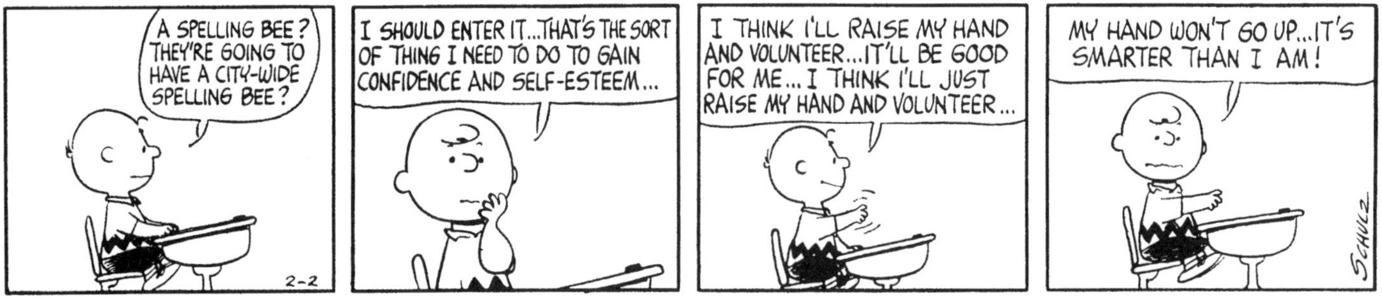
A SPELLING BEE? THEY'RE GOING TO HAVE A CITY-WIDE SPELLING BEE?
2-2
I SHOULD ENTER IT...THAT'S THE SORT OF THING I NEED TO DO TO GAIN CONFIDENCE AND SELF-ESTEEM...
I THINK I'LL RAISE MY HAND AND VOLUNTEER...IT'LL BE GOOD FOR ME... I THINK I'LL JUST RAISE MY HAND AND VOLUNTEER...
MY HAND WON'T GO UP...IT'S SMARTER THAN I AM!
SCHULZ

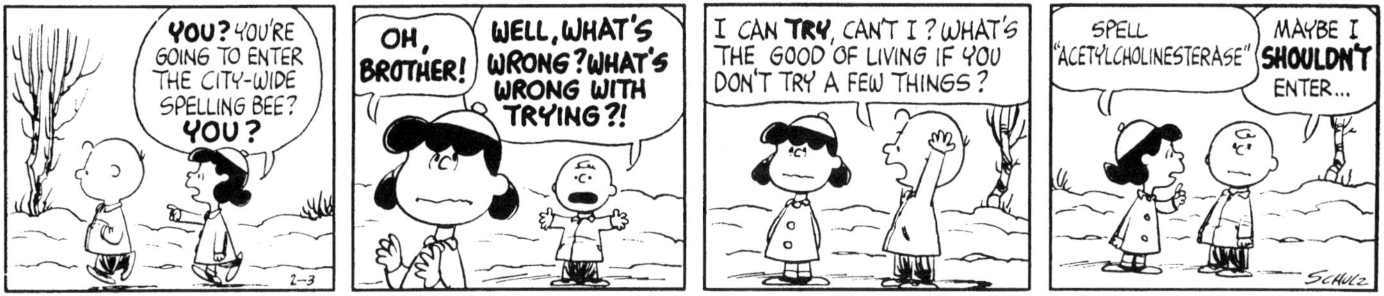
YOU? YOU'RE GOING TO ENTER THE CITY-WIDE SPELLING BEE? YOU?
2-3
OH, BROTHER!
WELL, WHAT'S WRONG? WHAT'S WRONG WITH TRYING?!
I CAN TRY, CAN'T I? WHAT'S THE GOOD OF LIVING IF YOU DON'T TRY A FEW THINGS?
SPELL "ACETYLCHOLINESTERASE"
MAYBE I SHOULDN'T ENTER...
SCHULZ

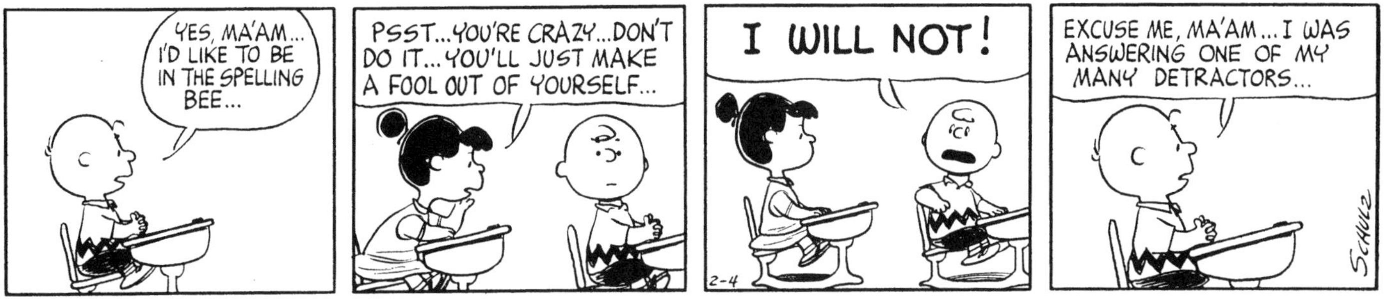
YES, MA'AM... I'D LIKE TO BE IN THE SPELLING BEE...
PSST...YOU'RE CRAZY...DON'T DO IT...YOU'LL JUST MAKE A FOOL OUT OF YOURSELF...
I WILL NOT!
2-4
EXCUSE ME, MA'AM... I WAS ANSWERING ONE OF MY MANY DETRACTORS...
SCHULZ

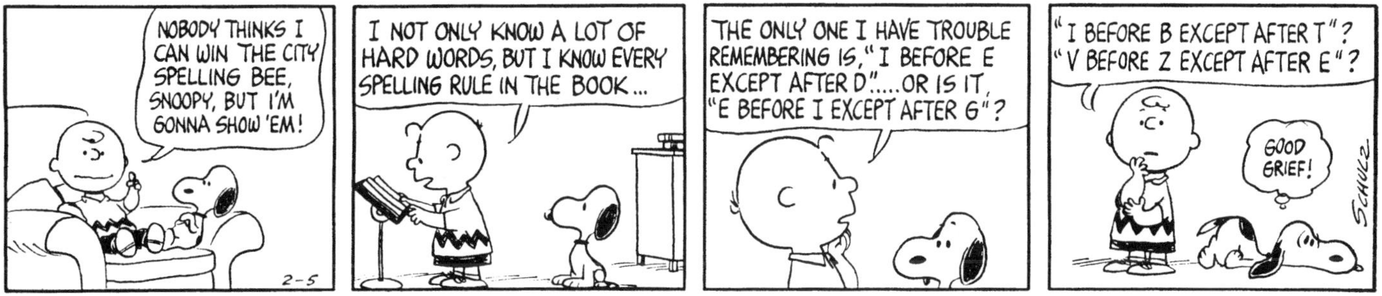
NOBODY THINKS I CAN WIN THE CITY SPELLING BEE, SNOOPY, BUT I'M GONNA SHOW 'EM!
2-5
I NOT ONLY KNOW A LOT OF HARD WORDS, BUT I KNOW EVERY SPELLING RULE IN THE BOOK...
THE ONLY ONE I HAVE TROUBLE REMEMBERING IS, "I BEFORE E EXCEPT AFTER D".....OR IS IT, "E BEFORE I EXCEPT AFTER G"?
"I BEFORE B EXCEPT AFTER T"? "V BEFORE Z EXCEPT AFTER E"?
GOOD GRIEF!
SCHULZ

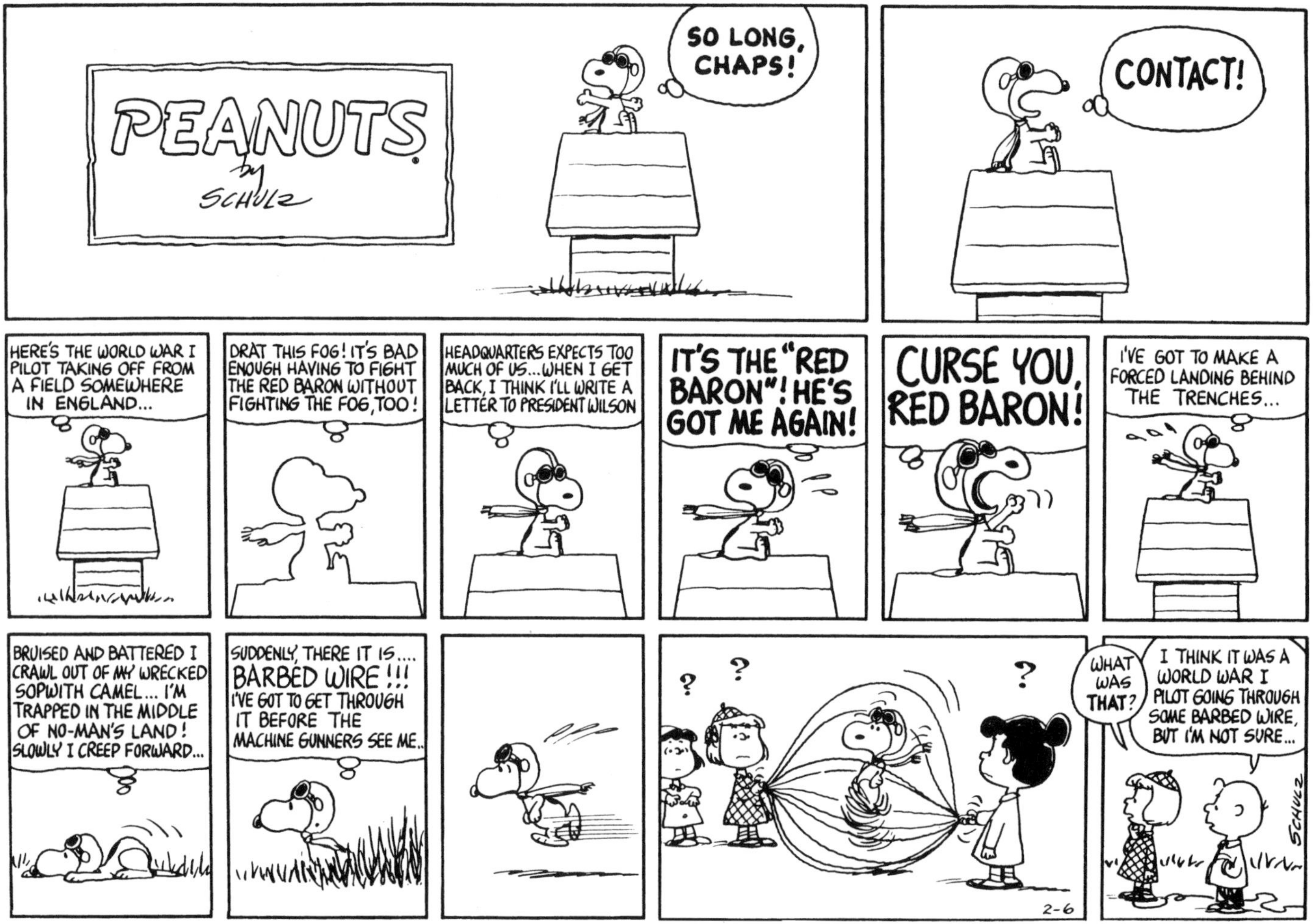
PEANUTS
by SCHULZ
SO LONG, CHAPS!
CONTACT!
HERE'S THE WORLD WAR I PILOT TAKING OFF FROM A FIELD SOMEWHERE IN ENGLAND...
DRAT THIS FOG! IT'S BAD ENOUGH HAVING TO FIGHT THE RED BARON WITHOUT FIGHTING THE FOG, TOO!
HEADQUARTERS EXPECTS TOO MUCH OF US...WHEN I GET BACK, I THINK I'LL WRITE A LETTER TO PRESIDENT WILSON
IT'S THE "RED BARON"! HE'S GOT ME AGAIN!
CURSE YOU, RED BARON!
I'VE GOT TO MAKE A FORCED LANDING BEHIND THE TRENCHES...
BRUISED AND BATTERED I CRAWL OUT OF MY WRECKED SOPWITH CAMEL... I'M TRAPPED IN THE MIDDLE OF NO-MAN'S LAND! SLOWLY I CREEP FORWARD...
SUDDENLY, THERE IT IS.... BARBED WIRE!!! I'VE GOT TO GET THROUGH IT BEFORE THE MACHINE GUNNERS SEE ME..
?
?
?
2-6
WHAT WAS THAT?
I THINK IT WAS A WORLD WAR I PILOT GOING THROUGH SOME BARBED WIRE, BUT I'M NOT SURE...
SCHULZ

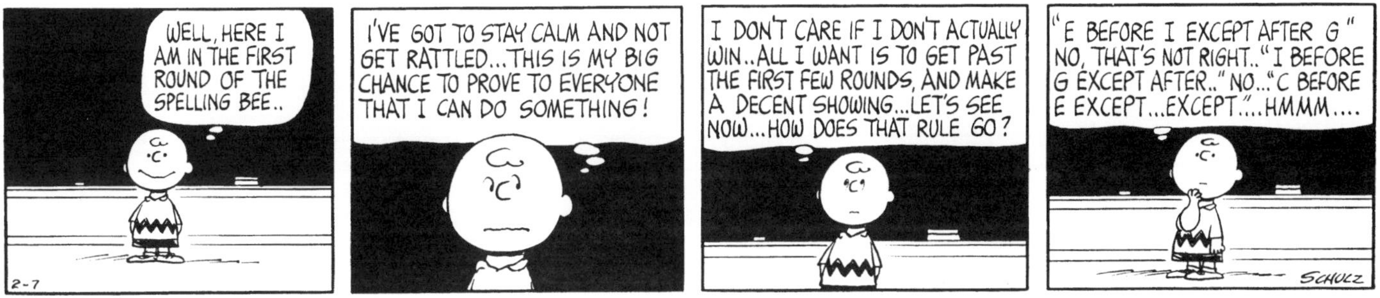
WELL, HERE I AM IN THE FIRST ROUND OF THE SPELLING BEE..
2-7
I'VE GOT TO STAY CALM AND NOT GET RATTLED... THIS IS MY BIG CHANCE TO PROVE TO EVERYONE THAT I CAN DO SOMETHING!
I DON'T CARE IF I DON'T ACTUALLY WIN.. ALL I WANT IS TO GET PAST THE FIRST FEW ROUNDS, AND MAKE A DECENT SHOWING... LET'S SEE NOW... HOW DOES THAT RULE GO?
"E BEFORE I EXCEPT AFTER G" NO, THAT'S NOT RIGHT.. "I BEFORE G EXCEPT AFTER.." NO... "C BEFORE E EXCEPT... EXCEPT."... HMMM....
SCHULZ

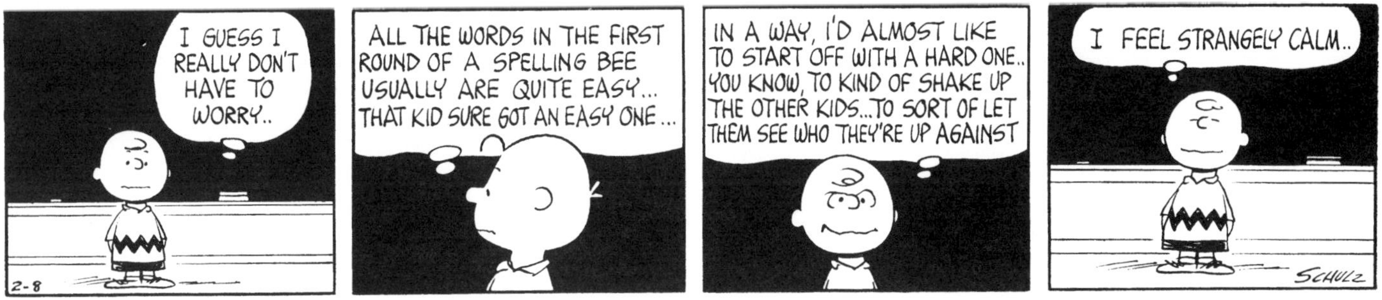
I GUESS I REALLY DON'T HAVE TO WORRY..
2-8
ALL THE WORDS IN THE FIRST ROUND OF A SPELLING BEE USUALLY ARE QUITE EASY... THAT KID SURE GOT AN EASY ONE...
IN A WAY, I'D ALMOST LIKE TO START OFF WITH A HARD ONE.. YOU KNOW, TO KIND OF SHAKE UP THE OTHER KIDS... TO SORT OF LET THEM SEE WHO THEY'RE UP AGAINST
I FEEL STRANGELY CALM..
SCHULZ

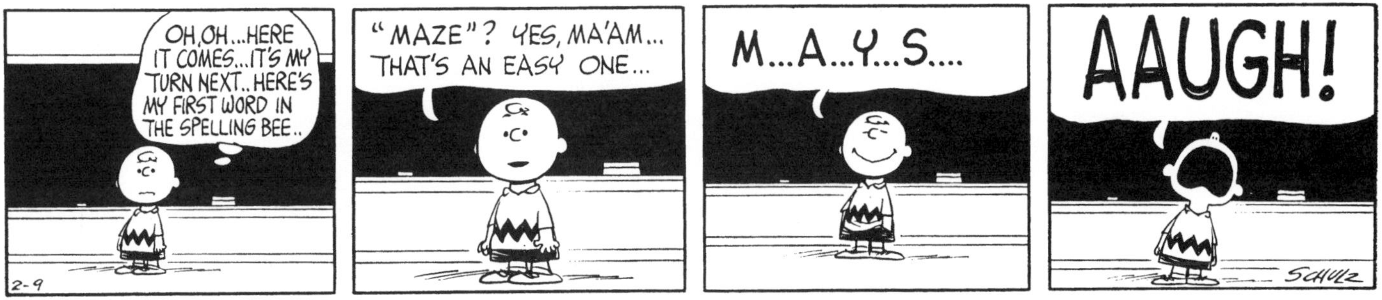
OH, OH... HERE IT COMES... IT'S MY TURN NEXT.. HERE'S MY FIRST WORD IN THE SPELLING BEE..
2-9
"MAZE"? YES, MA'AM... THAT'S AN EASY ONE...
M...A...Y...S....
AAUGH!
SCHULZ

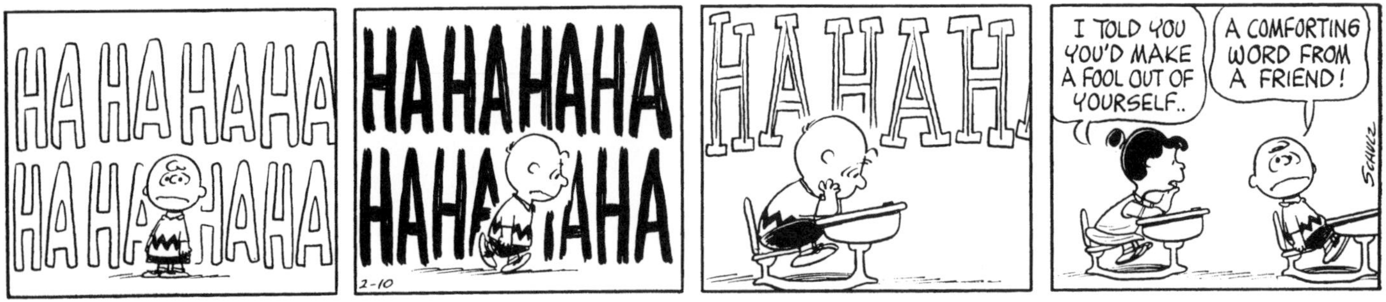
HA HA HA HA HA HA HA HA HA HA
HAHAHAHA HAHA HAHA
HAHAH
I TOLD YOU YOU'D MAKE A FOOL OUT OF YOURSELF..
A COMFORTING WORD FROM A FRIEND!
2-10
SCHULZ

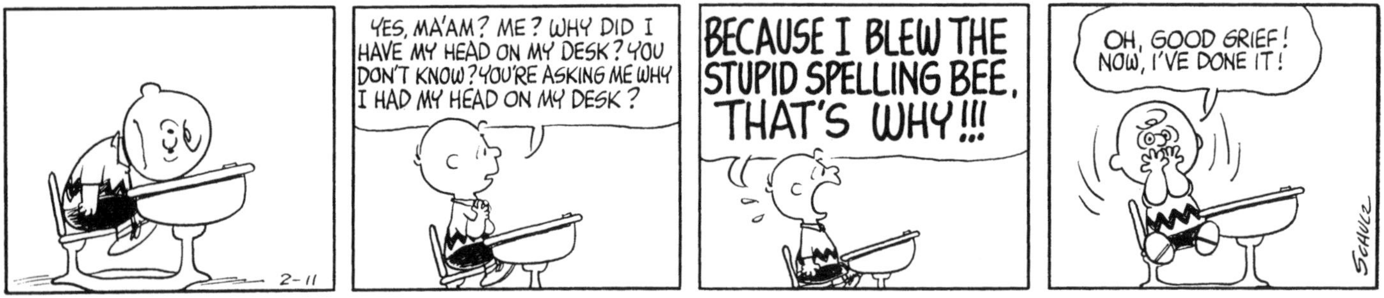
YES, MA'AM? ME? WHY DID I HAVE MY HEAD ON MY DESK? YOU DON'T KNOW? YOU'RE ASKING ME WHY I HAD MY HEAD ON MY DESK?
BECAUSE I BLEW THE STUPID SPELLING BEE, THAT'S WHY!!!
OH, GOOD GRIEF! NOW, I'VE DONE IT!
2-11
SCHULZ

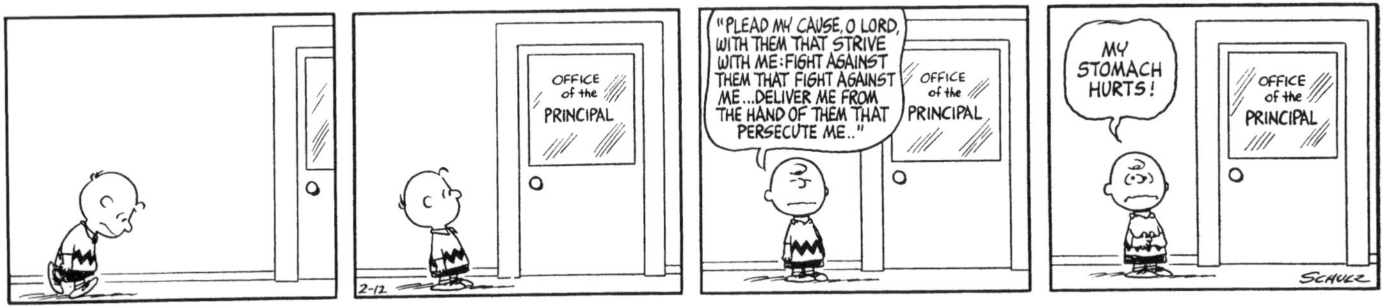
OFFICE of the PRINCIPAL
"PLEAD MY CAUSE, O LORD, WITH THEM THAT STRIVE WITH ME: FIGHT AGAINST THEM THAT FIGHT AGAINST ME...DELIVER ME FROM THE HAND OF THEM THAT PERSECUTE ME.."
OFFICE of the PRINCIPAL
MY STOMACH HURTS!
OFFICE of the PRINCIPAL
2-12
SCHULZ

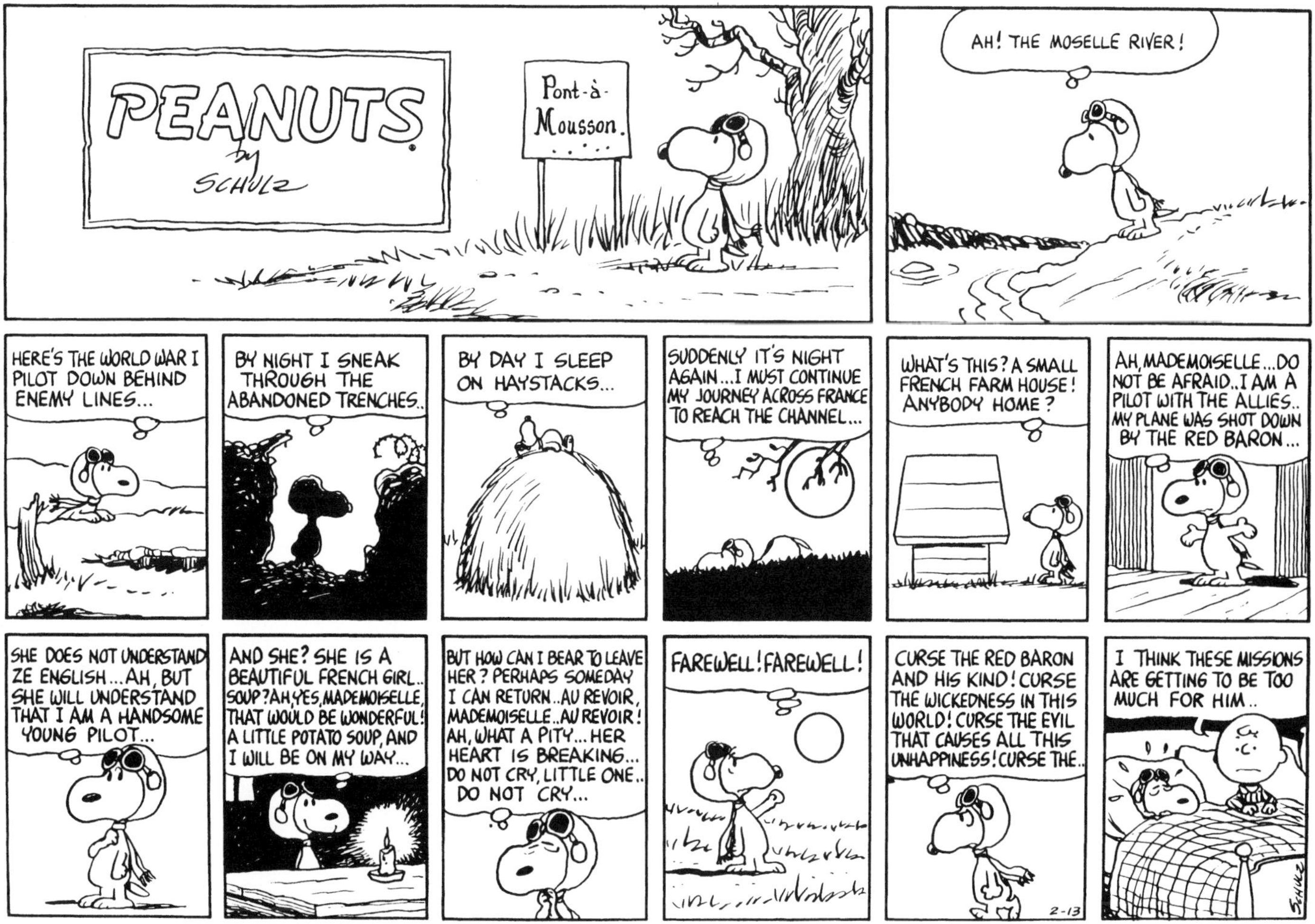
PEANUTS
by
SCHULZ
Pont-à-
Mousson
AH! THE MOSELLE RIVER!
HERE'S THE WORLD WAR I PILOT DOWN BEHIND ENEMY LINES...
BY NIGHT I SNEAK THROUGH THE ABANDONED TRENCHES..
BY DAY I SLEEP ON HAYSTACKS...
SUDDENLY IT'S NIGHT AGAIN...I MUST CONTINUE MY JOURNEY ACROSS FRANCE TO REACH THE CHANNEL...
WHAT'S THIS? A SMALL FRENCH FARM HOUSE! ANYBODY HOME?
AH, MADEMOISELLE...DO NOT BE AFRAID..I AM A PILOT WITH THE ALLIES.. MY PLANE WAS SHOT DOWN BY THE RED BARON...
SHE DOES NOT UNDERSTAND ZE ENGLISH...AH, BUT SHE WILL UNDERSTAND THAT I AM A HANDSOME YOUNG PILOT...
AND SHE? SHE IS A BEAUTIFUL FRENCH GIRL.. SOUP? AH, YES, MADEMOISELLE, THAT WOULD BE WONDERFUL! A LITTLE POTATO SOUP, AND I WILL BE ON MY WAY...
BUT HOW CAN I BEAR TO LEAVE HER? PERHAPS SOMEDAY I CAN RETURN..AU REVOIR, MADEMOISELLE..AU REVOIR! AH, WHAT A PITY... HER HEART IS BREAKING... DO NOT CRY, LITTLE ONE.. DO NOT CRY...
FAREWELL! FAREWELL!
2-13
CURSE THE RED BARON AND HIS KIND! CURSE THE WICKEDNESS IN THIS WORLD! CURSE THE EVIL THAT CAUSES ALL THIS UNHAPPINESS! CURSE THE..
I THINK THESE MISSIONS ARE GETTING TO BE TOO MUCH FOR HIM..
SCHULZ

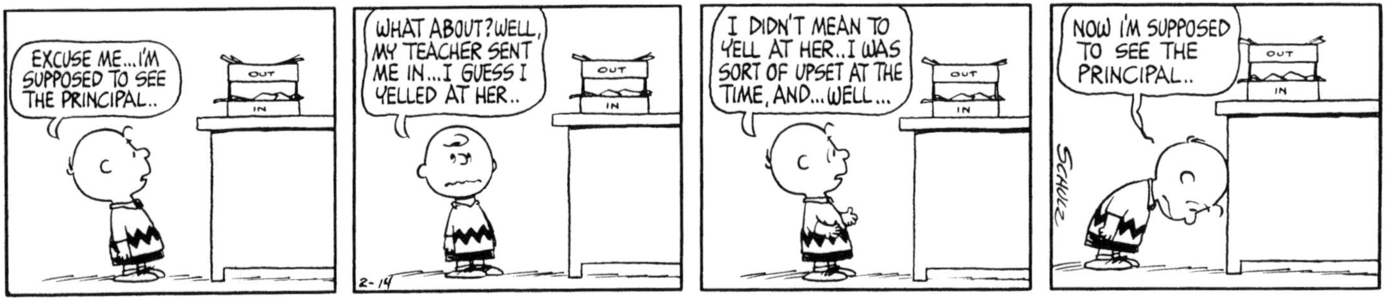
EXCUSE ME...I'M SUPPOSED TO SEE THE PRINCIPAL..
WHAT ABOUT? WELL, MY TEACHER SENT ME IN...I GUESS I YELLED AT HER..
2-14
I DIDN'T MEAN TO YELL AT HER..I WAS SORT OF UPSET AT THE TIME, AND...WELL...
NOW I'M SUPPOSED TO SEE THE PRINCIPAL..
SCHULZ

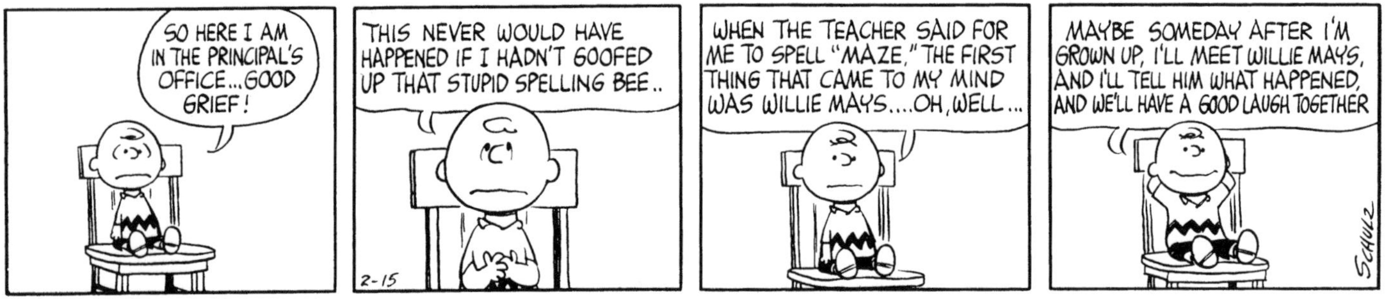
SO HERE I AM IN THE PRINCIPAL'S OFFICE...GOOD GRIEF!
THIS NEVER WOULD HAVE HAPPENED IF I HADN'T GOOFED UP THAT STUPID SPELLING BEE..
2-15
WHEN THE TEACHER SAID FOR ME TO SPELL "MAZE," THE FIRST THING THAT CAME TO MY MIND WAS WILLIE MAYS....OH, WELL...
MAYBE SOMEDAY AFTER I'M GROWN UP, I'LL MEET WILLIE MAYS, AND I'LL TELL HIM WHAT HAPPENED, AND WE'LL HAVE A GOOD LAUGH TOGETHER
SCHULZ

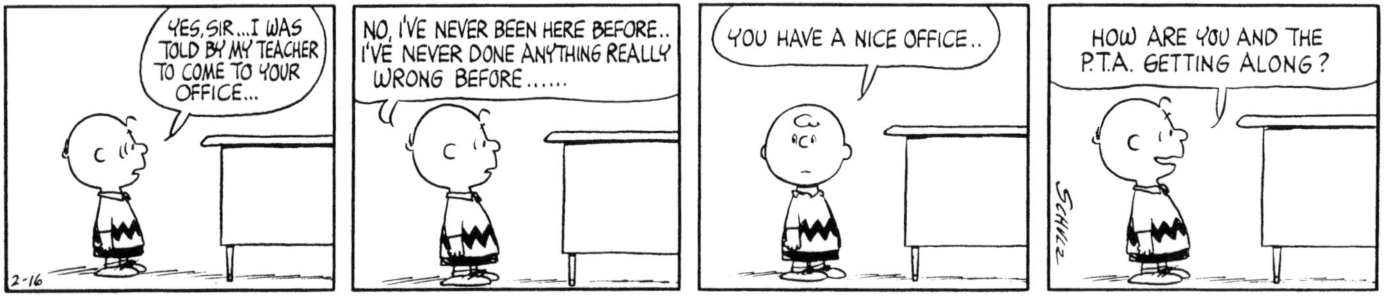
YES, SIR...I WAS TOLD BY MY TEACHER TO COME TO YOUR OFFICE...
2-16
NO, I'VE NEVER BEEN HERE BEFORE.. I'VE NEVER DONE ANYTHING REALLY WRONG BEFORE......
YOU HAVE A NICE OFFICE..
HOW ARE YOU AND THE P.T.A. GETTING ALONG?
SCHULZ

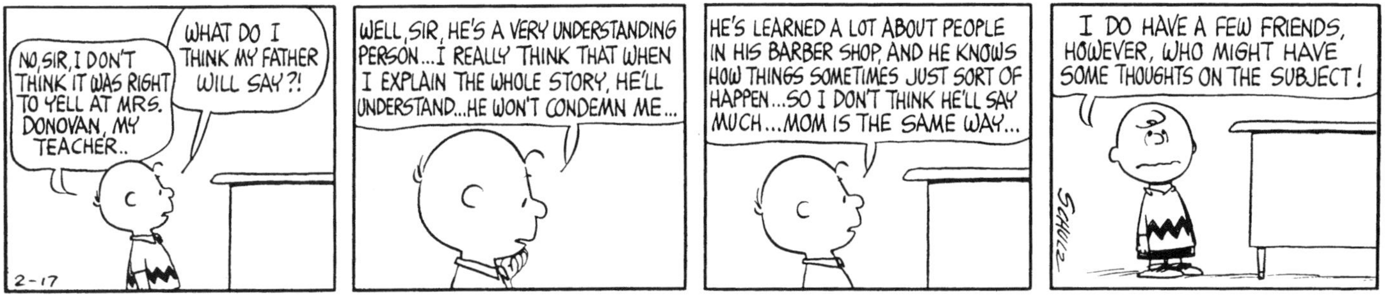
NO, SIR, I DON'T THINK IT WAS RIGHT TO YELL AT MRS. DONOVAN, MY TEACHER..
WHAT DO I THINK MY FATHER WILL SAY?!
2-17
WELL, SIR, HE'S A VERY UNDERSTANDING PERSON... I REALLY THINK THAT WHEN I EXPLAIN THE WHOLE STORY, HE'LL UNDERSTAND...HE WON'T CONDEMN ME...
HE'S LEARNED A LOT ABOUT PEOPLE IN HIS BARBER SHOP, AND HE KNOWS HOW THINGS SOMETIMES JUST SORT OF HAPPEN... SO I DON'T THINK HE'LL SAY MUCH... MOM IS THE SAME WAY...
I DO HAVE A FEW FRIENDS, HOWEVER, WHO MIGHT HAVE SOME THOUGHTS ON THE SUBJECT!
SCHULZ

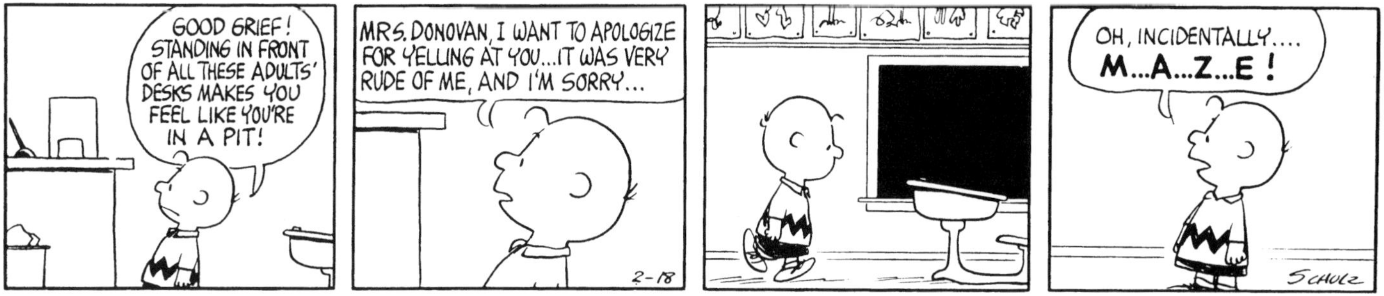
GOOD GRIEF! STANDING IN FRONT OF ALL THESE ADULTS' DESKS MAKES YOU FEEL LIKE YOU'RE IN A PIT!
MRS. DONOVAN, I WANT TO APOLOGIZE FOR YELLING AT YOU... IT WAS VERY RUDE OF ME, AND I'M SORRY...
2-18
OH, INCIDENTALLY.... M...A...Z...E!
SCHULZ

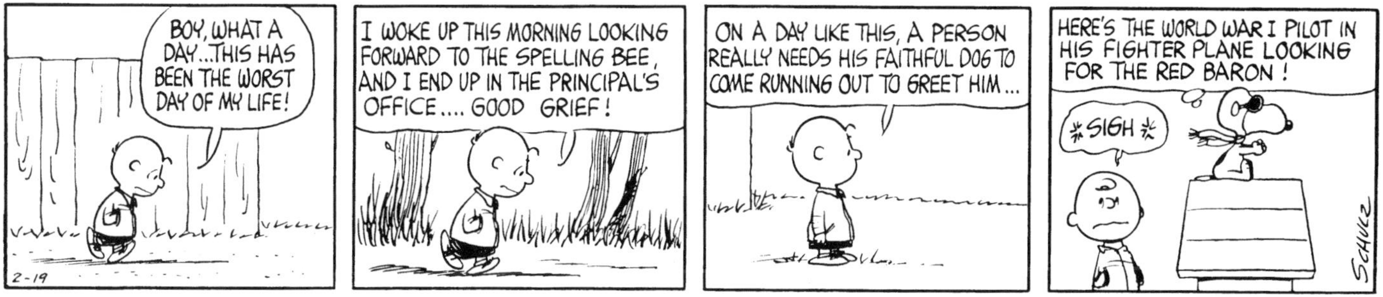
BOY, WHAT A DAY...THIS HAS BEEN THE WORST DAY OF MY LIFE!
2-19
I WOKE UP THIS MORNING LOOKING FORWARD TO THE SPELLING BEE, AND I END UP IN THE PRINCIPAL'S OFFICE.... GOOD GRIEF!
ON A DAY LIKE THIS, A PERSON REALLY NEEDS HIS FAITHFUL DOG TO COME RUNNING OUT TO GREET HIM...
HERE'S THE WORLD WAR I PILOT IN HIS FIGHTER PLANE LOOKING FOR THE RED BARON!
SIGH
SCHULZ

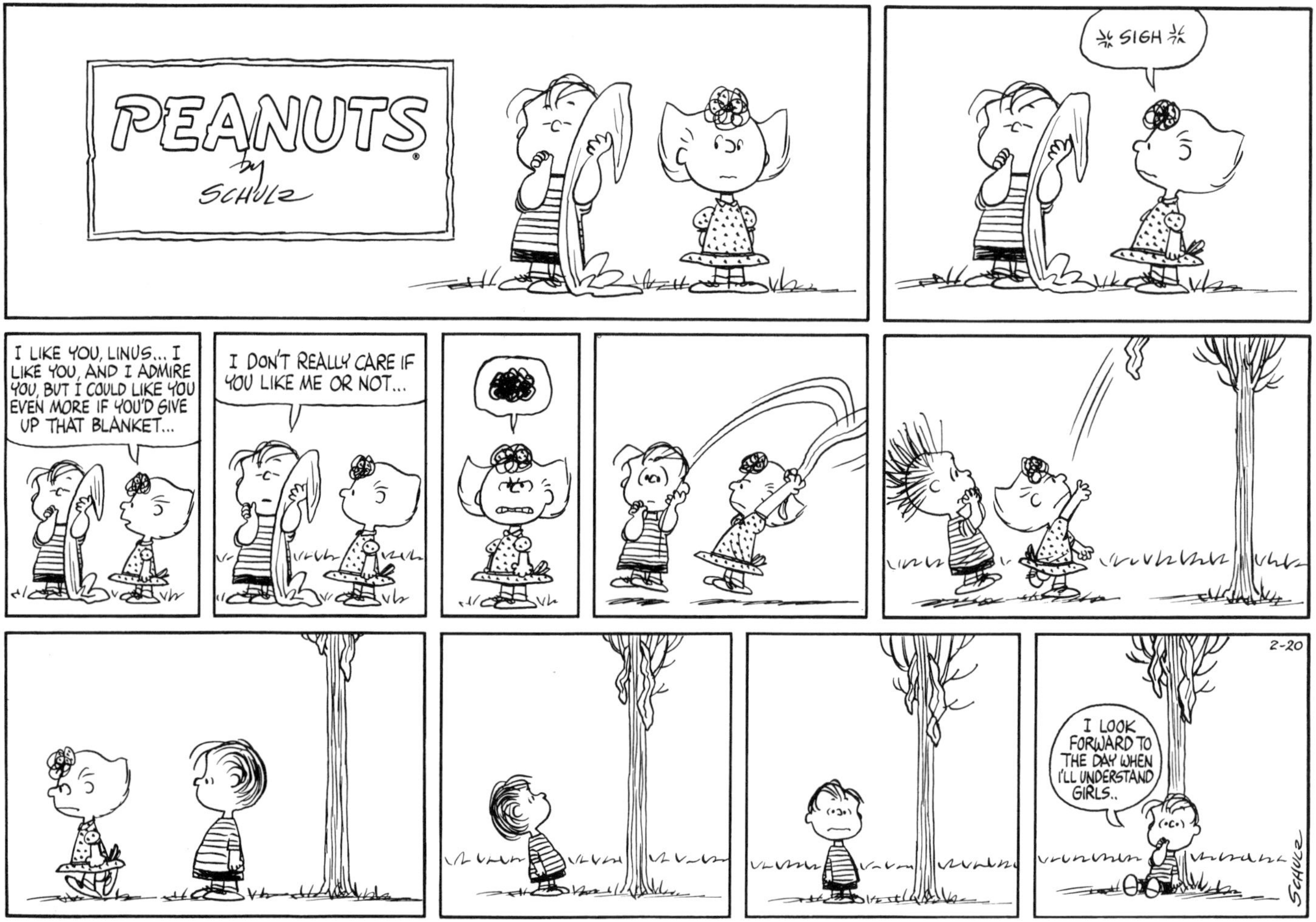
PEANUTS
by
SCHULZ
SIGH
I LIKE YOU, LINUS... I LIKE YOU, AND I ADMIRE YOU, BUT I COULD LIKE YOU EVEN MORE IF YOU'D GIVE UP THAT BLANKET...
I DON'T REALLY CARE IF YOU LIKE ME OR NOT...
2-20
I LOOK FORWARD TO THE DAY WHEN I'LL UNDERSTAND GIRLS..
SCHULZ

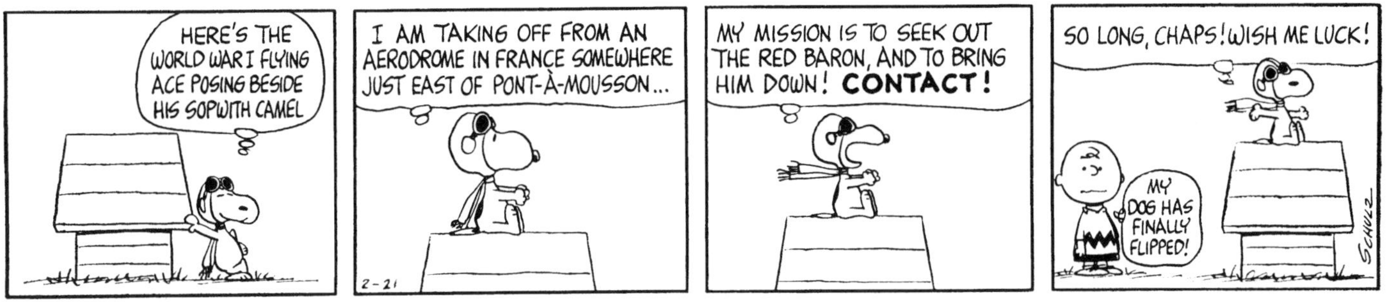
HERE'S THE WORLD WAR I FLYING ACE POSING BESIDE HIS SOPWITH CAMEL
I AM TAKING OFF FROM AN AERODROME IN FRANCE SOMEWHERE JUST EAST OF PONT-À-MOUSSON...
2-21
MY MISSION IS TO SEEK OUT THE RED BARON, AND TO BRING HIM DOWN! CONTACT!
SO LONG, CHAPS! WISH ME LUCK!
MY DOG HAS FINALLY FLIPPED!
SCHULZ

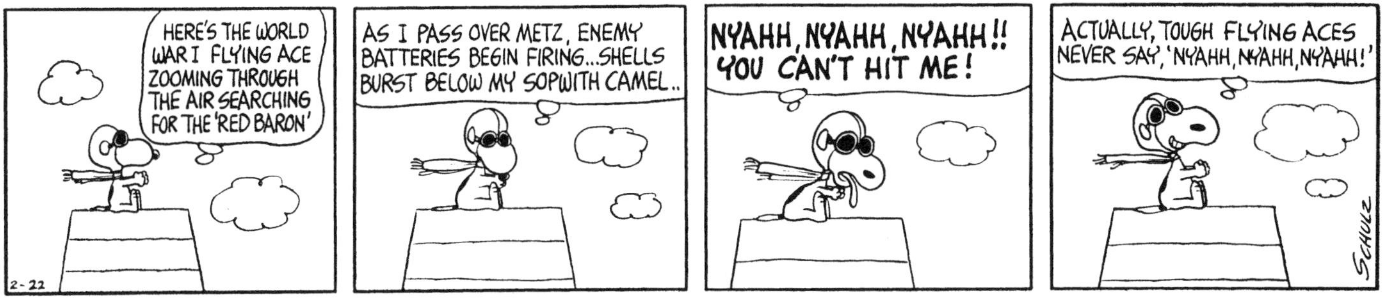
HERE'S THE WORLD WAR I FLYING ACE ZOOMING THROUGH THE AIR SEARCHING FOR THE 'RED BARON'
2-22
AS I PASS OVER METZ, ENEMY BATTERIES BEGIN FIRING...SHELLS BURST BELOW MY SOPWITH CAMEL..
NYAHH, NYAHH, NYAHH!! YOU CAN'T HIT ME!
ACTUALLY, TOUGH FLYING ACES NEVER SAY, 'NYAHH, NYAHH, NYAHH!'
SCHULZ

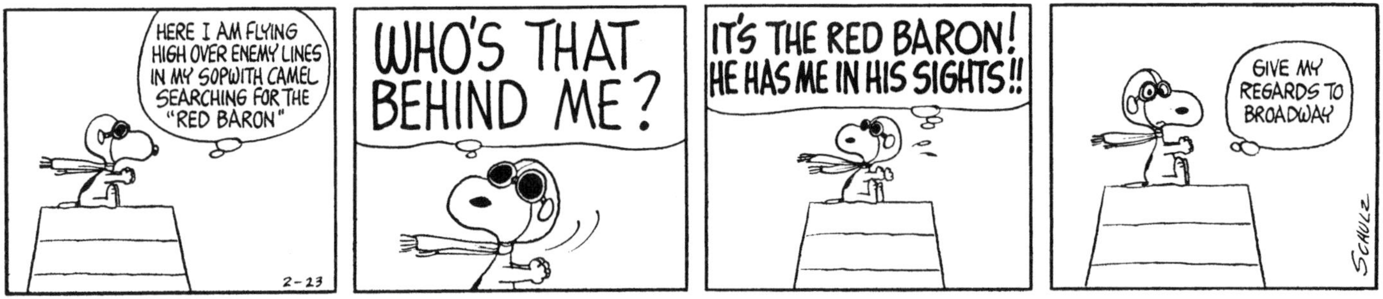
HERE I AM FLYING HIGH OVER ENEMY LINES IN MY SOPWITH CAMEL SEARCHING FOR THE "RED BARON"
2-23
WHO'S THAT BEHIND ME?
IT'S THE RED BARON! HE HAS ME IN HIS SIGHTS!!
GIVE MY REGARDS TO BROADWAY
SCHULZ

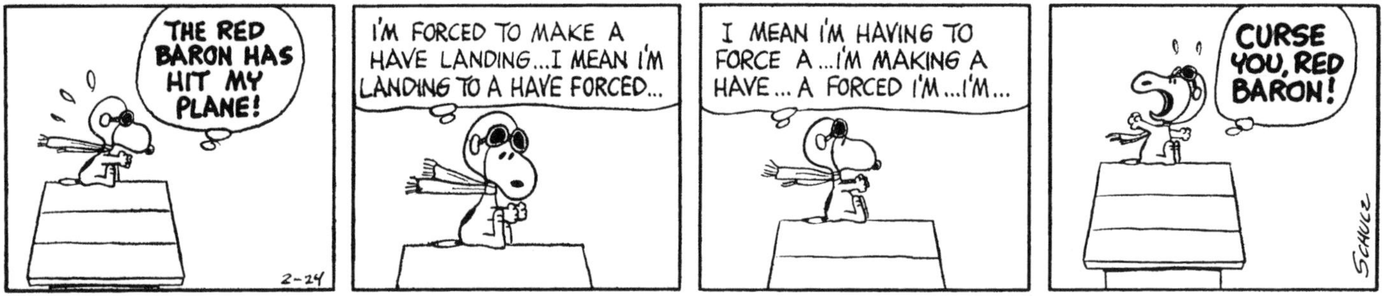
THE RED BARON HAS HIT MY PLANE!
2-24
I'M FORCED TO MAKE A HAVE LANDING...I MEAN I'M LANDING TO A HAVE FORCED...
I MEAN I'M HAVING TO FORCE A...I'M MAKING A HAVE... A FORCED I'M...I'M...
CURSE YOU, RED BARON!
SCHULZ

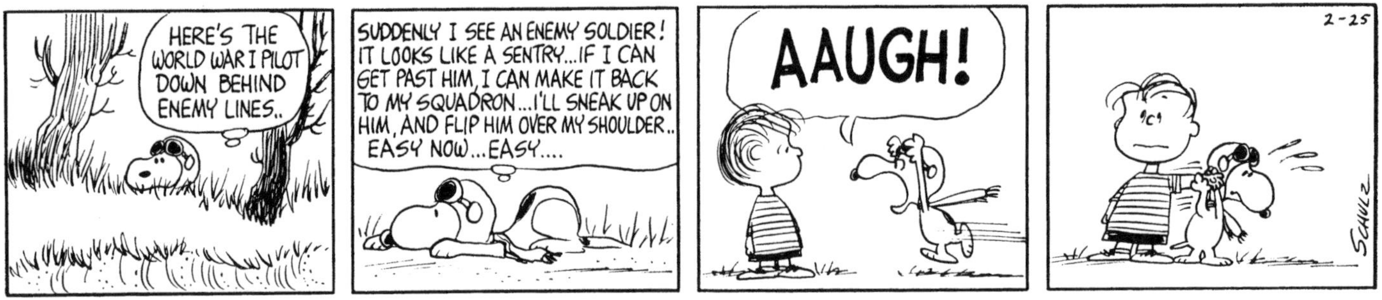
HERE'S THE WORLD WAR I PILOT DOWN BEHIND ENEMY LINES..
SUDDENLY I SEE AN ENEMY SOLDIER! IT LOOKS LIKE A SENTRY...IF I CAN GET PAST HIM, I CAN MAKE IT BACK TO MY SQUADRON...I'LL SNEAK UP ON HIM, AND FLIP HIM OVER MY SHOULDER.. EASY NOW...EASY....
AAUGH!
2-25
SCHULZ

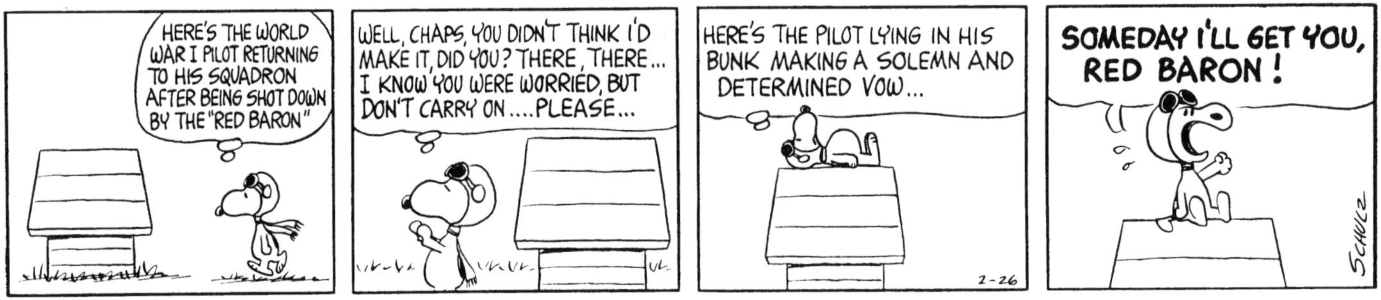
HERE'S THE WORLD WAR I PILOT RETURNING TO HIS SQUADRON AFTER BEING SHOT DOWN BY THE "RED BARON"
WELL, CHAPS, YOU DIDN'T THINK I'D MAKE IT, DID YOU? THERE, THERE... I KNOW YOU WERE WORRIED, BUT DON'T CARRY ON....PLEASE...
HERE'S THE PILOT LYING IN HIS BUNK MAKING A SOLEMN AND DETERMINED VOW...
2-26
SOMEDAY I'LL GET YOU, RED BARON!
SCHULZ

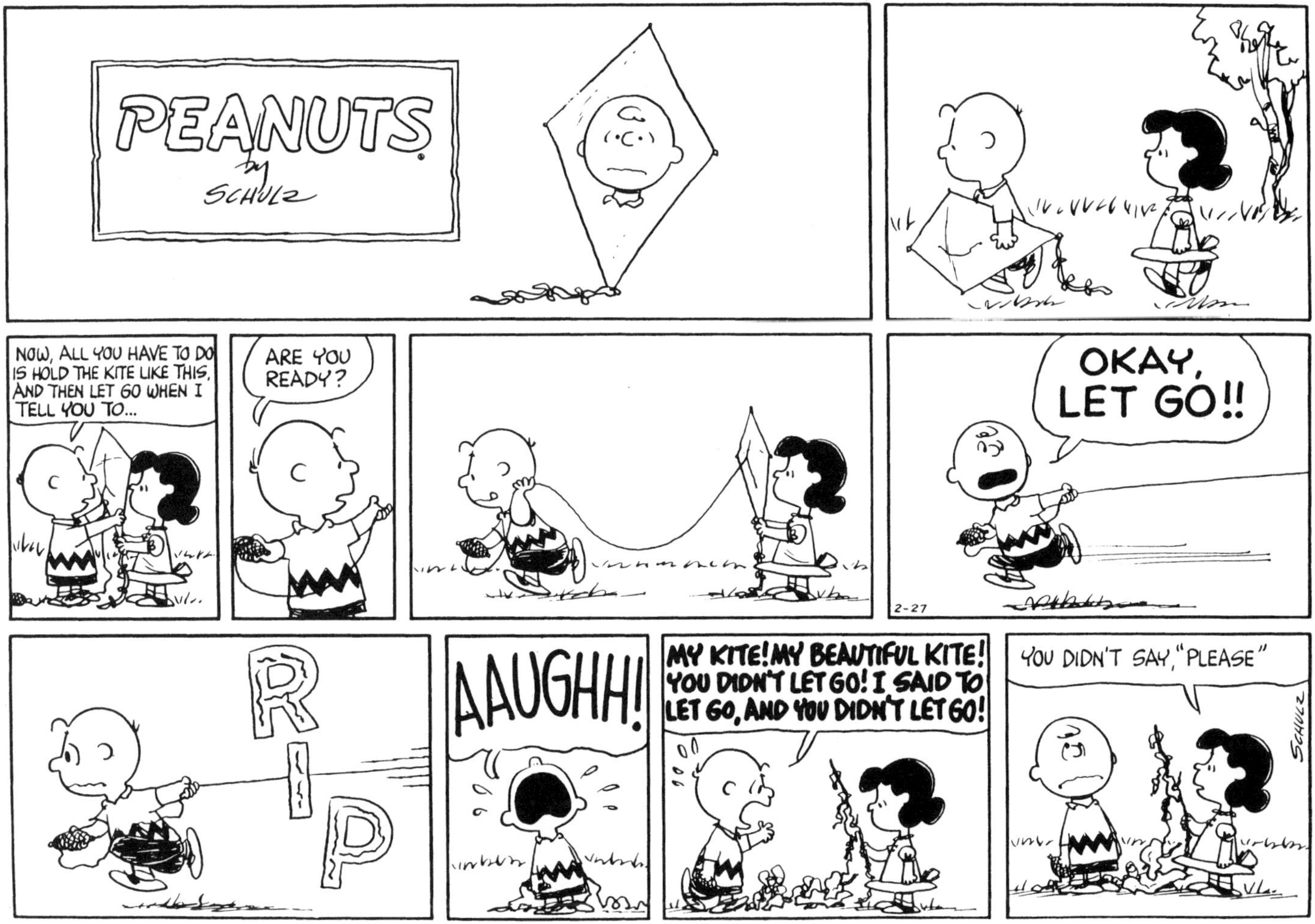
PEANUTS
by SCHULZ
NOW, ALL YOU HAVE TO DO IS HOLD THE KITE LIKE THIS, AND THEN LET GO WHEN I TELL YOU TO...
ARE YOU READY?
OKAY, LET GO!!
2-27
RIP
AAUGHH!
MY KITE! MY BEAUTIFUL KITE! YOU DIDN'T LET GO! I SAID TO LET GO, AND YOU DIDN'T LET GO!
YOU DIDN'T SAY, "PLEASE"
SCHULZ

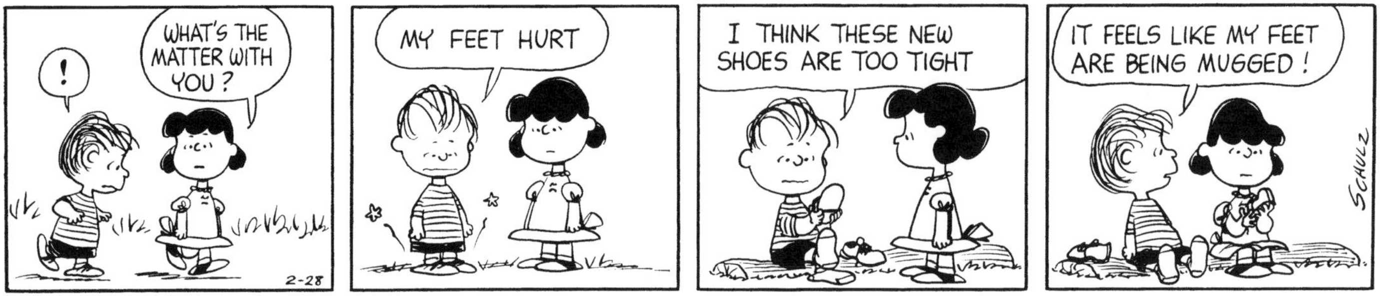
!
WHAT'S THE MATTER WITH YOU ?
2-28
MY FEET HURT
I THINK THESE NEW SHOES ARE TOO TIGHT
IT FEELS LIKE MY FEET ARE BEING MUGGED !
SCHULZ

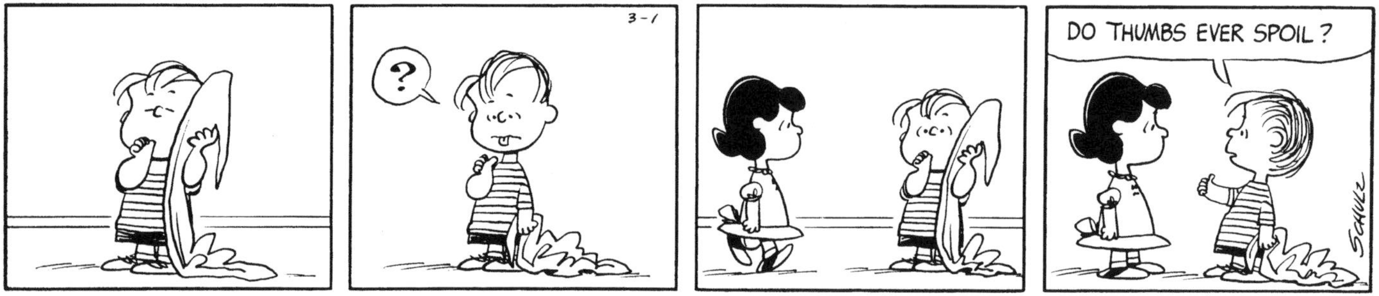
3-1
?
DO THUMBS EVER SPOIL ?
SCHULZ

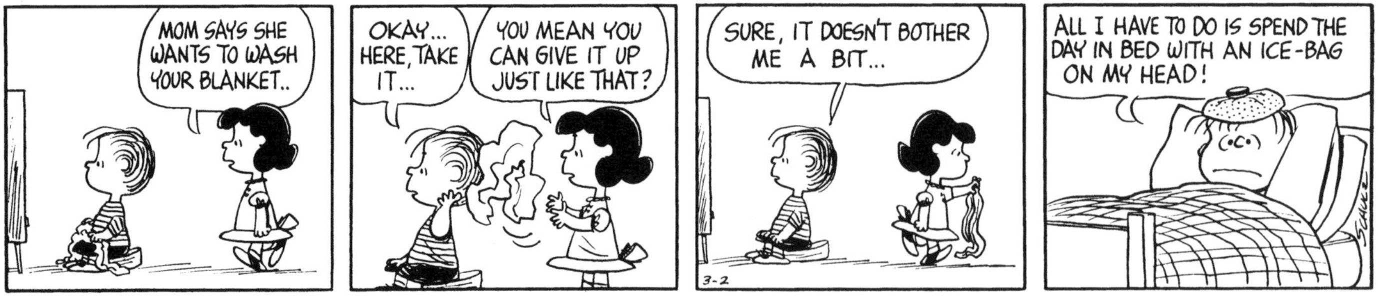
MOM SAYS SHE WANTS TO WASH YOUR BLANKET..
OKAY... HERE, TAKE IT...
YOU MEAN YOU CAN GIVE IT UP JUST LIKE THAT ?
SURE, IT DOESN'T BOTHER ME A BIT...
3-2
ALL I HAVE TO DO IS SPEND THE DAY IN BED WITH AN ICE-BAG ON MY HEAD !
SCHULZ

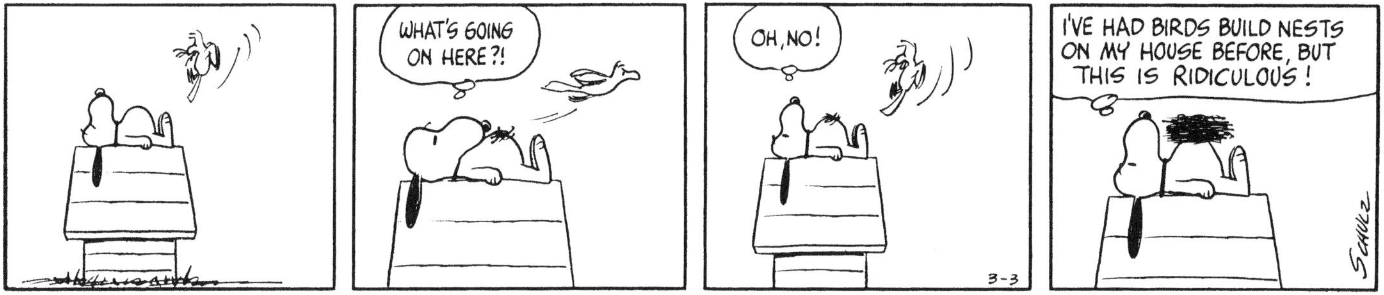
WHAT'S GOING ON HERE?!
OH, NO!
3-3
I'VE HAD BIRDS BUILD NESTS ON MY HOUSE BEFORE, BUT THIS IS RIDICULOUS!
SCHULZ

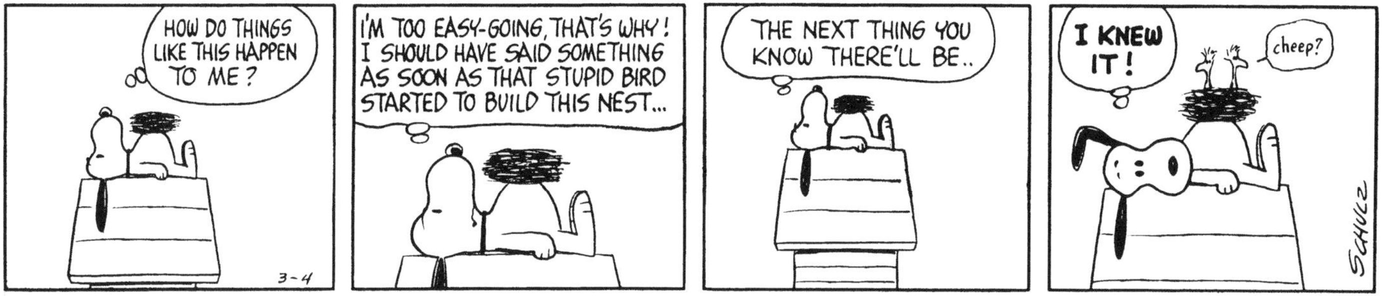
HOW DO THINGS LIKE THIS HAPPEN TO ME?
3-4
I'M TOO EASY-GOING, THAT'S WHY! I SHOULD HAVE SAID SOMETHING AS SOON AS THAT STUPID BIRD STARTED TO BUILD THIS NEST...
THE NEXT THING YOU KNOW THERE'LL BE..
I KNEW IT!
cheep?
SCHULZ

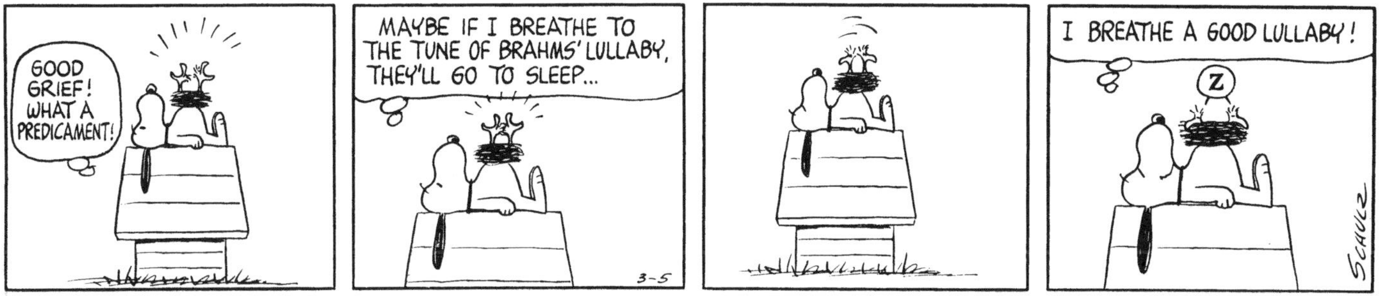
GOOD GRIEF! WHAT A PREDICAMENT!
MAYBE IF I BREATHE TO THE TUNE OF BRAHMS' LULLABY, THEY'LL GO TO SLEEP...
3-5
I BREATHE A GOOD LULLABY!
Z
SCHULZ

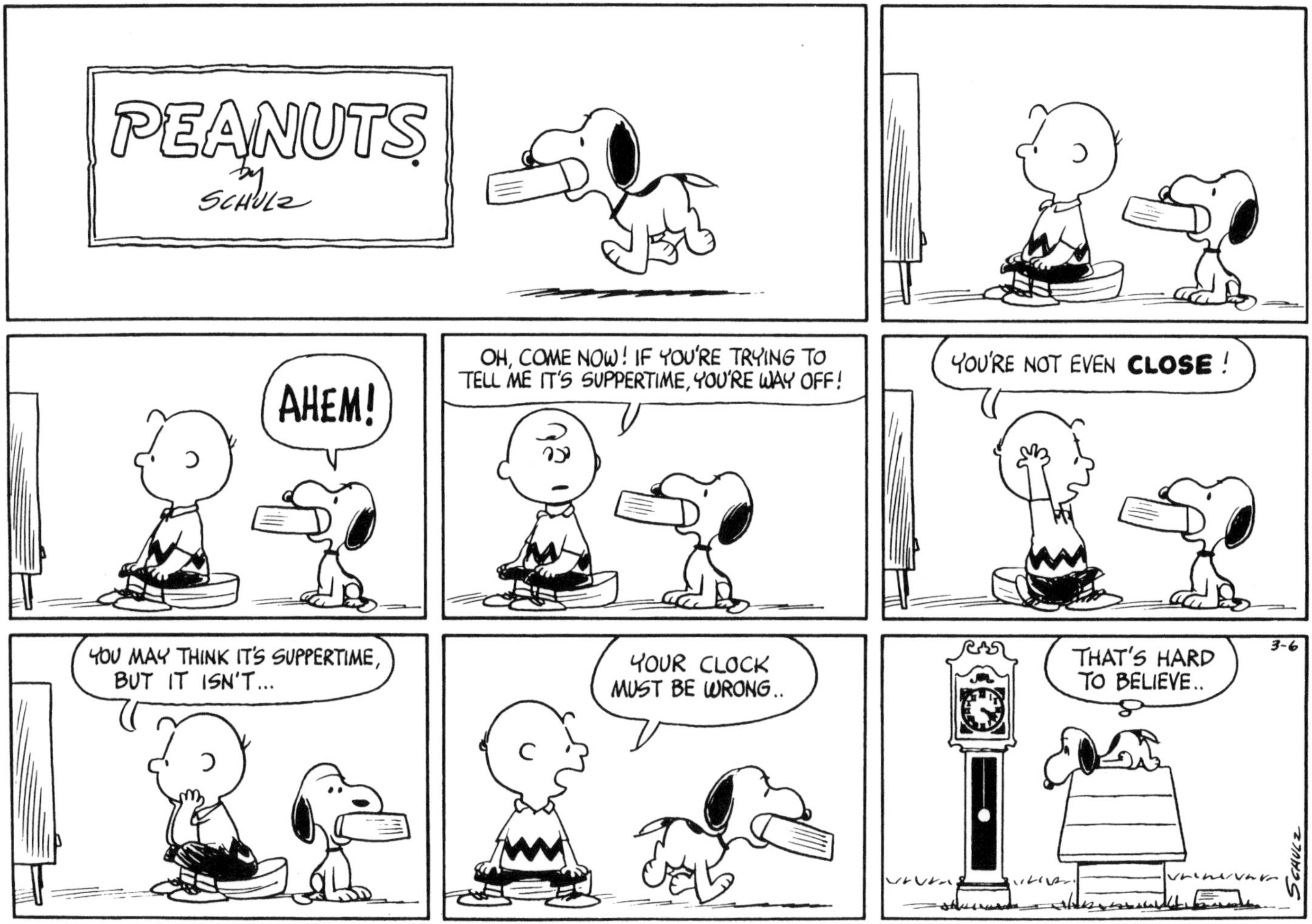
PEANUTS
by SCHULZ
AHEM!
OH, COME NOW! IF YOU'RE TRYING TO TELL ME IT'S SUPPERTIME, YOU'RE WAY OFF!
YOU'RE NOT EVEN CLOSE!
YOU MAY THINK IT'S SUPPERTIME, BUT IT ISN'T...
YOUR CLOCK MUST BE WRONG..
THAT'S HARD TO BELIEVE..
3-6
SCHULZ

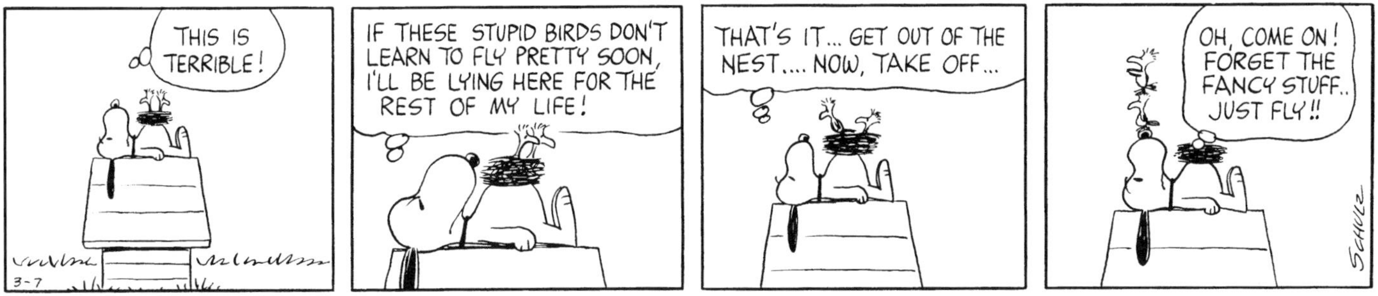
THIS IS TERRIBLE!
3-7
IF THESE STUPID BIRDS DON'T LEARN TO FLY PRETTY SOON, I'LL BE LYING HERE FOR THE REST OF MY LIFE!
THAT'S IT... GET OUT OF THE NEST.... NOW, TAKE OFF...
OH, COME ON! FORGET THE FANCY STUFF.. JUST FLY!!
SCHULZ

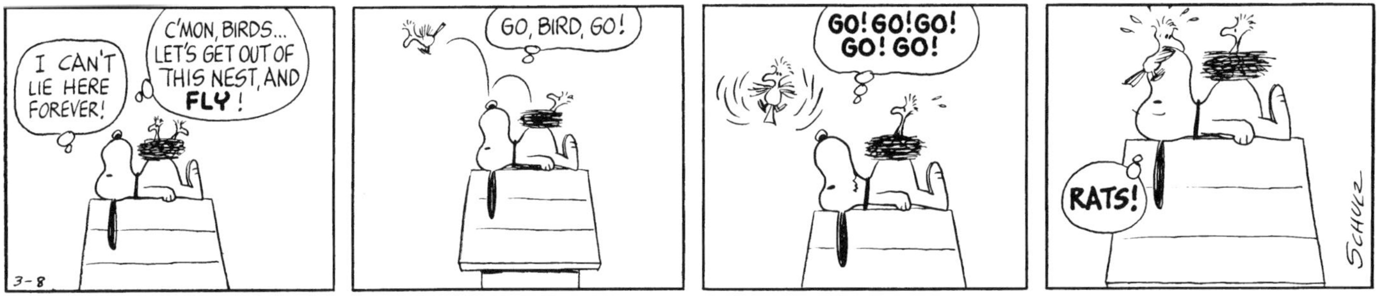
I CAN'T LIE HERE FOREVER!
C'MON, BIRDS... LET'S GET OUT OF THIS NEST, AND FLY!
3-8
GO, BIRD, GO!
GO! GO! GO! GO! GO!
RATS!
SCHULZ

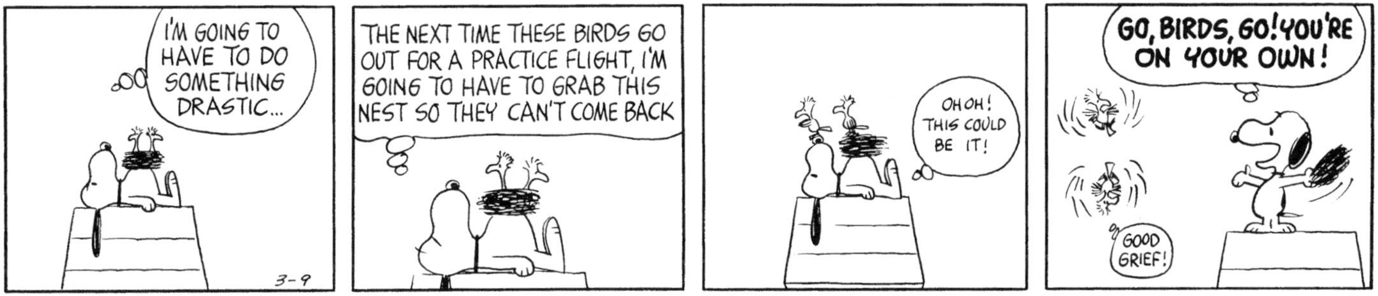
I'M GOING TO HAVE TO DO SOMETHING DRASTIC...
3-9
THE NEXT TIME THESE BIRDS GO OUT FOR A PRACTICE FLIGHT, I'M GOING TO HAVE TO GRAB THIS NEST SO THEY CAN'T COME BACK
OH OH! THIS COULD BE IT!
GO, BIRDS, GO! YOU'RE ON YOUR OWN!
GOOD GRIEF!

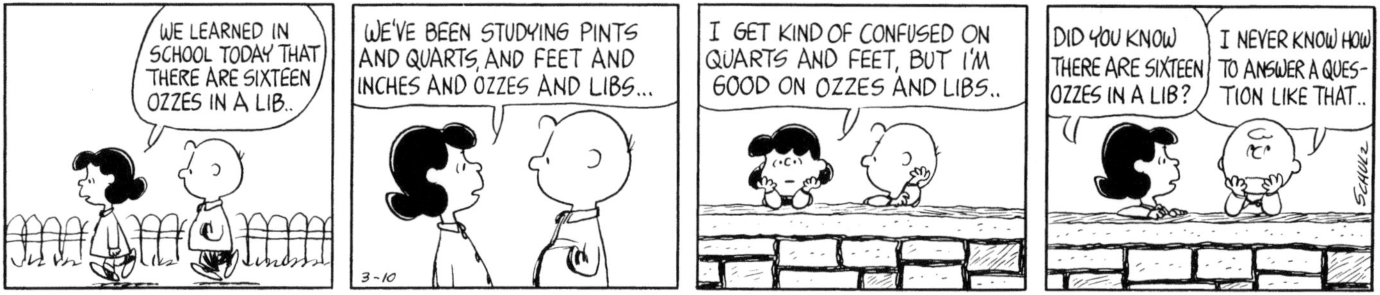
WE LEARNED IN SCHOOL TODAY THAT THERE ARE SIXTEEN OZZES IN A LIB..
WE'VE BEEN STUDYING PINTS AND QUARTS, AND FEET AND INCHES AND OZZES AND LIBS...
3-10
I GET KIND OF CONFUSED ON QUARTS AND FEET, BUT I'M GOOD ON OZZES AND LIBS..
DID YOU KNOW THERE ARE SIXTEEN OZZES IN A LIB?
I NEVER KNOW HOW TO ANSWER A QUESTION LIKE THAT..
SCHULZ

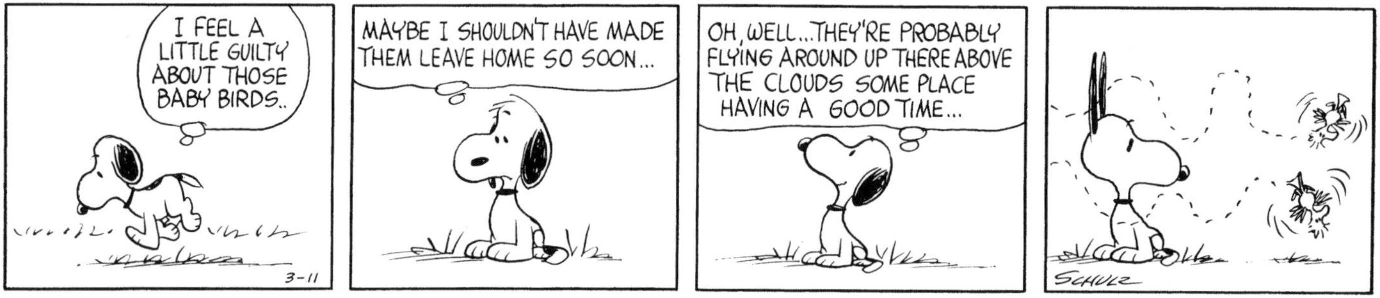
I FEEL A LITTLE GUILTY ABOUT THOSE BABY BIRDS..
3-11
MAYBE I SHOULDN'T HAVE MADE THEM LEAVE HOME SO SOON...
OH, WELL...THEY'RE PROBABLY FLYING AROUND UP THERE ABOVE THE CLOUDS SOME PLACE HAVING A GOOD TIME...
SCHULZ

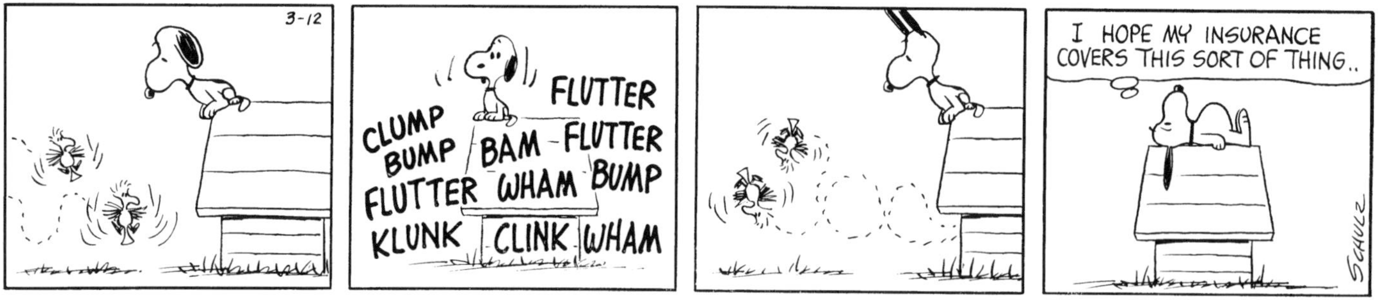
3-12
FLUTTER
CLUMP
BUMP
BAM
FLUTTER
FLUTTER
WHAM
BUMP
KLUNK
CLINK
WHAM
I HOPE MY INSURANCE COVERS THIS SORT OF THING..
SCHULZ

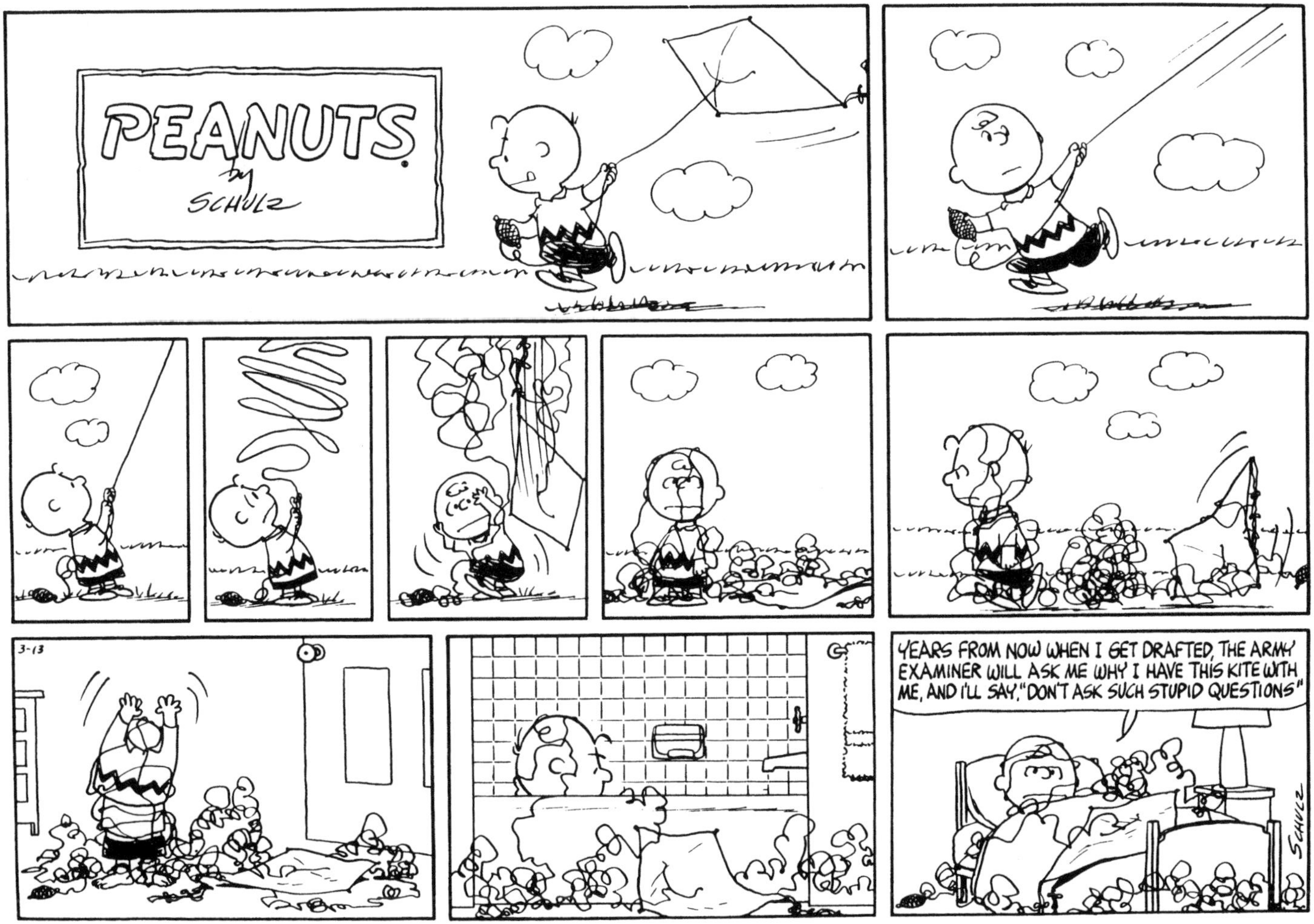
PEANUTS
by SCHULZ
3-13
YEARS FROM NOW WHEN I GET DRAFTED, THE ARMY EXAMINER WILL ASK ME WHY I HAVE THIS KITE WITH ME, AND I'LL SAY, "DON'T ASK SUCH STUPID QUESTIONS"
SCHULZ

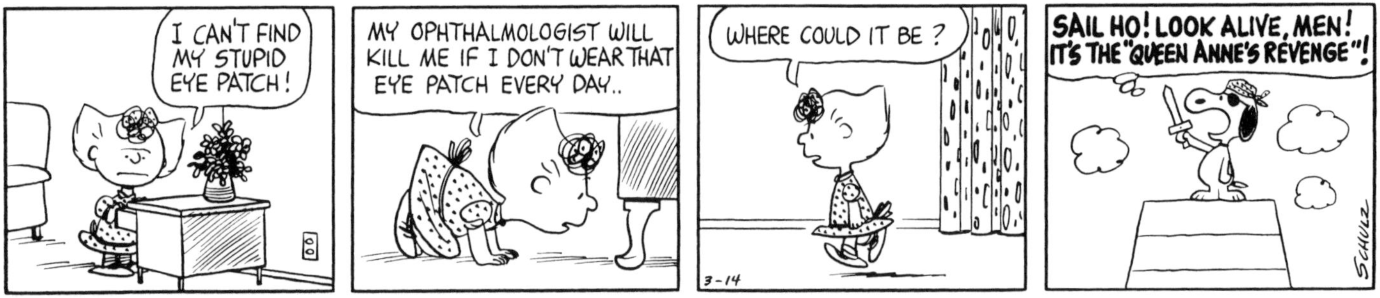
I CAN'T FIND MY STUPID EYE PATCH!
MY OPHTHALMOLOGIST WILL KILL ME IF I DON'T WEAR THAT EYE PATCH EVERY DAY..
WHERE COULD IT BE ?
3-14
SAIL HO! LOOK ALIVE, MEN! IT'S THE "QUEEN ANNE'S REVENGE"!
SCHULZ

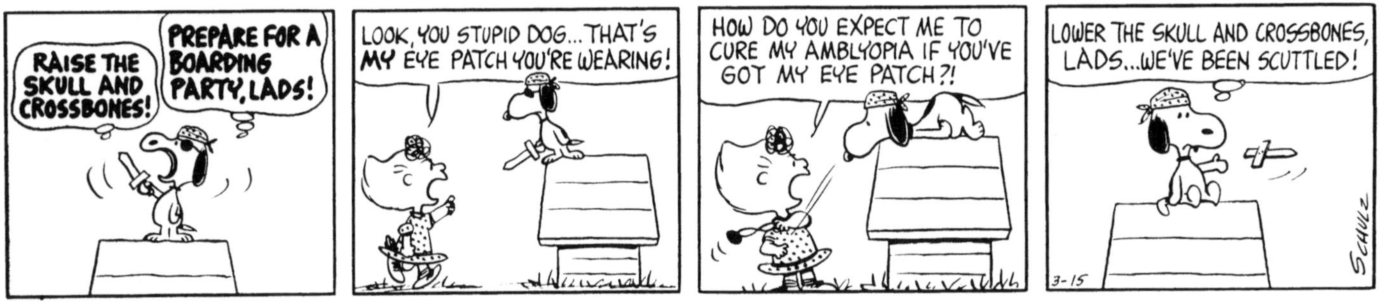
RAISE THE SKULL AND CROSSBONES!
PREPARE FOR A BOARDING PARTY, LADS!
LOOK, YOU STUPID DOG... THAT'S MY EYE PATCH YOU'RE WEARING!
HOW DO YOU EXPECT ME TO CURE MY AMBLYOPIA IF YOU'VE GOT MY EYE PATCH?!
LOWER THE SKULL AND CROSSBONES, LADS...WE'VE BEEN SCUTTLED!
SCHULZ
3-15

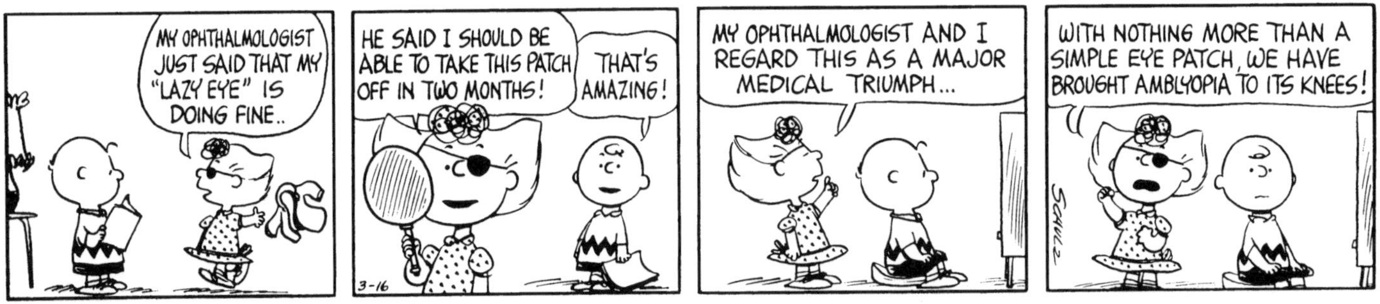
MY OPHTHALMOLOGIST JUST SAID THAT MY "LAZY EYE" IS DOING FINE..
HE SAID I SHOULD BE ABLE TO TAKE THIS PATCH OFF IN TWO MONTHS!
THAT'S AMAZING!
3-16
MY OPHTHALMOLOGIST AND I REGARD THIS AS A MAJOR MEDICAL TRIUMPH...
SCHULZ
WITH NOTHING MORE THAN A SIMPLE EYE PATCH, WE HAVE BROUGHT AMBLYOPIA TO ITS KNEES!

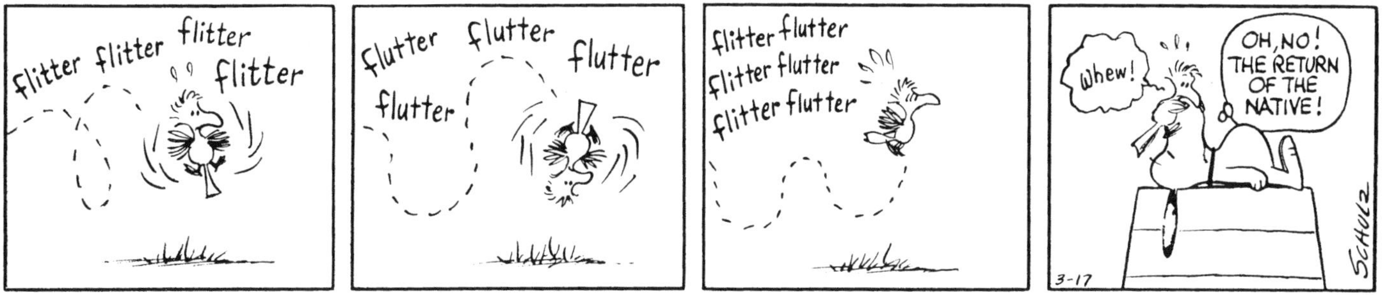
flitter flitter flitter flitter
flutter flutter flutter flutter
flitter flutter
flitter flutter
flitter flutter
Whew!
OH, NO! THE RETURN OF THE NATIVE!
3-17
SCHULZ

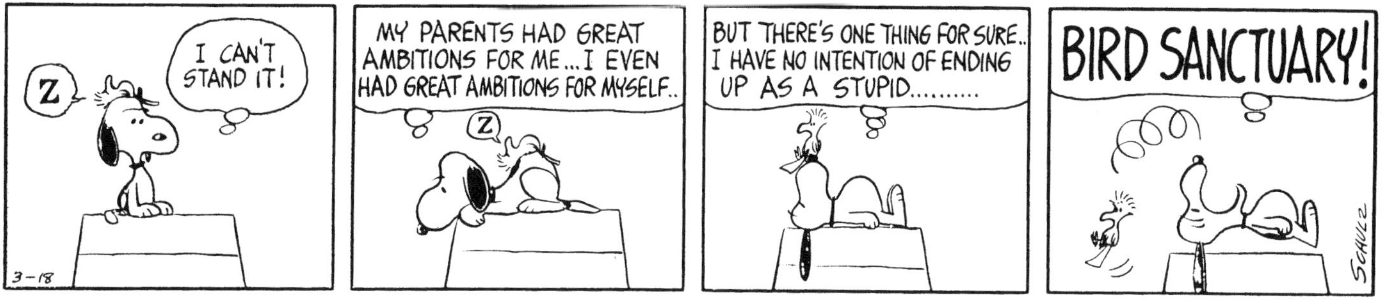
Z
I CAN'T STAND IT!
3-18
Z
MY PARENTS HAD GREAT AMBITIONS FOR ME...I EVEN HAD GREAT AMBITIONS FOR MYSELF..
BUT THERE'S ONE THING FOR SURE.. I HAVE NO INTENTION OF ENDING UP AS A STUPID.........
BIRD SANCTUARY!
SCHULZ

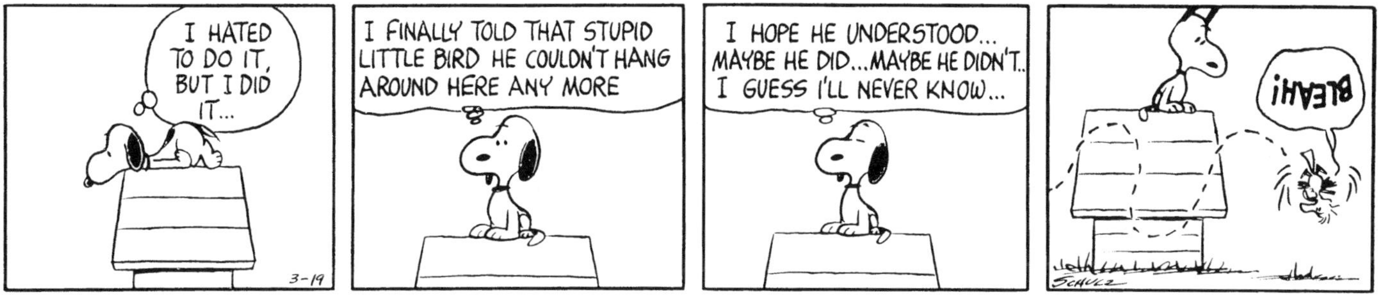
I HATED TO DO IT, BUT I DID IT...
3-19
I FINALLY TOLD THAT STUPID LITTLE BIRD HE COULDN'T HANG AROUND HERE ANY MORE
I HOPE HE UNDERSTOOD... MAYBE HE DID...MAYBE HE DIDN'T.. I GUESS I'LL NEVER KNOW...
BLEAH!
SCHULZ

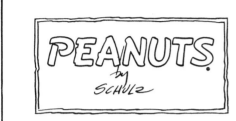

PEANUTS by SCHULZ

GOOD MORNING..

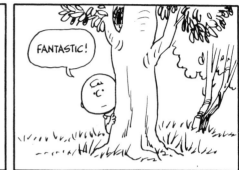

FANTASTIC!

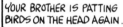

YOUR BROTHER IS PATTING BIRDS ON THE HEAD AGAIN..

OH, GOOD GRIEF!

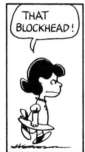

THAT BLOCKHEAD!

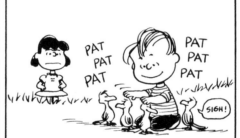

PAT PAT PAT

PAT PAT PAT

SIGH!

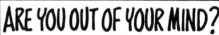

ARE YOU OUT OF YOUR MIND?

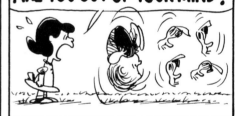

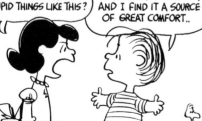

DON'T YOU REALIZE WHAT HAPPENS WHEN YOU DO STUPID THINGS LIKE THIS?

PATTING BIRDS ISN'T STUPID...THEY ENJOY IT, AND I FIND IT A SOURCE OF GREAT COMFORT..

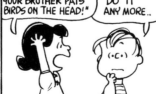

BUT WHAT ABOUT **ME**?! I'M THE ONE WHO HAS TO FACE THOSE KIDS AT SCHOOL WHO SAY,"HA! YOUR BROTHER PATS BIRDS ON THE HEAD!"

I SEE YOUR POINT...WELL, I GUESS I'D BETTER NOT DO IT ANY MORE..

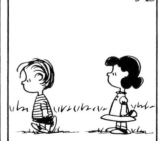

3-20

SCHULZ

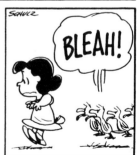

BLEAH!

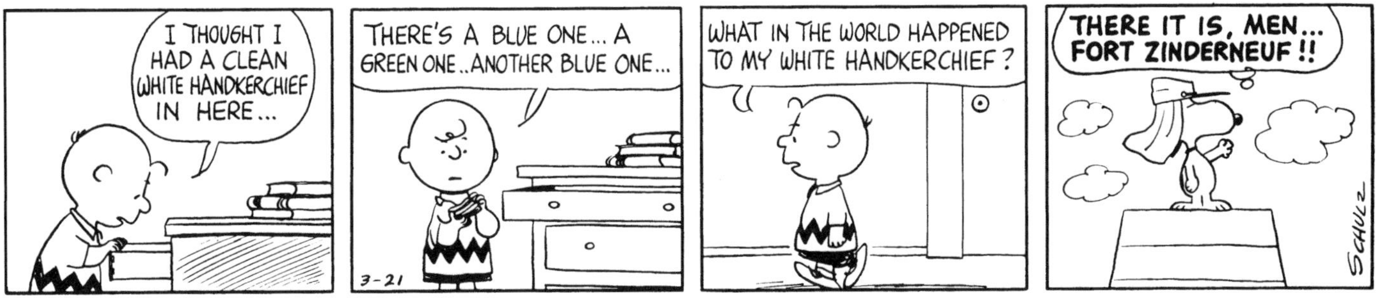
I THOUGHT I HAD A CLEAN WHITE HANDKERCHIEF IN HERE...
THERE'S A BLUE ONE... A GREEN ONE.. ANOTHER BLUE ONE...
3-21
WHAT IN THE WORLD HAPPENED TO MY WHITE HANDKERCHIEF?
THERE IT IS, MEN... FORT ZINDERNEUF!!
SCHULZ

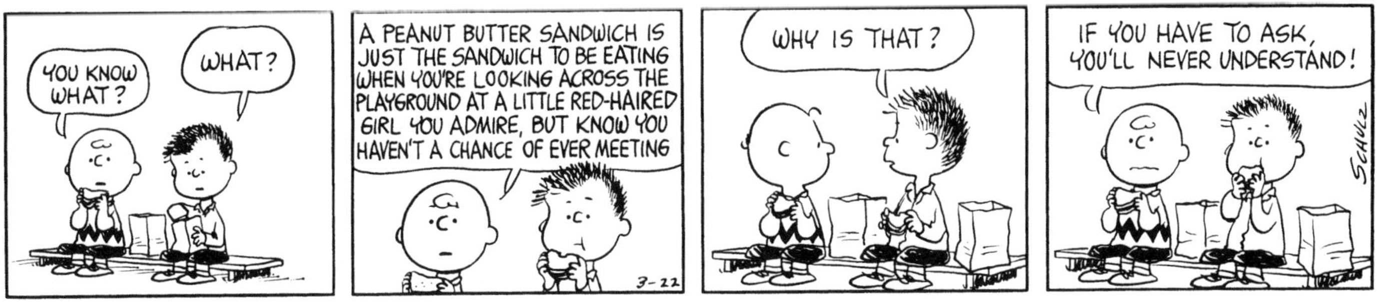
YOU KNOW WHAT?
WHAT?
A PEANUT BUTTER SANDWICH IS JUST THE SANDWICH TO BE EATING WHEN YOU'RE LOOKING ACROSS THE PLAYGROUND AT A LITTLE RED-HAIRED GIRL YOU ADMIRE, BUT KNOW YOU HAVEN'T A CHANCE OF EVER MEETING
3-22
WHY IS THAT?
IF YOU HAVE TO ASK, YOU'LL NEVER UNDERSTAND!
SCHULZ

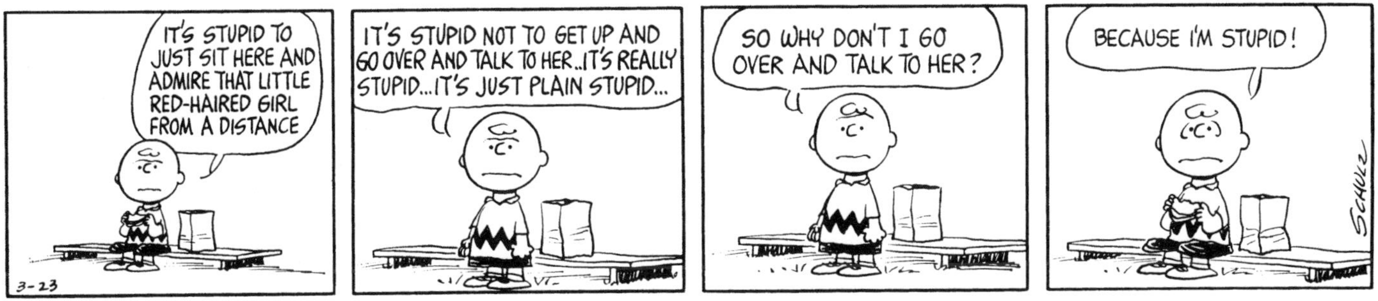
IT'S STUPID TO JUST SIT HERE AND ADMIRE THAT LITTLE RED-HAIRED GIRL FROM A DISTANCE
3-23
IT'S STUPID NOT TO GET UP AND GO OVER AND TALK TO HER..IT'S REALLY STUPID...IT'S JUST PLAIN STUPID...
SO WHY DON'T I GO OVER AND TALK TO HER?
BECAUSE I'M STUPID!
SCHULZ

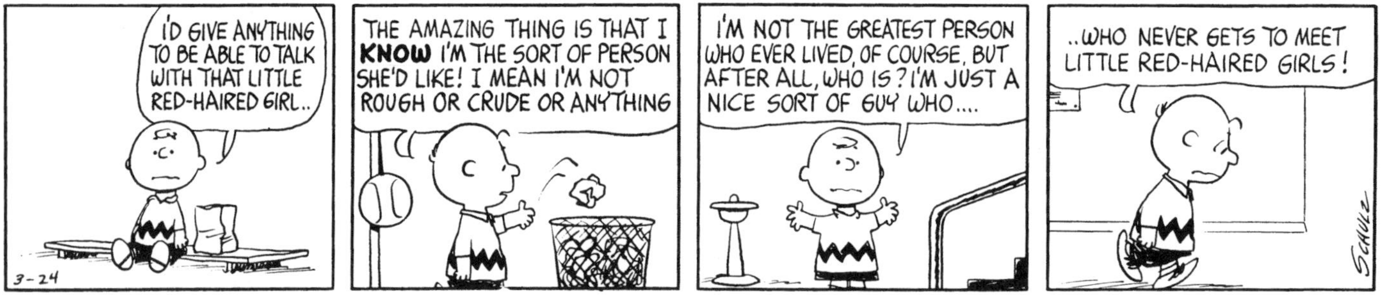
I'D GIVE ANYTHING TO BE ABLE TO TALK WITH THAT LITTLE RED-HAIRED GIRL..
THE AMAZING THING IS THAT I **KNOW** I'M THE SORT OF PERSON SHE'D LIKE! I MEAN I'M NOT ROUGH OR CRUDE OR ANYTHING
I'M NOT THE GREATEST PERSON WHO EVER LIVED, OF COURSE, BUT AFTER ALL, WHO IS? I'M JUST A NICE SORT OF GUY WHO....
..WHO NEVER GETS TO MEET LITTLE RED-HAIRED GIRLS!

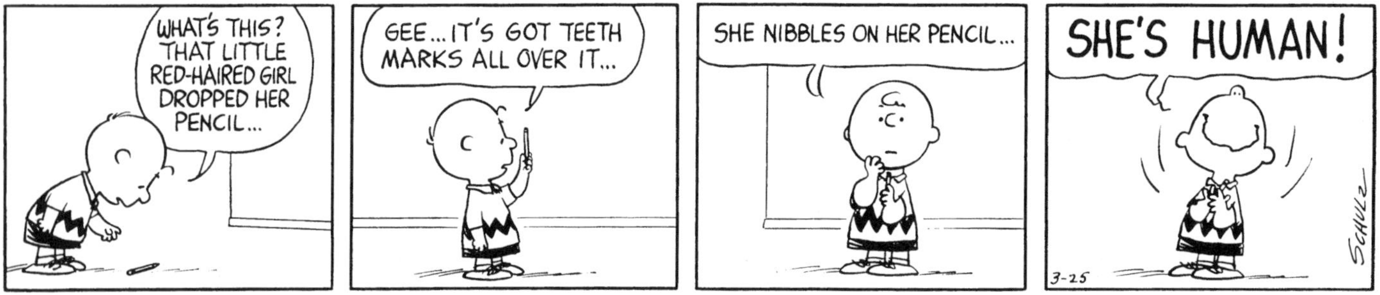
WHAT'S THIS? THAT LITTLE RED-HAIRED GIRL DROPPED HER PENCIL...
GEE... IT'S GOT TEETH MARKS ALL OVER IT...
SHE NIBBLES ON HER PENCIL...
SHE'S HUMAN!

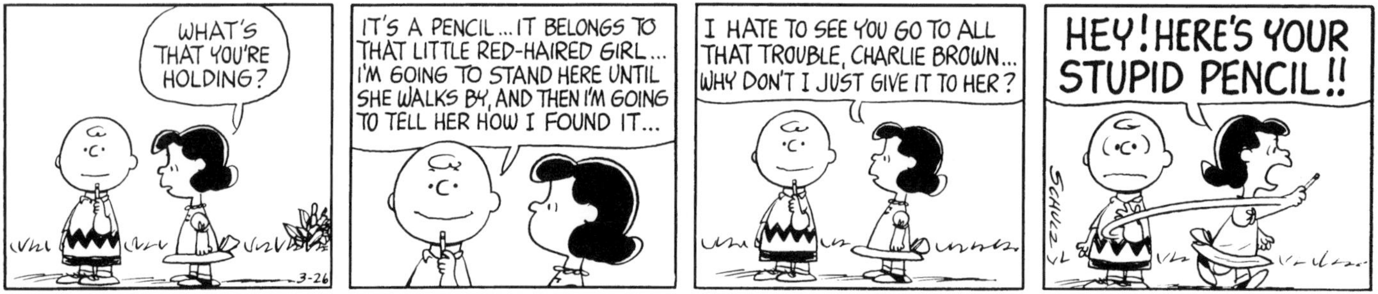
WHAT'S THAT YOU'RE HOLDING?
IT'S A PENCIL... IT BELONGS TO THAT LITTLE RED-HAIRED GIRL... I'M GOING TO STAND HERE UNTIL SHE WALKS BY, AND THEN I'M GOING TO TELL HER HOW I FOUND IT...
I HATE TO SEE YOU GO TO ALL THAT TROUBLE, CHARLIE BROWN... WHY DON'T I JUST GIVE IT TO HER?
HEY! HERE'S YOUR STUPID PENCIL!!

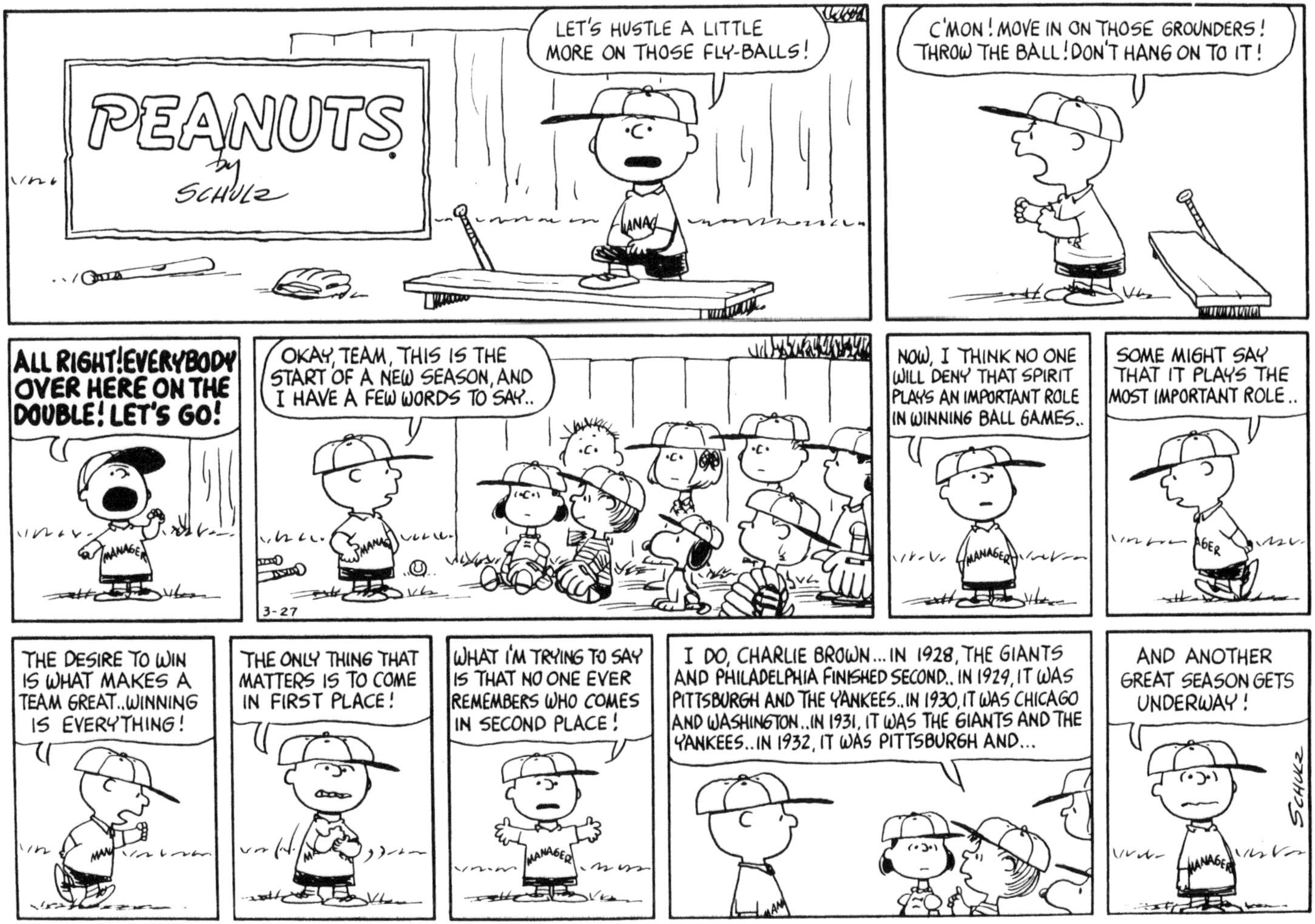
PEANUTS
by SCHULZ
LET'S HUSTLE A LITTLE MORE ON THOSE FLY-BALLS!
C'MON! MOVE IN ON THOSE GROUNDERS! THROW THE BALL! DON'T HANG ON TO IT!
ALL RIGHT! EVERYBODY OVER HERE ON THE DOUBLE! LET'S GO!
MANAGER
OKAY, TEAM, THIS IS THE START OF A NEW SEASON, AND I HAVE A FEW WORDS TO SAY..
3-27
NOW, I THINK NO ONE WILL DENY THAT SPIRIT PLAYS AN IMPORTANT ROLE IN WINNING BALL GAMES..
MANAGER
SOME MIGHT SAY THAT IT PLAYS THE MOST IMPORTANT ROLE..
THE DESIRE TO WIN IS WHAT MAKES A TEAM GREAT..WINNING IS EVERYTHING!
THE ONLY THING THAT MATTERS IS TO COME IN FIRST PLACE!
WHAT I'M TRYING TO SAY IS THAT NO ONE EVER REMEMBERS WHO COMES IN SECOND PLACE!
MANAGER
I DO, CHARLIE BROWN... IN 1928, THE GIANTS AND PHILADELPHIA FINISHED SECOND.. IN 1929, IT WAS PITTSBURGH AND THE YANKEES.. IN 1930, IT WAS CHICAGO AND WASHINGTON.. IN 1931, IT WAS THE GIANTS AND THE YANKEES.. IN 1932, IT WAS PITTSBURGH AND...
SCHULZ
AND ANOTHER GREAT SEASON GETS UNDERWAY!
MANAGER

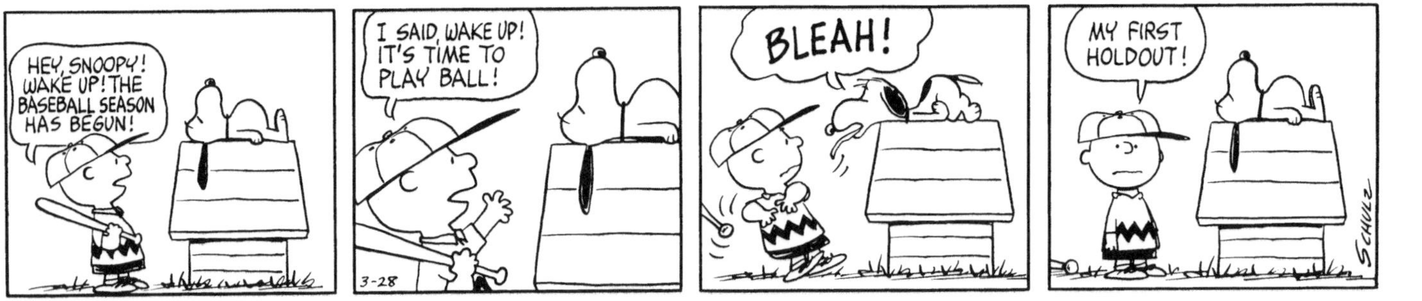
HEY, SNOOPY! WAKE UP! THE BASEBALL SEASON HAS BEGUN!
I SAID, WAKE UP! IT'S TIME TO PLAY BALL!
3-28
BLEAH!
MY FIRST HOLDOUT!
SCHULZ

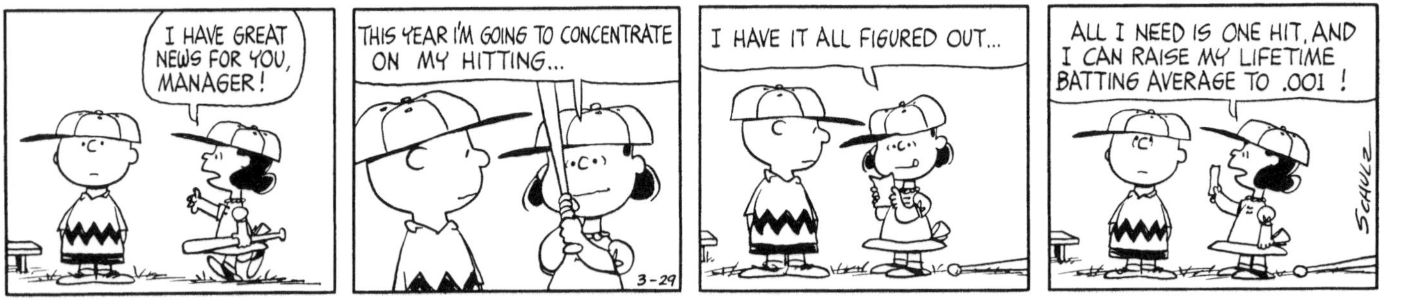
I HAVE GREAT NEWS FOR YOU, MANAGER!
THIS YEAR I'M GOING TO CONCENTRATE ON MY HITTING...
3-29
I HAVE IT ALL FIGURED OUT...
ALL I NEED IS ONE HIT, AND I CAN RAISE MY LIFETIME BATTING AVERAGE TO .001 !
SCHULZ

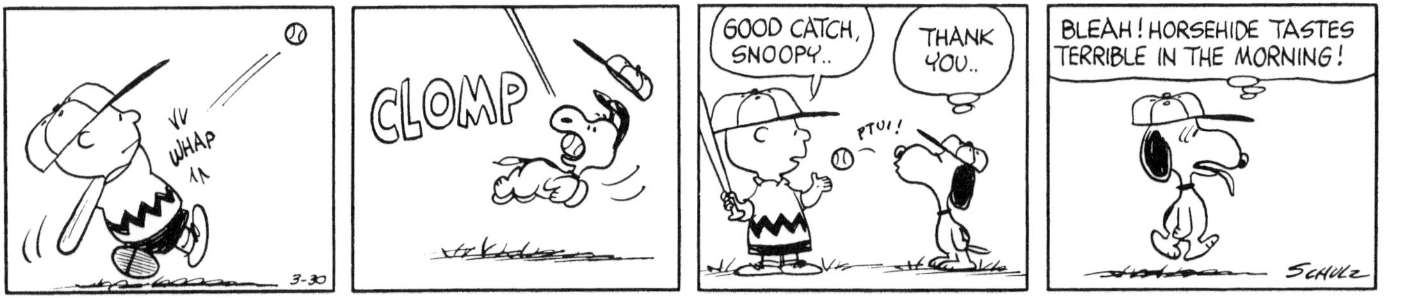
WHAP
3-30
CLOMP
GOOD CATCH, SNOOPY..
PTUI!
THANK YOU..
BLEAH! HORSEHIDE TASTES TERRIBLE IN THE MORNING!
SCHULZ

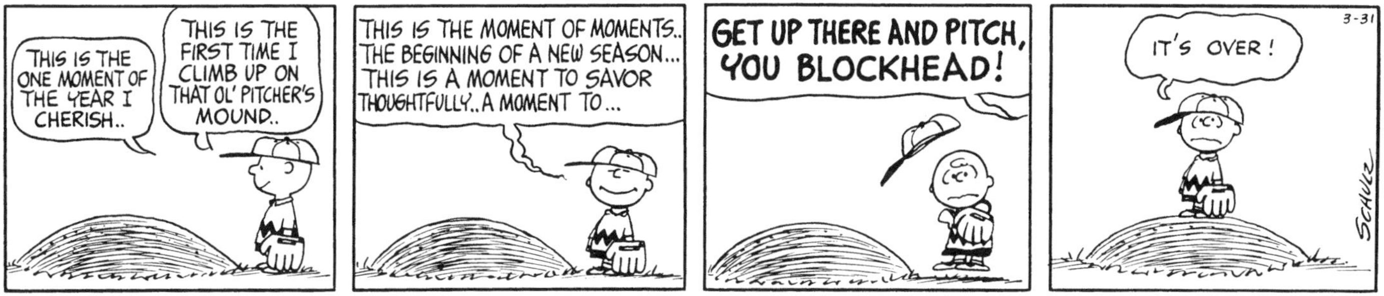
THIS IS THE ONE MOMENT OF THE YEAR I CHERISH..
THIS IS THE FIRST TIME I CLIMB UP ON THAT OL' PITCHER'S MOUND..
THIS IS THE MOMENT OF MOMENTS.. THE BEGINNING OF A NEW SEASON... THIS IS A MOMENT TO SAVOR THOUGHTFULLY.. A MOMENT TO...
GET UP THERE AND PITCH, YOU BLOCKHEAD!
3-31
IT'S OVER!
SCHULZ

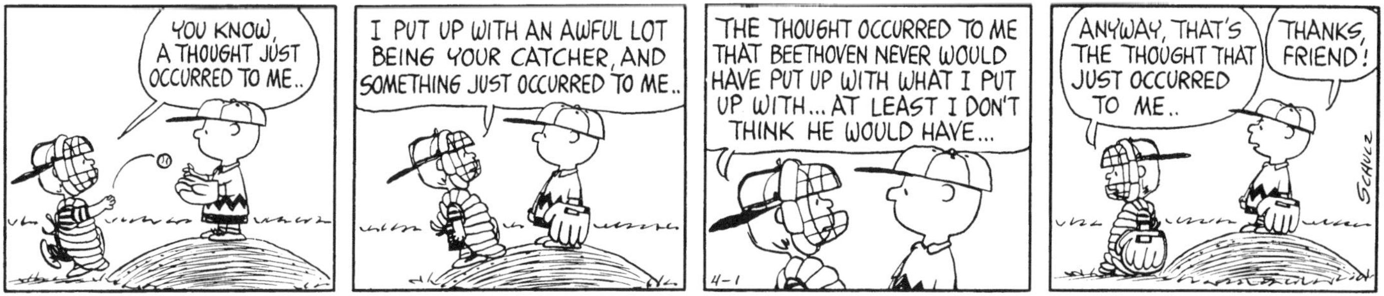
YOU KNOW, A THOUGHT JUST OCCURRED TO ME..
I PUT UP WITH AN AWFUL LOT BEING YOUR CATCHER, AND SOMETHING JUST OCCURRED TO ME..
THE THOUGHT OCCURRED TO ME THAT BEETHOVEN NEVER WOULD HAVE PUT UP WITH WHAT I PUT UP WITH... AT LEAST I DON'T THINK HE WOULD HAVE...
4-1
ANYWAY, THAT'S THE THOUGHT THAT JUST OCCURRED TO ME..
THANKS, FRIEND!
SCHULZ

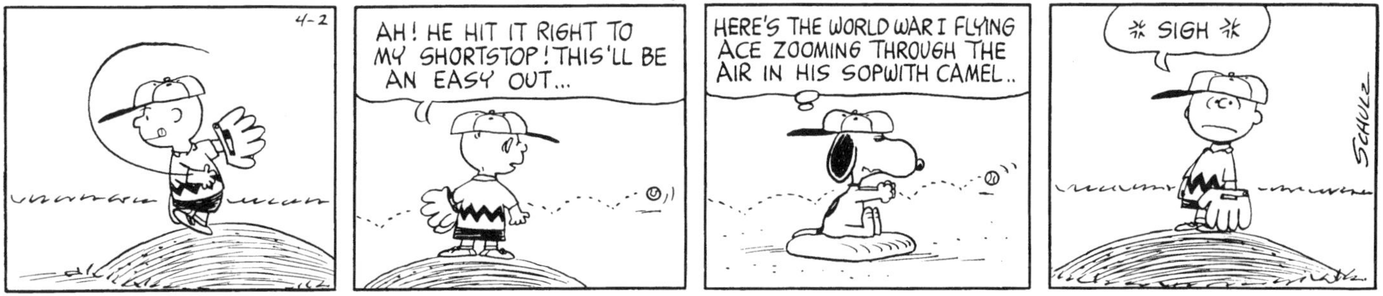
4-2
AH! HE HIT IT RIGHT TO MY SHORTSTOP! THIS'LL BE AN EASY OUT...
HERE'S THE WORLD WAR I FLYING ACE ZOOMING THROUGH THE AIR IN HIS SOPWITH CAMEL..
SIGH
SCHULZ

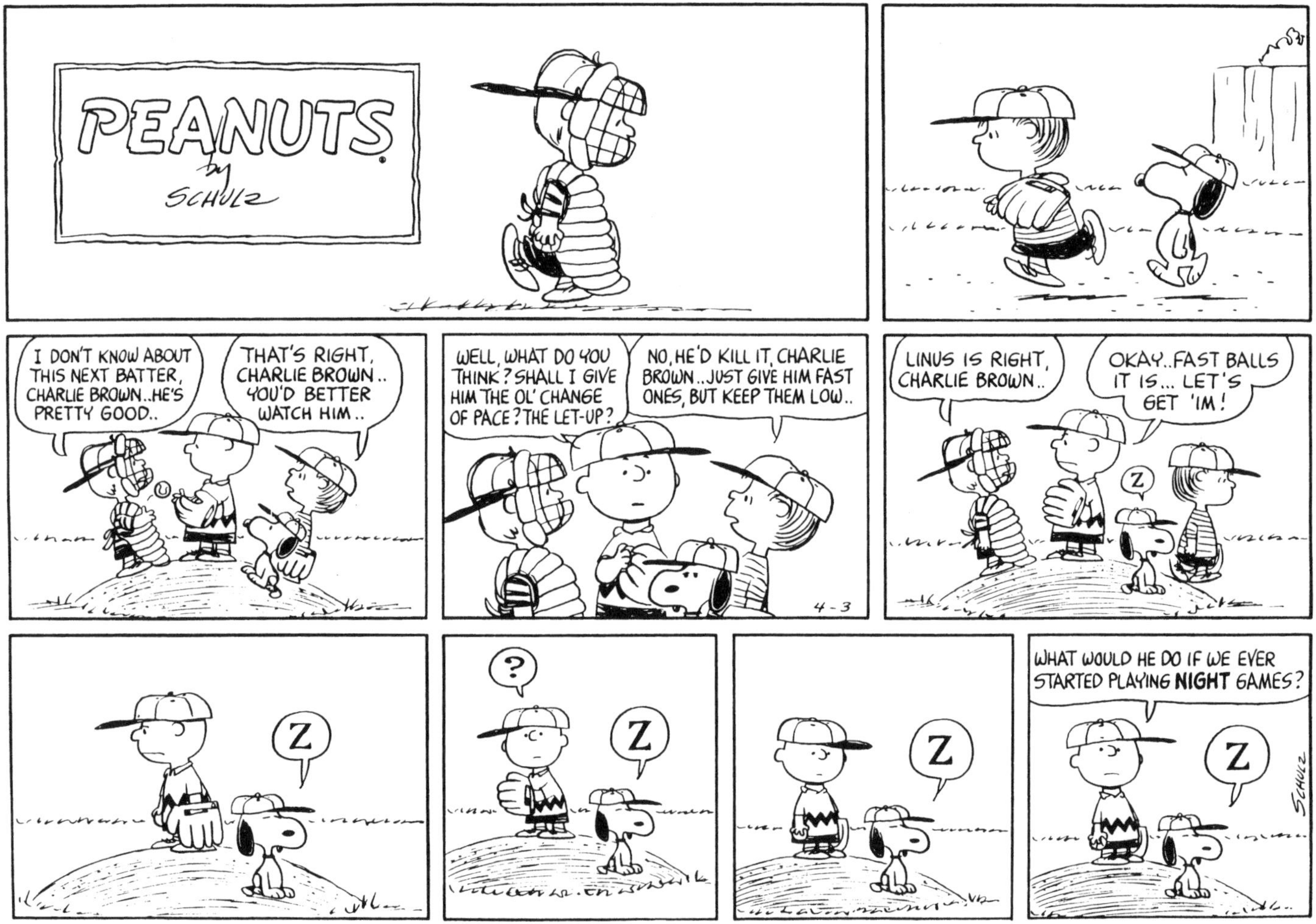
PEANUTS
by SCHULZ
I DON'T KNOW ABOUT THIS NEXT BATTER, CHARLIE BROWN..HE'S PRETTY GOOD..
THAT'S RIGHT, CHARLIE BROWN.. YOU'D BETTER WATCH HIM..
WELL, WHAT DO YOU THINK? SHALL I GIVE HIM THE OL' CHANGE OF PACE? THE LET-UP?
NO, HE'D KILL IT, CHARLIE BROWN..JUST GIVE HIM FAST ONES, BUT KEEP THEM LOW..
4-3
LINUS IS RIGHT, CHARLIE BROWN..
OKAY..FAST BALLS IT IS... LET'S GET 'IM!
Z
Z
?
Z
Z
WHAT WOULD HE DO IF WE EVER STARTED PLAYING **NIGHT** GAMES?
Z
SCHULZ

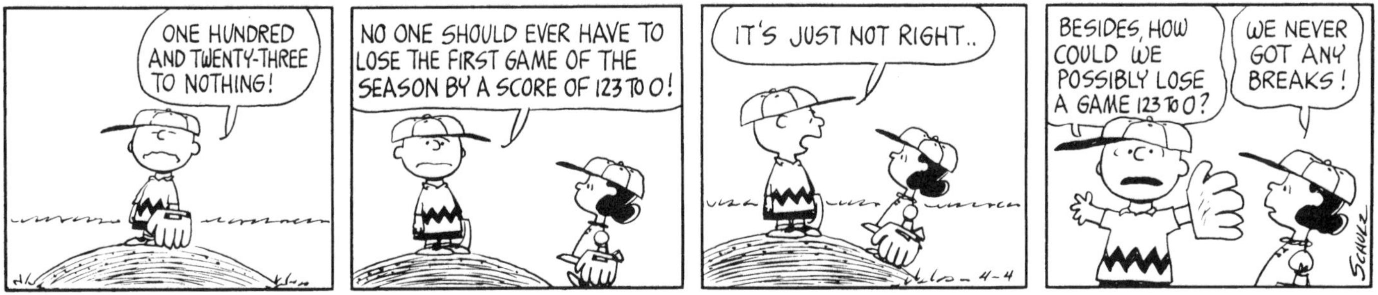
ONE HUNDRED AND TWENTY-THREE TO NOTHING!
NO ONE SHOULD EVER HAVE TO LOSE THE FIRST GAME OF THE SEASON BY A SCORE OF 123 TO 0!
IT'S JUST NOT RIGHT..
4-4
BESIDES, HOW COULD WE POSSIBLY LOSE A GAME 123 TO 0?
WE NEVER GOT ANY BREAKS!
SCHULZ

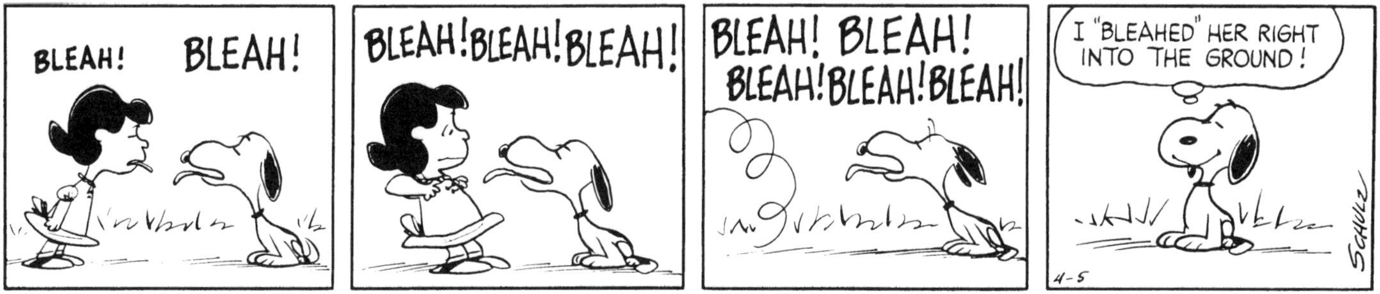
BLEAH!
BLEAH!
BLEAH! BLEAH! BLEAH!
BLEAH! BLEAH! BLEAH! BLEAH! BLEAH!
I "BLEAHED" HER RIGHT INTO THE GROUND!
4-5
SCHULZ

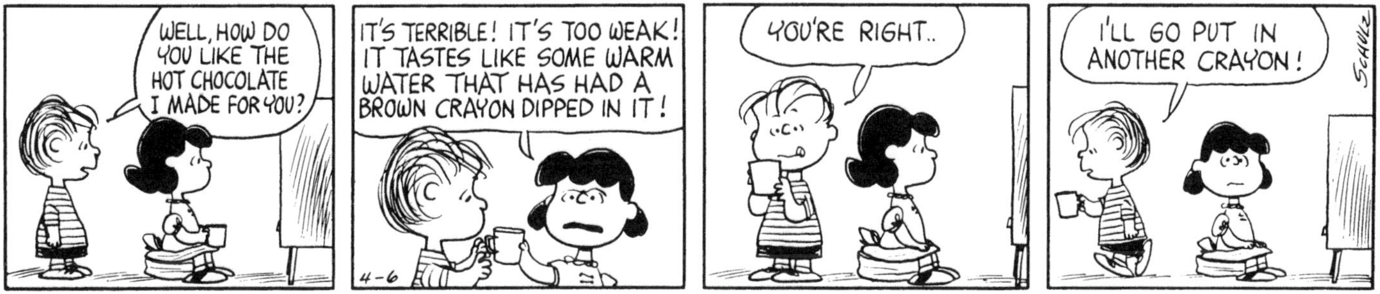
WELL, HOW DO YOU LIKE THE HOT CHOCOLATE I MADE FOR YOU?
IT'S TERRIBLE! IT'S TOO WEAK! IT TASTES LIKE SOME WARM WATER THAT HAS HAD A BROWN CRAYON DIPPED IN IT!
4-6
YOU'RE RIGHT..
I'LL GO PUT IN ANOTHER CRAYON!
SCHULZ

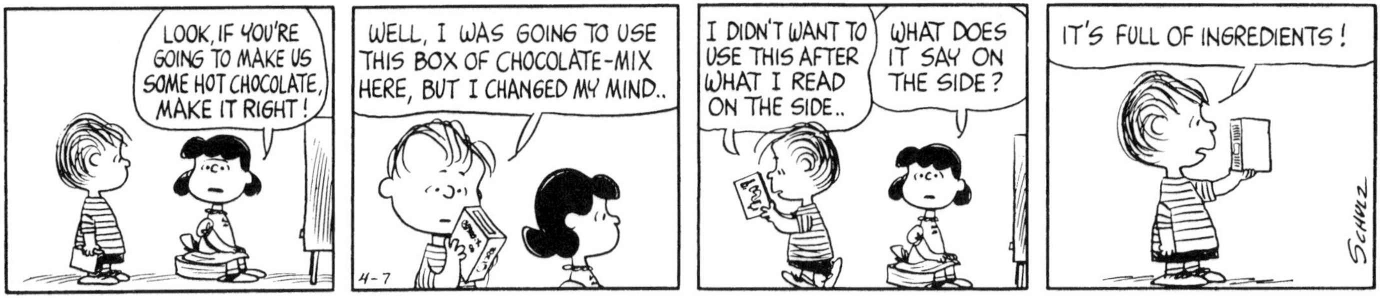
LOOK, IF YOU'RE GOING TO MAKE US SOME HOT CHOCOLATE, MAKE IT RIGHT!
WELL, I WAS GOING TO USE THIS BOX OF CHOCOLATE-MIX HERE, BUT I CHANGED MY MIND..
I DIDN'T WANT TO USE THIS AFTER WHAT I READ ON THE SIDE..
WHAT DOES IT SAY ON THE SIDE?
IT'S FULL OF INGREDIENTS!

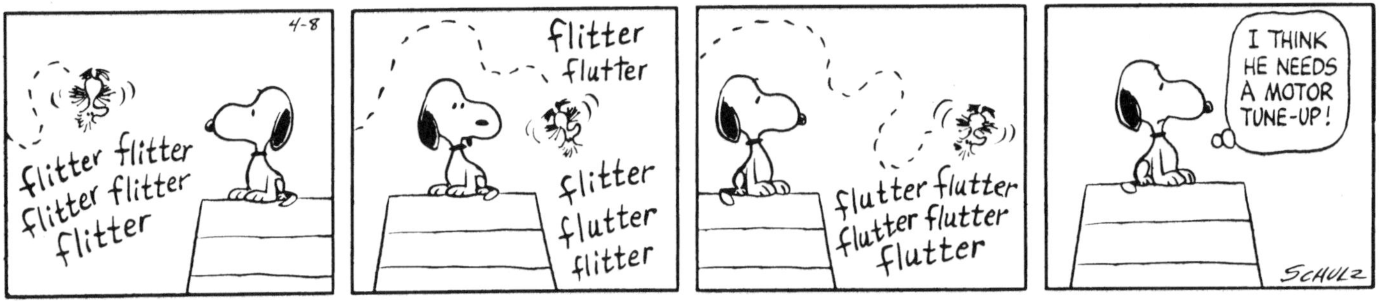
flitter flitter flitter flitter flitter
flitter flutter
flitter flutter flitter
flutter flutter flutter flutter flutter
I THINK HE NEEDS A MOTOR TUNE-UP!

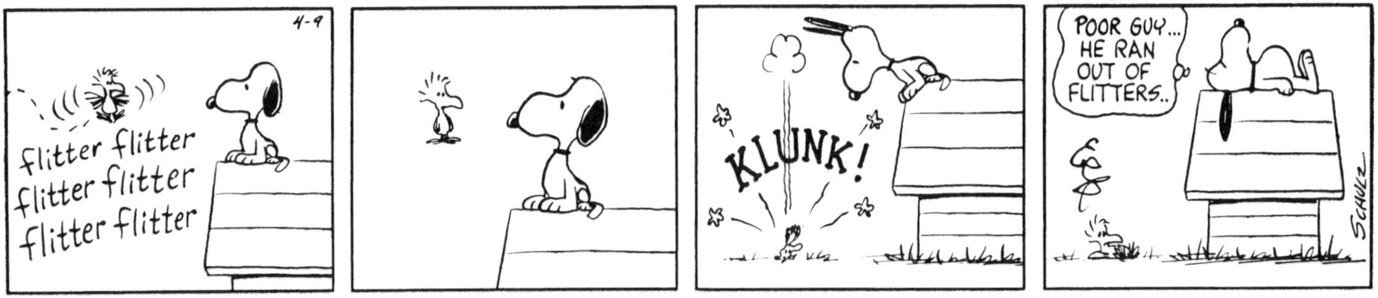
flitter flitter flitter flitter flitter flitter
KLUNK!
POOR GUY... HE RAN OUT OF FLITTERS..

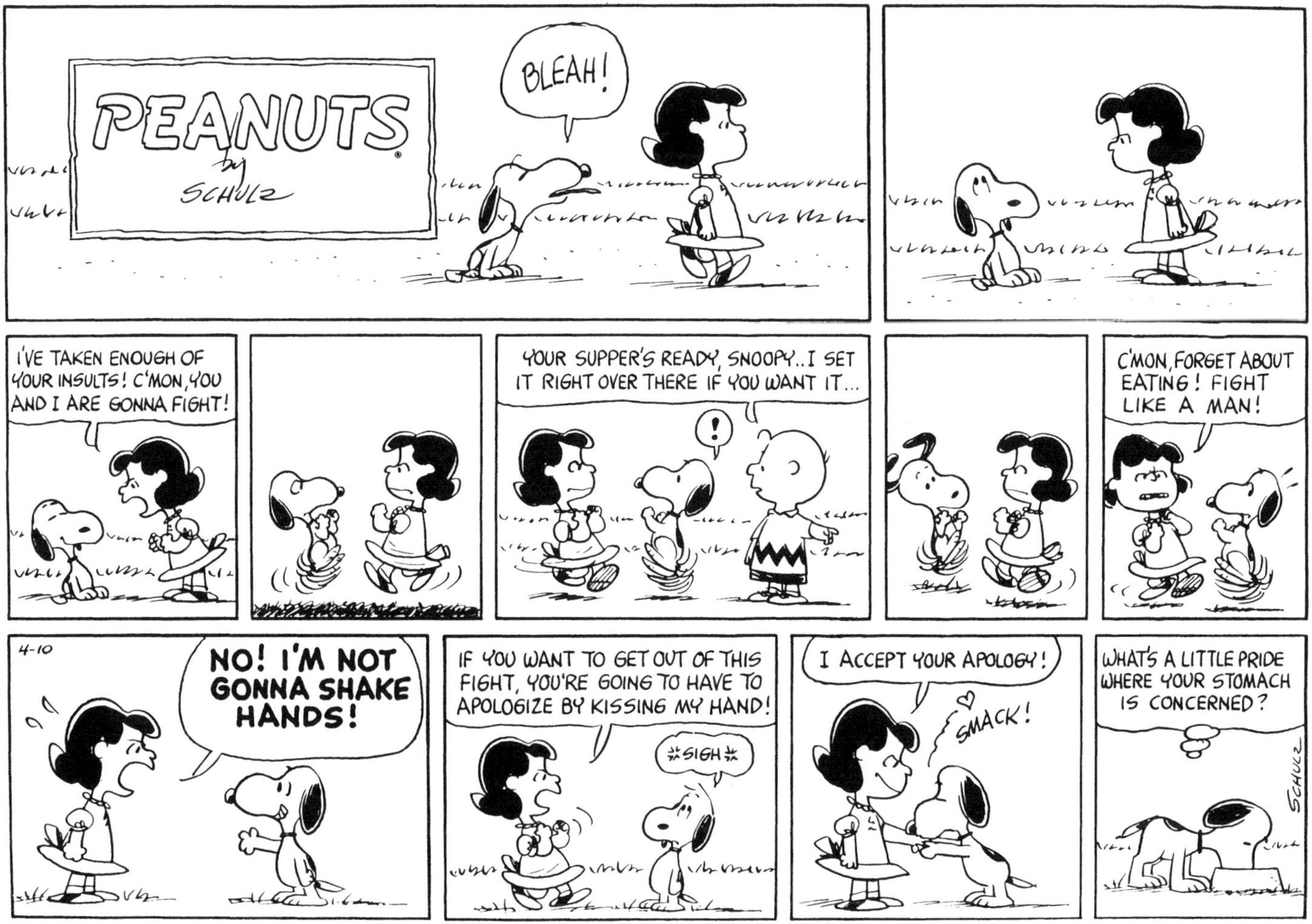
PEANUTS
by SCHULZ
BLEAH!
I'VE TAKEN ENOUGH OF YOUR INSULTS! C'MON, YOU AND I ARE GONNA FIGHT!
YOUR SUPPER'S READY, SNOOPY..I SET IT RIGHT OVER THERE IF YOU WANT IT...
!
C'MON, FORGET ABOUT EATING! FIGHT LIKE A MAN!
4-10
NO! I'M NOT GONNA SHAKE HANDS!
IF YOU WANT TO GET OUT OF THIS FIGHT, YOU'RE GOING TO HAVE TO APOLOGIZE BY KISSING MY HAND!
SIGH
I ACCEPT YOUR APOLOGY!
SMACK!
WHAT'S A LITTLE PRIDE WHERE YOUR STOMACH IS CONCERNED?
SCHULZ

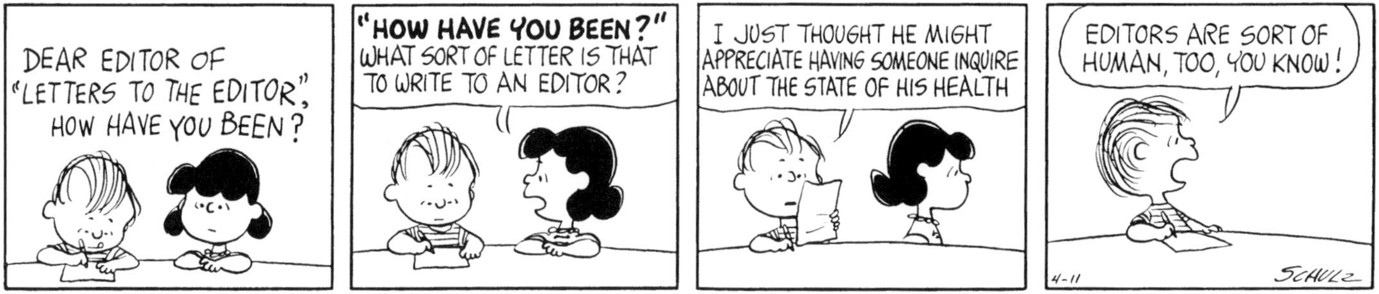
DEAR EDITOR OF "LETTERS TO THE EDITOR", HOW HAVE YOU BEEN?
"HOW HAVE YOU BEEN?" WHAT SORT OF LETTER IS THAT TO WRITE TO AN EDITOR?
I JUST THOUGHT HE MIGHT APPRECIATE HAVING SOMEONE INQUIRE ABOUT THE STATE OF HIS HEALTH
EDITORS ARE SORT OF HUMAN, TOO, YOU KNOW!
4-11
SCHULZ

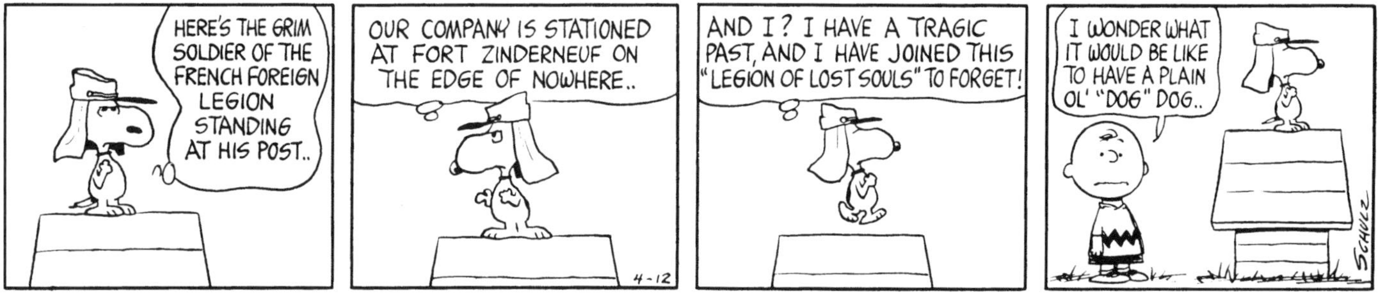
HERE'S THE GRIM SOLDIER OF THE FRENCH FOREIGN LEGION STANDING AT HIS POST..
OUR COMPANY IS STATIONED AT FORT ZINDERNEUF ON THE EDGE OF NOWHERE..
4-12
AND I? I HAVE A TRAGIC PAST, AND I HAVE JOINED THIS "LEGION OF LOST SOULS" TO FORGET!
I WONDER WHAT IT WOULD BE LIKE TO HAVE A PLAIN OL' "DOG" DOG..
SCHULZ

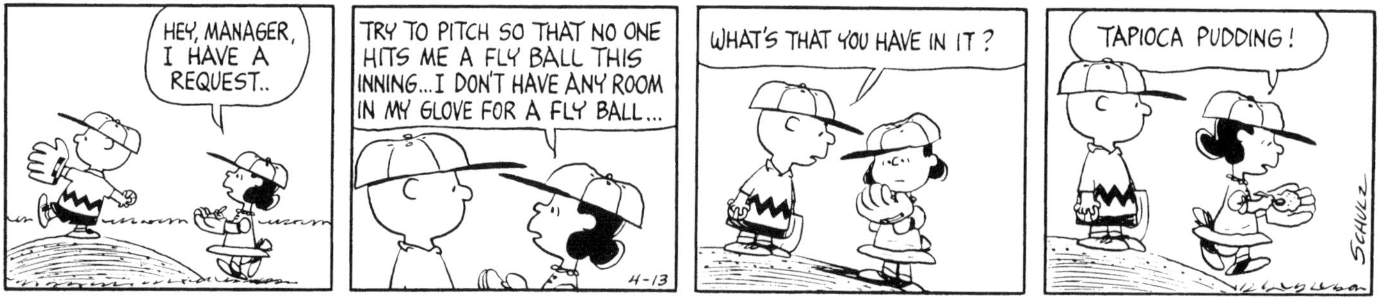
HEY, MANAGER, I HAVE A REQUEST..
TRY TO PITCH SO THAT NO ONE HITS ME A FLY BALL THIS INNING...I DON'T HAVE ANY ROOM IN MY GLOVE FOR A FLY BALL...
4-13
WHAT'S THAT YOU HAVE IN IT?
TAPIOCA PUDDING!
SCHULZ

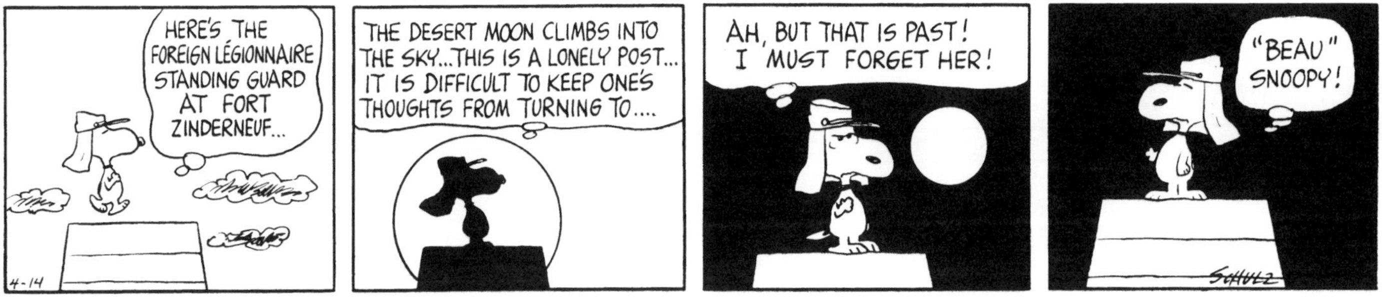
HERE'S THE FOREIGN LÉGIONNAIRE STANDING GUARD AT FORT ZINDERNEUF...
4-14
THE DESERT MOON CLIMBS INTO THE SKY...THIS IS A LONELY POST... IT IS DIFFICULT TO KEEP ONE'S THOUGHTS FROM TURNING TO....
AH, BUT THAT IS PAST! I MUST FORGET HER!
"BEAU" SNOOPY!
SCHULZ

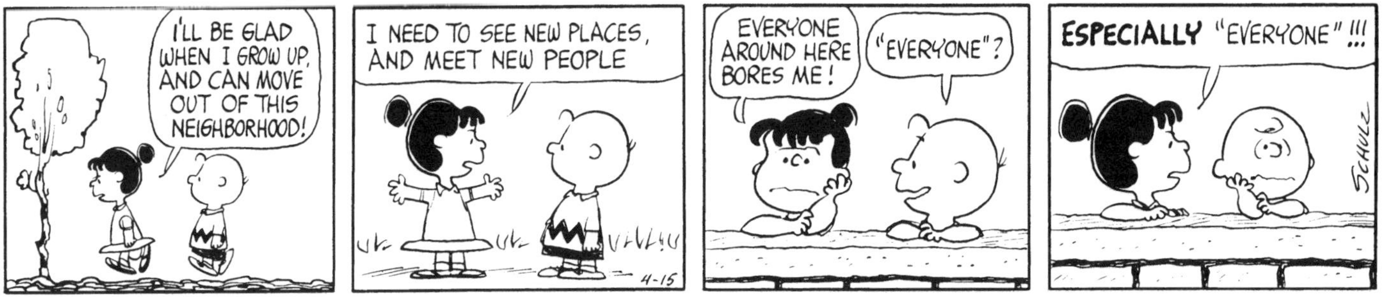
I'LL BE GLAD WHEN I GROW UP, AND CAN MOVE OUT OF THIS NEIGHBORHOOD!
I NEED TO SEE NEW PLACES, AND MEET NEW PEOPLE
4-15
EVERYONE AROUND HERE BORES ME!
"EVERYONE"?
ESPECIALLY "EVERYONE"!!!
SCHULZ

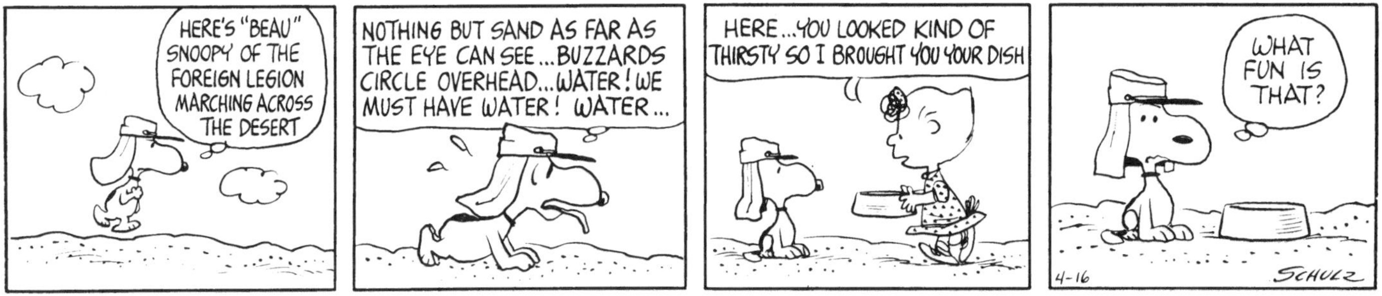
HERE'S "BEAU" SNOOPY OF THE FOREIGN LEGION MARCHING ACROSS THE DESERT
NOTHING BUT SAND AS FAR AS THE EYE CAN SEE...BUZZARDS CIRCLE OVERHEAD...WATER! WE MUST HAVE WATER! WATER...
HERE...YOU LOOKED KIND OF THIRSTY SO I BROUGHT YOU YOUR DISH
WHAT FUN IS THAT?
4-16
SCHULZ

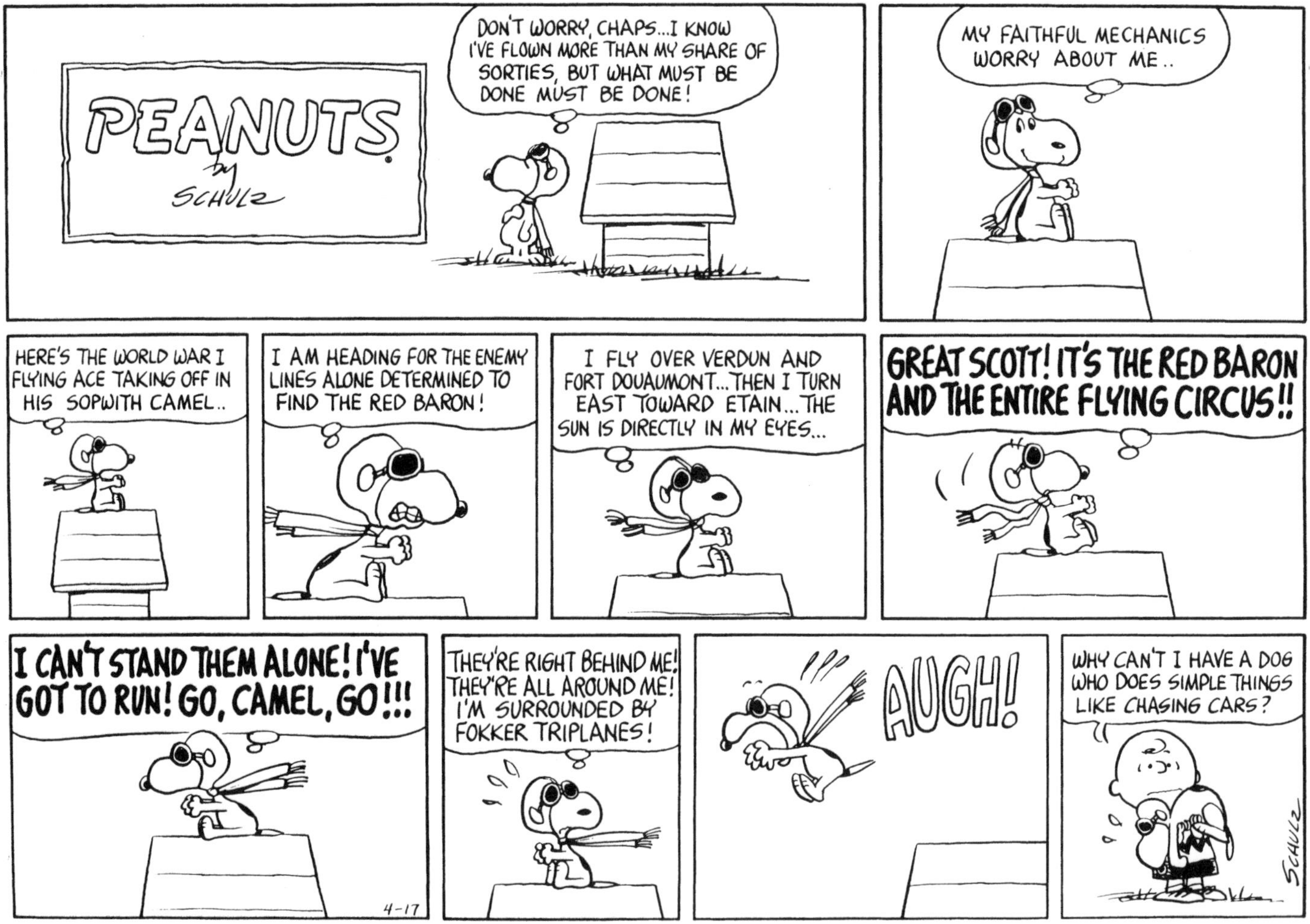
PEANUTS
by SCHULZ
DON'T WORRY, CHAPS...I KNOW I'VE FLOWN MORE THAN MY SHARE OF SORTIES, BUT WHAT MUST BE DONE MUST BE DONE!
MY FAITHFUL MECHANICS WORRY ABOUT ME..
HERE'S THE WORLD WAR I FLYING ACE TAKING OFF IN HIS SOPWITH CAMEL..
I AM HEADING FOR THE ENEMY LINES ALONE DETERMINED TO FIND THE RED BARON!
I FLY OVER VERDUN AND FORT DOUAUMONT...THEN I TURN EAST TOWARD ETAIN...THE SUN IS DIRECTLY IN MY EYES...
GREAT SCOTT! IT'S THE RED BARON AND THE ENTIRE FLYING CIRCUS!!
I CAN'T STAND THEM ALONE! I'VE GOT TO RUN! GO, CAMEL, GO!!!
4-17
THEY'RE RIGHT BEHIND ME! THEY'RE ALL AROUND ME! I'M SURROUNDED BY FOKKER TRIPLANES!
AUGH!
WHY CAN'T I HAVE A DOG WHO DOES SIMPLE THINGS LIKE CHASING CARS?
SCHULZ

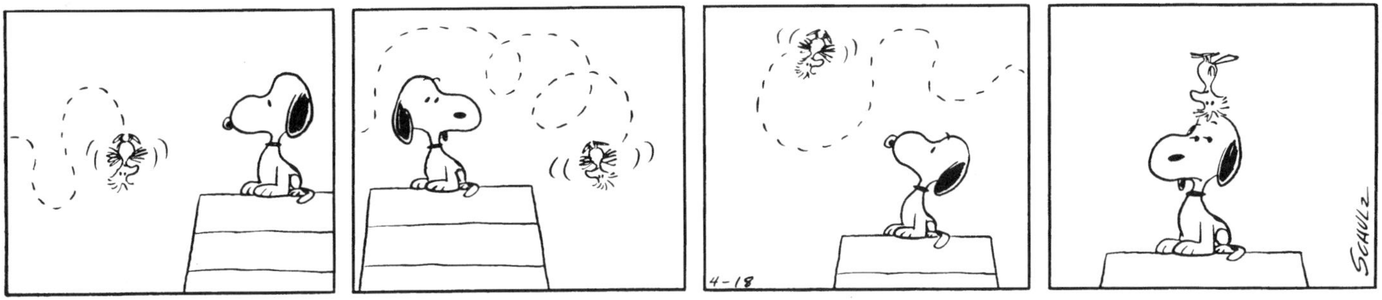
4-18
SCHULZ

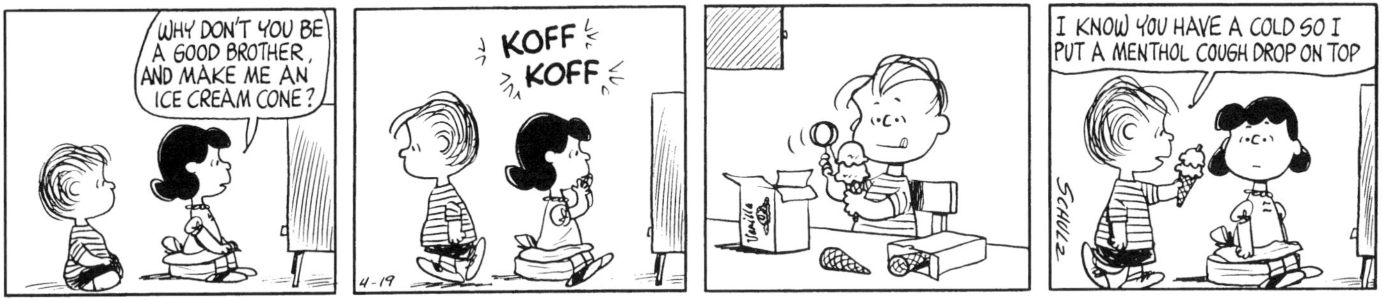
WHY DON'T YOU BE A GOOD BROTHER, AND MAKE ME AN ICE CREAM CONE?
KOFF KOFF
4-19
I KNOW YOU HAVE A COLD SO I PUT A MENTHOL COUGH DROP ON TOP
SCHULZ

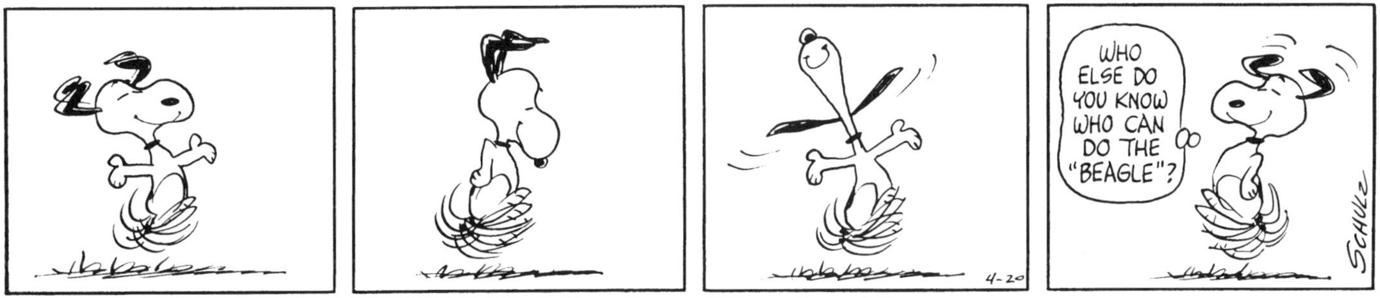
4-20
WHO ELSE DO YOU KNOW WHO CAN DO THE "BEAGLE"?
SCHULZ

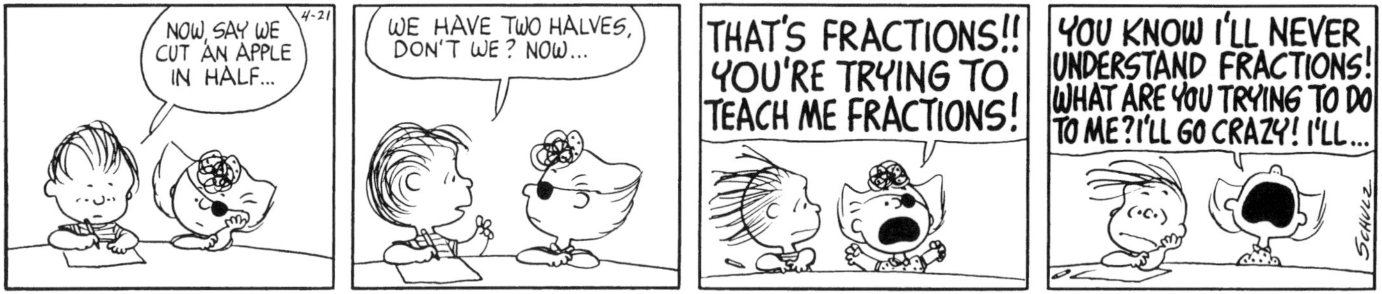
NOW, SAY WE CUT AN APPLE IN HALF...
WE HAVE TWO HALVES, DON'T WE? NOW...
THAT'S FRACTIONS!! YOU'RE TRYING TO TEACH ME FRACTIONS!
YOU KNOW I'LL NEVER UNDERSTAND FRACTIONS! WHAT ARE YOU TRYING TO DO TO ME? I'LL GO CRAZY! I'LL...

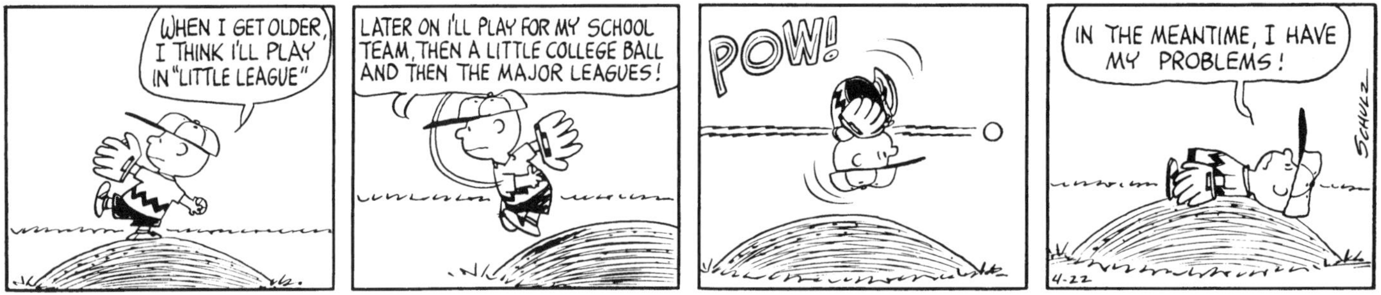
WHEN I GET OLDER, I THINK I'LL PLAY IN "LITTLE LEAGUE"
LATER ON I'LL PLAY FOR MY SCHOOL TEAM, THEN A LITTLE COLLEGE BALL AND THEN THE MAJOR LEAGUES!
POW!
IN THE MEANTIME, I HAVE MY PROBLEMS!

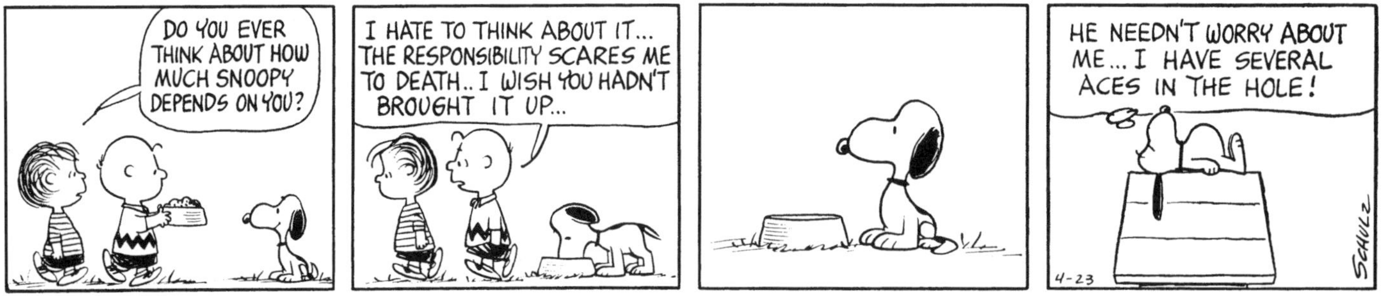
DO YOU EVER THINK ABOUT HOW MUCH SNOOPY DEPENDS ON YOU?
I HATE TO THINK ABOUT IT... THE RESPONSIBILITY SCARES ME TO DEATH.. I WISH YOU HADN'T BROUGHT IT UP...
HE NEEDN'T WORRY ABOUT ME... I HAVE SEVERAL ACES IN THE HOLE!

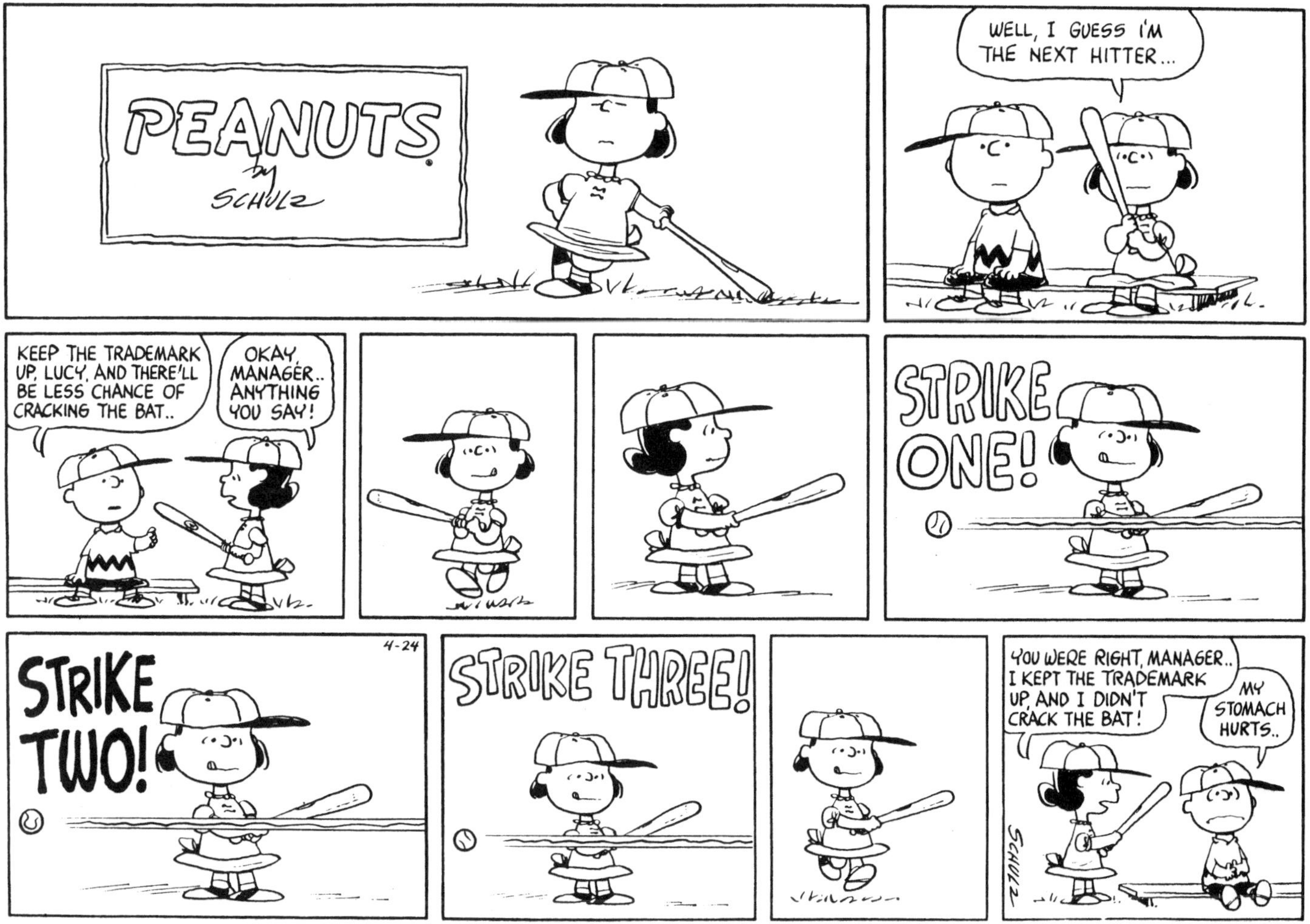
PEANUTS
by SCHULZ
WELL, I GUESS I'M THE NEXT HITTER...
KEEP THE TRADEMARK UP, LUCY, AND THERE'LL BE LESS CHANCE OF CRACKING THE BAT..
OKAY, MANAGER.. ANYTHING YOU SAY!
STRIKE ONE!
4-24
STRIKE TWO!
STRIKE THREE!
SCHULZ
YOU WERE RIGHT, MANAGER.. I KEPT THE TRADEMARK UP, AND I DIDN'T CRACK THE BAT!
MY STOMACH HURTS..

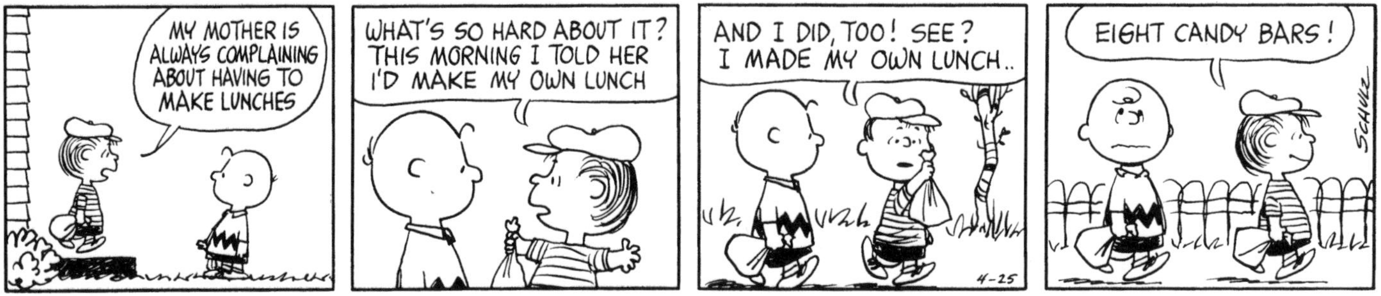
MY MOTHER IS ALWAYS COMPLAINING ABOUT HAVING TO MAKE LUNCHES
WHAT'S SO HARD ABOUT IT? THIS MORNING I TOLD HER I'D MAKE MY OWN LUNCH
AND I DID, TOO! SEE? I MADE MY OWN LUNCH..
4-25
EIGHT CANDY BARS!
SCHULZ

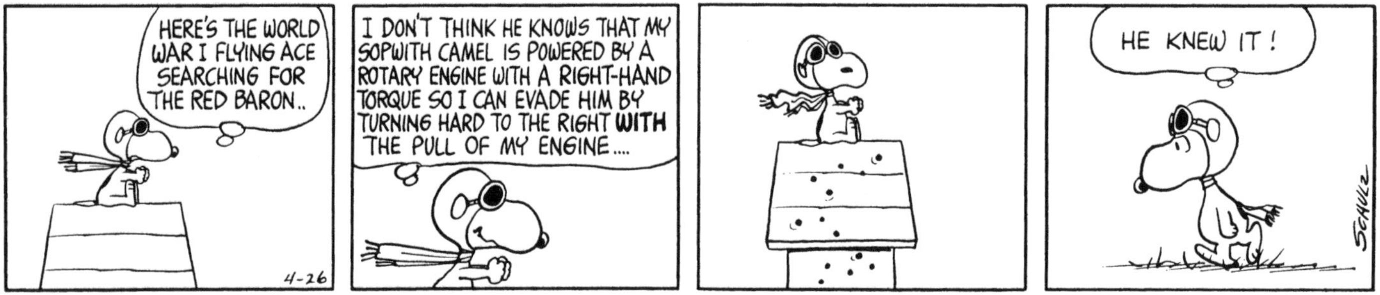
HERE'S THE WORLD WAR I FLYING ACE SEARCHING FOR THE RED BARON..
4-26
I DON'T THINK HE KNOWS THAT MY SOPWITH CAMEL IS POWERED BY A ROTARY ENGINE WITH A RIGHT-HAND TORQUE SO I CAN EVADE HIM BY TURNING HARD TO THE RIGHT WITH THE PULL OF MY ENGINE....
HE KNEW IT!
SCHULZ

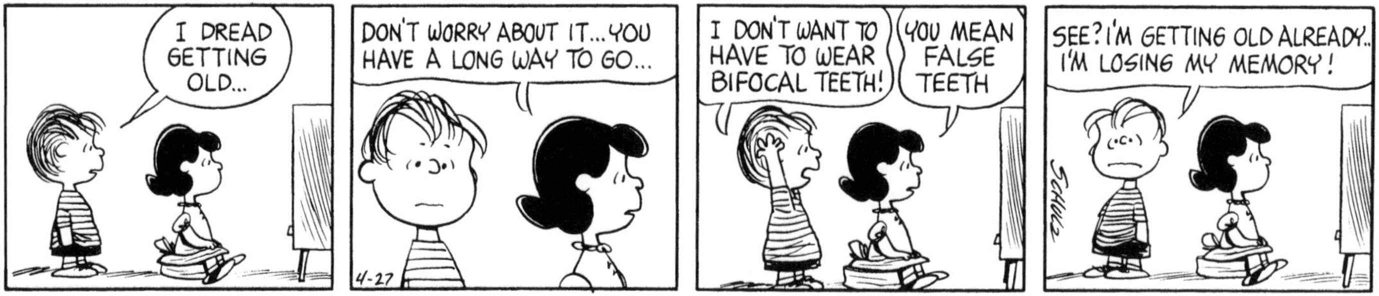
I DREAD GETTING OLD...
DON'T WORRY ABOUT IT...YOU HAVE A LONG WAY TO GO...
4-27
I DON'T WANT TO HAVE TO WEAR BIFOCAL TEETH!
YOU MEAN FALSE TEETH
SCHULZ
SEE? I'M GETTING OLD ALREADY.. I'M LOSING MY MEMORY!

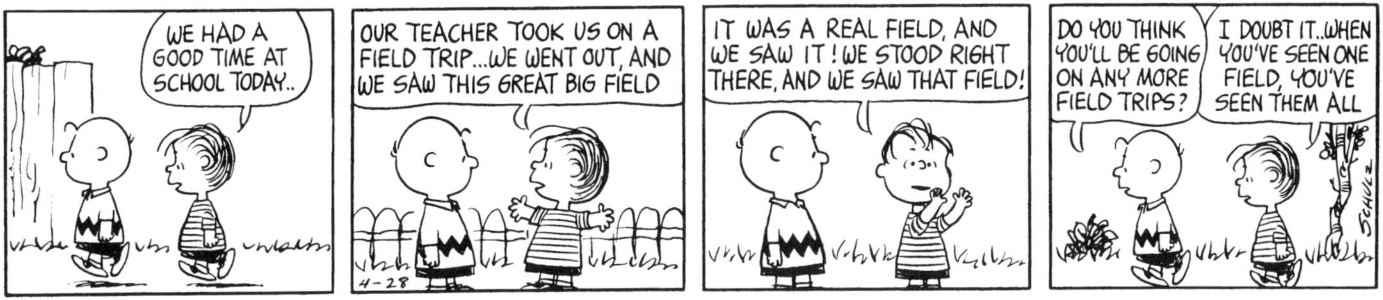
WE HAD A GOOD TIME AT SCHOOL TODAY..
OUR TEACHER TOOK US ON A FIELD TRIP...WE WENT OUT, AND WE SAW THIS GREAT BIG FIELD
IT WAS A REAL FIELD, AND WE SAW IT! WE STOOD RIGHT THERE, AND WE SAW THAT FIELD!
DO YOU THINK YOU'LL BE GOING ON ANY MORE FIELD TRIPS?
I DOUBT IT..WHEN YOU'VE SEEN ONE FIELD, YOU'VE SEEN THEM ALL

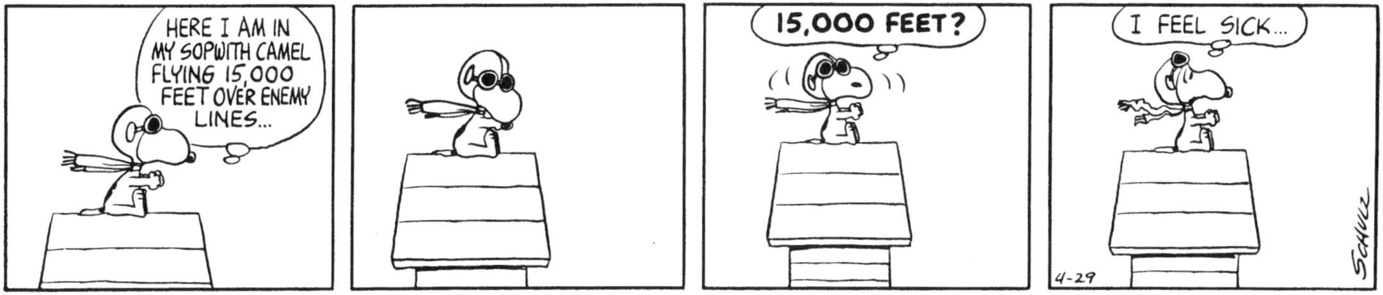
HERE I AM IN MY SOPWITH CAMEL FLYING 15,000 FEET OVER ENEMY LINES...
15,000 FEET?
I FEEL SICK...

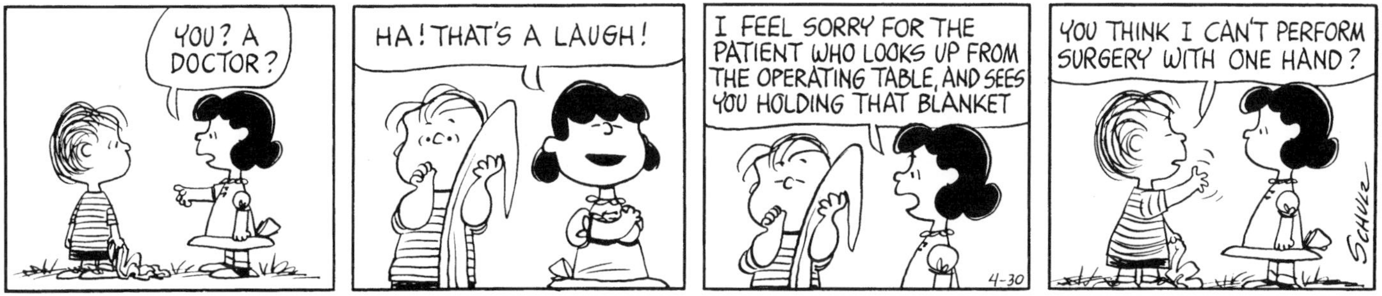
YOU? A DOCTOR?
HA! THAT'S A LAUGH!
I FEEL SORRY FOR THE PATIENT WHO LOOKS UP FROM THE OPERATING TABLE, AND SEES YOU HOLDING THAT BLANKET
YOU THINK I CAN'T PERFORM SURGERY WITH ONE HAND?

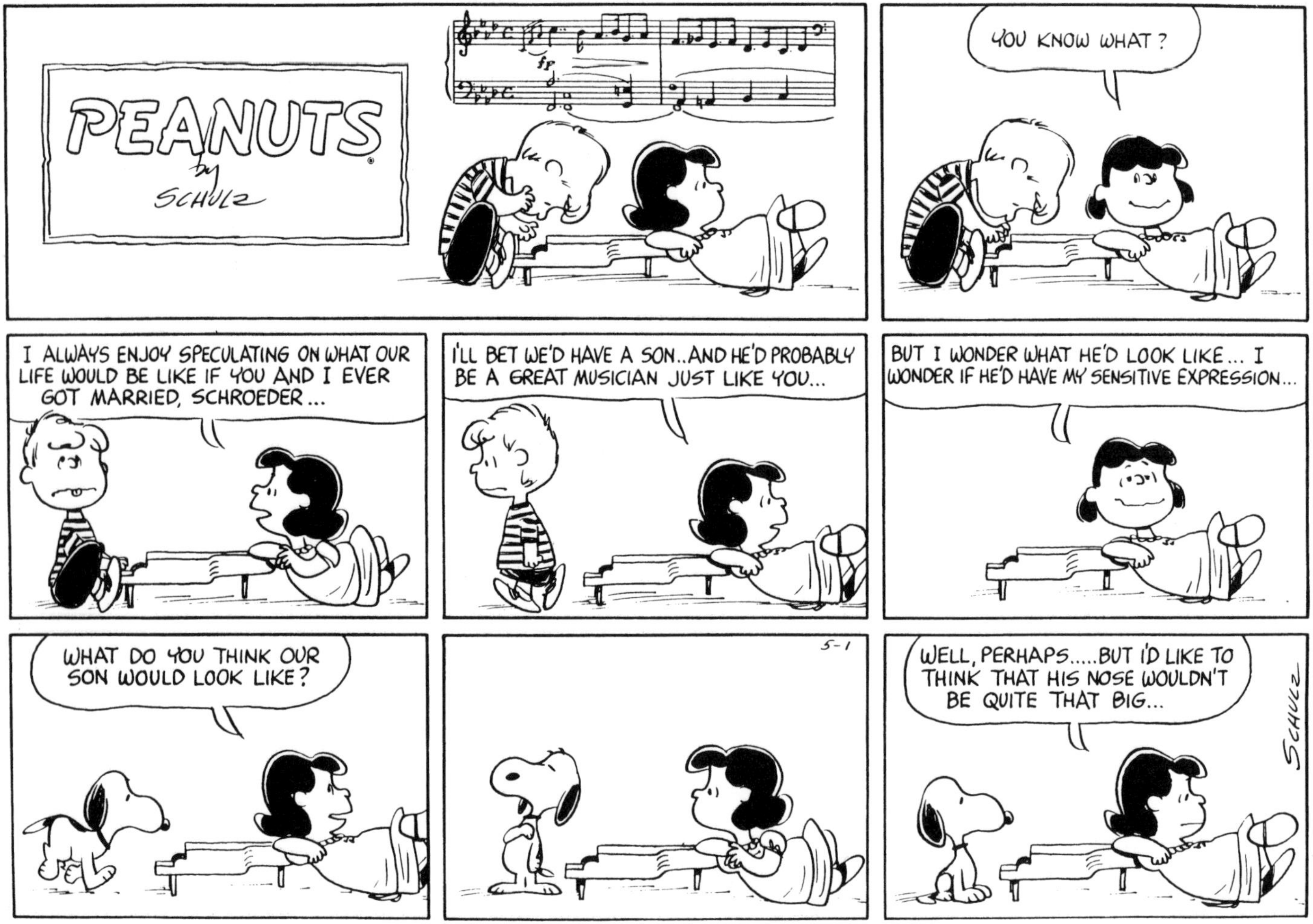
PEANUTS
by SCHULZ
YOU KNOW WHAT?
I ALWAYS ENJOY SPECULATING ON WHAT OUR LIFE WOULD BE LIKE IF YOU AND I EVER GOT MARRIED, SCHROEDER...
I'LL BET WE'D HAVE A SON..AND HE'D PROBABLY BE A GREAT MUSICIAN JUST LIKE YOU...
BUT I WONDER WHAT HE'D LOOK LIKE... I WONDER IF HE'D HAVE MY SENSITIVE EXPRESSION...
WHAT DO YOU THINK OUR SON WOULD LOOK LIKE?
5-1
WELL, PERHAPS.....BUT I'D LIKE TO THINK THAT HIS NOSE WOULDN'T BE QUITE THAT BIG...
SCHULZ

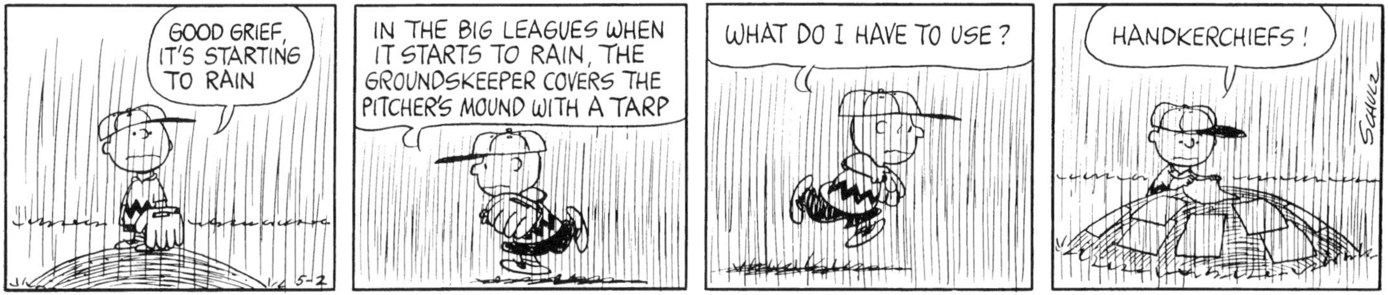
GOOD GRIEF, IT'S STARTING TO RAIN
IN THE BIG LEAGUES WHEN IT STARTS TO RAIN, THE GROUNDSKEEPER COVERS THE PITCHER'S MOUND WITH A TARP
WHAT DO I HAVE TO USE ?
HANDKERCHIEFS !

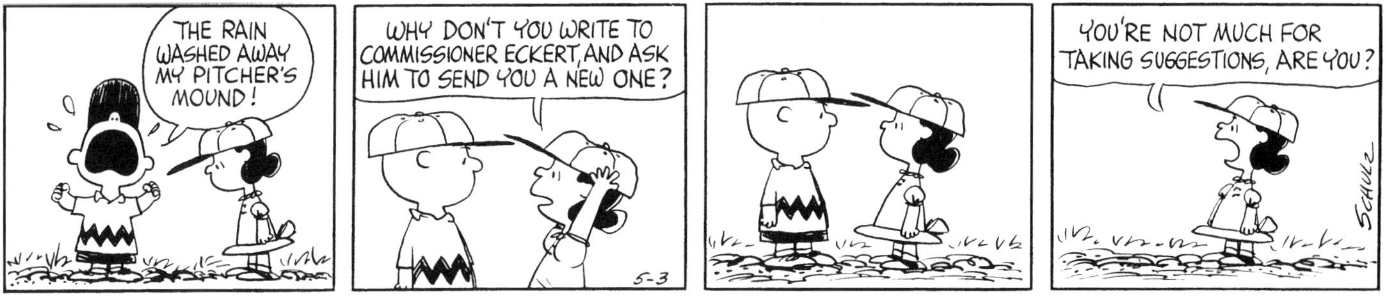
THE RAIN WASHED AWAY MY PITCHER'S MOUND !
WHY DON'T YOU WRITE TO COMMISSIONER ECKERT, AND ASK HIM TO SEND YOU A NEW ONE ?
YOU'RE NOT MUCH FOR TAKING SUGGESTIONS, ARE YOU ?

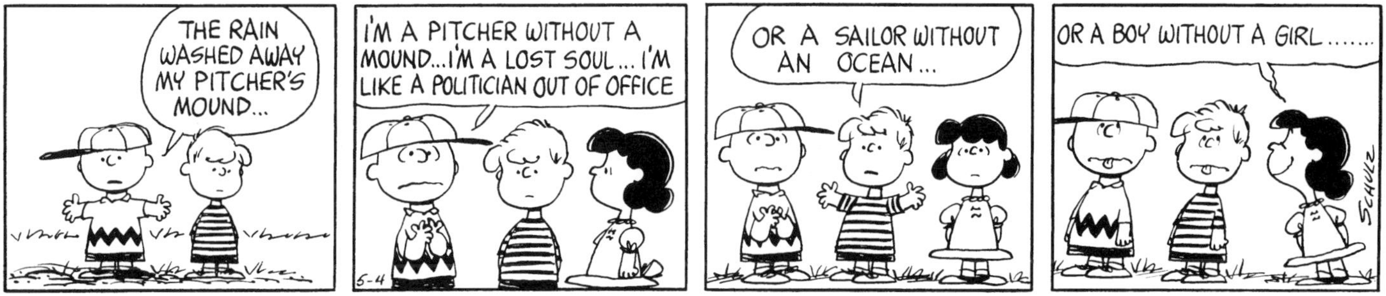
THE RAIN WASHED AWAY MY PITCHER'S MOUND...
I'M A PITCHER WITHOUT A MOUND...I'M A LOST SOUL ... I'M LIKE A POLITICIAN OUT OF OFFICE
OR A SAILOR WITHOUT AN OCEAN...
OR A BOY WITHOUT A GIRL.......

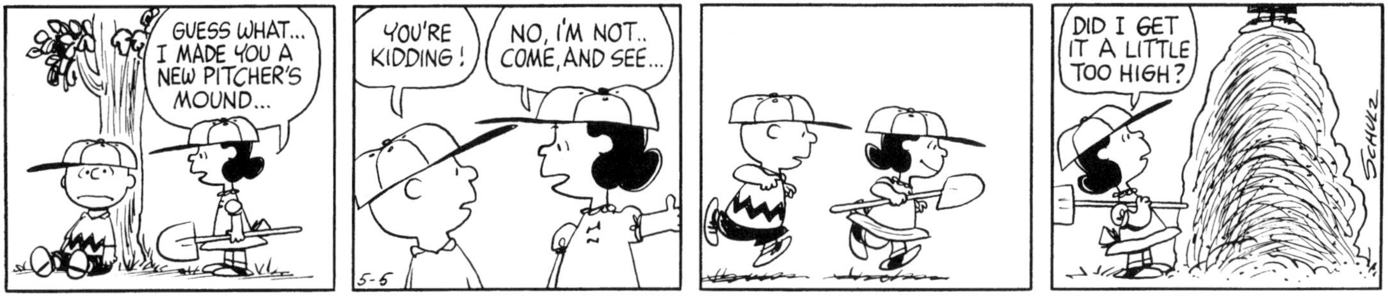
GUESS WHAT... I MADE YOU A NEW PITCHER'S MOUND...
YOU'RE KIDDING!
NO, I'M NOT.. COME, AND SEE...
5-5
DID I GET IT A LITTLE TOO HIGH?
SCHULZ

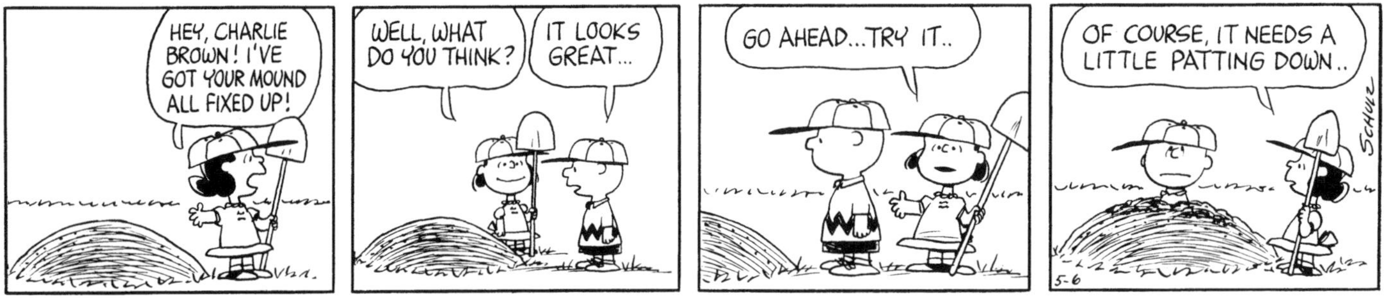
HEY, CHARLIE BROWN! I'VE GOT YOUR MOUND ALL FIXED UP!
WELL, WHAT DO YOU THINK?
IT LOOKS GREAT...
GO AHEAD...TRY IT..
OF COURSE, IT NEEDS A LITTLE PATTING DOWN..
SCHULZ
5-6

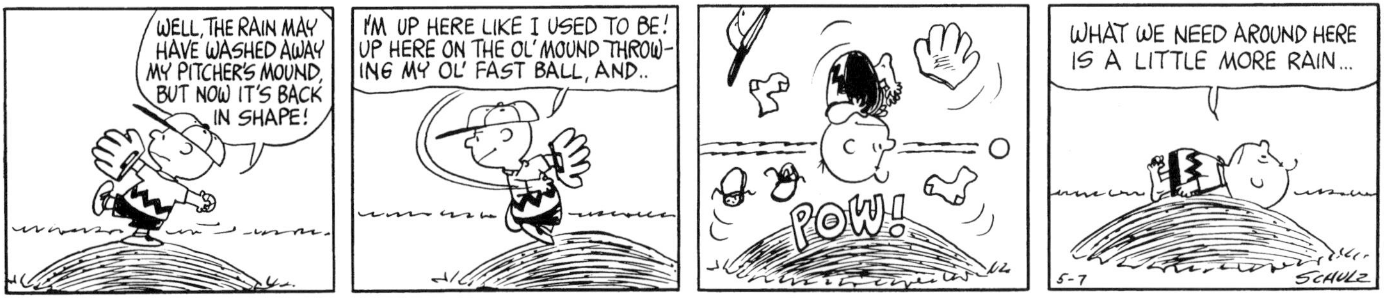
WELL, THE RAIN MAY HAVE WASHED AWAY MY PITCHER'S MOUND, BUT NOW IT'S BACK IN SHAPE!
I'M UP HERE LIKE I USED TO BE! UP HERE ON THE OL' MOUND THROWING MY OL' FAST BALL, AND..
POW!
WHAT WE NEED AROUND HERE IS A LITTLE MORE RAIN...
5-7
SCHULZ

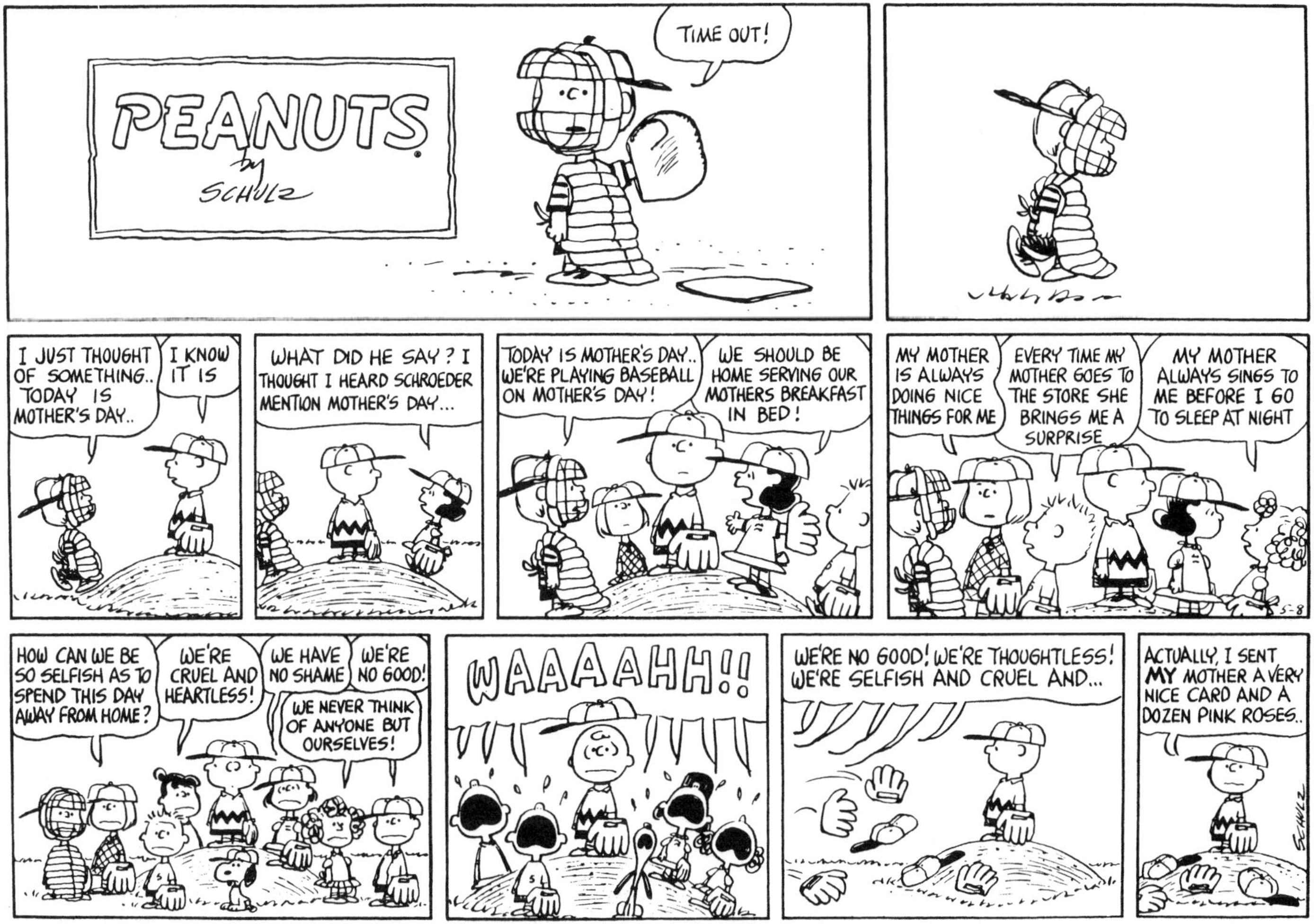
PEANUTS
by SCHULZ
TIME OUT!
I JUST THOUGHT OF SOMETHING.. TODAY IS MOTHER'S DAY..
I KNOW IT IS
WHAT DID HE SAY? I THOUGHT I HEARD SCHROEDER MENTION MOTHER'S DAY...
TODAY IS MOTHER'S DAY.. WE'RE PLAYING BASEBALL ON MOTHER'S DAY!
WE SHOULD BE HOME SERVING OUR MOTHERS BREAKFAST IN BED!
MY MOTHER IS ALWAYS DOING NICE THINGS FOR ME
EVERY TIME MY MOTHER GOES TO THE STORE SHE BRINGS ME A SURPRISE
MY MOTHER ALWAYS SINGS TO ME BEFORE I GO TO SLEEP AT NIGHT
5-8
HOW CAN WE BE SO SELFISH AS TO SPEND THIS DAY AWAY FROM HOME?
WE'RE CRUEL AND HEARTLESS!
WE HAVE NO SHAME
WE'RE NO GOOD!
WE NEVER THINK OF ANYONE BUT OURSELVES!
WAAAAAHH!!
WE'RE NO GOOD! WE'RE THOUGHTLESS! WE'RE SELFISH AND CRUEL AND...
ACTUALLY, I SENT **MY** MOTHER A VERY NICE CARD AND A DOZEN PINK ROSES..
SCHULZ

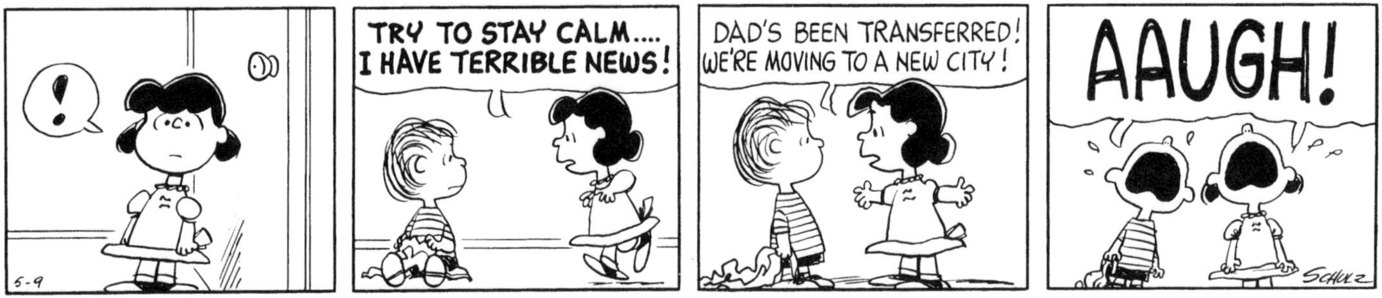
!
TRY TO STAY CALM.... I HAVE TERRIBLE NEWS!
DAD'S BEEN TRANSFERRED! WE'RE MOVING TO A NEW CITY!
AAUGH!

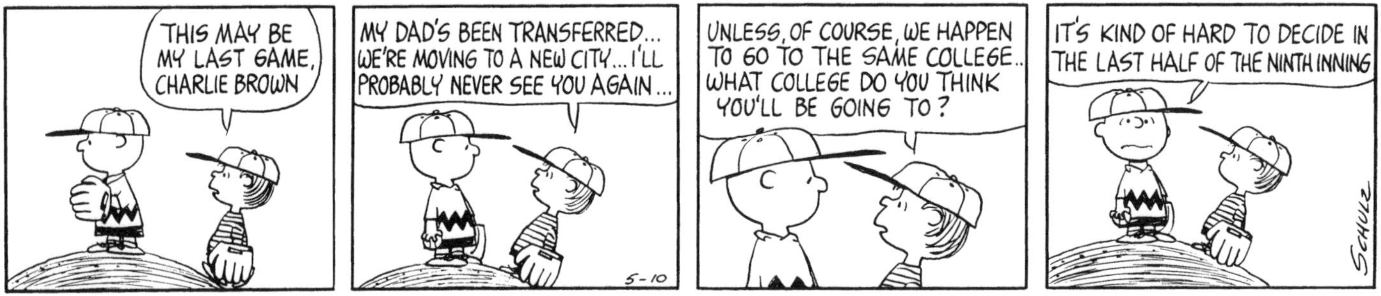
THIS MAY BE MY LAST GAME, CHARLIE BROWN
MY DAD'S BEEN TRANSFERRED... WE'RE MOVING TO A NEW CITY... I'LL PROBABLY NEVER SEE YOU AGAIN...
UNLESS, OF COURSE, WE HAPPEN TO GO TO THE SAME COLLEGE.. WHAT COLLEGE DO YOU THINK YOU'LL BE GOING TO?
IT'S KIND OF HARD TO DECIDE IN THE LAST HALF OF THE NINTH INNING

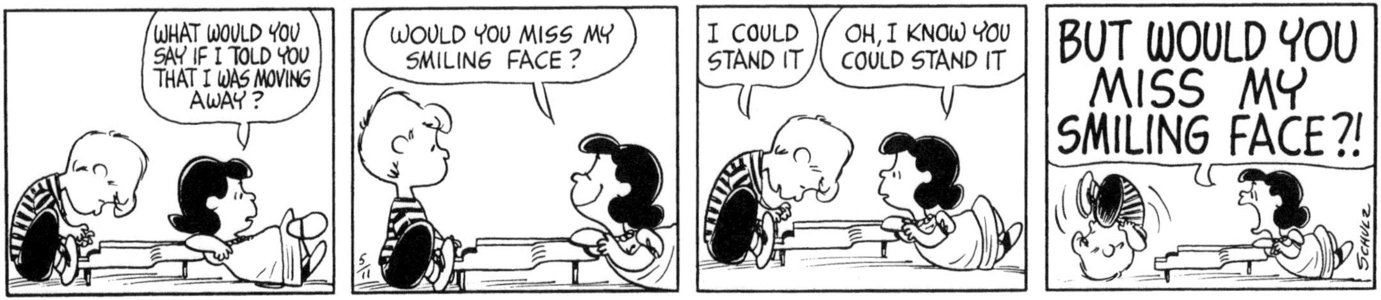
WHAT WOULD YOU SAY IF I TOLD YOU THAT I WAS MOVING AWAY?
WOULD YOU MISS MY SMILING FACE?
I COULD STAND IT
OH, I KNOW YOU COULD STAND IT
BUT WOULD YOU MISS MY SMILING FACE?!

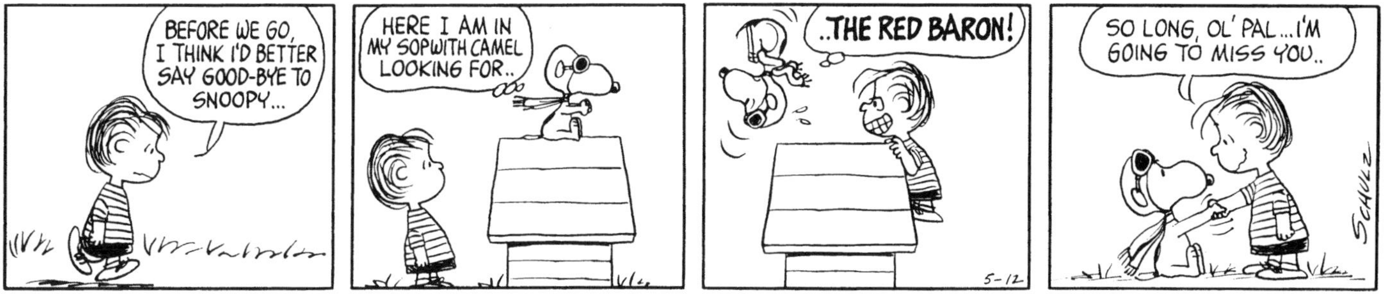
BEFORE WE GO, I THINK I'D BETTER SAY GOOD-BYE TO SNOOPY...
HERE I AM IN MY SOPWITH CAMEL LOOKING FOR..
..THE RED BARON!
SO LONG, OL' PAL...I'M GOING TO MISS YOU..

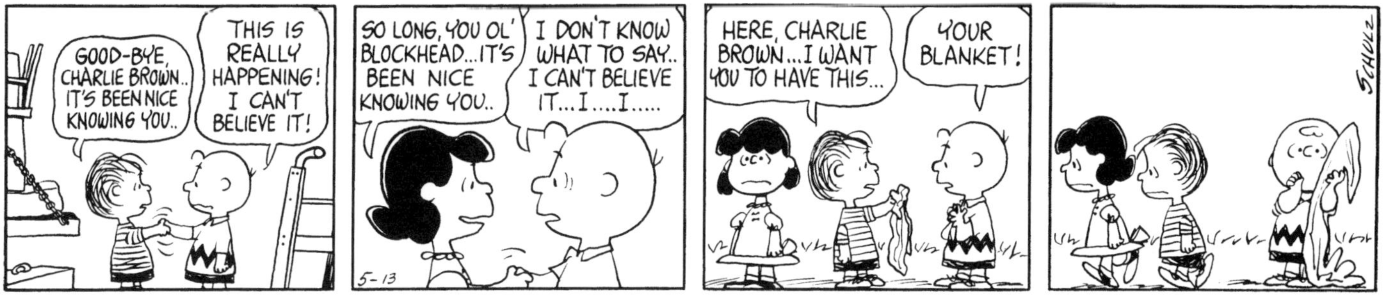
GOOD-BYE, CHARLIE BROWN.. IT'S BEEN NICE KNOWING YOU..
THIS IS REALLY HAPPENING! I CAN'T BELIEVE IT!
SO LONG, YOU OL' BLOCKHEAD...IT'S BEEN NICE KNOWING YOU..
I DON'T KNOW WHAT TO SAY.. I CAN'T BELIEVE IT...I....I.....
HERE, CHARLIE BROWN...I WANT YOU TO HAVE THIS...
YOUR BLANKET!

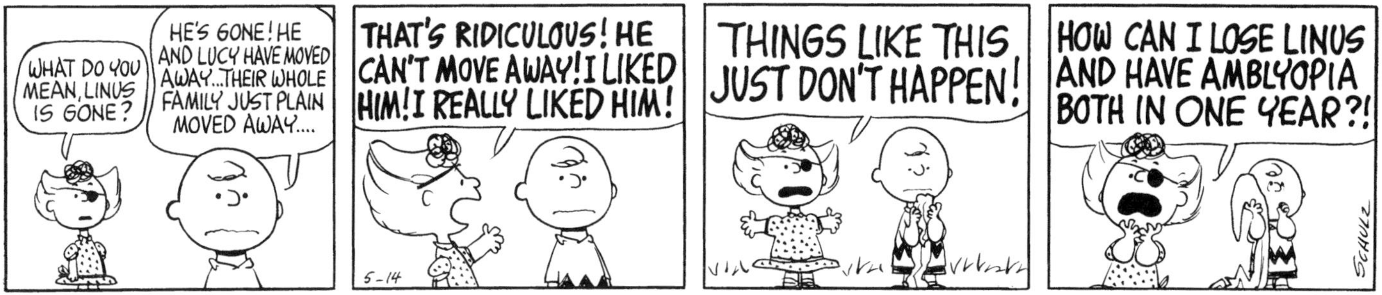
WHAT DO YOU MEAN, LINUS IS GONE?
HE'S GONE! HE AND LUCY HAVE MOVED AWAY...THEIR WHOLE FAMILY JUST PLAIN MOVED AWAY....
THAT'S RIDICULOUS! HE CAN'T MOVE AWAY! I LIKED HIM! I REALLY LIKED HIM!
THINGS LIKE THIS JUST DON'T HAPPEN!
HOW CAN I LOSE LINUS AND HAVE AMBLYOPIA BOTH IN ONE YEAR?!

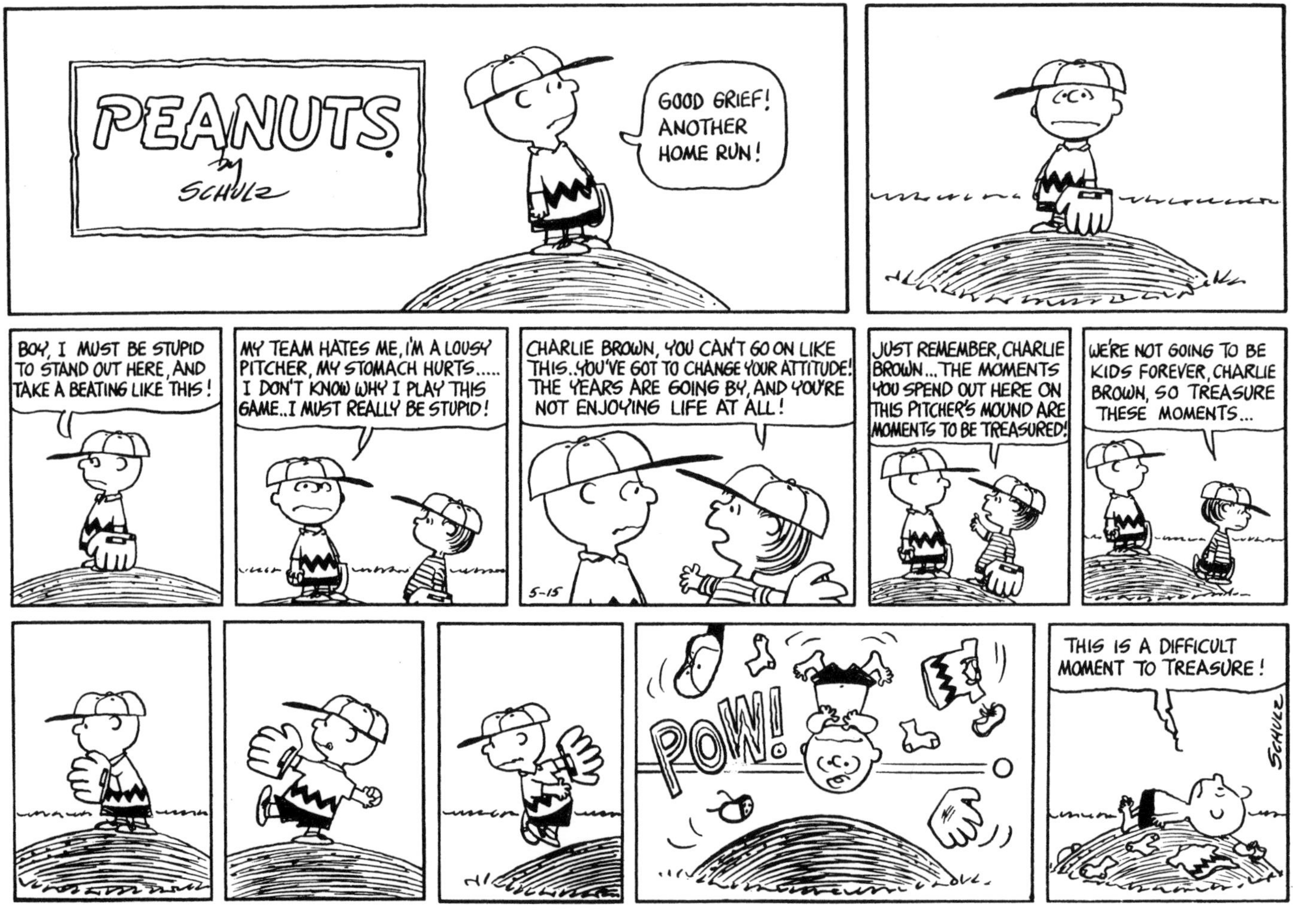
PEANUTS
by SCHULZ
GOOD GRIEF! ANOTHER HOME RUN!
BOY, I MUST BE STUPID TO STAND OUT HERE, AND TAKE A BEATING LIKE THIS!
MY TEAM HATES ME, I'M A LOUSY PITCHER, MY STOMACH HURTS..... I DON'T KNOW WHY I PLAY THIS GAME..I MUST REALLY BE STUPID!
CHARLIE BROWN, YOU CAN'T GO ON LIKE THIS..YOU'VE GOT TO CHANGE YOUR ATTITUDE! THE YEARS ARE GOING BY, AND YOU'RE NOT ENJOYING LIFE AT ALL!
5-15
JUST REMEMBER, CHARLIE BROWN... THE MOMENTS YOU SPEND OUT HERE ON THIS PITCHER'S MOUND ARE MOMENTS TO BE TREASURED!
WE'RE NOT GOING TO BE KIDS FOREVER, CHARLIE BROWN, SO TREASURE THESE MOMENTS...
POW!
THIS IS A DIFFICULT MOMENT TO TREASURE!
SCHULZ

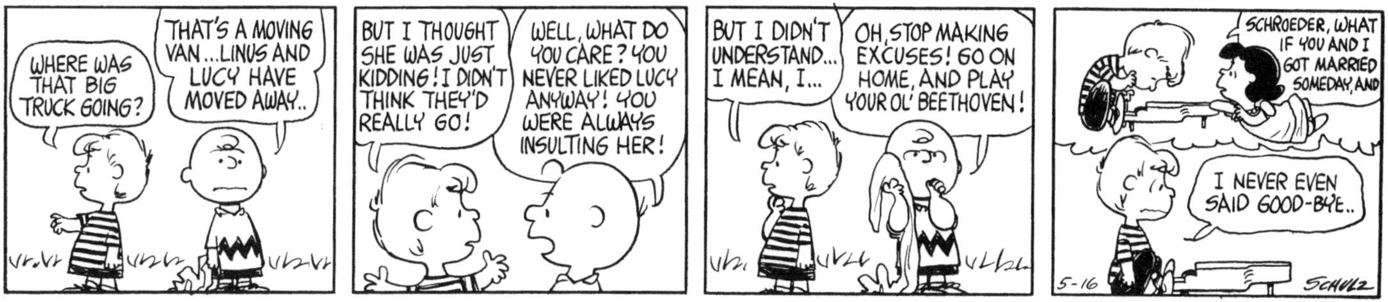
WHERE WAS THAT BIG TRUCK GOING?
THAT'S A MOVING VAN...LINUS AND LUCY HAVE MOVED AWAY..
BUT I THOUGHT SHE WAS JUST KIDDING! I DIDN'T THINK THEY'D REALLY GO!
WELL, WHAT DO YOU CARE? YOU NEVER LIKED LUCY ANYWAY! YOU WERE ALWAYS INSULTING HER!
BUT I DIDN'T UNDERSTAND... I MEAN, I...
OH, STOP MAKING EXCUSES! GO ON HOME, AND PLAY YOUR OL' BEETHOVEN!
SCHROEDER, WHAT IF YOU AND I GOT MARRIED SOMEDAY, AND
I NEVER EVEN SAID GOOD-BYE..
5-16
SCHULZ

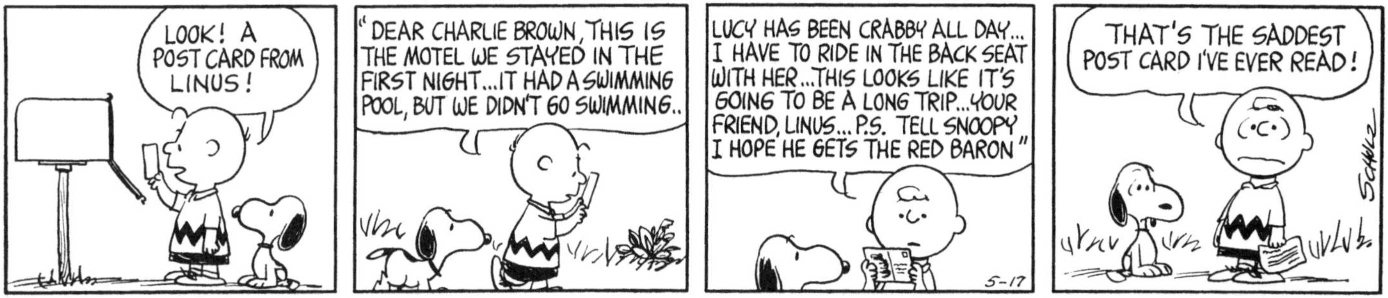
LOOK! A POST CARD FROM LINUS!
"DEAR CHARLIE BROWN, THIS IS THE MOTEL WE STAYED IN THE FIRST NIGHT...IT HAD A SWIMMING POOL, BUT WE DIDN'T GO SWIMMING..
LUCY HAS BEEN CRABBY ALL DAY... I HAVE TO RIDE IN THE BACK SEAT WITH HER...THIS LOOKS LIKE IT'S GOING TO BE A LONG TRIP...YOUR FRIEND, LINUS... P.S. TELL SNOOPY I HOPE HE GETS THE RED BARON"
5-17
THAT'S THE SADDEST POST CARD I'VE EVER READ!
SCHULZ

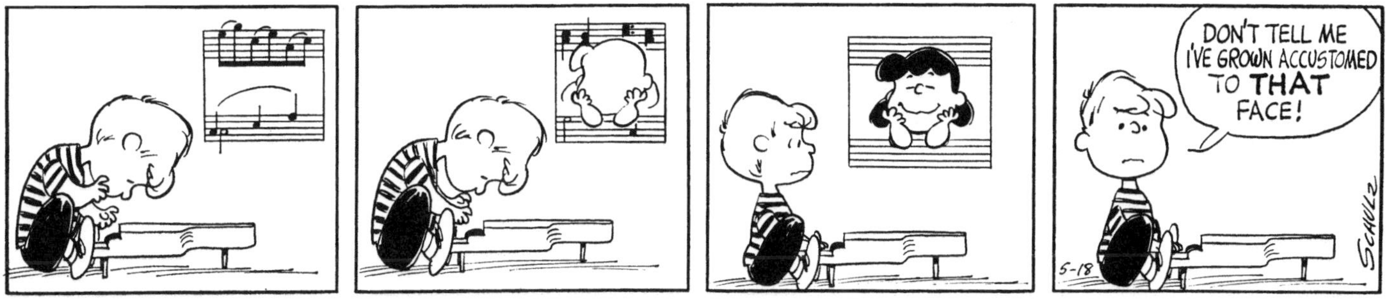
DON'T TELL ME I'VE GROWN ACCUSTOMED TO **THAT** FACE!
5-18
SCHULZ

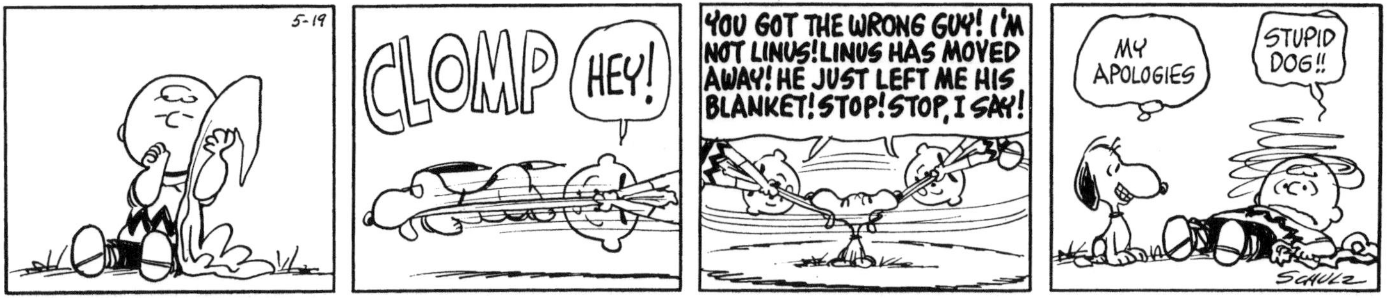
5-19
CLOMP
HEY!
YOU GOT THE WRONG GUY! I'M NOT LINUS! LINUS HAS MOVED AWAY! HE JUST LEFT ME HIS BLANKET! STOP! STOP, I SAY!
MY APOLOGIES
STUPID DOG!!
SCHULZ

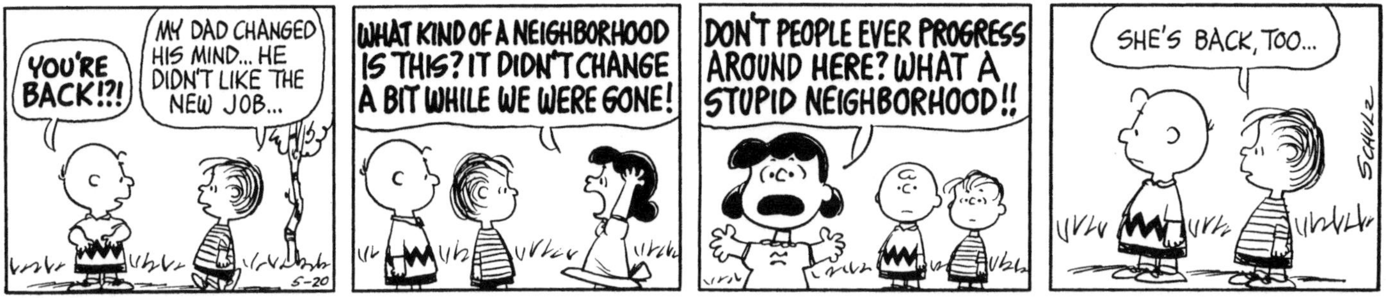
YOU'RE BACK!?!
MY DAD CHANGED HIS MIND... HE DIDN'T LIKE THE NEW JOB...
5-20
WHAT KIND OF A NEIGHBORHOOD IS THIS? IT DIDN'T CHANGE A BIT WHILE WE WERE GONE!
DON'T PEOPLE EVER PROGRESS AROUND HERE? WHAT A STUPID NEIGHBORHOOD!!
SHE'S BACK, TOO...
SCHULZ

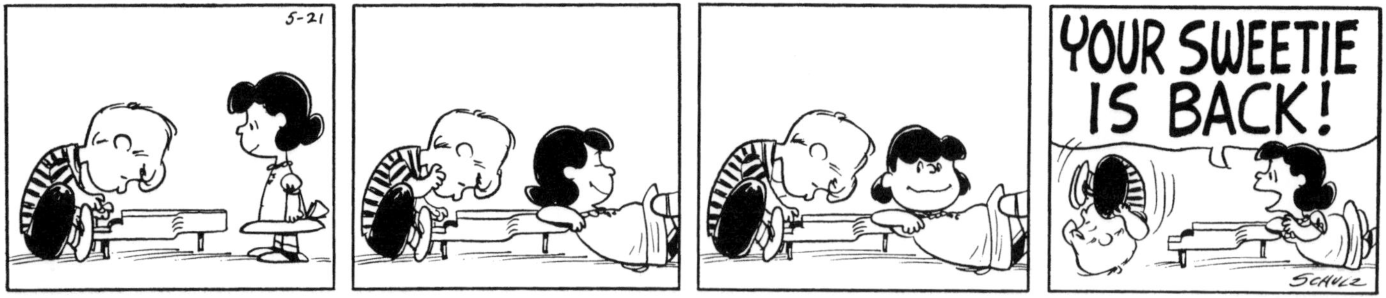
5-21
YOUR SWEETIE IS BACK!
SCHULZ

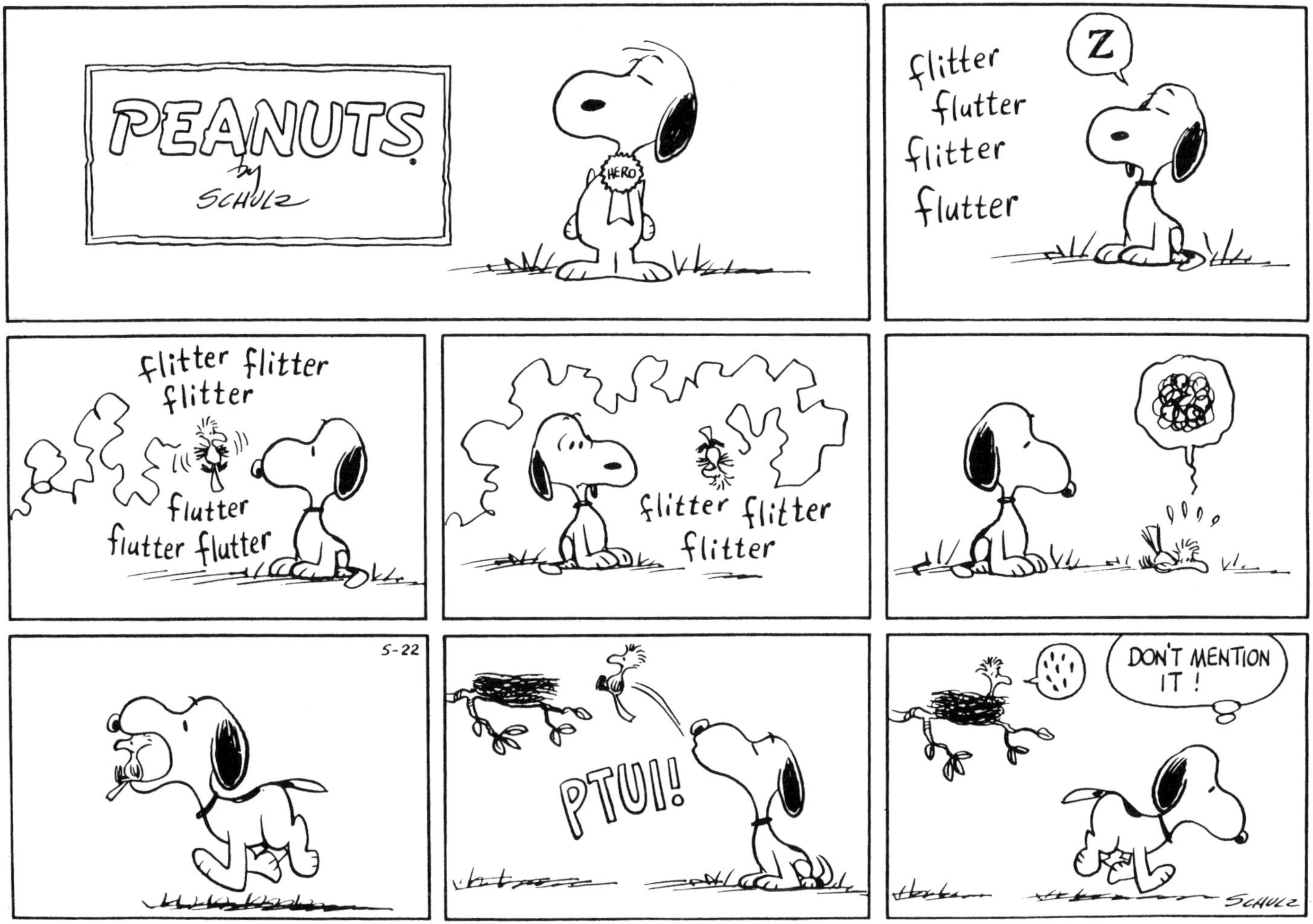
PEANUTS
by SCHULZ
HERO
flitter flutter flitter flutter
Z
flitter flitter flitter
flutter flutter flutter
flitter flitter flitter
5-22
PTUI!
DON'T MENTION IT!
SCHULZ

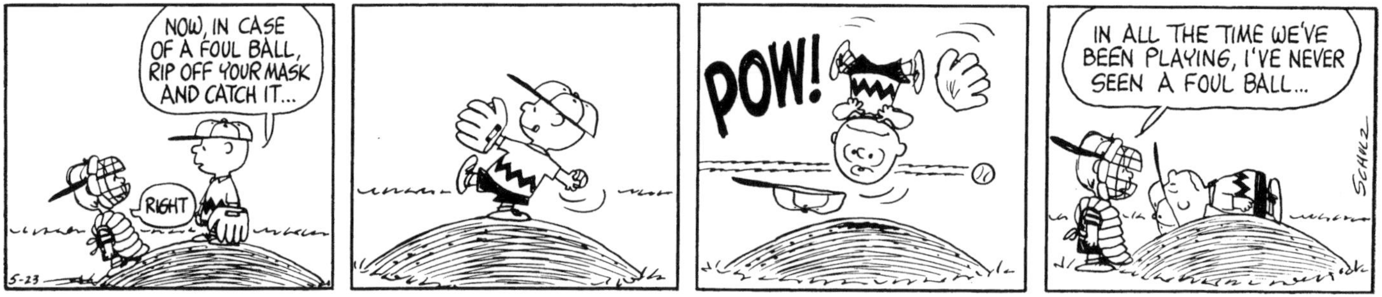
NOW, IN CASE OF A FOUL BALL, RIP OFF YOUR MASK AND CATCH IT...
RIGHT
POW!
IN ALL THE TIME WE'VE BEEN PLAYING, I'VE NEVER SEEN A FOUL BALL...
SCHULZ
5-23

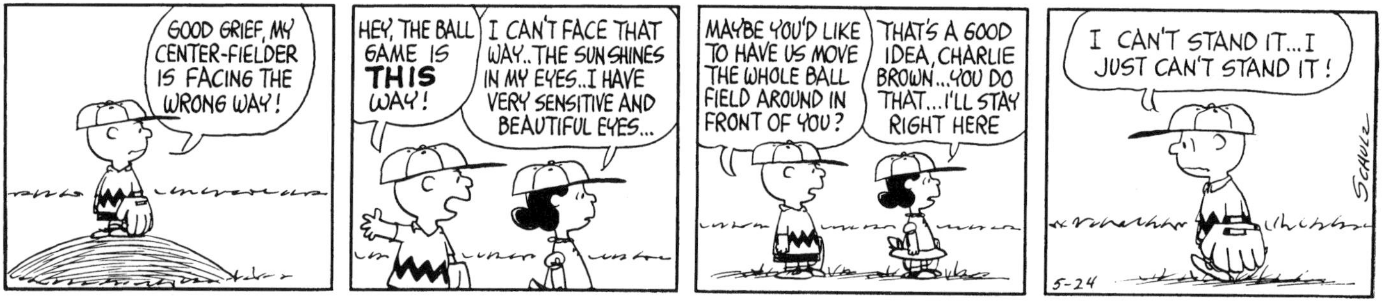
GOOD GRIEF, MY CENTER-FIELDER IS FACING THE WRONG WAY!
HEY, THE BALL GAME IS **THIS** WAY!
I CAN'T FACE THAT WAY.. THE SUN SHINES IN MY EYES.. I HAVE VERY SENSITIVE AND BEAUTIFUL EYES...
MAYBE YOU'D LIKE TO HAVE US MOVE THE WHOLE BALL FIELD AROUND IN FRONT OF YOU?
THAT'S A GOOD IDEA, CHARLIE BROWN...YOU DO THAT...I'LL STAY RIGHT HERE
I CAN'T STAND IT...I JUST CAN'T STAND IT!
SCHULZ
5-24

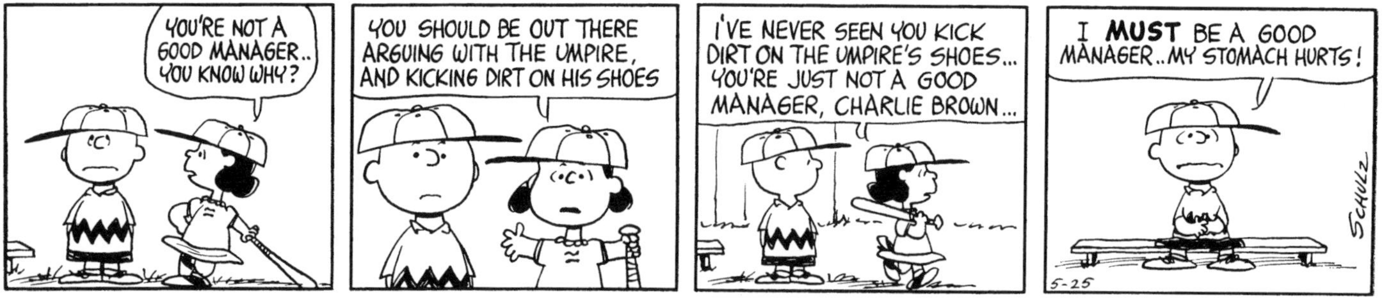
YOU'RE NOT A GOOD MANAGER.. YOU KNOW WHY?
YOU SHOULD BE OUT THERE ARGUING WITH THE UMPIRE, AND KICKING DIRT ON HIS SHOES
I'VE NEVER SEEN YOU KICK DIRT ON THE UMPIRE'S SHOES... YOU'RE JUST NOT A GOOD MANAGER, CHARLIE BROWN...
I **MUST** BE A GOOD MANAGER.. MY STOMACH HURTS!
SCHULZ
5-25

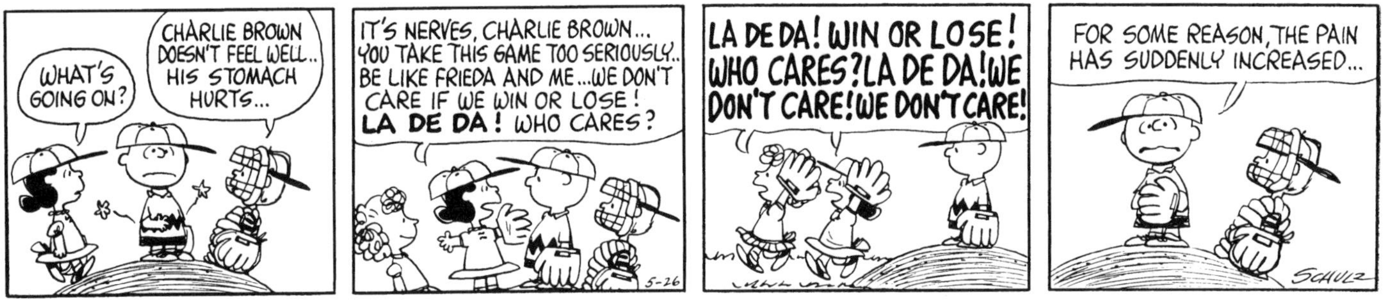
WHAT'S GOING ON?
CHARLIE BROWN DOESN'T FEEL WELL.. HIS STOMACH HURTS...
IT'S NERVES, CHARLIE BROWN... YOU TAKE THIS GAME TOO SERIOUSLY.. BE LIKE FRIEDA AND ME...WE DON'T CARE IF WE WIN OR LOSE! LA DE DA! WHO CARES?
5-26
LA DE DA! WIN OR LOSE! WHO CARES? LA DE DA! WE DON'T CARE! WE DON'T CARE!
FOR SOME REASON, THE PAIN HAS SUDDENLY INCREASED...
SCHULZ

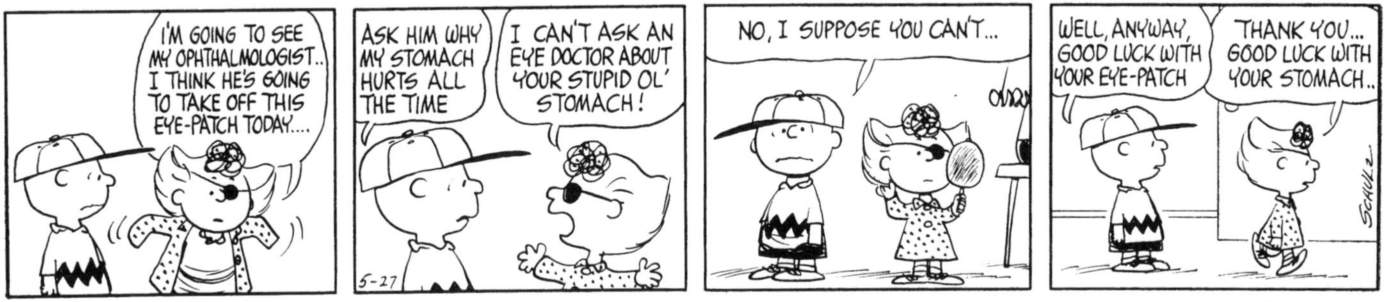
I'M GOING TO SEE MY OPHTHALMOLOGIST.. I THINK HE'S GOING TO TAKE OFF THIS EYE-PATCH TODAY....
ASK HIM WHY MY STOMACH HURTS ALL THE TIME
I CAN'T ASK AN EYE DOCTOR ABOUT YOUR STUPID OL' STOMACH!
5-27
NO, I SUPPOSE YOU CAN'T...
WELL, ANYWAY, GOOD LUCK WITH YOUR EYE-PATCH
THANK YOU... GOOD LUCK WITH YOUR STOMACH..
SCHULZ

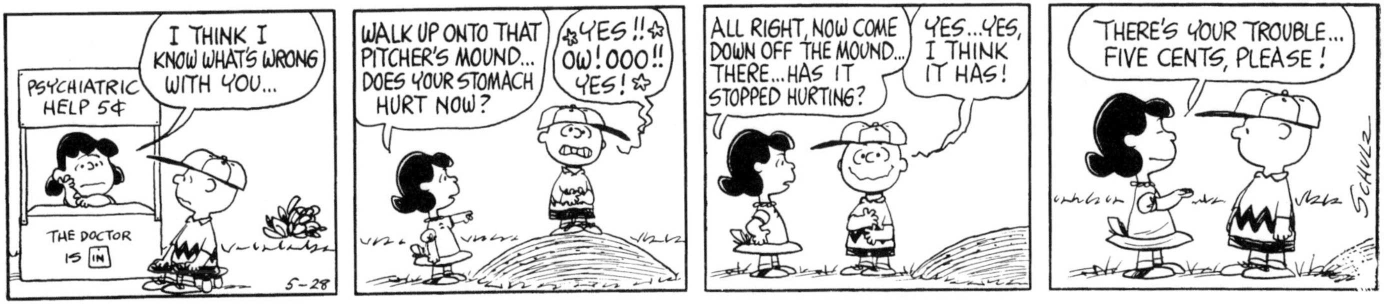
PSYCHIATRIC HELP 5¢
THE DOCTOR IS IN
I THINK I KNOW WHAT'S WRONG WITH YOU...
5-28
WALK UP ONTO THAT PITCHER'S MOUND... DOES YOUR STOMACH HURT NOW?
YES!! OW! OOO!! YES!
ALL RIGHT, NOW COME DOWN OFF THE MOUND... THERE...HAS IT STOPPED HURTING?
YES...YES, I THINK IT HAS!
THERE'S YOUR TROUBLE... FIVE CENTS, PLEASE!
SCHULZ

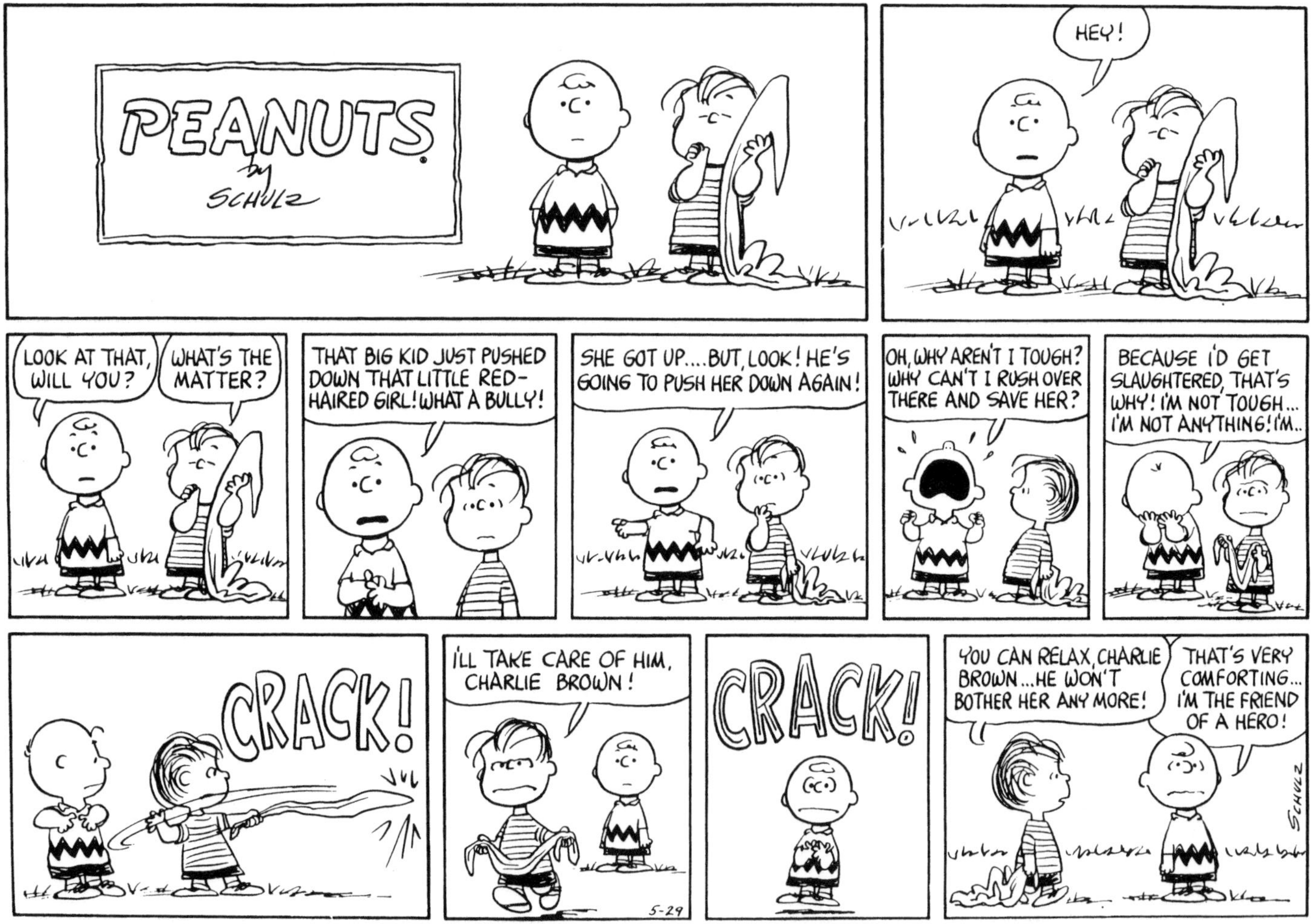
PEANUTS
by SCHULZ
HEY!
LOOK AT THAT, WILL YOU?
WHAT'S THE MATTER?
THAT BIG KID JUST PUSHED DOWN THAT LITTLE RED-HAIRED GIRL! WHAT A BULLY!
SHE GOT UP....BUT, LOOK! HE'S GOING TO PUSH HER DOWN AGAIN!
OH, WHY AREN'T I TOUGH? WHY CAN'T I RUSH OVER THERE AND SAVE HER?
BECAUSE I'D GET SLAUGHTERED, THAT'S WHY! I'M NOT TOUGH... I'M NOT ANYTHING! I'M..
CRACK!
I'LL TAKE CARE OF HIM, CHARLIE BROWN!
5-29
CRACK!
YOU CAN RELAX, CHARLIE BROWN...HE WON'T BOTHER HER ANY MORE!
THAT'S VERY COMFORTING... I'M THE FRIEND OF A HERO!
SCHULZ

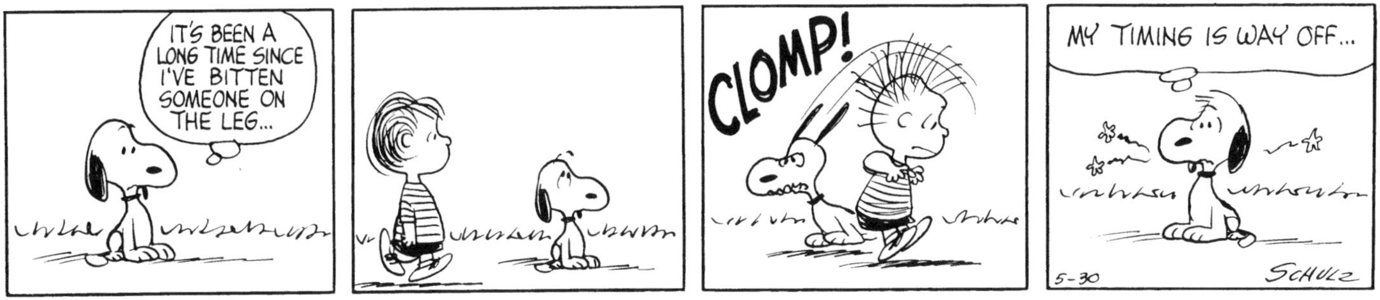
IT'S BEEN A LONG TIME SINCE I'VE BITTEN SOMEONE ON THE LEG...
CLOMP!
MY TIMING IS WAY OFF...
5-30
SCHULZ

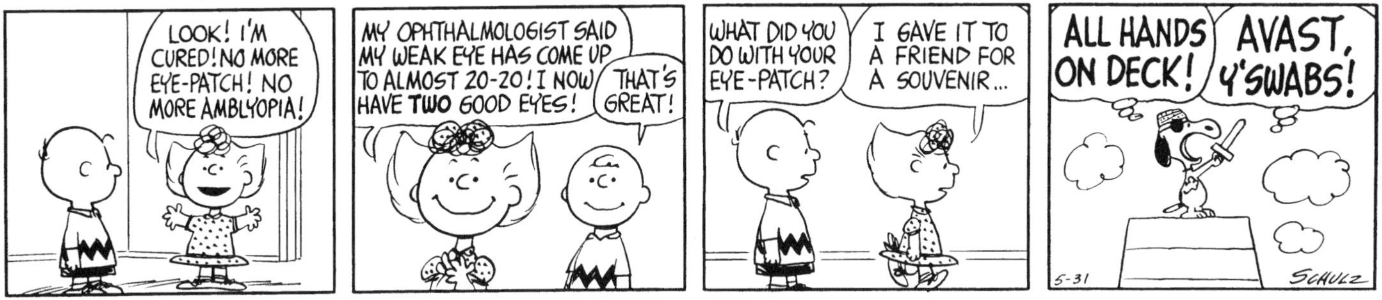
LOOK! I'M CURED! NO MORE EYE-PATCH! NO MORE AMBLYOPIA!
MY OPHTHALMOLOGIST SAID MY WEAK EYE HAS COME UP TO ALMOST 20-20! I NOW HAVE **TWO** GOOD EYES!
THAT'S GREAT!
WHAT DID YOU DO WITH YOUR EYE-PATCH?
I GAVE IT TO A FRIEND FOR A SOUVENIR...
ALL HANDS ON DECK!
AVAST, Y'SWABS!
5-31
SCHULZ

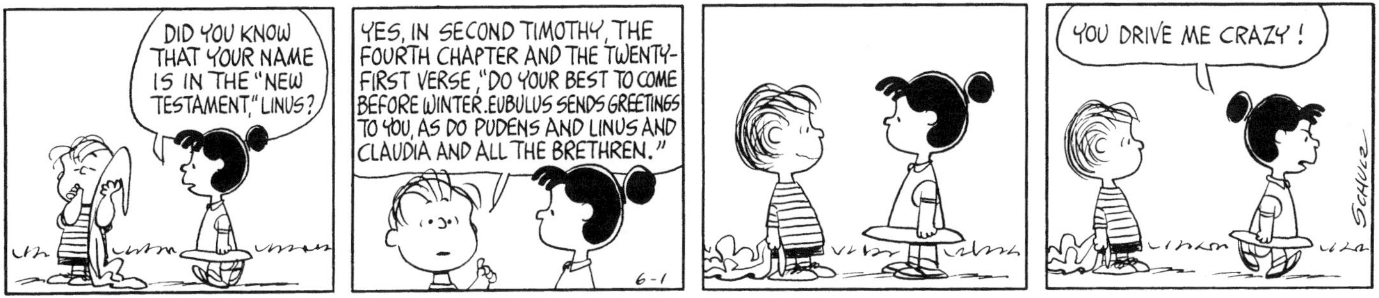
DID YOU KNOW THAT YOUR NAME IS IN THE "NEW TESTAMENT," LINUS?
YES, IN SECOND TIMOTHY, THE FOURTH CHAPTER AND THE TWENTY-FIRST VERSE, "DO YOUR BEST TO COME BEFORE WINTER. EUBULUS SENDS GREETINGS TO YOU, AS DO PUDENS AND LINUS AND CLAUDIA AND ALL THE BRETHREN."
6-1
YOU DRIVE ME CRAZY!
SCHULZ

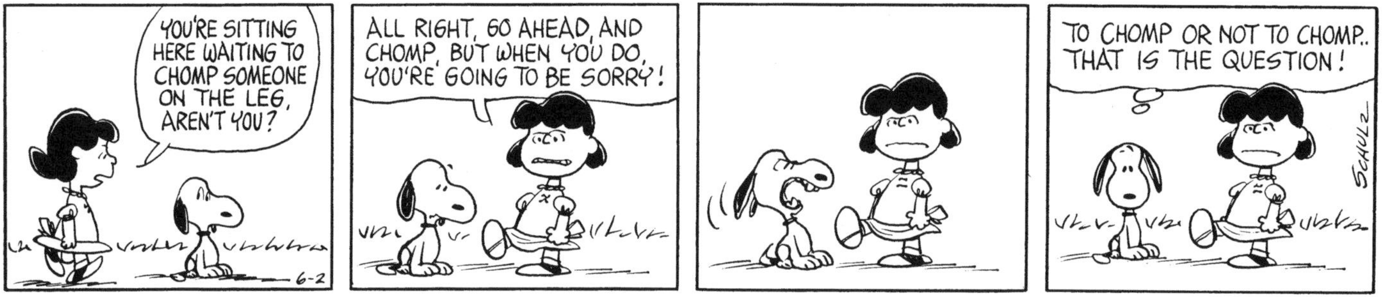
YOU'RE SITTING HERE WAITING TO CHOMP SOMEONE ON THE LEG, AREN'T YOU?
6-2
ALL RIGHT, GO AHEAD, AND CHOMP, BUT WHEN YOU DO, YOU'RE GOING TO BE SORRY!
TO CHOMP OR NOT TO CHOMP.. THAT IS THE QUESTION!
SCHULZ

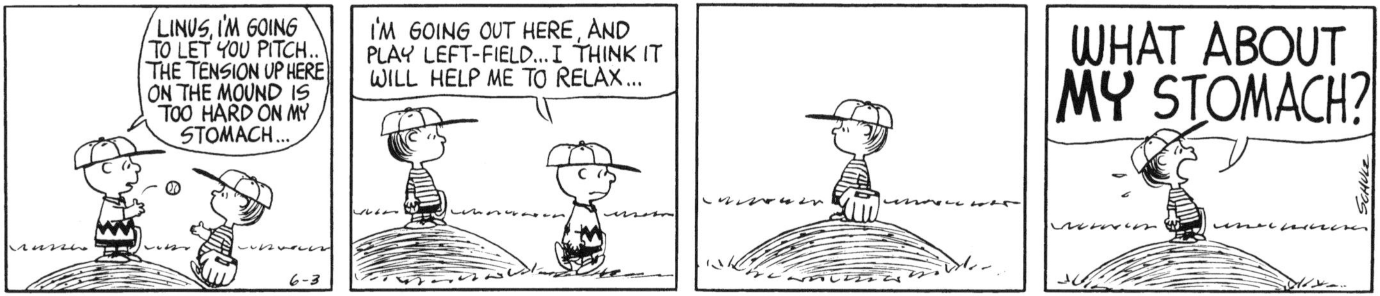
LINUS, I'M GOING TO LET YOU PITCH.. THE TENSION UP HERE ON THE MOUND IS TOO HARD ON MY STOMACH...
6-3
I'M GOING OUT HERE, AND PLAY LEFT-FIELD... I THINK IT WILL HELP ME TO RELAX...
WHAT ABOUT **MY** STOMACH?
SCHULZ

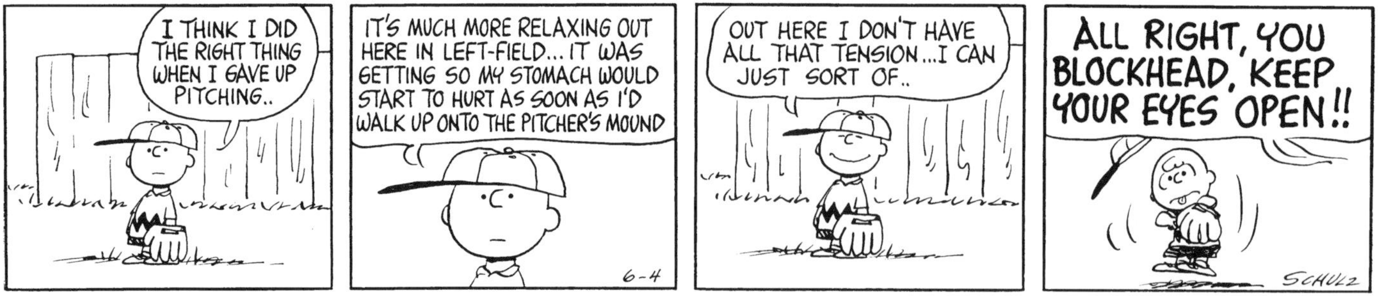
I THINK I DID THE RIGHT THING WHEN I GAVE UP PITCHING..
IT'S MUCH MORE RELAXING OUT HERE IN LEFT-FIELD... IT WAS GETTING SO MY STOMACH WOULD START TO HURT AS SOON AS I'D WALK UP ONTO THE PITCHER'S MOUND
6-4
OUT HERE I DON'T HAVE ALL THAT TENSION... I CAN JUST SORT OF..
ALL RIGHT, YOU BLOCKHEAD, KEEP YOUR EYES OPEN!!
SCHULZ

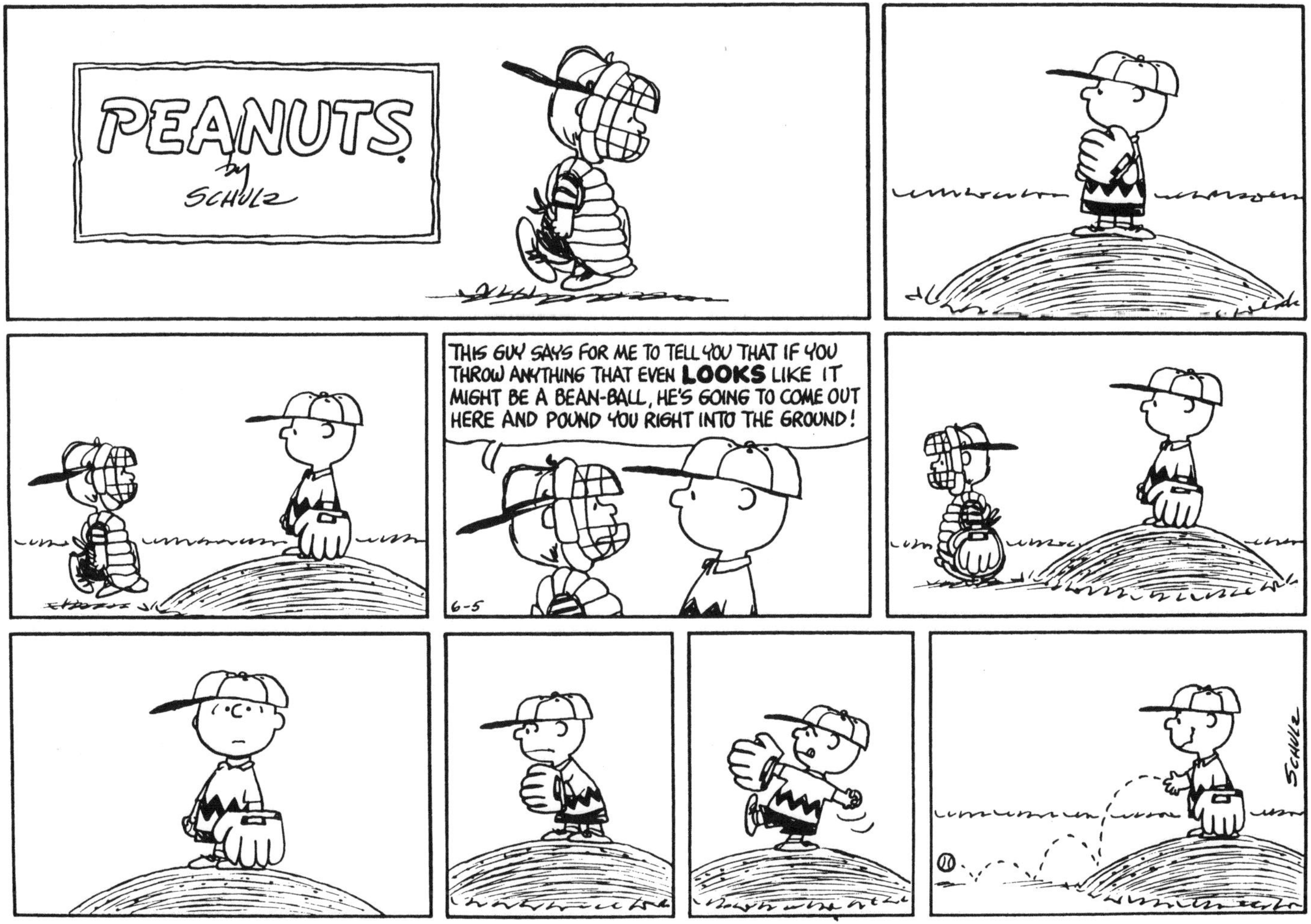
PEANUTS
by SCHULZ
THIS GUY SAYS FOR ME TO TELL YOU THAT IF YOU THROW ANYTHING THAT EVEN LOOKS LIKE IT MIGHT BE A BEAN-BALL, HE'S GOING TO COME OUT HERE AND POUND YOU RIGHT INTO THE GROUND!
6-5
SCHULZ

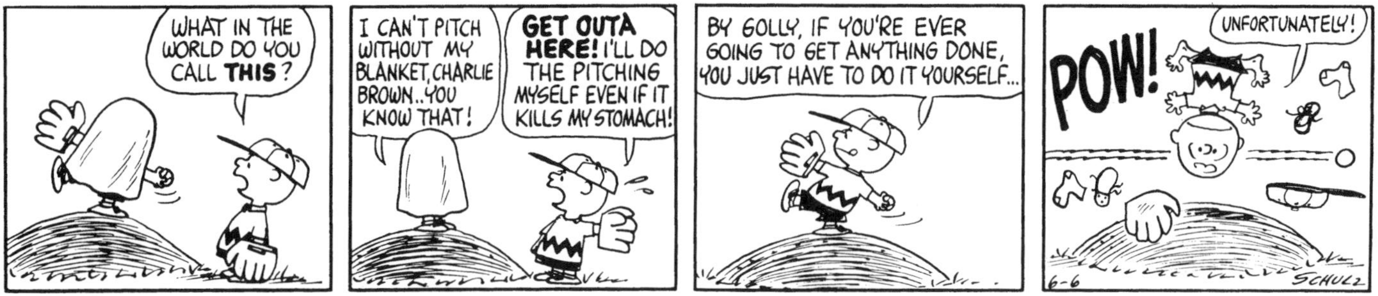
WHAT IN THE WORLD DO YOU CALL THIS?
I CAN'T PITCH WITHOUT MY BLANKET, CHARLIE BROWN..YOU KNOW THAT!
GET OUTA HERE! I'LL DO THE PITCHING MYSELF EVEN IF IT KILLS MY STOMACH!
BY GOLLY, IF YOU'RE EVER GOING TO GET ANYTHING DONE, YOU JUST HAVE TO DO IT YOURSELF...
POW!
UNFORTUNATELY!
6-6
SCHULZ

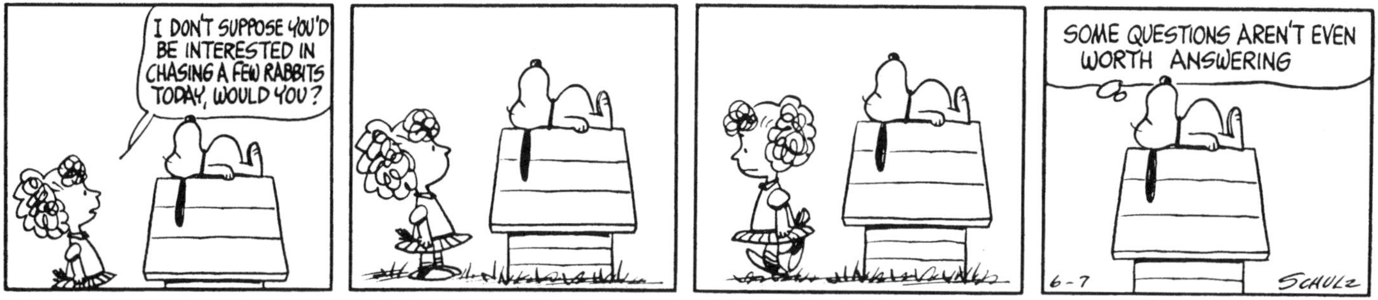
I DON'T SUPPOSE YOU'D BE INTERESTED IN CHASING A FEW RABBITS TODAY, WOULD YOU?
SOME QUESTIONS AREN'T EVEN WORTH ANSWERING
6-7
SCHULZ

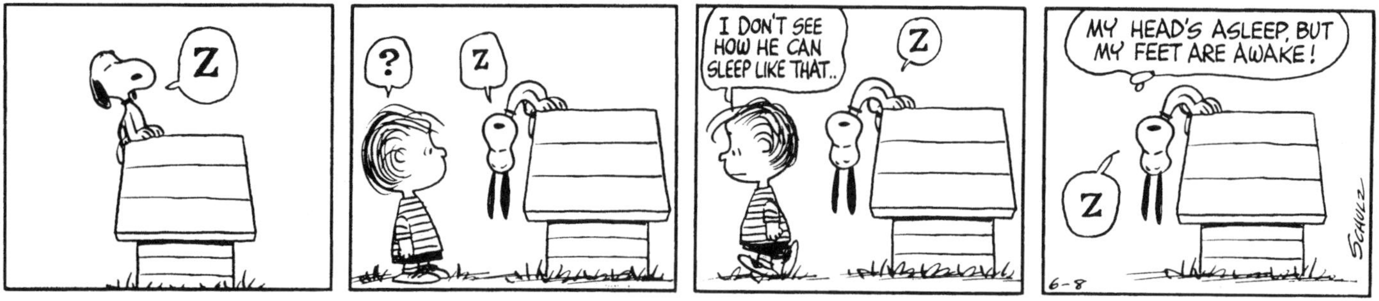
Z
?
Z
I DON'T SEE HOW HE CAN SLEEP LIKE THAT..
Z
MY HEAD'S ASLEEP, BUT MY FEET ARE AWAKE!
Z
SCHULZ
6-8

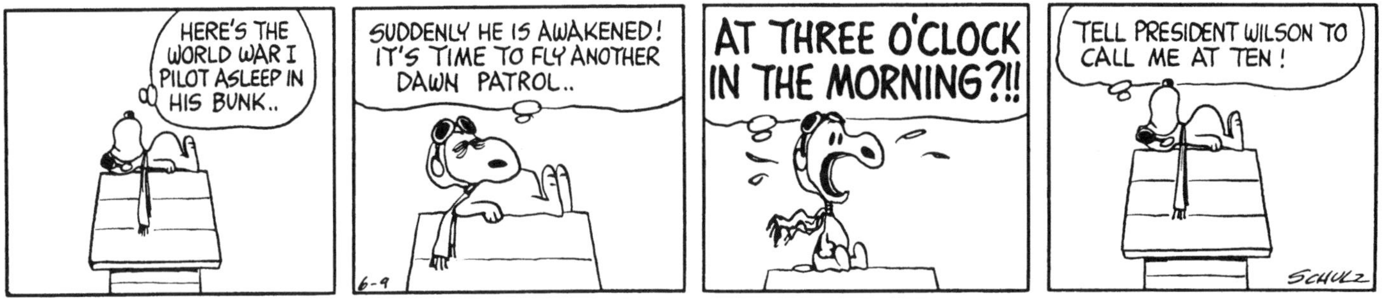
HERE'S THE WORLD WAR I PILOT ASLEEP IN HIS BUNK..
SUDDENLY HE IS AWAKENED! IT'S TIME TO FLY ANOTHER DAWN PATROL..
6-9
AT THREE O'CLOCK IN THE MORNING?!!
TELL PRESIDENT WILSON TO CALL ME AT TEN!
SCHULZ

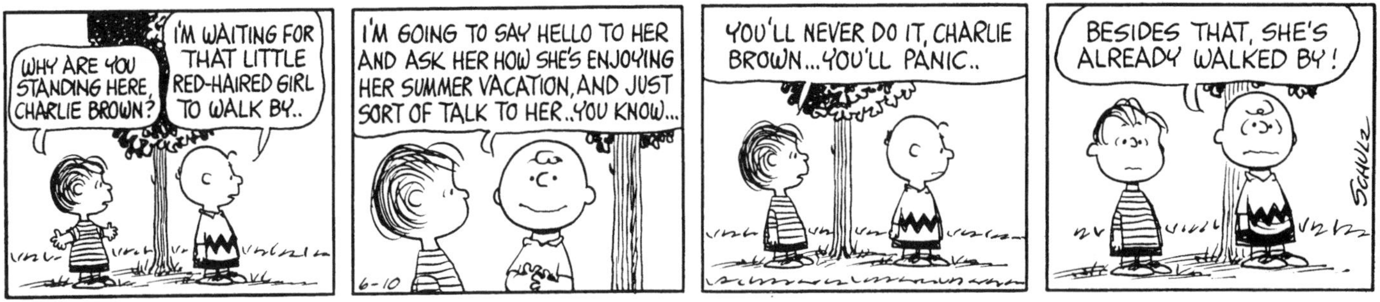
WHY ARE YOU STANDING HERE, CHARLIE BROWN?
I'M WAITING FOR THAT LITTLE RED-HAIRED GIRL TO WALK BY..
I'M GOING TO SAY HELLO TO HER AND ASK HER HOW SHE'S ENJOYING HER SUMMER VACATION, AND JUST SORT OF TALK TO HER..YOU KNOW...
6-10
YOU'LL NEVER DO IT, CHARLIE BROWN...YOU'LL PANIC..
BESIDES THAT, SHE'S ALREADY WALKED BY!
SCHULZ

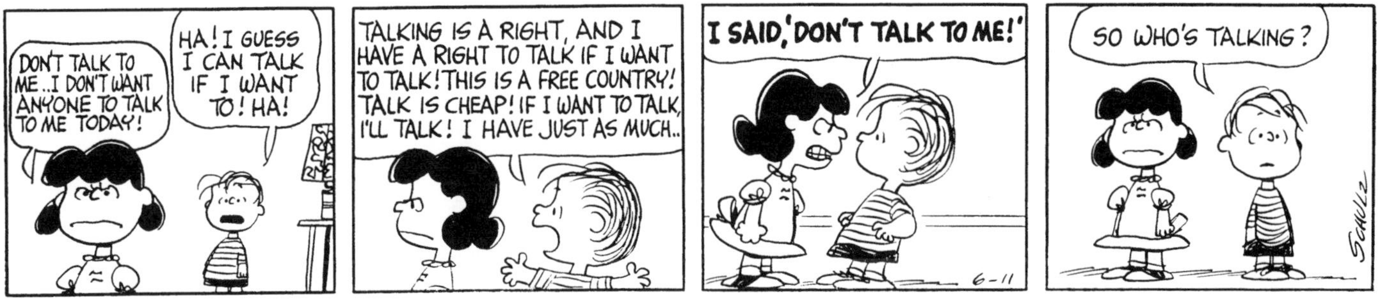
DON'T TALK TO ME..I DON'T WANT ANYONE TO TALK TO ME TODAY!
HA! I GUESS I CAN TALK IF I WANT TO! HA!
TALKING IS A RIGHT, AND I HAVE A RIGHT TO TALK IF I WANT TO TALK! THIS IS A FREE COUNTRY! TALK IS CHEAP! IF I WANT TO TALK, I'LL TALK! I HAVE JUST AS MUCH..
I SAID, 'DON'T TALK TO ME!'
6-11
SO WHO'S TALKING?
SCHULZ

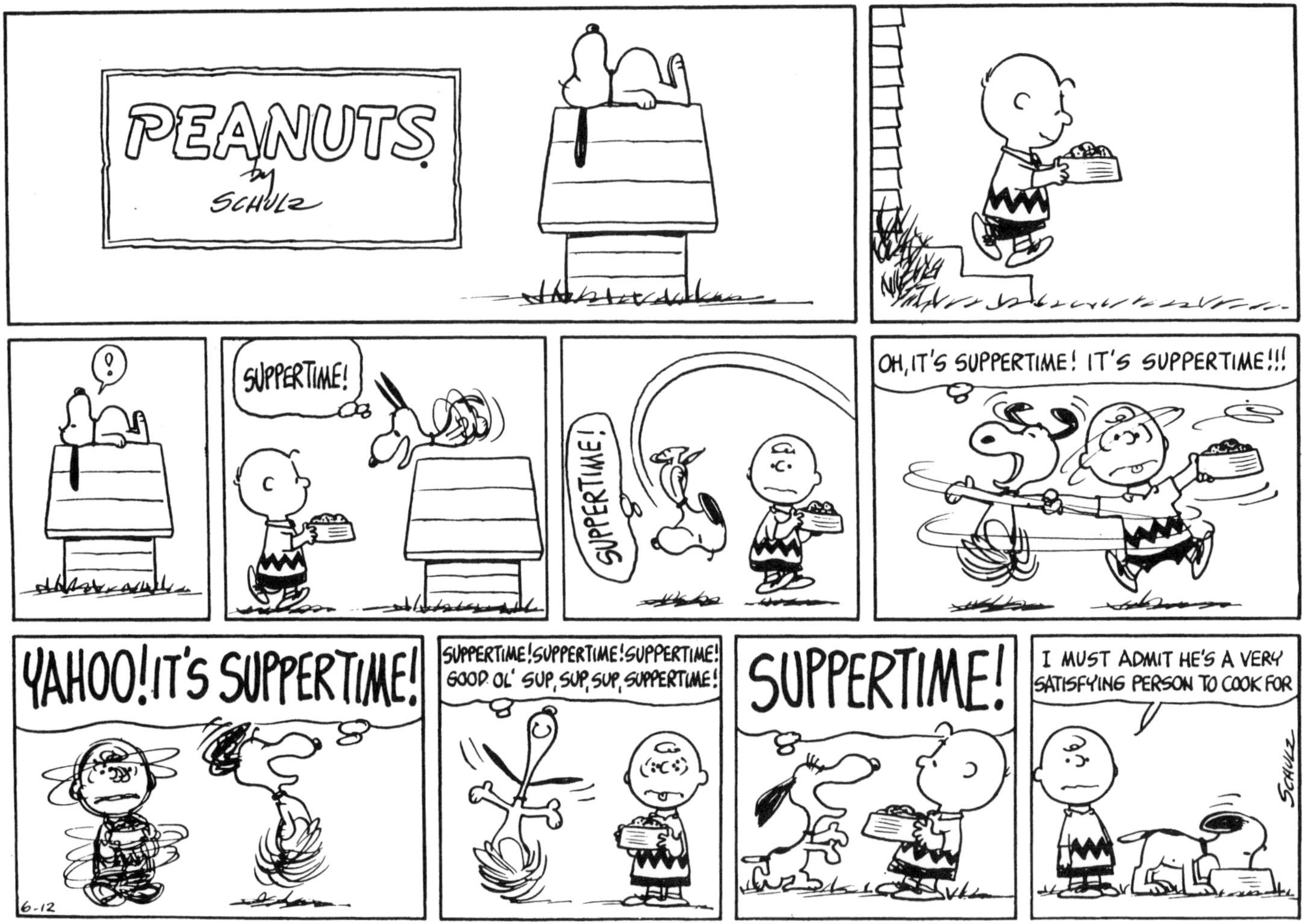
PEANUTS
by SCHULZ
!
SUPPERTIME!
SUPPERTIME!
OH, IT'S SUPPERTIME! IT'S SUPPERTIME!!!
YAHOO! IT'S SUPPERTIME!
6-12
SUPPERTIME! SUPPERTIME! SUPPERTIME! GOOD OL' SUP, SUP, SUP, SUPPERTIME!
SUPPERTIME!
I MUST ADMIT HE'S A VERY SATISFYING PERSON TO COOK FOR
SCHULZ

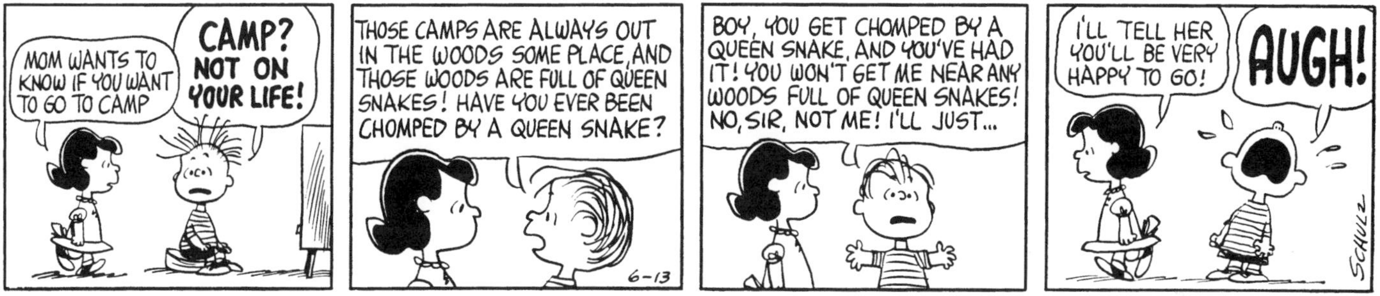
MOM WANTS TO KNOW IF YOU WANT TO GO TO CAMP
CAMP? NOT ON YOUR LIFE!
THOSE CAMPS ARE ALWAYS OUT IN THE WOODS SOME PLACE, AND THOSE WOODS ARE FULL OF QUEEN SNAKES! HAVE YOU EVER BEEN CHOMPED BY A QUEEN SNAKE?
6-13
BOY, YOU GET CHOMPED BY A QUEEN SNAKE, AND YOU'VE HAD IT! YOU WON'T GET ME NEAR ANY WOODS FULL OF QUEEN SNAKES! NO, SIR, NOT ME! I'LL JUST...
I'LL TELL HER YOU'LL BE VERY HAPPY TO GO!
AUGH!
SCHULZ

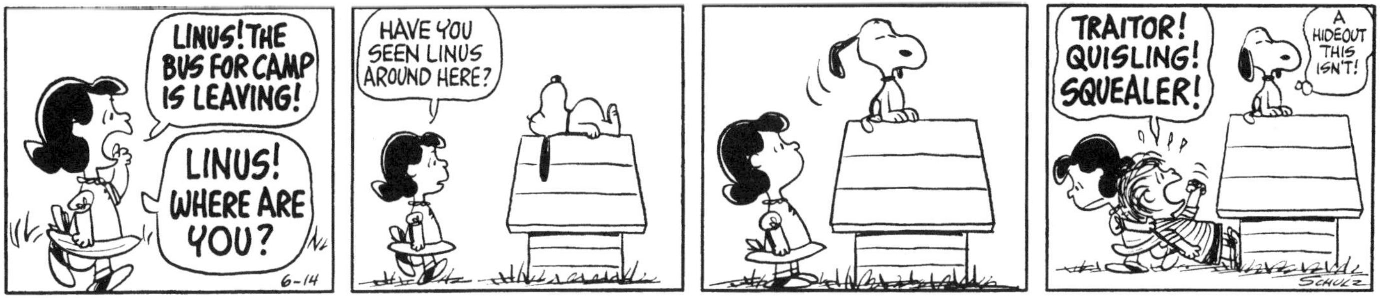
LINUS! THE BUS FOR CAMP IS LEAVING!
LINUS! WHERE ARE YOU?
6-14
HAVE YOU SEEN LINUS AROUND HERE?
TRAITOR! QUISLING! SQUEALER!
A HIDEOUT THIS ISN'T!
SCHULZ

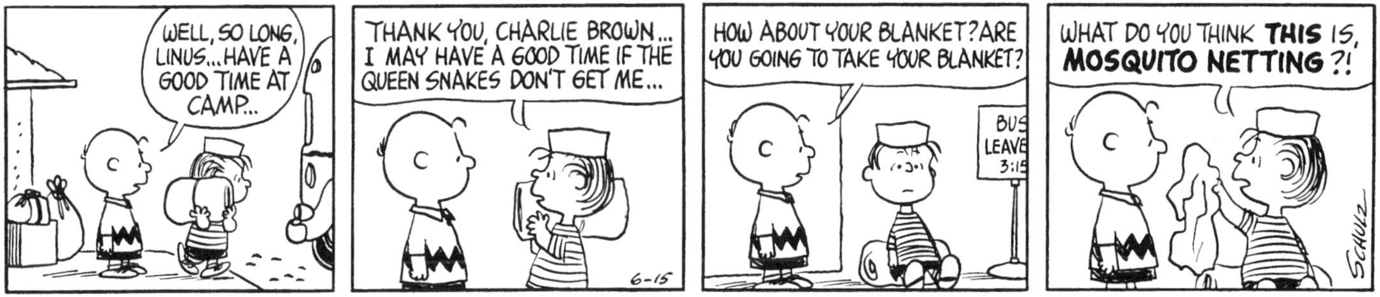
WELL, SO LONG, LINUS... HAVE A GOOD TIME AT CAMP...
THANK YOU, CHARLIE BROWN... I MAY HAVE A GOOD TIME IF THE QUEEN SNAKES DON'T GET ME...
6-15
HOW ABOUT YOUR BLANKET? ARE YOU GOING TO TAKE YOUR BLANKET?
BUS LEAVE 3:15
WHAT DO YOU THINK THIS IS, MOSQUITO NETTING?!
SCHULZ

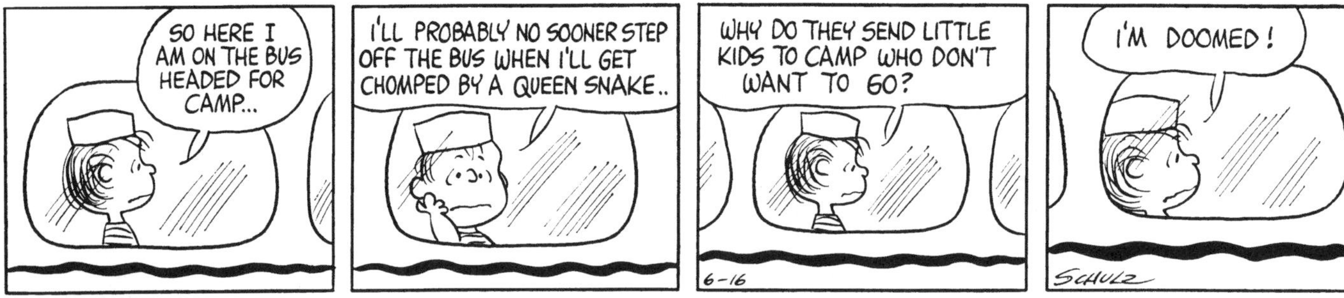
SO HERE I AM ON THE BUS HEADED FOR CAMP...
I'LL PROBABLY NO SOONER STEP OFF THE BUS WHEN I'LL GET CHOMPED BY A QUEEN SNAKE..
WHY DO THEY SEND LITTLE KIDS TO CAMP WHO DON'T WANT TO GO?
6-16
I'M DOOMED!
SCHULZ

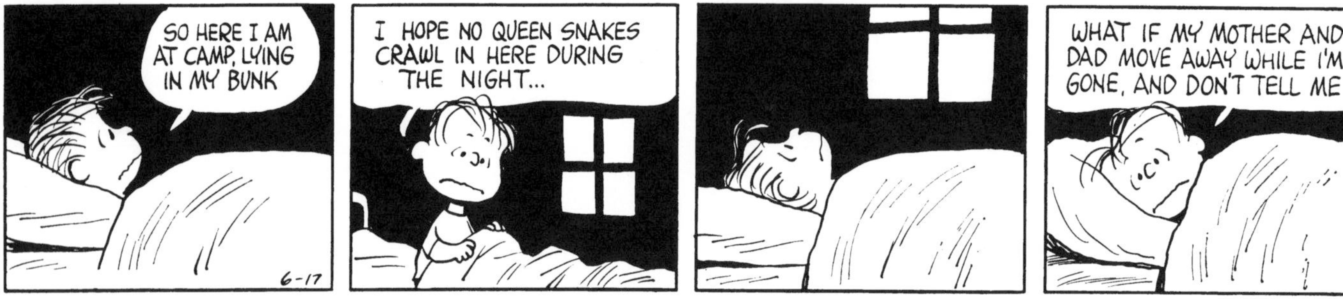
SO HERE I AM AT CAMP, LYING IN MY BUNK
6-17
I HOPE NO QUEEN SNAKES CRAWL IN HERE DURING THE NIGHT...
WHAT IF MY MOTHER AND DAD MOVE AWAY WHILE I'M GONE, AND DON'T TELL ME?
SCHULZ

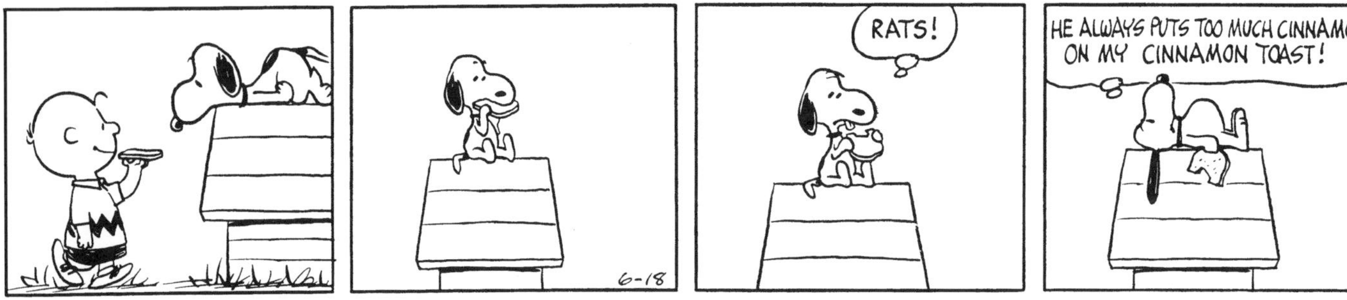
6-18
RATS!
HE ALWAYS PUTS TOO MUCH CINNAMON ON MY CINNAMON TOAST!
SCHULZ

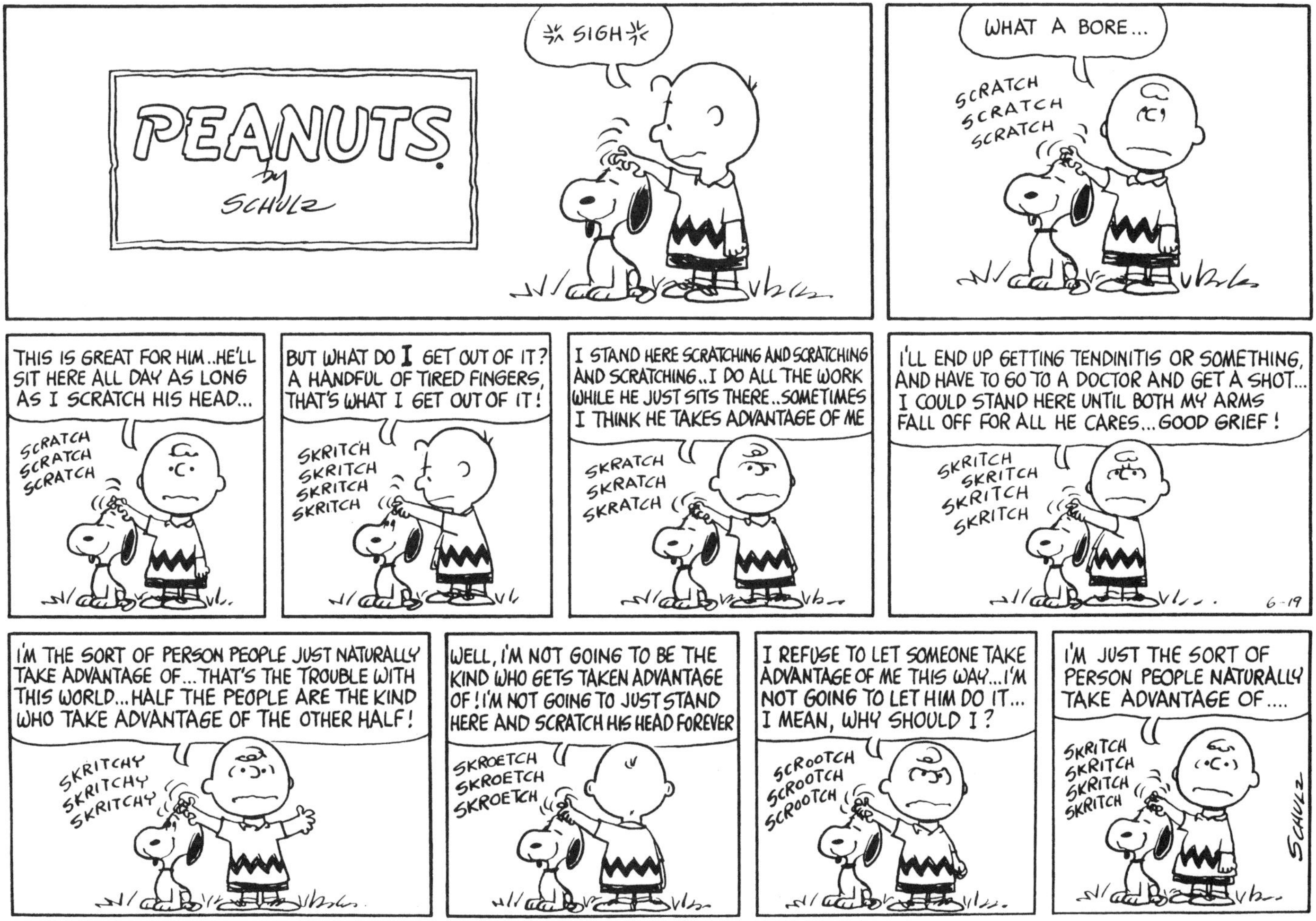
PEANUTS
by
SCHULZ
☼ SIGH ☼
WHAT A BORE...
SCRATCH
SCRATCH
SCRATCH
THIS IS GREAT FOR HIM..HE'LL SIT HERE ALL DAY AS LONG AS I SCRATCH HIS HEAD...
SCRATCH
SCRATCH
SCRATCH
BUT WHAT DO I GET OUT OF IT? A HANDFUL OF TIRED FINGERS, THAT'S WHAT I GET OUT OF IT!
SKRITCH
SKRITCH
SKRITCH
SKRITCH
I STAND HERE SCRATCHING AND SCRATCHING AND SCRATCHING..I DO ALL THE WORK WHILE HE JUST SITS THERE..SOMETIMES I THINK HE TAKES ADVANTAGE OF ME
SKRATCH
SKRATCH
SKRATCH
I'LL END UP GETTING TENDINITIS OR SOMETHING, AND HAVE TO GO TO A DOCTOR AND GET A SHOT... I COULD STAND HERE UNTIL BOTH MY ARMS FALL OFF FOR ALL HE CARES... GOOD GRIEF!
SKRITCH
SKRITCH
SKRITCH
SKRITCH
6-19
I'M THE SORT OF PERSON PEOPLE JUST NATURALLY TAKE ADVANTAGE OF... THAT'S THE TROUBLE WITH THIS WORLD... HALF THE PEOPLE ARE THE KIND WHO TAKE ADVANTAGE OF THE OTHER HALF!
SKRITCHY
SKRITCHY
SKRITCHY
WELL, I'M NOT GOING TO BE THE KIND WHO GETS TAKEN ADVANTAGE OF! I'M NOT GOING TO JUST STAND HERE AND SCRATCH HIS HEAD FOREVER
SKROETCH
SKROETCH
SKROETCH
I REFUSE TO LET SOMEONE TAKE ADVANTAGE OF ME THIS WAY... I'M NOT GOING TO LET HIM DO IT... I MEAN, WHY SHOULD I?
SCROOTCH
SCROOTCH
SCROOTCH
I'M JUST THE SORT OF PERSON PEOPLE NATURALLY TAKE ADVANTAGE OF....
SKRITCH
SKRITCH
SKRITCH
SKRITCH
SCHULZ

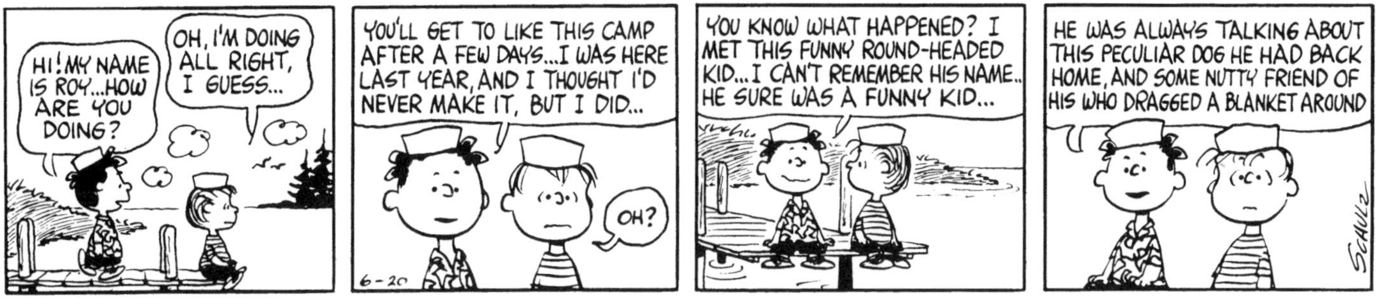
HI! MY NAME IS ROY...HOW ARE YOU DOING?
OH, I'M DOING ALL RIGHT, I GUESS...
YOU'LL GET TO LIKE THIS CAMP AFTER A FEW DAYS...I WAS HERE LAST YEAR, AND I THOUGHT I'D NEVER MAKE IT, BUT I DID...
OH?
6-20
YOU KNOW WHAT HAPPENED? I MET THIS FUNNY ROUND-HEADED KID...I CAN'T REMEMBER HIS NAME.. HE SURE WAS A FUNNY KID...
HE WAS ALWAYS TALKING ABOUT THIS PECULIAR DOG HE HAD BACK HOME, AND SOME NUTTY FRIEND OF HIS WHO DRAGGED A BLANKET AROUND
SCHULZ

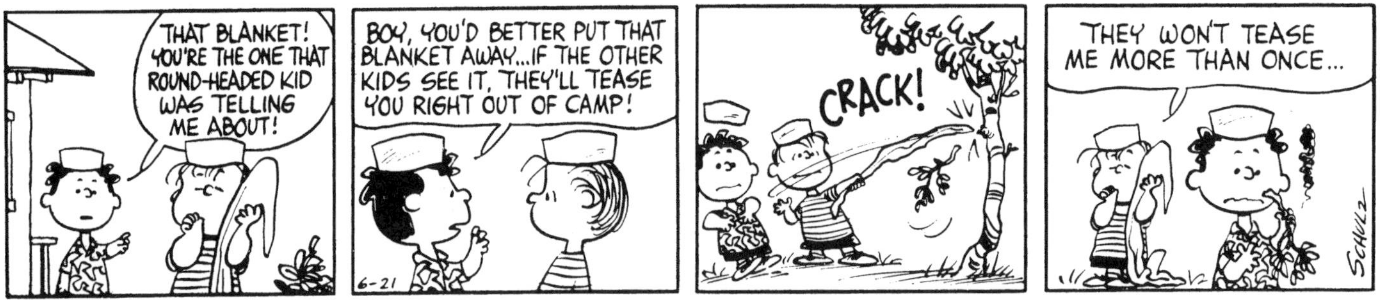
THAT BLANKET! YOU'RE THE ONE THAT ROUND-HEADED KID WAS TELLING ME ABOUT!
BOY, YOU'D BETTER PUT THAT BLANKET AWAY...IF THE OTHER KIDS SEE IT, THEY'LL TEASE YOU RIGHT OUT OF CAMP!
6-21
CRACK!
THEY WON'T TEASE ME MORE THAN ONCE...
SCHULZ

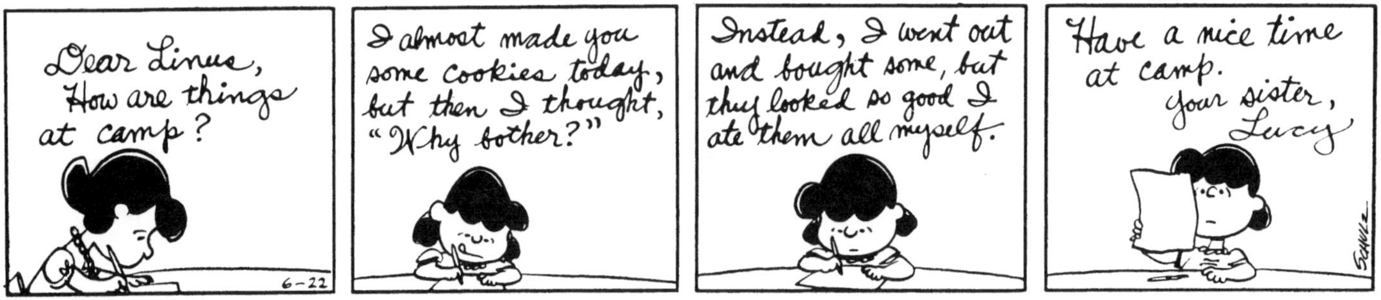
Dear Linus,
How are things at camp?
6-22
I almost made you some cookies today, but then I thought, "Why bother?"
Instead, I went out and bought some, but they looked so good I ate them all myself.
Have a nice time at camp.
Your sister,
Lucy
SCHULZ

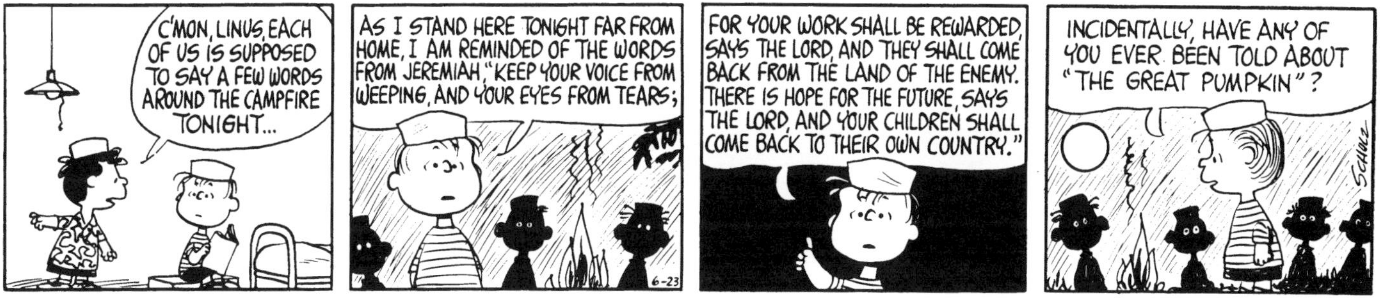
C'MON, LINUS, EACH OF US IS SUPPOSED TO SAY A FEW WORDS AROUND THE CAMPFIRE TONIGHT...
AS I STAND HERE TONIGHT FAR FROM HOME, I AM REMINDED OF THE WORDS FROM JEREMIAH, "KEEP YOUR VOICE FROM WEEPING, AND YOUR EYES FROM TEARS;
6-23
FOR YOUR WORK SHALL BE REWARDED, SAYS THE LORD, AND THEY SHALL COME BACK FROM THE LAND OF THE ENEMY. THERE IS HOPE FOR THE FUTURE, SAYS THE LORD, AND YOUR CHILDREN SHALL COME BACK TO THEIR OWN COUNTRY."
INCIDENTALLY, HAVE ANY OF YOU EVER BEEN TOLD ABOUT "THE GREAT PUMPKIN"?
SCHULZ

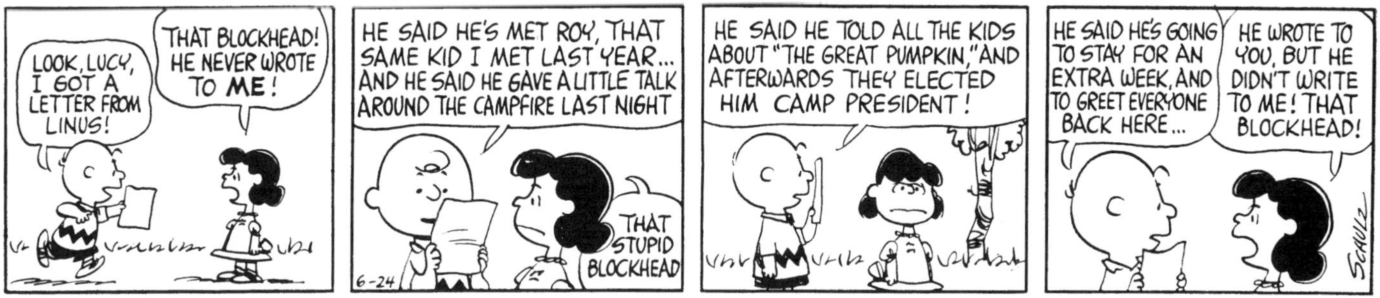
LOOK, LUCY, I GOT A LETTER FROM LINUS!
THAT BLOCKHEAD! HE NEVER WROTE TO ME!
HE SAID HE'S MET ROY, THAT SAME KID I MET LAST YEAR... AND HE SAID HE GAVE A LITTLE TALK AROUND THE CAMPFIRE LAST NIGHT
THAT STUPID BLOCKHEAD
6-24
HE SAID HE TOLD ALL THE KIDS ABOUT "THE GREAT PUMPKIN," AND AFTERWARDS THEY ELECTED HIM CAMP PRESIDENT!
HE SAID HE'S GOING TO STAY FOR AN EXTRA WEEK, AND TO GREET EVERYONE BACK HERE...
HE WROTE TO YOU, BUT HE DIDN'T WRITE TO ME! THAT BLOCKHEAD!
SCHULZ

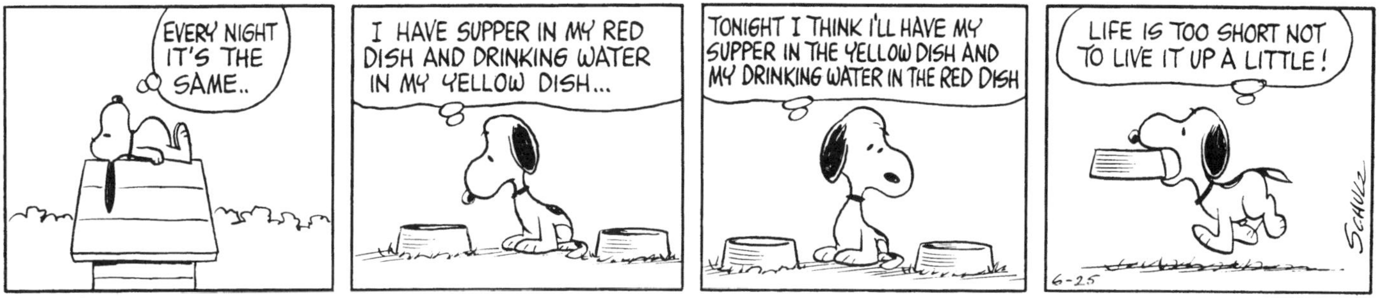
EVERY NIGHT IT'S THE SAME..
I HAVE SUPPER IN MY RED DISH AND DRINKING WATER IN MY YELLOW DISH...
TONIGHT I THINK I'LL HAVE MY SUPPER IN THE YELLOW DISH AND MY DRINKING WATER IN THE RED DISH
LIFE IS TOO SHORT NOT TO LIVE IT UP A LITTLE!
SCHULZ
6-25

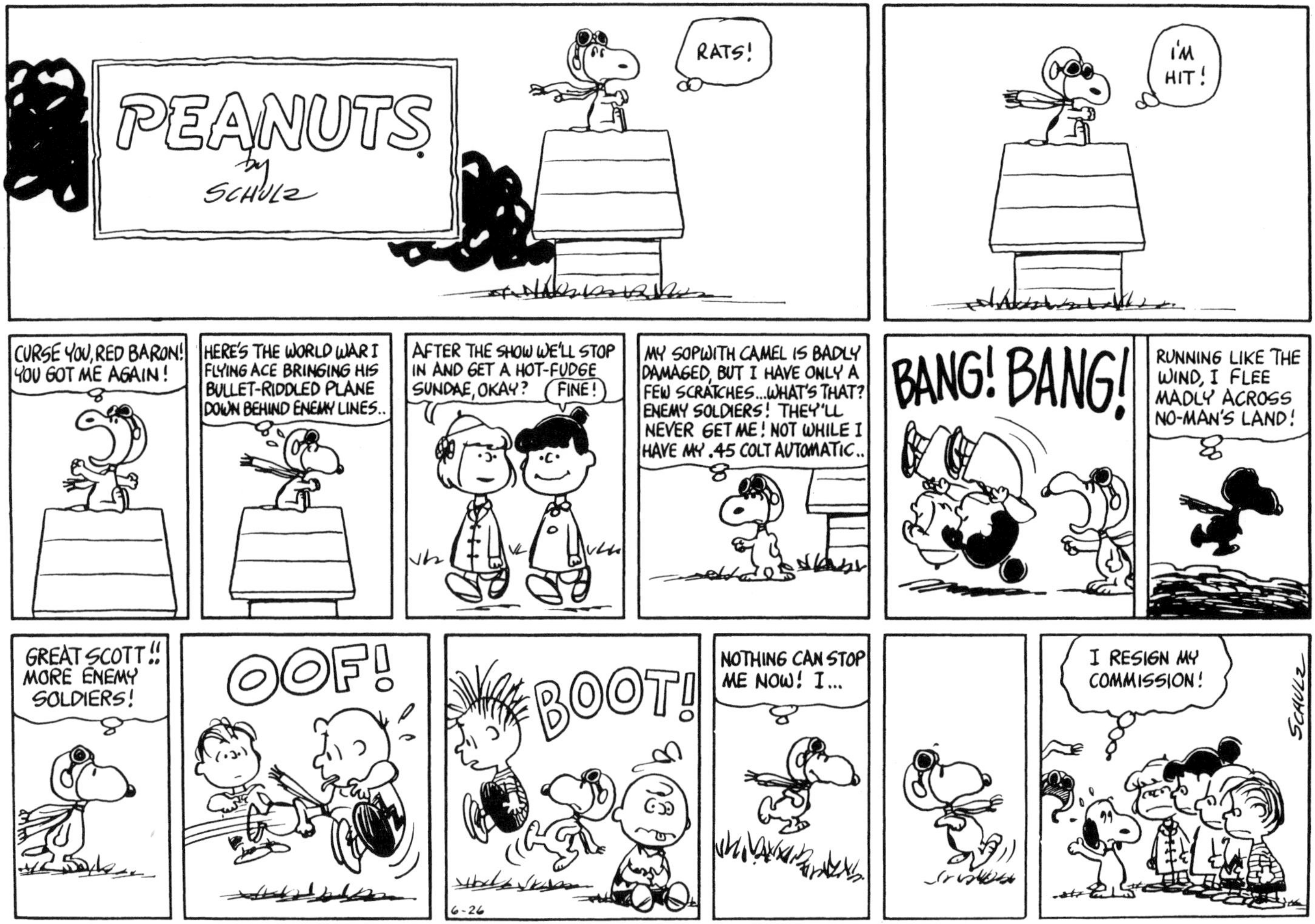
PEANUTS
by SCHULZ
RATS!
I'M HIT!
CURSE YOU, RED BARON! YOU GOT ME AGAIN!
HERE'S THE WORLD WAR I FLYING ACE BRINGING HIS BULLET-RIDDLED PLANE DOWN BEHIND ENEMY LINES..
AFTER THE SHOW WE'LL STOP IN AND GET A HOT-FUDGE SUNDAE, OKAY?
FINE!
MY SOPWITH CAMEL IS BADLY DAMAGED, BUT I HAVE ONLY A FEW SCRATCHES...WHAT'S THAT? ENEMY SOLDIERS! THEY'LL NEVER GET ME! NOT WHILE I HAVE MY .45 COLT AUTOMATIC..
BANG! BANG!
RUNNING LIKE THE WIND, I FLEE MADLY ACROSS NO-MAN'S LAND!
GREAT SCOTT!! MORE ENEMY SOLDIERS!
OOF!
BOOT!
6-26
NOTHING CAN STOP ME NOW! I...
I RESIGN MY COMMISSION!
SCHULZ

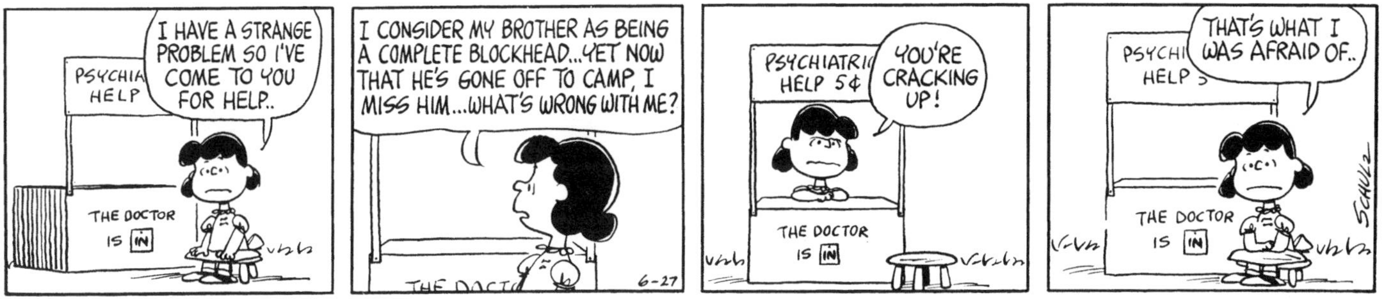
PSYCHIA HELP
I HAVE A STRANGE PROBLEM SO I'VE COME TO YOU FOR HELP..
THE DOCTOR IS IN
I CONSIDER MY BROTHER AS BEING A COMPLETE BLOCKHEAD...YET NOW THAT HE'S GONE OFF TO CAMP, I MISS HIM...WHAT'S WRONG WITH ME?
6-27
PSYCHIATRIC HELP 5¢
YOU'RE CRACKING UP!
THE DOCTOR IS IN
THAT'S WHAT I WAS AFRAID OF..
THE DOCTOR IS IN
SCHULZ

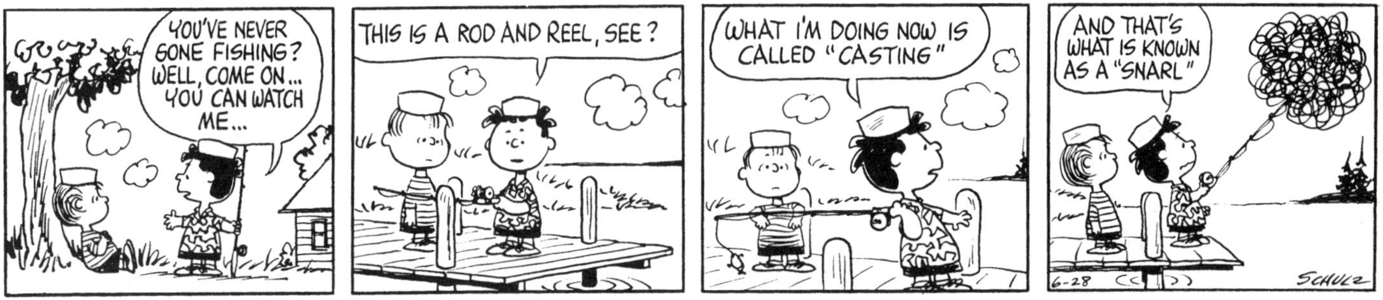
YOU'VE NEVER GONE FISHING? WELL, COME ON... YOU CAN WATCH ME...
THIS IS A ROD AND REEL, SEE?
WHAT I'M DOING NOW IS CALLED "CASTING"
AND THAT'S WHAT IS KNOWN AS A "SNARL"
6-28
SCHULZ

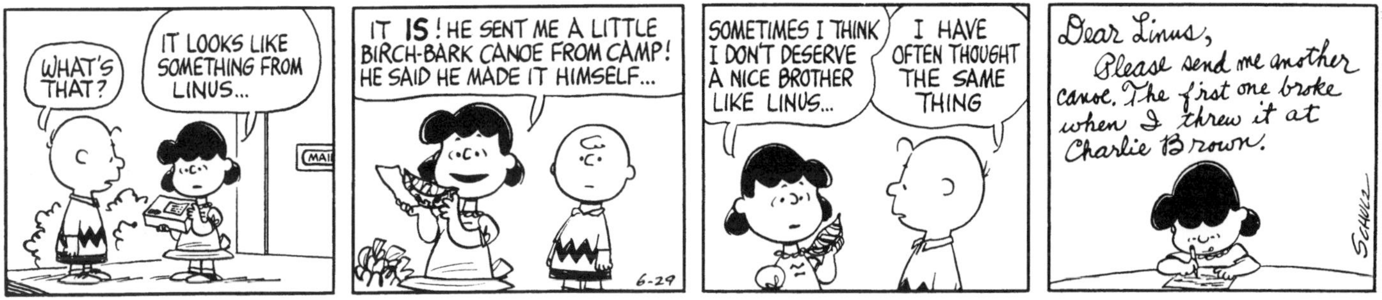
WHAT'S THAT?
IT LOOKS LIKE SOMETHING FROM LINUS...
IT IS! HE SENT ME A LITTLE BIRCH-BARK CANOE FROM CAMP! HE SAID HE MADE IT HIMSELF...
6-29
SOMETIMES I THINK I DON'T DESERVE A NICE BROTHER LIKE LINUS...
I HAVE OFTEN THOUGHT THE SAME THING
Dear Linus,
Please send me another canoe. The first one broke when I threw it at Charlie Brown.
SCHULZ

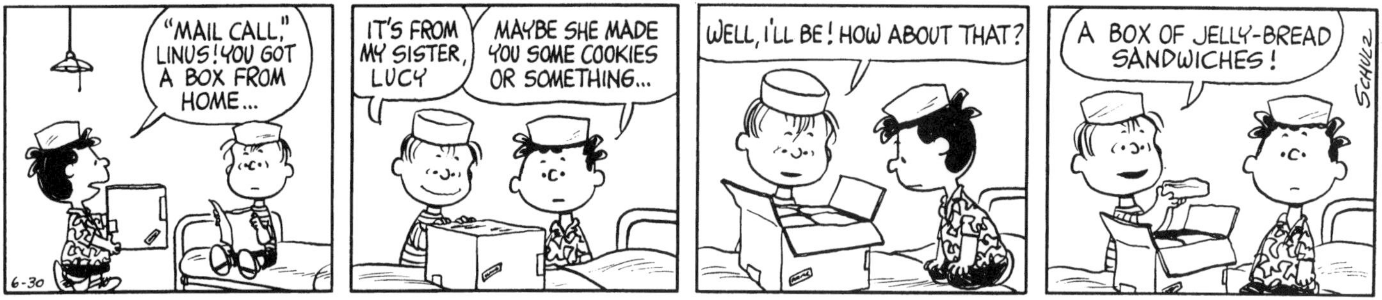
"MAIL CALL," LINUS! YOU GOT A BOX FROM HOME...
6-30
IT'S FROM MY SISTER, LUCY
MAYBE SHE MADE YOU SOME COOKIES OR SOMETHING...
WELL, I'LL BE! HOW ABOUT THAT?
A BOX OF JELLY-BREAD SANDWICHES!
SCHULZ

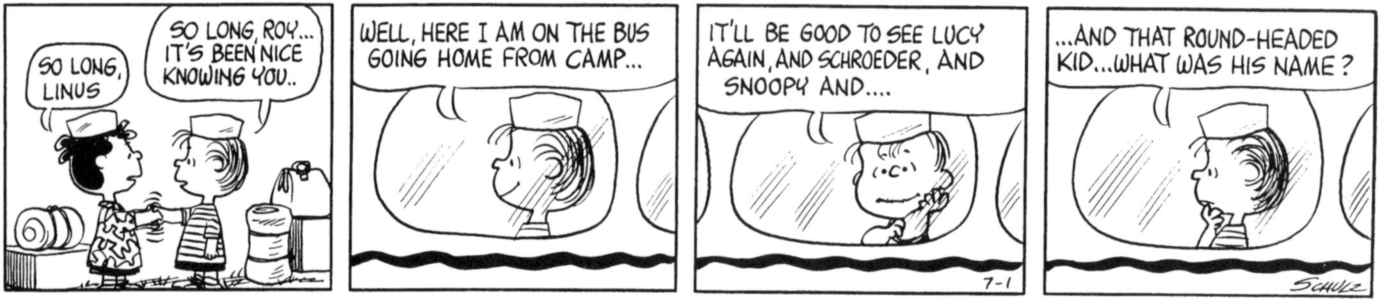
SO LONG, LINUS
SO LONG, ROY... IT'S BEEN NICE KNOWING YOU..
WELL, HERE I AM ON THE BUS GOING HOME FROM CAMP...
IT'LL BE GOOD TO SEE LUCY AGAIN, AND SCHROEDER, AND SNOOPY AND....
7-1
...AND THAT ROUND-HEADED KID...WHAT WAS HIS NAME?
SCHULZ

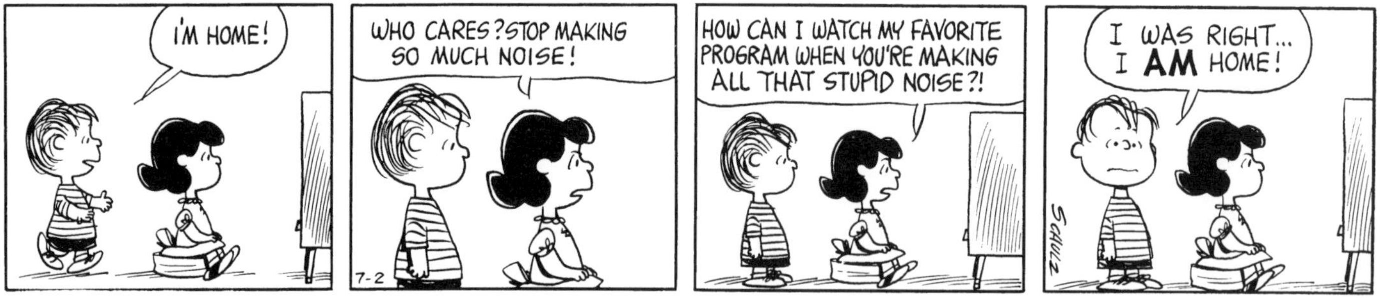
I'M HOME!
WHO CARES? STOP MAKING SO MUCH NOISE!
7-2
HOW CAN I WATCH MY FAVORITE PROGRAM WHEN YOU'RE MAKING ALL THAT STUPID NOISE?!
SCHULZ
I WAS RIGHT... I **AM** HOME!

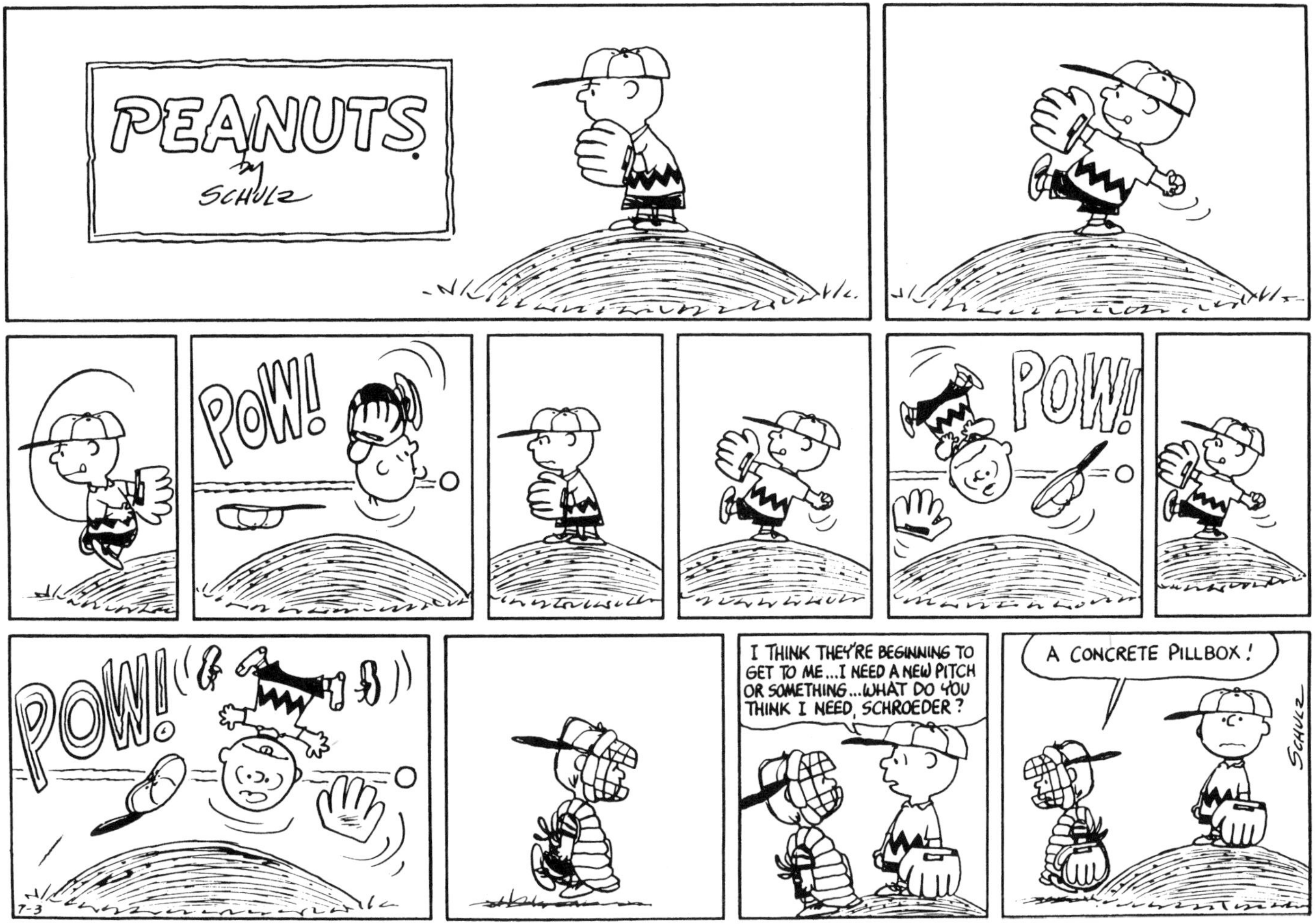
PEANUTS
by SCHULZ
POW!
POW!
POW!
I THINK THEY'RE BEGINNING TO GET TO ME...I NEED A NEW PITCH OR SOMETHING...WHAT DO YOU THINK I NEED, SCHROEDER?
A CONCRETE PILLBOX!
SCHULZ

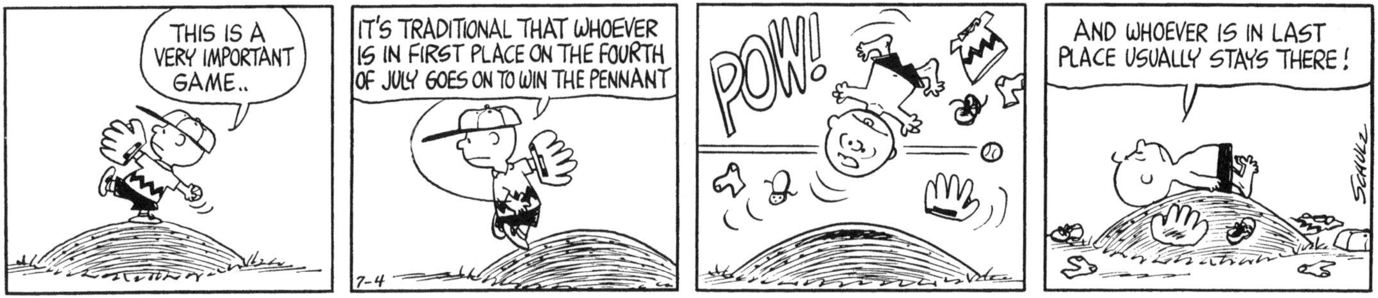
THIS IS A VERY IMPORTANT GAME..
IT'S TRADITIONAL THAT WHOEVER IS IN FIRST PLACE ON THE FOURTH OF JULY GOES ON TO WIN THE PENNANT
POW!
AND WHOEVER IS IN LAST PLACE USUALLY STAYS THERE!

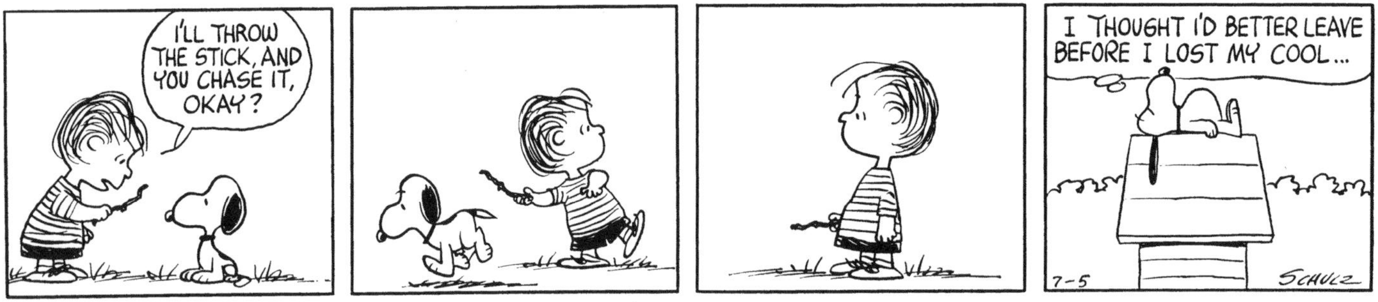
I'LL THROW THE STICK, AND YOU CHASE IT, OKAY?
I THOUGHT I'D BETTER LEAVE BEFORE I LOST MY COOL...

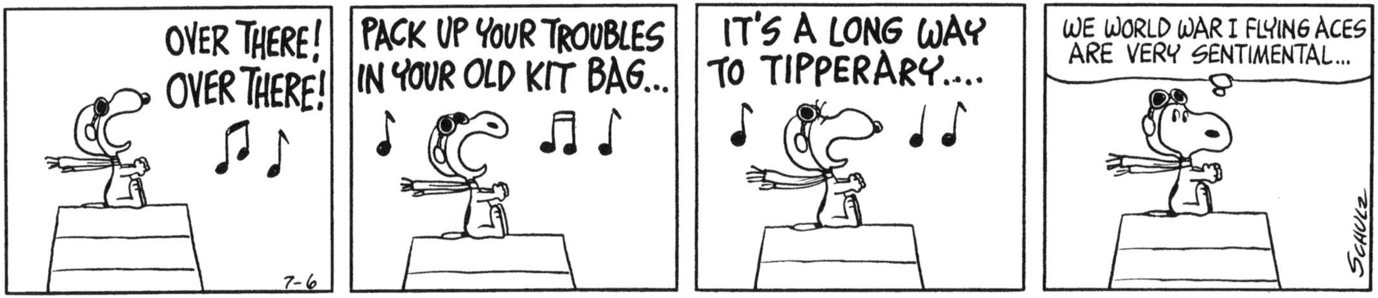
OVER THERE! OVER THERE!
PACK UP YOUR TROUBLES IN YOUR OLD KIT BAG...
IT'S A LONG WAY TO TIPPERARY....
WE WORLD WAR I FLYING ACES ARE VERY SENTIMENTAL...

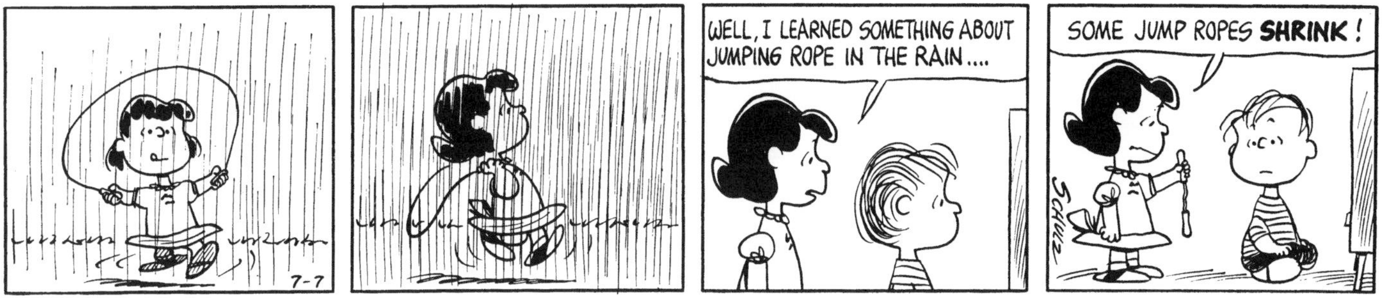
WELL, I LEARNED SOMETHING ABOUT JUMPING ROPE IN THE RAIN....
SOME JUMP ROPES **SHRINK**!
7-7
SCHULZ

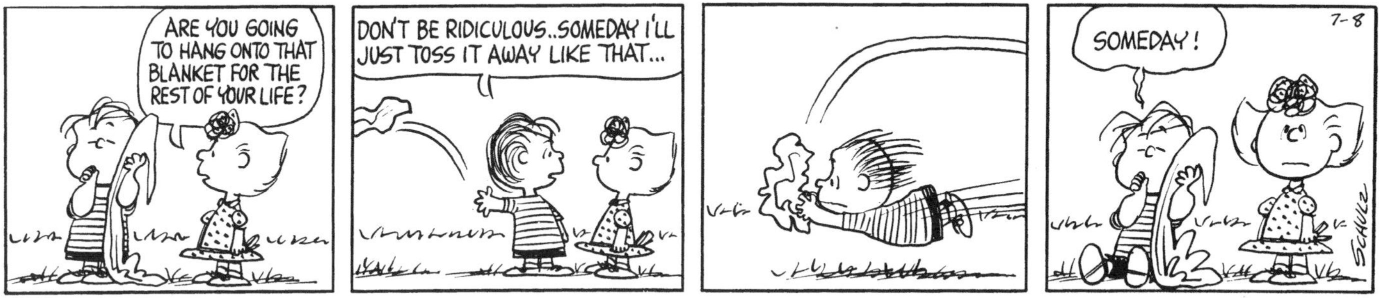
ARE YOU GOING TO HANG ONTO THAT BLANKET FOR THE REST OF YOUR LIFE?
DON'T BE RIDICULOUS..SOMEDAY I'LL JUST TOSS IT AWAY LIKE THAT...
SOMEDAY!
7-8
SCHULZ

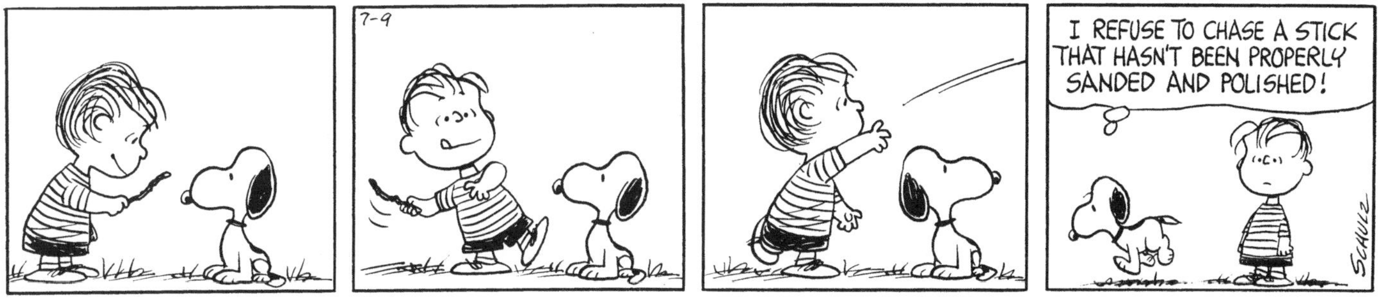
7-9
I REFUSE TO CHASE A STICK THAT HASN'T BEEN PROPERLY SANDED AND POLISHED!
SCHULZ

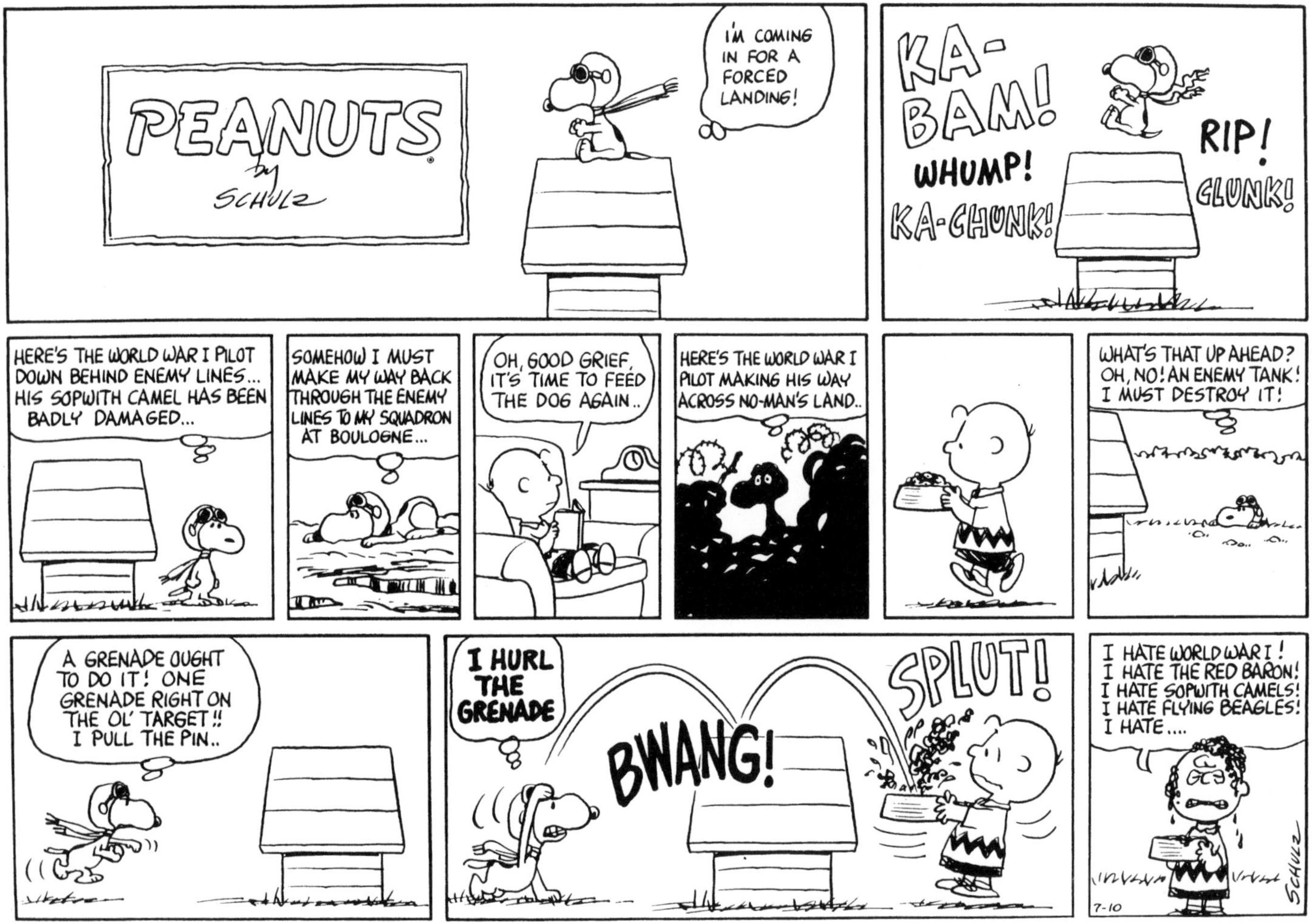
PEANUTS
by SCHULZ
I'M COMING IN FOR A FORCED LANDING!
KA-BAM!
WHUMP!
KA-CHUNK!
RIP!
CLUNK!
HERE'S THE WORLD WAR I PILOT DOWN BEHIND ENEMY LINES... HIS SOPWITH CAMEL HAS BEEN BADLY DAMAGED...
SOMEHOW I MUST MAKE MY WAY BACK THROUGH THE ENEMY LINES TO MY SQUADRON AT BOULOGNE...
OH, GOOD GRIEF, IT'S TIME TO FEED THE DOG AGAIN..
HERE'S THE WORLD WAR I PILOT MAKING HIS WAY ACROSS NO-MAN'S LAND..
WHAT'S THAT UP AHEAD? OH, NO! AN ENEMY TANK! I MUST DESTROY IT!
A GRENADE OUGHT TO DO IT! ONE GRENADE RIGHT ON THE OL' TARGET!! I PULL THE PIN..
I HURL THE GRENADE
BWANG!
SPLUT!
I HATE WORLD WAR I! I HATE THE RED BARON! I HATE SOPWITH CAMELS! I HATE FLYING BEAGLES! I HATE....
7-10
SCHULZ

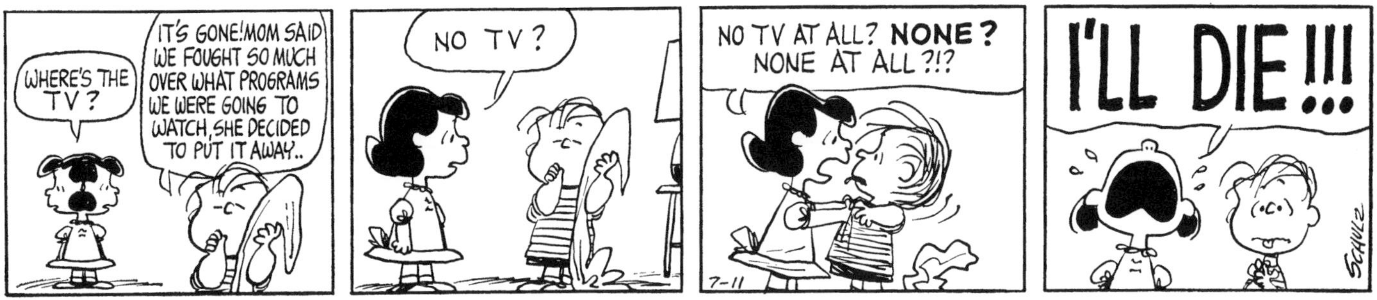
WHERE'S THE TV?
IT'S GONE! MOM SAID WE FOUGHT SO MUCH OVER WHAT PROGRAMS WE WERE GOING TO WATCH, SHE DECIDED TO PUT IT AWAY..
NO TV?
NO TV AT ALL? **NONE?** NONE AT ALL?!?
7-11
I'LL DIE!!!
SCHULZ

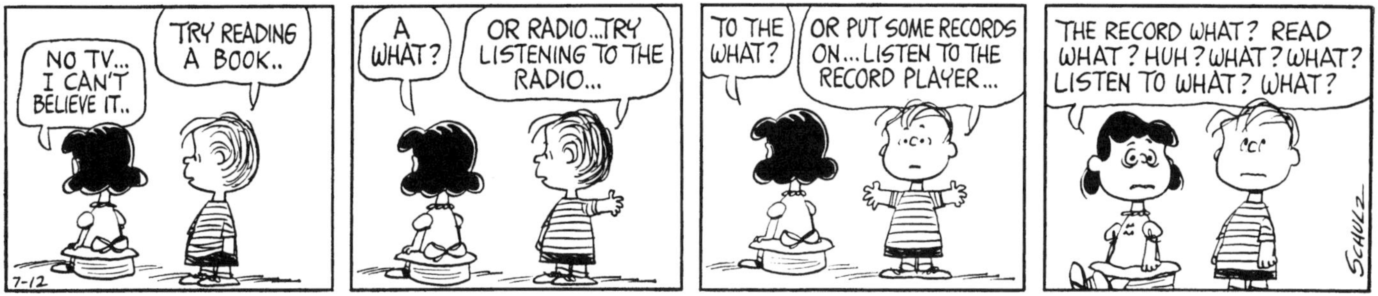
NO TV... I CAN'T BELIEVE IT..
TRY READING A BOOK..
7-12
A WHAT?
OR RADIO...TRY LISTENING TO THE RADIO...
TO THE WHAT?
OR PUT SOME RECORDS ON... LISTEN TO THE RECORD PLAYER...
THE RECORD WHAT? READ WHAT? HUH? WHAT? WHAT? LISTEN TO WHAT? WHAT?
SCHULZ

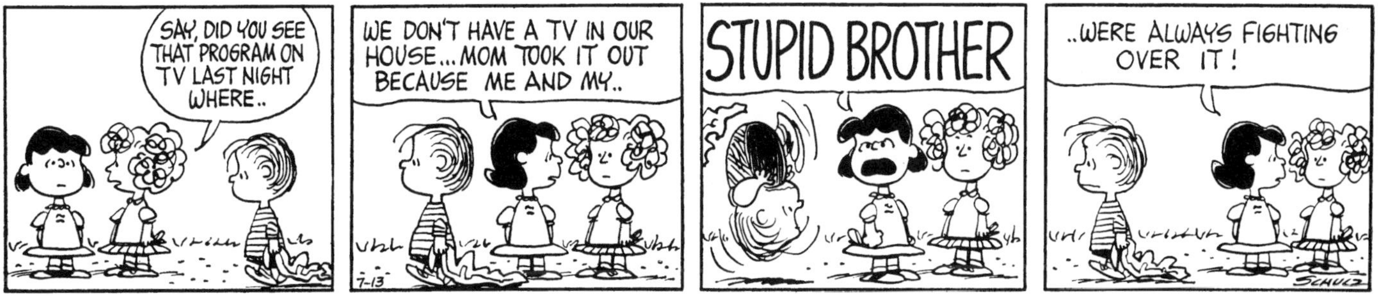
SAY, DID YOU SEE THAT PROGRAM ON TV LAST NIGHT WHERE..
WE DON'T HAVE A TV IN OUR HOUSE... MOM TOOK IT OUT BECAUSE ME AND MY..
7-13
STUPID BROTHER
..WERE ALWAYS FIGHTING OVER IT!
SCHULZ

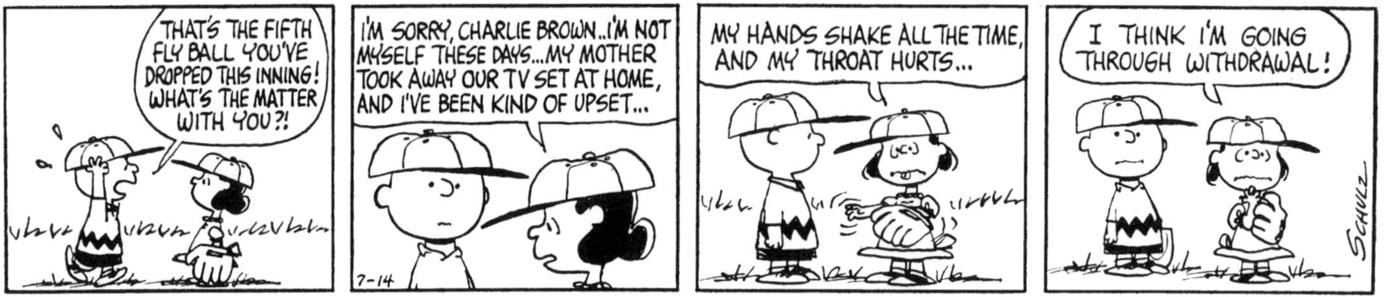
THAT'S THE FIFTH FLY BALL YOU'VE DROPPED THIS INNING! WHAT'S THE MATTER WITH YOU?!
I'M SORRY, CHARLIE BROWN..I'M NOT MYSELF THESE DAYS...MY MOTHER TOOK AWAY OUR TV SET AT HOME, AND I'VE BEEN KIND OF UPSET...
7-14
MY HANDS SHAKE ALL THE TIME, AND MY THROAT HURTS...
I THINK I'M GOING THROUGH WITHDRAWAL!
SCHULZ

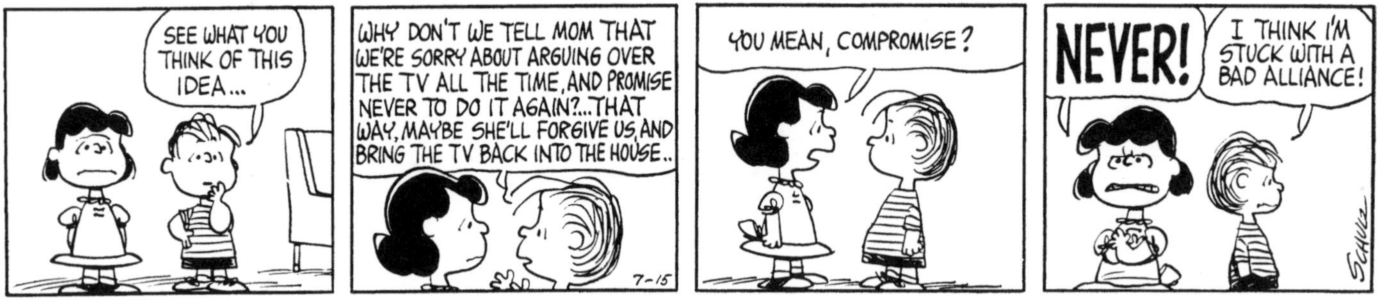
SEE WHAT YOU THINK OF THIS IDEA...
WHY DON'T WE TELL MOM THAT WE'RE SORRY ABOUT ARGUING OVER THE TV ALL THE TIME, AND PROMISE NEVER TO DO IT AGAIN?...THAT WAY, MAYBE SHE'LL FORGIVE US, AND BRING THE TV BACK INTO THE HOUSE..
7-15
YOU MEAN, COMPROMISE?
NEVER!
I THINK I'M STUCK WITH A BAD ALLIANCE!
SCHULZ

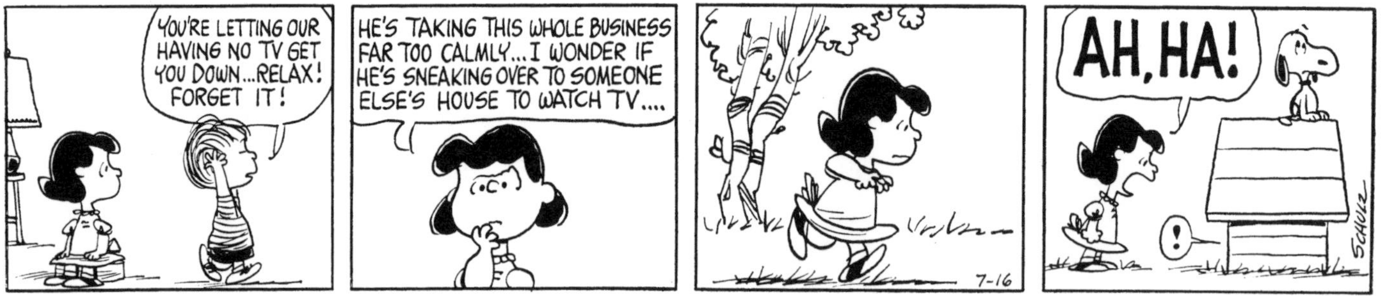
YOU'RE LETTING OUR HAVING NO TV GET YOU DOWN...RELAX! FORGET IT!
HE'S TAKING THIS WHOLE BUSINESS FAR TOO CALMLY...I WONDER IF HE'S SNEAKING OVER TO SOMEONE ELSE'S HOUSE TO WATCH TV....
7-16
AH, HA!
!
SCHULZ

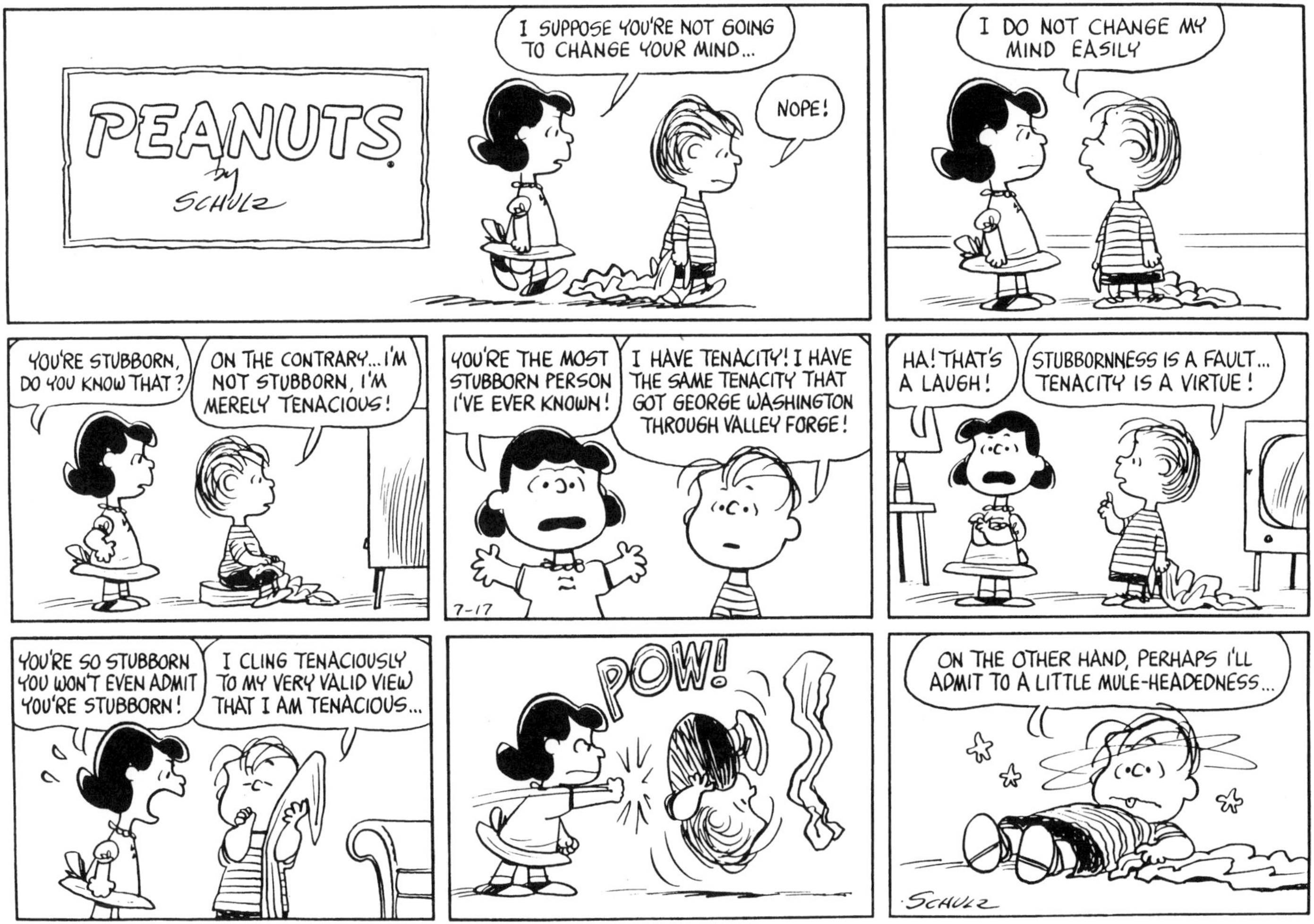
PEANUTS
by SCHULZ
I SUPPOSE YOU'RE NOT GOING TO CHANGE YOUR MIND...
NOPE!
I DO NOT CHANGE MY MIND EASILY
YOU'RE STUBBORN, DO YOU KNOW THAT?
ON THE CONTRARY...I'M NOT STUBBORN, I'M MERELY TENACIOUS!
YOU'RE THE MOST STUBBORN PERSON I'VE EVER KNOWN!
I HAVE TENACITY! I HAVE THE SAME TENACITY THAT GOT GEORGE WASHINGTON THROUGH VALLEY FORGE!
7-17
HA! THAT'S A LAUGH!
STUBBORNNESS IS A FAULT... TENACITY IS A VIRTUE!
YOU'RE SO STUBBORN YOU WON'T EVEN ADMIT YOU'RE STUBBORN!
I CLING TENACIOUSLY TO MY VERY VALID VIEW THAT I AM TENACIOUS...
POW!
ON THE OTHER HAND, PERHAPS I'LL ADMIT TO A LITTLE MULE-HEADEDNESS...
SCHULZ

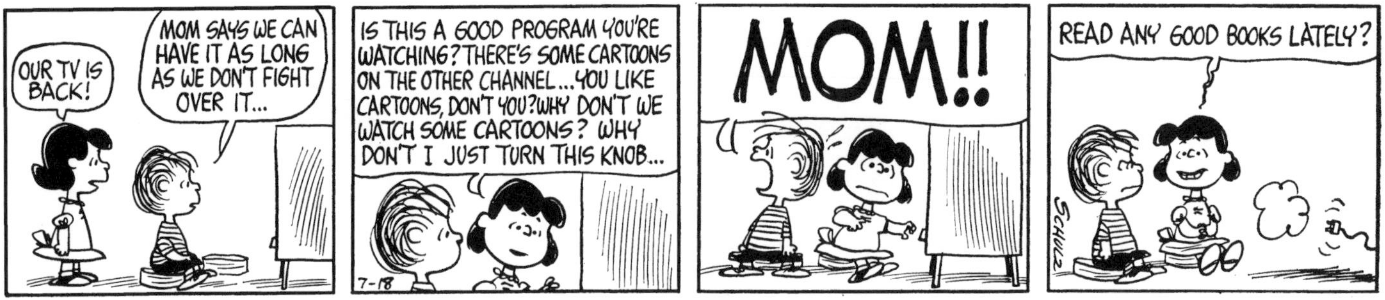
OUR TV IS BACK!
MOM SAYS WE CAN HAVE IT AS LONG AS WE DON'T FIGHT OVER IT...
IS THIS A GOOD PROGRAM YOU'RE WATCHING? THERE'S SOME CARTOONS ON THE OTHER CHANNEL...YOU LIKE CARTOONS, DON'T YOU? WHY DON'T WE WATCH SOME CARTOONS? WHY DON'T I JUST TURN THIS KNOB...
7-18
MOM!!
READ ANY GOOD BOOKS LATELY?
SCHULZ

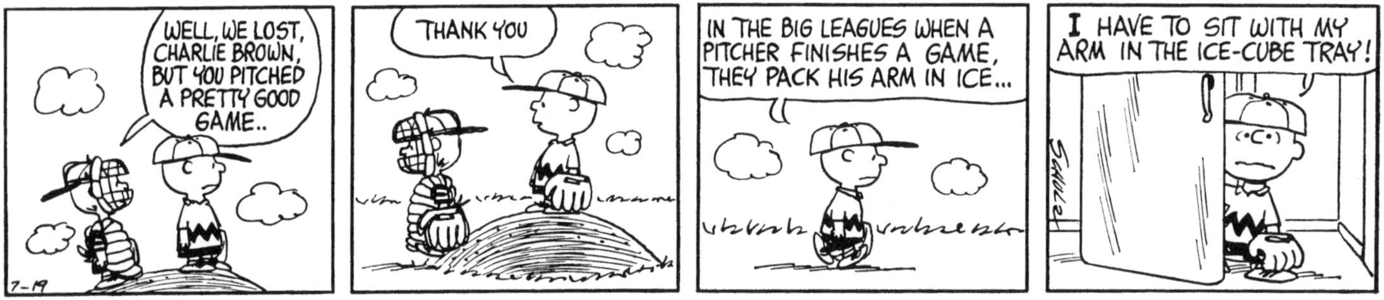
WELL, WE LOST, CHARLIE BROWN, BUT YOU PITCHED A PRETTY GOOD GAME..
7-19
THANK YOU
IN THE BIG LEAGUES WHEN A PITCHER FINISHES A GAME, THEY PACK HIS ARM IN ICE...
I HAVE TO SIT WITH MY ARM IN THE ICE-CUBE TRAY!
SCHULZ

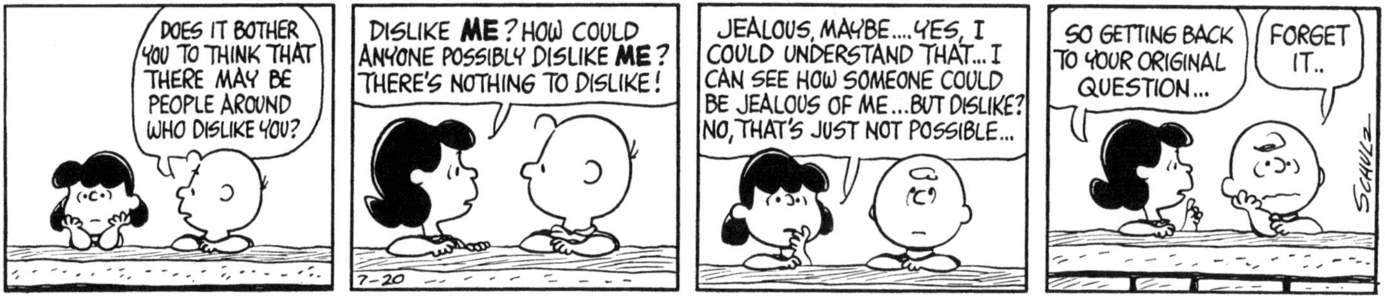
DOES IT BOTHER YOU TO THINK THAT THERE MAY BE PEOPLE AROUND WHO DISLIKE YOU?
DISLIKE ME? HOW COULD ANYONE POSSIBLY DISLIKE ME? THERE'S NOTHING TO DISLIKE!
7-20
JEALOUS, MAYBE....YES, I COULD UNDERSTAND THAT...I CAN SEE HOW SOMEONE COULD BE JEALOUS OF ME...BUT DISLIKE? NO, THAT'S JUST NOT POSSIBLE...
SO GETTING BACK TO YOUR ORIGINAL QUESTION...
FORGET IT..
SCHULZ

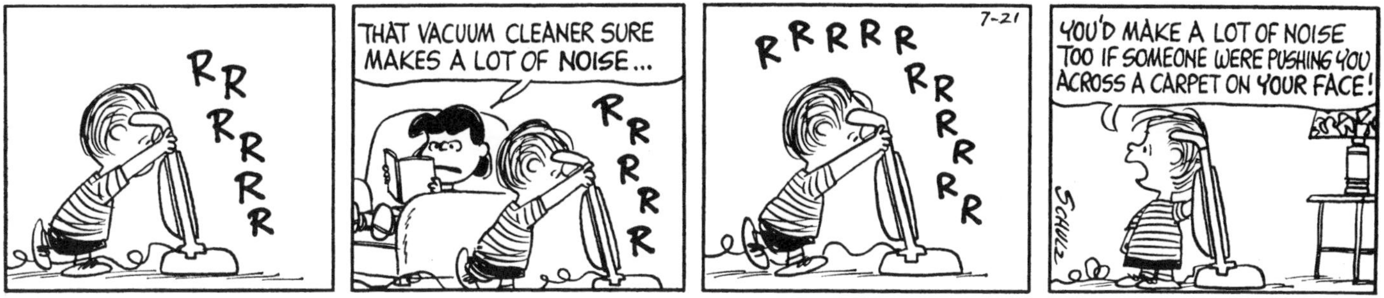
RRRRRR
THAT VACUUM CLEANER SURE MAKES A LOT OF NOISE...
RRRRRR
7-21
RRRRRRRRRRR
YOU'D MAKE A LOT OF NOISE TOO IF SOMEONE WERE PUSHING YOU ACROSS A CARPET ON YOUR FACE!
SCHULZ

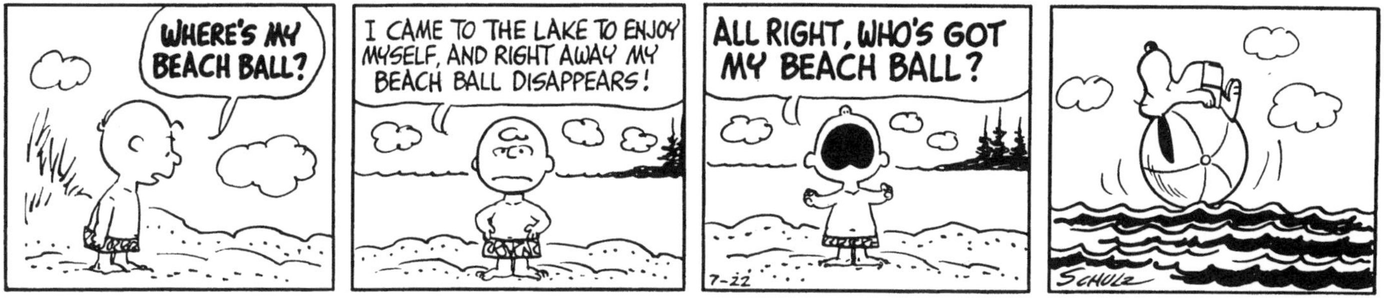
WHERE'S MY BEACH BALL?
I CAME TO THE LAKE TO ENJOY MYSELF, AND RIGHT AWAY MY BEACH BALL DISAPPEARS!
ALL RIGHT, WHO'S GOT MY BEACH BALL?
7-22
SCHULZ

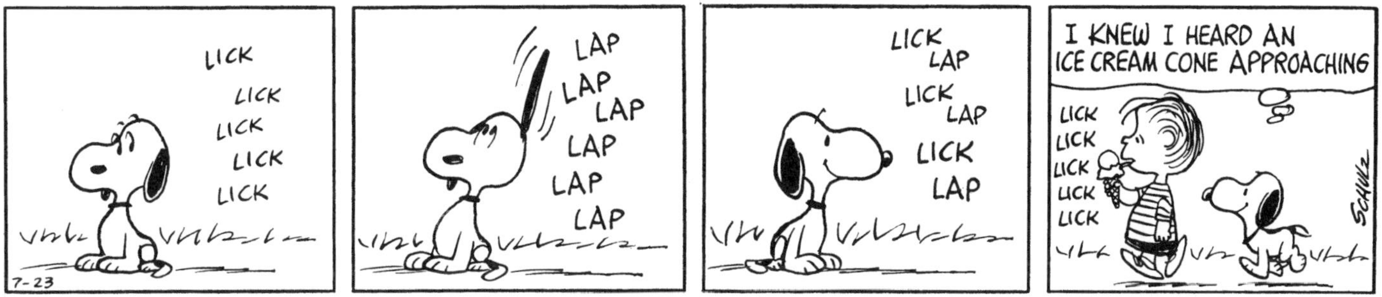
LICK
LICK
LICK
LICK
LICK
7-23
LAP
LAP
LAP
LAP
LAP
LAP
LICK
LAP
LICK
LAP
LICK
LAP
I KNEW I HEARD AN ICE CREAM CONE APPROACHING
LICK
LICK
LICK
LICK
LICK
SCHULZ

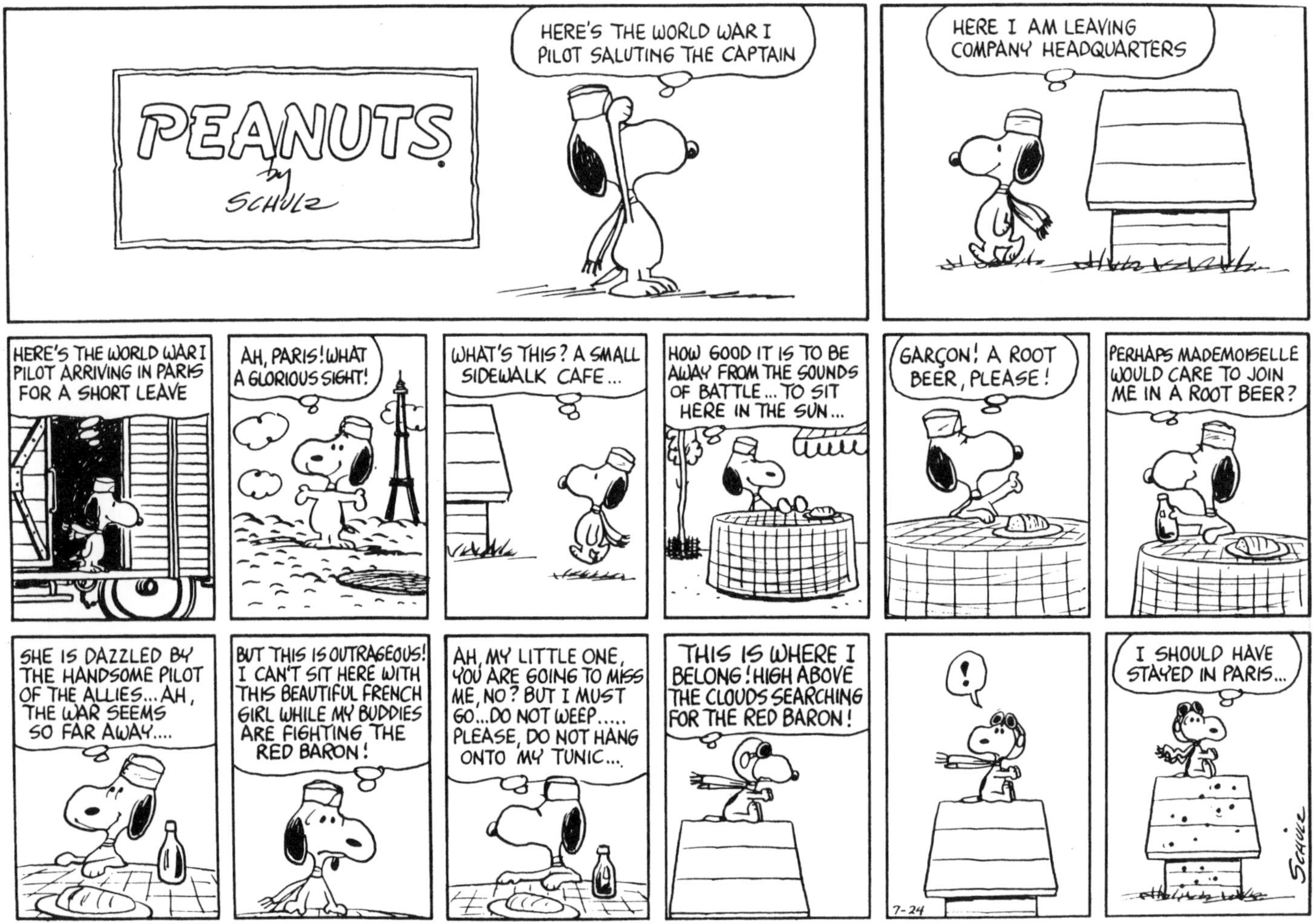
PEANUTS
by SCHULZ
HERE'S THE WORLD WAR I PILOT SALUTING THE CAPTAIN
HERE I AM LEAVING COMPANY HEADQUARTERS
HERE'S THE WORLD WAR I PILOT ARRIVING IN PARIS FOR A SHORT LEAVE
AH, PARIS! WHAT A GLORIOUS SIGHT!
WHAT'S THIS? A SMALL SIDEWALK CAFE...
HOW GOOD IT IS TO BE AWAY FROM THE SOUNDS OF BATTLE... TO SIT HERE IN THE SUN...
GARÇON! A ROOT BEER, PLEASE!
PERHAPS MADEMOISELLE WOULD CARE TO JOIN ME IN A ROOT BEER?
SHE IS DAZZLED BY THE HANDSOME PILOT OF THE ALLIES... AH, THE WAR SEEMS SO FAR AWAY....
BUT THIS IS OUTRAGEOUS! I CAN'T SIT HERE WITH THIS BEAUTIFUL FRENCH GIRL WHILE MY BUDDIES ARE FIGHTING THE RED BARON!
AH, MY LITTLE ONE, YOU ARE GOING TO MISS ME, NO? BUT I MUST GO... DO NOT WEEP..... PLEASE, DO NOT HANG ONTO MY TUNIC....
THIS IS WHERE I BELONG! HIGH ABOVE THE CLOUDS SEARCHING FOR THE RED BARON!
!
7-24
I SHOULD HAVE STAYED IN PARIS...
SCHULZ

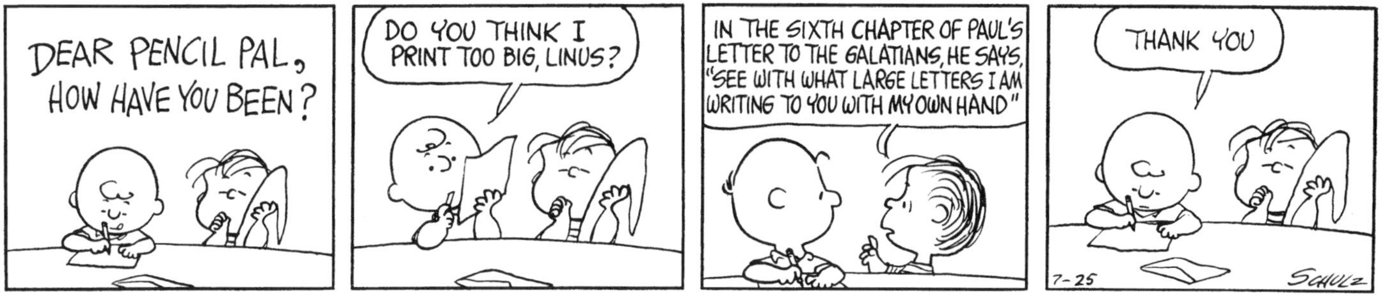
DEAR PENCIL PAL, HOW HAVE YOU BEEN?
DO YOU THINK I PRINT TOO BIG, LINUS?
IN THE SIXTH CHAPTER OF PAUL'S LETTER TO THE GALATIANS, HE SAYS, "SEE WITH WHAT LARGE LETTERS I AM WRITING TO YOU WITH MY OWN HAND"
THANK YOU
7-25
SCHULZ

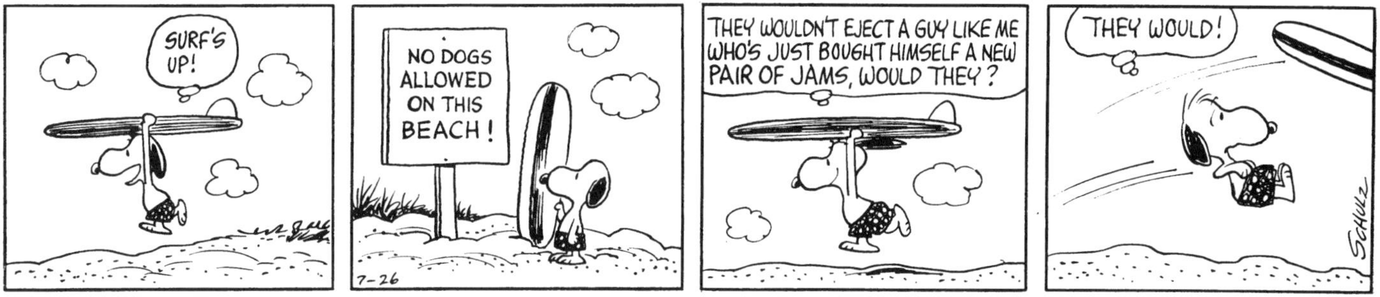
SURF'S UP!
NO DOGS ALLOWED ON THIS BEACH!
7-26
THEY WOULDN'T EJECT A GUY LIKE ME WHO'S JUST BOUGHT HIMSELF A NEW PAIR OF JAMS, WOULD THEY?
THEY WOULD!
SCHULZ

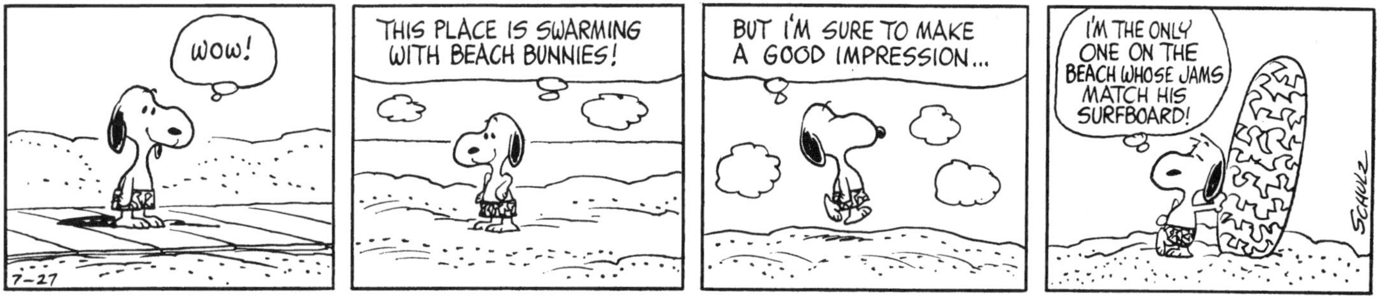
WOW!
7-27
THIS PLACE IS SWARMING WITH BEACH BUNNIES!
BUT I'M SURE TO MAKE A GOOD IMPRESSION...
I'M THE ONLY ONE ON THE BEACH WHOSE JAMS MATCH HIS SURFBOARD!
SCHULZ

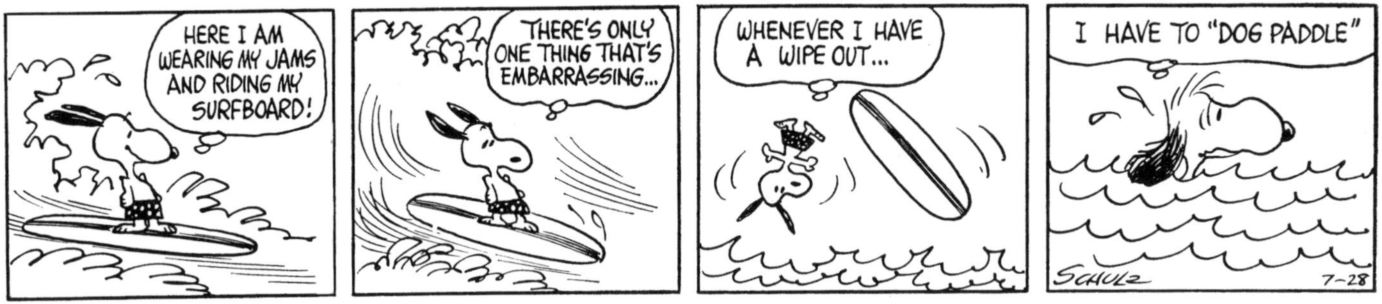
HERE I AM WEARING MY JAMS AND RIDING MY SURFBOARD!
THERE'S ONLY ONE THING THAT'S EMBARRASSING...
WHENEVER I HAVE A WIPE OUT...
I HAVE TO "DOG PADDLE"
SCHULZ
7-28

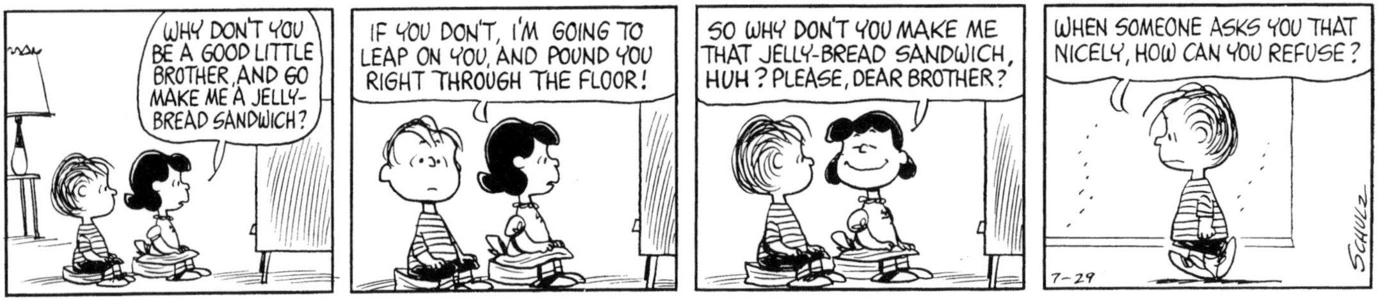
WHY DON'T YOU BE A GOOD LITTLE BROTHER, AND GO MAKE ME A JELLY-BREAD SANDWICH?
IF YOU DON'T, I'M GOING TO LEAP ON YOU, AND POUND YOU RIGHT THROUGH THE FLOOR!
SO WHY DON'T YOU MAKE ME THAT JELLY-BREAD SANDWICH, HUH? PLEASE, DEAR BROTHER?
WHEN SOMEONE ASKS YOU THAT NICELY, HOW CAN YOU REFUSE?
7-29
SCHULZ

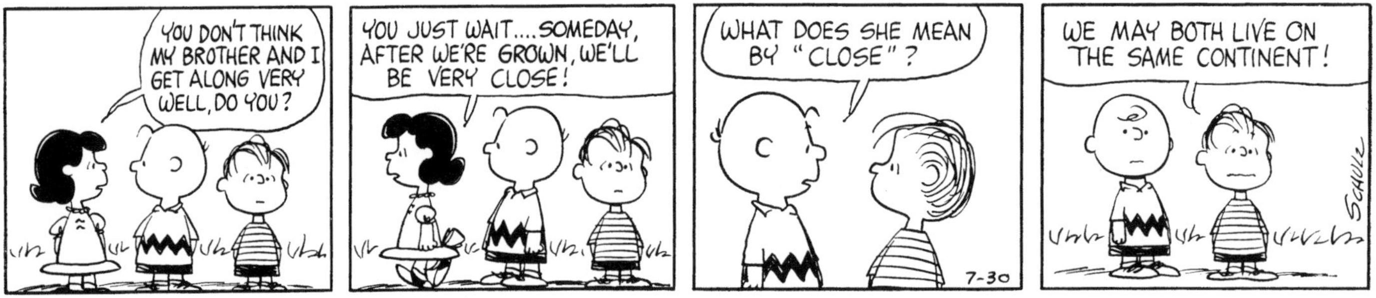
YOU DON'T THINK MY BROTHER AND I GET ALONG VERY WELL, DO YOU?
YOU JUST WAIT.... SOMEDAY, AFTER WE'RE GROWN, WE'LL BE VERY CLOSE!
WHAT DOES SHE MEAN BY "CLOSE"?
7-30
WE MAY BOTH LIVE ON THE SAME CONTINENT!
SCHULZ

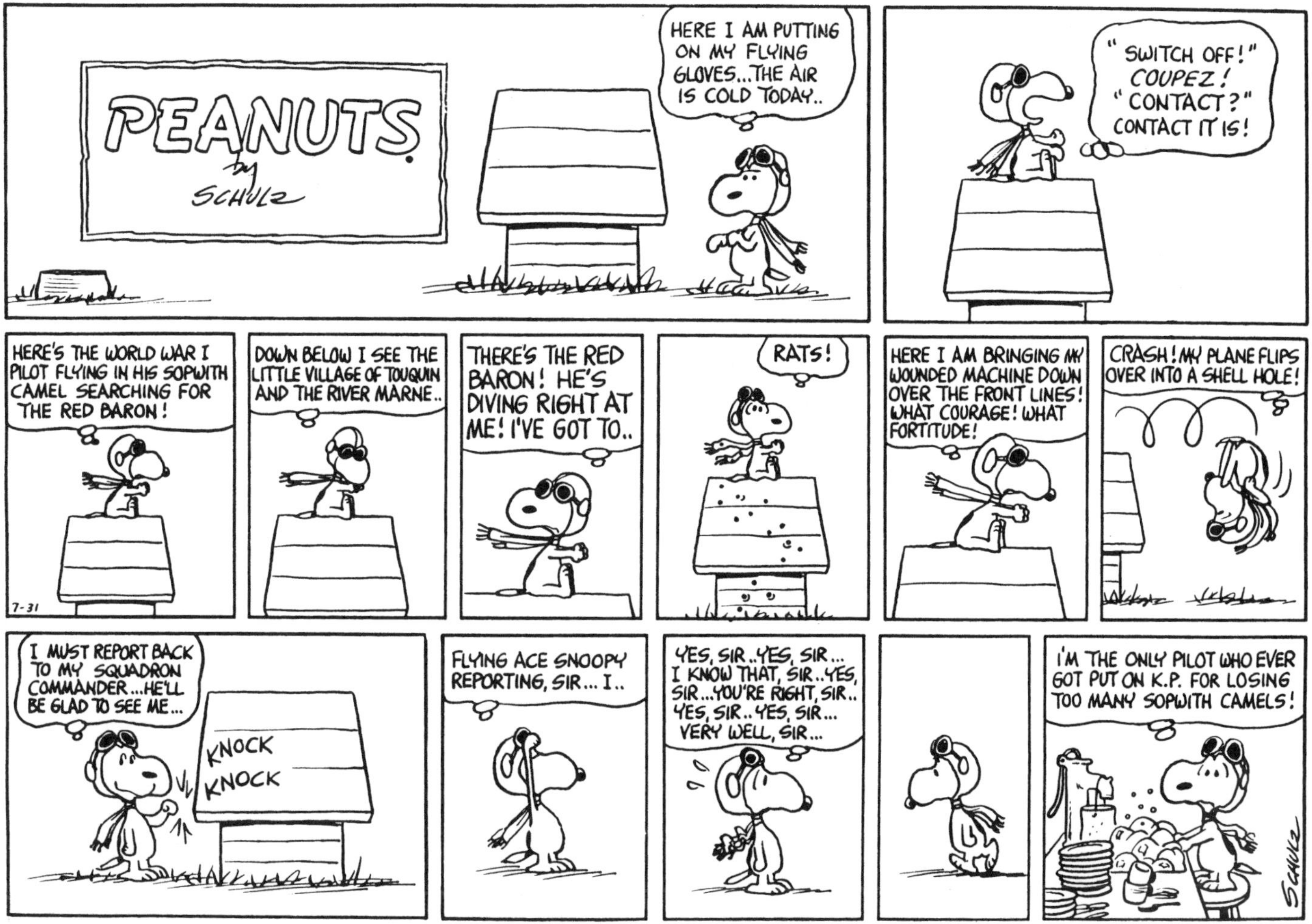
PEANUTS
by SCHULZ
HERE I AM PUTTING ON MY FLYING GLOVES...THE AIR IS COLD TODAY..
"SWITCH OFF!" COUPEZ! "CONTACT?" CONTACT IT IS!
HERE'S THE WORLD WAR I PILOT FLYING IN HIS SOPWITH CAMEL SEARCHING FOR THE RED BARON!
7-31
DOWN BELOW I SEE THE LITTLE VILLAGE OF TOUQUIN AND THE RIVER MARNE..
THERE'S THE RED BARON! HE'S DIVING RIGHT AT ME! I'VE GOT TO..
RATS!
HERE I AM BRINGING MY WOUNDED MACHINE DOWN OVER THE FRONT LINES! WHAT COURAGE! WHAT FORTITUDE!
CRASH! MY PLANE FLIPS OVER INTO A SHELL HOLE!
I MUST REPORT BACK TO MY SQUADRON COMMANDER...HE'LL BE GLAD TO SEE ME...
KNOCK
KNOCK
FLYING ACE SNOOPY REPORTING, SIR... I..
YES, SIR..YES, SIR... I KNOW THAT, SIR..YES, SIR...YOU'RE RIGHT, SIR.. YES, SIR..YES, SIR... VERY WELL, SIR...
I'M THE ONLY PILOT WHO EVER GOT PUT ON K.P. FOR LOSING TOO MANY SOPWITH CAMELS!
SCHULZ

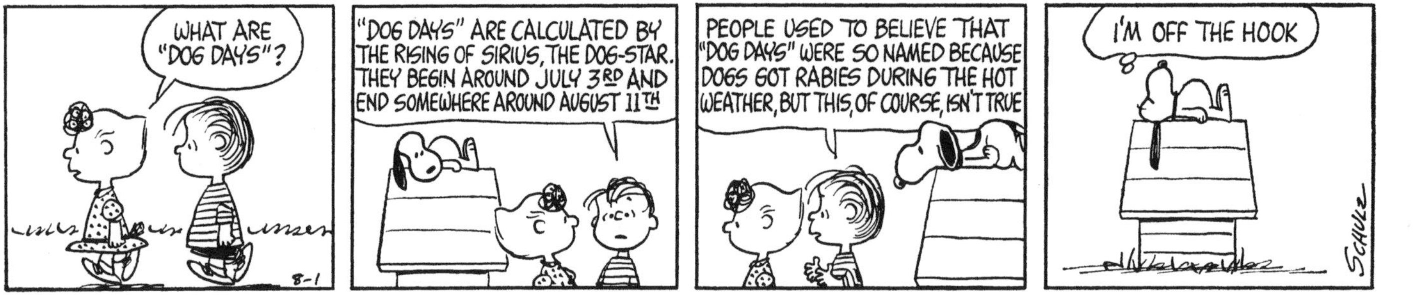
WHAT ARE "DOG DAYS"?
8-1
"DOG DAYS" ARE CALCULATED BY THE RISING OF SIRIUS, THE DOG-STAR. THEY BEGIN AROUND JULY 3RD AND END SOMEWHERE AROUND AUGUST 11TH
PEOPLE USED TO BELIEVE THAT "DOG DAYS" WERE SO NAMED BECAUSE DOGS GOT RABIES DURING THE HOT WEATHER, BUT THIS, OF COURSE, ISN'T TRUE
I'M OFF THE HOOK
SCHULZ

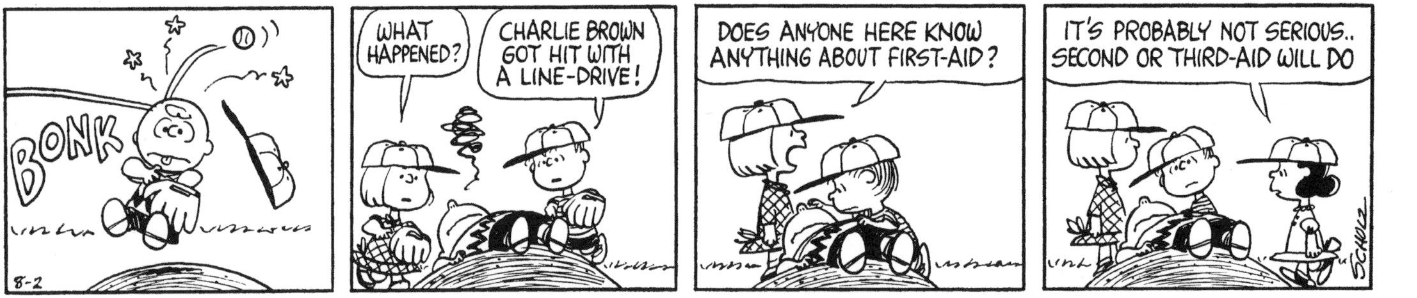
BONK
8-2
WHAT HAPPENED?
CHARLIE BROWN GOT HIT WITH A LINE-DRIVE!
DOES ANYONE HERE KNOW ANYTHING ABOUT FIRST-AID?
IT'S PROBABLY NOT SERIOUS.. SECOND OR THIRD-AID WILL DO
SCHULZ

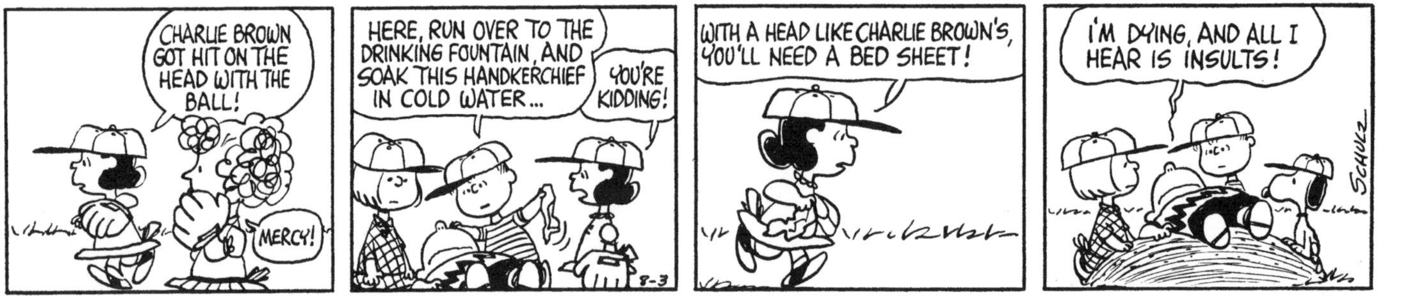
CHARLIE BROWN GOT HIT ON THE HEAD WITH THE BALL!
MERCY!
HERE, RUN OVER TO THE DRINKING FOUNTAIN, AND SOAK THIS HANDKERCHIEF IN COLD WATER...
YOU'RE KIDDING!
8-3
WITH A HEAD LIKE CHARLIE BROWN'S, YOU'LL NEED A BED SHEET!
I'M DYING, AND ALL I HEAR IS INSULTS!
SCHULZ

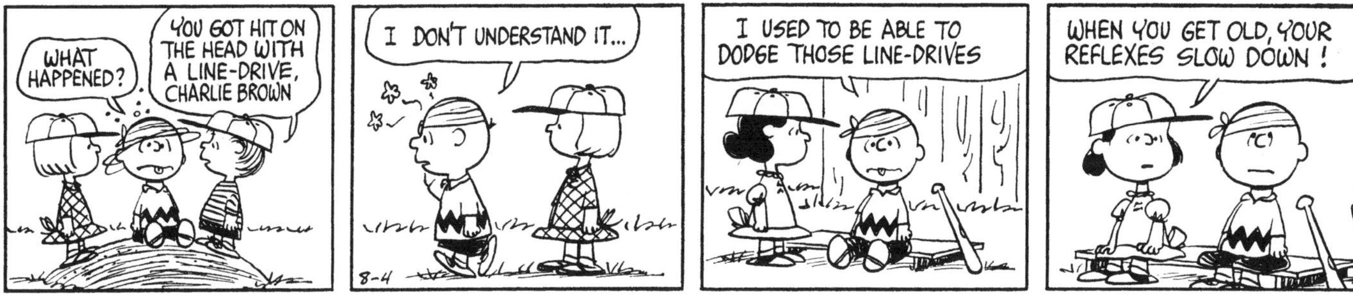
WHAT HAPPENED?
YOU GOT HIT ON THE HEAD WITH A LINE-DRIVE, CHARLIE BROWN
I DON'T UNDERSTAND IT...
8-4
I USED TO BE ABLE TO DODGE THOSE LINE-DRIVES
WHEN YOU GET OLD, YOUR REFLEXES SLOW DOWN!
SCHULZ

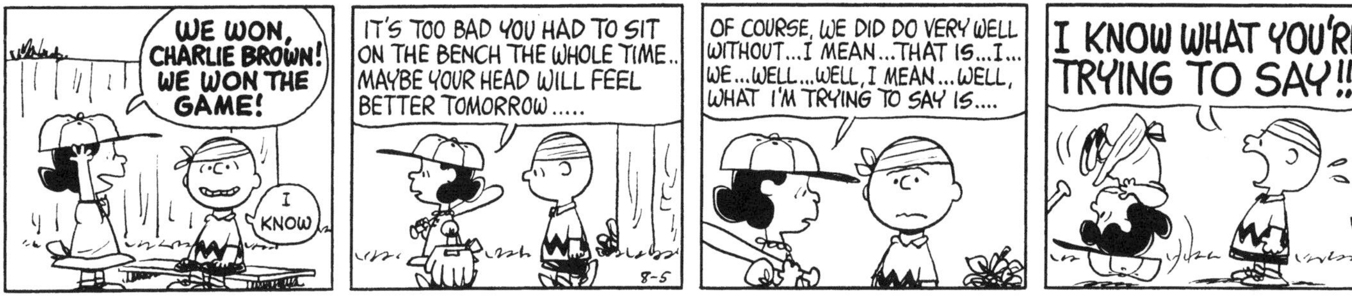
WE WON, CHARLIE BROWN! WE WON THE GAME!
I KNOW
IT'S TOO BAD YOU HAD TO SIT ON THE BENCH THE WHOLE TIME.. MAYBE YOUR HEAD WILL FEEL BETTER TOMORROW.....
8-5
OF COURSE, WE DID DO VERY WELL WITHOUT...I MEAN...THAT IS...I... WE...WELL...WELL, I MEAN...WELL, WHAT I'M TRYING TO SAY IS....
I KNOW WHAT YOU'RE TRYING TO SAY!!!
SCHULZ

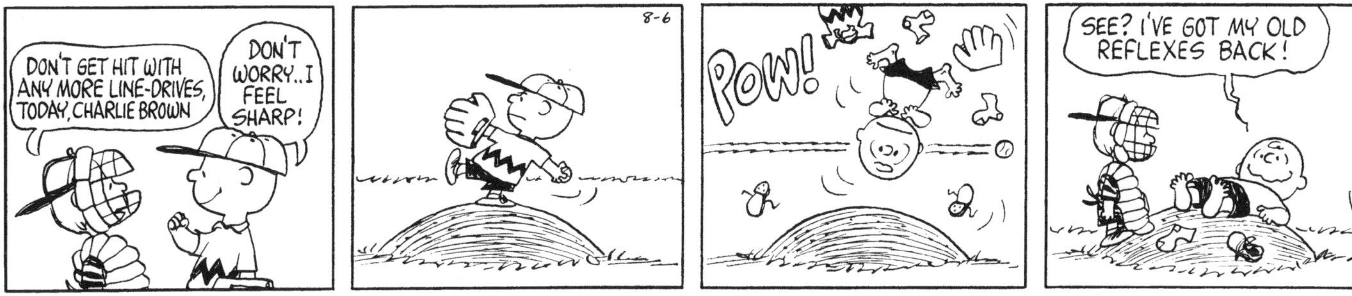
DON'T GET HIT WITH ANY MORE LINE-DRIVES, TODAY, CHARLIE BROWN
DON'T WORRY..I FEEL SHARP!
8-6
POW!
SEE? I'VE GOT MY OLD REFLEXES BACK!
SCHULZ

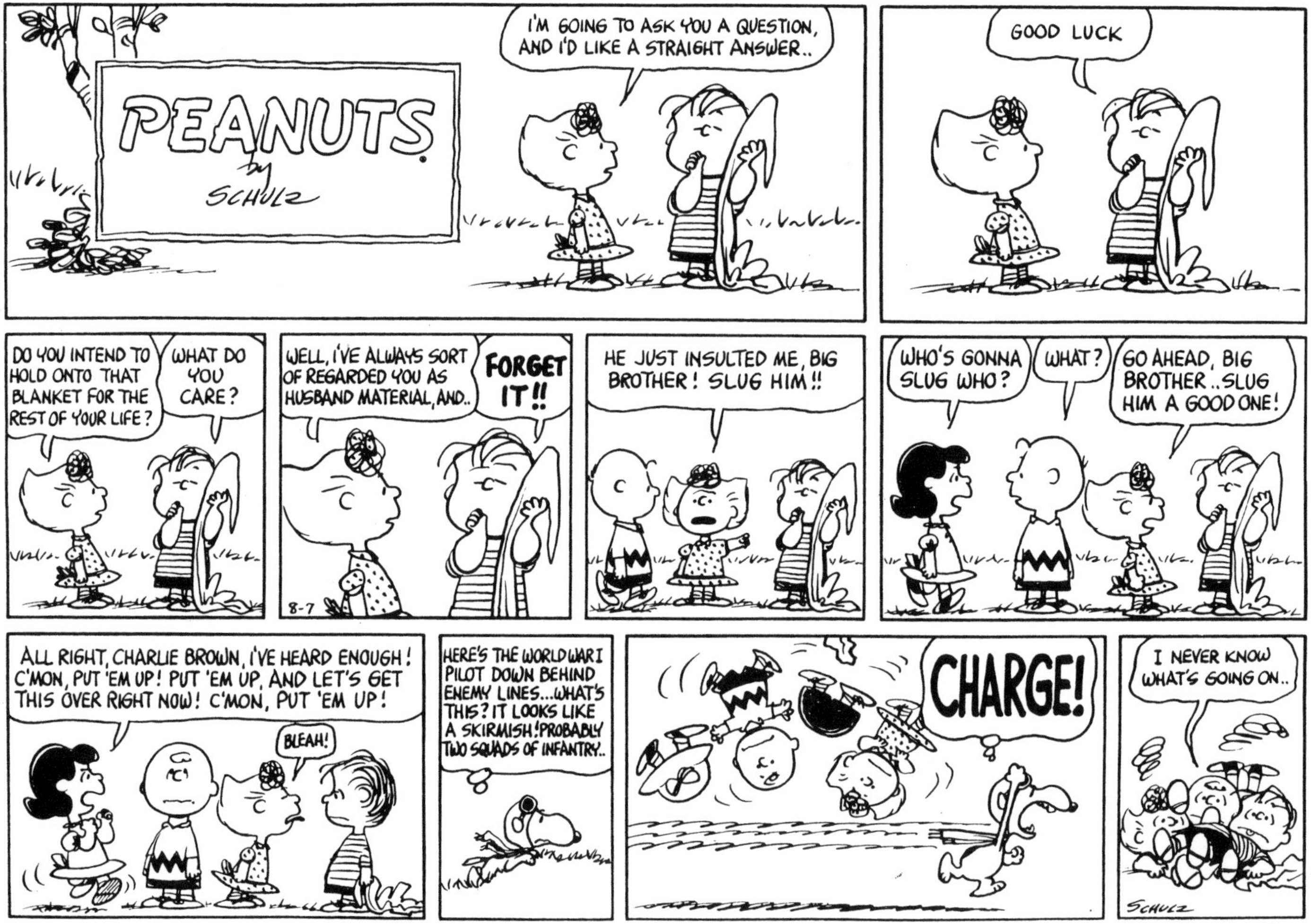
PEANUTS by SCHULZ
I'M GOING TO ASK YOU A QUESTION, AND I'D LIKE A STRAIGHT ANSWER..
GOOD LUCK
DO YOU INTEND TO HOLD ONTO THAT BLANKET FOR THE REST OF YOUR LIFE?
WHAT DO YOU CARE?
WELL, I'VE ALWAYS SORT OF REGARDED YOU AS HUSBAND MATERIAL, AND..
FORGET IT!!
8-7
HE JUST INSULTED ME, BIG BROTHER! SLUG HIM!!
WHO'S GONNA SLUG WHO?
WHAT?
GO AHEAD, BIG BROTHER..SLUG HIM A GOOD ONE!
ALL RIGHT, CHARLIE BROWN, I'VE HEARD ENOUGH! C'MON, PUT 'EM UP! PUT 'EM UP, AND LET'S GET THIS OVER RIGHT NOW! C'MON, PUT 'EM UP!
BLEAH!
HERE'S THE WORLD WAR I PILOT DOWN BEHIND ENEMY LINES...WHAT'S THIS? IT LOOKS LIKE A SKIRMISH! PROBABLY TWO SQUADS OF INFANTRY..
CHARGE!
I NEVER KNOW WHAT'S GOING ON..
SCHULZ

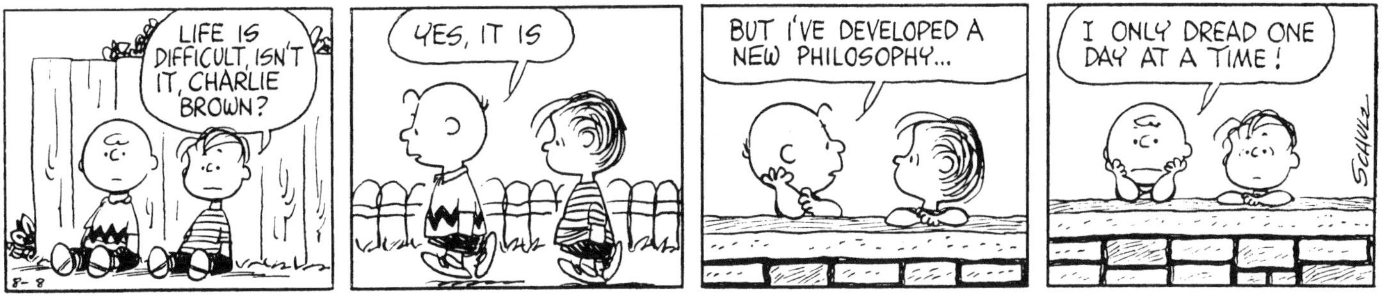
LIFE IS DIFFICULT, ISN'T IT, CHARLIE BROWN?
8-8
YES, IT IS
BUT I'VE DEVELOPED A NEW PHILOSOPHY...
I ONLY DREAD ONE DAY AT A TIME!
SCHULZ

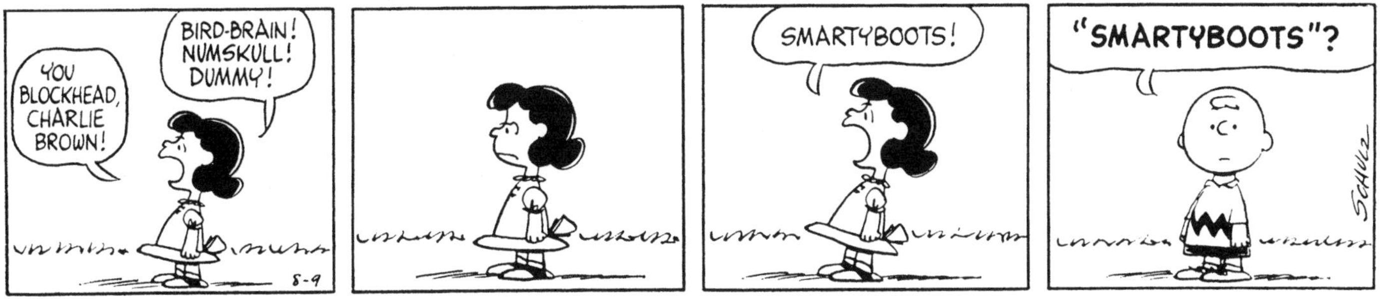
YOU BLOCKHEAD, CHARLIE BROWN!
BIRD-BRAIN! NUMSKULL! DUMMY!
8-9
SMARTYBOOTS!
"SMARTYBOOTS"?
SCHULZ

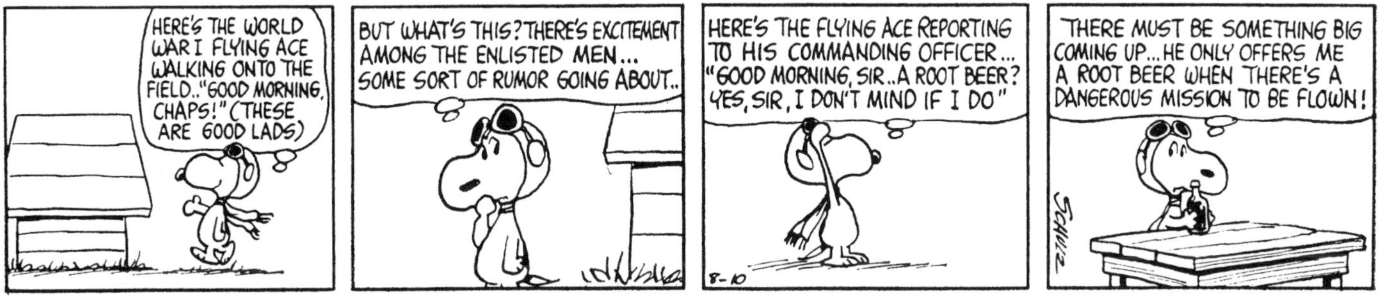
HERE'S THE WORLD WAR I FLYING ACE WALKING ONTO THE FIELD.."GOOD MORNING, CHAPS!" (THESE ARE GOOD LADS)
BUT WHAT'S THIS? THERE'S EXCITEMENT AMONG THE ENLISTED MEN... SOME SORT OF RUMOR GOING ABOUT..
HERE'S THE FLYING ACE REPORTING TO HIS COMMANDING OFFICER... "GOOD MORNING, SIR..A ROOT BEER? YES, SIR, I DON'T MIND IF I DO"
8-10
THERE MUST BE SOMETHING BIG COMING UP... HE ONLY OFFERS ME A ROOT BEER WHEN THERE'S A DANGEROUS MISSION TO BE FLOWN!
SCHULZ

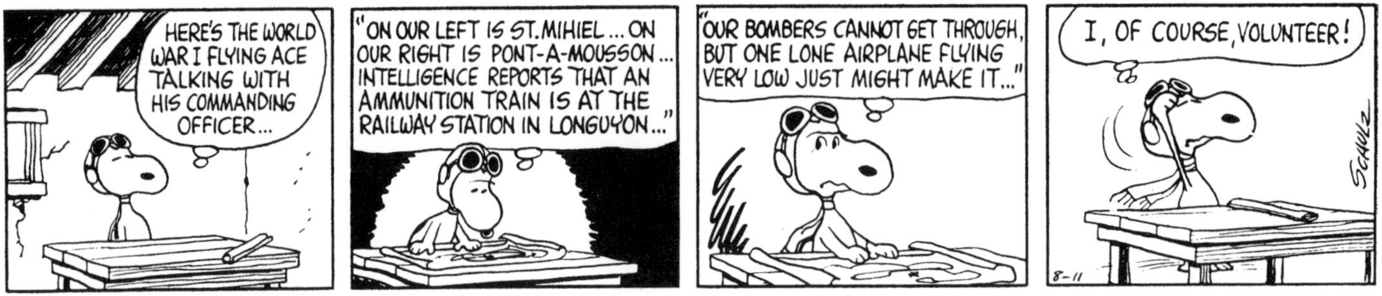
HERE'S THE WORLD WAR I FLYING ACE TALKING WITH HIS COMMANDING OFFICER...
"ON OUR LEFT IS ST. MIHIEL ... ON OUR RIGHT IS PONT-A-MOUSSON ... INTELLIGENCE REPORTS THAT AN AMMUNITION TRAIN IS AT THE RAILWAY STATION IN LONGUYON..."
"OUR BOMBERS CANNOT GET THROUGH, BUT ONE LONE AIRPLANE FLYING VERY LOW JUST MIGHT MAKE IT..."
I, OF COURSE, VOLUNTEER!
SCHULZ
8-11

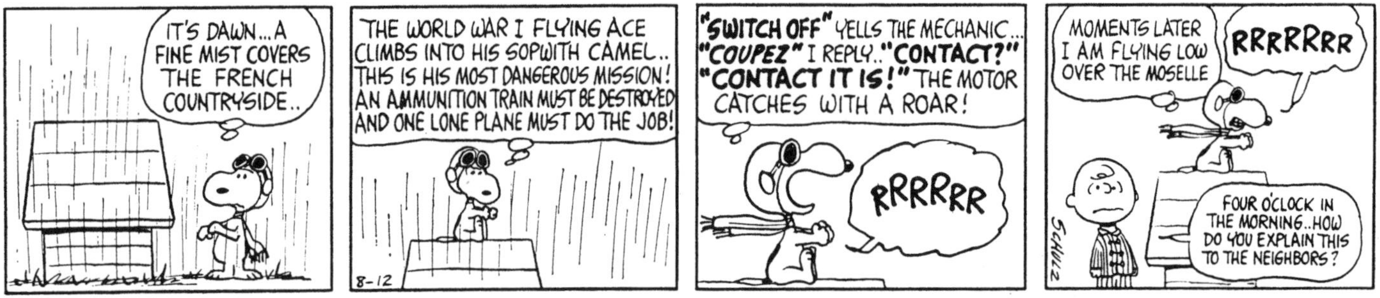
IT'S DAWN...A FINE MIST COVERS THE FRENCH COUNTRYSIDE..
THE WORLD WAR I FLYING ACE CLIMBS INTO HIS SOPWITH CAMEL.. THIS IS HIS MOST DANGEROUS MISSION! AN AMMUNITION TRAIN MUST BE DESTROYED AND ONE LONE PLANE MUST DO THE JOB!
8-12
"SWITCH OFF" YELLS THE MECHANIC... "COUPEZ" I REPLY.."CONTACT?" "CONTACT IT IS!" THE MOTOR CATCHES WITH A ROAR!
RRRRRR
MOMENTS LATER I AM FLYING LOW OVER THE MOSELLE
RRRRRRR
FOUR O'CLOCK IN THE MORNING..HOW DO YOU EXPLAIN THIS TO THE NEIGHBORS?
SCHULZ

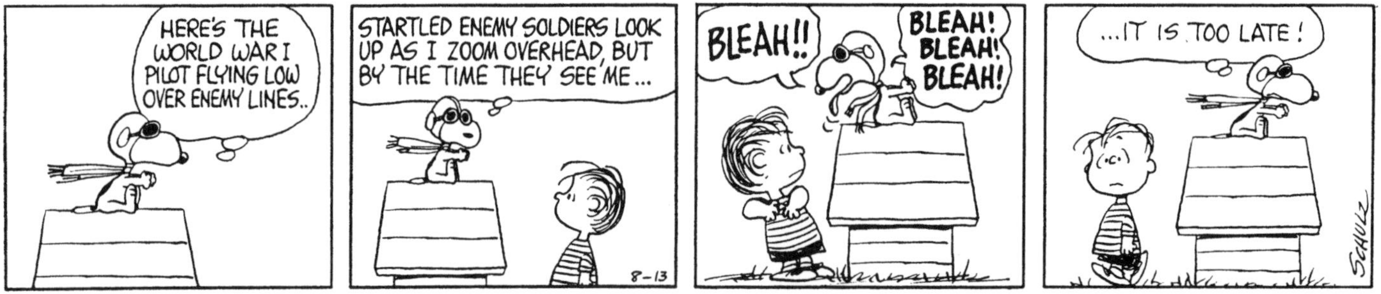
HERE'S THE WORLD WAR I PILOT FLYING LOW OVER ENEMY LINES..
STARTLED ENEMY SOLDIERS LOOK UP AS I ZOOM OVERHEAD, BUT BY THE TIME THEY SEE ME...
8-13
BLEAH!!
BLEAH! BLEAH! BLEAH!
...IT IS TOO LATE!
SCHULZ

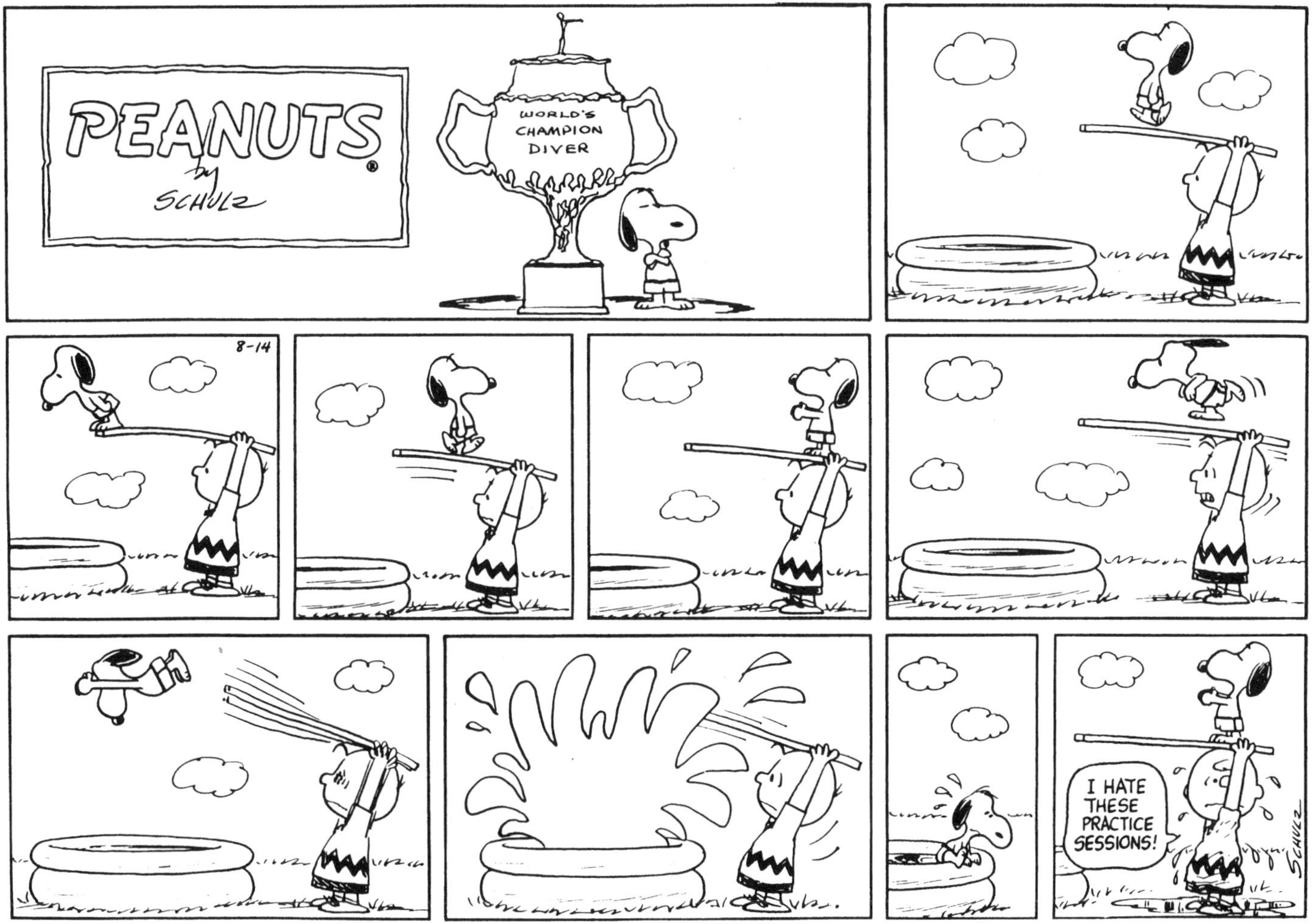
PEANUTS
by
SCHULZ
WORLD'S
CHAMPION
DIVER
8-14
I HATE THESE PRACTICE SESSIONS!
SCHULZ

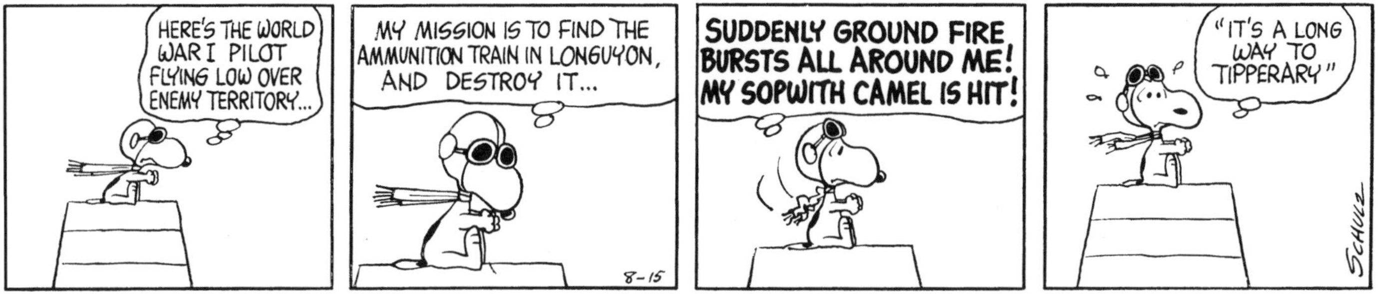
HERE'S THE WORLD WAR I PILOT FLYING LOW OVER ENEMY TERRITORY...
MY MISSION IS TO FIND THE AMMUNITION TRAIN IN LONGUYON, AND DESTROY IT...
8-15
SUDDENLY GROUND FIRE BURSTS ALL AROUND ME! MY SOPWITH CAMEL IS HIT!
"IT'S A LONG WAY TO TIPPERARY"
SCHULZ

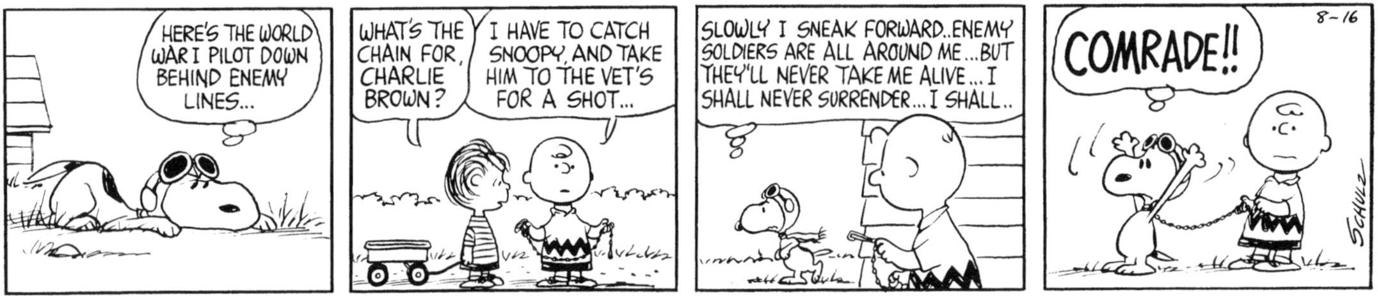
HERE'S THE WORLD WAR I PILOT DOWN BEHIND ENEMY LINES...
WHAT'S THE CHAIN FOR, CHARLIE BROWN?
I HAVE TO CATCH SNOOPY, AND TAKE HIM TO THE VET'S FOR A SHOT...
SLOWLY I SNEAK FORWARD..ENEMY SOLDIERS ARE ALL AROUND ME...BUT THEY'LL NEVER TAKE ME ALIVE...I SHALL NEVER SURRENDER...I SHALL..
8-16
COMRADE!!
SCHULZ

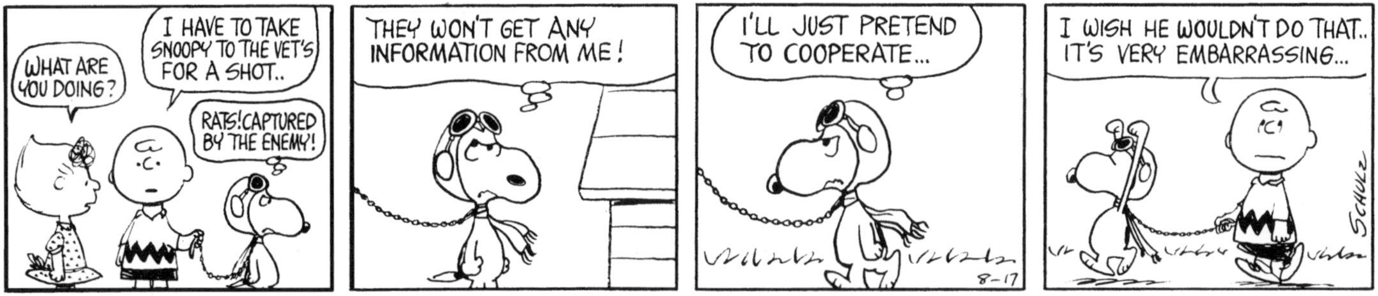
WHAT ARE YOU DOING?
I HAVE TO TAKE SNOOPY TO THE VET'S FOR A SHOT..
RATS! CAPTURED BY THE ENEMY!
THEY WON'T GET ANY INFORMATION FROM ME!
I'LL JUST PRETEND TO COOPERATE...
8-17
I WISH HE WOULDN'T DO THAT.. IT'S VERY EMBARRASSING...
SCHULZ

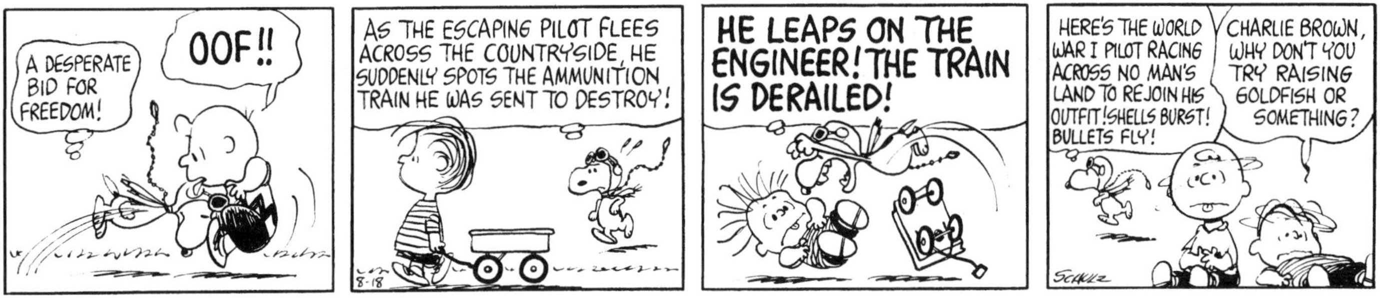
A DESPERATE BID FOR FREEDOM!
OOF!!
AS THE ESCAPING PILOT FLEES ACROSS THE COUNTRYSIDE, HE SUDDENLY SPOTS THE AMMUNITION TRAIN HE WAS SENT TO DESTROY!
8-18
HE LEAPS ON THE ENGINEER! THE TRAIN IS DERAILED!
HERE'S THE WORLD WAR I PILOT RACING ACROSS NO MAN'S LAND TO REJOIN HIS OUTFIT! SHELLS BURST! BULLETS FLY!
CHARLIE BROWN, WHY DON'T YOU TRY RAISING GOLDFISH OR SOMETHING?
SCHULZ

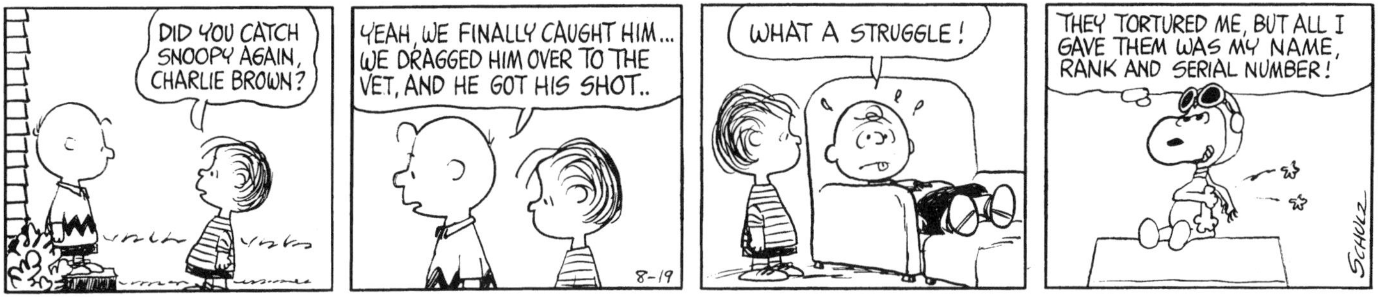
DID YOU CATCH SNOOPY AGAIN, CHARLIE BROWN?
YEAH, WE FINALLY CAUGHT HIM... WE DRAGGED HIM OVER TO THE VET, AND HE GOT HIS SHOT..
8-19
WHAT A STRUGGLE!
THEY TORTURED ME, BUT ALL I GAVE THEM WAS MY NAME, RANK AND SERIAL NUMBER!
SCHULZ

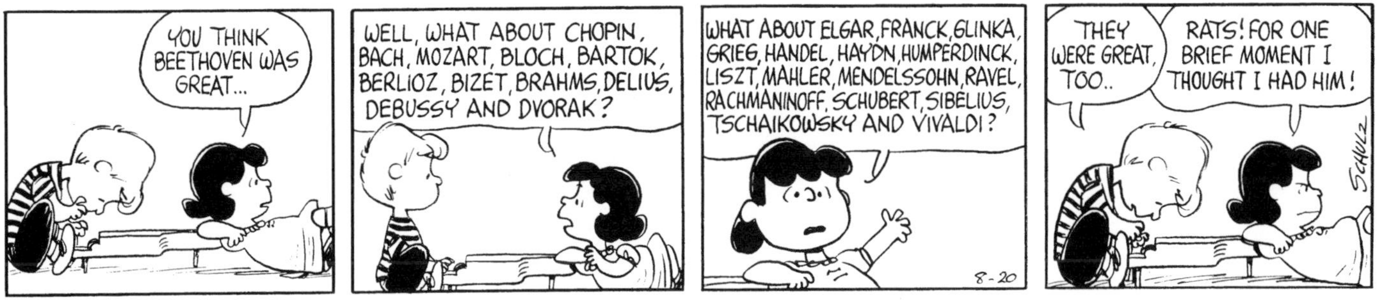
YOU THINK BEETHOVEN WAS GREAT...
WELL, WHAT ABOUT CHOPIN, BACH, MOZART, BLOCH, BARTOK, BERLIOZ, BIZET, BRAHMS, DELIUS, DEBUSSY AND DVORAK?
WHAT ABOUT ELGAR, FRANCK, GLINKA, GRIEG, HANDEL, HAYDN, HUMPERDINCK, LISZT, MAHLER, MENDELSSOHN, RAVEL, RACHMANINOFF, SCHUBERT, SIBELIUS, TSCHAIKOWSKY AND VIVALDI?
8-20
THEY WERE GREAT, TOO..
RATS! FOR ONE BRIEF MOMENT I THOUGHT I HAD HIM!
SCHULZ

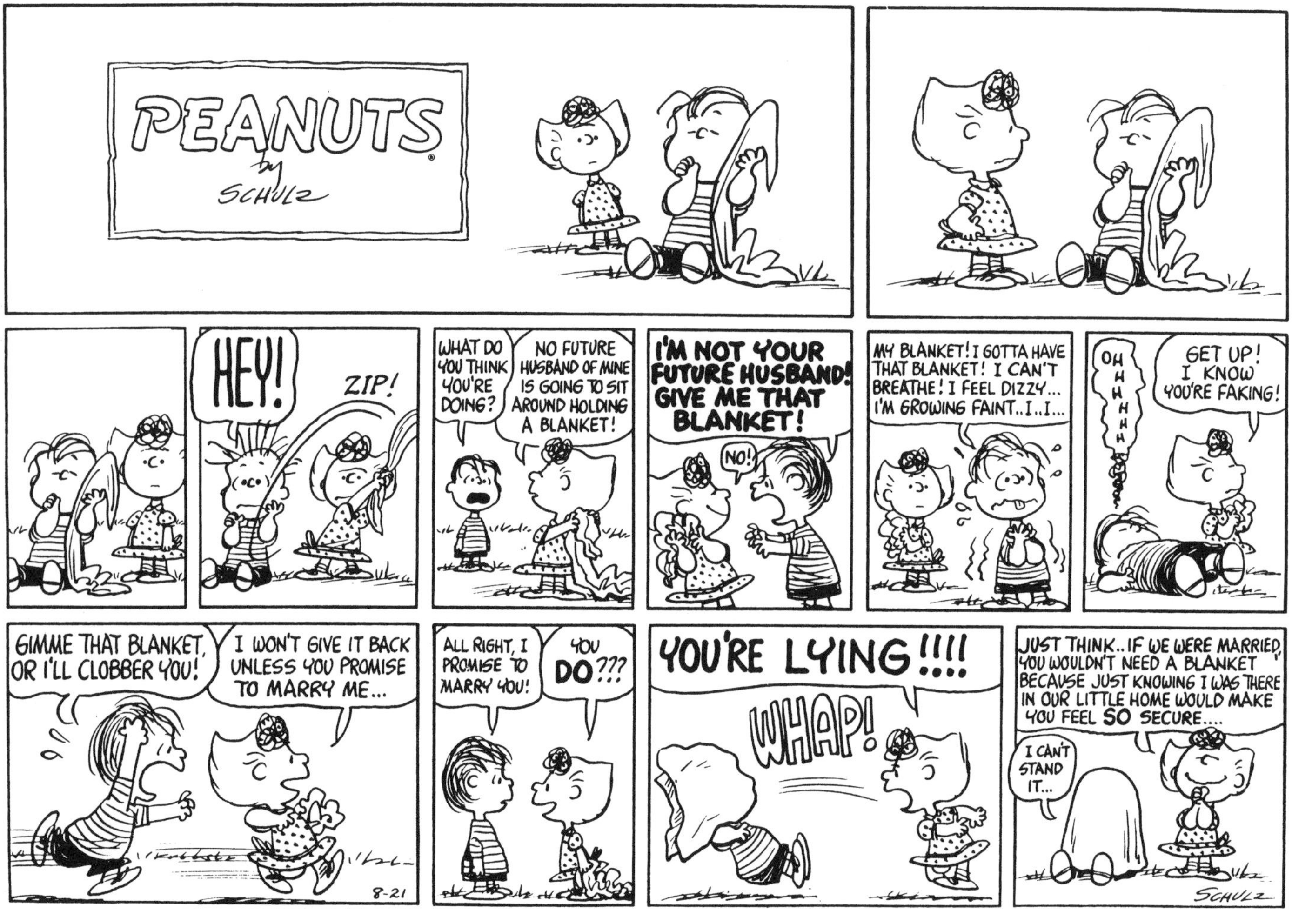
PEANUTS
by SCHULZ
HEY!
ZIP!
WHAT DO YOU THINK YOU'RE DOING?
NO FUTURE HUSBAND OF MINE IS GOING TO SIT AROUND HOLDING A BLANKET!
I'M NOT YOUR FUTURE HUSBAND! GIVE ME THAT BLANKET!
NO!
MY BLANKET! I GOTTA HAVE THAT BLANKET! I CAN'T BREATHE! I FEEL DIZZY... I'M GROWING FAINT..I..I...
OHHHHHH
GET UP! I KNOW YOU'RE FAKING!
GIMME THAT BLANKET, OR I'LL CLOBBER YOU!
I WON'T GIVE IT BACK UNLESS YOU PROMISE TO MARRY ME...
8-21
ALL RIGHT, I PROMISE TO MARRY YOU!
YOU DO???
YOU'RE LYING!!!!
WHAP!
JUST THINK..IF WE WERE MARRIED, YOU WOULDN'T NEED A BLANKET BECAUSE JUST KNOWING I WAS THERE IN OUR LITTLE HOME WOULD MAKE YOU FEEL SO SECURE....
I CAN'T STAND IT...
SCHULZ

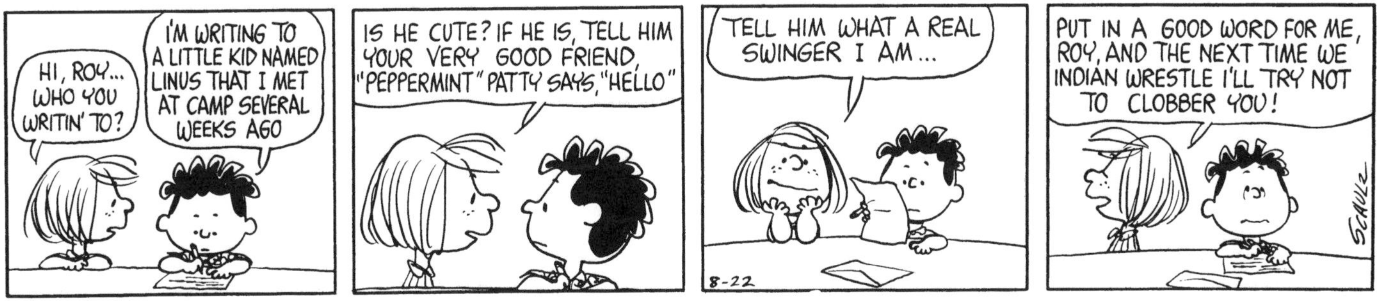
HI, ROY... WHO YOU WRITIN' TO?
I'M WRITING TO A LITTLE KID NAMED LINUS THAT I MET AT CAMP SEVERAL WEEKS AGO
IS HE CUTE? IF HE IS, TELL HIM YOUR VERY GOOD FRIEND, "PEPPERMINT" PATTY SAYS, "HELLO"
TELL HIM WHAT A REAL SWINGER I AM...
8-22
PUT IN A GOOD WORD FOR ME, ROY, AND THE NEXT TIME WE INDIAN WRESTLE I'LL TRY NOT TO CLOBBER YOU!
SCHULZ

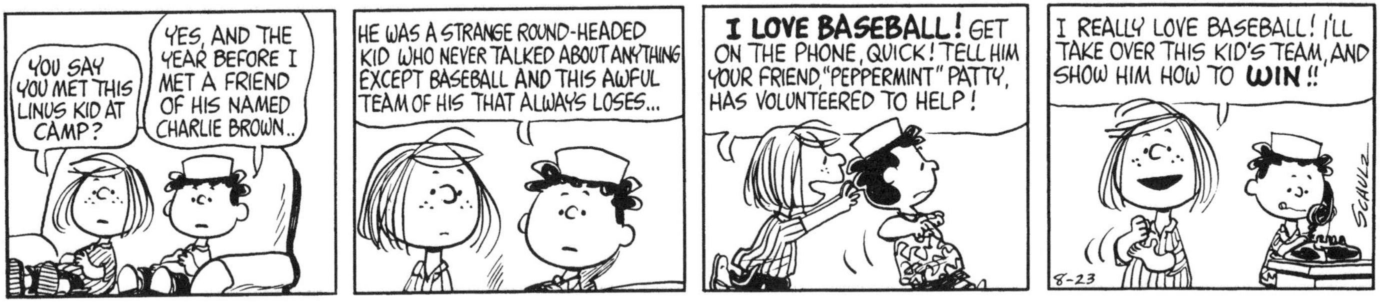
YOU SAY YOU MET THIS LINUS KID AT CAMP?
YES, AND THE YEAR BEFORE I MET A FRIEND OF HIS NAMED CHARLIE BROWN..
HE WAS A STRANGE ROUND-HEADED KID WHO NEVER TALKED ABOUT ANYTHING EXCEPT BASEBALL AND THIS AWFUL TEAM OF HIS THAT ALWAYS LOSES...
I LOVE BASEBALL! GET ON THE PHONE, QUICK! TELL HIM YOUR FRIEND, "PEPPERMINT" PATTY, HAS VOLUNTEERED TO HELP!
I REALLY LOVE BASEBALL! I'LL TAKE OVER THIS KID'S TEAM, AND SHOW HIM HOW TO WIN!!
SCHULZ
8-23

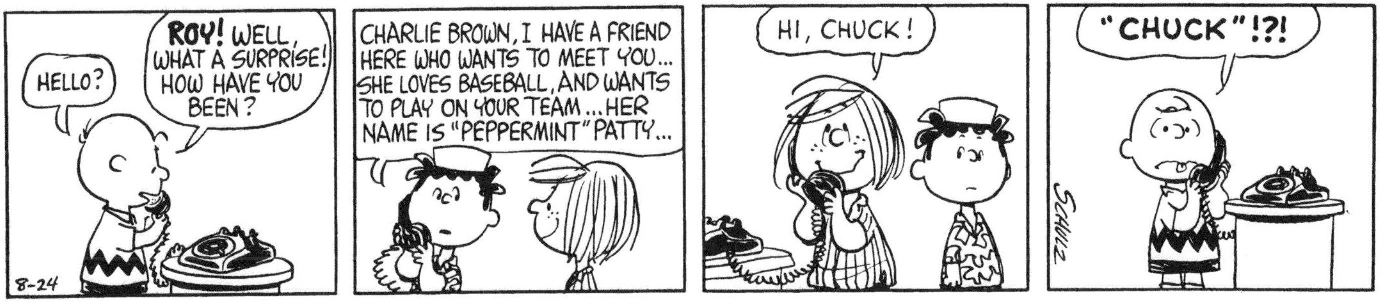
HELLO?
ROY! WELL, WHAT A SURPRISE! HOW HAVE YOU BEEN?
8-24
CHARLIE BROWN, I HAVE A FRIEND HERE WHO WANTS TO MEET YOU... SHE LOVES BASEBALL, AND WANTS TO PLAY ON YOUR TEAM... HER NAME IS "PEPPERMINT" PATTY...
HI, CHUCK!
SCHULZ
"CHUCK"!?!

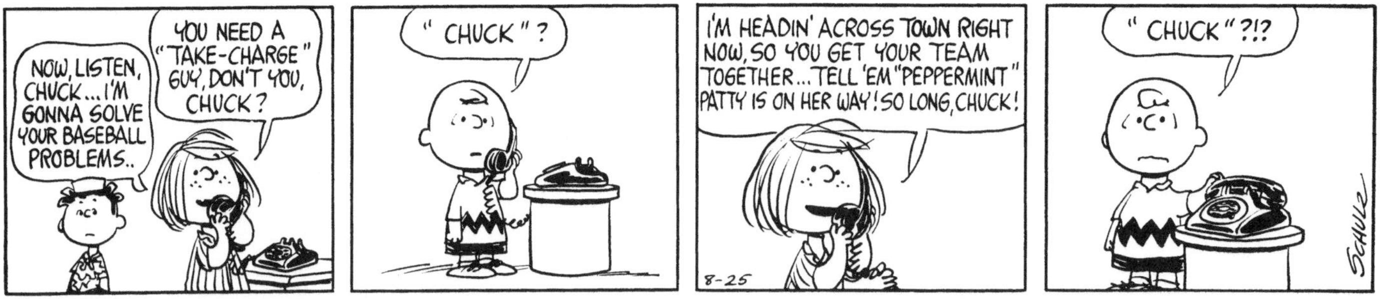
NOW, LISTEN, CHUCK...I'M GONNA SOLVE YOUR BASEBALL PROBLEMS..
YOU NEED A "TAKE-CHARGE" GUY, DON'T YOU, CHUCK?
"CHUCK"?
I'M HEADIN' ACROSS TOWN RIGHT NOW, SO YOU GET YOUR TEAM TOGETHER...TELL 'EM "PEPPERMINT" PATTY IS ON HER WAY! SO LONG, CHUCK!
8-25
"CHUCK"?!?
SCHULZ

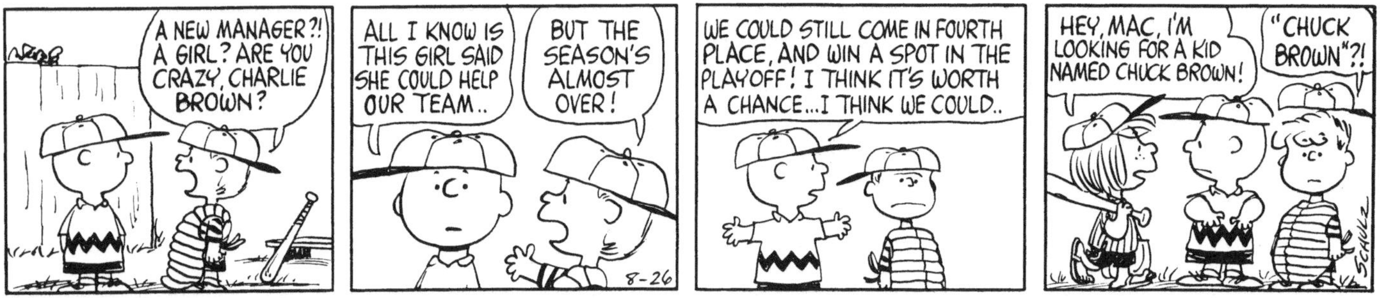
A NEW MANAGER?! A GIRL? ARE YOU CRAZY, CHARLIE BROWN?
ALL I KNOW IS THIS GIRL SAID SHE COULD HELP OUR TEAM..
BUT THE SEASON'S ALMOST OVER!
8-26
WE COULD STILL COME IN FOURTH PLACE, AND WIN A SPOT IN THE PLAYOFF! I THINK IT'S WORTH A CHANCE...I THINK WE COULD..
HEY, MAC, I'M LOOKING FOR A KID NAMED CHUCK BROWN!
"CHUCK BROWN"?!
SCHULZ

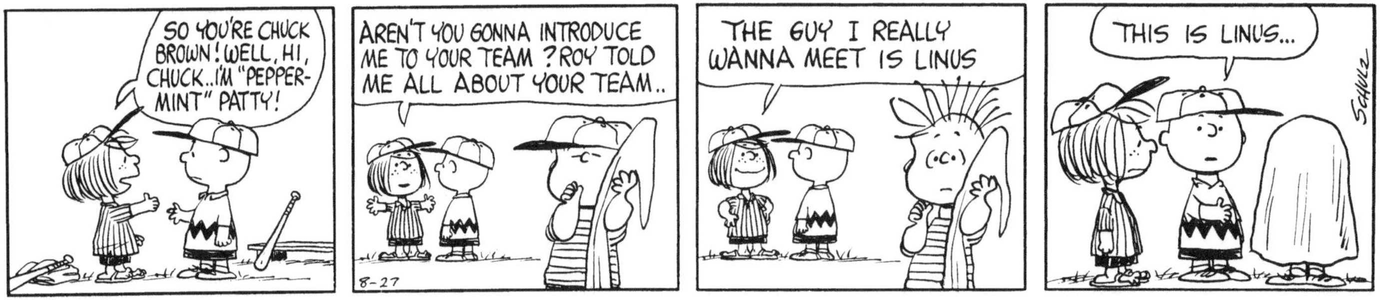
SO YOU'RE CHUCK BROWN! WELL, HI, CHUCK..I'M "PEPPERMINT" PATTY!
AREN'T YOU GONNA INTRODUCE ME TO YOUR TEAM? ROY TOLD ME ALL ABOUT YOUR TEAM..
8-27
THE GUY I REALLY WANNA MEET IS LINUS
THIS IS LINUS...
SCHULZ

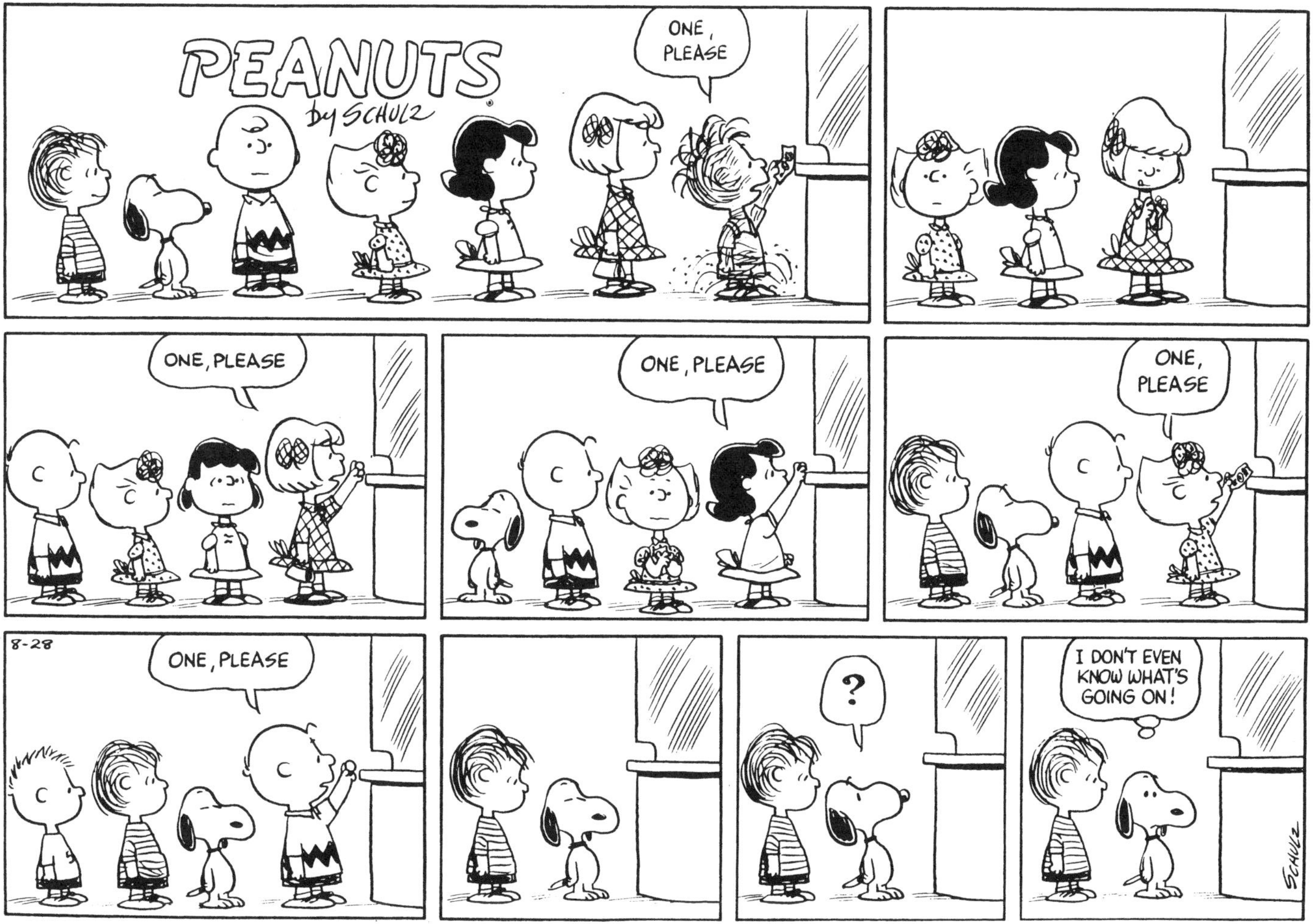
PEANUTS
by SCHULZ
ONE, PLEASE
ONE, PLEASE
ONE, PLEASE
ONE, PLEASE
8-28
ONE, PLEASE
?
I DON'T EVEN KNOW WHAT'S GOING ON!
SCHULZ

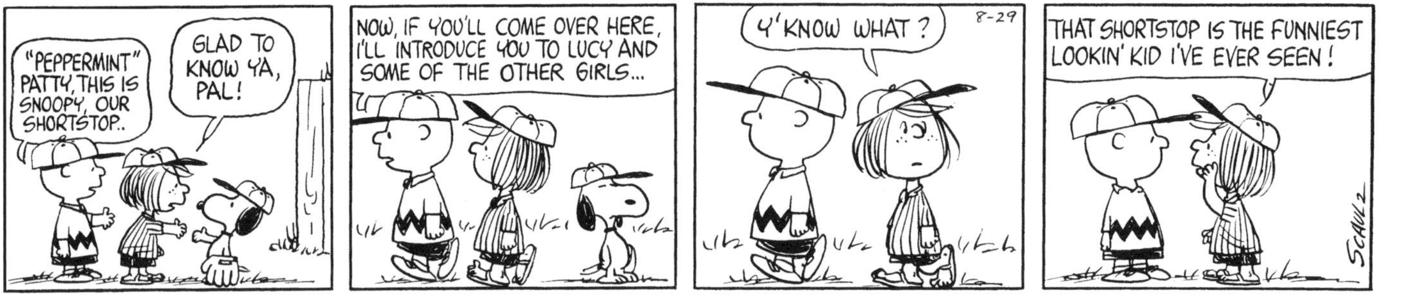
"PEPPERMINT" PATTY, THIS IS SNOOPY, OUR SHORTSTOP..
GLAD TO KNOW YA, PAL!
NOW, IF YOU'LL COME OVER HERE, I'LL INTRODUCE YOU TO LUCY AND SOME OF THE OTHER GIRLS...
Y'KNOW WHAT?
8-29
THAT SHORTSTOP IS THE FUNNIEST LOOKIN' KID I'VE EVER SEEN!
SCHULZ

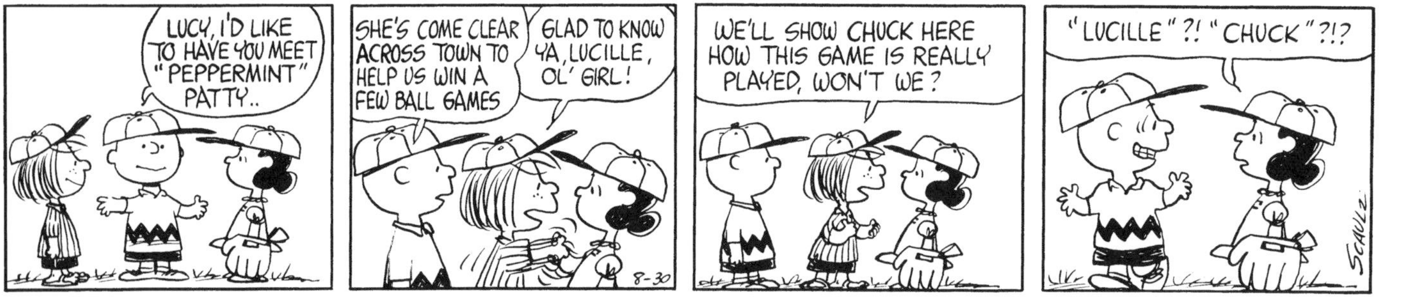
LUCY, I'D LIKE TO HAVE YOU MEET "PEPPERMINT" PATTY..
SHE'S COME CLEAR ACROSS TOWN TO HELP US WIN A FEW BALL GAMES
GLAD TO KNOW YA, LUCILLE, OL' GIRL!
8-30
WE'LL SHOW CHUCK HERE HOW THIS GAME IS REALLY PLAYED, WON'T WE?
"LUCILLE"?! "CHUCK"?!?
SCHULZ

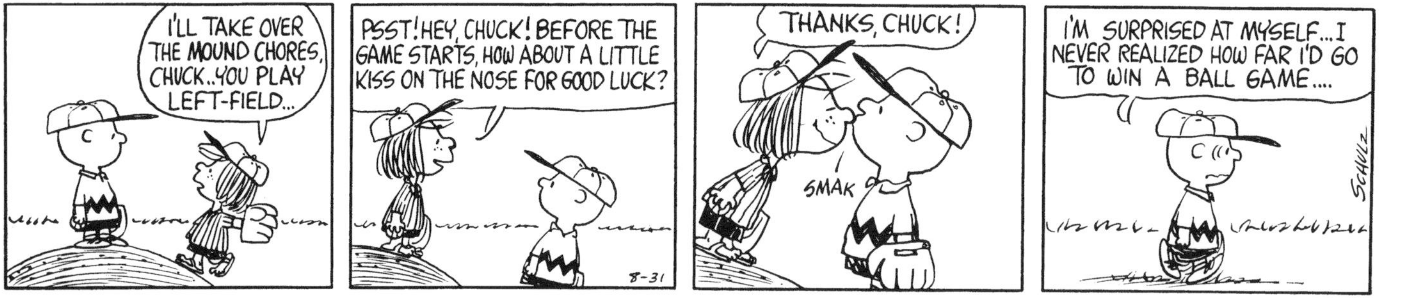
I'LL TAKE OVER THE MOUND CHORES, CHUCK..YOU PLAY LEFT-FIELD...
PSST! HEY, CHUCK! BEFORE THE GAME STARTS, HOW ABOUT A LITTLE KISS ON THE NOSE FOR GOOD LUCK?
8-31
THANKS, CHUCK!
SMAK
I'M SURPRISED AT MYSELF...I NEVER REALIZED HOW FAR I'D GO TO WIN A BALL GAME....
SCHULZ

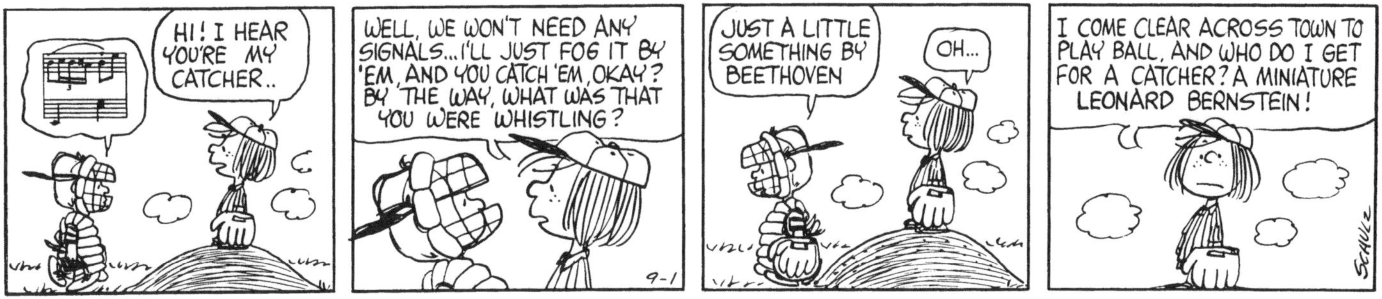
HI! I HEAR YOU'RE MY CATCHER..
WELL, WE WON'T NEED ANY SIGNALS...I'LL JUST FOG IT BY 'EM, AND YOU CATCH 'EM, OKAY? BY THE WAY, WHAT WAS THAT YOU WERE WHISTLING?
9-1
JUST A LITTLE SOMETHING BY BEETHOVEN
OH...
I COME CLEAR ACROSS TOWN TO PLAY BALL, AND WHO DO I GET FOR A CATCHER? A MINIATURE LEONARD BERNSTEIN!
SCHULZ

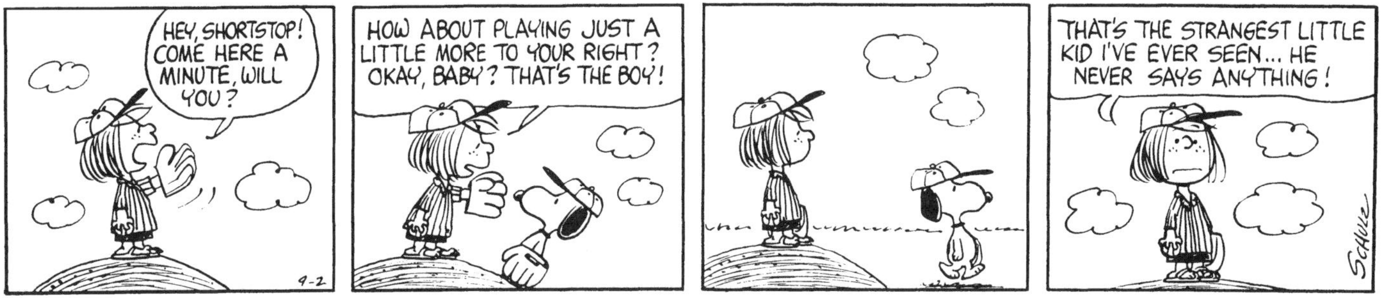
HEY, SHORTSTOP! COME HERE A MINUTE, WILL YOU?
9-2
HOW ABOUT PLAYING JUST A LITTLE MORE TO YOUR RIGHT? OKAY, BABY? THAT'S THE BOY!
THAT'S THE STRANGEST LITTLE KID I'VE EVER SEEN... HE NEVER SAYS ANYTHING!
SCHULZ

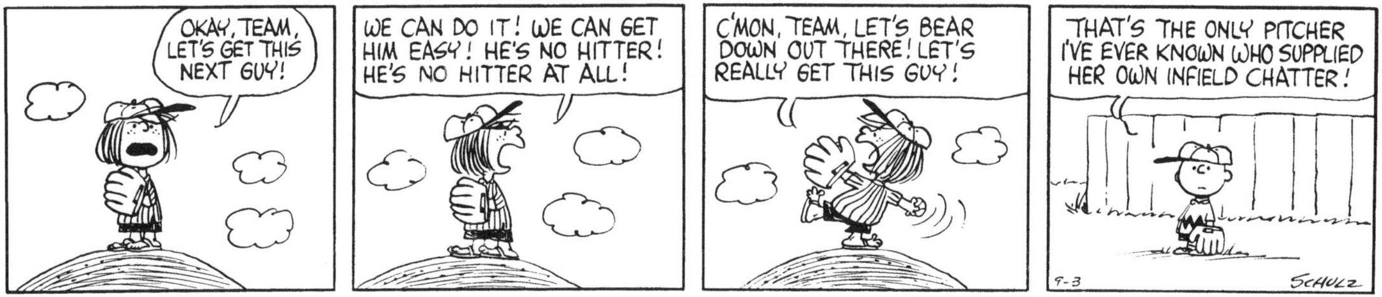
OKAY, TEAM, LET'S GET THIS NEXT GUY!
WE CAN DO IT! WE CAN GET HIM EASY! HE'S NO HITTER! HE'S NO HITTER AT ALL!
C'MON, TEAM, LET'S BEAR DOWN OUT THERE! LET'S REALLY GET THIS GUY!
THAT'S THE ONLY PITCHER I'VE EVER KNOWN WHO SUPPLIED HER OWN INFIELD CHATTER!
9-3
SCHULZ

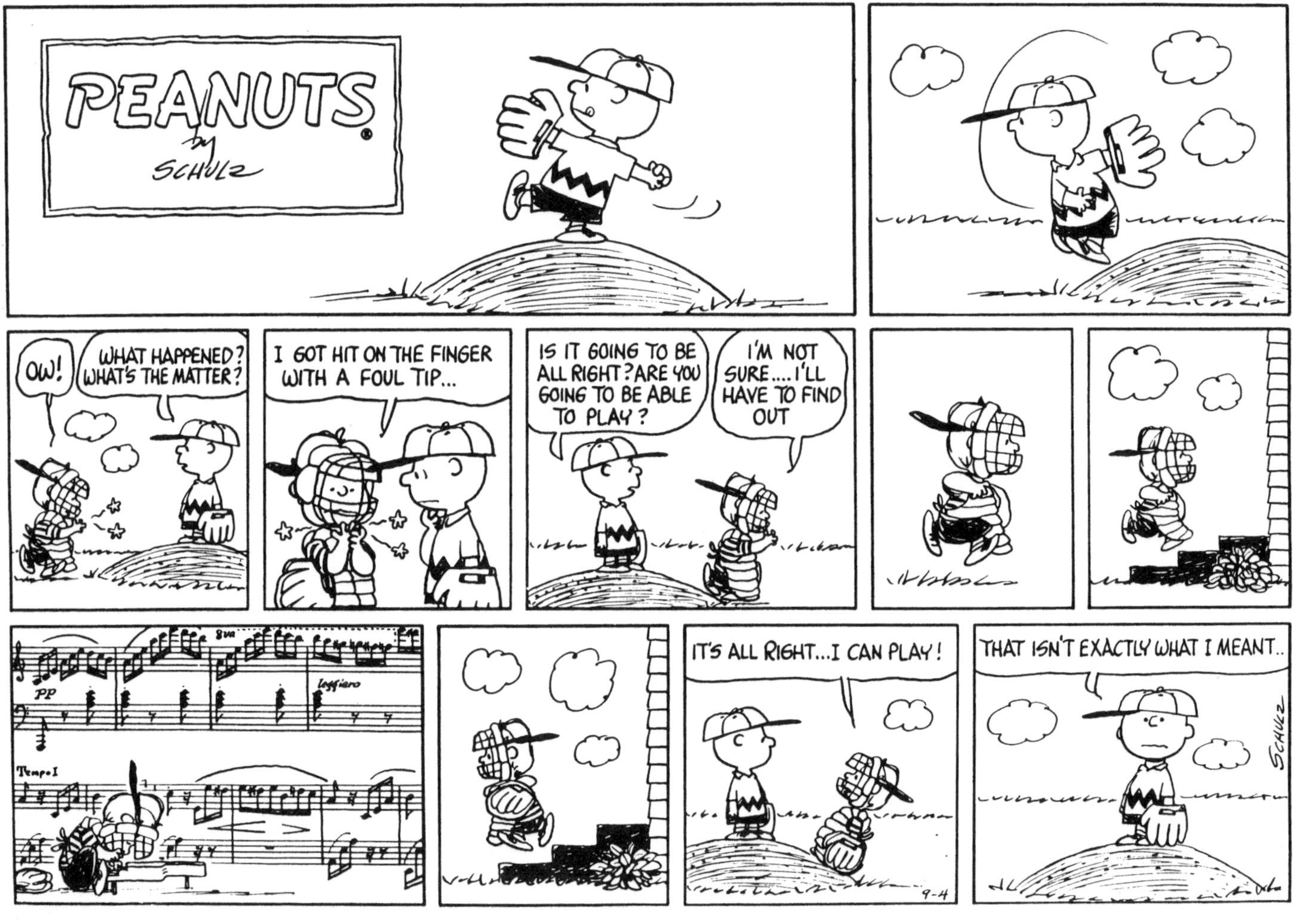
PEANUTS
by SCHULZ
OW!
WHAT HAPPENED? WHAT'S THE MATTER?
I GOT HIT ON THE FINGER WITH A FOUL TIP...
IS IT GOING TO BE ALL RIGHT? ARE YOU GOING TO BE ABLE TO PLAY?
I'M NOT SURE.... I'LL HAVE TO FIND OUT
leggiero
Tempo I
IT'S ALL RIGHT...I CAN PLAY!
9-4
THAT ISN'T EXACTLY WHAT I MEANT..
SCHULZ

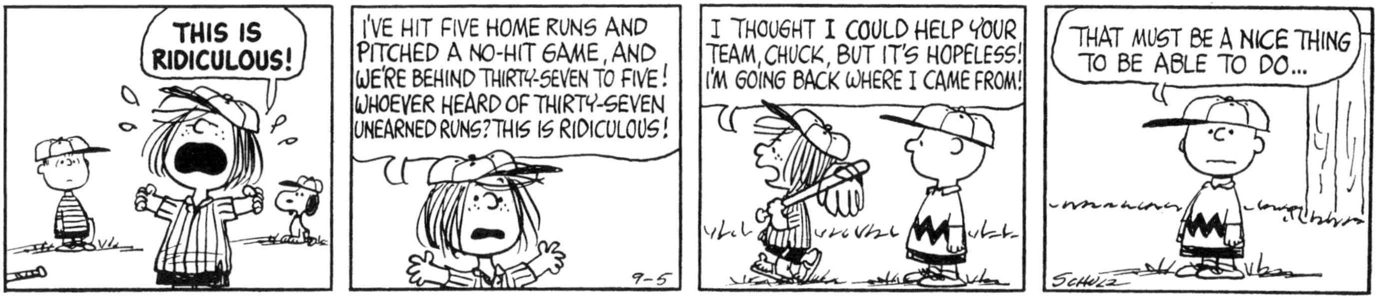
THIS IS RIDICULOUS!
I'VE HIT FIVE HOME RUNS AND PITCHED A NO-HIT GAME, AND WE'RE BEHIND THIRTY-SEVEN TO FIVE! WHOEVER HEARD OF THIRTY-SEVEN UNEARNED RUNS? THIS IS RIDICULOUS!
I THOUGHT I COULD HELP YOUR TEAM, CHUCK, BUT IT'S HOPELESS! I'M GOING BACK WHERE I CAME FROM!
THAT MUST BE A NICE THING TO BE ABLE TO DO...

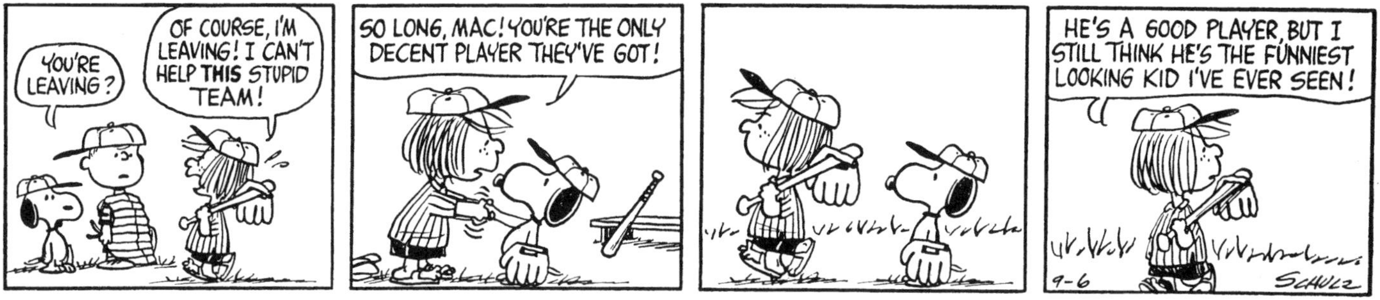
YOU'RE LEAVING?
OF COURSE, I'M LEAVING! I CAN'T HELP THIS STUPID TEAM!
SO LONG, MAC! YOU'RE THE ONLY DECENT PLAYER THEY'VE GOT!
HE'S A GOOD PLAYER, BUT I STILL THINK HE'S THE FUNNIEST LOOKING KID I'VE EVER SEEN!

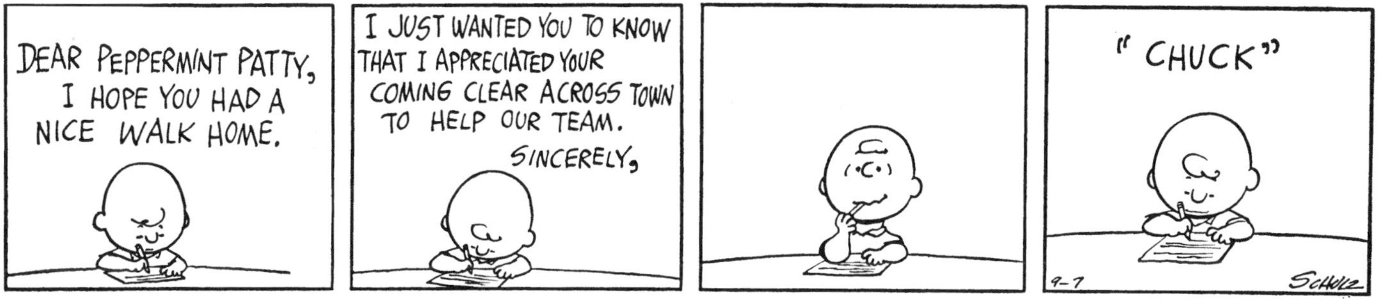
DEAR PEPPERMINT PATTY, I HOPE YOU HAD A NICE WALK HOME.
I JUST WANTED YOU TO KNOW THAT I APPRECIATED YOUR COMING CLEAR ACROSS TOWN TO HELP OUR TEAM.
SINCERELY,
"CHUCK"

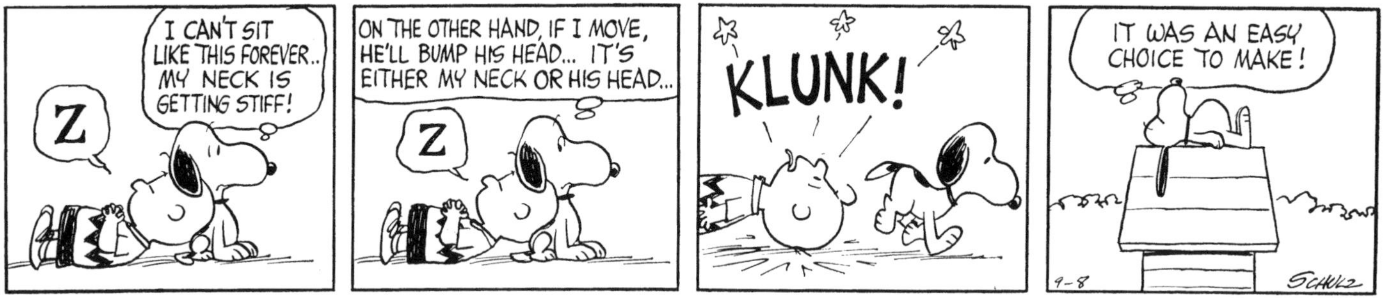
Z
I CAN'T SIT LIKE THIS FOREVER.. MY NECK IS GETTING STIFF!
ON THE OTHER HAND, IF I MOVE, HE'LL BUMP HIS HEAD... IT'S EITHER MY NECK OR HIS HEAD...
Z
KLUNK!
IT WAS AN EASY CHOICE TO MAKE!
9-8
SCHULZ

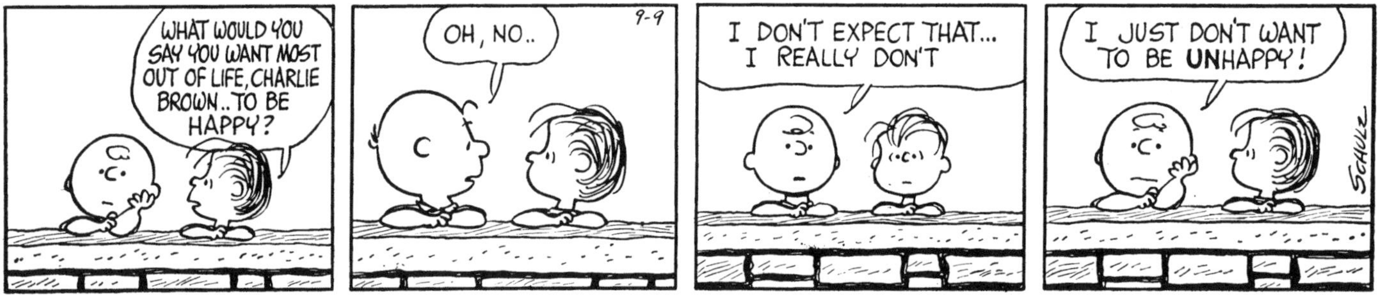
WHAT WOULD YOU SAY YOU WANT MOST OUT OF LIFE, CHARLIE BROWN.. TO BE HAPPY?
9-9
OH, NO..
I DON'T EXPECT THAT... I REALLY DON'T
I JUST DON'T WANT TO BE **UN**HAPPY!
SCHULZ

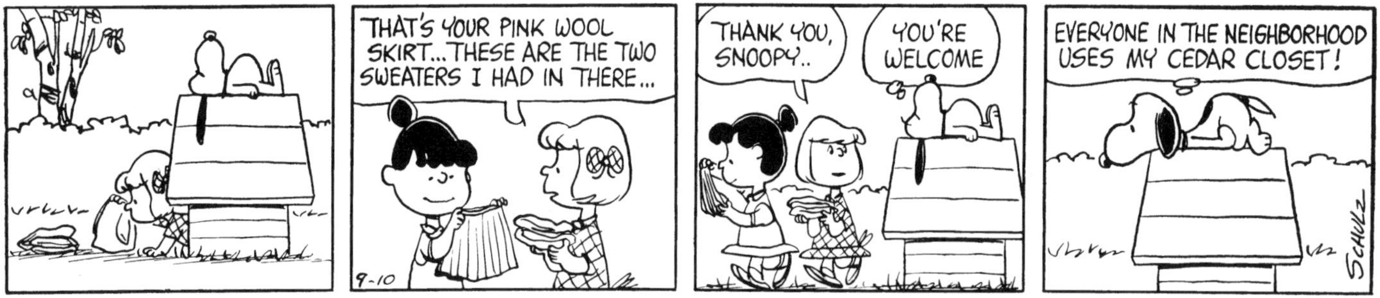
THAT'S YOUR PINK WOOL SKIRT... THESE ARE THE TWO SWEATERS I HAD IN THERE...
9-10
THANK YOU, SNOOPY..
YOU'RE WELCOME
EVERYONE IN THE NEIGHBORHOOD USES MY CEDAR CLOSET!
SCHULZ

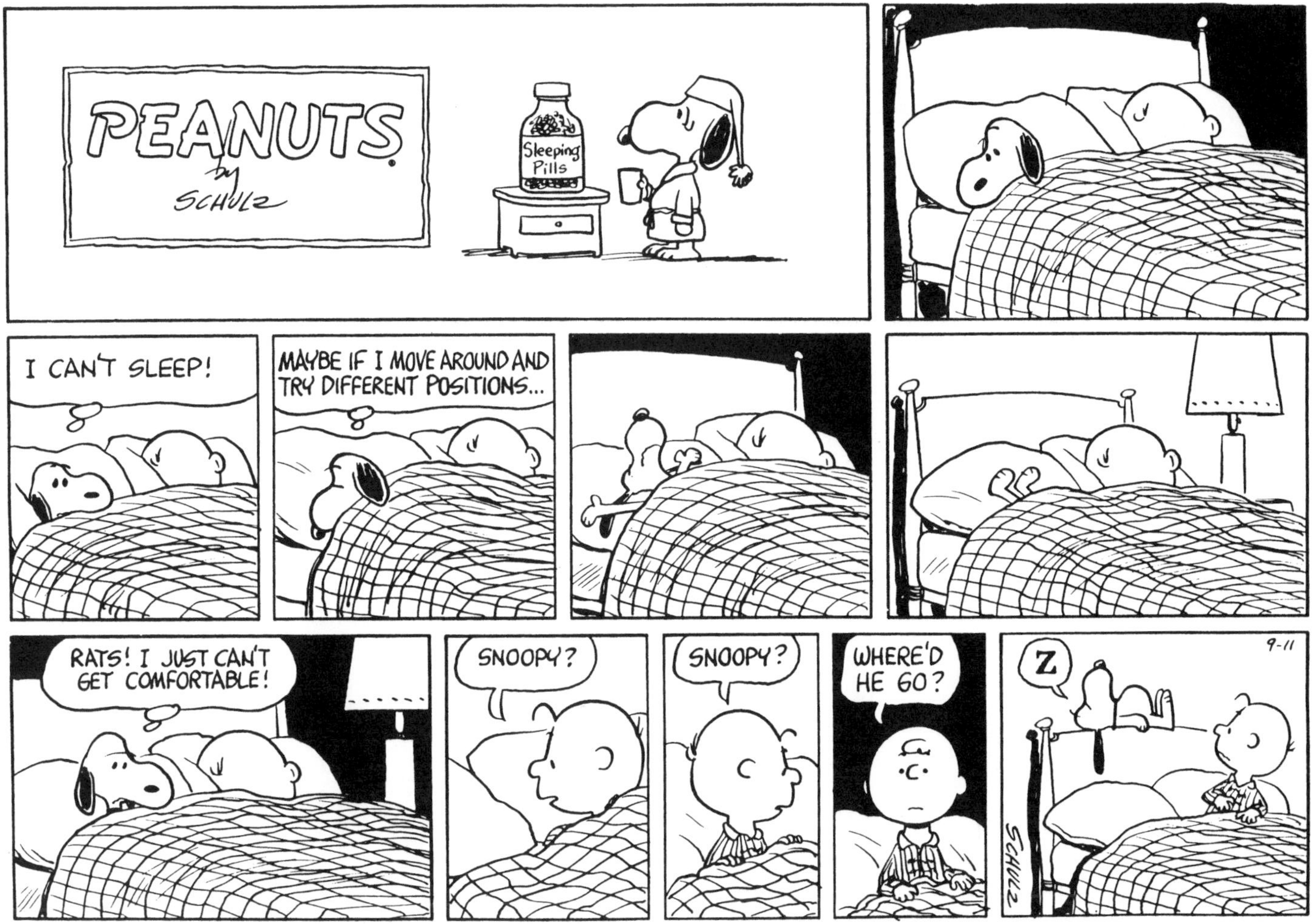
PEANUTS
by SCHULZ
Sleeping Pills
I CAN'T SLEEP!
MAYBE IF I MOVE AROUND AND TRY DIFFERENT POSITIONS...
RATS! I JUST CAN'T GET COMFORTABLE!
SNOOPY?
SNOOPY?
WHERE'D HE GO?
Z
9-11
SCHULZ

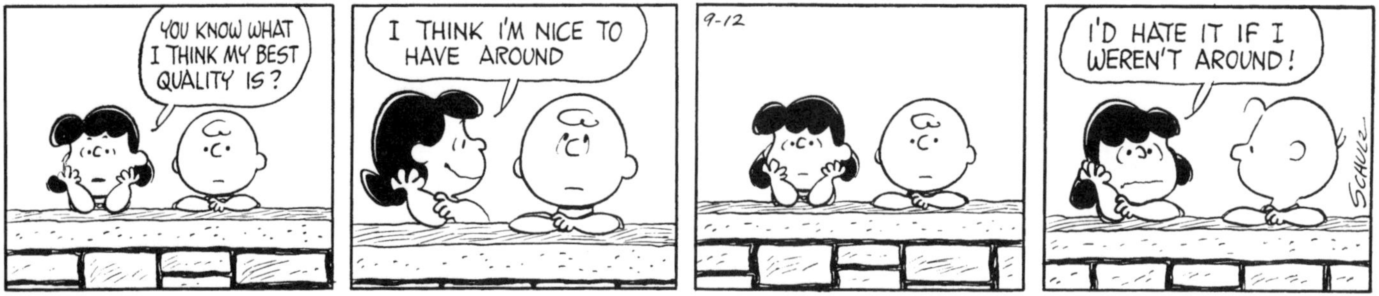
YOU KNOW WHAT I THINK MY BEST QUALITY IS?
I THINK I'M NICE TO HAVE AROUND
I'D HATE IT IF I WEREN'T AROUND!

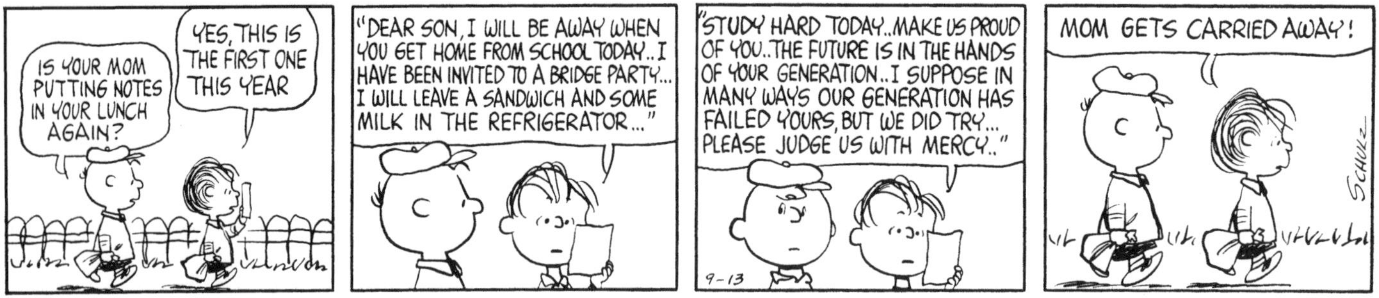
IS YOUR MOM PUTTING NOTES IN YOUR LUNCH AGAIN?
YES, THIS IS THE FIRST ONE THIS YEAR
"DEAR SON, I WILL BE AWAY WHEN YOU GET HOME FROM SCHOOL TODAY.. I HAVE BEEN INVITED TO A BRIDGE PARTY... I WILL LEAVE A SANDWICH AND SOME MILK IN THE REFRIGERATOR..."
"STUDY HARD TODAY.. MAKE US PROUD OF YOU.. THE FUTURE IS IN THE HANDS OF YOUR GENERATION.. I SUPPOSE IN MANY WAYS OUR GENERATION HAS FAILED YOURS, BUT WE DID TRY... PLEASE JUDGE US WITH MERCY.."
MOM GETS CARRIED AWAY!

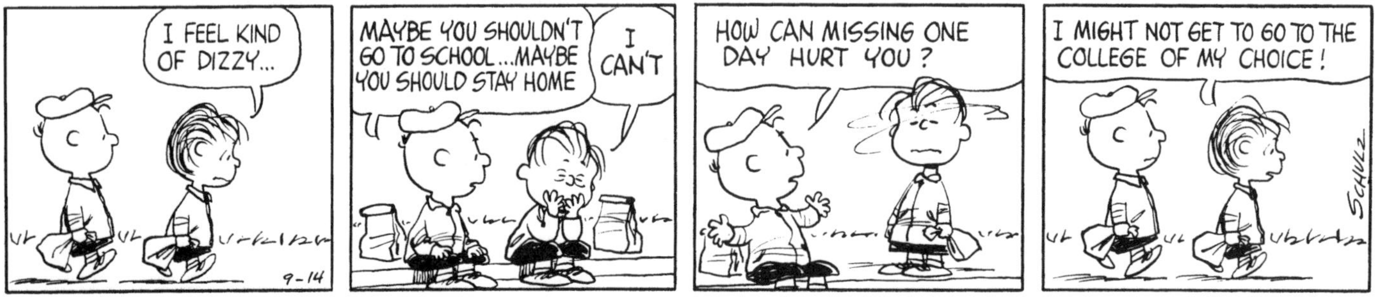
I FEEL KIND OF DIZZY...
MAYBE YOU SHOULDN'T GO TO SCHOOL... MAYBE YOU SHOULD STAY HOME
I CAN'T
HOW CAN MISSING ONE DAY HURT YOU?
I MIGHT NOT GET TO GO TO THE COLLEGE OF MY CHOICE!

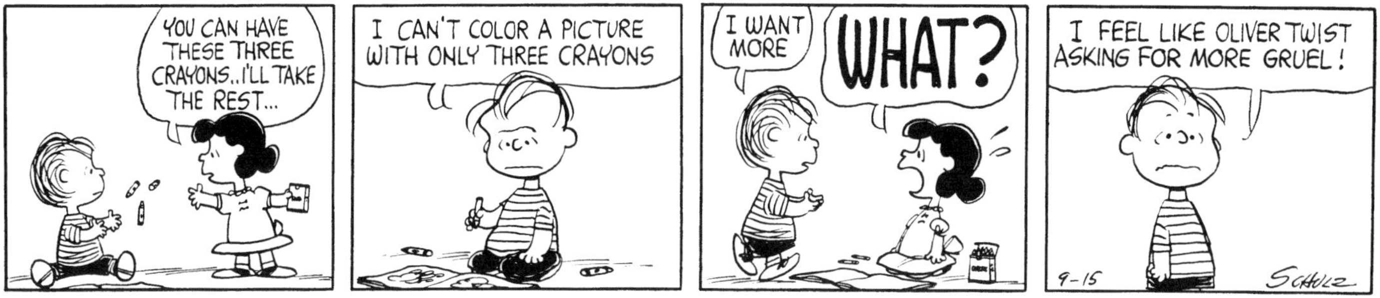
YOU CAN HAVE THESE THREE CRAYONS..I'LL TAKE THE REST...
I CAN'T COLOR A PICTURE WITH ONLY THREE CRAYONS
I WANT MORE
WHAT?
I FEEL LIKE OLIVER TWIST ASKING FOR MORE GRUEL!
9-15
SCHULZ

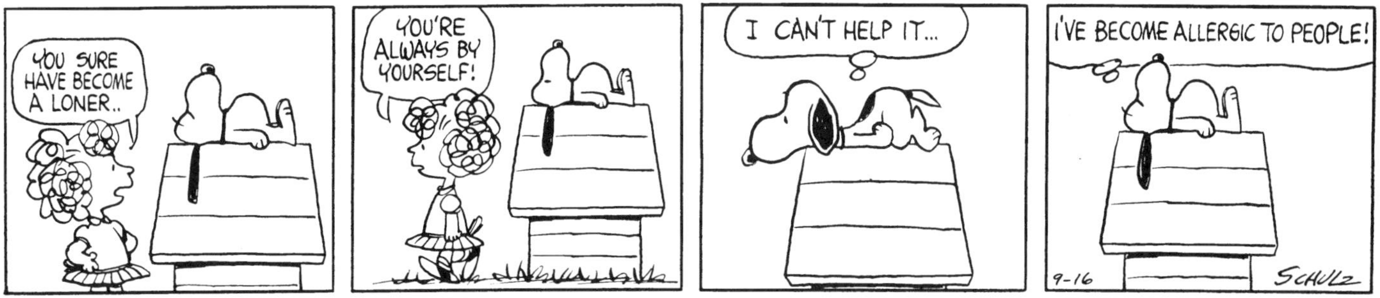
YOU SURE HAVE BECOME A LONER..
YOU'RE ALWAYS BY YOURSELF!
I CAN'T HELP IT...
I'VE BECOME ALLERGIC TO PEOPLE!
9-16
SCHULZ

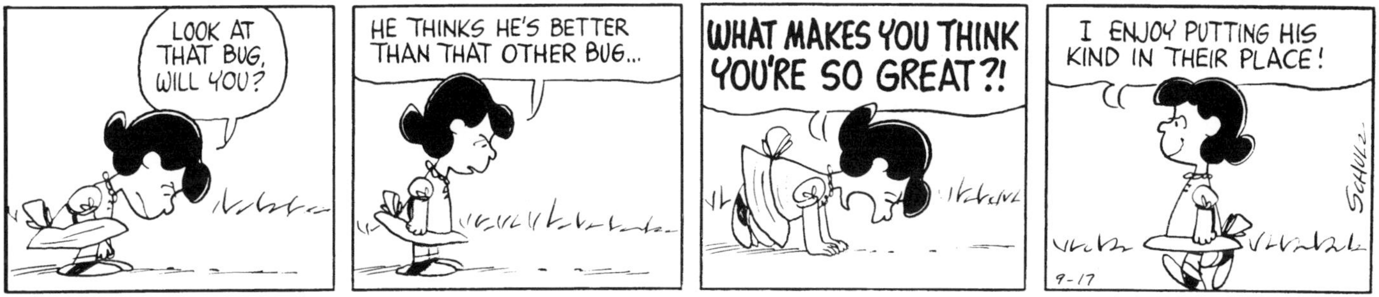
LOOK AT THAT BUG, WILL YOU?
HE THINKS HE'S BETTER THAN THAT OTHER BUG...
WHAT MAKES YOU THINK YOU'RE SO GREAT?!
I ENJOY PUTTING HIS KIND IN THEIR PLACE!
9-17
SCHULZ

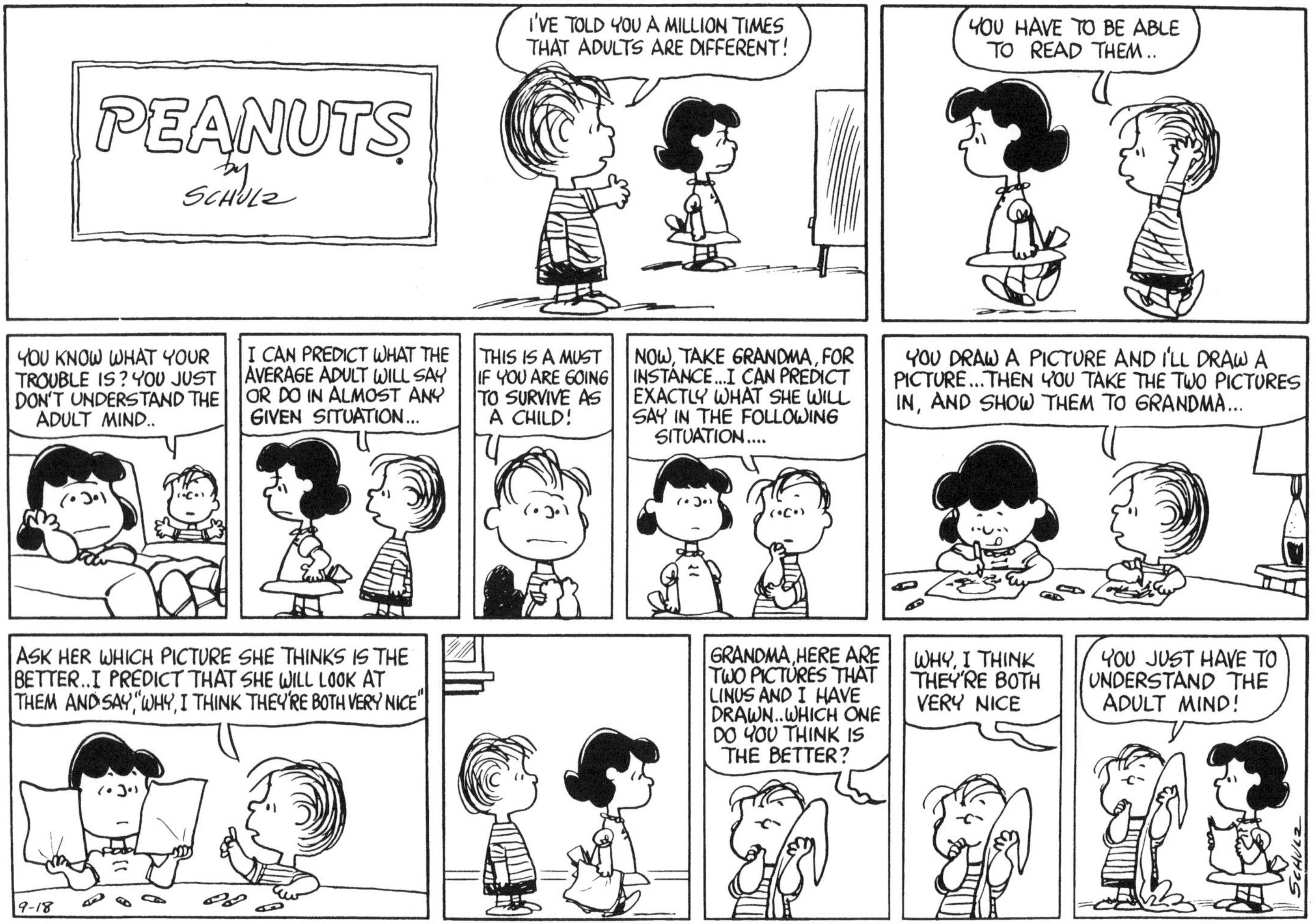
PEANUTS
by SCHULZ
I'VE TOLD YOU A MILLION TIMES THAT ADULTS ARE DIFFERENT!
YOU HAVE TO BE ABLE TO READ THEM..
YOU KNOW WHAT YOUR TROUBLE IS? YOU JUST DON'T UNDERSTAND THE ADULT MIND..
I CAN PREDICT WHAT THE AVERAGE ADULT WILL SAY OR DO IN ALMOST ANY GIVEN SITUATION...
THIS IS A MUST IF YOU ARE GOING TO SURVIVE AS A CHILD!
NOW, TAKE GRANDMA, FOR INSTANCE...I CAN PREDICT EXACTLY WHAT SHE WILL SAY IN THE FOLLOWING SITUATION....
YOU DRAW A PICTURE AND I'LL DRAW A PICTURE...THEN YOU TAKE THE TWO PICTURES IN, AND SHOW THEM TO GRANDMA...
ASK HER WHICH PICTURE SHE THINKS IS THE BETTER..I PREDICT THAT SHE WILL LOOK AT THEM AND SAY, "WHY, I THINK THEY'RE BOTH VERY NICE"
9-18
GRANDMA, HERE ARE TWO PICTURES THAT LINUS AND I HAVE DRAWN..WHICH ONE DO YOU THINK IS THE BETTER?
WHY, I THINK THEY'RE BOTH VERY NICE
YOU JUST HAVE TO UNDERSTAND THE ADULT MIND!
SCHULZ

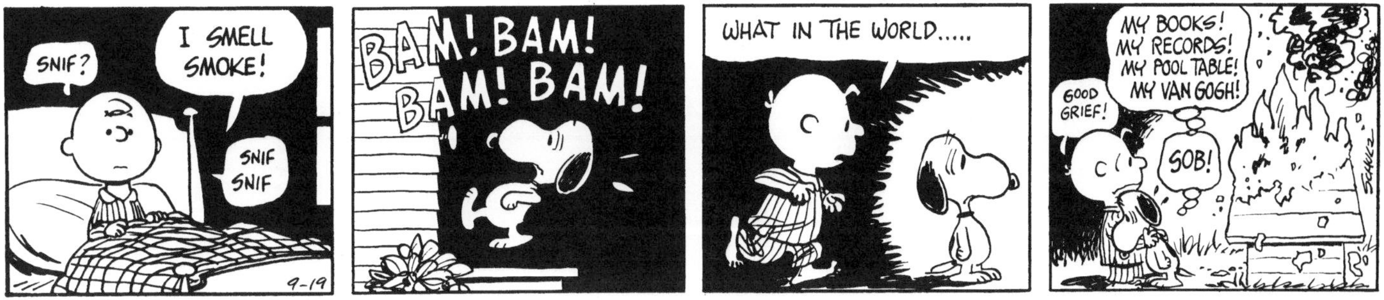
SNIF?
I SMELL SMOKE!
SNIF SNIF
9-19
BAM! BAM! BAM! BAM!
WHAT IN THE WORLD.....
GOOD GRIEF!
MY BOOKS! MY RECORDS! MY POOL TABLE! MY VAN GOGH!
SOB!
SCHULZ

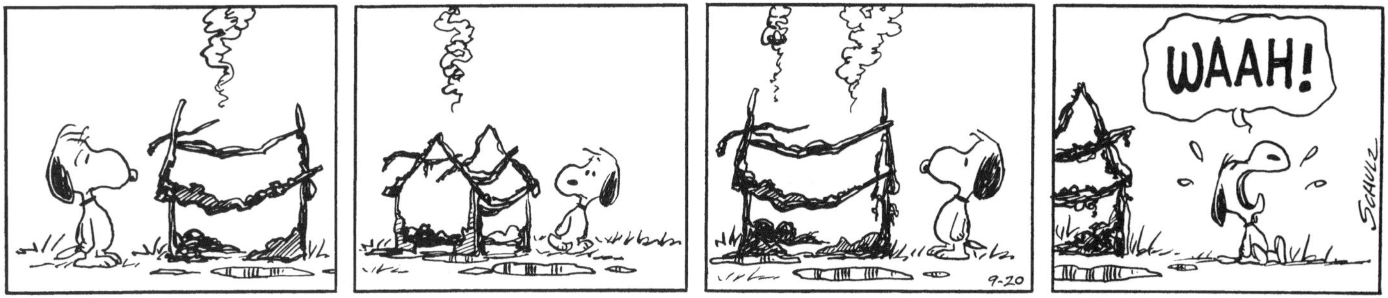
9-20
WAAH!
SCHULZ

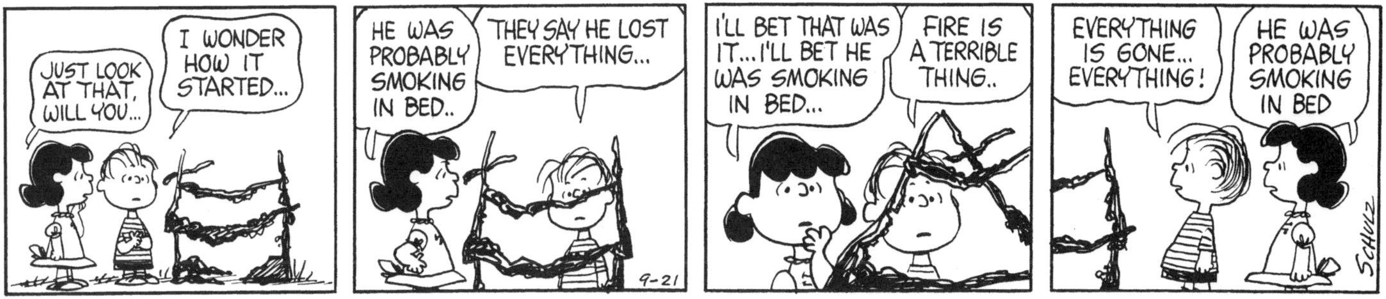
JUST LOOK AT THAT, WILL YOU...
I WONDER HOW IT STARTED...
HE WAS PROBABLY SMOKING IN BED..
THEY SAY HE LOST EVERYTHING...
9-21
I'LL BET THAT WAS IT...I'LL BET HE WAS SMOKING IN BED...
FIRE IS A TERRIBLE THING..
EVERYTHING IS GONE... EVERYTHING!
HE WAS PROBABLY SMOKING IN BED
SCHULZ

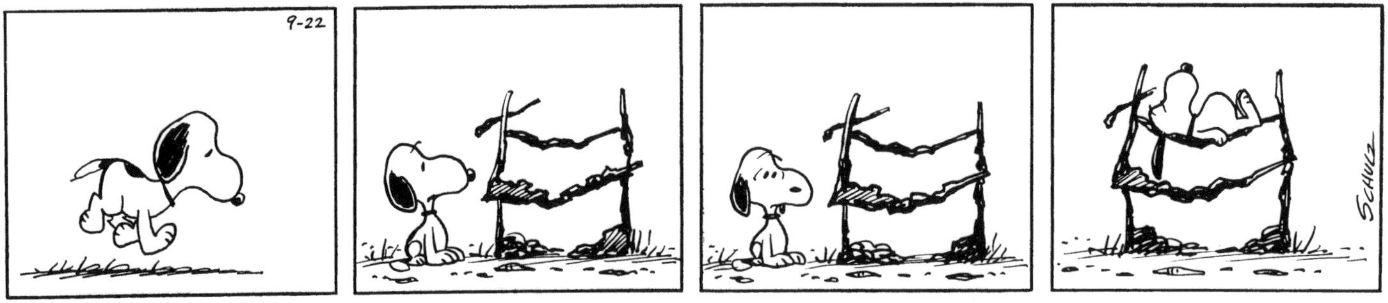
9-22
SCHULZ

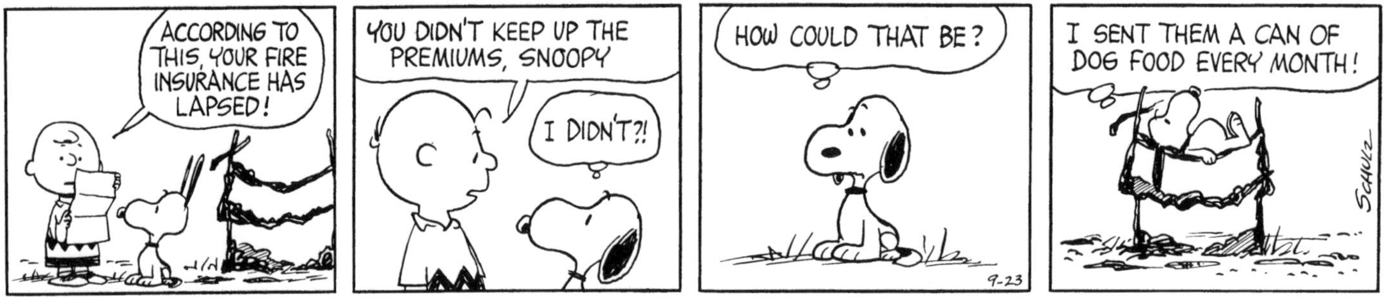
ACCORDING TO THIS, YOUR FIRE INSURANCE HAS LAPSED!
YOU DIDN'T KEEP UP THE PREMIUMS, SNOOPY
I DIDN'T?!
HOW COULD THAT BE?
9-23
I SENT THEM A CAN OF DOG FOOD EVERY MONTH!
SCHULZ

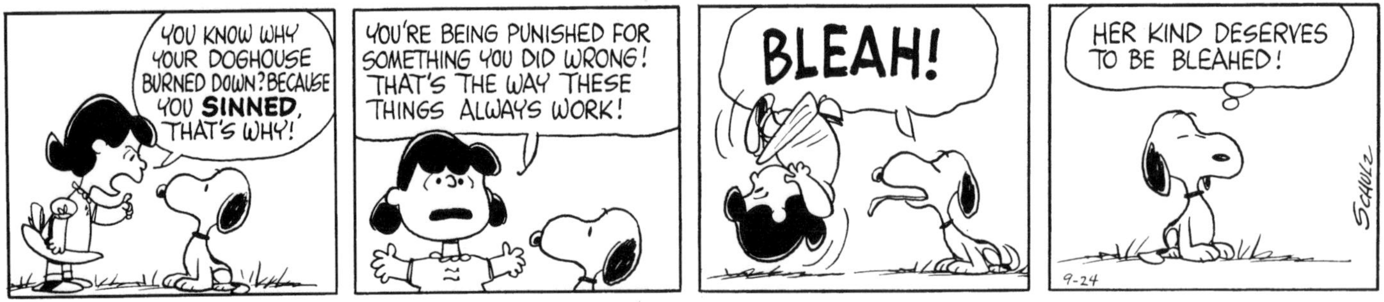
YOU KNOW WHY YOUR DOGHOUSE BURNED DOWN? BECAUSE YOU **SINNED**, THAT'S WHY!
YOU'RE BEING PUNISHED FOR SOMETHING YOU DID WRONG! THAT'S THE WAY THESE THINGS ALWAYS WORK!
BLEAH!
HER KIND DESERVES TO BE BLEAHED!
SCHULZ
9-24

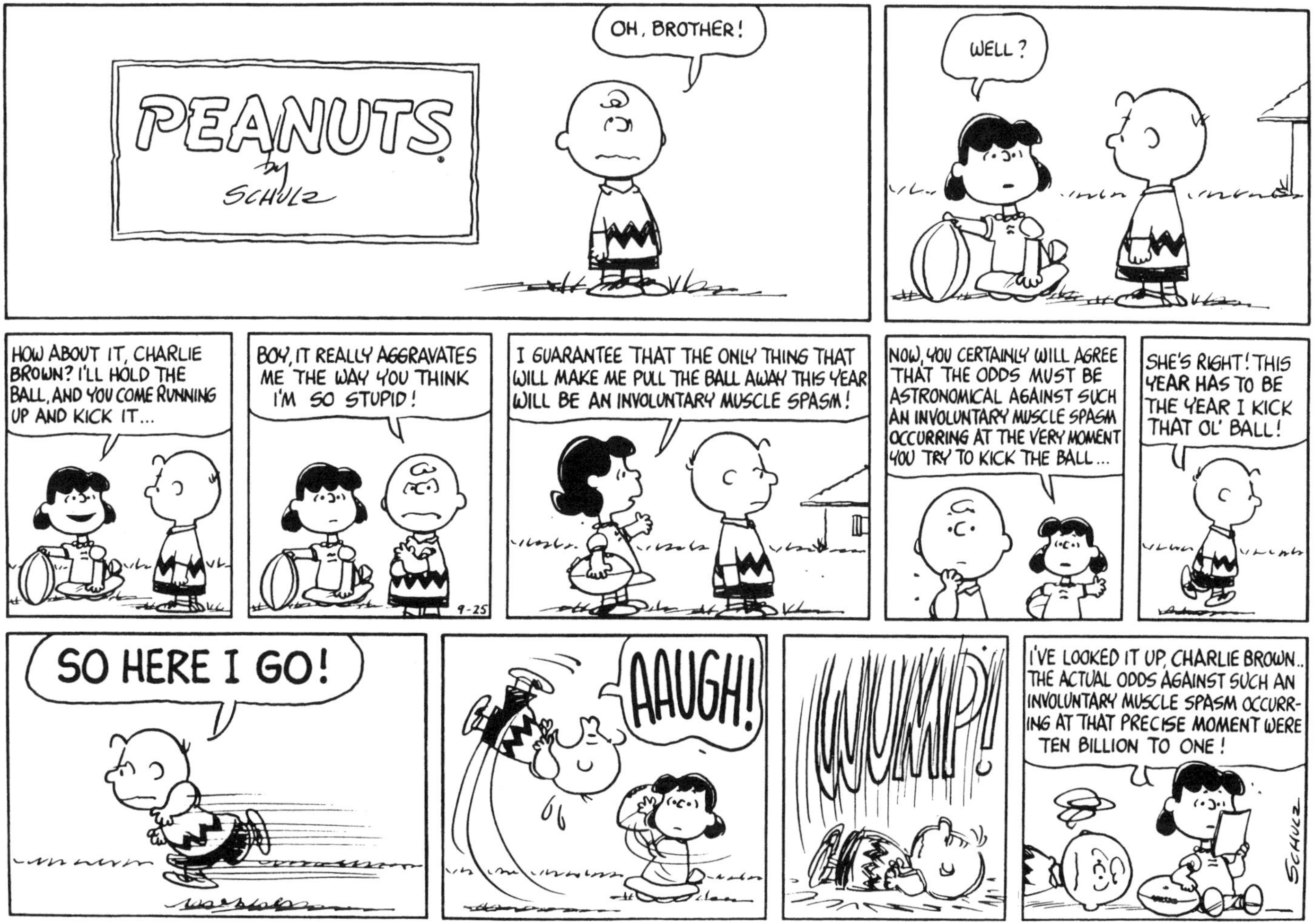
PEANUTS
by SCHULZ
OH, BROTHER!
WELL?
HOW ABOUT IT, CHARLIE BROWN? I'LL HOLD THE BALL, AND YOU COME RUNNING UP AND KICK IT...
BOY, IT REALLY AGGRAVATES ME THE WAY YOU THINK I'M SO STUPID!
9-25
I GUARANTEE THAT THE ONLY THING THAT WILL MAKE ME PULL THE BALL AWAY THIS YEAR WILL BE AN INVOLUNTARY MUSCLE SPASM!
NOW, YOU CERTAINLY WILL AGREE THAT THE ODDS MUST BE ASTRONOMICAL AGAINST SUCH AN INVOLUNTARY MUSCLE SPASM OCCURRING AT THE VERY MOMENT YOU TRY TO KICK THE BALL...
SHE'S RIGHT! THIS YEAR HAS TO BE THE YEAR I KICK THAT OL' BALL!
SO HERE I GO!
AAUGH!
WUMP!
I'VE LOOKED IT UP, CHARLIE BROWN.. THE ACTUAL ODDS AGAINST SUCH AN INVOLUNTARY MUSCLE SPASM OCCURRING AT THAT PRECISE MOMENT WERE TEN BILLION TO ONE!
SCHULZ

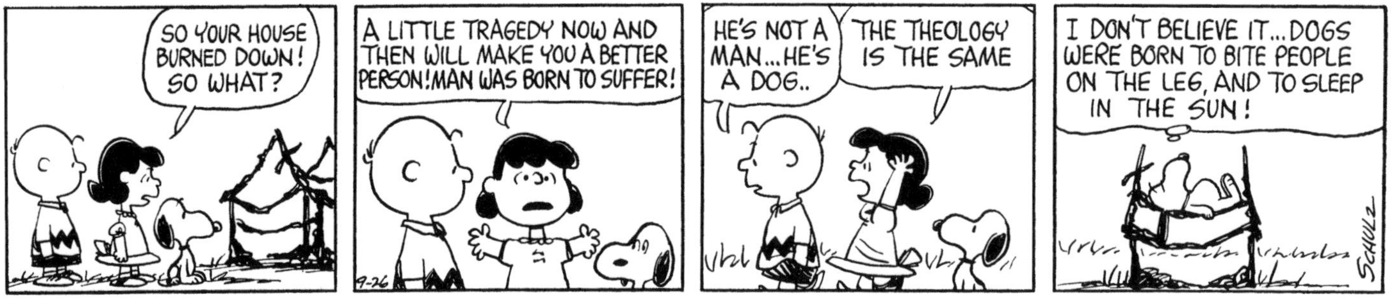
SO YOUR HOUSE BURNED DOWN! SO WHAT?
9-26
A LITTLE TRAGEDY NOW AND THEN WILL MAKE YOU A BETTER PERSON! MAN WAS BORN TO SUFFER!
HE'S NOT A MAN...HE'S A DOG..
THE THEOLOGY IS THE SAME
I DON'T BELIEVE IT...DOGS WERE BORN TO BITE PEOPLE ON THE LEG, AND TO SLEEP IN THE SUN!
SCHULZ

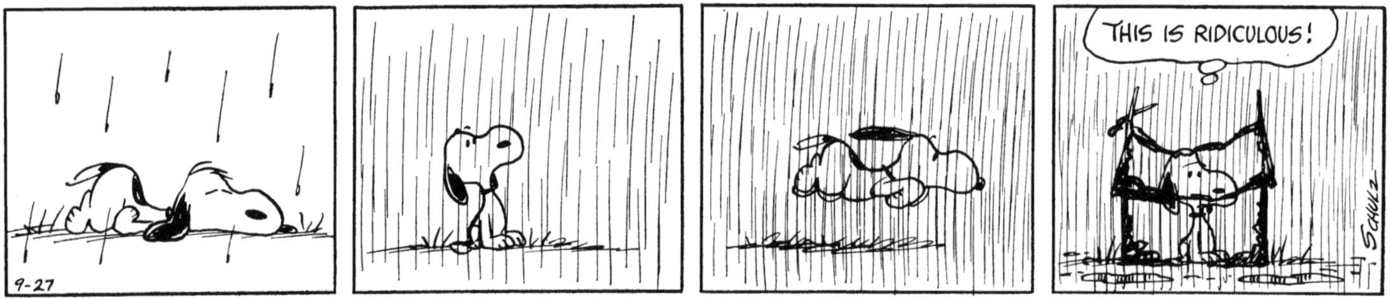
9-27
THIS IS RIDICULOUS!
SCHULZ

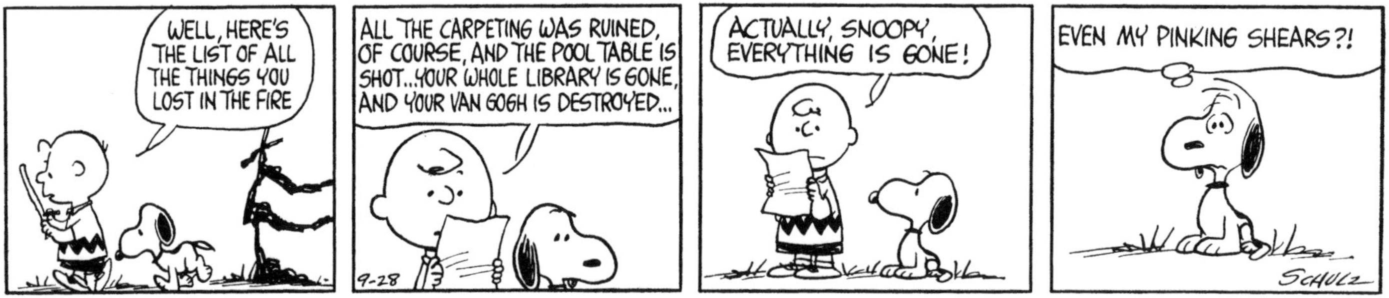
WELL, HERE'S THE LIST OF ALL THE THINGS YOU LOST IN THE FIRE
ALL THE CARPETING WAS RUINED, OF COURSE, AND THE POOL TABLE IS SHOT...YOUR WHOLE LIBRARY IS GONE, AND YOUR VAN GOGH IS DESTROYED...
9-28
ACTUALLY, SNOOPY, EVERYTHING IS GONE!
EVEN MY PINKING SHEARS?!
SCHULZ

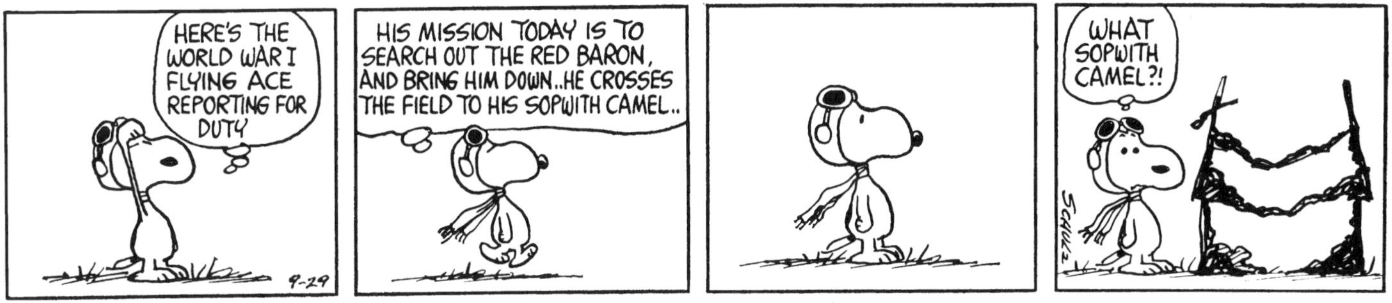
HERE'S THE WORLD WAR I FLYING ACE REPORTING FOR DUTY
9-29
HIS MISSION TODAY IS TO SEARCH OUT THE RED BARON, AND BRING HIM DOWN..HE CROSSES THE FIELD TO HIS SOPWITH CAMEL..
WHAT SOPWITH CAMEL?!
SCHULZ

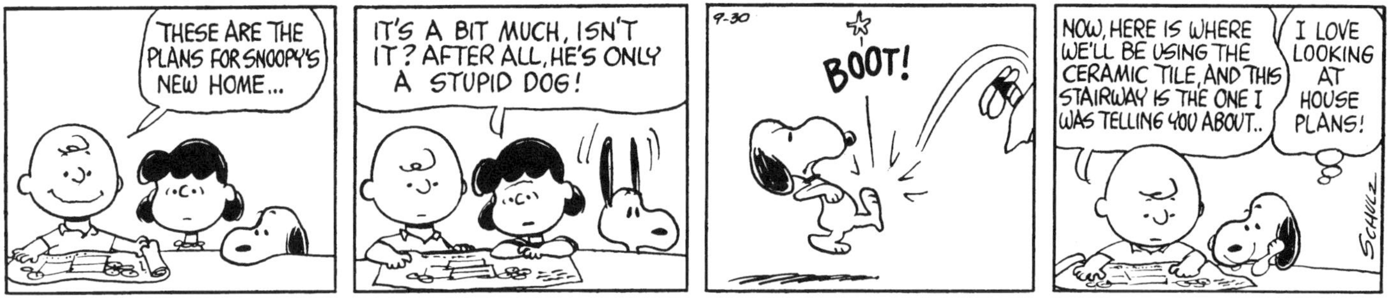
THESE ARE THE PLANS FOR SNOOPY'S NEW HOME...
IT'S A BIT MUCH, ISN'T IT? AFTER ALL, HE'S ONLY A STUPID DOG!
9-30
BOOT!
NOW, HERE IS WHERE WE'LL BE USING THE CERAMIC TILE, AND THIS STAIRWAY IS THE ONE I WAS TELLING YOU ABOUT..
I LOVE LOOKING AT HOUSE PLANS!
SCHULZ

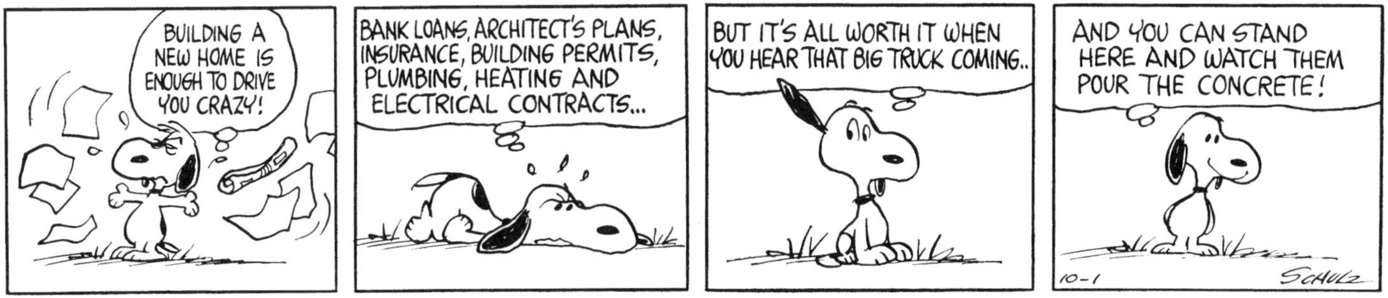
BUILDING A NEW HOME IS ENOUGH TO DRIVE YOU CRAZY!
BANK LOANS, ARCHITECT'S PLANS, INSURANCE, BUILDING PERMITS, PLUMBING, HEATING AND ELECTRICAL CONTRACTS...
BUT IT'S ALL WORTH IT WHEN YOU HEAR THAT BIG TRUCK COMING..
AND YOU CAN STAND HERE AND WATCH THEM POUR THE CONCRETE!
10-1
SCHULZ

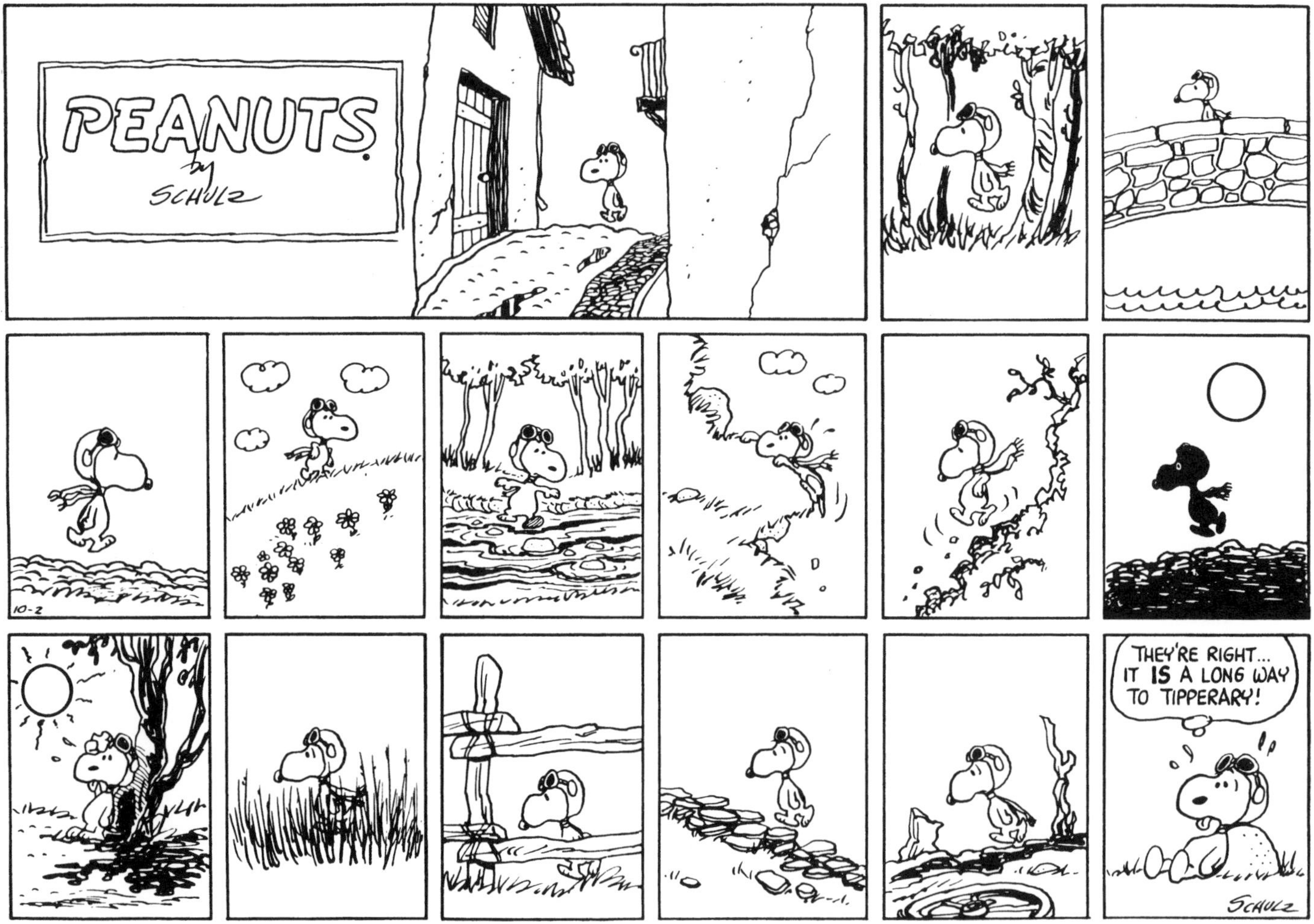
PEANUTS
by
SCHULZ
10-2
THEY'RE RIGHT...
IT **IS** A LONG WAY
TO TIPPERARY!
SCHULZ

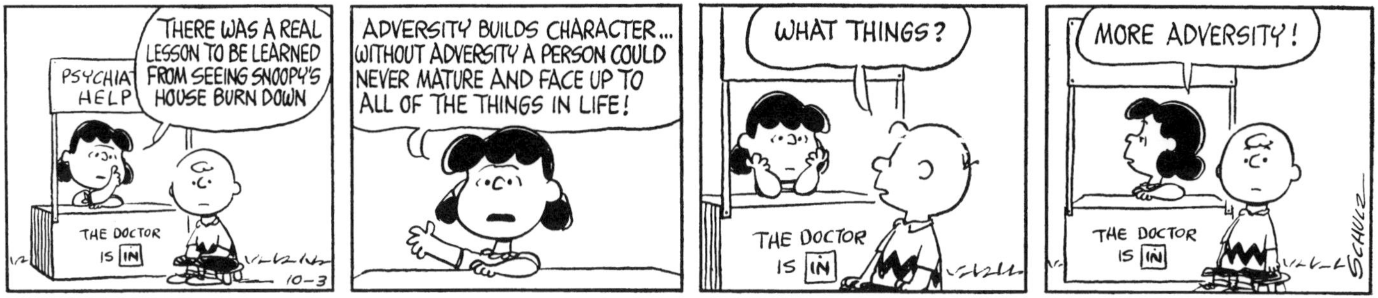
PSYCHIAT HELP
THERE WAS A REAL LESSON TO BE LEARNED FROM SEEING SNOOPY'S HOUSE BURN DOWN
THE DOCTOR IS IN
10-3
ADVERSITY BUILDS CHARACTER... WITHOUT ADVERSITY A PERSON COULD NEVER MATURE AND FACE UP TO ALL OF THE THINGS IN LIFE!
WHAT THINGS?
THE DOCTOR IS IN
MORE ADVERSITY!
THE DOCTOR IS IN
SCHULZ

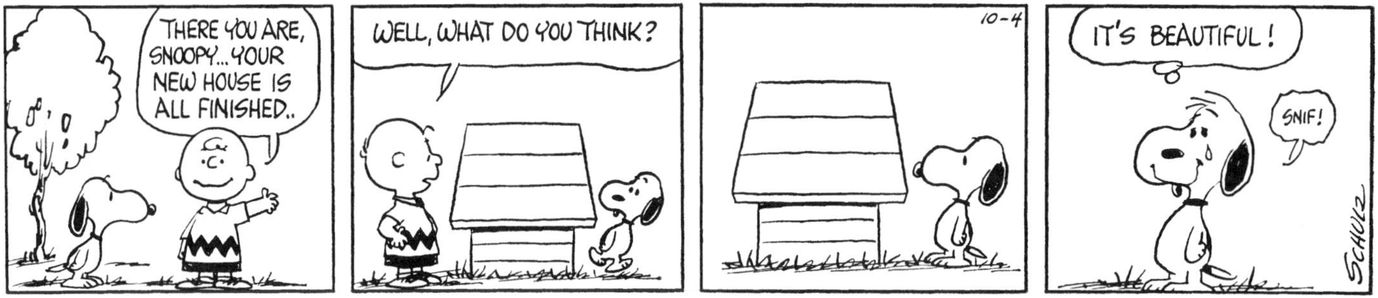
THERE YOU ARE, SNOOPY... YOUR NEW HOUSE IS ALL FINISHED..
WELL, WHAT DO YOU THINK?
10-4
IT'S BEAUTIFUL!
SNIF!
SCHULZ

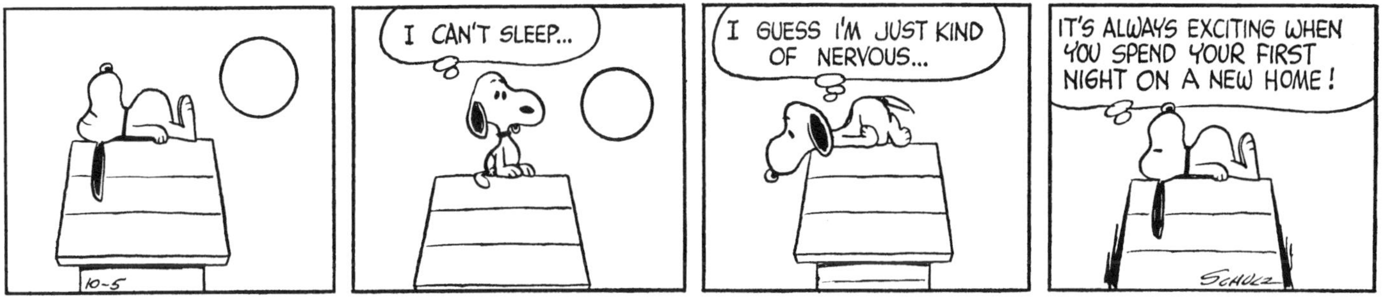
10-5
I CAN'T SLEEP...
I GUESS I'M JUST KIND OF NERVOUS...
IT'S ALWAYS EXCITING WHEN YOU SPEND YOUR FIRST NIGHT ON A NEW HOME!
SCHULZ

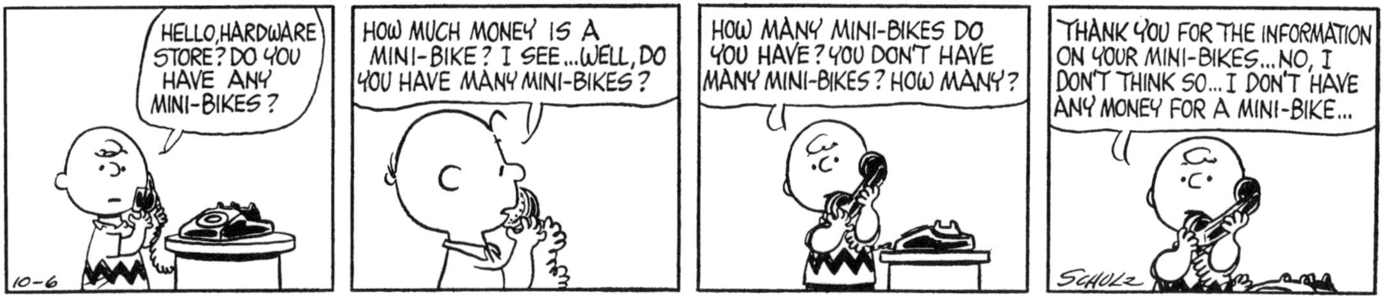
10-6
HELLO, HARDWARE STORE? DO YOU HAVE ANY MINI-BIKES?
HOW MUCH MONEY IS A MINI-BIKE? I SEE...WELL, DO YOU HAVE MANY MINI-BIKES?
HOW MANY MINI-BIKES DO YOU HAVE? YOU DON'T HAVE MANY MINI-BIKES? HOW MANY?
THANK YOU FOR THE INFORMATION ON YOUR MINI-BIKES...NO, I DON'T THINK SO...I DON'T HAVE ANY MONEY FOR A MINI-BIKE...

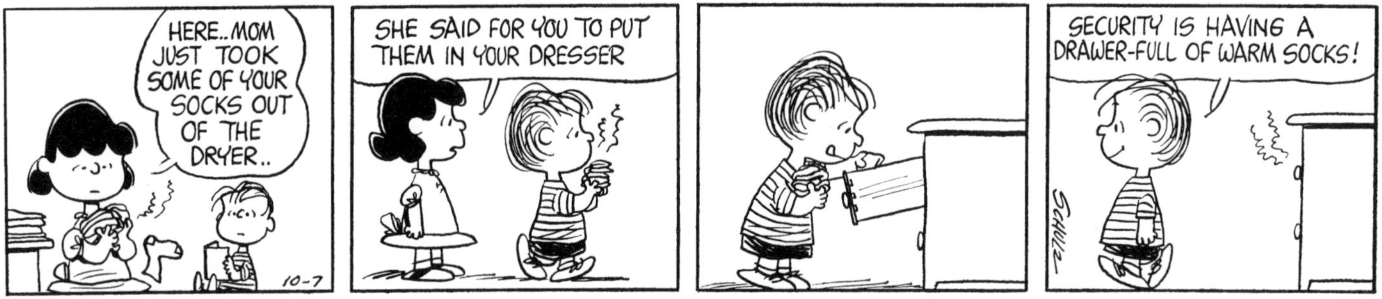
HERE..MOM JUST TOOK SOME OF YOUR SOCKS OUT OF THE DRYER..
10-7
SHE SAID FOR YOU TO PUT THEM IN YOUR DRESSER
SECURITY IS HAVING A DRAWER-FULL OF WARM SOCKS!

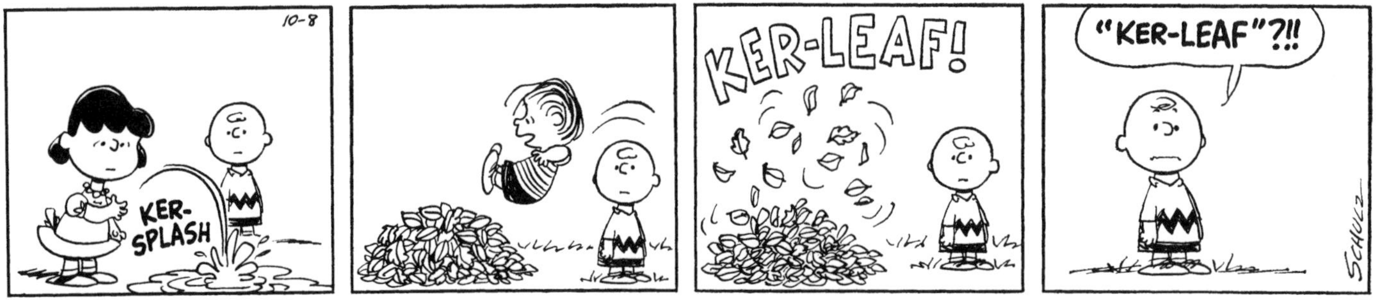
10-8
KER-SPLASH
KER-LEAF!
"KER-LEAF"?!!

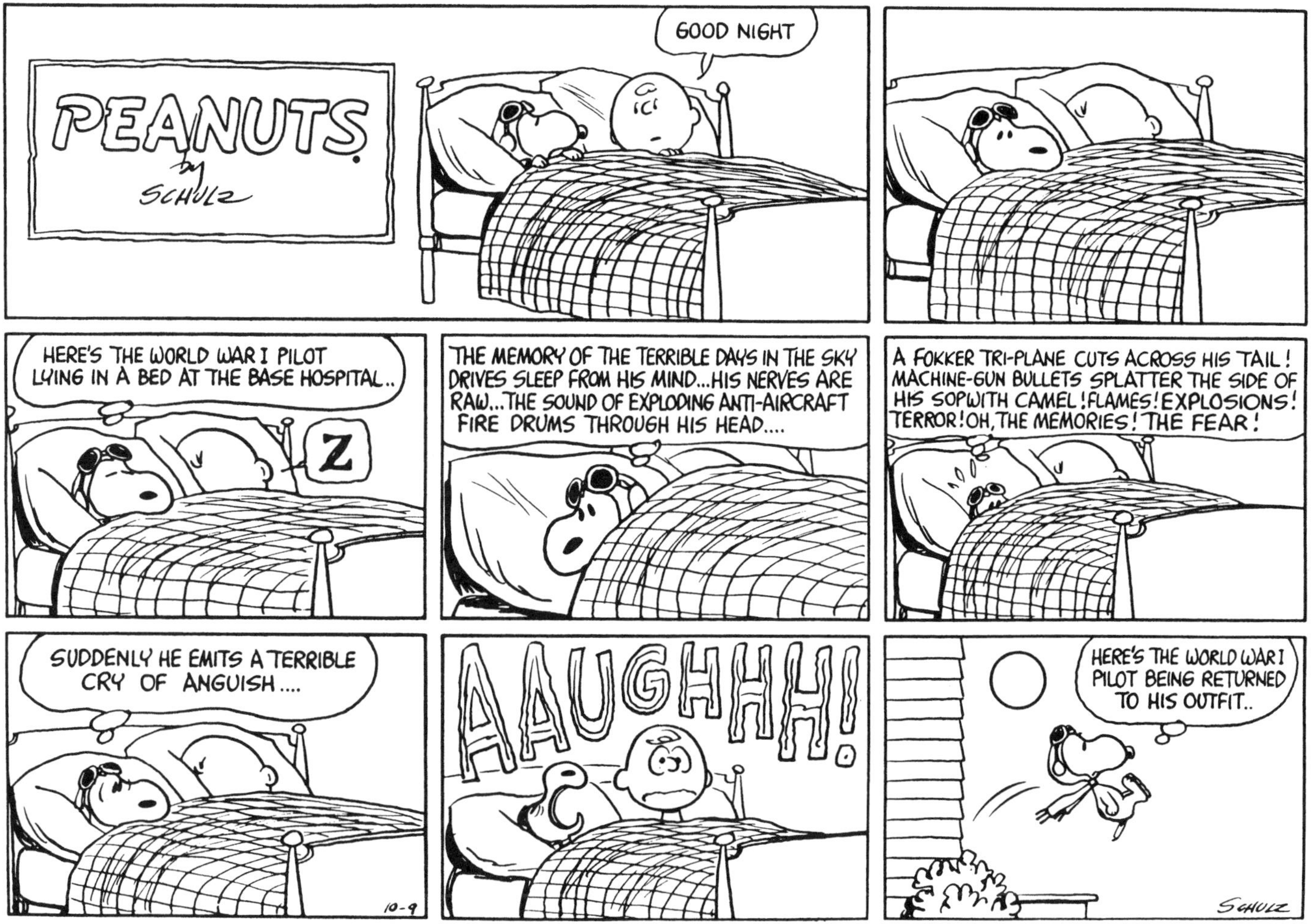
PEANUTS
by SCHULZ
GOOD NIGHT
HERE'S THE WORLD WAR I PILOT LYING IN A BED AT THE BASE HOSPITAL..
Z
THE MEMORY OF THE TERRIBLE DAYS IN THE SKY DRIVES SLEEP FROM HIS MIND...HIS NERVES ARE RAW...THE SOUND OF EXPLODING ANTI-AIRCRAFT FIRE DRUMS THROUGH HIS HEAD....
A FOKKER TRI-PLANE CUTS ACROSS HIS TAIL! MACHINE-GUN BULLETS SPLATTER THE SIDE OF HIS SOPWITH CAMEL! FLAMES! EXPLOSIONS! TERROR! OH, THE MEMORIES! THE FEAR!
SUDDENLY HE EMITS A TERRIBLE CRY OF ANGUISH....
10-9
AAUGHHH!
HERE'S THE WORLD WAR I PILOT BEING RETURNED TO HIS OUTFIT..
SCHULZ

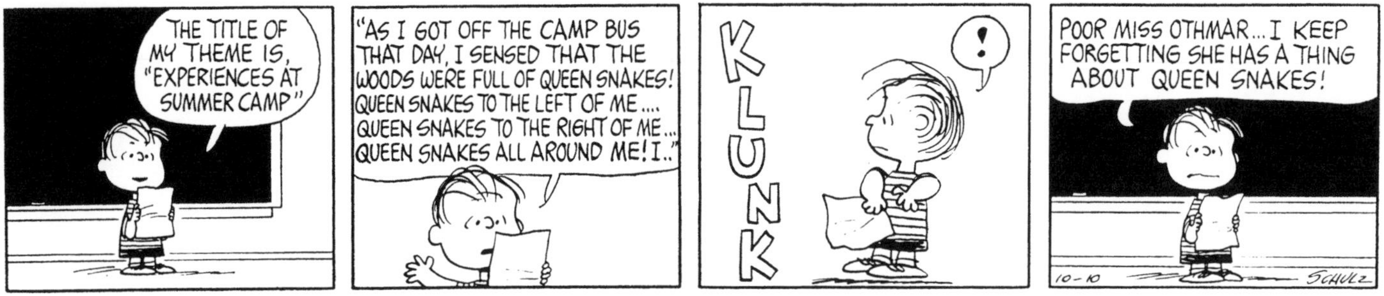
THE TITLE OF MY THEME IS, "EXPERIENCES AT SUMMER CAMP"
"AS I GOT OFF THE CAMP BUS THAT DAY, I SENSED THAT THE WOODS WERE FULL OF QUEEN SNAKES! QUEEN SNAKES TO THE LEFT OF ME.... QUEEN SNAKES TO THE RIGHT OF ME... QUEEN SNAKES ALL AROUND ME! I.."
KLUNK
!
POOR MISS OTHMAR...I KEEP FORGETTING SHE HAS A THING ABOUT QUEEN SNAKES!
10-10
SCHULZ

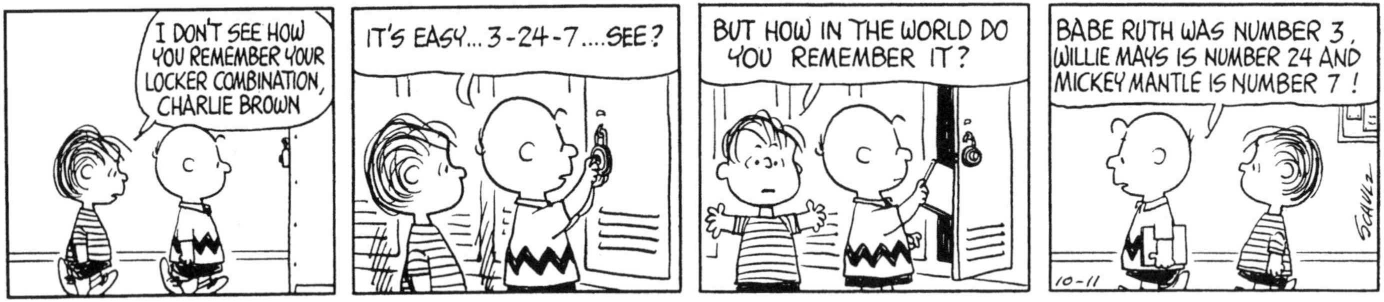
I DON'T SEE HOW YOU REMEMBER YOUR LOCKER COMBINATION, CHARLIE BROWN
IT'S EASY...3-24-7....SEE?
BUT HOW IN THE WORLD DO YOU REMEMBER IT?
BABE RUTH WAS NUMBER 3, WILLIE MAYS IS NUMBER 24 AND MICKEY MANTLE IS NUMBER 7!
SCHULZ
10-11

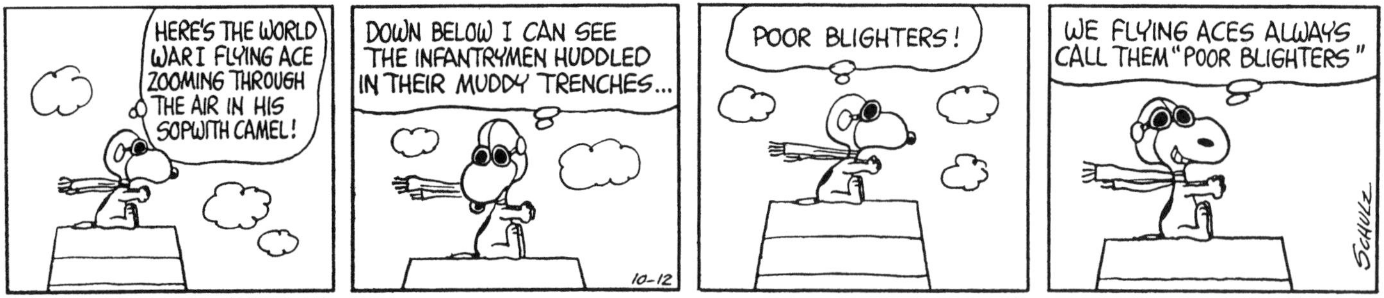
HERE'S THE WORLD WAR I FLYING ACE ZOOMING THROUGH THE AIR IN HIS SOPWITH CAMEL!
DOWN BELOW I CAN SEE THE INFANTRYMEN HUDDLED IN THEIR MUDDY TRENCHES...
10-12
POOR BLIGHTERS!
WE FLYING ACES ALWAYS CALL THEM "POOR BLIGHTERS"
SCHULZ

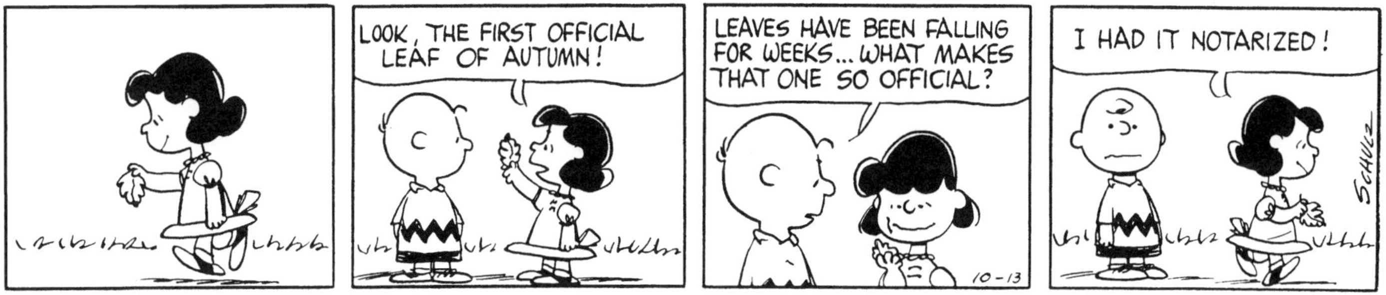
LOOK, THE FIRST OFFICIAL LEAF OF AUTUMN!
LEAVES HAVE BEEN FALLING FOR WEEKS... WHAT MAKES THAT ONE SO OFFICIAL?
10-13
I HAD IT NOTARIZED!
SCHULZ

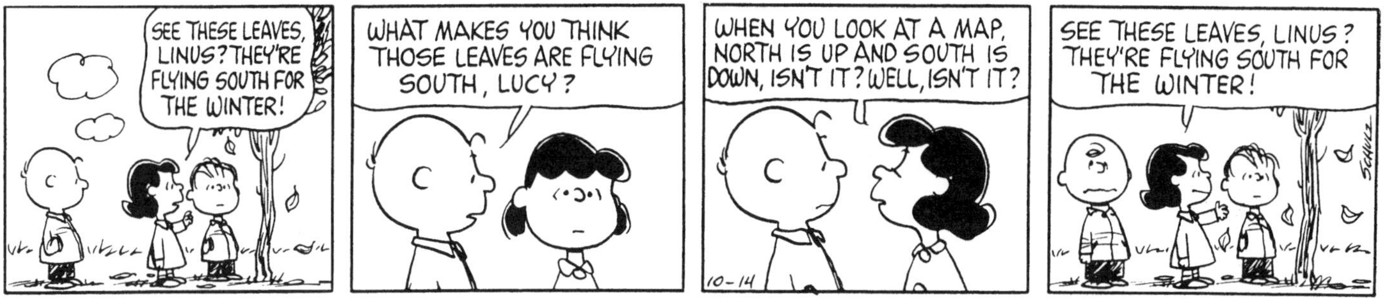
SEE THESE LEAVES, LINUS? THEY'RE FLYING SOUTH FOR THE WINTER!
WHAT MAKES YOU THINK THOSE LEAVES ARE FLYING SOUTH, LUCY?
WHEN YOU LOOK AT A MAP, NORTH IS UP AND SOUTH IS DOWN, ISN'T IT? WELL, ISN'T IT?
10-14
SEE THESE LEAVES, LINUS? THEY'RE FLYING SOUTH FOR THE WINTER!
SCHULZ

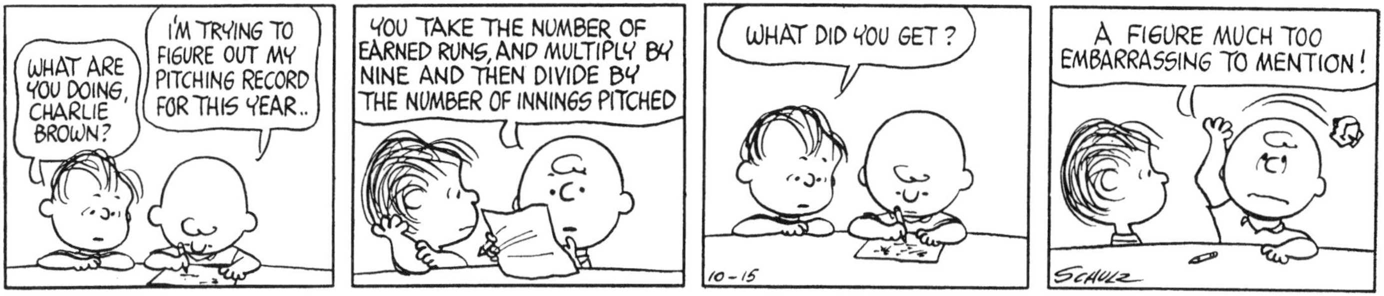
WHAT ARE YOU DOING, CHARLIE BROWN?
I'M TRYING TO FIGURE OUT MY PITCHING RECORD FOR THIS YEAR..
YOU TAKE THE NUMBER OF EARNED RUNS, AND MULTIPLY BY NINE AND THEN DIVIDE BY THE NUMBER OF INNINGS PITCHED
WHAT DID YOU GET?
10-15
A FIGURE MUCH TOO EMBARRASSING TO MENTION!
SCHULZ

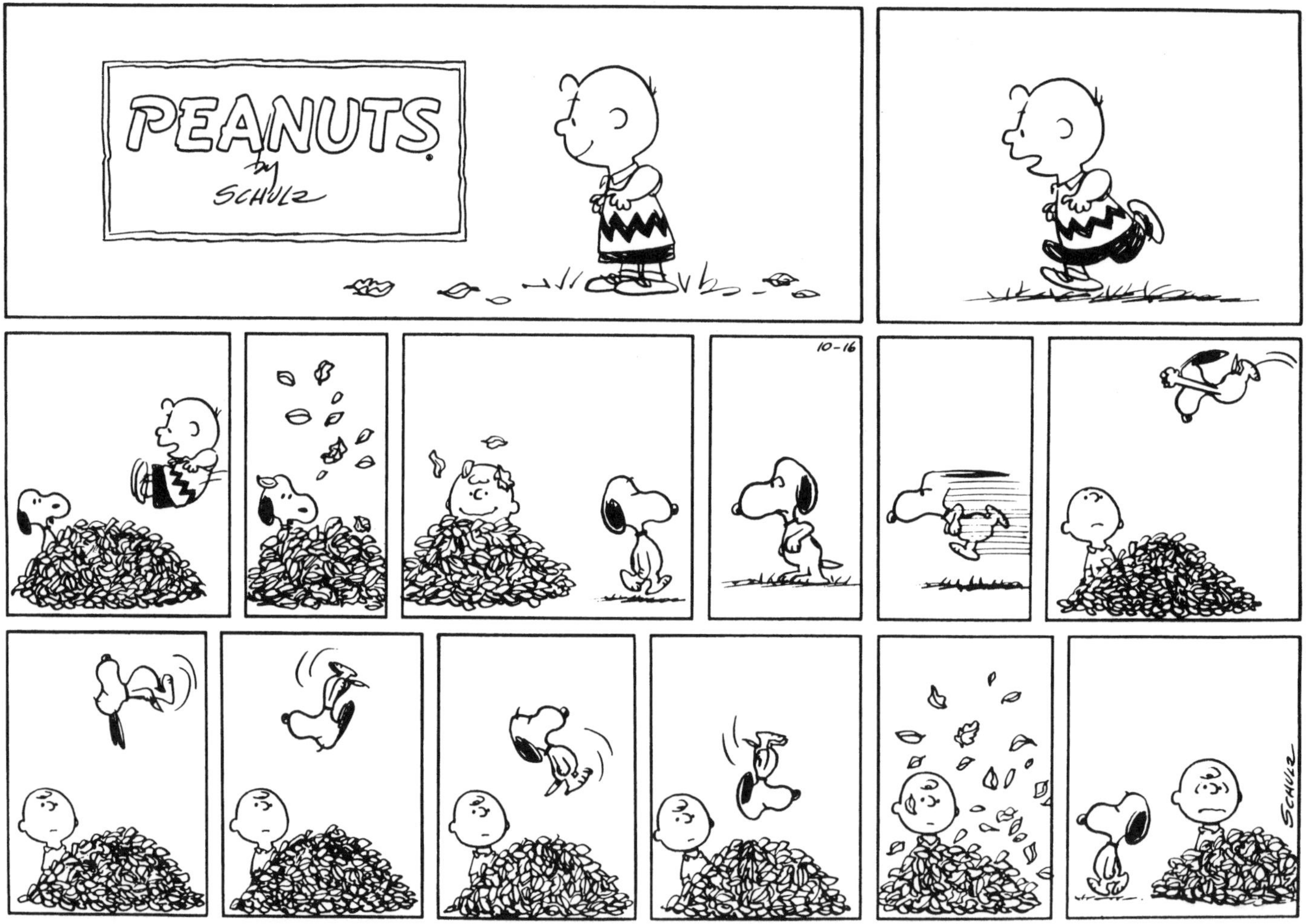
PEANUTS
by
SCHULZ
10-16
SCHULZ

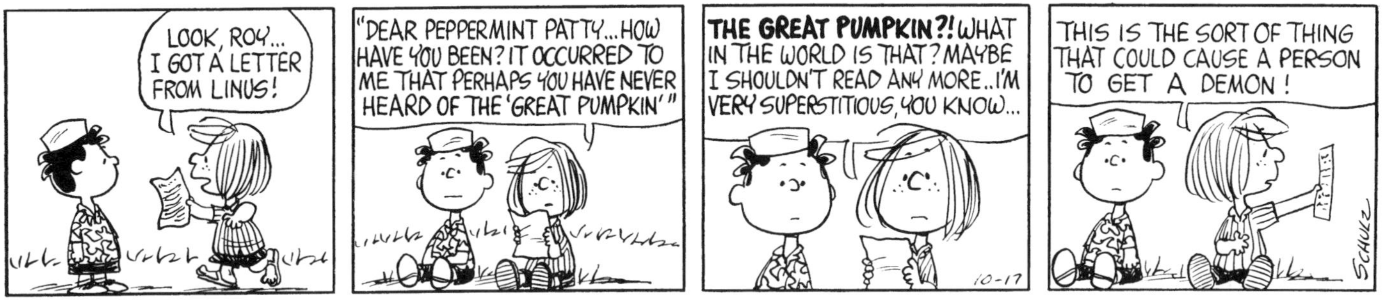
LOOK, ROY... I GOT A LETTER FROM LINUS!
"DEAR PEPPERMINT PATTY...HOW HAVE YOU BEEN? IT OCCURRED TO ME THAT PERHAPS YOU HAVE NEVER HEARD OF THE 'GREAT PUMPKIN'"
THE GREAT PUMPKIN?! WHAT IN THE WORLD IS THAT? MAYBE I SHOULDN'T READ ANY MORE..I'M VERY SUPERSTITIOUS, YOU KNOW...
10-17
THIS IS THE SORT OF THING THAT COULD CAUSE A PERSON TO GET A DEMON!
SCHULZ

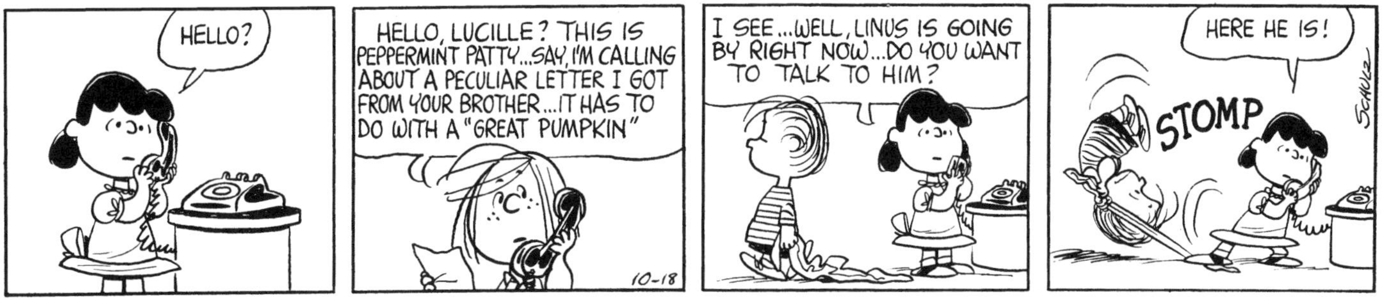
HELLO?
HELLO, LUCILLE? THIS IS PEPPERMINT PATTY...SAY, I'M CALLING ABOUT A PECULIAR LETTER I GOT FROM YOUR BROTHER...IT HAS TO DO WITH A "GREAT PUMPKIN"
10-18
I SEE...WELL, LINUS IS GOING BY RIGHT NOW...DO YOU WANT TO TALK TO HIM?
HERE HE IS!
SCHULZ
STOMP

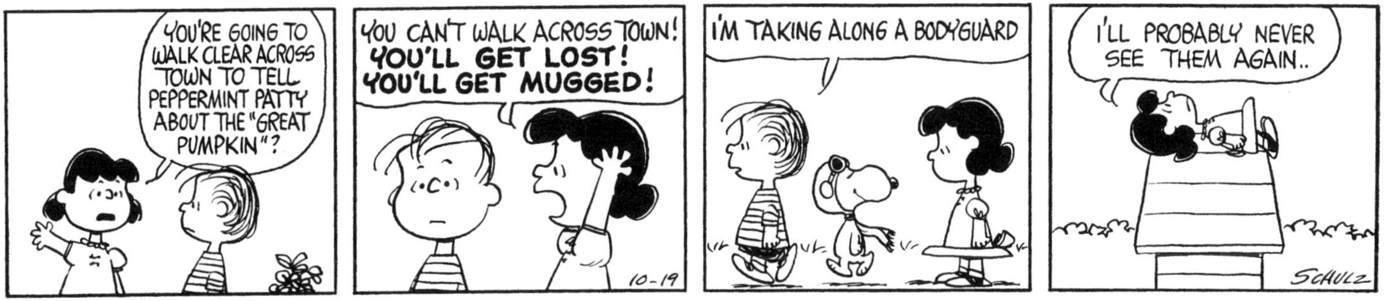
YOU'RE GOING TO WALK CLEAR ACROSS TOWN TO TELL PEPPERMINT PATTY ABOUT THE "GREAT PUMPKIN"?
YOU CAN'T WALK ACROSS TOWN! YOU'LL GET LOST! YOU'LL GET MUGGED!
10-19
I'M TAKING ALONG A BODYGUARD
I'LL PROBABLY NEVER SEE THEM AGAIN..
SCHULZ

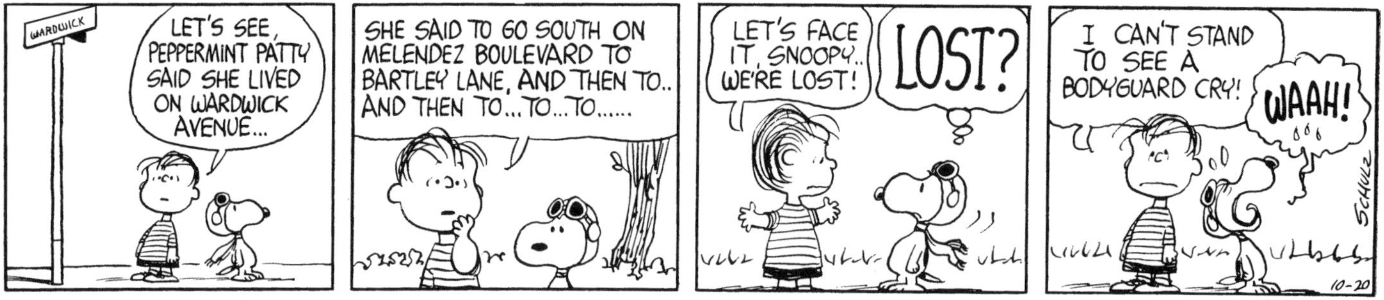
WARDWICK
LET'S SEE, PEPPERMINT PATTY SAID SHE LIVED ON WARDWICK AVENUE...
SHE SAID TO GO SOUTH ON MELENDEZ BOULEVARD TO BARTLEY LANE, AND THEN TO.. AND THEN TO... TO... TO......
LET'S FACE IT, SNOOPY.. WE'RE LOST!
LOST?
I CAN'T STAND TO SEE A BODYGUARD CRY!
WAAH!
SCHULZ
10-20

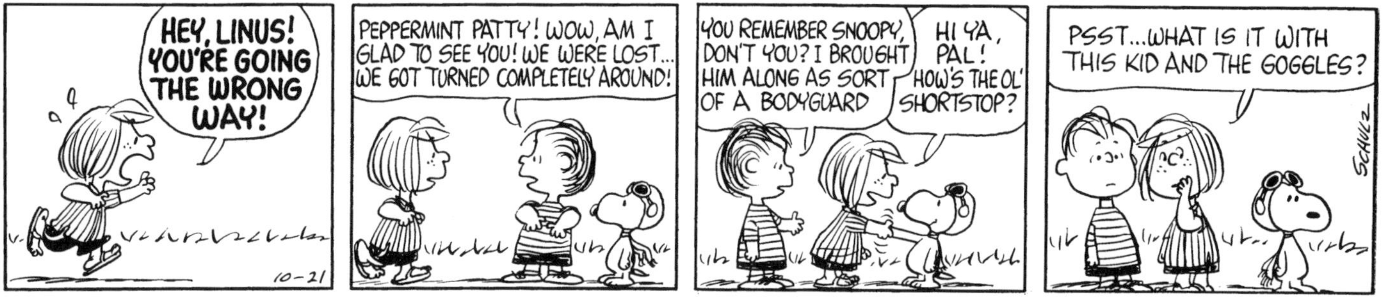
HEY, LINUS! YOU'RE GOING THE WRONG WAY!
10-21
PEPPERMINT PATTY! WOW, AM I GLAD TO SEE YOU! WE WERE LOST... WE GOT TURNED COMPLETELY AROUND!
YOU REMEMBER SNOOPY, DON'T YOU? I BROUGHT HIM ALONG AS SORT OF A BODYGUARD
HI YA, PAL! HOW'S THE OL' SHORTSTOP?
PSST...WHAT IS IT WITH THIS KID AND THE GOGGLES?
SCHULZ

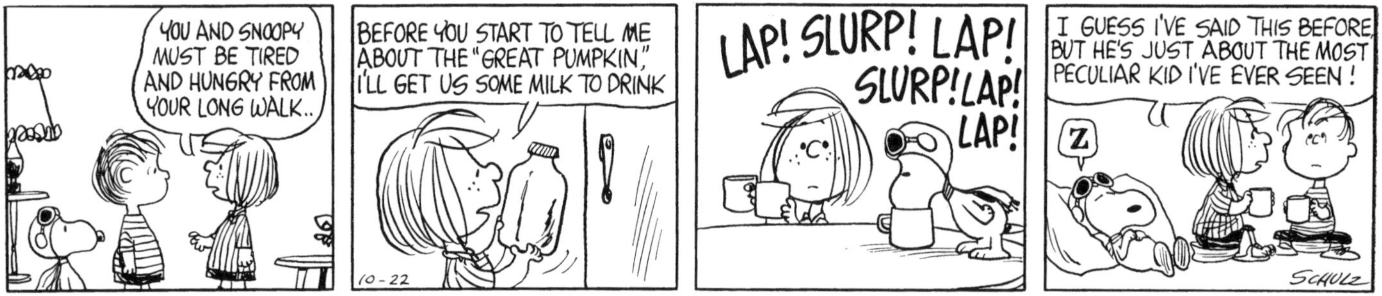
YOU AND SNOOPY MUST BE TIRED AND HUNGRY FROM YOUR LONG WALK..
BEFORE YOU START TO TELL ME ABOUT THE "GREAT PUMPKIN," I'LL GET US SOME MILK TO DRINK
10-22
LAP! SLURP! LAP! SLURP! LAP! LAP!
I GUESS I'VE SAID THIS BEFORE, BUT HE'S JUST ABOUT THE MOST PECULIAR KID I'VE EVER SEEN!
Z
SCHULZ

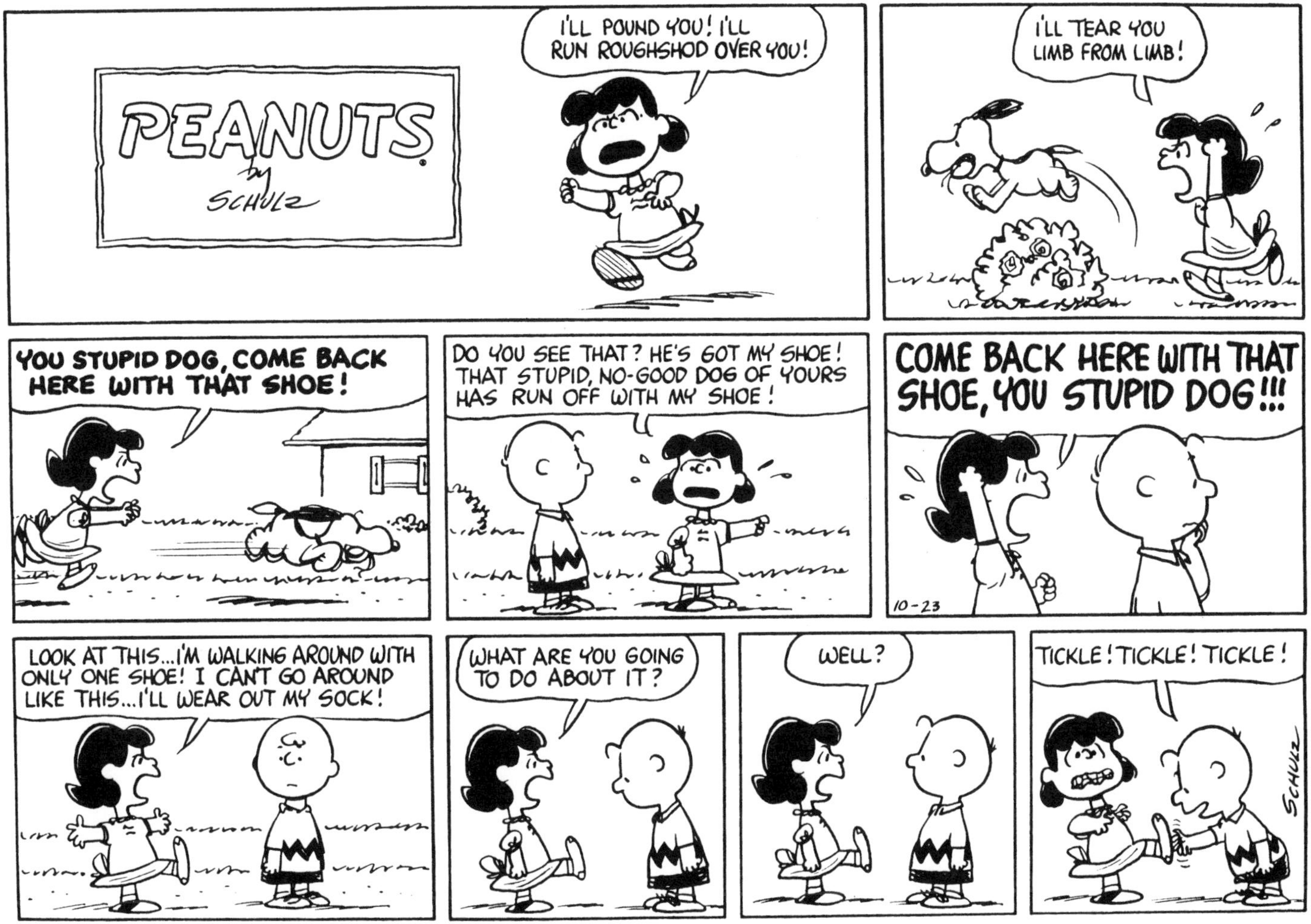
PEANUTS
by SCHULZ
I'LL POUND YOU! I'LL RUN ROUGHSHOD OVER YOU!
I'LL TEAR YOU LIMB FROM LIMB!
YOU STUPID DOG, COME BACK HERE WITH THAT SHOE!
DO YOU SEE THAT? HE'S GOT MY SHOE! THAT STUPID, NO-GOOD DOG OF YOURS HAS RUN OFF WITH MY SHOE!
COME BACK HERE WITH THAT SHOE, YOU STUPID DOG!!!
10-23
LOOK AT THIS...I'M WALKING AROUND WITH ONLY ONE SHOE! I CAN'T GO AROUND LIKE THIS...I'LL WEAR OUT MY SOCK!
WHAT ARE YOU GOING TO DO ABOUT IT?
WELL?
TICKLE! TICKLE! TICKLE!
SCHULZ

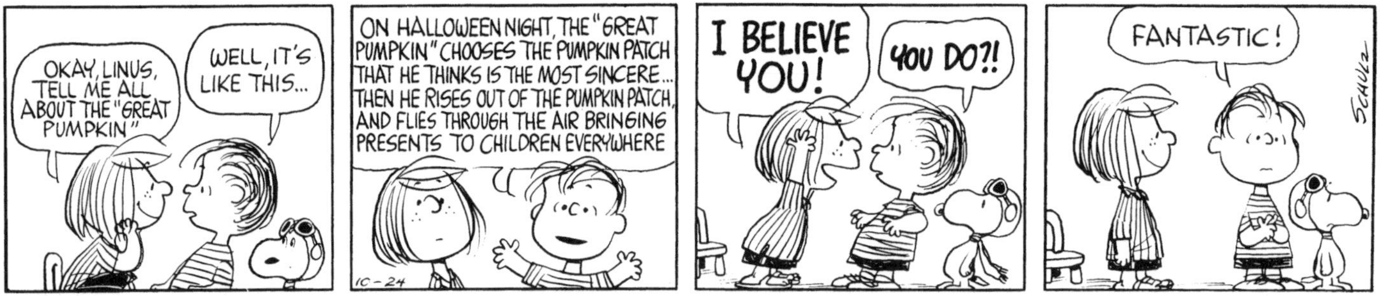
OKAY, LINUS, TELL ME ALL ABOUT THE "GREAT PUMPKIN"
WELL, IT'S LIKE THIS...
ON HALLOWEEN NIGHT, THE "GREAT PUMPKIN" CHOOSES THE PUMPKIN PATCH THAT HE THINKS IS THE MOST SINCERE... THEN HE RISES OUT OF THE PUMPKIN PATCH, AND FLIES THROUGH THE AIR BRINGING PRESENTS TO CHILDREN EVERYWHERE
10-24
I BELIEVE YOU!
YOU DO?!
FANTASTIC!
SCHULZ

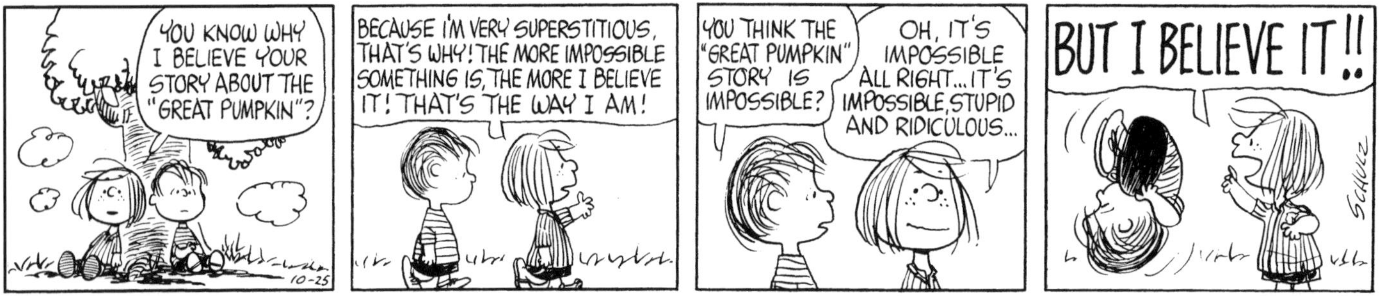
YOU KNOW WHY I BELIEVE YOUR STORY ABOUT THE "GREAT PUMPKIN"?
10-25
BECAUSE I'M VERY SUPERSTITIOUS, THAT'S WHY! THE MORE IMPOSSIBLE SOMETHING IS, THE MORE I BELIEVE IT! THAT'S THE WAY I AM!
YOU THINK THE "GREAT PUMPKIN" STORY IS IMPOSSIBLE?
OH, IT'S IMPOSSIBLE ALL RIGHT... IT'S IMPOSSIBLE, STUPID AND RIDICULOUS...
BUT I BELIEVE IT!!
SCHULZ

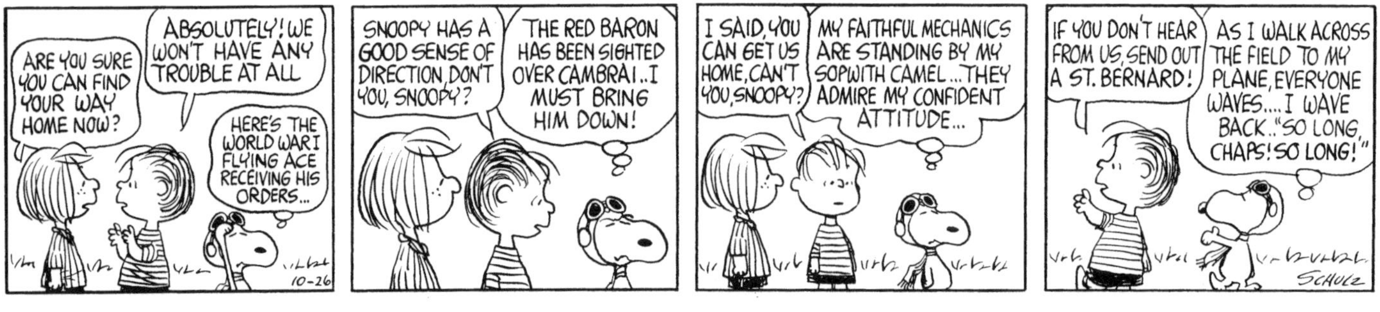
ARE YOU SURE YOU CAN FIND YOUR WAY HOME NOW?
ABSOLUTELY! WE WON'T HAVE ANY TROUBLE AT ALL
HERE'S THE WORLD WAR I FLYING ACE RECEIVING HIS ORDERS...
10-26
SNOOPY HAS A GOOD SENSE OF DIRECTION, DON'T YOU, SNOOPY?
THE RED BARON HAS BEEN SIGHTED OVER CAMBRAI.. I MUST BRING HIM DOWN!
I SAID, YOU CAN GET US HOME, CAN'T YOU, SNOOPY?
MY FAITHFUL MECHANICS ARE STANDING BY MY SOPWITH CAMEL... THEY ADMIRE MY CONFIDENT ATTITUDE...
IF YOU DON'T HEAR FROM US, SEND OUT A ST. BERNARD!
AS I WALK ACROSS THE FIELD TO MY PLANE, EVERYONE WAVES.... I WAVE BACK.."SO LONG, CHAPS! SO LONG!"
SCHULZ

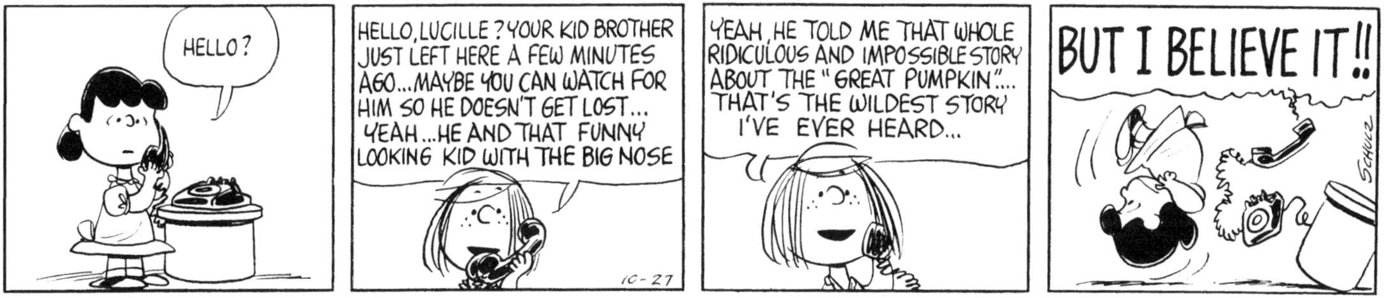
HELLO?
HELLO, LUCILLE? YOUR KID BROTHER JUST LEFT HERE A FEW MINUTES AGO...MAYBE YOU CAN WATCH FOR HIM SO HE DOESN'T GET LOST... YEAH...HE AND THAT FUNNY LOOKING KID WITH THE BIG NOSE
YEAH, HE TOLD ME THAT WHOLE RIDICULOUS AND IMPOSSIBLE STORY ABOUT THE "GREAT PUMPKIN"... THAT'S THE WILDEST STORY I'VE EVER HEARD...
BUT I BELIEVE IT!!

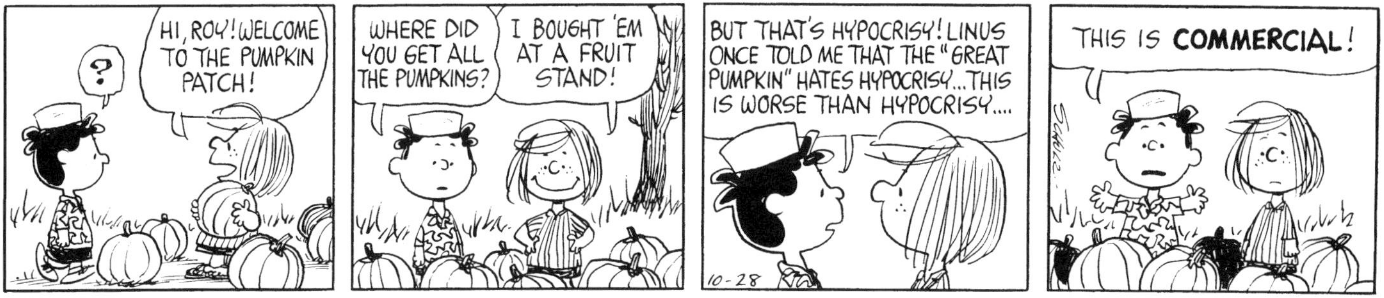
?
HI, ROY! WELCOME TO THE PUMPKIN PATCH!
WHERE DID YOU GET ALL THE PUMPKINS?
I BOUGHT 'EM AT A FRUIT STAND!
BUT THAT'S HYPOCRISY! LINUS ONCE TOLD ME THAT THE "GREAT PUMPKIN" HATES HYPOCRISY...THIS IS WORSE THAN HYPOCRISY....
THIS IS COMMERCIAL!

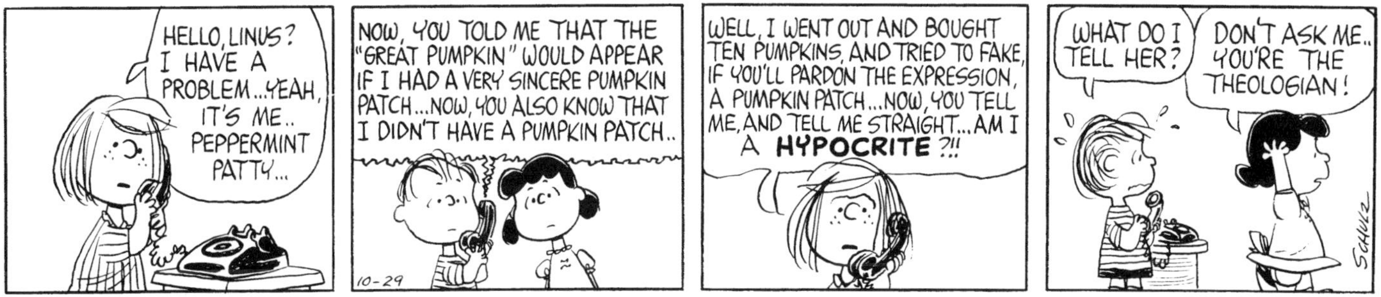
HELLO, LINUS? I HAVE A PROBLEM...YEAH, IT'S ME.. PEPPERMINT PATTY...
NOW, YOU TOLD ME THAT THE "GREAT PUMPKIN" WOULD APPEAR IF I HAD A VERY SINCERE PUMPKIN PATCH...NOW, YOU ALSO KNOW THAT I DIDN'T HAVE A PUMPKIN PATCH..
WELL, I WENT OUT AND BOUGHT TEN PUMPKINS, AND TRIED TO FAKE, IF YOU'LL PARDON THE EXPRESSION, A PUMPKIN PATCH...NOW, YOU TELL ME, AND TELL ME STRAIGHT...AM I A HYPOCRITE?!!
WHAT DO I TELL HER?
DON'T ASK ME.. YOU'RE THE THEOLOGIAN!

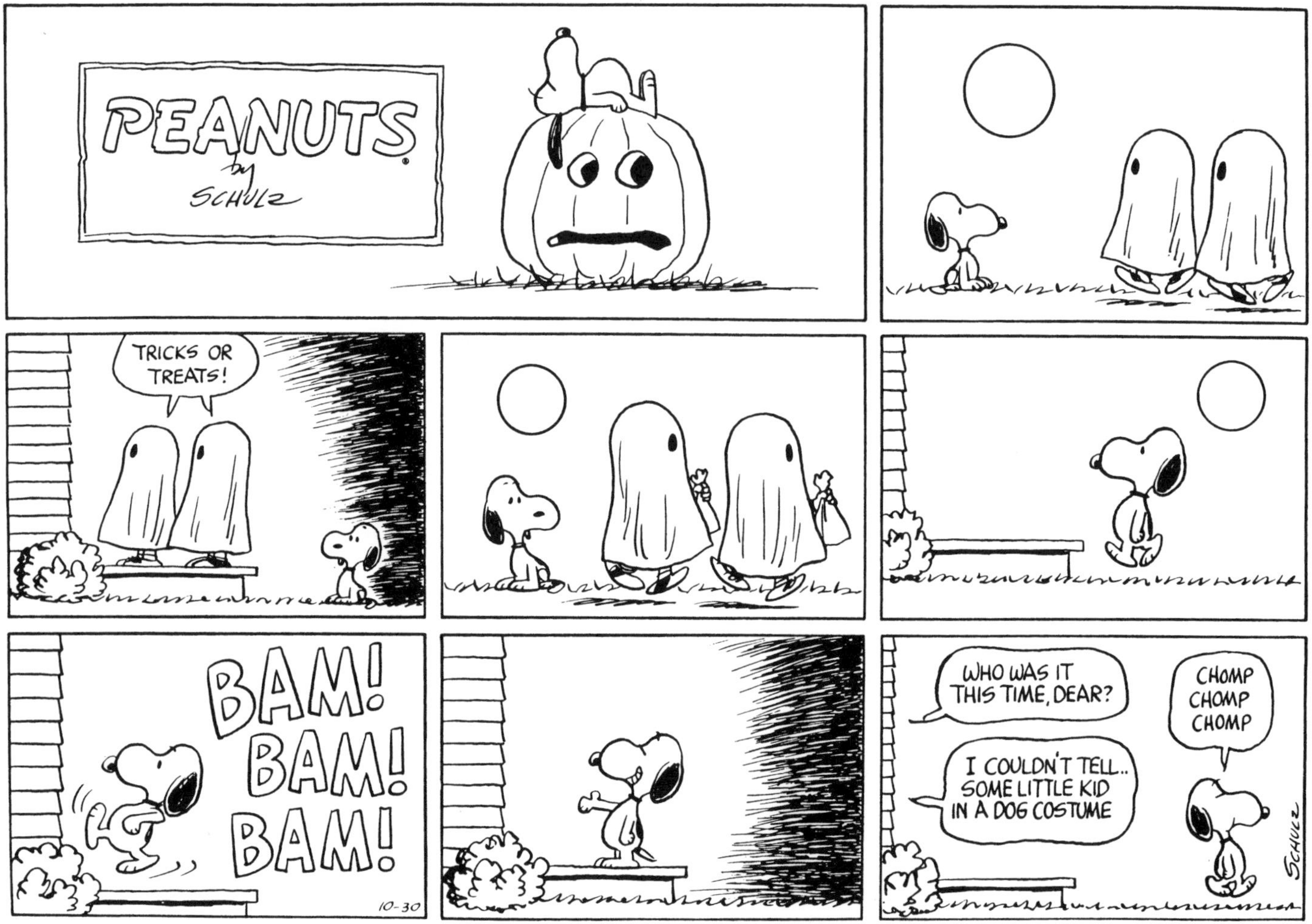
PEANUTS
by
SCHULZ
TRICKS OR TREATS!
BAM! BAM! BAM!
10-30
WHO WAS IT THIS TIME, DEAR?
CHOMP CHOMP CHOMP
I COULDN'T TELL.. SOME LITTLE KID IN A DOG COSTUME
SCHULZ

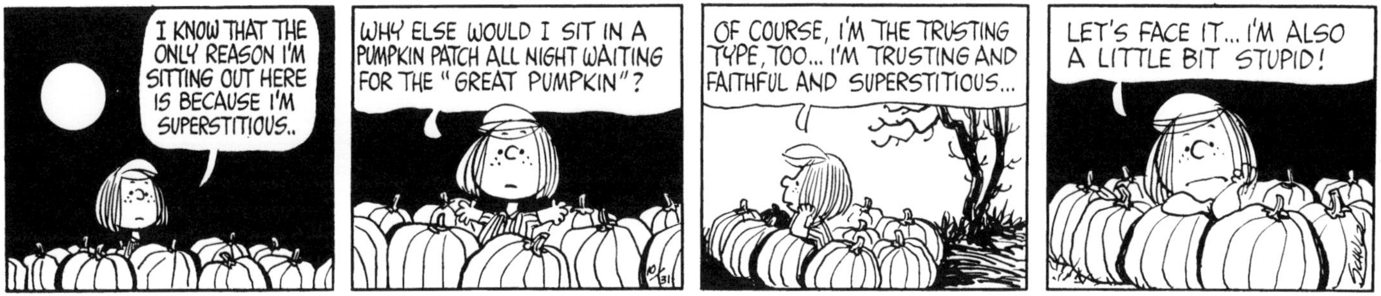
I KNOW THAT THE ONLY REASON I'M SITTING OUT HERE IS BECAUSE I'M SUPERSTITIOUS..
WHY ELSE WOULD I SIT IN A PUMPKIN PATCH ALL NIGHT WAITING FOR THE "GREAT PUMPKIN"?
OF COURSE, I'M THE TRUSTING TYPE, TOO... I'M TRUSTING AND FAITHFUL AND SUPERSTITIOUS...
LET'S FACE IT... I'M ALSO A LITTLE BIT STUPID!

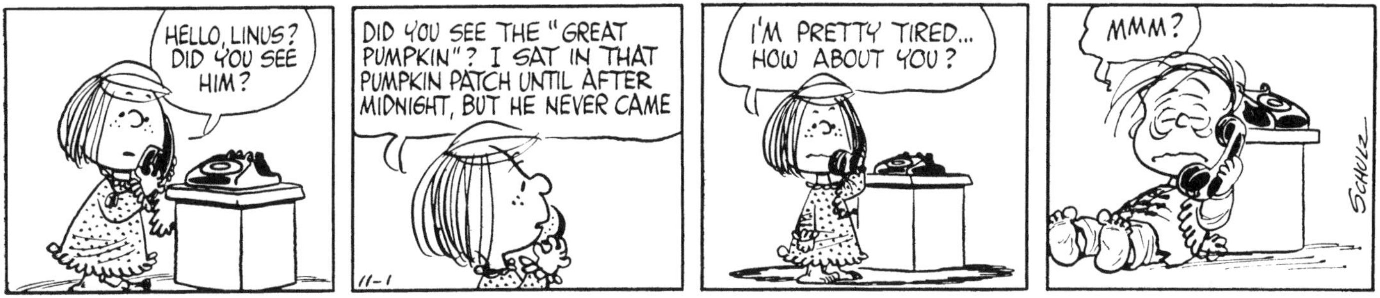
HELLO, LINUS? DID YOU SEE HIM?
DID YOU SEE THE "GREAT PUMPKIN"? I SAT IN THAT PUMPKIN PATCH UNTIL AFTER MIDNIGHT, BUT HE NEVER CAME
I'M PRETTY TIRED... HOW ABOUT YOU?
MMM?

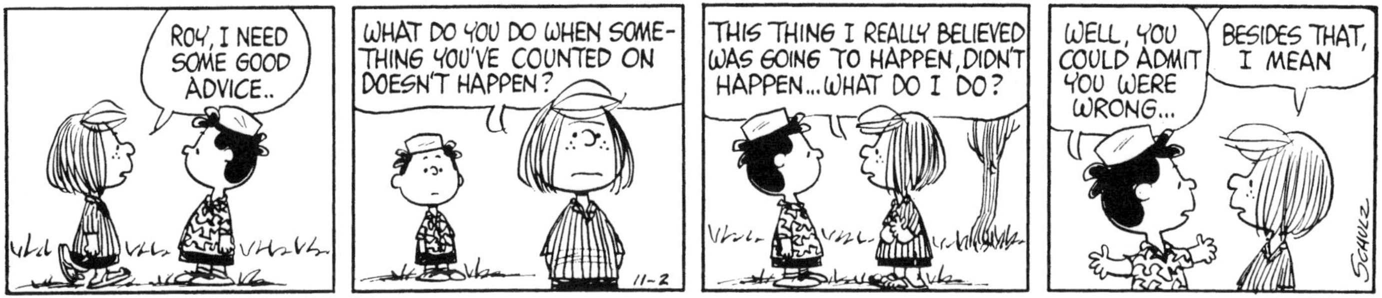
ROY, I NEED SOME GOOD ADVICE..
WHAT DO YOU DO WHEN SOMETHING YOU'VE COUNTED ON DOESN'T HAPPEN?
THIS THING I REALLY BELIEVED WAS GOING TO HAPPEN, DIDN'T HAPPEN... WHAT DO I DO?
WELL, YOU COULD ADMIT YOU WERE WRONG...
BESIDES THAT, I MEAN

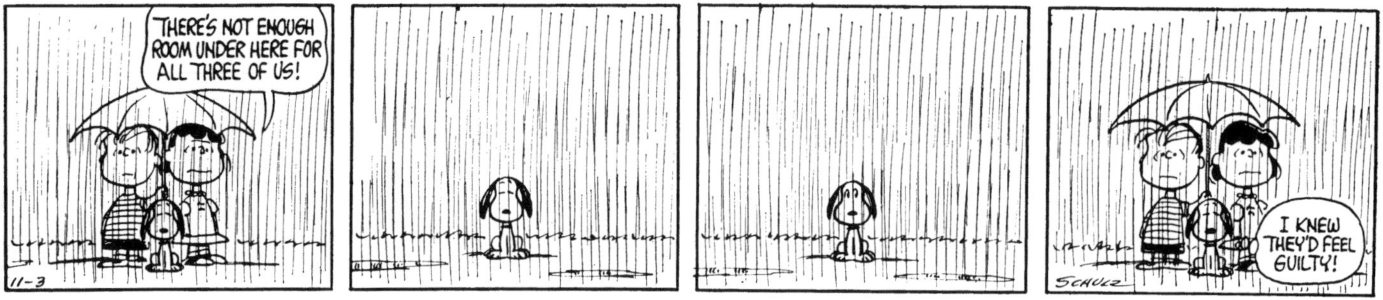
11-3
THERE'S NOT ENOUGH ROOM UNDER HERE FOR ALL THREE OF US!
I KNEW THEY'D FEEL GUILTY!
SCHULZ

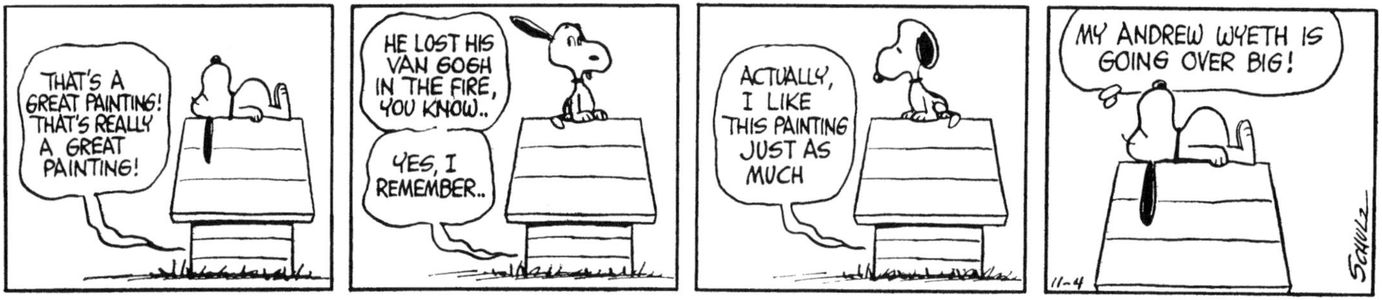
THAT'S A GREAT PAINTING! THAT'S REALLY A GREAT PAINTING!
HE LOST HIS VAN GOGH IN THE FIRE, YOU KNOW..
YES, I REMEMBER..
ACTUALLY, I LIKE THIS PAINTING JUST AS MUCH
MY ANDREW WYETH IS GOING OVER BIG!
11-4
SCHULZ

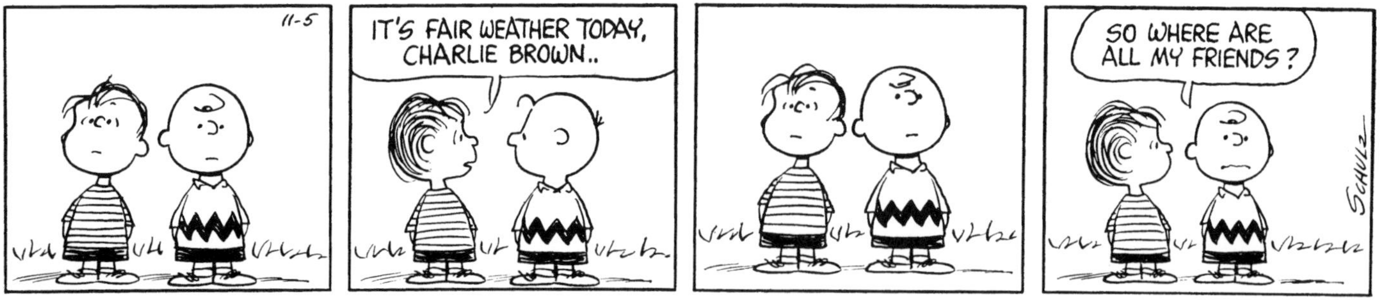
11-5
IT'S FAIR WEATHER TODAY, CHARLIE BROWN..
SO WHERE ARE ALL MY FRIENDS?
SCHULZ

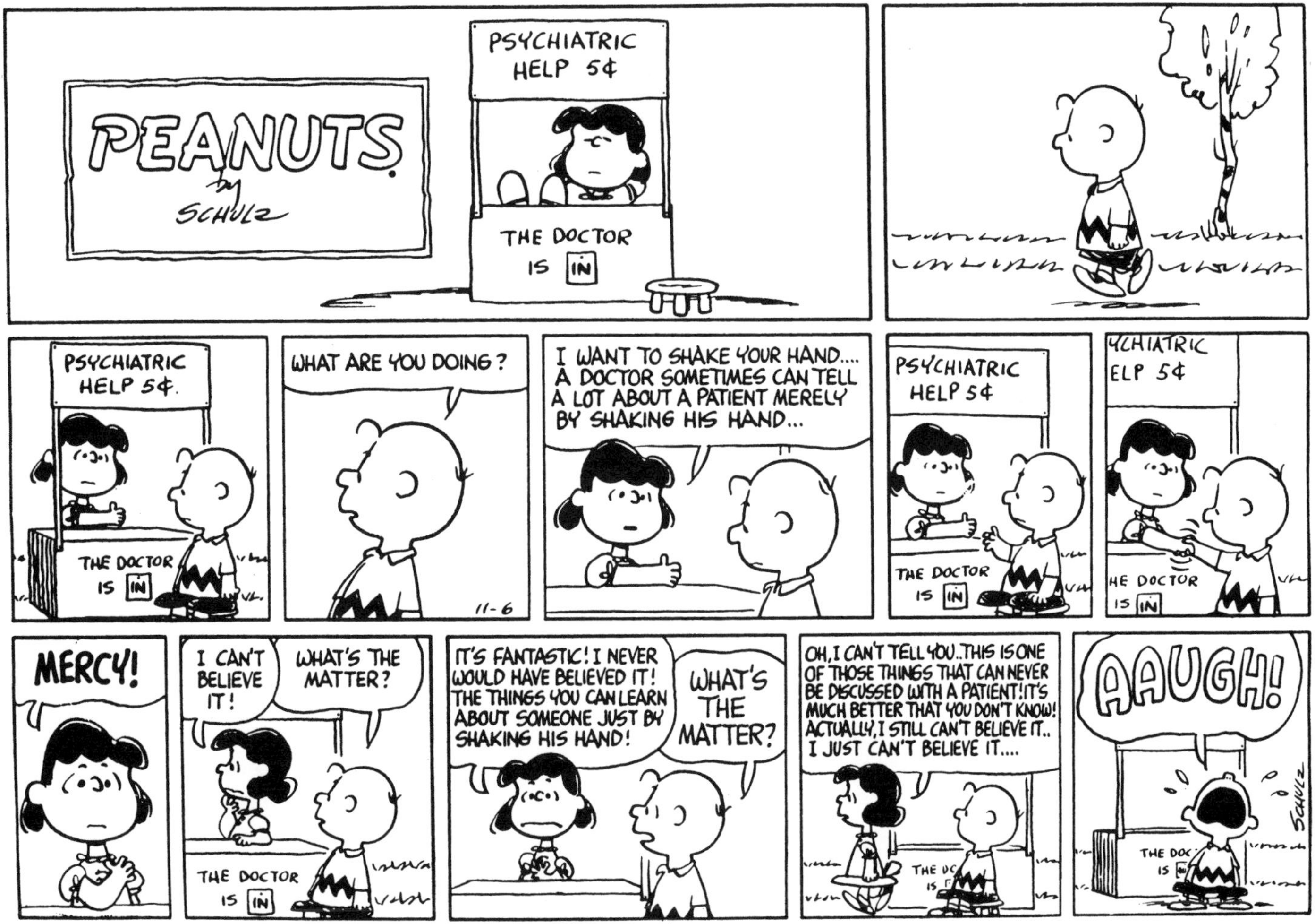

PEANUTS
by SCHULZ
PSYCHIATRIC HELP 5¢
THE DOCTOR IS IN
PSYCHIATRIC HELP 5¢
THE DOCTOR IS IN
WHAT ARE YOU DOING?
11-6
I WANT TO SHAKE YOUR HAND.... A DOCTOR SOMETIMES CAN TELL A LOT ABOUT A PATIENT MERELY BY SHAKING HIS HAND...
PSYCHIATRIC HELP 5¢
THE DOCTOR IS IN
YCHIATRIC ELP 5¢
HE DOCTOR IS IN
MERCY!
I CAN'T BELIEVE IT!
WHAT'S THE MATTER?
THE DOCTOR IS IN
IT'S FANTASTIC! I NEVER WOULD HAVE BELIEVED IT! THE THINGS YOU CAN LEARN ABOUT SOMEONE JUST BY SHAKING HIS HAND!
WHAT'S THE MATTER?
OH, I CAN'T TELL YOU..THIS IS ONE OF THOSE THINGS THAT CAN NEVER BE DISCUSSED WITH A PATIENT! IT'S MUCH BETTER THAT YOU DON'T KNOW! ACTUALLY, I STILL CAN'T BELIEVE IT.. I JUST CAN'T BELIEVE IT....
AAUGH!
SCHULZ

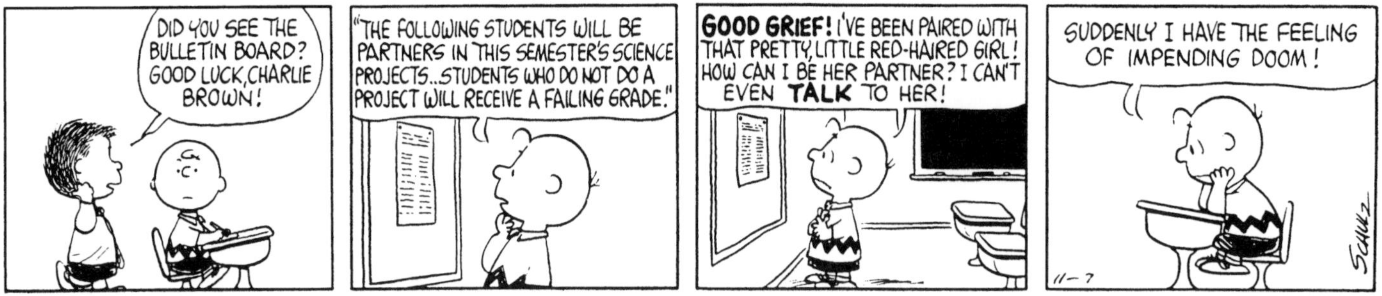
DID YOU SEE THE BULLETIN BOARD? GOOD LUCK, CHARLIE BROWN!
"THE FOLLOWING STUDENTS WILL BE PARTNERS IN THIS SEMESTER'S SCIENCE PROJECTS...STUDENTS WHO DO NOT DO A PROJECT WILL RECEIVE A FAILING GRADE."
GOOD GRIEF! I'VE BEEN PAIRED WITH THAT PRETTY, LITTLE RED-HAIRED GIRL! HOW CAN I BE HER PARTNER? I CAN'T EVEN TALK TO HER!
SUDDENLY I HAVE THE FEELING OF IMPENDING DOOM!
11-7
SCHULZ

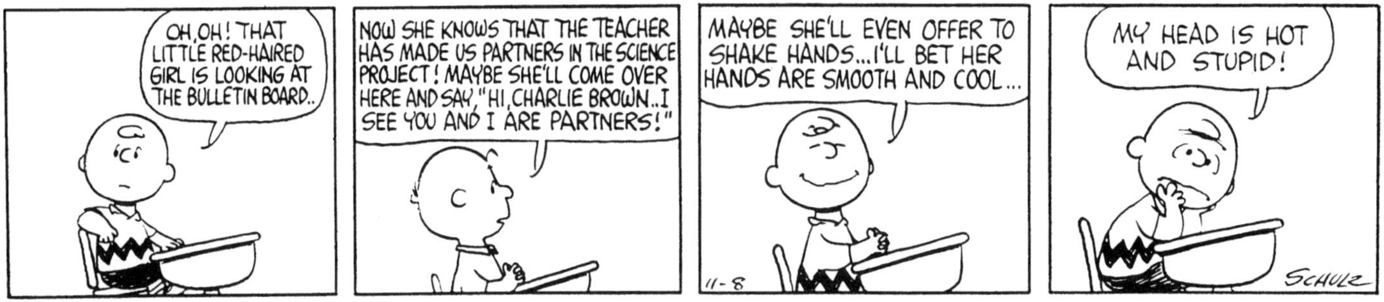
OH, OH! THAT LITTLE RED-HAIRED GIRL IS LOOKING AT THE BULLETIN BOARD..
NOW SHE KNOWS THAT THE TEACHER HAS MADE US PARTNERS IN THE SCIENCE PROJECT! MAYBE SHE'LL COME OVER HERE AND SAY, "HI, CHARLIE BROWN..I SEE YOU AND I ARE PARTNERS!"
MAYBE SHE'LL EVEN OFFER TO SHAKE HANDS...I'LL BET HER HANDS ARE SMOOTH AND COOL...
11-8
MY HEAD IS HOT AND STUPID!
SCHULZ

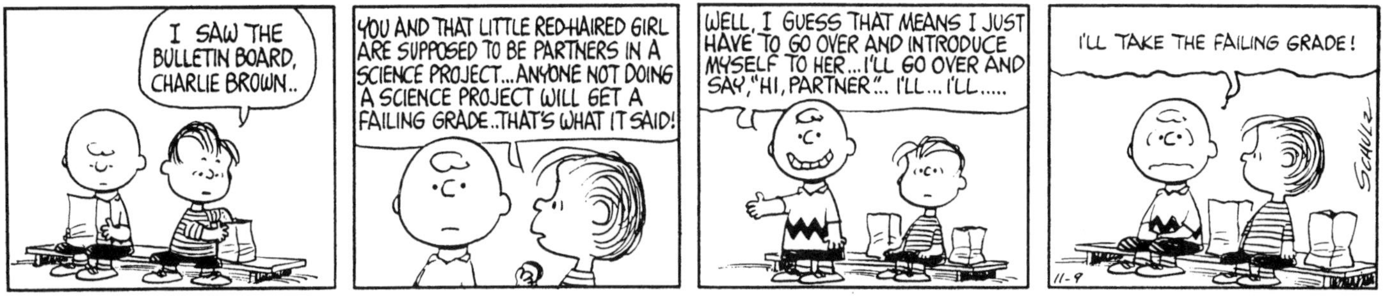
I SAW THE BULLETIN BOARD, CHARLIE BROWN..
YOU AND THAT LITTLE RED-HAIRED GIRL ARE SUPPOSED TO BE PARTNERS IN A SCIENCE PROJECT...ANYONE NOT DOING A SCIENCE PROJECT WILL GET A FAILING GRADE..THAT'S WHAT IT SAID!
WELL, I GUESS THAT MEANS I JUST HAVE TO GO OVER AND INTRODUCE MYSELF TO HER...I'LL GO OVER AND SAY, "HI, PARTNER"... I'LL... I'LL.....
I'LL TAKE THE FAILING GRADE!
11-9
SCHULZ

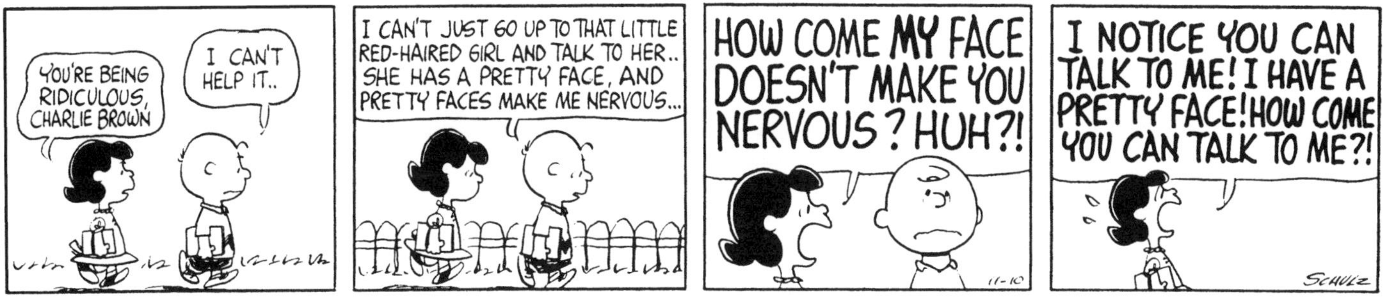
YOU'RE BEING RIDICULOUS, CHARLIE BROWN
I CAN'T HELP IT..
I CAN'T JUST GO UP TO THAT LITTLE RED-HAIRED GIRL AND TALK TO HER.. SHE HAS A PRETTY FACE, AND PRETTY FACES MAKE ME NERVOUS...
HOW COME **MY** FACE DOESN'T MAKE YOU NERVOUS? HUH?!
11-10
I NOTICE YOU CAN TALK TO ME! I HAVE A PRETTY FACE! HOW COME YOU CAN TALK TO ME?!
SCHULZ

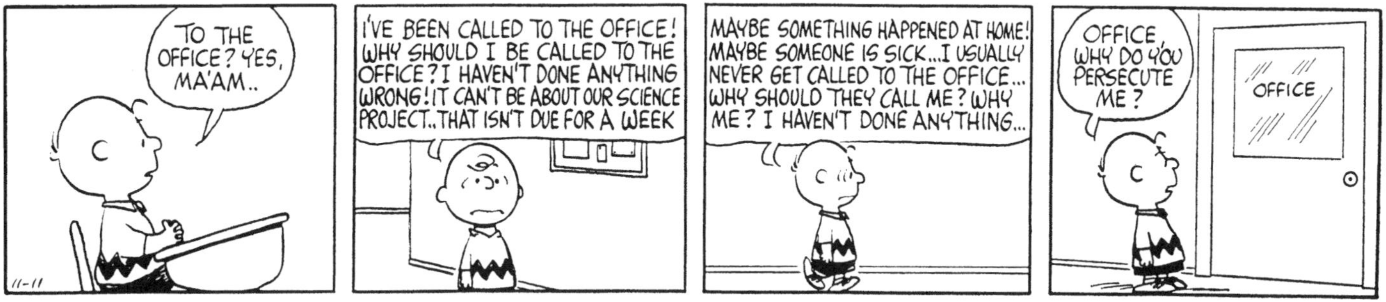
11-11
TO THE OFFICE? YES, MA'AM..
I'VE BEEN CALLED TO THE OFFICE! WHY SHOULD I BE CALLED TO THE OFFICE? I HAVEN'T DONE ANYTHING WRONG! IT CAN'T BE ABOUT OUR SCIENCE PROJECT.. THAT ISN'T DUE FOR A WEEK
MAYBE SOMETHING HAPPENED AT HOME! MAYBE SOMEONE IS SICK...I USUALLY NEVER GET CALLED TO THE OFFICE... WHY SHOULD THEY CALL ME? WHY ME? I HAVEN'T DONE ANYTHING...
OFFICE, WHY DO YOU PERSECUTE ME?
OFFICE

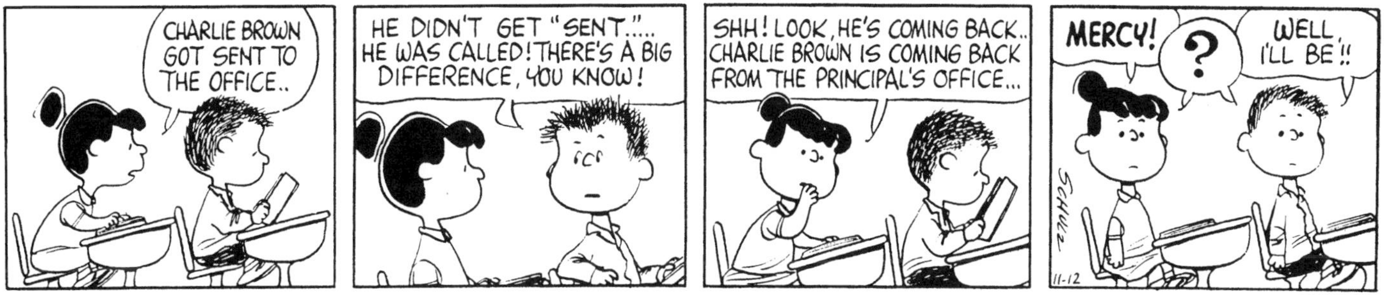
CHARLIE BROWN GOT SENT TO THE OFFICE..
HE DIDN'T GET "SENT."... HE WAS CALLED! THERE'S A BIG DIFFERENCE, YOU KNOW!
SHH! LOOK, HE'S COMING BACK.. CHARLIE BROWN IS COMING BACK FROM THE PRINCIPAL'S OFFICE...
MERCY!
?
WELL, I'LL BE!!
SCHULZ
11-12

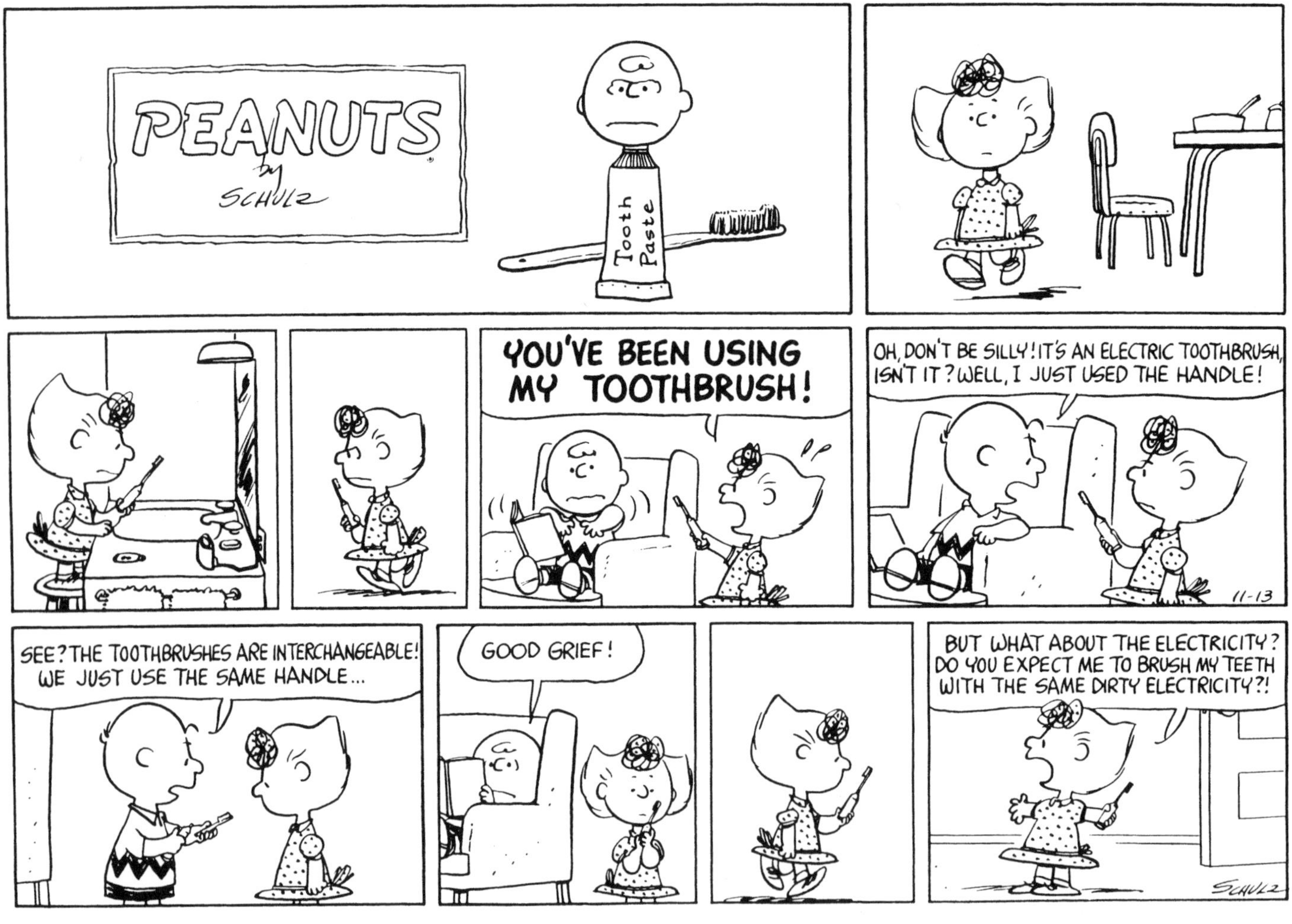
PEANUTS
by SCHULZ
Tooth Paste
YOU'VE BEEN USING MY TOOTHBRUSH!
OH, DON'T BE SILLY! IT'S AN ELECTRIC TOOTHBRUSH, ISN'T IT? WELL, I JUST USED THE HANDLE!
11-13
SEE? THE TOOTHBRUSHES ARE INTERCHANGEABLE! WE JUST USE THE SAME HANDLE...
GOOD GRIEF!
BUT WHAT ABOUT THE ELECTRICITY? DO YOU EXPECT ME TO BRUSH MY TEETH WITH THE SAME DIRTY ELECTRICITY?!
SCHULZ

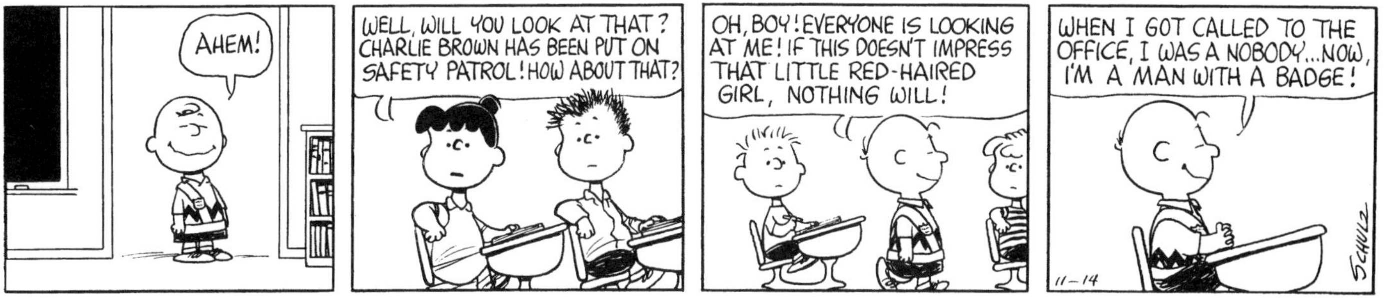
AHEM!
WELL, WILL YOU LOOK AT THAT? CHARLIE BROWN HAS BEEN PUT ON SAFETY PATROL! HOW ABOUT THAT?
OH, BOY! EVERYONE IS LOOKING AT ME! IF THIS DOESN'T IMPRESS THAT LITTLE RED-HAIRED GIRL, NOTHING WILL!
WHEN I GOT CALLED TO THE OFFICE, I WAS A NOBODY...NOW, I'M A MAN WITH A BADGE!
SCHULZ
11-14

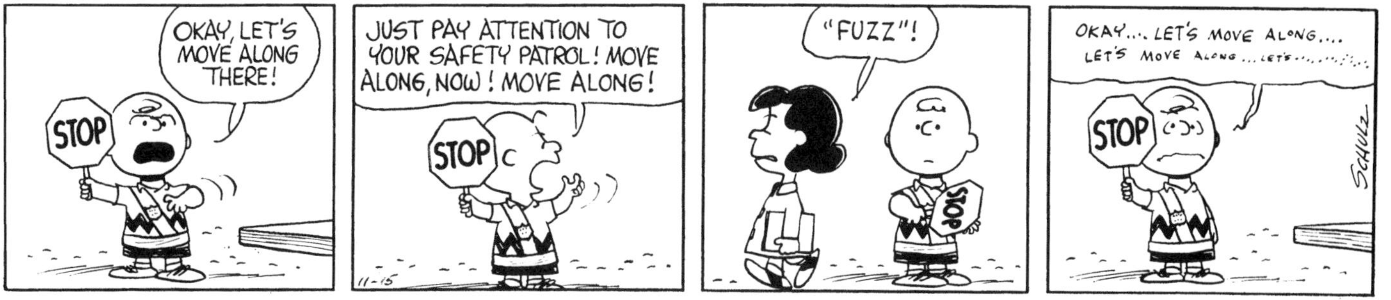
STOP
OKAY, LET'S MOVE ALONG THERE!
JUST PAY ATTENTION TO YOUR SAFETY PATROL! MOVE ALONG, NOW! MOVE ALONG!
STOP
11-15
"FUZZ"!
STOP
OKAY.... LET'S MOVE ALONG.... LET'S MOVE ALONG... LET'S...
STOP
SCHULZ

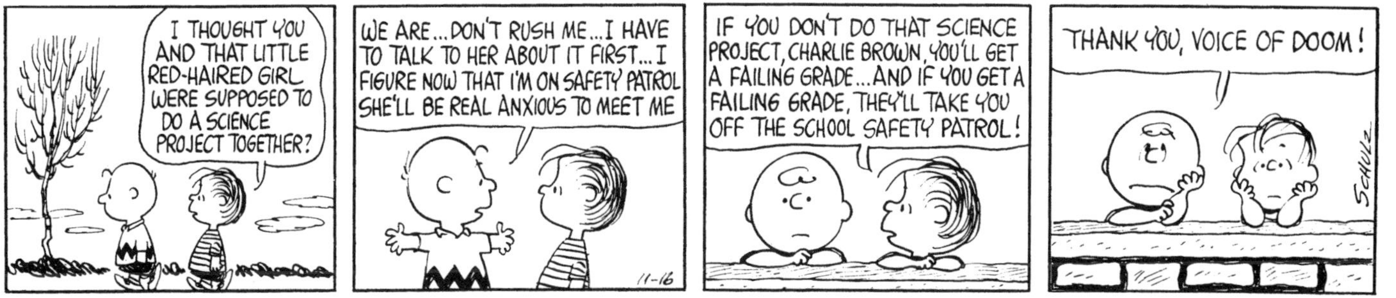
I THOUGHT YOU AND THAT LITTLE RED-HAIRED GIRL WERE SUPPOSED TO DO A SCIENCE PROJECT TOGETHER?
WE ARE...DON'T RUSH ME...I HAVE TO TALK TO HER ABOUT IT FIRST...I FIGURE NOW THAT I'M ON SAFETY PATROL SHE'LL BE REAL ANXIOUS TO MEET ME
11-16
IF YOU DON'T DO THAT SCIENCE PROJECT, CHARLIE BROWN, YOU'LL GET A FAILING GRADE...AND IF YOU GET A FAILING GRADE, THEY'LL TAKE YOU OFF THE SCHOOL SAFETY PATROL!
THANK YOU, VOICE OF DOOM!
SCHULZ

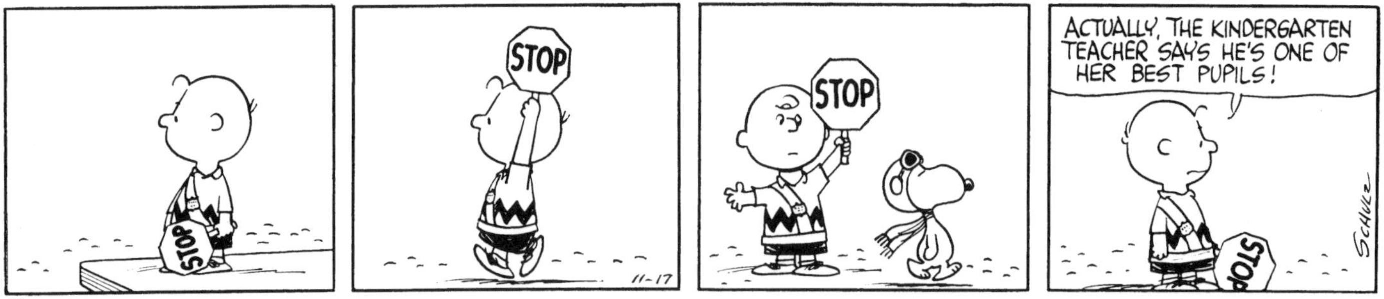
STOP
STOP
11-17
STOP
ACTUALLY, THE KINDERGARTEN TEACHER SAYS HE'S ONE OF HER BEST PUPILS!
STOP
SCHULZ

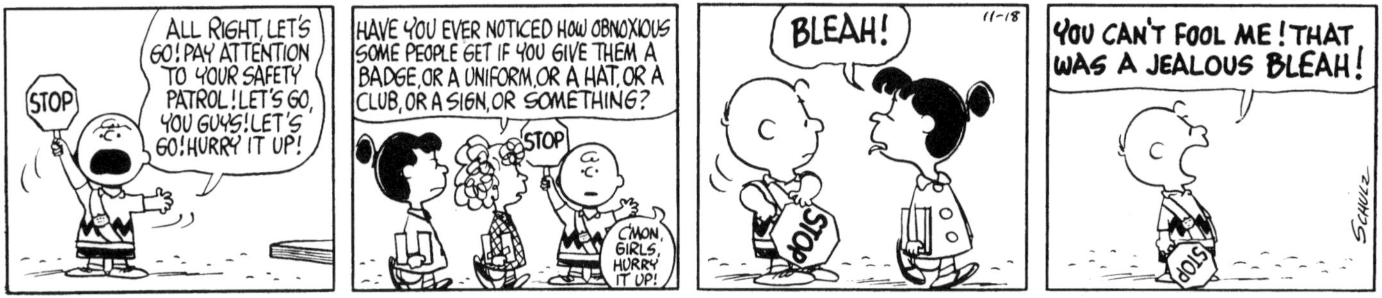
STOP
ALL RIGHT, LET'S GO! PAY ATTENTION TO YOUR SAFETY PATROL! LET'S GO, YOU GUYS! LET'S GO! HURRY IT UP!
HAVE YOU EVER NOTICED HOW OBNOXIOUS SOME PEOPLE GET IF YOU GIVE THEM A BADGE, OR A UNIFORM, OR A HAT, OR A CLUB, OR A SIGN, OR SOMETHING?
STOP
C'MON, GIRLS, HURRY IT UP!
11-18
BLEAH!
STOP
YOU CAN'T FOOL ME! THAT WAS A JEALOUS BLEAH!
STOP
SCHULZ

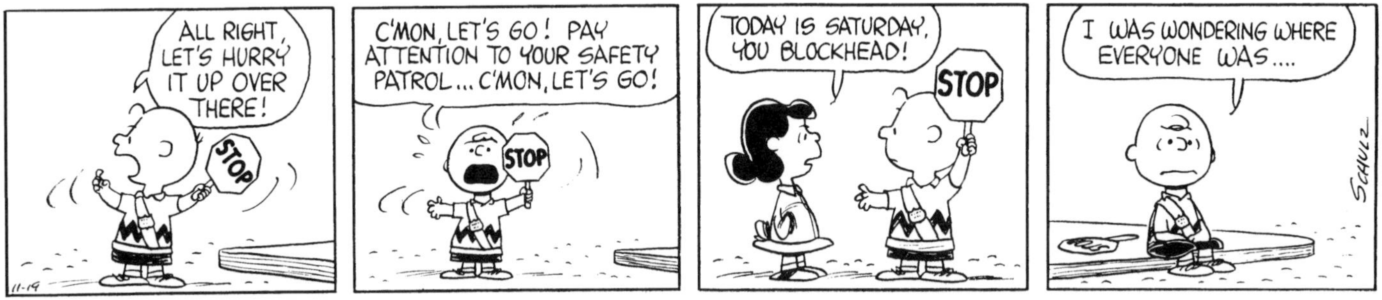
ALL RIGHT, LET'S HURRY IT UP OVER THERE!
STOP
11-19
C'MON, LET'S GO! PAY ATTENTION TO YOUR SAFETY PATROL... C'MON, LET'S GO!
STOP
TODAY IS SATURDAY, YOU BLOCKHEAD!
STOP
I WAS WONDERING WHERE EVERYONE WAS....
SCHULZ

PEANUTS
featuring
"Good ol' Charlie Brown"
BY SCHULZ
PSYCHIAT HELP 5¢
SIT DOWN, PLEASE
THANK YOU
THE DOCTOR IS IN
PSYCHIATRIC HELP 5¢
I'M GOING TO ASK YOU A QUESTION, AND I WANT YOU TO ANSWER ME TRUTHFULLY
THE DOCTOR IS IN
11-20
YOU SEE, PHYSICIANS CAN LEARN A LOT ABOUT A PATIENT BY ASKING WHAT MAY EVEN SOUND LIKE A VERY SIMPLE QUESTION..
ALL RIGHT, NOW ANSWER ME TRUTHFULLY... WHICH DO YOU PREFER, A SUNRISE OR A SUNSET?
WELL, A SUNSET, I GUESS..
THE DOCTOR IS IN
I THOUGHT SO! YOU'RE JUST THE TYPE! I MIGHT HAVE KNOWN! WHAT A DISAPPOINTMENT!
THE DOCTOR IS IN
PEOPLE WHO PREFER SUNSETS ARE DREAMERS! THEY ALWAYS GIVE UP! THEY ALWAYS LOOK BACK INSTEAD OF FORWARD! I JUST MIGHT HAVE KNOWN YOU WEREN'T A SUNRISE PERSON!
SUNRISERS ARE GO-GETTERS! THEY HAVE AMBITION AND DRIVE! GIVE ME A PERSON WHO LIKES A SUNRISE EVERY TIME! YES, SIR!
HE DOCTOR IS IN
I'M SORRY, CHARLIE BROWN...IF YOU PREFER SUNSETS TO SUNRISES, I CAN'T TAKE YOUR CASE...YOU'RE HOPELESS!
HE DOCTOR IS IN
ACTUALLY, I'VE ALWAYS SORT OF PREFERRED NOON!
THE DOCTOR IS IN
SCHULZ

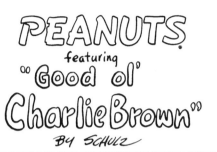

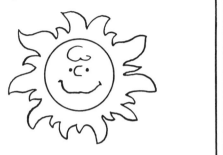

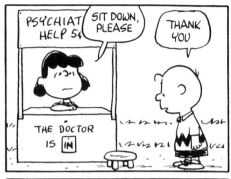

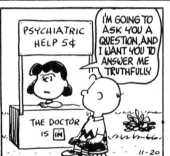

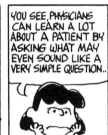

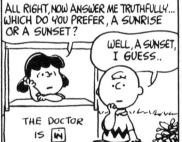

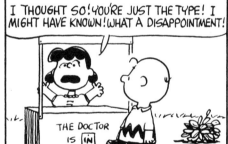

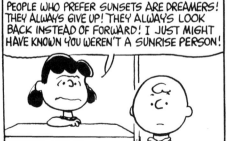

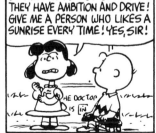

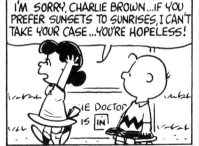

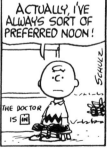

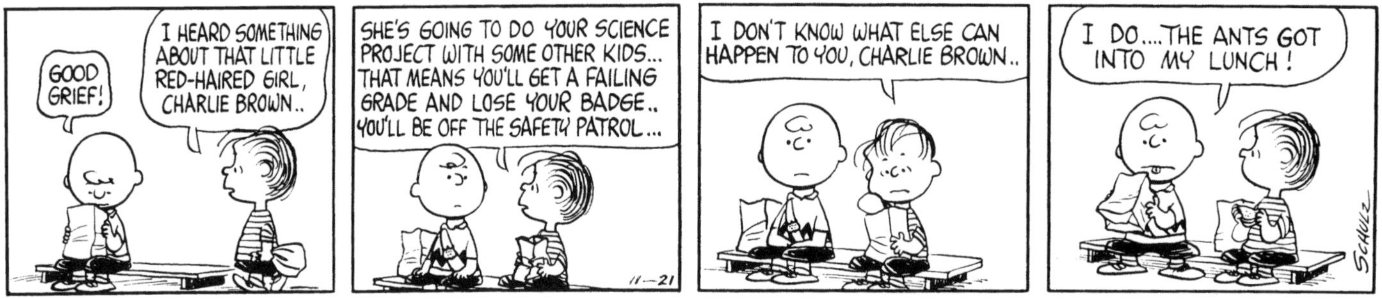
I HEARD SOMETHING ABOUT THAT LITTLE RED-HAIRED GIRL, CHARLIE BROWN..
GOOD GRIEF!
SHE'S GOING TO DO YOUR SCIENCE PROJECT WITH SOME OTHER KIDS... THAT MEANS YOU'LL GET A FAILING GRADE AND LOSE YOUR BADGE.. YOU'LL BE OFF THE SAFETY PATROL...
11-21
I DON'T KNOW WHAT ELSE CAN HAPPEN TO YOU, CHARLIE BROWN..
I DO....THE ANTS GOT INTO MY LUNCH!
SCHULZ

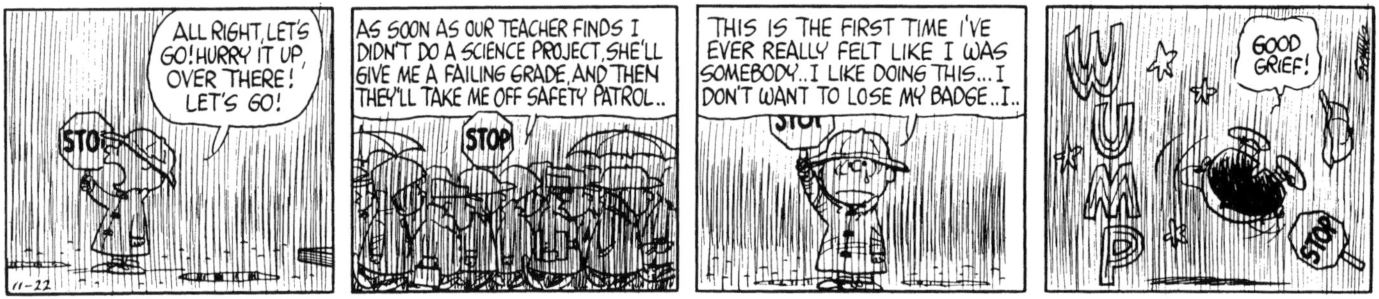
ALL RIGHT, LET'S GO! HURRY IT UP, OVER THERE! LET'S GO!
11-22
AS SOON AS OUR TEACHER FINDS I DIDN'T DO A SCIENCE PROJECT, SHE'LL GIVE ME A FAILING GRADE, AND THEN THEY'LL TAKE ME OFF SAFETY PATROL..
STOP
THIS IS THE FIRST TIME I'VE EVER REALLY FELT LIKE I WAS SOMEBODY.. I LIKE DOING THIS... I DON'T WANT TO LOSE MY BADGE.. I..
WUMP
GOOD GRIEF!
STOP
SCHULZ

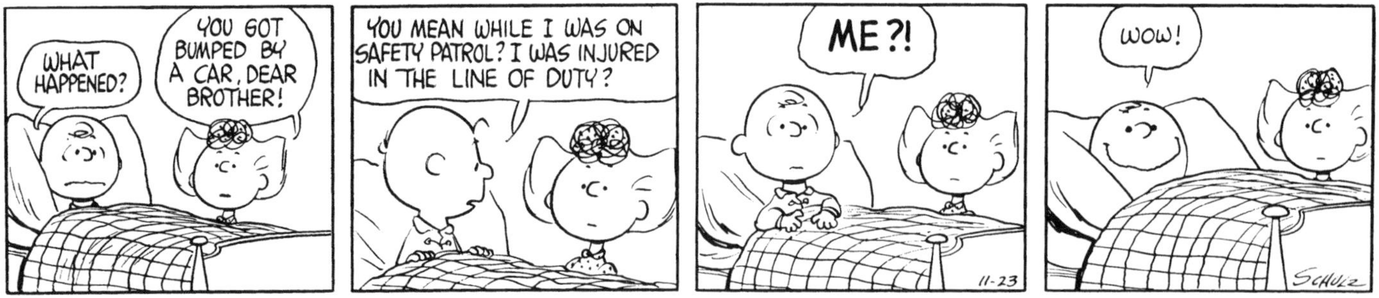
WHAT HAPPENED?
YOU GOT BUMPED BY A CAR, DEAR BROTHER!
YOU MEAN WHILE I WAS ON SAFETY PATROL? I WAS INJURED IN THE LINE OF DUTY?
ME?!
11-23
WOW!
SCHULZ

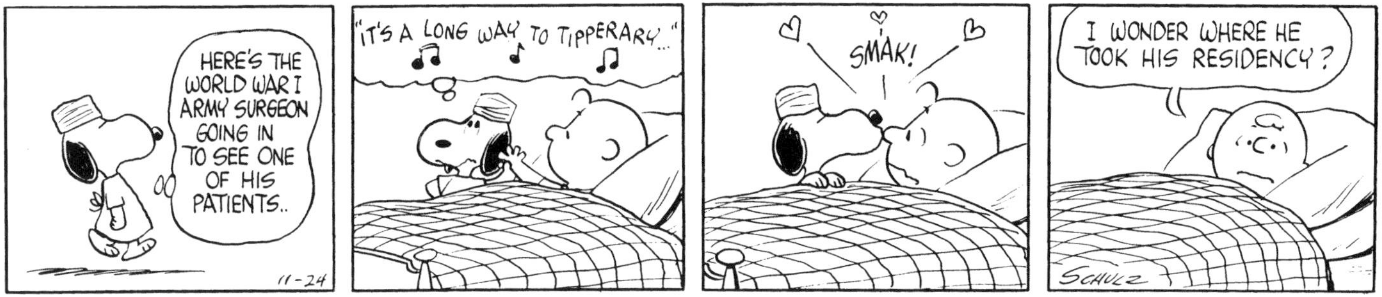
HERE'S THE WORLD WAR I ARMY SURGEON GOING IN TO SEE ONE OF HIS PATIENTS..
11-24
"IT'S A LONG WAY TO TIPPERARY..."
SMAK!
I WONDER WHERE HE TOOK HIS RESIDENCY?
SCHULZ

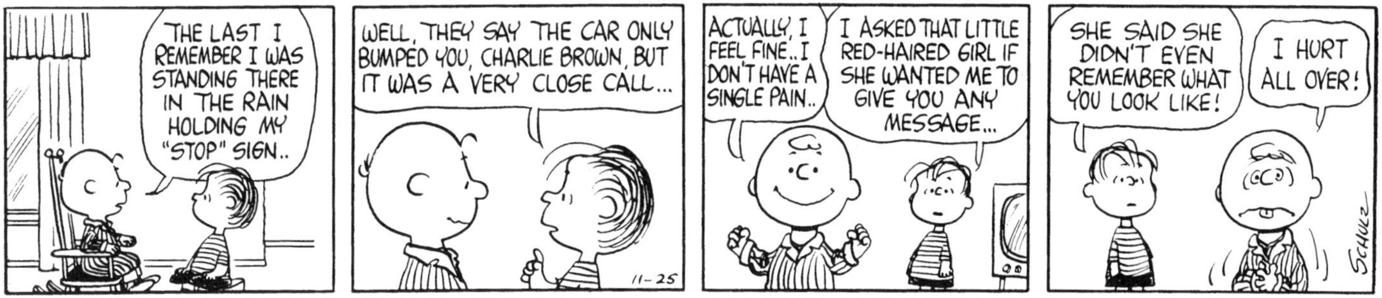
THE LAST I REMEMBER I WAS STANDING THERE IN THE RAIN HOLDING MY "STOP" SIGN..
WELL, THEY SAY THE CAR ONLY BUMPED YOU, CHARLIE BROWN, BUT IT WAS A VERY CLOSE CALL...
11-25
ACTUALLY, I FEEL FINE.. I DON'T HAVE A SINGLE PAIN..
I ASKED THAT LITTLE RED-HAIRED GIRL IF SHE WANTED ME TO GIVE YOU ANY MESSAGE...
SHE SAID SHE DIDN'T EVEN REMEMBER WHAT YOU LOOK LIKE!
I HURT ALL OVER!
SCHULZ

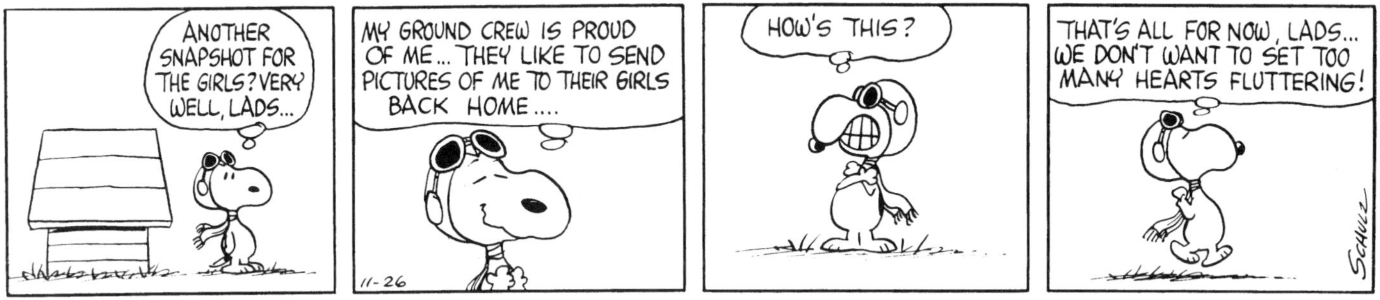
ANOTHER SNAPSHOT FOR THE GIRLS? VERY WELL, LADS...
MY GROUND CREW IS PROUD OF ME... THEY LIKE TO SEND PICTURES OF ME TO THEIR GIRLS BACK HOME....
11-26
HOW'S THIS?
THAT'S ALL FOR NOW, LADS... WE DON'T WANT TO SET TOO MANY HEARTS FLUTTERING!
SCHULZ

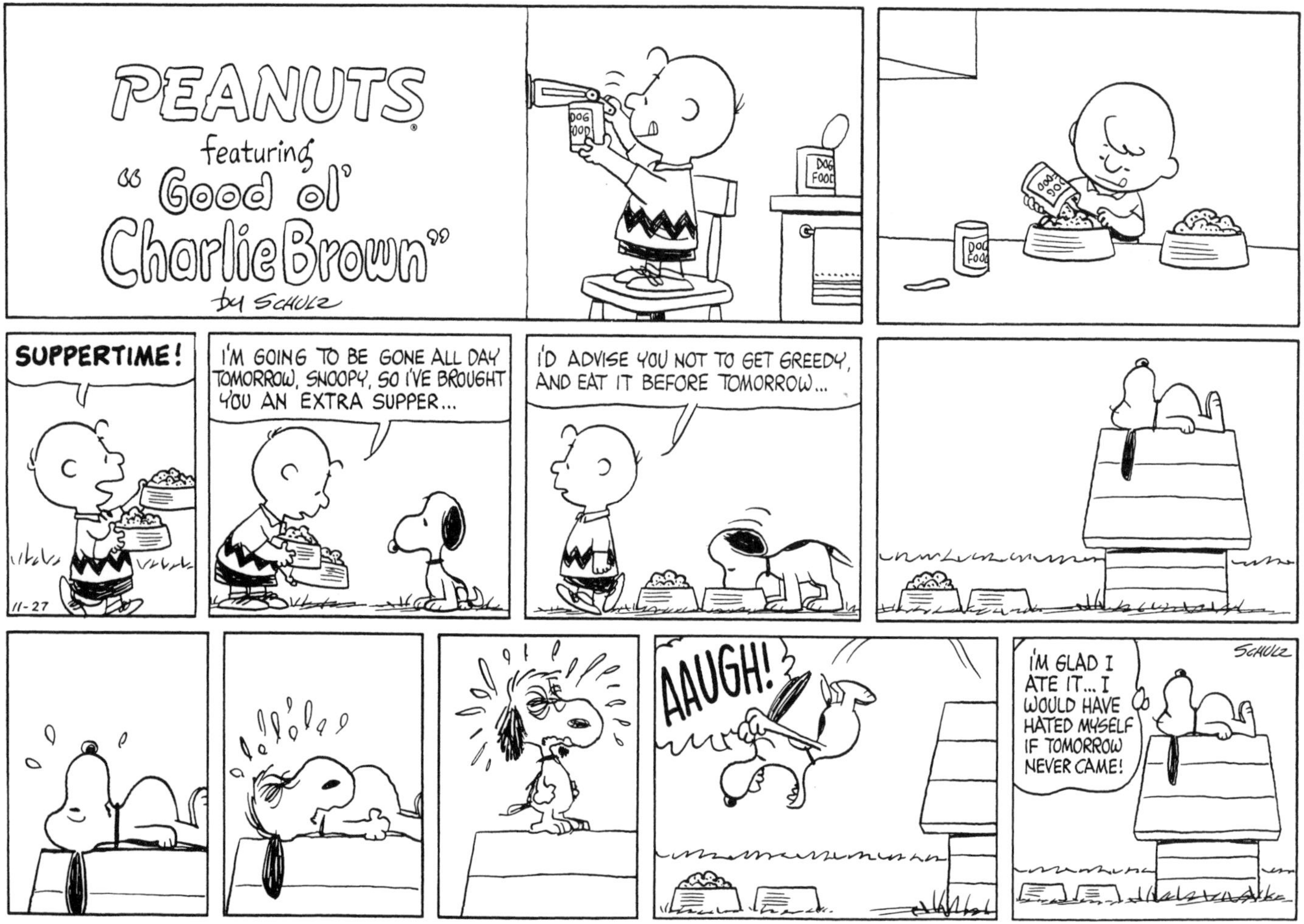

PEANUTS
featuring "Good ol' Charlie Brown"
by SCHULZ
DOG FOOD
DOG FOOD
DOG FOOD
DOG FOOD
SUPPERTIME!
11-27
I'M GOING TO BE GONE ALL DAY TOMORROW, SNOOPY, SO I'VE BROUGHT YOU AN EXTRA SUPPER...
I'D ADVISE YOU NOT TO GET GREEDY, AND EAT IT BEFORE TOMORROW...
AAUGH!
SCHULZ
I'M GLAD I ATE IT... I WOULD HAVE HATED MYSELF IF TOMORROW NEVER CAME!

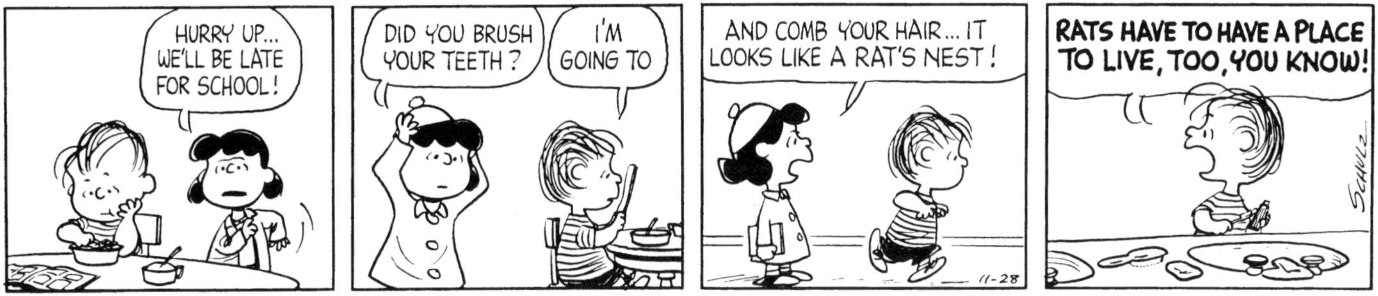
HURRY UP... WE'LL BE LATE FOR SCHOOL!
DID YOU BRUSH YOUR TEETH?
I'M GOING TO
AND COMB YOUR HAIR... IT LOOKS LIKE A RAT'S NEST!
11-28
RATS HAVE TO HAVE A PLACE TO LIVE, TOO, YOU KNOW!
SCHULZ

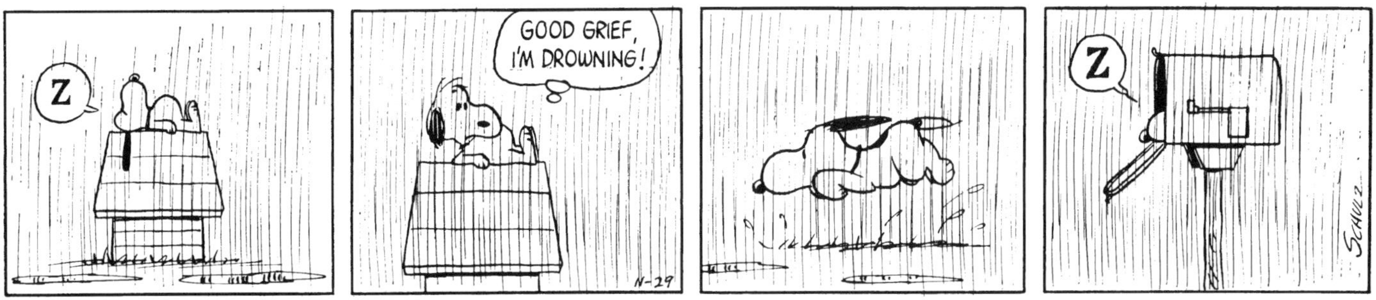
Z
GOOD GRIEF, I'M DROWNING!
11-29
Z
SCHULZ

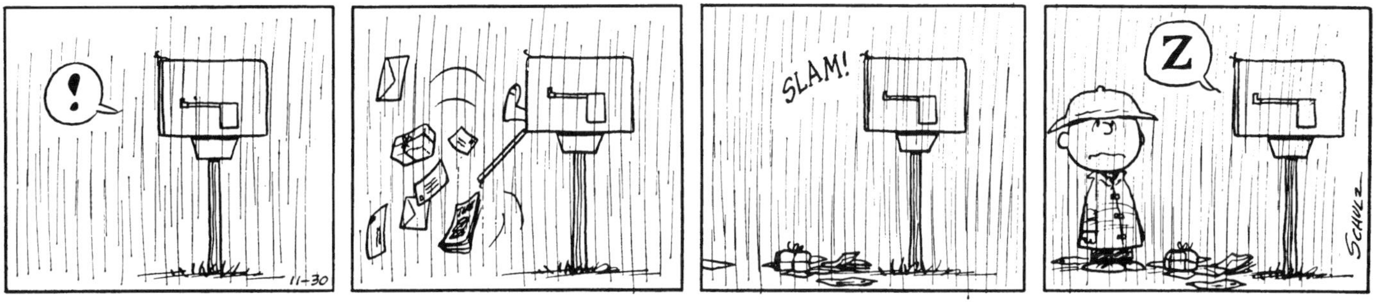
!
11-30
SLAM!
Z
SCHULZ

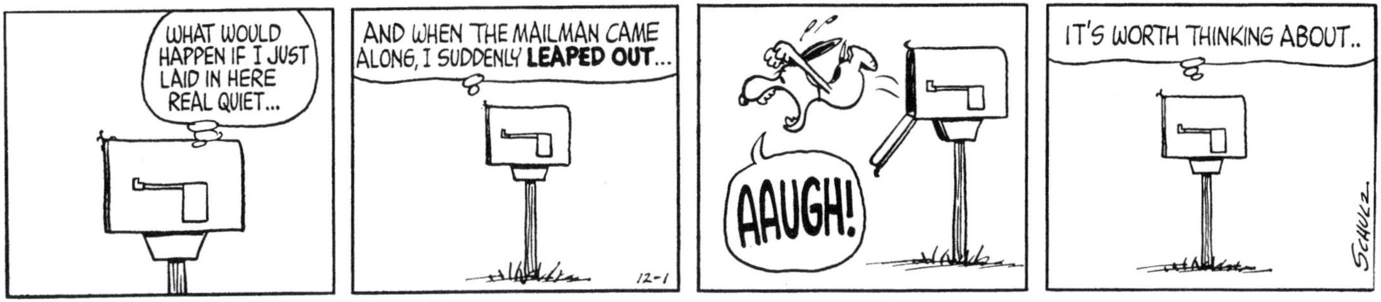
WHAT WOULD HAPPEN IF I JUST LAID IN HERE REAL QUIET...
AND WHEN THE MAILMAN CAME ALONG, I SUDDENLY **LEAPED OUT**...
AAUGH!
IT'S WORTH THINKING ABOUT..

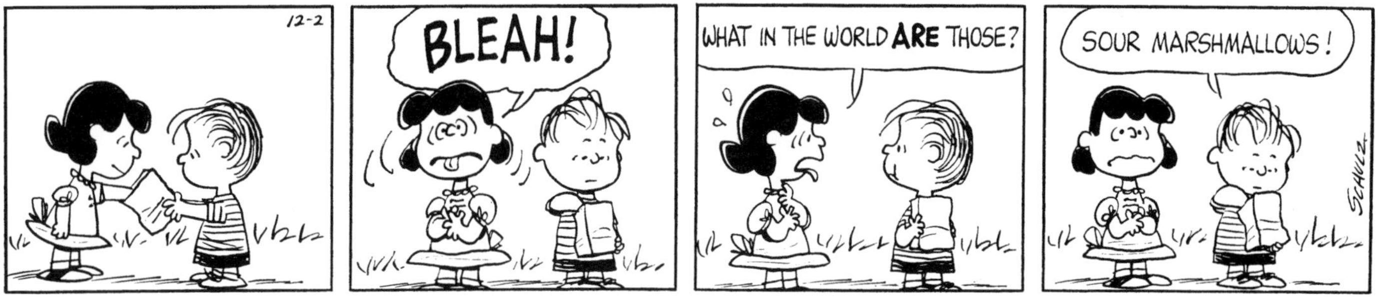
BLEAH!
WHAT IN THE WORLD **ARE** THOSE?
SOUR MARSHMALLOWS!

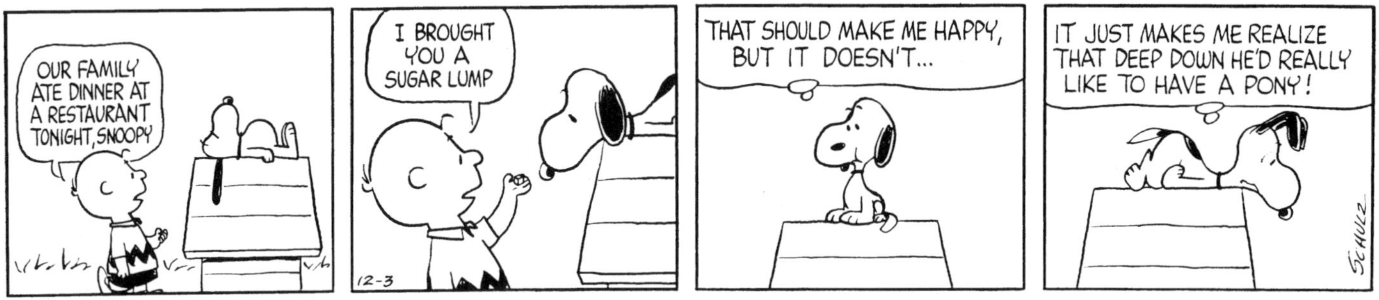
OUR FAMILY ATE DINNER AT A RESTAURANT TONIGHT, SNOOPY
I BROUGHT YOU A SUGAR LUMP
THAT SHOULD MAKE ME HAPPY, BUT IT DOESN'T...
IT JUST MAKES ME REALIZE THAT DEEP DOWN HE'D REALLY LIKE TO HAVE A PONY!

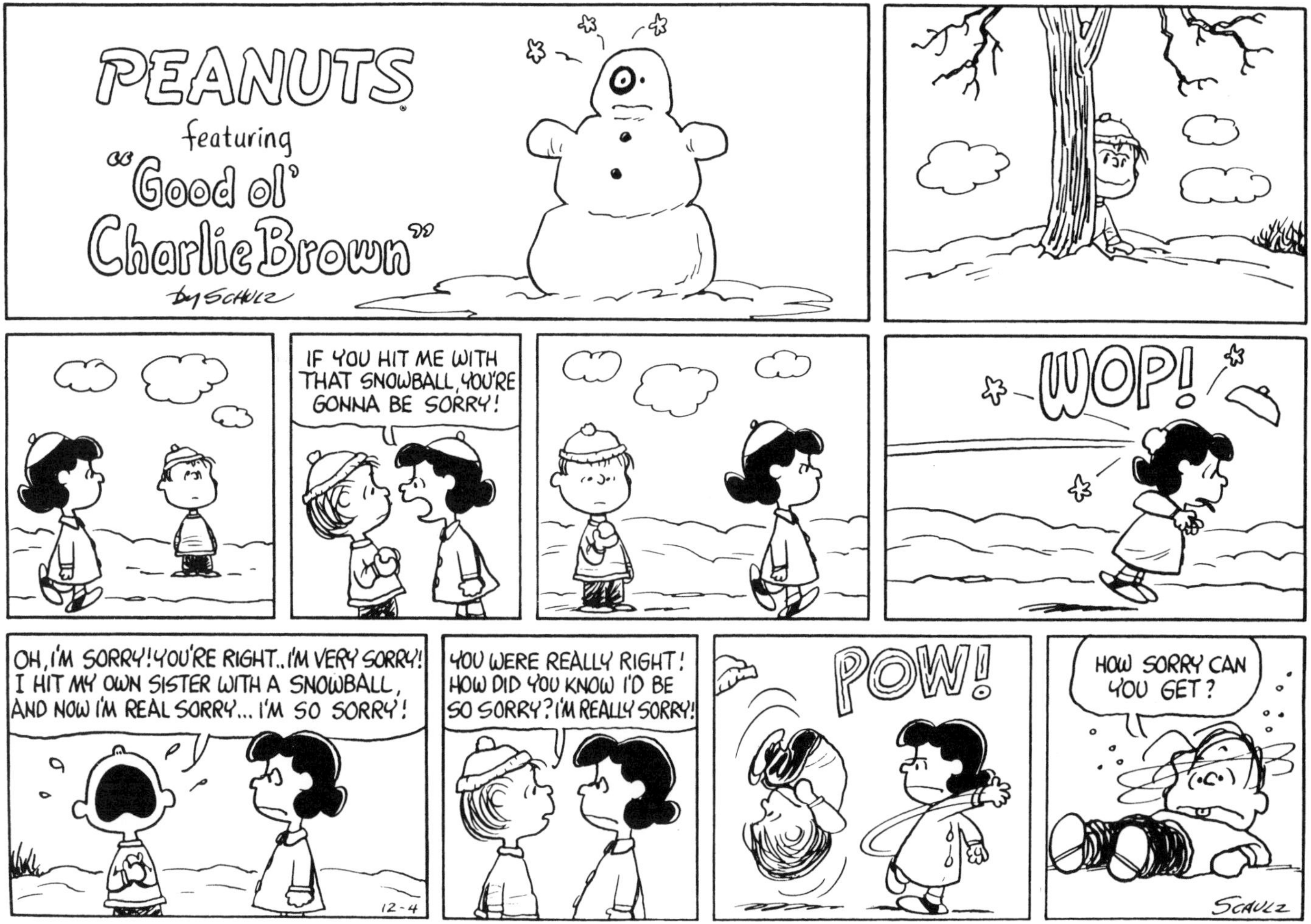
PEANUTS featuring "Good ol' Charlie Brown"
by SCHULZ
IF YOU HIT ME WITH THAT SNOWBALL, YOU'RE GONNA BE SORRY!
WOP!
OH, I'M SORRY! YOU'RE RIGHT.. I'M VERY SORRY! I HIT MY OWN SISTER WITH A SNOWBALL, AND NOW I'M REAL SORRY... I'M SO SORRY!
12-4
YOU WERE REALLY RIGHT! HOW DID YOU KNOW I'D BE SO SORRY? I'M REALLY SORRY!
POW!
HOW SORRY CAN YOU GET?
SCHULZ

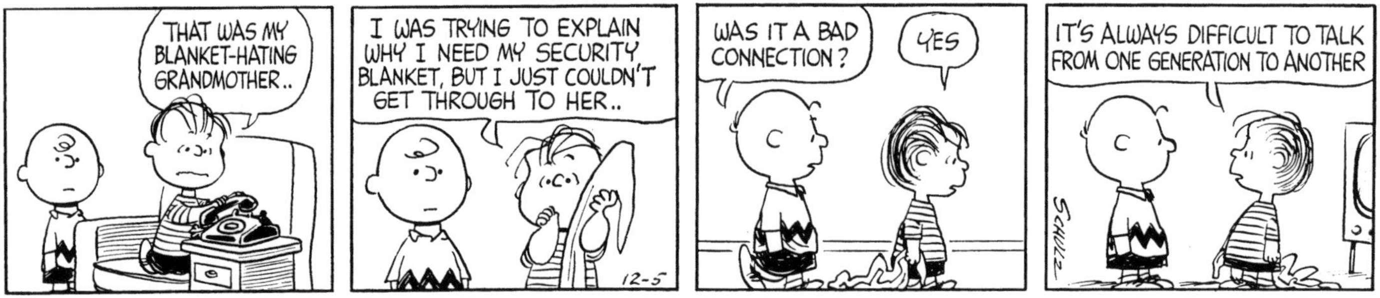
THAT WAS MY BLANKET-HATING GRANDMOTHER..
I WAS TRYING TO EXPLAIN WHY I NEED MY SECURITY BLANKET, BUT I JUST COULDN'T GET THROUGH TO HER..
12-5
WAS IT A BAD CONNECTION?
YES
IT'S ALWAYS DIFFICULT TO TALK FROM ONE GENERATION TO ANOTHER
SCHULZ

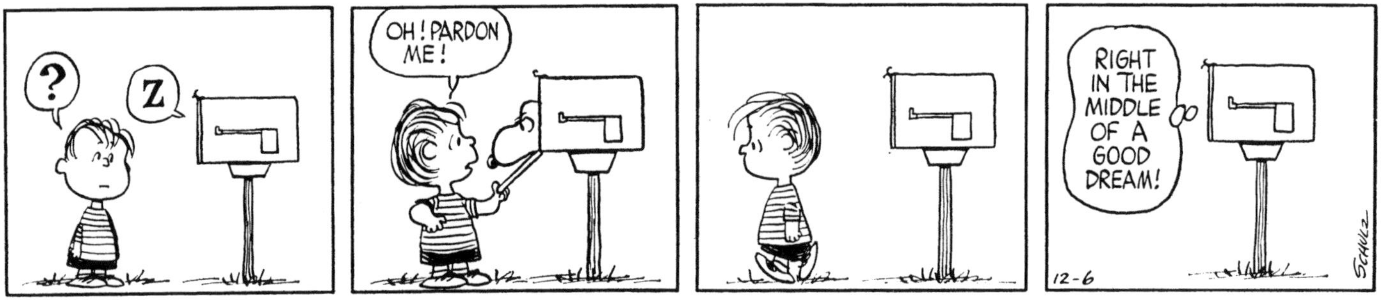
?
Z
OH! PARDON ME!
RIGHT IN THE MIDDLE OF A GOOD DREAM!
12-6
SCHULZ

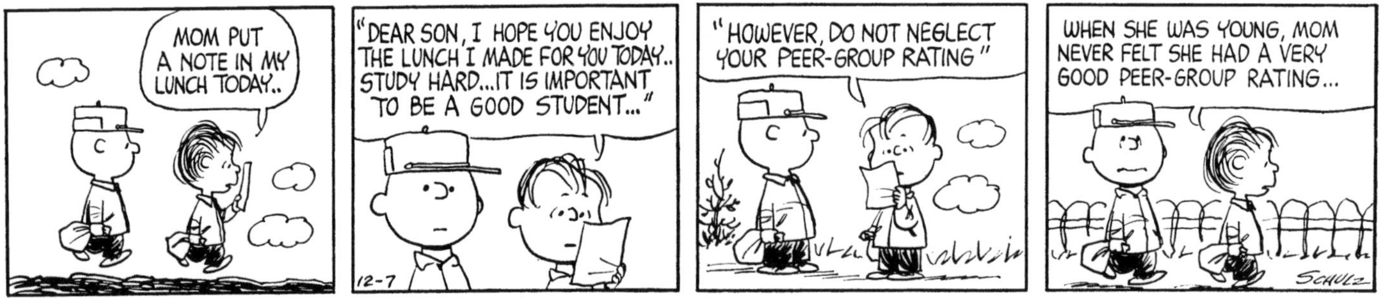
MOM PUT A NOTE IN MY LUNCH TODAY..
"DEAR SON, I HOPE YOU ENJOY THE LUNCH I MADE FOR YOU TODAY.. STUDY HARD...IT IS IMPORTANT TO BE A GOOD STUDENT..."
12-7
"HOWEVER, DO NOT NEGLECT YOUR PEER-GROUP RATING"
WHEN SHE WAS YOUNG, MOM NEVER FELT SHE HAD A VERY GOOD PEER-GROUP RATING...
SCHULZ

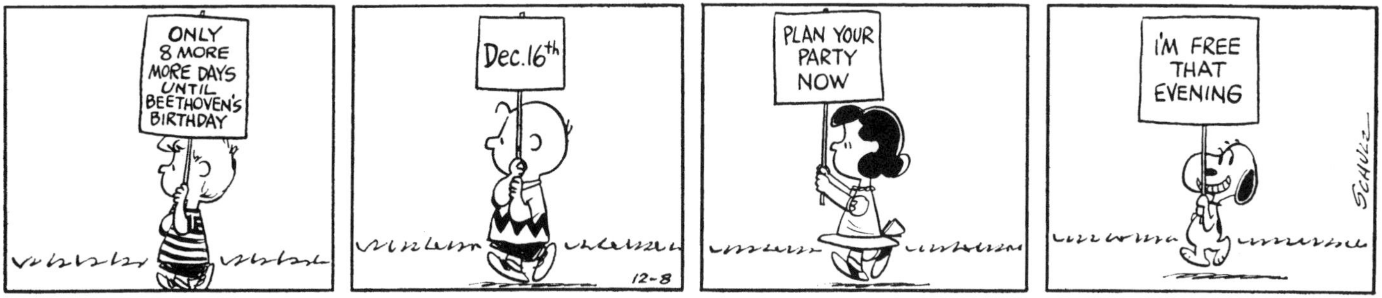
ONLY 8 MORE MORE DAYS UNTIL BEETHOVEN'S BIRTHDAY
Dec. 16th
12-8
PLAN YOUR PARTY NOW
I'M FREE THAT EVENING
SCHULZ

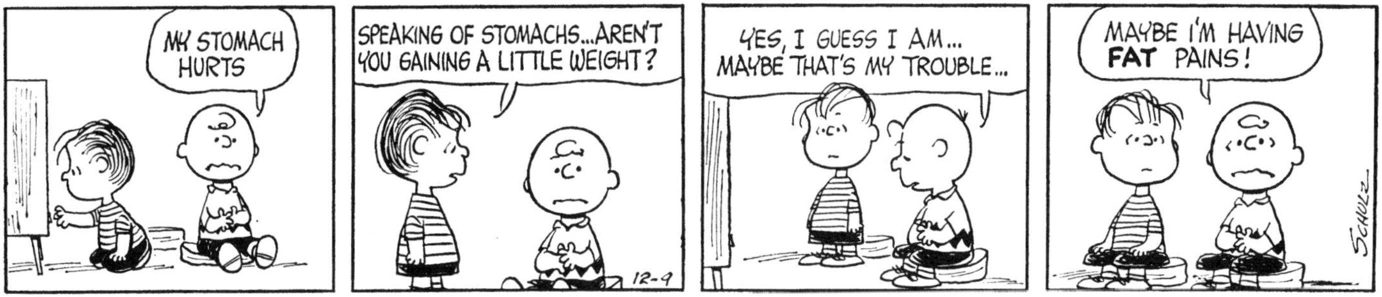
MY STOMACH HURTS
SPEAKING OF STOMACHS...AREN'T YOU GAINING A LITTLE WEIGHT?
12-9
YES, I GUESS I AM... MAYBE THAT'S MY TROUBLE...
MAYBE I'M HAVING **FAT** PAINS!
SCHULZ

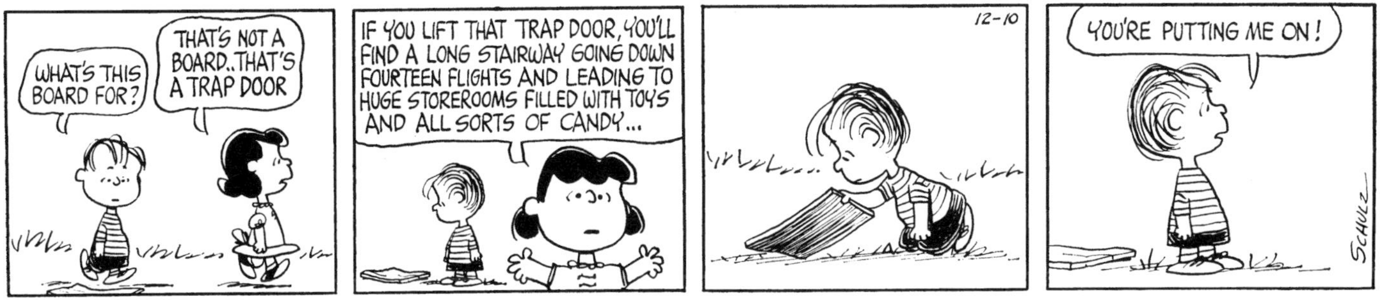
WHAT'S THIS BOARD FOR?
THAT'S NOT A BOARD..THAT'S A TRAP DOOR
IF YOU LIFT THAT TRAP DOOR, YOU'LL FIND A LONG STAIRWAY GOING DOWN FOURTEEN FLIGHTS AND LEADING TO HUGE STOREROOMS FILLED WITH TOYS AND ALL SORTS OF CANDY...
12-10
SCHULZ
YOU'RE PUTTING ME ON!

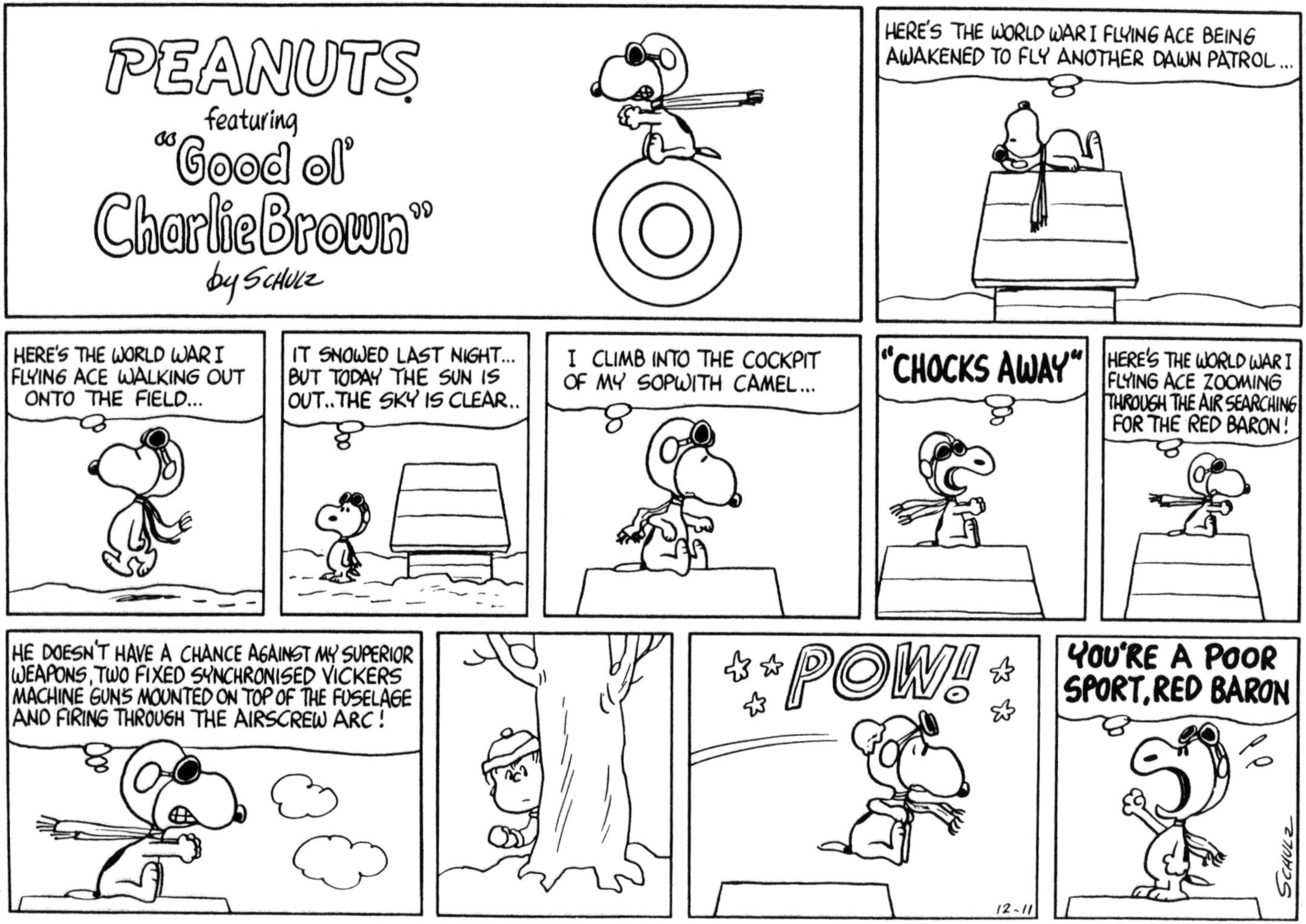
PEANUTS
featuring
"Good ol' CharlieBrown"
by SCHULZ
HERE'S THE WORLD WAR I FLYING ACE BEING AWAKENED TO FLY ANOTHER DAWN PATROL...
HERE'S THE WORLD WAR I FLYING ACE WALKING OUT ONTO THE FIELD...
IT SNOWED LAST NIGHT... BUT TODAY THE SUN IS OUT..THE SKY IS CLEAR..
I CLIMB INTO THE COCKPIT OF MY SOPWITH CAMEL...
"CHOCKS AWAY"
HERE'S THE WORLD WAR I FLYING ACE ZOOMING THROUGH THE AIR SEARCHING FOR THE RED BARON!
HE DOESN'T HAVE A CHANCE AGAINST MY SUPERIOR WEAPONS, TWO FIXED SYNCHRONISED VICKERS MACHINE GUNS MOUNTED ON TOP OF THE FUSELAGE AND FIRING THROUGH THE AIRSCREW ARC!
POW!
12-11
YOU'RE A POOR SPORT, RED BARON
SCHULZ

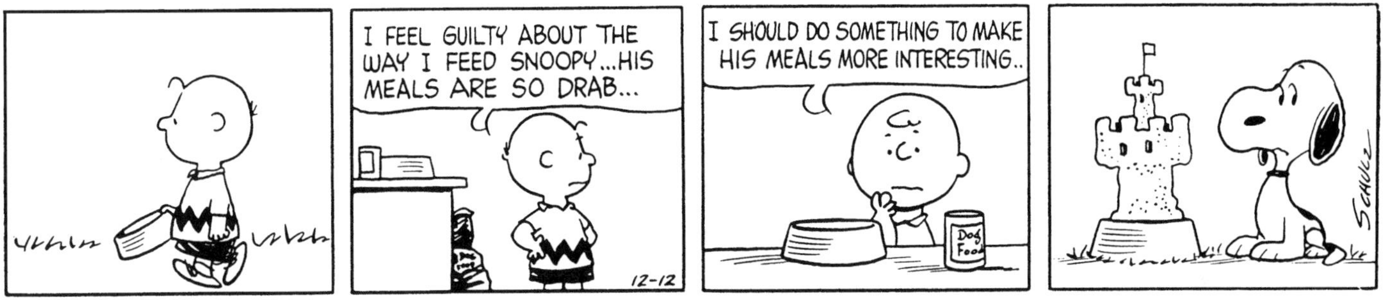
I FEEL GUILTY ABOUT THE WAY I FEED SNOOPY...HIS MEALS ARE SO DRAB...
12-12
I SHOULD DO SOMETHING TO MAKE HIS MEALS MORE INTERESTING..
Dog Food
SCHULZ

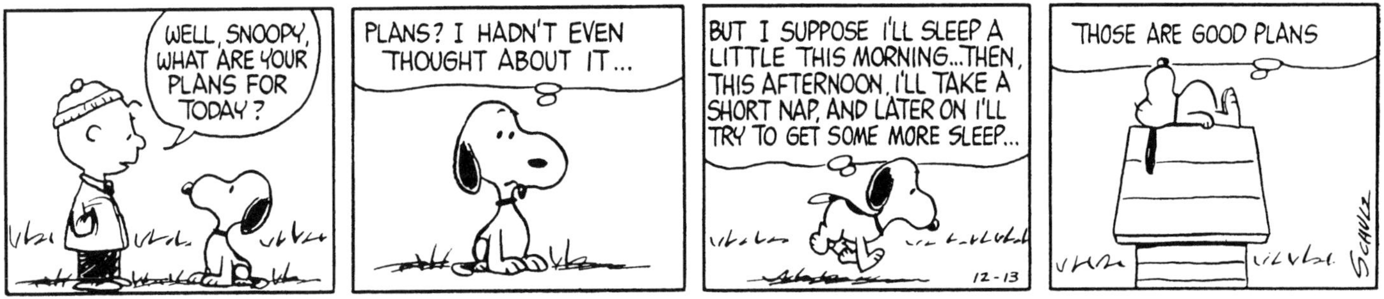
WELL, SNOOPY, WHAT ARE YOUR PLANS FOR TODAY?
PLANS? I HADN'T EVEN THOUGHT ABOUT IT...
BUT I SUPPOSE I'LL SLEEP A LITTLE THIS MORNING...THEN, THIS AFTERNOON, I'LL TAKE A SHORT NAP, AND LATER ON I'LL TRY TO GET SOME MORE SLEEP...
12-13
THOSE ARE GOOD PLANS
SCHULZ

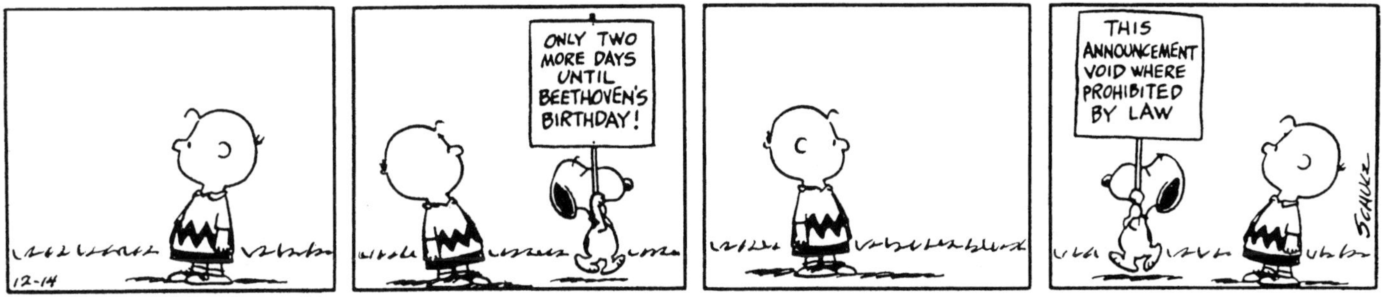
12-14
ONLY TWO MORE DAYS UNTIL BEETHOVEN'S BIRTHDAY!
THIS ANNOUNCEMENT VOID WHERE PROHIBITED BY LAW
SCHULZ

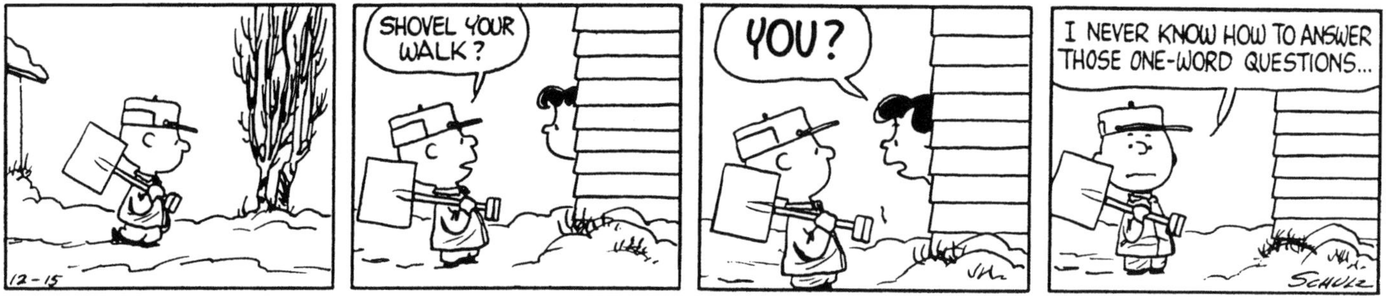
12-15
SHOVEL YOUR WALK?
YOU?
I NEVER KNOW HOW TO ANSWER THOSE ONE-WORD QUESTIONS...
SCHULZ

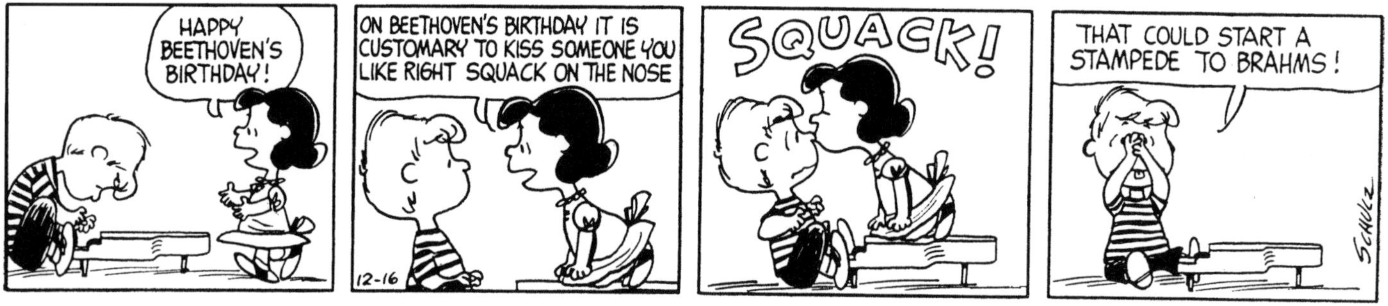
HAPPY BEETHOVEN'S BIRTHDAY!
ON BEETHOVEN'S BIRTHDAY IT IS CUSTOMARY TO KISS SOMEONE YOU LIKE RIGHT SQUACK ON THE NOSE
12-16
SQUACK!
THAT COULD START A STAMPEDE TO BRAHMS!
SCHULZ

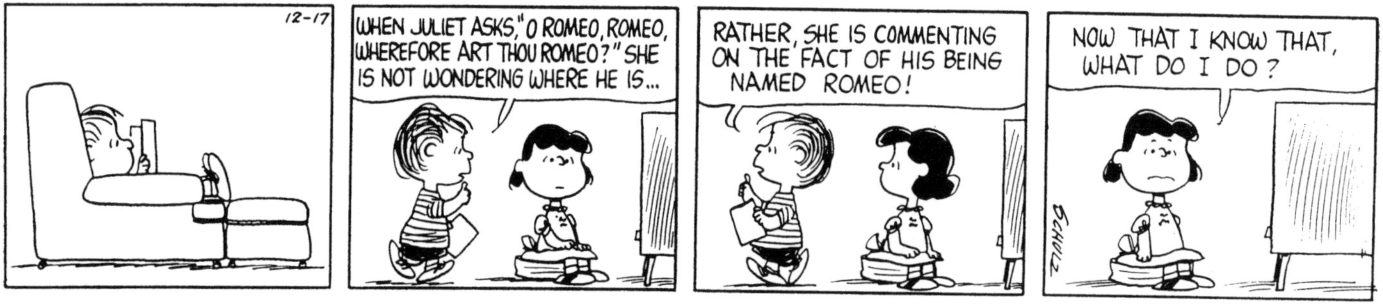
12-17
WHEN JULIET ASKS, "O ROMEO, ROMEO, WHEREFORE ART THOU ROMEO?" SHE IS NOT WONDERING WHERE HE IS...
RATHER, SHE IS COMMENTING ON THE FACT OF HIS BEING NAMED ROMEO!
SCHULZ
NOW THAT I KNOW THAT, WHAT DO I DO?

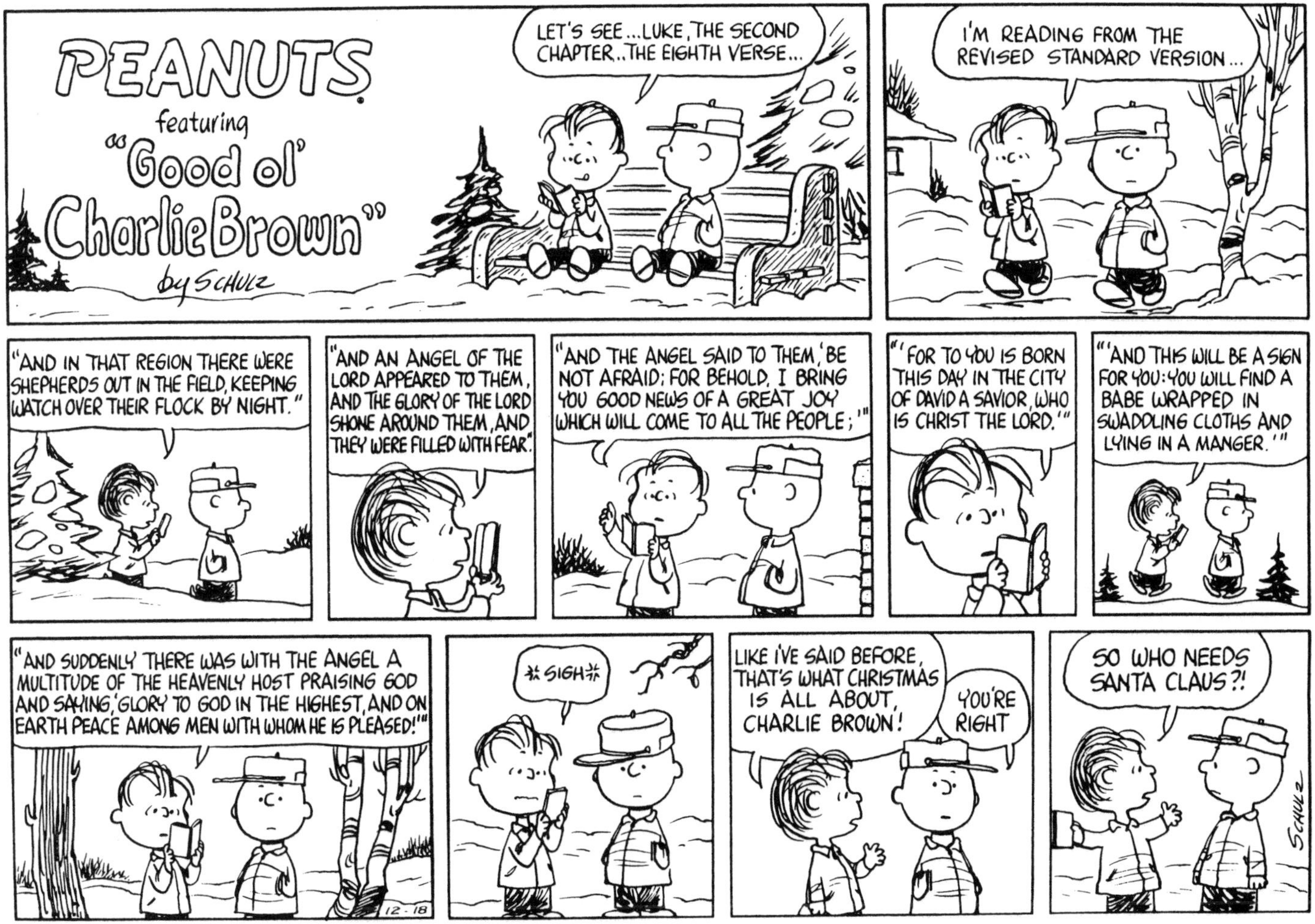
PEANUTS
featuring "Good ol' Charlie Brown"
by SCHULZ
LET'S SEE...LUKE, THE SECOND CHAPTER..THE EIGHTH VERSE...
I'M READING FROM THE REVISED STANDARD VERSION...
"AND IN THAT REGION THERE WERE SHEPHERDS OUT IN THE FIELD, KEEPING WATCH OVER THEIR FLOCK BY NIGHT."
"AND AN ANGEL OF THE LORD APPEARED TO THEM, AND THE GLORY OF THE LORD SHONE AROUND THEM, AND THEY WERE FILLED WITH FEAR."
"AND THE ANGEL SAID TO THEM, 'BE NOT AFRAID; FOR BEHOLD, I BRING YOU GOOD NEWS OF A GREAT JOY WHICH WILL COME TO ALL THE PEOPLE;'"
"'FOR TO YOU IS BORN THIS DAY IN THE CITY OF DAVID A SAVIOR, WHO IS CHRIST THE LORD.'"
"'AND THIS WILL BE A SIGN FOR YOU: YOU WILL FIND A BABE WRAPPED IN SWADDLING CLOTHS AND LYING IN A MANGER.'"
"AND SUDDENLY THERE WAS WITH THE ANGEL A MULTITUDE OF THE HEAVENLY HOST PRAISING GOD AND SAYING, 'GLORY TO GOD IN THE HIGHEST, AND ON EARTH PEACE AMONG MEN WITH WHOM HE IS PLEASED!'"
12-18
SIGH
LIKE I'VE SAID BEFORE, THAT'S WHAT CHRISTMAS IS ALL ABOUT, CHARLIE BROWN!
YOU'RE RIGHT
SO WHO NEEDS SANTA CLAUS?!
SCHULZ

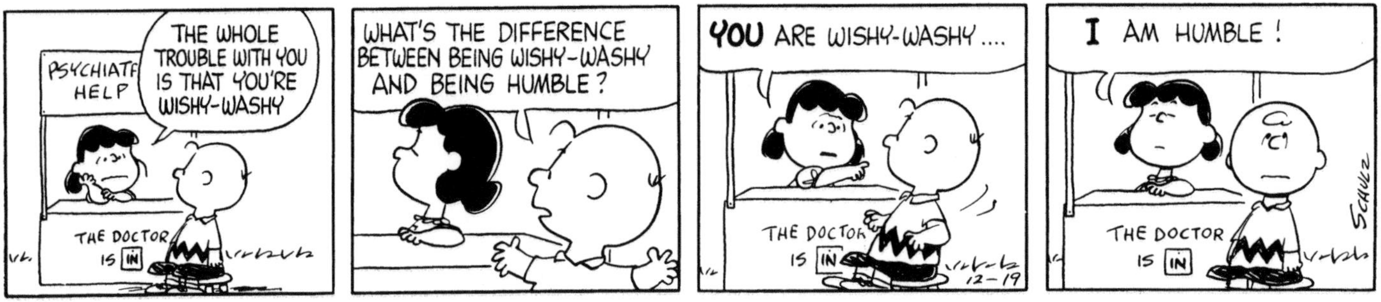
PSYCHIATF
HELP
THE WHOLE TROUBLE WITH YOU IS THAT YOU'RE WISHY-WASHY
THE DOCTOR IS IN
WHAT'S THE DIFFERENCE BETWEEN BEING WISHY-WASHY AND BEING HUMBLE?
YOU ARE WISHY-WASHY....
THE DOCTOR IS IN
12-19
I AM HUMBLE!
THE DOCTOR IS IN
SCHULZ

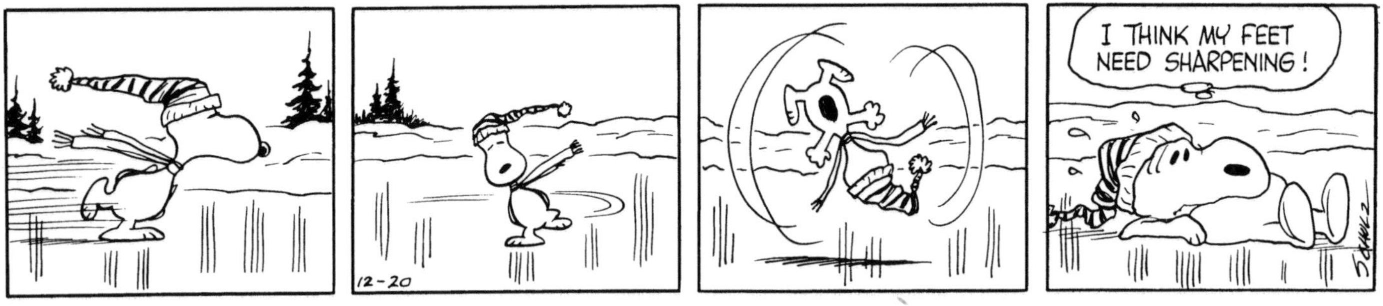
12-20
I THINK MY FEET NEED SHARPENING!
SCHULZ

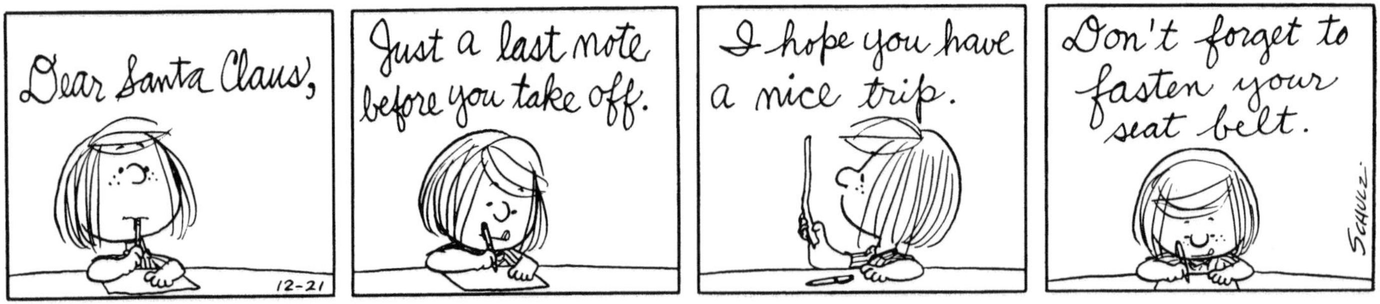
Dear Santa Claus,
12-21
Just a last note before you take off.
I hope you have a nice trip.
Don't forget to fasten your seat belt.
SCHULZ

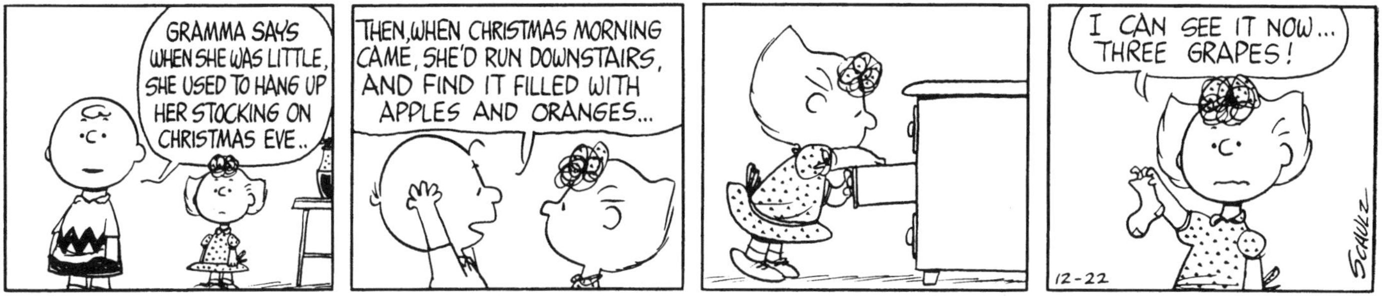
GRAMMA SAYS WHEN SHE WAS LITTLE, SHE USED TO HANG UP HER STOCKING ON CHRISTMAS EVE..
THEN, WHEN CHRISTMAS MORNING CAME, SHE'D RUN DOWNSTAIRS, AND FIND IT FILLED WITH APPLES AND ORANGES...
I CAN SEE IT NOW... THREE GRAPES!

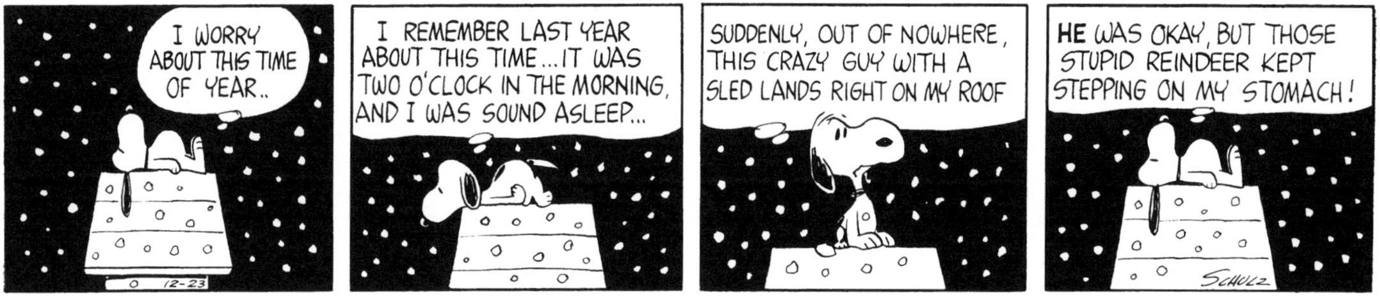
I WORRY ABOUT THIS TIME OF YEAR..
I REMEMBER LAST YEAR ABOUT THIS TIME... IT WAS TWO O'CLOCK IN THE MORNING, AND I WAS SOUND ASLEEP...
SUDDENLY, OUT OF NOWHERE, THIS CRAZY GUY WITH A SLED LANDS RIGHT ON MY ROOF
HE WAS OKAY, BUT THOSE STUPID REINDEER KEPT STEPPING ON MY STOMACH!

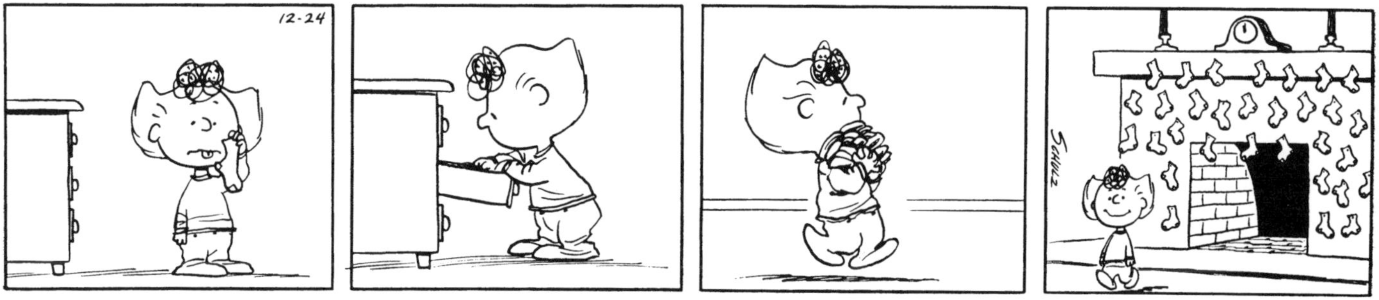

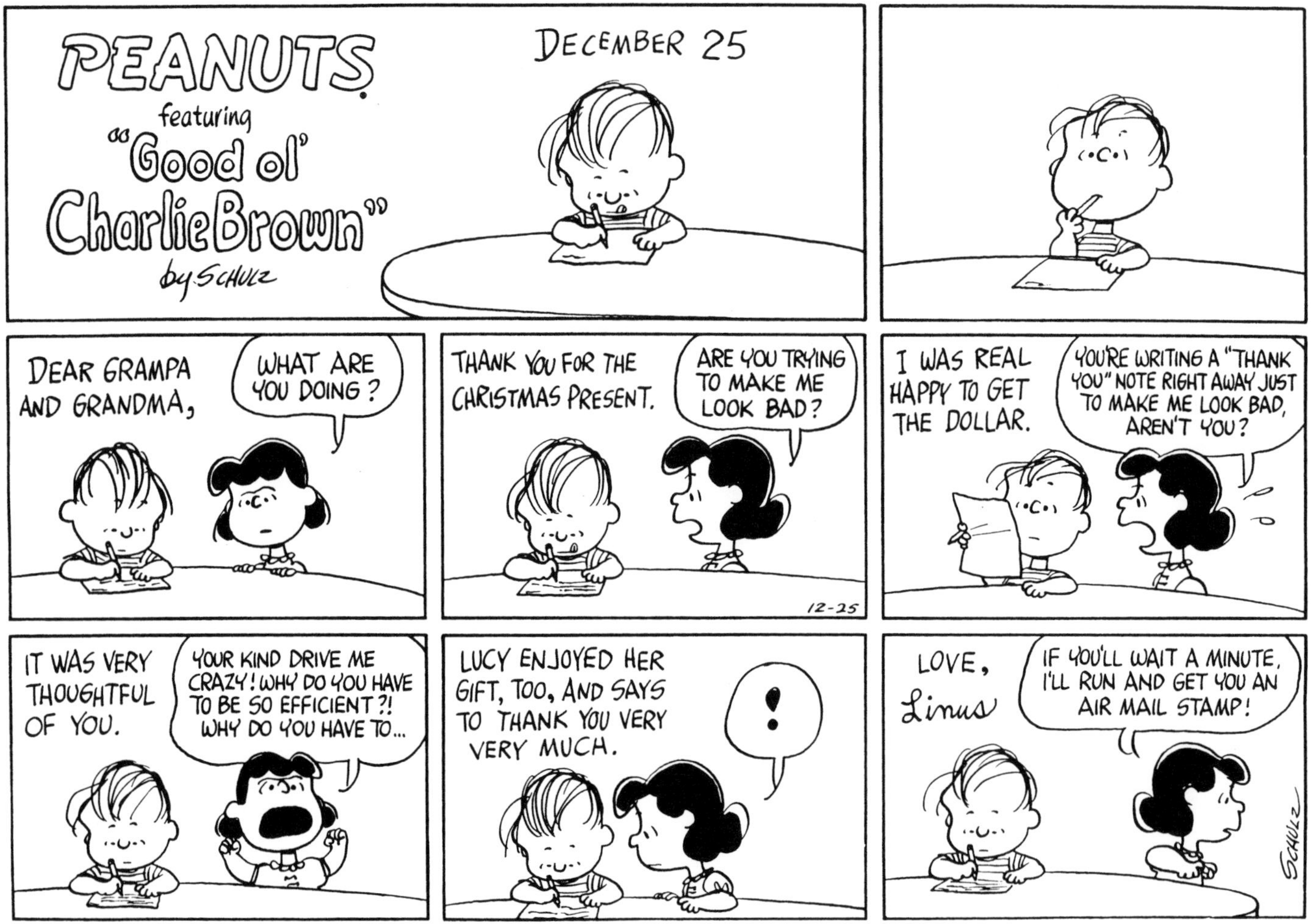
PEANUTS
featuring
"Good ol' Charlie Brown"
by SCHULZ
DECEMBER 25
DEAR GRAMPA AND GRANDMA,
WHAT ARE YOU DOING?
THANK YOU FOR THE CHRISTMAS PRESENT.
ARE YOU TRYING TO MAKE ME LOOK BAD?
12-25
I WAS REAL HAPPY TO GET THE DOLLAR.
YOU'RE WRITING A "THANK YOU" NOTE RIGHT AWAY JUST TO MAKE ME LOOK BAD, AREN'T YOU?
IT WAS VERY THOUGHTFUL OF YOU.
YOUR KIND DRIVE ME CRAZY! WHY DO YOU HAVE TO BE SO EFFICIENT?! WHY DO YOU HAVE TO...
LUCY ENJOYED HER GIFT, TOO, AND SAYS TO THANK YOU VERY VERY MUCH.
!
LOVE,
Linus
IF YOU'LL WAIT A MINUTE, I'LL RUN AND GET YOU AN AIR MAIL STAMP!
SCHULZ

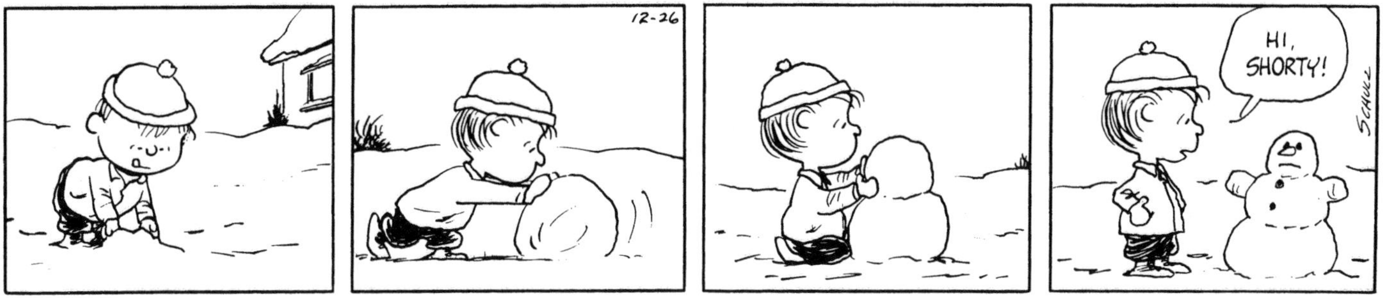
12-26
HI, SHORTY!
SCHULZ

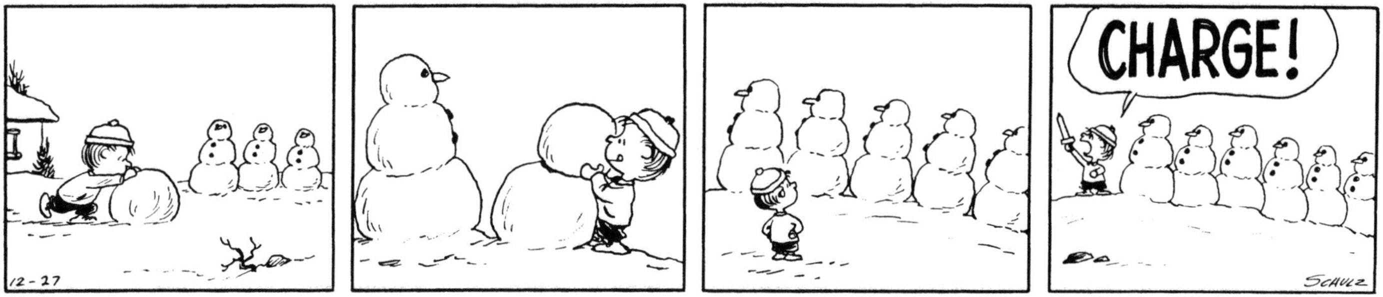
12-27
CHARGE!
SCHULZ

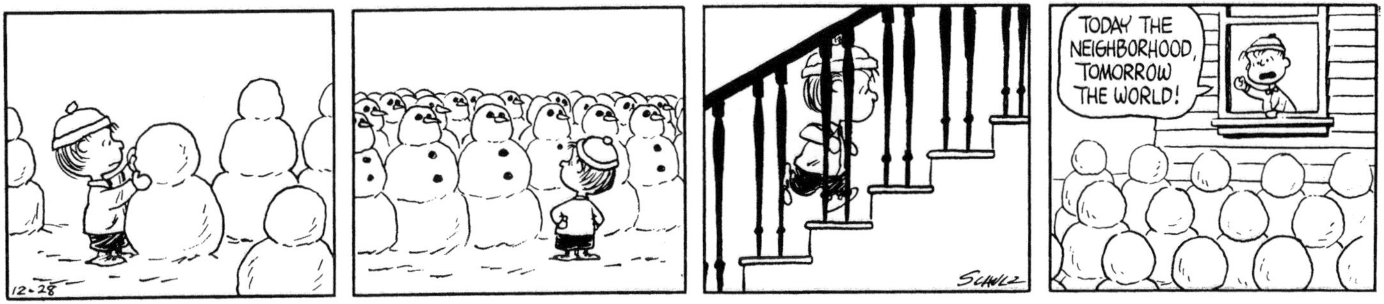
12-28
SCHULZ
TODAY THE NEIGHBORHOOD, TOMORROW THE WORLD!

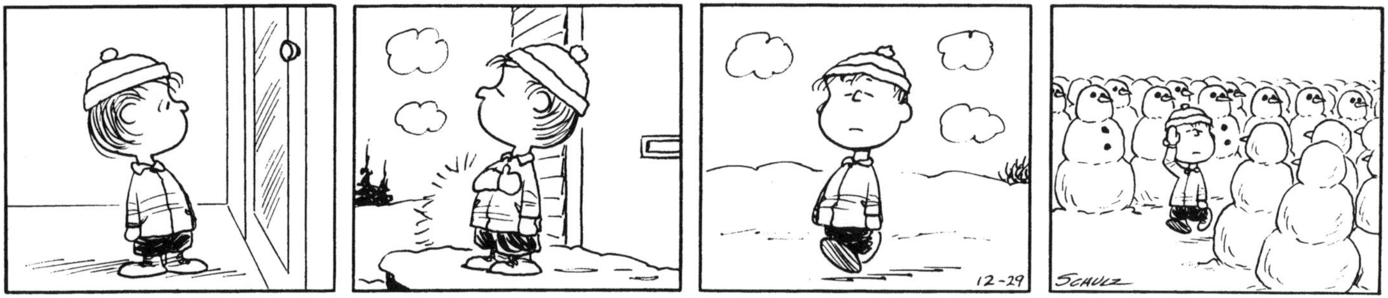
12-29
SCHULZ
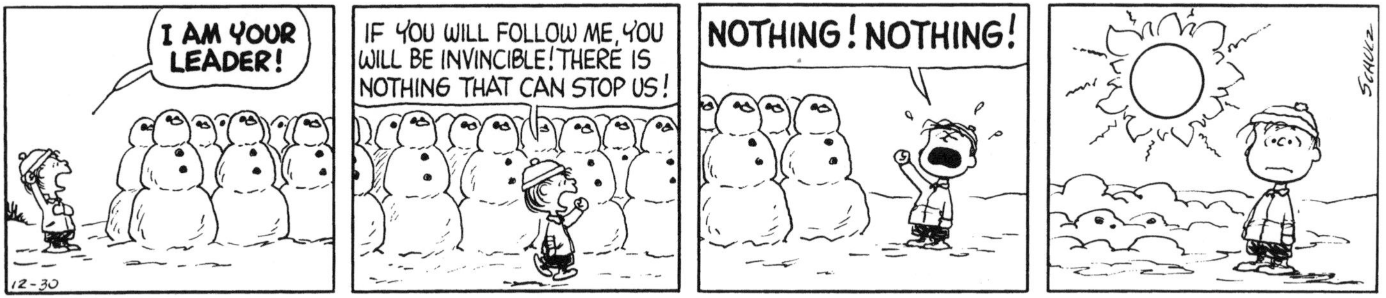
I AM YOUR LEADER!
12-30
IF YOU WILL FOLLOW ME, YOU WILL BE INVINCIBLE! THERE IS NOTHING THAT CAN STOP US!
NOTHING! NOTHING!
SCHULZ
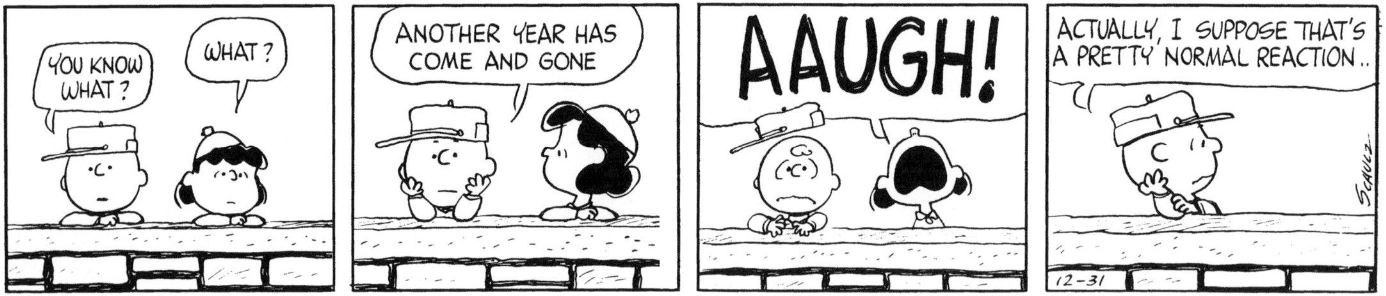
YOU KNOW WHAT?
WHAT?
ANOTHER YEAR HAS COME AND GONE
AAUGH!
ACTUALLY, I SUPPOSE THAT'S A PRETTY NORMAL REACTION..
SCHULZ
12-31

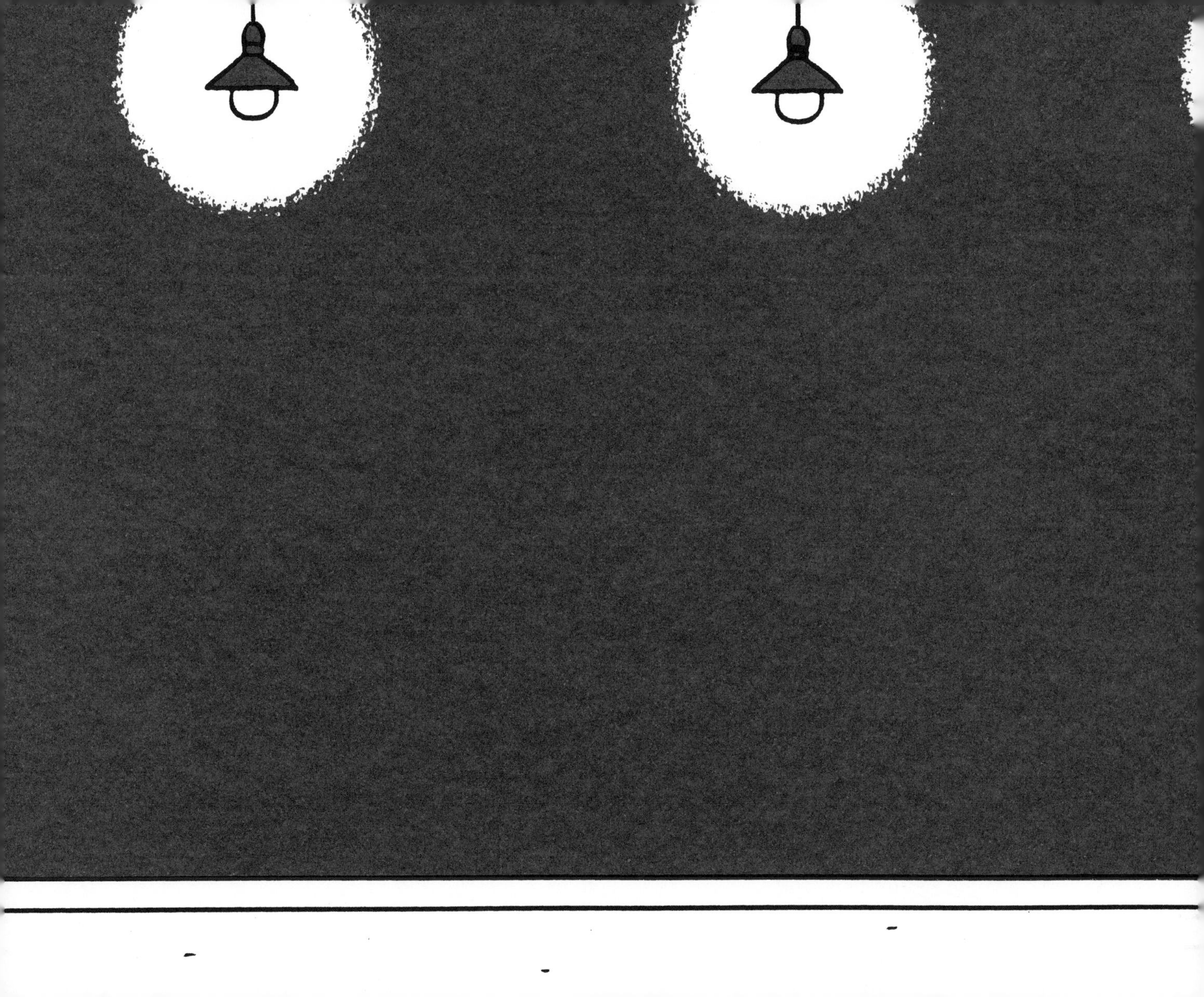

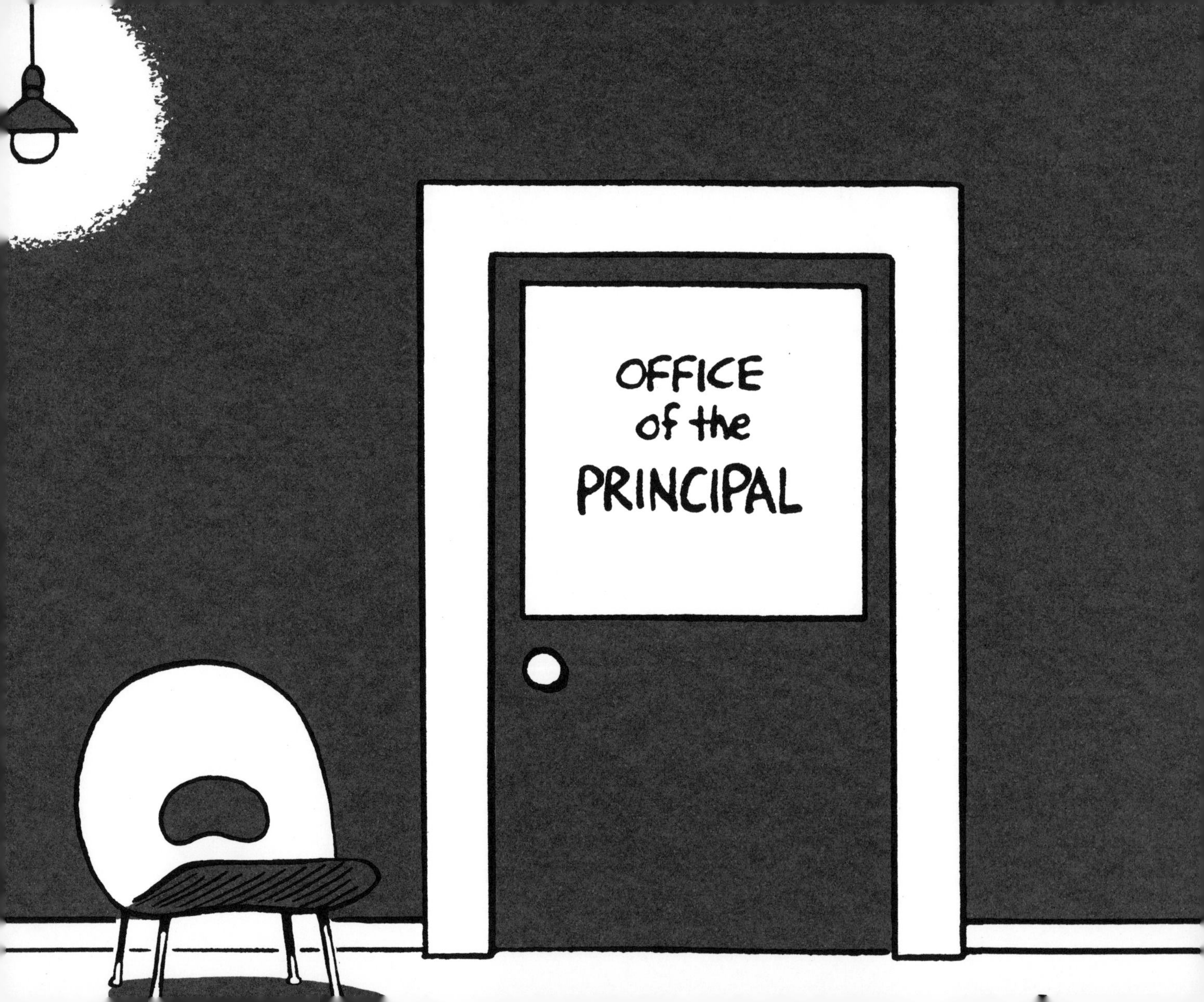
OFFICE
of the
PRINCIPAL

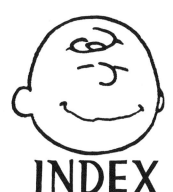

INDEX

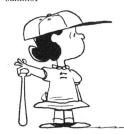

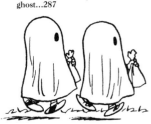

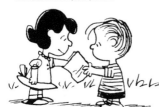

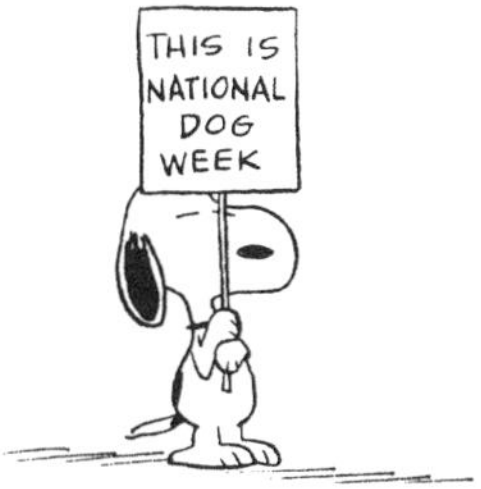
THIS IS
NATIONAL
DOG
WEEK

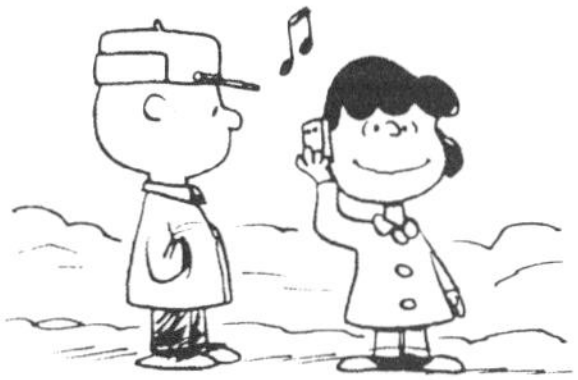

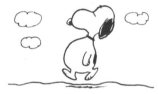
It was a dark
and stormy night.

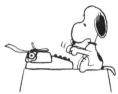

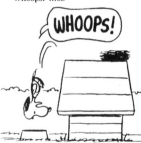

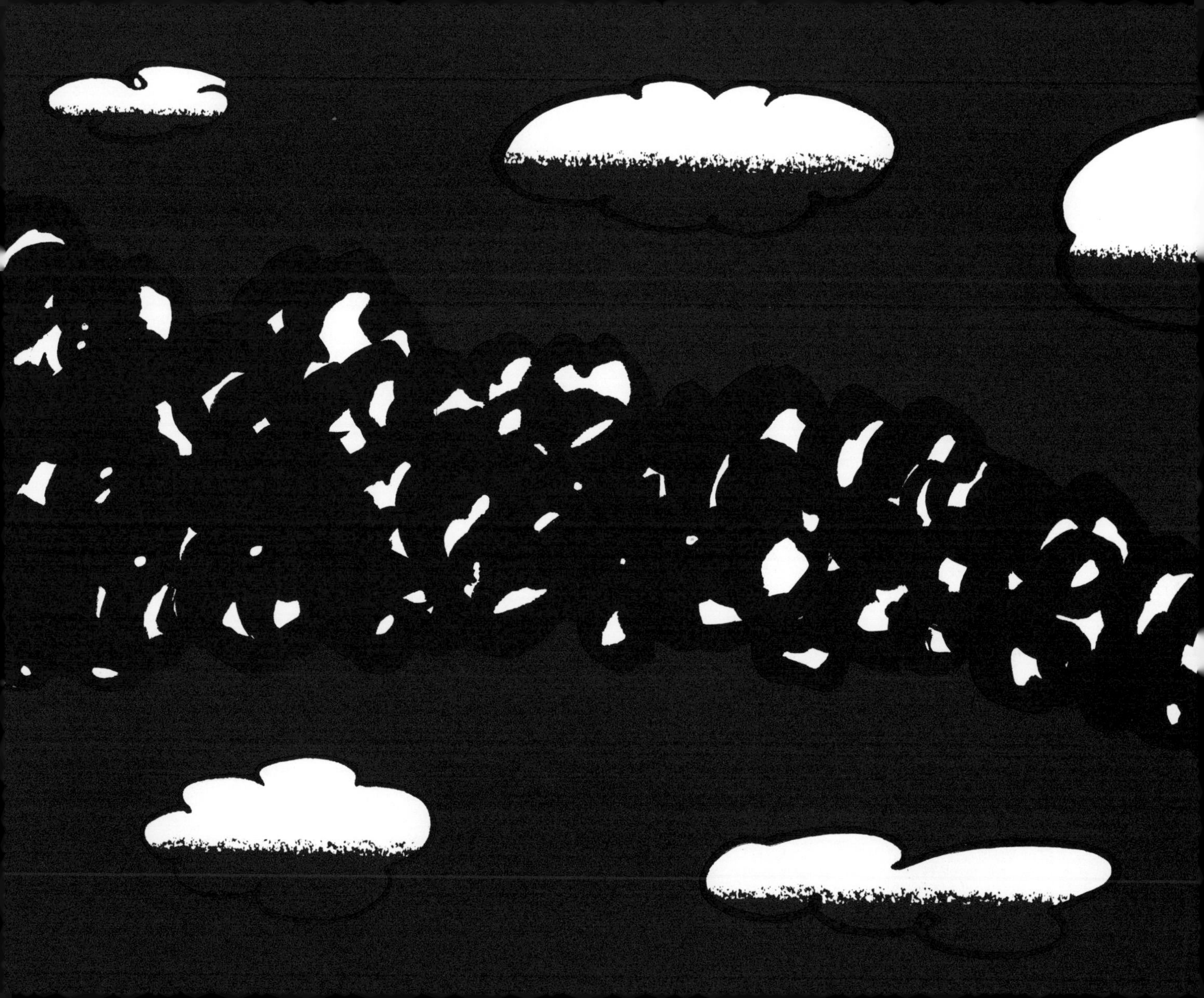

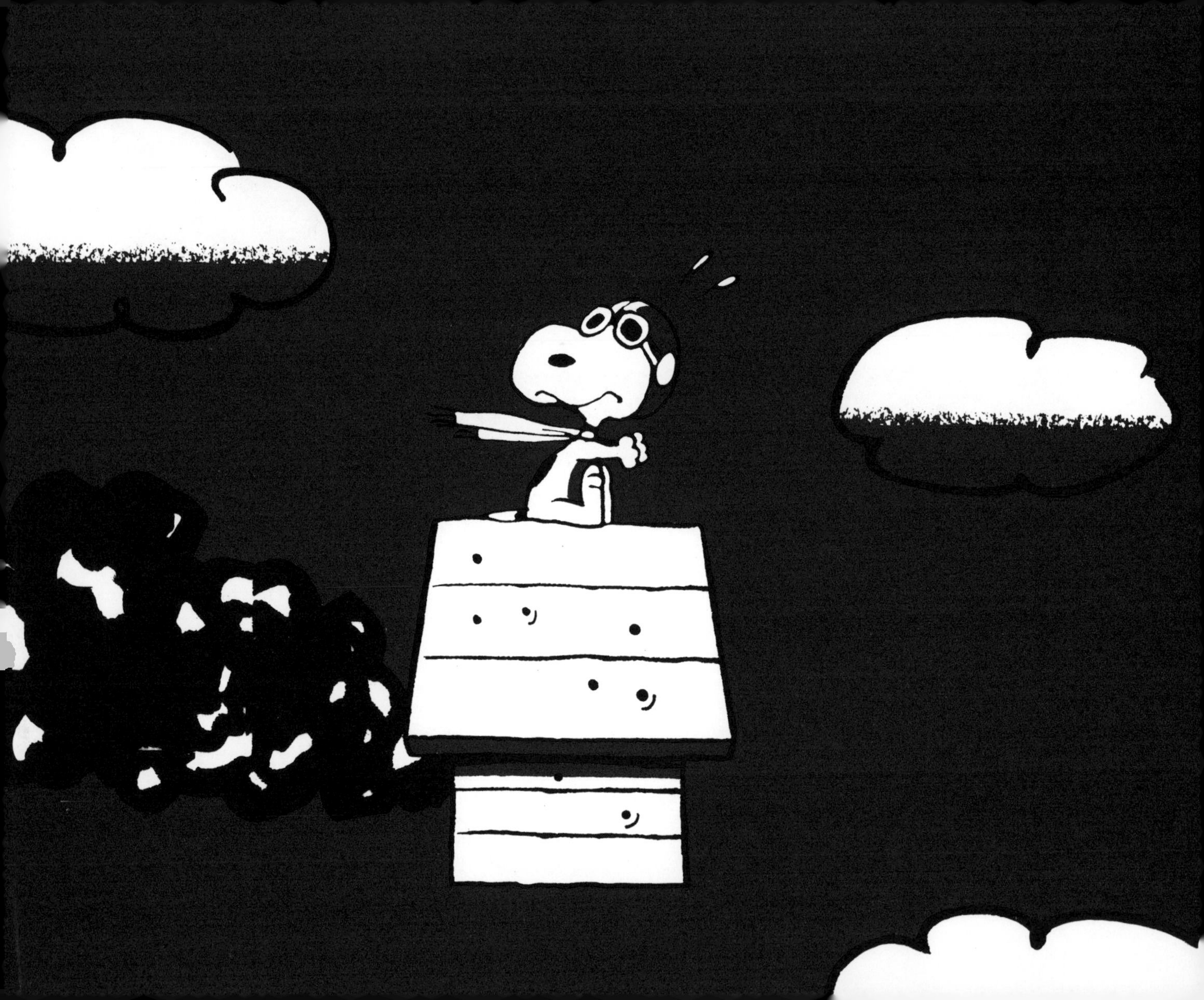

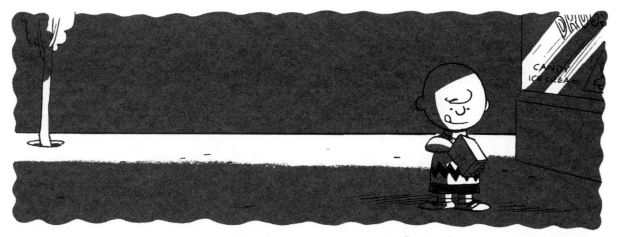

CHARLES M. SCHULZ · 1922 To 2000

Charles M. Schulz was born November 25, 1922 in Minneapolis. His destiny was foreshadowed when an uncle gave him, at the age of two days, the nickname Sparky (after the racehorse Spark Plug in the newspaper strip *Barney Google*).

Schulz grew up in St. Paul. By all accounts, he led an unremarkable, albeit sheltered, childhood. He was an only child, close to both parents, his eventual career path nurtured by his father, who bought four Sunday papers every week — just for the comics.

An outstanding student, he skipped two grades early on, but began to flounder in high school — perhaps not so coincidentally at the same time kids are going through their cruelest, most status-conscious period of socialization. The pain, bitterness, insecurity, and failures chronicled in *Peanuts* appear to have originated from this period of Schulz's life.

Although Schulz enjoyed sports, he also found refuge in solitary activities: reading, drawing, and watching movies. He bought comic books and Big Little Books, pored over the newspaper strips, and copied his favorites — *Buck Rogers*, the Walt Disney characters, *Popeye, Tim Tyler's Luck*. He quickly became a connoisseur; his heroes were Milton Caniff, Roy Crane, Hal Foster, and Alex Raymond.

In his senior year in high school, his mother noticed an ad in a local newspaper for a correspondence school, Federal Schools (later called Art

Instruction Schools). Schulz passed the talent test, completed the course and began trying, unsuccessfully, to sell gag cartoons to magazines. (His first published drawing was of his dog, Spike, and appeared in a 1937 *Ripley's Believe It Or Not!* installment.)

After World War II had ended and Schulz was discharged from the army, he started submitting gag cartoons to the various magazines of the time; his first breakthrough, however, came when an editor at *Timeless Topix* hired him to letter adventure comics. Soon after that, he was hired by his alma mater, Art Instruction, to correct student lessons returned by mail.

Between 1948 and 1950, he succeeded in selling 17 cartoons to the *Saturday Evening Post* — as well as, to the local *St. Paul Pioneer Press*, a weekly comic feature called *Li'l Folks*. It was run in the women's section and paid $10 a week. After writing and drawing the feature for two years, Schulz asked for a better location in the paper or for daily exposure, as well as a raise. When he was turned down on all three counts, he quit.

He started submitting strips to the newspaper syndicates. In the Spring of 1950, he received a letter from the United Feature Syndicate, announcing their interest in his submission, *Li'l Folks*. Schulz boarded a train in June for New York City; more interested in doing a strip than a panel, he also brought along the first installments of what would become *Peanuts* — and that was what sold. (The title, which Schulz loathed to his dying day, was imposed by the syndicate). The first *Peanuts* daily appeared October 2, 1950; the first Sunday, January 6, 1952.

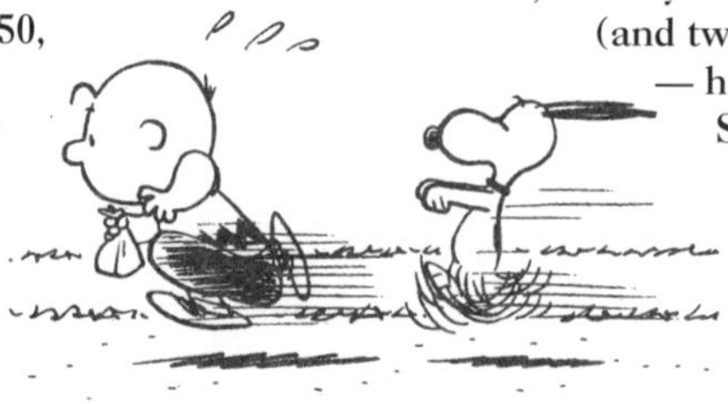

Prior to *Peanuts*, the province of the comics page had been that of gags, social and political observation, domestic comedy, soap opera, and various adventure genres. Although *Peanuts* changed, or evolved, during the 50 years Schulz wrote and drew it, it remained, as it began, an anomaly on the comics page — a comic strip about the interior crises of the cartoonist himself. After a painful divorce in 1973 from which he had not yet recovered, Schulz told a reporter, "Strangely, I've drawn better cartoons in the last six months — or as good as I've ever drawn. I don't know how the human mind works." Surely, it was this kind of humility in the face of profoundly irreducible human question that makes *Peanuts* as universally moving as it is.

Diagnosed with cancer, Schulz retired from *Peanuts* at the end of 1999. He died on February 12th 2000, the day before his last strip was published (and two days before Valentine's Day) — having completed 17,897 daily and Sunday strips, each and every one fully written, drawn, and lettered entirely by his own hand — an unmatched achievement in comics.

—Gary Groth

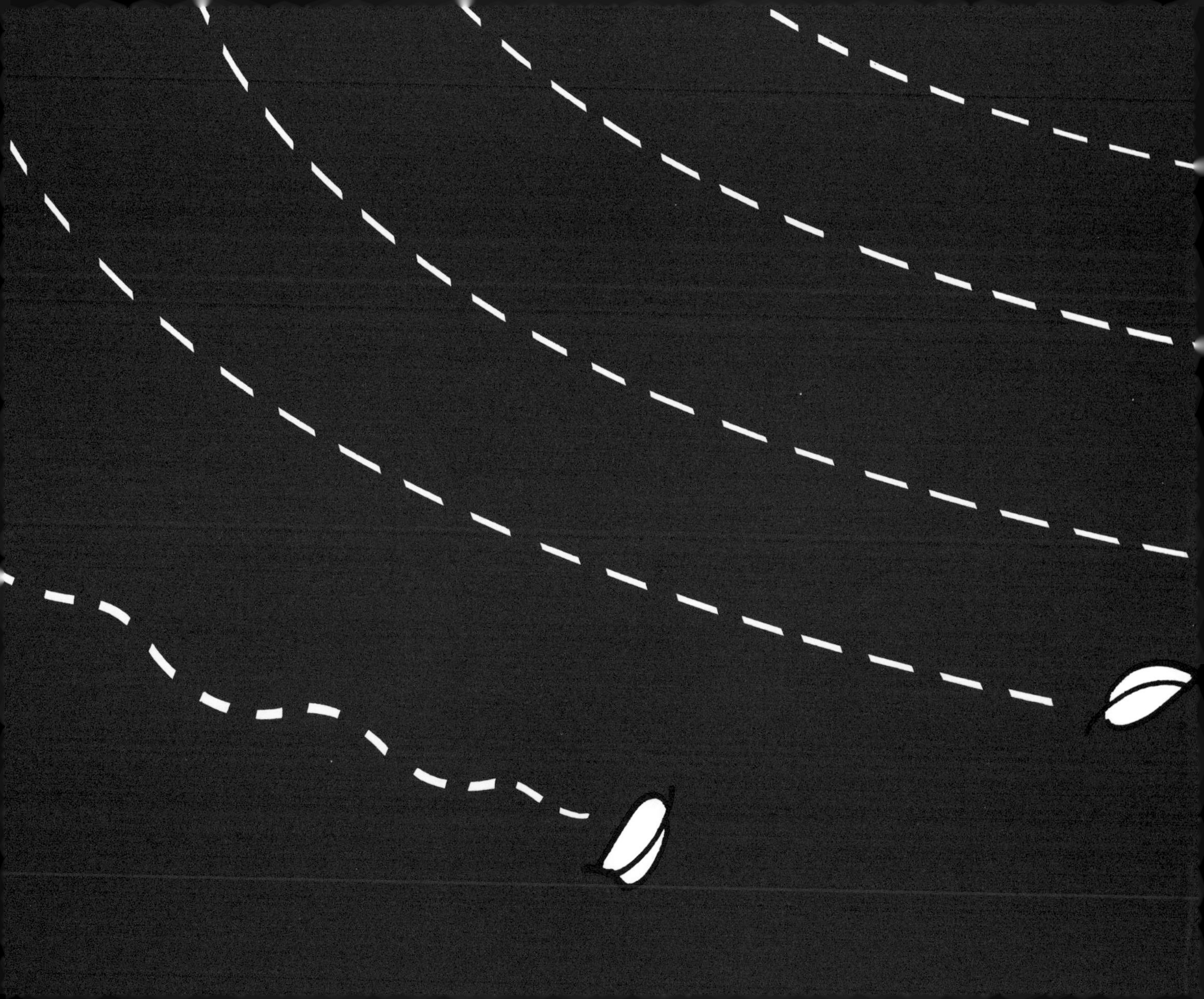

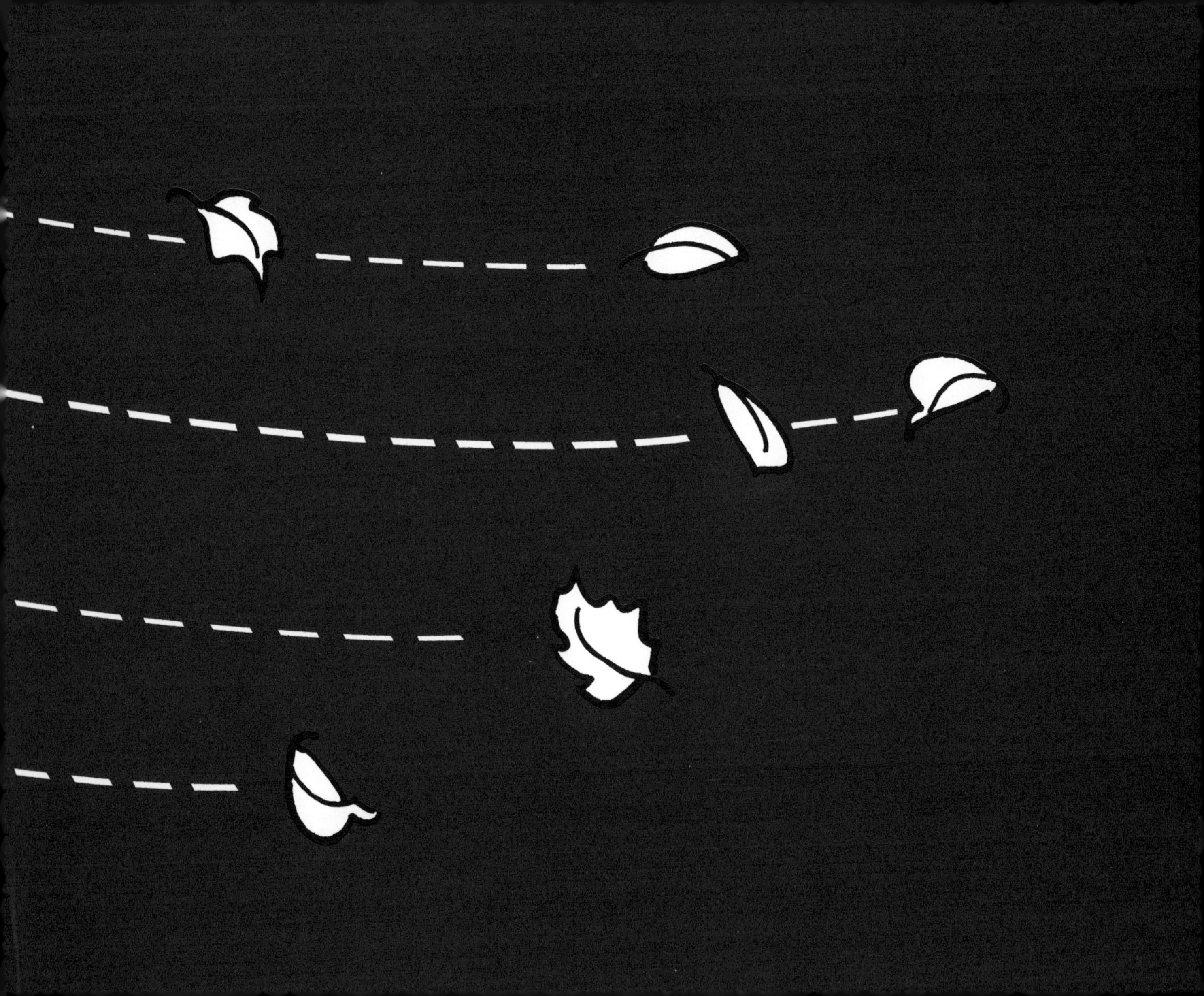

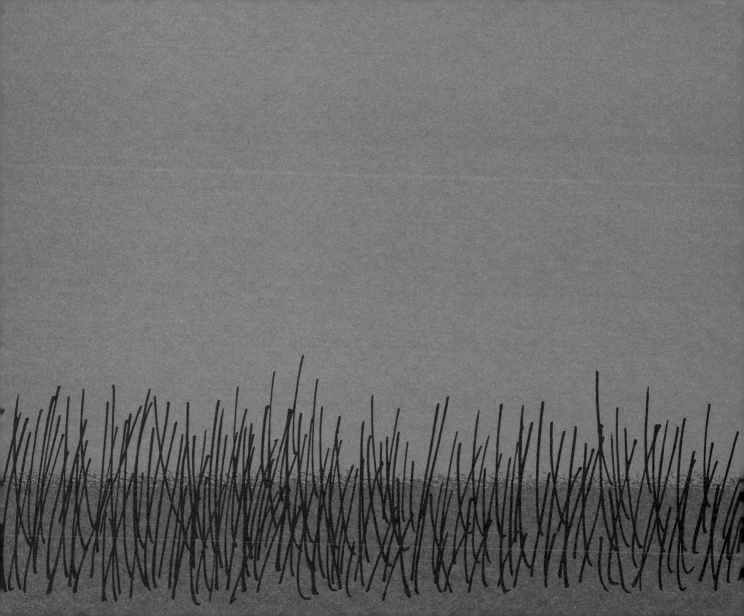

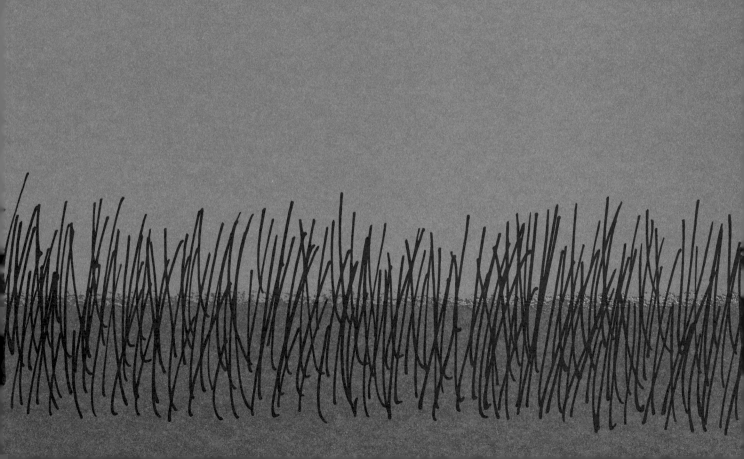

ALSO AVAILABLE FROM CANONGATE

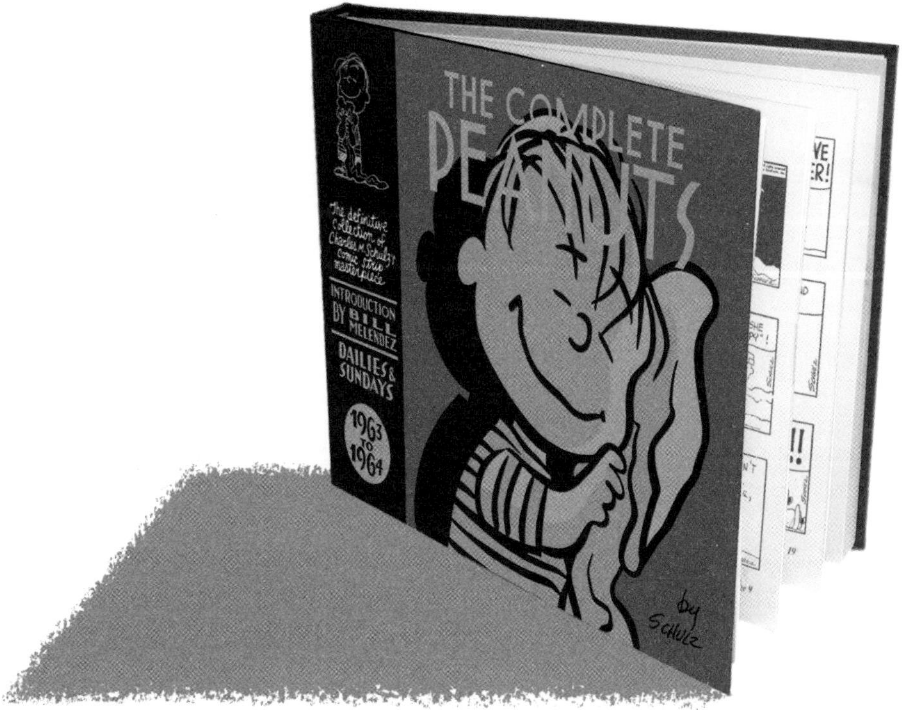
THE COMPLETE
INTRODUCTION BY BILL MELENDEZ
DAILIES & SUNDAYS
1963 TO 1964
by SCHULZ

THE COMPLETE PEANUTS: 1963–1964

A new character – in fact, three new characters – appear: the numerically monikered 555 95472 and his sisters 3 and 4 . . . Charlie Brown blows a baseball match with the little red-haired girl in attendance . . . Snoopy befriends bunnies and birds, and goes for a stay in the hospital . . . Linus's run for class president is derailed by his religious beliefs . . . Plus Dally vs. school, and Lucy's campaign to improve everyone but herself!

ISBN 978 1 84767 814 0

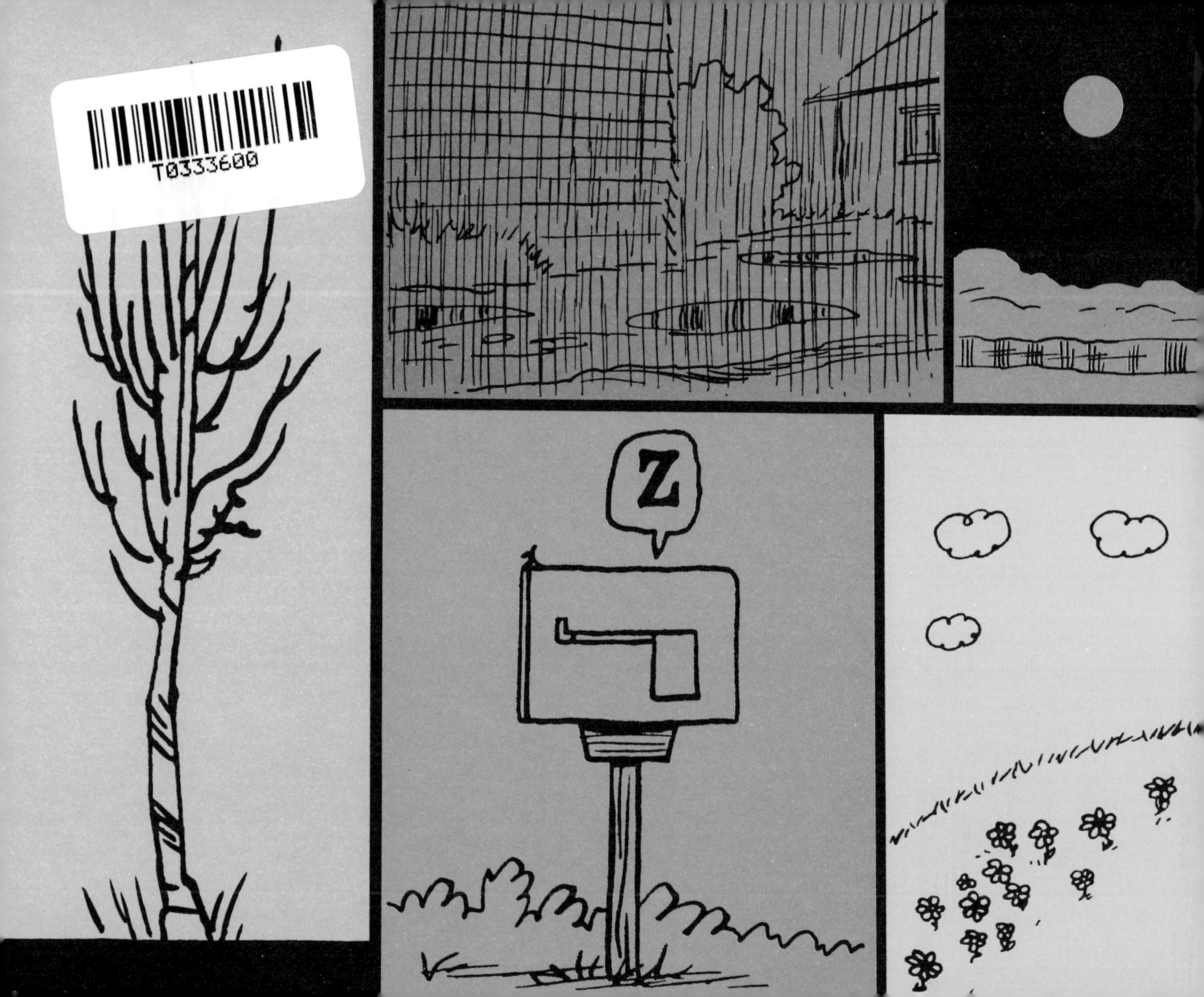
Z